World Business Travel Guide

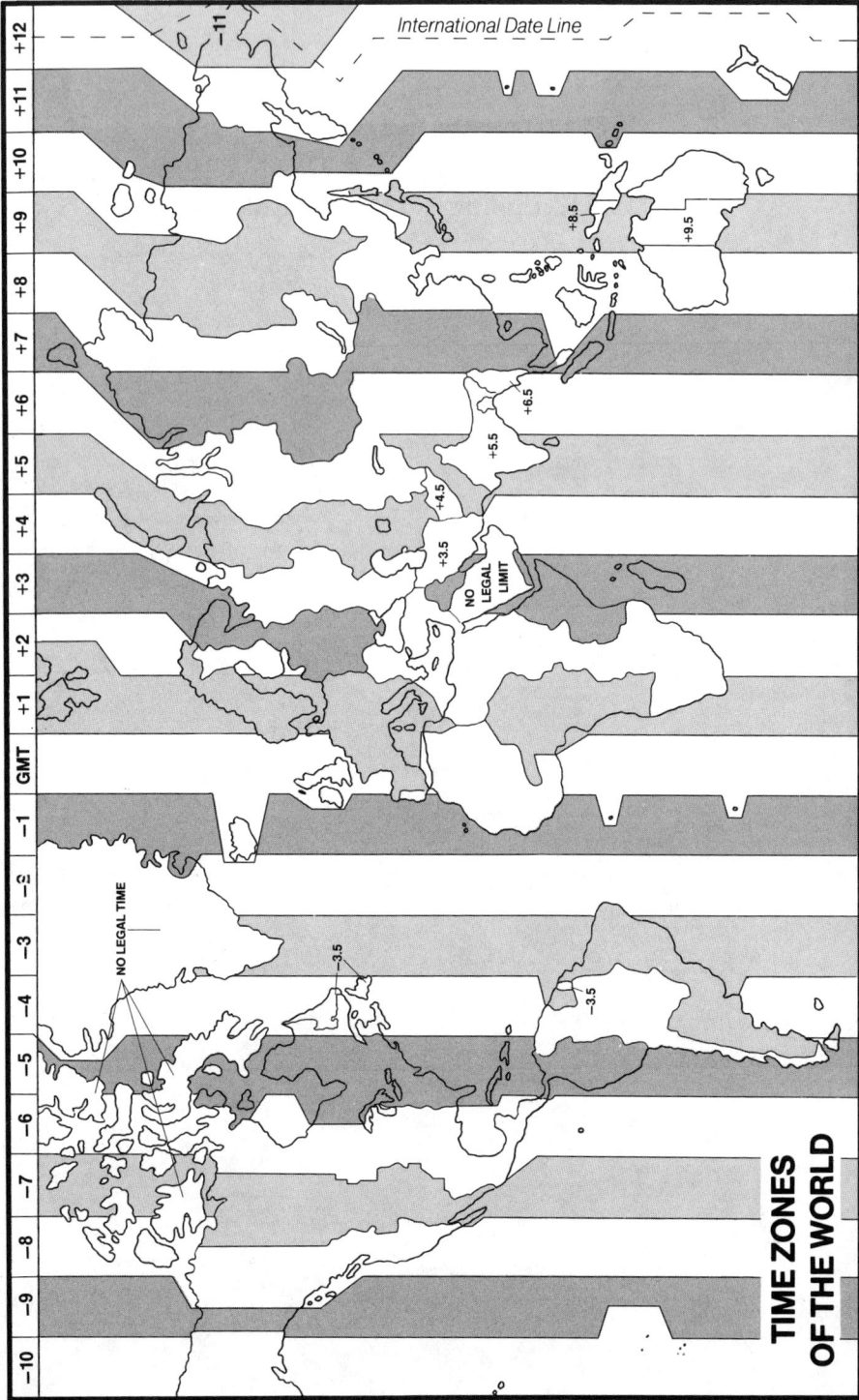

TIME ZONES
OF THE WORLD

International Date Line

NO LEGAL TIME

NO LEGAL LIMIT

+8.5
+9.5
+6.5
+5.5
+4.5
+3.5
-3.5
-3.5
-11

World Business Travel Guide

SP Travel Books
Toronto

© 1990 SP Travel Books

Published in North America by :
Summerhill Press Ltd.
52 Shaftesbury Avenue
Toronto, Ontario M4T 1A2

ISBN 0-929091-25-6

Editorial Contributors: David Densmore, Sandra Densmore, Judith Drynan, Mae Walker, Michael Miner, Doug McArthur, Linda Sharman, James Williamson.

Maps: Intercontinental Maps and Charts, Toronto

Distributed in Canada by:
University of Toronto Press
5201 Dufferin Street
Downsview, Ontario M3H 5T8

Distributed in the United States by:
Firefly Books
250 Sparks Avenue
Willowdale, Ontario M2H 2S4

Printed and bound in Canada

List of Advertisers

Table of Contents

Worldwide Business Travel Costs
International Flying Times
Passenger Aircraft Facts
World Currency and Exchange Rates
Worldwide Weather
Worldwide International Airports
International Telephone Codes
International Clothing Sizes
Metric Conversions
Foreign Language Vocabulary

Algeria	*Algiers (El Djazair)*
Egypt	*Cairo*
Israel	*Tel Aviv*
Kenya	*Nairobi*
Kuwait	
Morocco	*Casablanca*
Nigeria	*Lagos*
Saudi Arabia	*Riyadh*
South Africa	*Johannesberg*
Turkey	*Istanbul*
United Arab Emirates	*Dubai*

Australia	*Melbourne, Perth, Sydney*
China	*Bejing*
Hong Kong	
India	*Bombay, Dehli*
Indonesia	*Jakarta*
Japan	*Osaka, Tokyo*
Malaysia	*Kuala Lumpur*
New Zealand	*Aukland*
Pakistan	*Karachi*
Philippines	*Manila*
Singapore	
South Korea	*Seoul*

Taiwan	*Taipai*
Thailand	*Bangkok*

Austria	*Vienna*
Belgium	*Brussels*
Czechoslovakia	*Prague*
Denmark	*Copenhagen*
Finland	*Helsinki*
France	*Lyon, Paris*
Germany (West)	*Dusseldorf, Frankfurt,*
	Hamburg, Munich, West Berlin
Greece	*Athens*
Hungary	*Budapest*
Ireland	*Dublin*
Italy	*Milan, Rome*
Netherlands	*Amsterdam, Rotterdam*
Poland	*Warsaw*
Norway	*Oslo*
Portugal	*Lisbon*
Spain	*Barcelona, Madrid*
Sweden	*Stockholm*
Switzerland	*Geneva, Zurich*
USSR	*Moscow*
United Kingdom	*Birmingham, London,*
	Manchester
Yugoslavia	*Belgrade*

Argentina	*Buenos Aires*
Bolovia	*La Paz*
Brazil	*Rio di Janiero, Sao Paulo*
Canada	*Calgary, Edmonton, Ottawa,*
	Montreal, Toronto, Vancouver,
	Winnipeg
Chile	*Santiago*
Colombia	*Bogota*
Mexico	*Mexico City*
Peru	*Lima*
United States	*Atlanta, Boston, Chicago,*
	Cleveland, Dallas, Denver,
	Detroit, Houston, Los Angeles,
	Miami, Minneapolis, New Orleans
	New York, Philadelphia, Pittsburgh,
	St. Louis, San Francisco,
	Seattle, Washington D.C.
Venezuela	*Caracas*

Easy on
the long haul.

When business takes you halfway around the world, there's one airline that makes the trip easy.

United. Serving thirteen cities throughout Asia and the South Pacific from more of the U.S. than any other airline.

With service uniquely tailored to the special needs of the international business traveler including our exclusive First Class Concierge, great movies, great meals and generous Mileage Plus credit.

Rededicated to giving you the service you deserve. Come fly the friendly skies.

UNITED
A I R L I N E S

INTRODUCTION

Welcome to the second edition of the Uniglobe World Business Travel Guide. This updated edition includes new telephone numbers and addresses, current business data, and other changes that have occurred since the initial guide was published two years ago.

The basic format has remained unchanged. It has proven to be an easy-to-read and informative guide for business travellers and travel agents, and will continue to be the most comprehensive travel guide available for the business traveller.

How to Use the Guide

The World Business Travel Guide is organized in a logical manner which facilitates quick reference of any destination and any subject category.

The front chapters are articles of general information on currency exchange, airport and airline travel, health, and doing business in foreign cultures. The information is general but contains many pertinent points which every traveller should be aware of. In addition there are charts and graphs on flight times, airport information, currency, clothing sizes, metric conversions, and a foreign vocabulary guide for English, Spanish, French and German languages.

The country and city section is divided into four regions of the world: Africa/Middle East, Asia/Pacific, Europe, and North/South America. Each is separately tabbed for easy visual reference, and the countries and cities within are arranged alphabetically. The information is standardized so that once the system is understood, information can be retrieved very quickly.

The guide is written primarily for the English-speaking traveller who is a citizen of either the United States, Canada, Great Britain or a Commonwealth country. For this reason some of the categories give information only for these business travellers. Subject areas which require more explanation follow.

Visa Requirements

This section provides entry and exit requirements primarily for citizens of the United States, Canada, Great Britain and Commonwealth countries. Other travellers should consult the embassy or consulate of the country they intend to visit for visa or passport information.

Currency and Exchange

Because of the rapid fluctuations among world currencies, exchange rates should be obtained from daily sources such as the newspapers, or from currency exchange dealers such as Deak International. The currency and exchange chart in the *"Travellers Information"* section includes the latest exchange rates as this book went to press, and also blank spaces to update changes at later dates. In areas of the book where prices are quoted in $US, the change in rates should be taken into account, otherwise the prices are usually quoted in the currency of that country.

Addresses and Telephone Numbers
The information provided was as up-to-date as possible before this book went to press. However, moves and telephone number changes frequently occur and therefore some may not be valid in the future. These changes will be updated in future editions of this guide.

Business Data
The business data on GDP, trade, population, growth rates, etc., are acquired from govenment sources and are normally a year old, from 1988. Again, future editions will update this information.

Hotels
The hotels listed are not necessarily recommendations. Most travellers will have other sources for choosing hotels. For this reason the hotel listings are simply provided for address and telephone and do not include information on number of rooms, facilities, and prices.

The World Business Travel Guide is intended to provide as much information as any business traveller would ever need in a foreign country or city. However, it is not a substitute for good travel planning before departure. In this regard, each traveller should plan ahead, research the cities before going, and utilize the expertise of a good travel agent when booking airline, car rental and hotel reservations. That, along with the information in the guide will go a long way to ensuring that a business trip is as pleasant and trouble-free as possible.

The people at Uniglobe and the travel editors at SP Travel Books hope that you find this book useful in making your future business trips more enjoyable and profitable.

CURRENCY AND EXCHANGE

Reduce the hassles of dealing with unfamiliar currency on your next foreign business trip by taking action ahead of time.

Before leaving home, go to a currency exchange outlet in your home city and buy some of the money you'll be spending. Ask for a mixed packet including some bills of small denomination.

Take the peculiar looking currency and study it. Play games with it. Show it to your family. Get to know what each bill looks like and what each is worth in dollars. That way you won't get short-changed by the taxi driver going from the airport to your hotel.

Unfortunately, many business travellers wait until the airport to think about changing money. Keep in mind that airport locations often charge considerably more than the bank rate. They have to because rents are high. In addition, you might be delayed at the airline check-in and never make it to the exchange counter. Or you make it only to learn the currency you need is out of stock. Or just as bad, the smallest bill available is worth $35. That's an awfully big tip to hand to a bellboy.

There's a reason why airport exchange booths carry large bills. Much of their currency is purchased from arriving overseas visitors in exchange for dollars. Travellers usually bring large bills so that's what the airport booths have on hand to sell back to you.

You could have difficulty changing those large bills when you first arrive at your destination. For that reason many business travellers switch to Plan Two. They decide to wait until their arrival and use an airport bank or exchange booth at the other end. Now that you travel regularly you will know that that means more headaches. The booths are usually

outside the baggage claim area, leaving you with no local currency to tip a porter. Then you get to the bank and discover the line-up is 45 minutes long. The last thing you want to do—especially after an overnight flight, passport control and immigration checks—is face another line-up.

Even worse, you could arrive early in the morning, late at night or on a holiday and find the exchange counter closed. That can always make getting to your hotel tricky.

The smart traveller is the one who arrives with bills in assorted sizes and the knowledge of what each one is worth. Bring enough currency for the first two or three days ($50 to $100 a day, even if using credit cards) especially if arriving on a weekend or bank holiday.

But like all rules, this one has exceptions. Many Eastern Bloc and Third World countries prohibit the importation of their own currency or restrict the amount you can bring in. It may be possible to buy Russian roubles or Indian rupees at your local exchange house, but you could get in trouble bringing them with you. A reputable exchange dealer should warn you of the restrictions. If you're caught importing local currency in such a country, a number of things could happen. The money could be confiscated and returned as you leave, when it's no longer of any use. It might just be confiscated. Or, you might end up in jail. Don't take the risk. In countries with currency restrictions, grit your teeth and line-up at the airport bank when you get there.

For currency conversions after your arrival, your best bet is a bank. Hotels will accept your dollars, but since they don't deal with the bank every day, they usually charge you 5 to 10 per cent as protection against fluctuations. Keep in mind, however, that banking hours overseas are often shorter than at home. It's not unusual for foreign banks to close over lunchtime or to open only in the morning. If you are in meetings from 8:30 to 4:30 and the banks open from 8 to 10 and 2 to 4, you could have a problem.

How much money you bring along will depend on how much you plan to spend, on whether you are using a credit card and on whether any of your major expenses have been prepaid. Increasingly companies are asking travelling employees to use corporate charge cards whenever possible. When the bills come in, companies get detailed records of where their money was spent. However, if you have a company credit card which is billed to your home or if you use a personal credit card overseas, you could end up out of pocket. Charges are converted to dollars at the going rate on the day the bills reach your home city, not the rate on the day of purchase. Out-of-country bills can take weeks or sometimes months to reach you. If the dollar falls in the meantime, you'll be billed more than you expected. In addition, you may find service charges for foreign transactions added to your bill.

Using a credit card can also increase your costs in countries like Brazil which have an official exchange rate and a parallel grey market rate. All credit card transactions will be at the official rate but cash or traveller's cheques are often converted at the lower rate. In some countries credit card users can also leave themselves open to fraud. If a figure on a bill is altered after you sign it, it's hard to prove you were cheated when you're back home, thousands of miles away from the point of purchase.

Another way to cut down on the amount of cash to be carried is by paying some bills ahead of time. One way of doing this is with international travel vouchers which have been introduced in recent years by such companies as MasterCard, Visa and Citicorp Diners Club. The new vouchers are legal documents payable to a hotel or car rental firm, and can cover either the full bill or simply a deposit. If business travellers change plans and don't use all the services paid for, a refund will be transmitted through the booking travel agency. If you bring vouchers with you, guard them as carefully as your airline tickets. They are negotiable documents and someone else could use them.

But even with credit cards and travel vouchers, you'll still need some old-fashioned cash to pay for such things as taxis, and meals in the many excellent restaurants which don't accept plastic.

The best way to bring money with you is in the form of traveller's cheques. These are almost interchangeable with cash and have the advantage that they can be replaced if lost or stolen. And you'll save the most money by bringing traveller's cheques made out in the currency of the country you plan to visit. If you're off to Britain, bring traveller's cheques in pounds. For Germany bring marks. For Japan yen. Traveller's cheques are available in most major hard currencies.

The big advantage to local currency traveller's cheques is that they can be changed almost anywhere—in a store, a restaurant or taxi—with no service fee. Traveller's cheques in U.S. or Canadian funds may not be accepted outside of banks, hotels, exchange houses or branches of the issuing travel agency. If they are cashed, you could get a poor exchange rate and pay a steep fee to boot. In Europe, it's not unusual for banks to charge fees of more than $5 U.S. to cash a traveller's cheque in a foreign currency. Such charges are usually per transaction, not per cheque, so you could pay the same fee to cash one $20 traveller's cheque as for five worth $100 each.

If your trip covers a number of countries, you might bring some traveller's cheques in the currency of each country to be visited. Failing that, select the country with the strongest currency in the area—Germany or Switzerland for Europe, Japan or Hong Kong for the Orient.

Fall back on U.S. dollar traveller's cheques for Taiwan, Korea and countries in Eastern Europe or the Third World which have currency prohibitions or restrictions. The U.S. dollar is still the currency of international travel and countries with soft currencies are anxious to get their hands on it. Patriotic Canadians who insist on bringing cheques in Canadian rather than U.S. dollars may get fair rates in Western Europe. But in other parts of the world they could lose out. In many countries there is less demand for Canadian than U.S. dollars, and the exchange rate is based on how quickly the money can be resold. In countries like India or Burma, the rate for the Canadian dollar may change only once a month. If the Canadian dollar climbs in the meantime, the traveller won't get the benefit.

What about changing money on the black market? If you travel to the Third World, you'll no doubt be stopped by individuals on the street corner, at the airport or even in your hotel offering an exchange rate much better than the one at the bank. At the time of writing, Brazil's "parallel market" operates so openly that its rates are quoted in daily newspapers along with those for the official rate. But, a crackdown at any time could suddenly change the rules.

In most countries, if you know what you're doing and don't get caught, you can stretch your dollars by dealing on the street. But there are real risks. If it's your company's money you're spending, why bother?

First of all, if you aren't familiar with the local currency you could get swindled. You might end up with counterfeit bills or old currency which is no longer legal tender or which has been devalued. In many South American countries, currencies are devalued frequently with one new note equal to 1,000 old ones. Sometimes both are in circulation at the same time. Could you be sure of which notes you were getting in a fast transaction in a darkened alley?

Worse still, you could be jailed if the police catch you in the act. The person offering you the deal might be an enforcement officer setting you up. Penalties are severe in Eastern Europe, India and Burma. And a brush with authorities could ruin your reputation or even your career.

Keep in mind that there is always a difference between the buying and selling rate for currency. That's where banks or exchange houses make their profit. Even if there's no fluctuation, you'll lose out buying a currency one day and selling it back the next. The difference can be as little as 4 per cent on European currencies or 100 per cent or more on less requested currencies. You could spend $50 in Brazilian money one day and get only $20 selling it back the next.

If you are going off the beaten track or to countries with restrictions, it's advisable to end up with as little of the local currency as possible. Some countries refuse to change your money back into dollars. Some will change only a fixed amount and some will require you to produce official exchange receipts. Always hang on to your exchange receipts until you leave a country. In Eastern Europe you could be detained if you lose them. Bring along some $20 traveller's cheques to tide you through on the last day. If you end up with $4 or $5 worth of local currency you might as well spend it at the airport before you catch your flight home.

One final piece of advice. Take precautions that your money, traveller's cheques, documents and other valuables aren't stolen. Use the hotel safety deposit box and only carry with you what you really need. Women's swinging purses are prime targets for snatch-and-grab thieves who often operate from motorcycles. Don't walk in deserted areas of cities at night. Carry your cash in a money belt, shoulder holster or in your front pants pocket. And don't flaunt your wealth. Displaying an expensive watch, gold chains, and a bulging wallet in a poor nation could be asking for trouble.

AIR TRAVEL MADE EASY

Flying has become so commonplace for business travellers that advice on how to do it properly might seem unnecessary. Ironically, many frequent flyers still do all the wrong things, arriving at their destinations exhausted, uncomfortable and frazzled.

Perhaps they should listen to the advice of David Springbett, a Londoner who was dubbed the "fastest man in the atmosphere" a few years back by the British press. That was after he circled the globe by commercial air carriers in 44 hours and six minutes to win himself a spot in the *Guinness Book of World Records*.

While that trip was purely a stunt, Mr. Springbett was regularly crossing the Atlantic or flying to far-flung parts of the world almost on a weekly basis in his role as managing director of an insurance underwriting firm. He shared his travel tips with the press at the time, and all frequent flyers who want to arrive relaxed and refreshed should pay heed.

Start by flying the least fashionable flight, he recommended. The less crowded the plane, the more chance there is of getting a quiet seat by yourself. Before booking a flight, he said, he sometimes phoned an airline and asked if there would be difficulty getting six seats. If the answer was no he knew the plane was relatively empty.

Here are some of Mr. Springbett's other suggestions: Try and arrange for an empty seat beside you to allow privacy for sleeping or catching up on office work. Take only hand luggage whenever possible. Wear loose-fitting clothing and comfortable shoes because cabin pressure causes body swelling. Bring along an eye mask for sleeping, and drink plenty of water to avoid dehydration. For safety's sake watch the life jacket demonstration on every flight. About a dozen different types of life jackets are used around the world.

As for preventing jet lag, Mr. Springbett recommended avoiding all alcoholic beverages in the air and skipping the main course on airline meals. The stomach swells when off the ground and overeating only adds to the discomfort.

Of course, jet lag has given rise to a lot of other theories as well. Jet lag, caused by moving quickly through time zones, can last for up to seven days. Its symptoms include fatigue and disorientation, off-schedule bodily functions and loss of appetite. Scientists know that its effects are worse flying east than flying west. But jet lag continues to remain one of those mystery ailments like hiccups or warts. Everyone knows a remedy, but no one seems to have a definitive cure. Writer and television personality David Frost, who once crossed the Atlantic on a weekly basis, recommended adjusting your watch to the time of your destination city as soon as you get on an aircraft. That gets your mind adjusted to the realities of a different time zone. Former U.S. President Lyndon Johnson went to the other extreme. He kept his watch firmly on Washington time no matter where he went. That explains why his meeting with President Nguyen Van Thieu of South Vietnam, held in Guam, was scheduled for the middle of the night.

Another approach is described in the pocketbook *Overcoming Jet Lag* by Dr. Charles F. Ebret and Lynne Waller Scanlon which is based on 30 years of research with laboratory animals. The book describes a regimen of feasting and fasting on alternate days starting one to four days before the trip and continuing until the day of arrival with set types of food and activities at fixed times.

Ideally, one of the best ways to lessen the effects of jet lag is to schedule stopovers on a long flight. Unfortunately, that usually can't be done by a business traveller who must get to the Orient immediately. The next best approach is to get a good night's sleep before leaving and to take things as easy as possible in the air. Ask for a window seat so you can catch some sleep. Don't overeat and above all don't overdrink. Remember, two drinks in the air have the same effect as three or four at sea level. Don't smoke on an airplane and ask to sit in the no-smoking section. Breathing in smoke can only increase the effects of jet lag. Walking around the aircraft when permitted, or doing exercises in your seat will also help make you feel better.

Your flight experience starts the minute you leave for the airport, so anything you can do to ease the hassles of arriving at your seat is to the good. Phone ahead to make sure the flight is still leaving on time. There's nothing worse than getting to the airport and discovering the flight has been delayed two hours. Taking a taxi or limousine is less hectic than driving yourself. Arrive in lots of time to avoid panic. If you check in at the last minute, you may make the flight but your bag may not. A late arrival might also be "bumped" if the flight is oversold. Airlines say bumping is here to stay as long as there are no-shows—usually business travelers who make a number of bookings but show up for only one. Most North American airlines ask for volunteers if someone must be bumped, and since compensation is high there is usually no shortage of passengers willing to wait for the next flight. However, compensation is much lower or even non-existent in other parts of the world.

Select your seat and get your boarding pass at time of booking if it can be arranged. That way, if you travel with hand luggage you can avoid the line-ups at the check-in counter.

If you do check luggage, take precautions to lessen the chances of it being lost en route. Inspect your baggage claim check. If you suspect the three-letter airport code is not the one for the city you are headed to, tell the check-in person immediately. And make sure your name and address is on the inside of the bag as well as outside. Don't display your home address on your luggage tag. There's no point in advertising to would-be thieves that you are not at home. Instead use your work address and omit the company name.

Don't put your valuables in checked luggage. There's a limit on the amount of compensation you'll be paid if the bag is lost. And use your hand luggage for items you'll want in case your checked bag goes astray. High on the list should be your passport, medications, fresh socks and underwear. If your bag does get lost, report it immediately to the airline you arrived on and ask what daily compensation can be claimed for your expenses.

Still on the subject of luggage, inquire ahead of time about the rules if you have a connecting flight along the way. North American and western European airlines usually operate on the piece system which allows the traveller to bring along two bags with certain size and weight restrictions. Much of the rest of the world uses a weight system which allows any number of bags up to a set combined weight. Someone flying from North America to Africa via Europe could be well within the rules on the initial flight, but be stuck with a hefty excess baggage charge on the Europe-to-Africa segment.

Consider paying to join one of the membership clubs operated by most large North American airlines. Benefits vary from airline to airline, but they usually include use of the first or business class check-in counter, use of the carrier's private airport lounge—away from the milling throngs—and priority baggage treatment.

What class you fly will depend on your pocketbook or on your company's travel policy. If you have to ask the price you can't afford first class—unless you get upgraded through your frequent flyer program. First class offers roomy seating, gourmet meals, premium brand beverages and individual pampering. Best of all, many airlines now have first class sleeper seats on international flights. These allow passengers to stretch out and nod off in comfort. Business class, offering a separate quiet cabin with big seats, a choice of entrees and other extras, usually sells at a set percentage above the coach or economy fare.

The back of the plane—coach or economy class—usually means cramped seating and meals served on a tray. Coach or economy seats on any given flight sell at a variety of prices depending on the conditions attached to their sale. Vacationers

THE WORLD OF CANADIAN. THE ORIENT.

FAR MORE FLIGHTS TO THE FAR EAST THAN ANY OTHER AIRLINE.

We've introduced a new nonstop to Nagoya, new Alberta–Tokyo service and new Toronto–Tokyo nonstop service.* We'll be offering 24 flights weekly from Canada to the Orient this summer – 33% more than last year.

As well as local service between Tokyo and Hong Kong, we have excellent connections throughout the Far East. While we offer three classes – First Class, Canadian Business Class, and Canadian Class – we only have one standard of service. World-class.

The world of Canadian spans five continents, but it revolves around one person. You.

OUR WORLD REVOLVES AROUND YOU.

We are Canadi⟩n

*A joint venture with Japan Air Lines. Canadi⟩n is a registered trademark of Canadian Airlines International Ltd.
New services subject to government approval.

can take advantage of discount fares which often require booking ahead, staying a minimum number of days or being away over a Saturday night. Such fares are sometimes non-refundable if plans have to be changed. Since business travellers want to be home on weekends and need flexibility in their itineraries, the airlines would like to see them pay the full coach or economy fare. Increasingly, North American business travellers are planning their trips to fit the conditions of cheaper fares. The group which often gets hit with the full fare are those who must fly immediately to a funeral or to the bedside of a seriously ill friend or relative.

While long-distance international flights, and some flights within Canada, offer all three classes of service, long-distance flights within the United States have only first class and coach. And short flights most places in the world offer only coach or economy seating. First class on U.S. domestic flights is less luxurious than the overseas product.

While booking your airline seat, you might also consider ordering a special meal. Providing you ask in advance, you can opt for any of a range of meals prepared for those with dietary or religious requirements. Feel free to experiment, even if a special meal isn't a necessity. Often the special meals are better than those served the rest of the passengers. Options offered, depending on airline, can include low cholesterol, low calorie, hypoglycemic, infant, kosher, Muslim, low sodium, Hindu vegetarian, and non-vegetarian diabetic and gluten-free.

If you plan to sleep on the aircraft tell the flight attendant once you are seated. That way you won't be awakened for magazines, hot towels, duty-free bar sales, beverage carts and meals. If you want to read, bring along a battery-powered book light which you can buy in a travel specialty shop. Otherwise you may have difficulty seeing once the cabin lights are dimmed for sleep time or the movie. The best time to avoid line-ups at the washroom is often when everyone else is finishing their dessert just before the aisles get clogged by carts collecting dinner trays.

Most important, read the safety card in the seat pocket in front of you and listen intently to the safety demonstration. Know where the emergency exits are and how to open them. Being prepared can save your life.

Hertz has small rates for small vacations.

Affordable Weekends™

And small rates for big vacations.

Affordable Weekly™

With Hertz, you get a great low rate no matter how long you rent.

If you're getting away for just a few days, Hertz offers Affordable Weekend rates. No reservations required.

If you're staying away longer, we offer Affordable Weekly rates as well. To get these rates, just reserve your car in advance. And keep it 5, 6 or 7 days. Minimum rental period and other restrictions apply.

Hertz

Hertz rents Fords and other fine cars.

TRAVEL HEALTH TIPS

Mosquitos and unsafe drinking water are two of the greatest health hazards lurking in wait for the business traveller off to exotic locales.

Mosquitos can carry a host of deadly diseases, with malaria in particular becoming an increasing threat around the world. And all those armchair advisors who say "don't drink the water" are right on the mark for anyone straying away from the beaten track. An upset stomach or a case of "the runs" while trying to conduct business overseas can be inconvenient. With proper precautions, both can be avoided.

Only 20 years ago, health authorities were predicting that malaria would soon be on the list of conquered diseases. Instead, the microscopic animal which causes malaria is becoming resistant to drugs like chloraquine. And the *anopheles* mosquito—whose saliva can transmit the parasites into your bloodstream and thence to your liver—is becoming resistant to insecticides. Today the disease strikes hundreds of millions of people each year causing more than one million deaths in tropical Africa alone.

Symptoms, which can begin from 10 days to months after infection, include shaking, followed by a high fever, followed by profuse sweating and exhaustion. The deadly *falciparum malaria* can attack body systems causing anything from vomiting or coughing up blood to paralysis and death. Report any malaria symptoms to your doctor immediately along with details of where you've been. To reduce the risk of contracting malaria, take action well in advance of travel. If you are headed anywhere outside of the United States, Canada, Europe, Australia, Japan or Israel, check with the local infectious disease clinic or health department to find out if malaria pills are recommended. Give the specialists a complete itinerary as the risk of malaria often applies only to certain areas within a country. In some cases, major cities are safe, but a brief sidetrip into a rural area could be extremely hazardous. Just as important, find out which kind of malaria pills you need. A kind that works in one area of the world may be useless somewhere else. And don't wait until the last minute. To be effective, malaria pills must be started two weeks in advance of a trip, taken while you are away and continued for six to eight weeks after you return home. Pregnant women should seek a physician's advice before taking malaria pills.

Remember, even malaria pills aren't 100 per cent effective. When in high risk areas, sleep under mosquito netting and use insect repellent. After sunset wear long sleeves and long trousers and stay indoors when possible.

While you are checking with health authorities, find out what other shots are required or recommended. Under World

Health Organization regulations, vaccinations are mandatory for travel to many destinations and travellers to these areas are required to carry an International Certificate of Vaccination booklet. Whether shots are required can depend on what other countries are being visited on the way. Make inquiries— spelling out your full itinerary—a month ahead where possible to allow time in case a number of shots are required. Some inoculations, such as diptheria, polio and tetanus are often recommended by medical authorities even if not required.

Any business traveller with a chronic disease, such as cardiac problems, hypertension or gastric ulcers should get a thorough medical examination well in advance of travel.

Don't be embarrassed to bring along a medical kit with over-the-counter remedies similar to ones you stock at home. You might include something for motion sickness, indigestion and diarrhea plus a laxative, sun screen, antihistamines and analgesics. If you use glasses or contact lenses, bring an extra pair and a copy of the prescription. Make sure you have an adequate supply of any prescription drugs you are taking, plus written details from your doctor on the drugs, your treatment and your medical history. Keep medication in your hand luggage in case your checked bag goes astray.

Watch what you eat in tropical countries. Fruit is fine, provided you peel it or see it peeled in front of you by someone with clean hands. Eat only cooked vegetables and avoid ice cream and milk (which are likely unpasteurized and may contain untreated water), green salads (vegetables may be fertilized with "night soil"), and uncooked shellfish and prawns. Steering clear of highly-spiced foods and sticking as closely as possible to your normal diet can help avoid intestinal problems and traveller's diarrhea.

Always keep in mind that water in most tropical countries is inadequately treated and can be infected by sewage. Drinking it can expose your system to any number of diseasecausing organisms. Stick to mineral water, beer or soft drinks which have been professionally bottled and sealed, and are then opened in front of you. Don't trust jugs of water left in your room, even in a good hotel; if the maid has a busy day she might save time by refilling the vessel from the tap. And ask for all drinks without ice—too many travellers forget that the ice in their Scotch is made from the same tap water they are otherwise avoiding.

Tea and coffee are safe to drink because boiling water kills infectious agents. You can even sterilize water yourself using an immersion heater which can be purchased in a travel specialty shop. But make sure you use boiling water to wash the container which will hold the sterile water.

Not only is water unsafe to drink in many tropical countries, it is also unsafe for swimming. Salt water beaches are fine, but fresh-water lakes and rivers in much of South America, Asia, the Caribbean and Africa contain minute snails which can cause deadly bilharziasis or schistosomiasis. Also avoid walking barefoot in tropical countries except on ocean beaches as parasites can enter your body through your feet. After visits to some exotic and tropical locales it is advisable to get a checkup at a tropical diseases clinic. Some parasitic infections and diseases may have no obvious symptoms in the early stages when treatment is most effective.

Travellers heading from a North American winter to a hot climate should take precautions against dehydration. Limit activity and increase the intake of salt and fluids. Also reduce activity to prevent headache, dizziness and nausea if business takes you to high-altitude cities such as Mexico City or La Paz.

If you do fall sick in a foreign land, you should seek treatment from a doctor who speaks English, and who is familiar with the medical standards and practices you are used to at home. To find one in case of an emergency, take out a membership ahead of time in the International Association for Medical Assistance to Travelers (IAMAT). The inspiration to start the organization came from Dr. Vincenzo Marcolongo, a physician who was called to treat a Toronto woman who fell sick in Rome after taking an unfamiliar pain killer in 1960. The medication was one which can destroy the white blood cells of Anglo-Saxons and Scandinavians although it has no effect on Latins. The doctor recognized the cause of the illness and saved her life. He also realized that something had to be done to coordinate medical services throughout the world so that North Americans travelling abroad could have the same medical treatment as is available at home.

Today about a quarter-million travellers a year take out memberships in IAMAT. There is no charge for individuals, but tax-deductible donations are suggested for corporations signing up a number of employees.

Members get publications on immunization, malaria, schistosomiasis and world climates. In addition they get a booklet with IAMAT addresses and phone numbers in more than 100 countries. These local offices provide lists of approved doctors who can speak English or another language and who adhere to an approved fee schedule. Rates are $20 U.S. for office visits, $30 for house or hotel calls and $40 for night and holiday calls. Special services cost extra.

For information contact IAMAT at 188 Nicklin Road, Guelph, Ont., Canada N1H 7L5, or at 417 Center Street, Lewiston, N.Y. 14092. There are also membership offices in Zug, Switzerland and Christchurch, New Zealand.

Another must for anyone travelling abroad is health insurance. And just because you are travelling on company business don't assume your company has you covered. Before you leave get details of your company insurance plans, the company's pension plan and any private insurance policies held. Know exactly what protection would be provided in case of death, accident or illness while away. For example, would your company insurance pay for the return of a body? Would it pay for a family member to fly to your bedside if you become hospitalized abroad? Would it pay for you to be flown home by air ambulance with an attendant nurse? Then assess your needs, and your family's, in case of an emergency. If the existing policies are not adequate, additional trip insurance should be purchased either on a one-time or annual basis. Most travel insurance firms provide flight insurance, 24-hour accident insurance and supplementary medical and health coverage.

DOING BUSINESS ABROAD

Doing business outside of the United States and Canada presents a whole new set of problems for the business traveller.

Often there is a different language to contend with, different cultural values, different rules of social etiquette and different ways of doing business. As well, international corporate travellers must learn to find their way around strange cities and get accustomed to using unfamiliar currencies. They may also have to cope with inefficient telephone systems and the lack of office backup services taken for granted back home.

Doing homework is essential. Jumping on an airplane on a whim and trying to set up appointments on your arrival can be dangerous. In many parts of the world business grinds to a halt for weeks at a time. In Brazil most business people take holidays between Christmas and the annual pre-Lenten Carnival. In France, August is universal vacation month. In Moslem countries avoid the 30-day Ramadan fast period whose dates fluctuate from year to year.

Once you have established the best time to go, try and arrange approximate appointment times by writing in advance. Then phone on arrival to fix exact times for the meetings. Seek help in advance from your own government's trade department or from your embassies, consulates or trade missions overseas. In some cases government trade officials will suggest contacts, set up appointments and help arrange for a translator. They are also a prime source of information on local business conditions and economic prospects.

Other helpful sources are the trade offices of the countries you plan to visit. Governments anxious to sell their products to your firm will go out of their way to help with your trip arrangements. As well, many tourist boards, international airlines and hotel chains publish books filled with tips and background information on business practices and etiquette in specific countries. Other sources of advance information are companies already active in the area, international banks and law firms, trade magazines and universities.

The hotel you select to stay in may be dictated by company policy, by the size of your travel budget or by personal preference. In large cities with congested traffic it's best to stay close to the site of the majority of your appointments. Some security consultants are advising important VIPs to avoid American chain hotels overseas as an anti-terrorist measure. However, unless you speak the local language, you should choose a hotel with English speaking staff. You may also want a hotel with a business center which can provide secretarial, translation, photocopying and telex facilities. Keep in mind that many overseas hotels do not provide direct-dial telephones in the room, so you may be placing all your calls through the hotel operator.

Also be prepared for high service charges on phone calls placed from hotel rooms. Surcharges of 250 to 300 per cent are common overseas, particularly in Europe. It's not unusual for a business traveller to pay more on check-out for the phone bill than for the room. To avoid those unexpected costs, hotel guests have several choices. They can stay off the phone—not practical for someone on business. They can dial direct, call collect or use a credit card, if the hotel permits. They can place calls from a public telephone and telegraph building, where standard rates apply. Or they can stay at a hotel which participates in Teleplan, a fixed-cost program established by AT&T Communications. New Jersey-based AT&T runs ads promoting those hotels which have agreed to keep their phone surcharges below a fixed amount.

For important business meetings in a foreign language, bring your own interpreter—properly briefed in advance— who can verify what is being said and often add information.

The etiquette of doing business overseas is the most crucial skill to be mastered. The rules will vary from society to society. Nonetheless, some standard dictums apply. Respect the local customs. Take an interest in the culture. Be sensitive to the feelings of others. Don't boast about how you do things at home. The North American way may be different, but that doesn't make it better.

Avoid subjects which could be controversial such as the status of women, government corruption or religion. Don't take bribes and don't get involved in the black market. Adjust to the local time frame. Don't be impatient in countries where decision making can be a slow process. But also remember that in northern Europe you will be expected to arrive on time.

If you're planning serious negotiations in a country, take language lessons before setting out. English is the international language of business, but you'll win points for trying if you at least pick up a few key words. And a more thorough knowledge of the language could help you win out over the competition.

Business cards printed with the local language on the reverse side are a must in Japan and the Arab world, and a courtesy anywhere. If in doubt about what to wear, dress conservatively—a dark suit and tie for men, dress, skirt-suit or skirt, blouse and sweater for women. And be yourself. Trying to dress like the locals may make you look ridiculous. Also keep in mind that in much of the world first names are reserved for close friends and family.

In each place you travel you will find local customs, local social taboos and local concepts of what is polite and impolite. These vary between areas of the world, between countries

and sometimes even within countries. Find out ahead what is
socially acceptable and what is considered downright rude.

In the Moslem Middle East, keep your legs uncrossed; it is
impolite to make the sole of your shoe visible. Use your
right hand to accept anything handed to you or to pass something to someone else; the left hand is considered unclean.
Accept coffee if offered, and never offer alcohol or pork to a
Muslim. Women should avoid revealing clothing.

In Japan, avoid personal contact beyond an initial hand-
shake. Patting someone on the back or squeezing his arms just
isn't done. Expect to be entertained by business contacts at
a restaurant and nightclubs at night. North American busi-
nesswomen will be invited along, but if you are entertaining,
don't ask a Japanese businessman to bring his wife.

At a Chinese banquet, never take the last morsel from a
communal platter. That tells your host there wasn't enough
food. The host will make the first toast, then one should
be made by the guest of honor. Dinner guests should make
the first move to depart after the meal and should invite
the hosts to a return dinner.

Similar do's and don'ts apply wherever you go, so learn the
guidelines. Even a simple thing like bringing flowers if you
are invited to dinner can have its own protocol. Tradition in
Europe calls for flowers to be odd in number. And don't
bring red roses in Germany. That could indicate you are in
love with the wife of your host.

TRAVELER'S INFORMATION

Diners Club Can Open Doors Around The World.

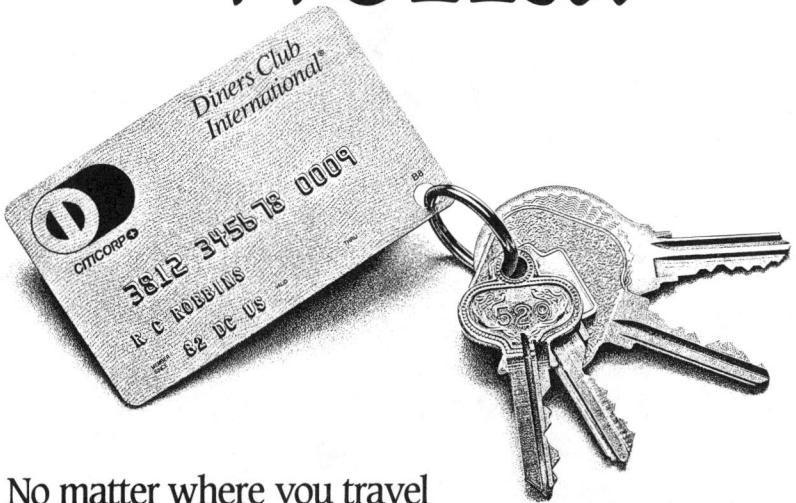

No matter where you travel
on business, carry the Diners Club Card.
And you'll carry the key to a world of doors.

WORLDWIDE BUSINESS TRAVEL COSTS

City, Country	Deluxe Hotel 1 Night/Single U.S. $	Deluxe Dinner One Person U.S. $	City Taxi Two Miles U.S. $
Abu Dhabi Dubai, UAE	160.00	75.00	7.00
Amsterdam, Netherlands	155.00	70.00	9.00
Athens, Greece	150.00	50.00	6.00
Auckland, New Zealand	160.00	80.00	10.00
Bangkok, Thailand	130.00	45.00	7.00
Beijing, China	145.00	45.00	5.00
Bombay, India	100.00	35.00	5.00
Buenos Aires, Argentina	160.00	50.00	8.00
Cairo, Egypt	90.00	55.00	7.00
Caracas, Venezuela	125.00	40.00	10.00
Copenhagen, Denmark	180.00	80.00	12.00
Frankfurt, Germany (Fed. Rep.)	175.00	75.00	10.00
Helsinki, Finland	160.00	80.00	15.00
Hong Kong, HK	170.00	90.00	10.00
Istanbul, Turkey	130.00	50.00	8.00
Jakarta, Indonesia	130.00	60.00	6.00
Jeddah, Saudi Arabia	150.00	55.00	8.00
Karachi, Pakistan	100.00	50.00	6.00
Kuala Lumpur, Malaysia	95.00	50.00	5.00
Kuwait City, Kuwait	95.00	50.00	5.00
Lagos, Nigeria	120.00	50.00	7.00
Lisbon, Portugal	125.00	55.00	6.00
London, UK	250.00	110.00	15.00
Madrid, Spain	160.00	80.00	10.00
Manila, Phillipines	100.00	50.00	7.00
Mexico City, Mexico	105.00	70.00	8.00
Moscow, USSR	150.00	60.00	8.00
Nairobi, Kenya	95.00	50.00	8.00
New York, N.Y.	210.00	90.00	14.00
Oslo, Norway	190.00	90.00	15.00
Paris, France	200.00	110.00	14.00
Rio de Janeiro, Brazil	160.00	60.00	9.00
Rome, Italy	180.00	80.00	9.00
Santiago, Chile	120.00	55.00	8.00
Seoul, Korea	180.00	100.00	10.00
Singapore, Singapore	140.00	70.00	8.00
Stockholm, Sweden	190.00	80.00	14.00
Sydney, Australia	170.00	85.00	8.00
Taipai, Taiwan	165.00	90.00	10.00
Tel Aviv, Israel	130.00	60.00	8.00
Tokyo, Japan	260.00	140.00	20.00
Toronto, Canada	160.00	70.00	10.00
Vienna, Austria	170.00	80.00	12.00
Zurich, Switzerland	180.00	85.00	15.00

INTERNATIONAL FLYING TIMES

	Amsterdam	Bangkok	Buenos Aires	Cairo	Delhi	Frankfurt	Geneva	Hong Kong	Johannesburg
Amsterdam	—	15	18	5	10	1	1	18	14
Bangkok	17	—	25	12	4	14	15	3	16
Buenos Aires	17	25	—	20	28	17	17	34	15
Cairo	5	11	19	—	7	5	5	14	11
Delhi	13	4	28	8	—	9	9	7	15
Frankfurt	1	13	9	5	9	—	1	17	14
Geneva	1	16	9	5	9	1	—	17	14
Hong Kong	17	3	34	15	7	18	18	—	16
Johannesburg	15	15	15	10	14	14	14	15	—
Karachi	11	5	26	6	2	9	9	7	10½
London	1	15	18	5	11	2	2	15	13
Manila	20	3	38	15	8	19	19	2	21
Moscow	4	13	25	15	6	3	3	15	15
New York	7	25	15	14	19	9	9	22	16
Paris	1	15	18	5	10	1	1	18	13
Rio de Janeiro	13	23	4	14	25	13	13	30	9
Rome	3	13	16	3	9	2	2	15	13
San Francisco	13	18	16	19	19	14	14	15	19
Sydney	25	12	24	25	15	26	26	9	21
Tokyo	20	8	26	20	12	21	21	5	18
Toronto	7	24	16	14	19	8	8	22	17

Note: Approximate flying times. Some airline connections may provide faster services.

Karachi	London	Manila	Moscow	New York	Paris	Rio de Janeiro	Rome	San Francisco	Sydney	Tokyo	Toronto
11	1	19	3	7	1	13	2	13	24	20	7
5	16	4	13	26	16	24	14	18	11	7	24
25	17	36	24	14	16	3½	15	16	25	26	16
6	5½	15	4½	15	5	15	4	19	24	20	14
2	13	8	8½	22	11	26	10½	19	15	11	19
9	1	19	3	9	1	14	2	14	24	20	8
9	1	19	3	9	1	14	2	14	24	20	8
7	17	2	16	20	19	32	16	15	9	4	22
10	14	21	15	17	14	10	13½	18	16	21	17
—	11	10	6	22	11	16	10	18	15	12	20
10	—	19	3	7	1	13	2½	13	24	20	6
10	20	—	17	21	21	35	17	17	8	4	24
6	4	16	—	10	4	18	4	15	25	10	9
20	6	24	9	—	6	10	8	6	25	16	1
11	1	9½	4	7	—	12	2	13	26	17	7
14	12	34	17	9	11	—	12	16	28	31	10
10	3	17	4	9	2	13	—	14	25	20	8
18	13	17	15	6	13	10	14	—	18	12	6
14	25	8	24	21	28	28	26	18	—	9	25
13	20	5	10	14	17	26	21	12	9	—	16
20	6	24	9	1	7	10	8	6	25	16	—

PASSENGER AIRCRAFT FACTS

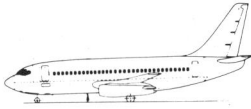

B-737

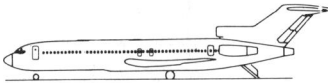

B-727

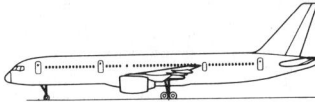

B-757

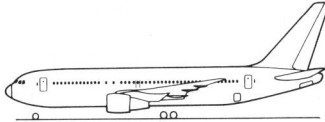

B-767

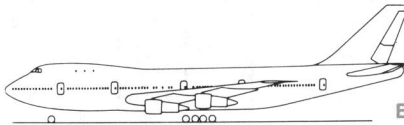

B-747

BOEING	Advanced B-737	Advanced B-727-200	Basic B-757-200	Basic B-767-200	B-747-200B	B-747SP
Fuselage length	100'2"	153'2"	155'3"	159'2"	231'10"	184'9"
Wing span	93'	108'	124'6"	156'1"	195'8"	195'8"
Number of engines	2	3	2	2	4	4
Max. gross takeoff weight (pounds)	128,100	209,500	220,000	315,000	785,000	630,000
Passenger capacity (seats)	115	189	178	218	496	352
Payload (pounds)	30,400	42,500	54,940	68,918	147,440	85,980
Cruise speed (mph)	480	550	525	525	550	565
Range (statute miles)	2,130	2,800	2,865	4,100	5,500-6,500	6,000-6,900

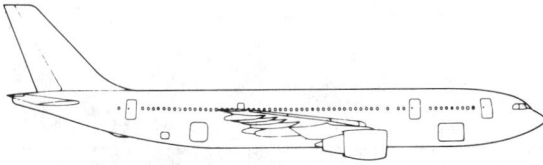

A300

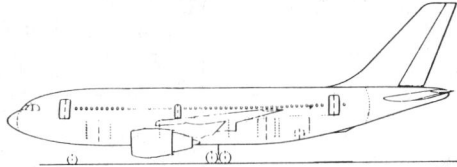

A310

AIRBUS	A300 B2-200	A300 B4-200	A300-600	A310-200	A310-300
Fuselage length	175'11"	175'11"	177'5"	153'1"	153'1"
Wing span	147'1"	147'1"	147'1"	144'	144'
Number of engines	2	2	2	2	2
Max. gross takeoff weight (pounds)	313,000	363,800	363,800	313,050	337,300
Passenger capacity (seats)	220-345	220-345	220-345	210-265	200-280
Payload (pounds)	74,800	82,000	94,600	77,060	80,250
Cruise speed (mph)	520-550	520-550	520-550	520-550	520-550
Range (statute miles)	1,900	3,200	3,800	4,380	5,300

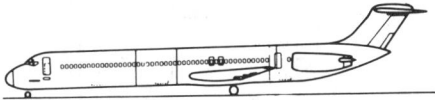

DC-9

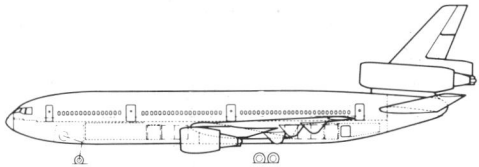

DC-10

McDonnell Douglas	DC-9-20	DC-9-30	DC-9-40	DC-9-50	Super 80	DC-10-30	DC-10-40
Fuselage length	104'5"	119'4"	125'7"	133'7"	147'10"	181'7"	180'7"
Wing span	93'4"	93'4"	93'4"	93'4"	107'10"	165'4"	165'4"
Number of engines	2	2	2	2	2	3	3
Max. gross takeoff weight (pounds)	90,700	108,000	114,000	121,000	140,000	572,000	572,000
Passenger capacity (seats)	90	119	132	139	172	255-380	255-380
Payload (pounds)	20,850	24,000	27,925	32,615	41,000	106,541	101,935
Cruise speed (mph)	560	560	560	560	580	600	600
Range (statute miles)	1,584	1,368	1,674	1,044	2,053	6,600	6,500

WORLD CURRENCY AND EXCHANGE RATES

	Country	Monetary Unit	Value per US$	Rate Updates Date/Rate		
North/South America	Argentina	Austral	196.0			
	Brazil	Cuzeiro	1.35			
	Canada	Dollar	1.21			
	Chile	Peso	255.0			
	Colombia	Peso	371.0			
	Costa Rica	Colon	80.5			
	Mexico	Peso	2467.0			
	Peru	Inti	3250.0			
	United States	Dollar	1.00			
	Venezuela	Bolivar	38.6			
Asia/Pacific	Australia	Dollar	1.32			
	China	Yuan	3.72			
	Hong Kong	Dollar	7.78			
	India	Rupee	16.5			
	Indonesia	Rupiah	1773.0			
	Japan	Yen	141.0			
	Korea (South)	Won	662.0			
	Malaysia	Ringgit	2.71			
	New Zealand	Dollar	1.75			
	Pakistan	Rupee	20.9			
	Phillipines	Peso	21.6			
	Singapore	Dollar	1.96			
	Taiwan	Dollar	26.2			
	Thailand	Baht	25.9			
Europe	Austria	Schilling	14.0			
	Belgium	Franc	41.8			
	Czechoslovakia	Koruna	10.4			
	Denmark	Krone	7.75			
	Finland	Markka	4.44			
	France	Franc	6.76			

TRAVELLER'S INFORMATION

	Country	Monetary Unit	Value per US$	Rate Updates Date/Rate		
Europe	Germany (East)	Mark	1.99			
	German (West)	Deutsche Mark	1.99			
	Greece	Drachma	171.0			
	Hungary	Forint	64.1			
	Ireland	Punt	0.75			
	Italy	Lira	1445.0			
	Netherlands	Guilder	2.24			
	Norway	Kroner	7.22			
	Poland	Zloty	868.0			
	Portugal	Escudo	166.2			
	Romania	Leu	9.68			
	Spain	Peseta	128.2			
	Sweden	Krona	6.71			
	Switzerland	Franc	1.72			
	USSR	Rouble	0.66			
	United Kingdom	Pound	0.65			
	Yugoslavia	Dinar	$568.5			
Africa/Middle East	Algeria	Dinar	7.62			
	Egypt	Pound	2.49			
	Israel	Schekel	1.94			
	Jordan	Dinar	0.57			
	Kenya	Shilling	21.4			
	Kuwait	Dinar	0.29			
	Morocco	Dirham	8.70			
	Nigeria	Naira	7.40			
	Saudi Arabia	Riyal	3.75			
	South Africa	Rand	2.81			
	Turkey	Lira	2136.2			
	United Arab Emirates	Dirham	3.67			

WORLDWIDE WEATHER

City	Average Hi/Lo Temp (°F)				Dry Months	Wet Months
	January	April	July	October		
Amsterdam	39/34	52/43	70/59	55/48	Feb/Apr	Aug/Oct
Anchorage	20/5	44/27	65/50	42/28	Jan/June	July/Oct
Athens	54/43	66/52	90/72	73/61	June/Sept	Nov/Jan
Atlanta	51/33	71/50	86/69	72/52	Aug/Nov	Jan/July
Auckland	73/59	66/55	57/46	63/52	Dec/Mar	May/Aug
Bangkok	90/68	95/77	90/75	88/75	Dec/Feb	May/Oct
Beijing	34/16	68/45	90/70	68/43	Oct/Mar	July/Aug
Belgrade	37/27	64/45	82/63	64/46	Jan/Mar	May/June
Berlin	35/26	55/39	74/56	55/42	May/June	Nov/Mar
Bombay	82/66	90/75	84/77	90/75	Dec/Apr	June/Sept
Boston	36/19	54/37	81/63	63/46	May/Oct	Nov/Mar
Brussels	39/30	57/41	73/54	59/45	February	July/Jan
Budapest	34/25	63/43	82/61	61/45	September	July
Buenos Aires	84/63	72/54	57/43	72/43	Jan/May	Aug/Nov
Cairo	64/46	82/57	97/70	86/64	Jan/Dec	—
Calgary	24/2	53/27	76/47	54/29	Nov/Dec	May/Aug
Caracas	75/65	78/68	79/70	76/68	Jan/Apr	June/Sept
Casablanca	63/45	70/52	79/64	75/57	May/Sept	Nov/Mar
Chicago	32/18	55/39	81/66	61/46	July/Oct	Feb/June
Dallas	55/35	76/54	95/74	79/56	July/Aug	Apr/May
Dubai	61/48	82/68	102/86	91/73	Jan/Dec	—
Frankfurt	37/28	61/43	77/59	57/45	Feb/Apr	June/Aug
Hong Kong	64/55	75/66	88/79	81/73	Nov/Jan	May/Sept
Honolulu	76/69	78/68	82/73	82/72	Feb/Mar	July/Dec
Istanbul	46/37	61/45	82/64	68/55	July/Aug	Dec/Feb
Jakarta	84/74	87/75	87/73	87/74	—	Jan/Dec
Jeddah	84/66	91/70	99/79	95/73	Jan/Dec	—
Johannesburg	79/57	72/50	63/39	77/54	May/Sept	Nov/Mar
Karachi	77/55	84/73	91/81	91/72	Oct/May	July/Aug
Kuala Lumpur	90/72	91/73	90/73	90/73	July	Sept/Apr
Kuwait	61/48	82/68	102/86	91/73	Jan/Dec	—
Lagos	88/74	89/77	83/74	85/74	Nov/Mar	May/July
Lima	82/66	80/63	67/57	71/58	Jan/Dec	—

City	Average Hi/Lo Temp (°F)				Dry Months	Wet Months
	January	April	July	October		
Lisbon	57/46	68/54	81/63	72/57	June/Aug	Nov/Mar
London	43/36	55/41	72/55	57/46	Feb/May	Oct/Dec
Los Angeles	64/46	70/52	81/59	77/55	July/Nov	February
Madrid	48/36	64/45	93/63	66/50	July/Aug	Oct/Nov
Manila	86/70	93/73	88/75	88/73	Nov/May	June/Oct
Mexico City	66/42	77/51	73/53	70/50	Nov/Mar	June/Sept
Miami	75/58	82/62	89/75	84/71	Feb/Apr	June/Oct
Milan	39/28	66/46	84/64	64/48	July/Aug	February
Montreal	21/7	50/34	79/61	54/39	April	July/Dec
Moscow	21/9	46/30	75/55	46/34	Feb/Mar	May/Oct
Nairobi	77/54	75/57	70/52	75/55	July/Sept	Mar-May/Nov
New York	37/25	57/43	82/66	64/48	Oct/Feb	July/Aug
Paris	43/34	59/43	77/59	59/46	June/Aug	Nov/Jan
Perth	84/63	75/57	63/48	70/54	Dec/Mar	June/Aug
Prague	34/27	54/39	73/57	54/43	Aug/Jan	June/July
Rio de Janeiro	84/73	81/70	75/63	77/66	June/Sept	Oct/Feb
Riyadh	84/66	91/70	99/79	95/73	Jan/Dec	—
Rome	52/41	66/50	86/68	72/55	July/Aug	Oct/Jan
San Francisco	55/39	63/45	70/52	70/48	June/Sept	Dec/Mar
Seattle	43/33	57/40	73/53	59/44	July/Aug	Nov/Jan
Seoul	32/16	63/41	84/70	66/45	Jan/Mar	July/Aug
Singapore	86/73	88/75	88/75	88/73	May/July	Nov/Jan
Stockholm	30/23	46/34	72/57	48/41	Mar/May	Aug/Dec
Sydney	79/64	72/57	61/46	72/55	July/Sept	Mar/May
Taipei	65/58	75/67	90/80	80/71	Feb/Apr	Oct/Jan
Tel Aviv	64/48	73/50	86/70	82/63	Apr/Sept	Dec/Jan
Tokyo	46/28	63/46	82/70	70/55	Dec/Jan	June/Oct
Toronto	30/16	50/34	79/59	56/40	July/Aug	Nov/Jan
Vancouver	41/32	58/40	74/54	57/44	July/Sept	Nov/Jan
Vienna	34/25	59/41	79/59	59/45	Oct/Mar	May/Sept
Warsaw	30/23	54/37	75/59	55/41	Sept/Nov	Jan/Apr
Washington	43/27	67/45	88/69	69/49	September	May-July/Dec
Zurich	36/27	59/34	77/57	57/43	Jan/Feb	May/Aug

WORLDWIDE INTERNATIONAL AIRPORTS

Country: City	Airport	Code	City Distance (miles)
ALGERIA: Algiers	Hovari Boumedienne Intl.	ALG	12
ARGENTINA: Buenos Aires	Ezeiza Intl.	EZE	31
AUSTRALIA: Melbourne	Tullamarine	MEL	14
Perth	Perth Intl.	PER	8
Sydney	Kingsford Smith Intl.	SYD	7
AUSTRIA: Vienna	Schwechat	VIE	11
BAHRAIN: Bahrain	Muharraq	BAH	4
BANGLADESH: Dacca	Zia Intl.	DAC	13
BELGIUM: Brussels	Brussels National	BRU	8
BRAZIL: Rio de Janeiro	Galeao Intl.	GIG	12
CANADA: Calgary	Calgary Intl.	YYC	5
Edmonton	Edmonton Intl.	YEG	17
Montreal	Mirabel	YMX	33
Toronto	Toronto Intl.	YYZ	18
Vancouver	Vancouver Intl.	YVR	11
CHILE: Santiago	Arturo Merino Benitez	SCL	10
CHINA: Peking (Beijing)	Capital	PEK	14
Shanghai	Hung' Chiao	SHA	7
COLOMBIA: Bogota	El Dorado	BOG	7
CYPRUS: Larnaca	Larnaca	LCA	5
CZECHOSLOVAKIA: Prague	Ruzyne	PRG	10
DENMARK: Copenhagen	Kastrup	CPH	5
EGYPT: Cairo	Cairo Intl.	CAI	15
FINLAND: Helsinki	Vantaa	HEL	11
FRANCE: Lyon	Satolas	LYS	16
Marseille	Marignane	MRS	17
Paris	Orly	OLY	10
Paris	Roissy Charles de Gaulle	CDG	16
GERMANY, EAST: Berlin	Schonefeld	SXF	12
GERMANY, WEST: Berlin	Tegei	TXL	5
Cologne	Cologne-Bonn	CGN	12
Dusseldorf	Dusseldorf	DUS	6
Frankfurt	Frankfurt	FRA	6
Hamburg	Fuhlsbutte	HAM	8
Munich	Riern	MUC	6
GREECE: Athens	Hellenikon	ATH	8
HONG KONG: Hong Kong	Kai Tak	HKG	5
HUNGARY: Budapest	Ferihegy	BUD	9
ICELAND: Reykjavik	Keflavik Intl.	REK	37
INDIA: Bombay	Bombay	BOM	23
Calcutta	Calcutta	CCU	7
Delhi	Delhi Intl.	DEL	9
INDONESIA: Jakarta	Halim Intl.	JKT	9
IRAQ: Baghdad	Baghdad Intl.	BGW	18
ISRAEL: Tel Aviv	Ben Gurion Intl.	TLV	12
IRELAND: Dublin	Dublin	DUB	6
Shannon	Shannon	SNN	15
ITALY: Milan	Linate	LIN	5
Rome	Fiumicino	FCO	22
JAPAN: Osaka	Itami	OSA	10
Tokyo	Narita	TYO	41
JORDAN: Amman	Amman	AMM	4
KENYA: Nairobi	Jomo Kenyatta Intl.	NBO	9
KOREA, SO: Seoul	Kimpo Intl.	SEL	16
KUWAIT: Kuwait	Kuwait	KWI	12
LUXEMBOURG: Luxembourg	Findel	LUX	4
MALAYSIA: Kuala Lumpur	Subang	KUL	14
MEXICO: Mexico City	Benito Juarez Intl.	MEX	5
MOROCCO: Casablanca	Nouasseur	CMN	19

Country: City	Airport	Code	City Distance (miles)
NETHERLANDS: Amsterdam	Schiphol	AMS	9
Rotterdam	Rotterdam	RTM	6
NEW ZEALAND: Auckland	Auckland Intl.	AKL	14
NIGERIA: Lagos	Murtala Muhammed	LOS	14
NORWAY: Oslo	Fornebu	OSL	6
PAKISTAN: Karachi	Karachi Intl.	KHI	10
PHILIPPINES: Manila	Manila Intl.	MNL	7
POLAND: Warsaw	Okecie	WAW	6
PORTUGAL: Lisbon	Portela	LIS	6
QATAR: Doha	Doha Intl.	DOH	4
SAUDI ARABIA: Jeddah	King Abdul Aziz Intl.	JED	25
Riyadh	Riyadh Intl.	RUH	4
SINGAPORE: Singapore	Changi	SIN	11
SOUTH AFRICA: Johannesburg	Jan Smuts	JNB	14
SPAIN: Barcelona	Barcelona	BCN	8
Madrid	Barajas	MAD	8
SRI LANKA: Colombo	Katunayake	CMB	20
SWEDEN: Stockholm	Arlanda	ARN	24
SWITZERLAND: Geneva	Colhtrin	GVA	3
Zurich	Kloten	ZRH	8
SYRIA: Damascus	Damascus Intl.	DAM	18
TAIWAN: Taipai	Chiang Kai-shek Intl.	TPE	25
THAILAND: Bangkok	Don Muang Intl.	BKK	16
TURKEY: Istanbul	Yesilkoy	IST	15
USSR: Moscow	Sheremetyevo	SVO	24
UNITED ARAB EMIRATES:			
Abu Dhabi	Abu Dhabi New Intl.	AUH	22
Dubai	Dubai Intl.	DXB	3
UNITED KINGDOM: Birmingham	Birmingham	BHX	6
Edinburgh	Edinburgh	EDI	6
Glasgow	Prestwick	PIK	9
London	Heathrow	LHR	15
London	Gatwick	LGW	28
Manchester	Manchester	MAN	10
UNITED STATES: Atlanta	Wm. Hartsfield Intl.	ATL	9
Boston	Logan Intl.	BOS	3
Chicago	O'Hare Intl.	ORD	21
Cleveland	Hopkins Intl.	CLE	12
Dallas	Dallas/Fort Worth	DAL	19
Denver	Stapleton Intl.	DEN	7
Detroit	Wayne County	DTT	20
Honolulu	Honolulu Intl.	HNL	4
Houston	Intercontinental	IAH	22
Los Angeles	Los Angeles Intl.	LAX	15
Miami	Miami Intl.	MIA	7
Minneapolis	Minn.-St. Paul Intl.	MSP	12
New York	J F Kennedy Intl.	JFK	13
New York	La Guardia	LGA	8
Philadelphia	Philadelphia Intl.	PHL	8
Pittsburgh	Pittsburgh Intl.	PIT	16
St. Louis	Lambert Intl.	STL	15
San Diego	Lindberg Intl.	SFO	14
San Francisco	San Francisco Intl.	SAN	2
Seattle	Sea-Tac Intl.	SEA	13
Washington	National	DCA	3
Washington DC	Dulles Intl.	IAD	26
VENEZUELA: Caracas	Simon Bolivar	CCS	14
YUGOSLAVIA: Belgrade	Belgrade	BEG	12

INTERNATIONAL TELEPHONE CODES

Algeria	213	France	33	Kuwait	965	Sri Lanka	94
All Cities	*	Lyon	7	All Cities	*	Colombo Central	1
Argentina	**54**	Marseille	91	**Luxembourg**	**352**	**Sweden**	**46**
Buenos Aires	1	Nice	93	All Cities	*	Goteborg	31
Cordoba	51	Paris	1	**Malaysia**	**60**	Karlstad	54
La Plata	21	Toulouse	61	Kuala Lumpur	3	Norrkoping	11
Mendoza	61	**Germany (East)**	**37**	**Monaco**	**33**	Stockholm	8
Rosario	41	Berlin	2	All Cities	93	Uppsala	18
Australia	**61**	Dresden	51	**Morocco**	**212**	**Switzerland**	**41**
Adelaide	8	Leipzig	41	Casablanca	*	Basel	61
Brisbane	7	**Germany (West)**	**49**	Tangiers	9	Bern	31
Melbourne	3	Berlin	30	**Netherlands**	**31**	Geneva	22
Perth	9	Dusseldorf	211	Amsterdam	20	Lausanne	21
Sydney	2	Essen	201	Eindhoven	40	Zurich	1
Austria	**43**	Frankfurt	611	Haarlem	23	**Taiwan**	**86**
Graz	316	Hamburg	40	Rotterdam	10	Taichung	42
Innsbruck	5222	Munich	89	The Hague	70	Tainan	62
Linz, Donau	732	**Greece**	**30**	Utrecht	30	Taipei	2
Salzburg	6222	Athens	1	**New Zealand**	**64**	**Thailand**	**66**
Vienna	222	Thessaloniki	31	Auckland	9	Bangkok	2
Belgium	**32**	Tripolis	71	Christchurch	3	**Turkey**	**90**
Antwerp	31	**Hong Kong**	**852**	Wellington	4	Ankara	41
Bruges	50	Hong Kong	5	**Nigeria**	**234**	Istanbul	11
Brussels	2	Kowloon	3	Lagos	1	Izmir	51
Ghent	91	**Iceland**	**354**	**Norway**	**47**	**U.S.S.R.**	**7**
Liege	41	Reykjavik	1	Bergen	5	Moscow	095
Bolivia	**591**	**Indonesia**	**62**	Oslo	2	**United Arab**	**971**
La Paz	2	Jakarta	21	**Pakistan**	**92**	**Emirates**	
Brazil	**55**	Padang	751	Karachi	21	Abu Dhabi	2
Belo Horizonte	31	Surabaya	31	**Paraguay**	**595**	Dubai	4
Brasilia	61	**Iraq**	**964**	Asuncion	21	**United Kingdom**	**44**
Rio de Janeiro	21	Baghdad	1	**Peru**	**51**	Belfast	232
Slavador	71	**Ireland**	**353**	Arequipa	54	Birmingham	21
Sao Paulo	11	Cork	21	Lima	14	Bristol	272
Chile	**56**	Dublin	1	Trujillo	44	Coventry	203
Santiago	2	Galway	91	**Phillipines**	**63**	Edinburgh	31
Valparaiso	31	Waterford	51	Cebu	32	Glasgow	41
Columbia	**57**	**Israel**	**972**	Davao	35	Leeds	532
Bogota	*	Haifa	4	Manila	2	Leicester	533
Bucaramanga	71	Jerusalem	2	**Portugal**	**351**	Liverpool	51
Cali	3	Tel Aviv	3	Coimbra	39	London	1
Cyprus	**357**	**Italy**	**39**	Lisbon	19	Manchester	61
Famagusta	31	Florence	55	**Romania**	**40**	Sheffield	742
Limassol	51	Milan	2	Bucharest	06	Southampton	703
Nicosia	21	Naples	81	**Saudi Arabia**	**966**	**Uruguay**	**598**
Denmark	**45**	Rome	6	Jeddah	21	Montevideo	2
Aalborg	8	Venice	41	Mecca	22	**Vatican City**	**39**
Copenhagen	1 or 2	**Japan**	**81**	Riyadh	1	All Cities	6
Esbjerg	5	Kobe	78	**Singapore**	**65**	**Venezuela**	**58**
Odense	9	Kyoto	75	All Cities	*	Caracas	2
Ecuador	**593**	Nagoya	52	**South Africa**	**27**	Maracaibo	61
Quito	2	Osaka	6	Cape Town	21	Valencia	41
Egypt	**20**	Tokyo	3	Durban	31	**Yugoslavia**	**38**
Alexandria	3	Yokohama	45	Johannesburg	11	Belgrade	11
Cairo	2	**Kenya**	**254**	**Spain**	**34**	Sarajevo	71
Luxor	95	Mombasa	11	Barcelona	3	Skoplje	91
Port Said	66	Nairobi	2	Madrid	1	Zagreb	41
Finland	**358**	**Korea, So.**	**82**	Valencia	6		
Helsinki	0	Inchon	32				
Tampere	31	Pusan	51				
		Seoul	2				

Dial 011 + Country Code + City Code + Local Number

*NO CITY CODE REQUIRED

INTERNATIONAL CLOTHING SIZES

MEN

Suits, Overcoats & Sweaters

American & British	34	36	38	40	42	44	46
Continental	44	46	48	50	52	54	56
Japanese	S	—	M	—	L	—	LL

Shirts

American & British	14	$14^1/_2$	15	$15^1/_2$	16	$16^1/_2$	17
Continental & Japanese	36	37	38	39	40	41	42

Hats

American	$6^5/_8$	$6^3/_4$	$6^7/_8$	7	$7^1/_8$	$7^1/_4$	$7^3/_8$	$7^1/_2$	$7^5/_8$
British	$6^1/_2$	$6^5/_8$	$6^3/_4$	$6^7/_8$	7	$7^1/_8$	$7^1/_4$	$7^3/_8$	$7^1/_2$
Continental & Japanese	53	54	55	56	57	58	59	60	61

Shoes

American	7	$7^1/_2$	8	$8^1/_2$	9	$9^1/_2$	10	$10^1/_2$	11
British	$6^1/_2$	7	$7^1/_2$	8	$8^1/_2$	9	$9^1/_2$	10	$10^1/_2$
Continental	39	40	41	42	43	43	44	44	45
Japanese	—	26	—	$26^3/_4$	—	$27^1/_2$	—	28	—

Socks

American & British	$9^1/_2$	10	$10^1/_2$	11	$11^1/_2$	12	$12^1/_2$
Continental	39	40	41	42	43	44	45
Japanese	24	25	26	28	29	—	—

WOMEN

Dresses & Coats

American	8	10	12	14	16	18	20
British	30	32	34	36	38	40	42
Continental	36	38	40	42	44	46	48
Japanese	—	9	11	13	15	17	19

Sweaters & Blouses

American	32	34	36	38	40	42	44
British	34	36	38	40	42	44	46
Continental	40	42	44	46	48	50	52
Japanese	M	M	L	L	LL	LL	LL

Shoes

American	5	6	7	8	$8^1/_2$	9	10
British	$3^1/_2$	$4^1/_2$	$5^1/_2$	$6^1/_2$	7	$7^1/_2$	$8^1/_2$
Continental	36	37	38	39	40	41	42
Japanese	—	23	24	25	$25^1/_2$	26	—

Hosiery

American & British	8	$8^1/_2$	9	$9^1/_2$	10	$10^1/_2$	11
Continental	0	1	2	3	4	5	6
Japanese	21	22	23	24	25	26	—

METRIC CONVERSION CHART

WEIGHTS

1 ounce = 28.350 grams	1 gram = .035 ounce
1 pound = .454 kilogram	1 kilogram = 2.204 pounds
1 ton = .907 metric ton	1 metric ton = 1.103 tons

LENGTH

1 inch = 2.54 centimeters (cm)	1 centimeter = .394 inch
1 foot = .305 meter (m)	1 meter = 39.370 inches
1 yard = .914 meter	= 3.281 feet
1 mile = 1.609 kilometers (km)	= 1.094 yards
	1 kilometer = .621 mile

LIQUID MEASURE

1 quart (dry) = 1.101 liters	1 liter = .908 quart (dry)
1 quart (liquid) = .946 liters	1 liter = 1.057 quarts (liquid)
1 U.S. gallon = 3.785 liters	1 liter = .264 U.S. gallon
1 U.S. gal. = .833 Imperial gallon	1 Imperial gal. = 1.201 U.S. gallons

TEMPERATURE

Fahrenheit   0   25 ^{32} 50   75   100   125   150   175   200 ^{212}

Centigrade -20   -10   0   10   20   30   40   50   60   70   80   90   100

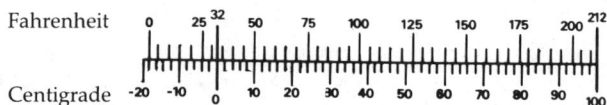

Notes: To convert into Fahrenheit, multiply °C by 1.8 and then add 32

To convert Fahrenheit into Centigrade, subtract 32 from °F and then divide by 1.8

FOREIGN LANGUAGE VOCABULARY
USEFUL PHRASES

ENGLISH	FRENCH	GERMAN	SPANISH
Do you speak English?	Parlez-vous Anglais?	Sprechen sie Englisch?	¿Habla usted Inglés
Excuse me	Excusez-moi	Entschuldigen Sie	Dispénseme
Good morning	Bonjour	Guten Morgen	Buenos días
Good afternoon	Bonjour	Guten Tag	Buenas tardes
Good evening	Bonsoir	Guten Abend	Buenas noches
Good night	Bonne nuit	Gute Nacht	Buenas noches
Good-bye	Au revoir	Auf Wiedersehen	Adiós
How are you?	Comment allez-vous?	Wie geht es Ihnen?	¿Cómo está usted
How far?	A quelle distance?	Wie weit?	¿Qué distancia
How many?	Combien?	Wie viele?	¿Cuántos
How much is it?	A quel prix?	Wieviel kostet es?	¿Cuanto vale
I do not understand.	Je ne comprends pas	Ich verstehe nicht	No entiendo
I understand	Je comprends	Ich verstehe	Comprendo
I would like . . .	J'aimerais . . .	Ich möchte . . .	Me gustaría . . .
Is there . . .?	Y a-t-il . . .?	Gibt es . . .?	¿Hay . . .
My name is . . .	Je m'apelle . . .	Mein Name ist	Me llamo
Please	S'il vous plait	Bitte	Por favor
Thank You	Merci	Danke	Gracias
Too big	Trop grand	Zu gross	Demasiado grande
Too much	Trop cher	Zu teuer	Demasiado
Too small	Trop petit	Zu klein	Demasiado pequeño
Yes; No	Oui; Non	Ja; Nein	Si; No
Your name?	Votre nom?	Ihr name bitte?	¿Su nombre
What time is it?	Quelle heure est-il?	Wieviel Uhr ist es?	¿Qué hora es
Where is . . .?	Ou se trouve . . .?	Wo ist . . .?	¿Dónde está . . .

USEFUL WORDS

ENGLISH	FRENCH	GERMAN	SPANISH
airport	aéroport	flugplatz; flughafen	aeropuerto
automobile; car	auto; voiture	auto	automovil; coche
bank	banque	bank	banco
barber	coiffeur	friseur	barbero
bath	bain	bad	baño
beauty salon/parlor	salon de beauté	friseursalon	salón de belleza
chambermaid	femme de chambre	zimmermädchen	camarera
change (coins)	monnaie	kleingeld	suelta; cambio
change (money)	changer	wechsein	cambiar
check (bill)	addition; note	rechnung	cuenta
checkroom	vestiaire	garderobe	vestuario
church	église	kirche	iglesia
clothes	habits	kleider	ropas
cold	froid	kalt	frío
dentist	dentiste	zahnarzt	dentista
doctor	docteur	arzt	médico
dry clean	nettoyer à sec	chemische reinigen	limpiar a seco
early	tôt	früh	temprano
elevator	ascenseur	fahrstuhl; aufzug	ascensor; elevator
envelope	enveloppe	briefumschlag	sobre
exit	sortie	ausgang	salida
gasoline; petrol	essence	benzin	gasolina
gift (present)	cadeau	geschenk	regalo
guide	guide	führer	guía
hospital	hôpital	krankenhaus	hospital
hot	chaud	heiss	caliente

USEFUL WORDS (*Continued*)

ENGLISH	FRENCH	GERMAN	SPANISH
information	renseignement	auskunft	informes
late	tard	spät	tarde
lavatory (toilet)	toilette; cabines	abort; toilette	retrete; excusado
left (direction)	gauche	links	izquierda
letter	lettre	brief	carta
mail	poste	post	correo
market	marché	markt	mercado
men (gentlemen)	hommes; messieurs	männer; herren	señores; caballeros
money	argent	geld	dinero
night club	boîte de nuit	nachtklub	cabaret; café
pharmacy	pharmacie	apotheke	farmacia
porter (baggage)	porteur	gepäckträger	mozo; maletero
postcard	carte postale	postkarte	tarjeta postal
post office	bureau de poste	postamt	casa de correos
press (iron)	repasser	bügeln	planchar
registered (letter)	recommandée	eingeschriebener	certificada
room (hotel)	chambre	zimmer	cuarto
smoking	fumer	rauchen	fumar
soap	savon	seife	jabón
stamp (postage)	timbre-poste	briefmarke	sello de correo
station (R.R.)	gare	bahnhof	estación
suitcase	valise	handkoffer	maleta
ticket (travel)	billet	fahrkarte	billete
ticket office	guichet	billettausgabe	despacho de billetes
today	aujourd'hui	heute	hoy
tomorrow	demain	morgen	mañana

USEFUL WORDS (Continued)

ENGLISH	FRENCH	GERMAN	SPANISH
towel	serviette	handtuch	toalla
train (R.R.)	train	zug	tren
trolley	trolleybus	oberleitungsbus	trolebús
umbrella	parapluie	regenschirm	paraguas
waiting room	salle d'attente	wartenzimmer	sala de espera
women (ladies)	femmes	frauen	mujeres
writing paper	papier à lettre	briefpapier	papel de escribir
yesterday	hier	gestern	ayer

Days

Sunday	dimanche	Sonntag	domingo
Monday	lundi	Montag	lunes
Tuesday	mardi	Dienstag	martes
Wednesday	mércredi	Mittwoch	miercoles
Thursday	jeudi	Donnerstag	jueves
Friday	vendredi	Freitag	viernes
Saturday	samedi	Sonnabend	sábado

Numbers

one	un, une	eins	uno, una
two	deux	zwei	dos
three	trois	drei	tres
four	quatre	vier	cuatro
five	cinq	fünf	cinco
six	six	sechs	seis
seven	sept	sieben	siete

USEFUL WORDS (*Continued*)

ENGLISH	FRENCH	GERMAN	SPANISH
eight	huit	acht	ocho
nine	neuf	neun	nueve
ten	dix	zehn	diez
eleven	onze	elf	once
twelve	douze	zwölf	doce
thirteen	treize	dreizehn	trece
fourteen	quatorze	vierzehn	catorce
fifteen	quinze	fünfzehn	quince
sixteen	seize	sechzehn	diez y seis
seventeen	dix-sept	siebzehn	diez y siete
eighteen	dix-huit	achtzehn	diez y ocho
nineteen	dix-neuf	neunzehn	diez y nueve
twenty	vingt	zwanzig	veinte
twenty-one	vingt-et-un	einundzwanzig	veinte y uno
twenty-two	vingt-deux	zweiundzwanzig	veinte dos
thirty	trente	dreissig	treinta
forty	quarante	vierzig	cuarenta
fifty	cinquante	fünfzig	cincuenta
sixty	soixante	sechzig	sesenta
seventy	soixante-dix	siebzig	setenta
eighty	quatre-vingt	achtzig	ochenta
ninety	quatre-vingt-dix	neunzig	noventa
one hundred	cent	hundert	cien
two hundred	deux cents	zweihundert	doscientos
one thousand	mille	tausend	mil

FOOD AND DRINK

ENGLISH	FRENCH	GERMAN	SPANISH
General	**Général**	**Allgemein**	**General**
baked	cuit au four	gebacken	asado
boiled	bouilli	gekocht	cocido
broiled (grilled)	grillé	gegrillt	a la parrilla
cold; hot	froid; chaud	kalt; heiss	frio; caliente
Check, please	L'addition, s'il vous plait	Die Rechnung, bitte	La cuenta, por favor
dining room	salle à manger	speisezimmer	comedor
fresh	frais	frisch	fresco
fried	frit	gebraten	frito
I would like . . .	J'aimerais . . .	Ich möchte	Me gustaría
Is service included?	Est-ce que le service est compris?	Ist die Bedienung einbegriffen?	¿Esta incluido el servicio
medium	à point	halb durchgebraten	Medio asada
napkin	serviette	serviette	servilleta
Nothing more, thank you	Rien d'autre, merci	Nichts weiter, danke	Nada más, gracias
rare	saignant	halbgebraten	poco asada
salt; pepper	sel; poivre	salz; pfeffer	sal; pimienta
steamed	à l'étuvee	gedämpft	cocido
waiter	garçon	kellner	camarero
waitress	mademoiselle	fräulein	camarera
well done	bien cuite	durchgebraten	bien asada
What is this charge for?	Pourriez-vous m'expliquer ceci?	Wofür ist dies?	?Que es esto que ha cargado a mi cuenta
Breakfast	**Le Petit Déjeuner**	**Fruhstuck**	**Desayuno**
bread	pain	brot	pan

FOOD AND DRINK *(Continued)*

ENGLISH	FRENCH	GERMAN	SPANISH
butter	beurre	butter	mantequilla
coffee	café	kaffee	café
corn flakes	cornflakes	geröstete maisflocken	hojuelas de maíz
cream	crème	sahne	crema
fried eggs	oeufs sur la plat	spiegeleier	huevos fritos
hot cereal	semoule	haferbrei	avena
hot chocolate	chocolat	heisser kakao	chocolate
marmalade (jam)	confiture	marmelade (konfiture)	mermelada
milk	lait	milch	leche
omelette	omelette	omelette	tortilla de huevos
orange juice	jus d'orange	orangensaft	jugo de naranja
pastries	gâteaux	gebäck	pasteles
poached eggs	oeufs pochés	verlorene eier	huevos blandos
rolls	petit pain	brötchen	panecillo
tea	thé	tee	té
toast	pain grillé	toast	tostado
scrambled eggs	oeufs brouilles	rühreier	huevos revueltos
soft (hard) boiled eggs	oeufs à la coque (oeufs durs)	weich (hart) gekochte eier	huevos pasados (huevos duro) por agua
sugar	sucre	zucker	azúcar
Lunch-Dinner	Déjeuner-Diner	Mittagessen-Abendessen	Almuerzo-Cena
bacon	lard	speck	tocino
beef	boeuf	rindfleisch	carne de vaca
beetroot	betterave	rote rubën	remolacha

FOOD AND DRINK (Continued)

ENGLISH	FRENCH	GERMAN	SPANISH
cabbage	chou	kohl	col (repollo)
carrots	carottes	mohrruben	zanahorias
chicken	poulet	huhn	pollo
clams	palourdes	sandmuschel	almejas
crabs	crabe	krabben	cangrejo
cucumber	concombre	gurke	pepino
eggplant	aubergine	aubergine	berenjena
endive	endive	endivie	endiva-escarola
frankfurter	hot dog	wiener würstchen	salchiha alemana
garlic	ail	knoblauch	ajo
green peppers	poivrons	paprikaschoten	pimientos verdes
ham	jambon	schinken	jamón
hamburger	hamburger	deutsches beefsteak	hamburguesa
herring	hareng	hering	arenque
lamb	agneau	lammfleisch	cordero
lettuce	laitue	kopfsalat	lechuga
liver	foie	leber	hígado
lobster	homard	hummer	langosta
mixed green	salade verte	gemischter	ensalada
mushrooms	champignons	pilze	hongos (setas)
noodles	nouilles	nudeln	fideos
oil & vinegar dressing	huile et vinaigre	ol und essig	aceite y vinagre (aderezo)
onions	oignons	zwiebeln	cebollas
oysters	huîtres	austern	ostras
peas	petits pois	erbsen	guisantes
pork	porc	schweinefleisch	puerco

FOOD AND DRINK (*Continued*)

ENGLISH	FRENCH	GERMAN	SPANISH
potatoes (french fries)	pommes de terre (pommes frites)	kartoffeln (pommes frites)	patatas (fritas)
ravioli	raviolis	ravioli	ravioli
rice	riz	reis	arroz
salad	salade	salate	ensaladas
salmon	saumon	lachs	salmón
sandwich	sandwich	belegtes brot	bocadillo
sauerkraut	choucroute	sauerkraut	choucroute
sausage	saucisse	wurst	salchicha
shrimp	crevettes	garnele	gambas
sole	sole	seezunge	lenguado
soup	soupe	suppe	sopa
spinach	épinards	spinat	espinaca
steak	bifteck (beefsteak)	steak	biftec
string beans	haricots verts	grüne bohnen	judías verdes
tomatoes	tomates	tomaten	tomates
trout	truite	forelle	trucha
veal	veau	kalbfleisch	ternera
Desserts	Dessert	Nachtisch	Postres
apple	pomme	apfel	manzana
cake	gâteau	kuchen	bizcocho
cheese	fromage	käse	queso
cheese of the region	fromage du pays	käse der gegend	queso de la región
crepes	crêpes	crêpes	crepés

FOOD AND DRINK *(Continued)*

ENGLISH	FRENCH	GERMAN	SPANISH
fresh fruit	fruits	frisches obst	fruta fresca
ice cream	crème à la glace	eis	helado
melon	melon	melone	melón
orange	orange	apfelsine	naranja
pear	poire	birne	pera
tart, pie	tarte, pâté	torte, pastete	tarta, pastel
whipped cream	crème chantilly	schlagsahne	nata

Drinks	Boissons	Getränke	Bebidas
Wine list, please	La carte des vins, S.V.P.	Die weinkarte, bitte	Lista de vinos, por favor
beer	biere	bier	cerveza
ice	glace	eis	hielo
mineral water	eau minérale	mineralwasser	agua mineral
red	rouge	rot	tinto
rose	rosé	rosé	clarete
water	eau	wasser	agua
white	blanc	weiss	blanco
wine	vin	wein	vino
wine of the region (in carafe)	vin du pays (en carafe)	hiesigen wein (in karaffe)	vina de la region (de la casa)

Africa/Middle East

ALGERIA

Essential Information

Type of Government
Republic

Area
2.4 million sq km
(918,497 sq mi)

Population
22 million

Annual Growth Rate
3.1%

Languages
Arabic (official), Berber
(indigenous), French and Arabic
(commercial)

Religion
Sunni Muslim (state religion)

Ethnic Groups
Arab 75%, Berbers 25%

Weights and Measures
Metric

Electrical Current
A.C. 50c 127/220V and 220/380V.
Plugs and outlets are all different
sizes.

Major Business Cities
Algiers (cap) 2,250,000
Oran 945,000
Constantine 650,000
Annaba 550,000

Currency
Algerian Dinar = 100 centimes
Notes 5, 10, 50, 100 dinars
Coins 1, 2, 5, 10, 20, 50
    centimes; 1, 5 dinars

Public Holidays
Jan 1 New Year
May 1 Labor Day
June 19 Sursaut Revolutionnaire
Many Muslim holidays and
observances, including the
month of fasting called
Ramadan, follow the lunar cycle
and advance 12-15 days every
year. Check tourist board for
current dates.

Travellers Information

Entry Requirements
Passport required by all except
Algerian nationals. Visa required
by most countries including
US, excepting Britain. Anyone
wishing to stay more than three
months needs to get a permit
from nearest "Wilaya".

Working Restrictions
Work permit is obtainable only if
there is a contact between your
country and Algeria and you are
coming as part of an agreed
work project.

Vaccination Required
None is required, but those for
typhoid, tetanus, polio, malaria,
and cholera are recommended.
There is malaria risk in some
areas in summer.

Customs and Duty Free
On arrival: 200 cigarets or 50
cigars or 400g/14oz tobacco;
1 bottle spirits; small amount of
perfume

Currency Restrictions
Foreign currency must be
declared at customs. No more
than 50 dinars may be brought
in or out. Currency declaration
forms should be filled out at
each successive money change
so that accurate records can be
handed in at departure. Credit
cards are not widely accepted
and French-franc travellers
checks are recommended.

Health Tips
Drink bottled water which is
readily available, be careful of
cold foods, and wash all fruit
and vegetables thoroughly. It is
a good idea to take antimalarial
tablets during your stay.

Climate and Clothing
Jun-Sept: inland temps 27-32c
(80-90F) and humid; coastal

regions (Algiers, Annaba, Oran) more temperate 13-24c (55-75F) and somewhat rainy.
Sahara desert very hot and dry. Light or tropical weight clothing. Light raincoat for coast, light jacket for evening.
Oct-May: rainy season, particularly on coast. Temperatures go down and winter clothing is worn between November and April; rainwear is advisable.

Tipping
Service charge of 10-15% is usually added to the bills in hotels and restuarants, but an additional 10% to the staff is appreciated. Tip 10% for taxis, 5 dinars per portered bag, and 2 dinar for small services.

Food and Drink
Berber and Arab dishes feature lemon chicken with rice, couscous, tajine (stew of meat, fish or poultry with dates, honey, almonds, raisins, and prunes), spit-roasted lamb, and seafood in coastal areas.
International food is available but is mainly expensive and in hotels.
Algeria makes highly alcoholic red wine. Local beer, mineral water, and fruit juices also available. Mint tea is customary at the end of the meal.

Business Brief

GDP
$32.3 billion
(per capita income $2,063)

Annual Growth Rate
11.1%

Natural Resources
Crude oil, natural gas, iron ore, phosphates, uranium, lead, zinc, mercury

Agriculture
Only about 3% of land is currently under cultivation and 65% of foodstuffs are imported. Crops are grapes, olives, dates, citrus fruits, tobacco, sugar beets, tomatoes.

Industry
Crude oil, natural gas, iron, steel, textiles, fertilizers, transportation equipment

Imports
Total $10.2 billion
Wheat, corn, soybeans, meat, milk, eggs, machinery and vehicles, aircraft

Exports
Total $7.8 billion
Crude oil and refined products, liquified natural gas, mercury, phosphates, wine

Major Trading Partners
US, France, West Germany, Netherlands, Canada, Italy, Belgium, Spain

Tips For Doing Business
English is spoken a little, but French is the preferred language for business. Even though a Muslim country, alcoholic drinks are available at hotels providing a usual place for business meetings. Wear conservative clothing (women should never wear anything revealing) and carry bilingual business cards printed in both Arabic and English, Arabic and French, or English and French. Business is conducted in a low-key manner. Make appointments ahead of time.

Best Months For Doing Business
Best months for business are October through May. Avoid trips in the weeks around Christmas, at Easter, and in the month of Ramadan. (This changes yearly so check with travel bureau or local consulate to find out time.) Algerian businessmen vacation during the summer months of July and August.

Business Hours

Government and Business
Sat-Thur 0800-1200, 1400-1730
(Fri closed and some half days in
summer and during Ramadan)

Banks
Sometimes closed on days before
and after holidays so check
dates. Sat-Wed 0900-1530/1600
(Thur-Fri closed)

Shops
Sat-Wed 0800-1200, 1430-1800

Telephone and Communications

Telephone country code: 213
Telephone city code: 0
Telex country code: 936
Public telephone boxes are in all
post offices and large hotels.
Enquiries dial 19, telegrams 13,
police 17. International direct
dialing code: 010213.
Telegrams can be sent from any
post office. The main post office
in Algiers, 5 Boulevard
Mohamed Khemisti, maintains a
24 hour telegraph service.
Telex facilities are also at the
main post office and at the El
Aurassi, El Alitti, El Djazair and
El Safir hotels.
You should rent a box at the
post office for incoming mail and
make sure all business
correspondence is sent airmail
and marked "Documentation
Technique-Sans Valeur
Commerciale."

Air Travel

There are routes operated by Air
Algerie from Algiers to all major
centers. Flights can be paid for
in local currency.

Other Transport

Cars can be rented in major
cities from airports and city
rental offices. An international
driving license and third-party
insurance are required.
Bus service throughout the
country is operated by SNTV
and ALTOUR. Book well in

advance and get confirmation.
Over a third of the roads are
paved and classed as main.
Trains are operated by SNTF.
There are two classes. Some
services have air-conditioning
and/or couchettes. Book in
advance and confirm.

ALGIERS (EL DJAZAIRO)

Airport Information

Time
GMT
GMT +1 May-Oct

Airport
Hovari Boumedienne ALG
Tel: 761018
21 km (13 mi) E of city

Airlines
Aeroflot 605661
Air Algerie 589505
Air France 631610
Alitalia 646850
Egyptair 630505
Iberia 612473
Interflug 665017
Kuwait Air 630458
Libyan 636383
Lufthansa 642736
Sabena 633214
SAS 590934
Saudia 664555
Swissair 633367
Syrian 639234

Transport To City
Taxi: readily available; costs
about 85-90 dinars.
Coach: to city (25 min) every 30
minutes from 0015-1945. Return
from Air Algerie (next to Hotel
Alleti,
rue Colonel Ben Abderreza)
every 90 minutes before flight
departure; 6-7 dinars.

Facilities
Restaurant, buffet, bank with
currency exchange, post office,

baggage deposit, barber shop, shops.

Duty-free shop sells cigarets, cigars, tobacco, wines, aperitifs, glass and china. Most currencies accepted.

Car rental at ALTOUR.

Airport Taxes
None

City Information

Weather
Mediterranean with rain between November and March and often between September and May.

Can get quite hot in the summer months.

Transportation
Taxis operate on a minimum-fare system and you should tip 10%. Radio cabs available (tel: 623333). Cabs identified by color codes can be hailed. All difficult to get in the rush hour. Car rental with self-drive cars available, but you must have an international driving license. Major agencies at ALTOUR.

Car Hire
Avis, 109 rue Didouche Mourad (tel: 668528/30)

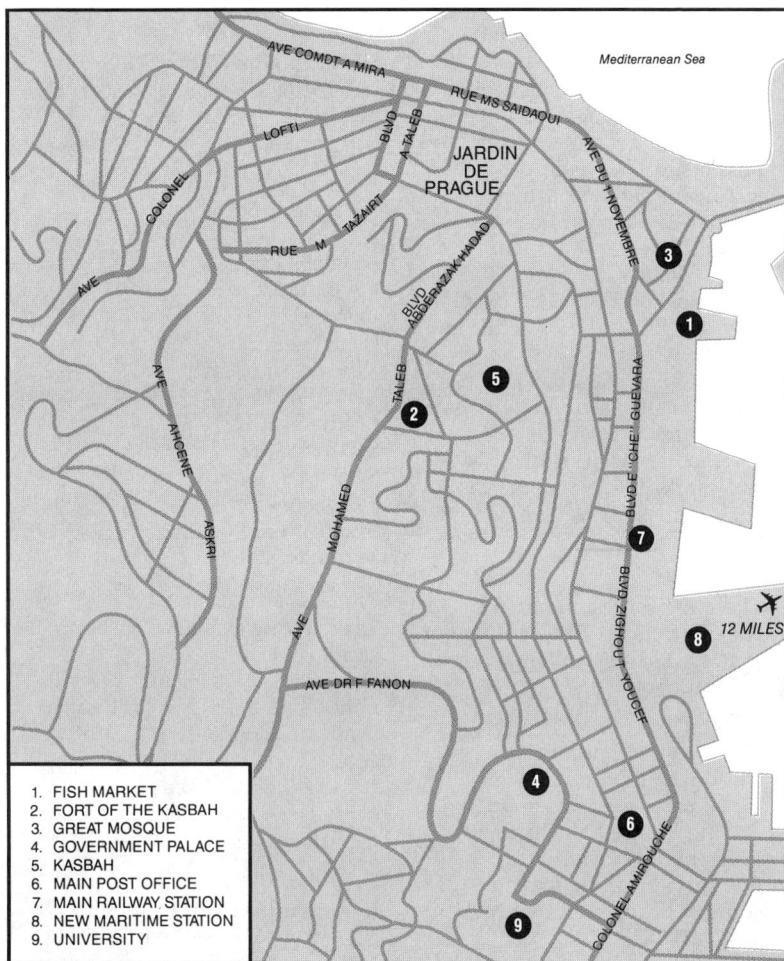

1. FISH MARKET
2. FORT OF THE KASBAH
3. GREAT MOSQUE
4. GOVERNMENT PALACE
5. KASBAH
6. MAIN POST OFFICE
7. MAIN RAILWAY STATION
8. NEW MARITIME STATION
9. UNIVERSITY

Algiers

Garage Yettou, 2 Boulevard des Martyrs (tel: 605429)

Hospitals
English-speaking doctor:
Dr. Larbi Ould-Aoudia
(tel: 771454)

Hotels
Book well in advance and get confirmation since accomodation, especially in Algiers, is expensive and difficult to get. Credit cards are not usually accepted. Bring warm clothing in winter as the rooms are sometimes not well-heated.
Albert 1, 5 Ave Pasteur
  (tel: 630020)
El Sofir, 1 Rue Asselah Hocine
  (tel: 635042 & 635040)
El Aurassi, Ave Frantz Fanon
  (tel: 648252)
Angleterre, Ben Boulaid
  (tel: 636540)
El Djazair, 24 Ave Souidani
  Boudjemaa (tel: 665300)

What to See and Do
West of Algiers are Phoenician, Punic and Roman sites of Tipaza and Cherchell. In the city are museums: Stephane Gsell has Roman objects and Islamic art, and the Bardo has clothing, jewellery and weapons. Restaurants and nightclubs have oriental cabaret: usually expensive. In Algiers visit the citadel, the Sidi-Abderahouane and Grand Mosques, and the Museum of Popular Arts which was once a Turkish palace.

Useful Addresses

Embassies and Consulates
American: 4 Chemin Cheich Bachir Brahimi (tel: 601425 & 601186)
Canadian: 27 bis rue D'Anjou, Hydra (tel: 606611)
British: Residence Cassiopee, Batiment B, 7 Chemin des Glycines (tel: 605601/411/038/831)

Business and Commerce
Central Post Office, 5 Boulevard Mohamed Khemisti
Central Bank (Banque Central d'Algerie), 8 Boulevard Zirout Josef (tel: 647500)
Chamber of Commerce: Chambre Francaise de Commerce, 1 rue du Languedo (tel: 632525)
Translators: Union Nationale des Interpreters et Traducteurs, 1 rue Sid-Ali Aouf (tel: 579072)
Algerian Commercial Trade Center: 24 Bordj El-Kiffan (tel: 627044)

Tourism and Travel
Algerian Tourist Agency, 2 Pl. Cheikh B. Badis
Algerian Travel Agency, 9 Blvd. Zirout Josef
Touring Club of Algeria, 1 rue Al-Idrissi (tel: 640837)
American Express, (Tipaza) Altour, Ghemoua Place, Blida, (tel: 461450/51)

EGYPT

Essential Information

Type of Government
Republic

Area
1,001,258 sq km
(386,650 sq mi)

Population
49.5 million

Annual Growth Rate
2.7%

Languages
Arabic (official), English, French

Religion
Sunni Muslim 90%, Coptic
Christian

Ethnic Groups
Egyptian, Bedouin Arabs,
Nubian

Weights and Measures
Metric

Electrical Current
A.C. 50c 110V & 220/380V

Major Business Cities
Cairo (cap) 12,500,000
Alexandria 3,250,000
Port Said 350,000
Ismailia 372,000
Suez 368,000

Currency
Egyptian Pound = 100 piasters
Notes 5, 10, 25 and 50 piasters;
  1, 5, 10, 20 and 100 pounds
Coins 1, 5, 10 and 20 piasters

Public Holidays
Offices and businesses may be
closed on holidays, but since
Muslim holidays (M.H.) change
yearly according to lunar cycles,
you should consult local
Egyptian consulate for current
dates before planning a business
trip.
M.H. Sham el Nessin
Apr 25 Sinai Liberation Day
May 1 Labor Day
Jun 18 Evacuation Day
M.H. Id al-Fitr
Jul 23 National Day
M.H. Id al-Adha
M.H. Islamic New Year
Oct 6 Armed Forces Day
M.H. Mouled al Nabi

Travellers Information

Entry Requirements
Passport, valid until at least 3
months after end of visit, is
required by all except those with
a laissez-passer from Arab
countries.
Visas are required by all except
those who will be continuing
their journey within 24 hours,
and should be obtained through
an Egyptian embassy or
consulate before arriving. Ticket
to leave required. An emergency
visa valid for one month can be
obtained at the airport. If on
business, letter from firm or
confirmed appointment in Egypt
is required. All visitors must
register with authorities within 7
days - those staying in a hotel
are automatically registered.
Nationals of Taiwan, South
Africa, Yemen and Libya
prohibited entry.

Vaccination Required
Cholera and yellow fever
vaccinations required if arriving
from infected area. Take
antimalerial pills in outlying
areas. Shots not required for
visitors coming from North
American or Europe. The
Department of State Medical
Division recommends that you
get shots for cholera, typhoid,
tetanus, polio and hepatitis
(gamma globulin).

Customs and Duty Free
On arrival: 200 cigarets or 25
cigars or 200g tobacco; 1 liter
spirits or 1 bottle wine.

Currency Restrictions
There is no restriction on the
import of foreign currency but a
currency declaration form must
be completed on arrival. The
amount declared can be taken
out on departure. You may be
asked to exchange the equivalent
of US$150 into local currency at
the official incentive exchange
rate on arrival. Import and
export of more than 20 Egyptian
pounds is prohibited.

Health Tips
Do not drink tapwater except in
Cairo and Alexandria. Cairo has
several well-equipped hospitals
with good doctors. Many doctors
speak English. Imported

pharmaceuticals are expensive and scarce. Bring special medication with you.

Climate and Clothing
Dress in a conservative and modest fashion in clothing suitable for hot summers and cool but temperate winters. Climate is warm and dry from November to March. Temperatures can rise to over 38c (100F) in Cairo and upper Egypt from April to October. Very cool to cool in evenings so take a light coat. Hot dusty wind from the Khamaseen desert blows in April and May, August and September.

Tipping
Give taxi drivers 10% of the fare, porters 50 piasters for each piece of luggage. In hotels, restaurants and nightspots, 10% is added to the bill but it is customary to leave an additional 5-10%. Small services 30 piasters.

Food and Drink
Egyptian food combines many elements of Middle Eastern cooking including the use of rice, fish, lamb, poultry and stuffed vegetables. Dips made from tomatoes, yogurt, cucumbers, chick peas and garlic are usually found on the table along with flat Egyptian breads and tahina (sesame seed paste). Western food is available at fast-food outlets in the major cities and at large hotels.

Business Brief

GDP
$23 billion — $32.44 billion at the official incentive exchange rate (per capita income $655)

Annual Growth Rate
5-7%

Natural Resources
Petroleum and natural gas, iron ore, phosphates, manganese, limestone, gypsum, talc, asbestos, lead, zinc

Agriculture
Cotton, rice, onions, beans, citrus fruits, wheat, corn, barley, sugar

Industry
Food processing, textile, chemicals, petrochemicals, construction, light manufacturing, iron and steel products, aluminum, cement, military equipment

Imports
Total $16.23 billion
Foodstuffs, machinery and transport equipment, paper and wood products

Exports
Total $4.35 billion
Cotton, manufactured goods, rice, fruits, cement

Major Trading Partners
USSR, US, Italy, West Germany, EEC countries

Workforce
13.4 million
Agriculture 50%, services 26%, industry 13%, trade and finance 11%

Tips for Doing Business
Prior appointments necessary for all government and business meetings and business cards printed in both English and Arabic would be helpful and courteous: they can be printed locally in two to three days. Many businesses in the export-import trade are nationalized and run by both governmental and private firms with the exception of cotton, rice, wheat and oil which are run exclusively by the government. Both English and French are spoken. Egyptian businessmen are friendly, generous and proud, and entertain lavishly. Courteous

bargaining is accepted. If a businessman has three names, address him by the last one. Avoid talking about the politics of the Middle East, especially those of Israel. Always remove your shoes when entering a mosque.

Best Months for Doing Business

As in all Muslim countries, things slow down in the month of the month of fasting called Ramadan. Check with a travel agent or local Egyptian consulate before planning your trip as Muslim holidays vary from year to year according to the lunar cycle. Business vacations are taken in June, July, August and September.

Business Hours

Government
Summer: Mon-Wed 0800-1400, Thu 0800-1300, Fri closed
Winter: Mon-Wed 0900-1300, 1600-l900, Thu 0900-1300, Fri closed

Business
Summer: Mon-Wed 0800-1400, Thu 0800-1300, Fri closed
Winter: Mon-Wed 0900-1300, 1600-l900, Thu 0900-1300, Fri closed

Banks
Mon-Thu 0800-1330
Sun 1000-1200

Shops
Summer 0900-2000
Winter 1000-1900

English Language Publications

Egyptian Gazette is the daily newspaper published in English.

Telephone and Communications

Telephone country code: 20
Telephone city code: Cairo 2, Alexandria 3, Asswan 97, Port Said 66, Suez 62
Telex country code: 927
Automatic telephone service in main towns. Expect delays. Book international calls well in advance. When calling internally, note that Egyptian residents and businesses are listed under the initial of their first name, non-Egyptians under initial of last name.

Telex facilities available in major hotels and post offices: a 24 hour service at Cairo Central Telegraph office. Domestic post is unreliable; airmail to Europe about 5 days.

Air Travel

International airports at Cairo (CAI) and Alexandria (ALY). Egyptair offers flights from Cairo to Luxor, Aswan, Abu Simel and Alexandria.
Air Sinai has services to North and South Sinai. Book well in advance, particularly in winter.

Other Transport

Taxis are available in most centers and air-conditioned limousines at airports and hotels. Fares to various places listed in hotels. Tip 10%.
Frequent bus service from Cairo to Alexandria and other major cities.
There are express trains from Cairo to Alexandria, Luxor and Aswan. Certain routes have air-conditioned cars and food service. Car hire available for good internal roads between major cities. International license plus third-party insurance needed. Negotiate rates in advance.

CAIRO

Airport Information

Time
GMT +2

Airport
Cairo International CAI

Tel: 968866
22.5 km (14 mi) NE of city

Airlines
Aeroflot 743132
Air Algerie 740688
Air France 750648
Alia 750876
Alitalia 753449
Austrian 742755
British Airways 772981
Egyptair 441460
El Al 3411429
Finnair 769571
Gulf Air 3484116
Iberia 749955
Interflug 919705
Iraqi 44300
JAL 740809
KLM 751306

Korean 747302
Kuwait Air 759874
Lufthansa 3930343
MEA 750984
Olympic 3931318
Pan Am 760307
PIA 3931604
Qantas 7491300
Sabena 751194
Saudia 741200
SAS 753955
Singapore 769681
Swissair 392522
TWA 749900
United 933950
Varig 933979

Transport to City
Taxis: navy and white taxis are
always available and take about
40 minutes to city. Rates

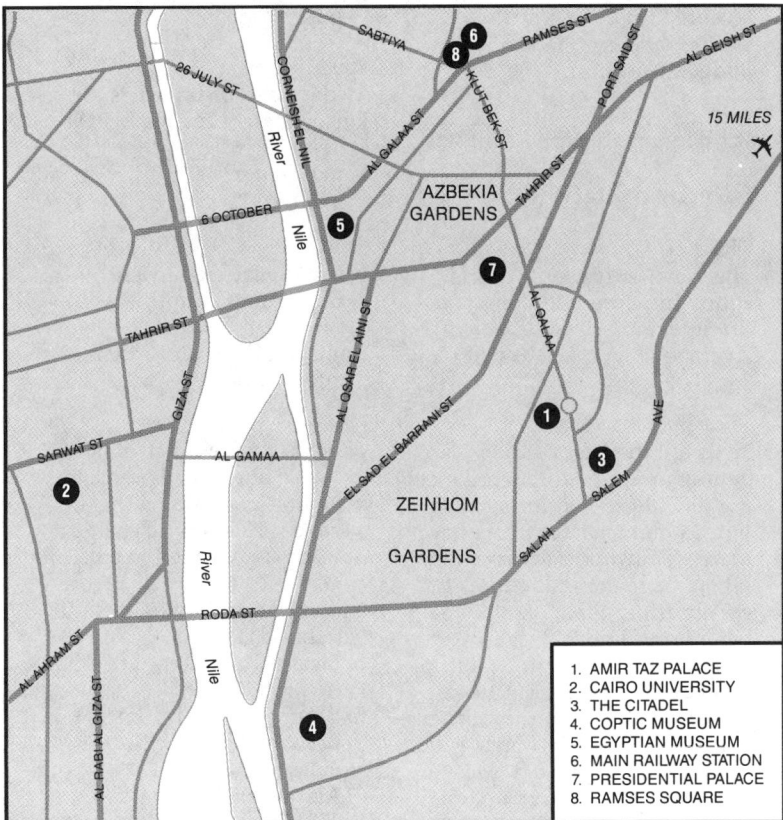

15 MILES

1. AMIR TAZ PALACE
2. CAIRO UNIVERSITY
3. THE CITADEL
4. COPTIC MUSEUM
5. EGYPTIAN MUSEUM
6. MAIN RAILWAY STATION
7. PRESIDENTIAL PALACE
8. RAMSES SQUARE

Cairo

negotiable but about US$5; not airconditioned.

Coach: Bank Nasser Limo buses cost US$2.50 to city and stop at hotels and on request; take about 45-55 minutes and meet most flights. Misr travel limos go to city center and major hotels every hour on the hour between October and May.

Transit: Local bus is inexpensive but takes nearly two hours.

Facilities

Currency exchange, hotel reservations, post office, restaurant, shops, conference rooms, first aid/medical.

Duty-free shop at airport sells tobaccos, spirits, wines, liqueurs, watches, jewellery. Shop is open to arrival passengers and convertible currencies are accepted.

Car rental desks: Hertz, Avis, Budget, Europcar

Airport Taxes

Per person: 5 Egyptian pounds

City Information

Weather

The weather is cool, dry and sunny in winter; very hot and dry in summer.

Average temps: Jan 13c(56F) July 38c(100F)

Transportation

Taxis are the best method of getting around, although they are difficult to get during rush hour. Often shared. Some have meters showing exact fare, but others have minimum fares for certain trips; agree on amount before setting out. Have destination written in Arabic to show to the driver. Tip 10%.

Air-conditioned limos available at airport and main hotels where fares are usually listed. Most are expensive but good in hot weather.

Cars can be rented (international driving licence required) but without a good knowledge of traffic and routes, it is better to use other forms of city transportation. There is an inexpensive train/bus service, and a metro service is being built.

Car Hire

Rental charges are usually based on a day-rate plus cost per km. Roads, although connecting most parts of the country, are not good.

Hertz, Cairo Airport (tel: 873241 & 3474172)

Avis, 16 Moamal El Sukar (tel: 666688 & 345081)

Budget, 5 Sh. El Makrizi (tel: 963270 & 400070)

Europcar, 9 A Sh. Champollion (tel: 753130)

Hospitals

Medical aid for travellers at:

Iamat Center, 11 Emad el Din St. (tel: 910816)

Iamat Center, 87, Road 9, Maadi (tel: 633105)

Trade Fairs

International Trade Fair, Exhibition Ground, Massar City (Mar)

Contact GOIEF for further information.

Hotels

There is a wide range of hotels available but it is advisable to book first-class rooms well in advance; 12% service charge and municipal tax added to bill. Tip 10%.

Atlas, 2 Sh Mohamed Rushdi (tel: 918311)

El Gezirah Sheraton, El Orman (tel: 988607)

El Salam Hyatt, Sh Abdel H. Badawy (tel: 691255)

Holiday Inn Pryamids, Alexandria Desert Rd (tel: 856477)

Marriott, Gezeira Island (tel: 650840)
Mena House Oberoi, Giza (tel: 855444)
Meridien Cairo, Corniche El Nil (tel: 845444)
Nile Hilton, Tahrir Sq (tel: 740777)
Novotel, Cairo Airport (tel: 661330)
President, 22 Sh Taha Hussein (tel: 816671)
Ramses Hilton, 1115 Corniche (tel: 744400)
Sheraton-Cairo, Galae Sq (tel: 3488700)
Sheraton-Heliopolis, Uruda Rd (tel: 665500)
Sonesta, El Tayaran St (tel: 609444)

What to See and Do
The three Great Pyramids of Giza (Menkaru, Chephren and Cheops) and the Sphinx are 9 miles west of Cairo. The step-pyramid of King Zosser is at Saqqara. In Cairo, visit the Egyptian Antiquities Museum which includes Tutankhamun's sarcophagus and funeral mask; the mosques of Al Azhar and Ibn Tulun, the Marble Mosque; the Coptic and Islamic museums; the Museum of Islamic Arts; the Khan el Khalili Bazaar.

Embassies and Consulates
American: 5 Sh Latin America (tel: 3557371)
Canadian: 6 Sh Muh. Fahmy El Sayed (tel: 3543110)
British: Sh Ahmed Raghab (tel: 3540852)

Business and Commerce
Central Post Office, Atava Sq
Central Bank of Egypt, 31 Kasr El Nil St. (tel: 751529)
Cairo Stock Exchange, El Shaerifein St. (tel: 54447)
Egyptian Chamber of Commerce, 4 Midan El Falaki St (tel: 22897)
Egyptian General Trade Organization, 9 Sh Talaat Harb
United Nations Information Office, Boite Postale 262 (tel: 25153)

Tourism and Travel
Egyptian State Tourist Office, Misr Travel Tower, Abbassia (tel: 826016)
Automobile Club of Egypt, Kasr El Nil St (tel: 743355)
American Express, 15 Sh Kasr El St (tel: 970138)
Thomas Cook, 4 Sh Champollion (Tel: 743955)

ISRAEL

Essential Information

Type of Government
Parliamentary Democracy

Area
20,325 sq km (7,850 sq mi)

Population
4.4 million

Annual Growth Rate
1.6%

Languages
Hebrew, Arabic, English

Religion
Judaism, Muslim, Christianity, Druze

Ethnic Groups
Jewish 83%, non-Jewish (mostly Arab) 17%

Weights and Measures
Metric

Electrical Current
A.C. 50c 230/400V & 220V

Major Business Cities
Jerusalem (cap) 457,000
Tel Aviv (most countries
maintain their embassies in Tel
Aviv) 385,000
Haifa 240,000

Currency
1 Shekel = 100 New Argorot
Notes 1, 5, 10, 15, 100, 500
  shekels
Coins 1, 5, 10, 50 new argorot

Public Holidays
Jewish holidays are determined
by lunar cycles. It is wise to
check before travelling.
Mar 15 Purim
Apr 14-24 Passover
May 14 Independence
Jun 3 Pentacost (Shavuot)
Sept 24 Rosh Hashanah
Oct 3 Yom Kippur
Oct 8 Sukkot
Oct 15 Simhat Torah
Dec 16 First Day of Chanukah

Travellers Information

Entry Requirements
Passport required by all. Visa is
not required by nationals of US,
Canada, Australia, New Zealand
or UK, who receive a free visa
on entry. Many other nationals
need visas, however, which
must be obtained before
departing for Israel. It is wise to
check. On arrival, everyone must
fill out entry form AL 17: if you
plan to go on to Arab countries,
ask to have your entry stamp on
this document rather than your
passport. If your have an entry
stamp from an Arab country in
your passport, you will be
refused entry. Regular travellers
to both Israel and Arab countries
often use two passports.

Working Restrictions
To get a work permit, apply to

the embassy in your home
country.

Vaccination Required
No vaccinations required.
Cholera and typhoid shots
recommended.

Customs and Duty Free
On arrival: 250 cigarets or 250g/
8oz tobacco; 1 liter liquor; 2 liters
wine; reasonable amount of
perfume

Currency Restrictions
Import of foreign currency is
unrestricted and no declaration
is necessary. Visitors may
reconvert Israel shekels up to the
equivalent of US$3000 on
departure.

Health Tips
Adequate health care facilities:
some doctors and dentists speak
English. Ask at government
tourist offices or hotels.
Water is purified in cities but
drink bottled water outside
main centers. Imported
pharmaceuticals are expensive.
Emergency care is free but other
services must be paid for.

Climate and Clothing
The climate is Mediterranean.
Between April and October it is
dry, sunny and hot. Wear
lightweight to tropical weight
clothes. November to March is
mild with a little rain; wear
medium weight clothes and take
a raincoat.

Tipping
Usually 15% is added to hotel,
restaurant, and nightclub bills; if
not, leave it yourself. Tip porters
the equivalent of 50 cents per
bag, chambermaids 50 cents per
day or $3 at the end of stay. Taxi
drivers do not expect a tip.

Food and Drink
There is a diversity of foods from
many parts of the world.
Kabobs, borscht and chicken

soup are all popular. Try gefilte fish, vegetable salad, and falafel (stuffed pita bread). Beef is usually eaten only on Fridays; chicken and fish are more common. Fruit and fruit juices are plentiful and usually part of every meal; alcohol is not as popular as in Europe and North America.

Business Brief

GDP
$32.6 billion
(per capita income $7,588)

Annual Growth Rate
1%

Natural Resources
Copper, phosphate, bromide, potash, clay, sand, sulphur, bitumen, manganese

Agriculture
Citrus and other fruits, vegetables, beef, dairy and poultry products

Industry
Food processing, diamond cutting and polishing, textiles and clothing, chemicals, metal products, transport equipment, electrical equipment, miscellaneous machinery, potash mining, high technology, electronics

Imports
Total $14.4 billion
Military equipment, rough diamonds, oil, chemicals, machinery, iron and steel, cereals, textiles, livestock, vehicles, ships and aircraft

Exports
Total $8.47 billion
Polished diamonds, citrus and other fruits, textiles and clothing, processed foods, fertilizer and chemical products, electronics. Tourism is also an important foreign-exchange earner.

Major Trading Partners
US, UK, West Germany, Netherlands, Belgium, France, Switzerland, Italy, Hong Kong, Japan

Workforce
1.2 million
Industry 25.3%, public services 32.8%, commerce 12.2%, agriculture 6.5%

Tips for Doing Business
A business suit is necessary for government visits but Israel is an informal country and suits and ties are rarely worn for business calls. Make prior appointments for visits to executives and government officials. You should make appointments for all other meetings as well: in an emergency, however, it is not considered impolite to phone and turn up. Most Israeli businessmen speak English and may seem a bit abrupt at first, but that is just their manner. When meeting or leaving use the phrase "shalom". Avoid the subjects of religion, Arabs and foreign aid. If invited to someone's home, take flowers or chocolates.

Best Months for Doing Business
October through June are best months for travel. Avoid the week of Purim, the week before and during Passover and the week of the Jewish New Year. Vacations are in July, August and September.

Business Hours

Government
Sept-May: Sun-Thurs 0700-1600
Fri 0730-1430
June-Aug: Sun-Thurs 0730-1430
Fri 0730-1300
Weekly holiday is Saturday

Business
Sept-May: Sun-Thurs 0730-1600
Fri 0730-1230
June-Aug: Sun-Thurs 0730-1430

Fri 0730-1230
Weekly holiday is Saturday

Banks
Sun-Fri 0830-1230
Weekly holiday is Saturday

Shops
Sun-Fri 0800-1300, 1600-1900
Arab shops closed on Friday and
Christian shops on Sunday

English Language Publications
Daily newspaper is the Jerusalem
Post; Ha'aretz is the daily with
business news.

Telephone and Communications
Telephone country code: 972
Telephone city code: Tel Aviv 03,
Haifa 4, Jerusalem 2
Telex country code: 922
Telephone and telegraph services
are generally good. Direct dialing
within the country and for
some international calls. Many
operators speak English. Public
telephones use tokens (called
Aseemonim) available at kiosks
and post offices.
Telex facilities are available at
major hotels in Tel Aviv and
Jerusalem.

Air Travel
Comprehensive domestic air
service is operated by Arkia
(tel: 03 426262)

Other Transport
Major cities are connected by
good roads. The National Bus
Company, Egged (03-331101),
has extensive service. Reliable,
but not too comfortable.
Travel by rail is best left for
sight-seeing.
City-to-city travel is often done
in "Sherut" taxis which operate
on fixed routes. Seats can be
booked or you can get a Sherut
from Central Bus Stations in
major cities at frequent intervals.
There is no public transportation
(including air) from sundown
Friday to sundown Saturday.

TEL AVIV

Airport Information

Time
GMT +2

Airport
Ben Gurian International TLV
Tel: 9711461
20 km (12 mi) E of city

Airlines
Aer Lingus 291980
Air Canada 247976
Air France 5103050
Air Sinai 246442
Alitalia 245353
Austrian 693535
British Airways 229251
Canadian International 03652163
El Al 625252
Eastern 227914
Iberian 290976
KLM 654141
Lufthansa 5101621
Northwest 295153
Olympic 294381
Pan Am 201906
Qantas 652163
Sabena 654411
SAS 5101177
Swissair 5102626
TWA 651212
UTA 297211
United 247224

Transport to City
Taxi: there are two types of
taxi, "Sherut" and private. Sherut
are Mercedes which carry seven
passengers and charge about
US$4 per person. Takes 15-20
minutes into the city and
operates 24 hours. Private taxis
cost about US$10 during the day,
25% more at night. Tip 10-15%.
Coach: a United Tours air-
conditioned bus has service
every hour from 0600-2200.
Meets all international flights
and takes 20-30 minutes to North
Tel Aviv Bus Terminal where
there are connecting taxis to
most hotels.

Transit: for those with little baggage, there are buses operated by National Israel Bus Company to Central Station every 15 minutes from 0500-2300 for a fare of $1.05.

Facilities
Bar, buffet, snack bar, restaurant, bank with currency exchange, insurance, hotel reservations, post office, baggage deposit, barber shop, nursery, synagogue, information desk, conference facilities, first aid/ medical, shops selling books, gifts, silver, ceramics. Duty-free shop sells cigarets, cigars, tobacco, liquors, wines, liqueurs, perfume, jewellery, glass, china, watches, radios. Australian, Belgian, Dutch, French, Swiss, British and US currencies accepted. Car rental desks: Hertz, Avis, InterRent, Europcar

Airport Taxes
Per person: equivalent of US$10 in shekels

City Information

Weather
Hot and humid in the summer months but there is virtually no rain from May to October. The winter months are temperate with occasional rains.

1. DIZENGOFF CENTER
2. F. MANN AUDITORIUM
3. HISTORICAL MUSEUM
4. KIKKAR HAMEDINA
5. OHEL HALL
6. OPERA
7. RAILWAY STATION
8. TEL AVIV MUSEUM

Tel Aviv

Average temps: Jan 14c (57F)
July 28c (82F)

Transportation

Taxis are metered but expensive and have a 25% surcharge at night. It is easier and more economical to take a "Sherut", a large shared taxi which follows main bus routes. No tips expected. Car hire is available with a day charge plus charge per kilometer. International or foreign drivers license.

Car Hire

All rental automobiles must be covered by unlimited third-party insurance.
Hertz, 10 Carleback St.
    (tel: 971165 & 9711350)
Avis, 80 Aamasger (tel: 971080 & 651093)
Champion InterRent, 160 Hayarkon St (tel: 240089)
Europcar, 198 Hayarkon St
    (tel: 230149)

Hospitals

Emergency number 101.
Medical aid for travellers at:
    Iamat Center, (tel: 756688)
Assutah Hospital, (tel: 245211 & 240697)

Hotels

Value-added tax 15%, exempt if paid in foreign currency.
Basel, 156 Hayarkon St
    (tel: 244161)
Carlton Penta, 10 Hayarkon St
    (tel: 291291)
City, 9 Mapu St (tel: 24653)
Dan, 99 Hayarkon St (tel: 24111)
Sheraton, 115 Hayarkon St
    (tel: 286222)
Tal, 287 Hayarkon St (tel: 455281)
Tel Aviv Hilton, Independence Park (tel: 244222)

What to See and Do

Visit some of the many museums: Ha'aretz Museum complex in Ramat Aviv for glass, ceramics and archeology; the Tel Aviv Museum on Shaul Hamelech for artists like Chagall and Modigliani; the Diaspara Museum in the University for history of the Jews. The Mann Auditorium houses the Israel Philharmonic. Atarim Square is a tourist mall with boutiques, restaurants and cinemas. Visit Old Jaffa for nightclubs and cabarets, and the cafes in Digengoff Street for coffee and ice cream.

Useful Addresses

Embassies and Consulates

American: 71 Rehov Hayarkon
    (tel: 54338)
Canadian: 220 Rehov Hayarkon
    (tel: 228122)
British: 192 Rehov Hayarkon
    (tel: 249171)

Business and Commerce

Central Bank (Bank of Israel) Mizpeh Bldg, 29 Jaffa Rd, Jerusalem (tel: 241611)
Tel Aviv Stock Exchange, 113 Allenby Rd
Tel Aviv Chamber of Commerce, 84 Hahashmoniam St
    (tel: 223235 & 288224)
American Chamber of Commerce, 35 Shaul Hamelech Blvd (tel: 252341/2)
British Chamber of Commerce, 99 Ahad Ha'Am St
    (tel: 229165)

Tourism and Travel

Ministry of Tourism, 7 Mendele St (tel: 223266)

KENYA

Essential Information

Type of Government
Republic

Area
582,646 sq km
(224,960 sq mi)

Population
21 million

Annual Growth Rate
3.9%

Languages
Swahili (official) Swahili and
English (commercial)

Religion
Protestant 38%, Roman Catholic
28%, Indigenous beliefs 26%,
Muslim 6%

Ethnic Groups
African: Kikuyu 21%, Luhya
14%, Luo 13%, Kalenjin 11%,
Kamba 11%, Kisii 6%, Meru 5%
Non-African: Asian, European,
Arab

Weights and Measures
Metric

Electrical Current
A.C. 50c 240/415V

Major Business Cities
Nairobi (cap) 1,250,000
Mombassa 450,000

Currency
1 Kenya Shilling = 100 cents
Notes 5, 10, 20, 100 shillings
Coins 5, 10, 50 cents, 1 shilling

Public Holidays
Jan 1 New Year
Apr 13-20 Easter Week
May 1 Labor Day
Jun 1 Madaraka Day
Oct 20 Kenyatta Day
Dec 12 Independence Day
Dec 25 Christmas Day
Dec 26 Boxing Day
There are Muslim holidays as
well as Christian and traditional,
but since these change yearly
according to lunar cycles it is
wise to consult local Kenyan
embassy for current dates before
planning a business trip.

Travellers Information

Entry Requirements
Passport required by all visitors.
Visa required by all except
Commonwealth citizens (with
the exception of Indians,
Ugandans and Tanzanians.)
Visas should be obtained in
advance from a local Kenyan
Embassy. All visitors need a
visitor's pass and a valid ticket
onward. Commonwealth
nationals may obtain them on
arrival. There are no special
restrictions for business visitors.
Entry restricted for South African
passport holders.

Vaccination Required
Certificates of yellow fever and
cholera vaccinations required if
arriving from infected areas, Asia
or the Middle East. Vaccinations
are recommended for polio,
typhoid and tetanus. Check
yellow fever vaccination
requirements for the next
country to be visited. You may
require a certificate for entry.

Customs and Duty Free
On arrival: 200 cigarets or 50
cigars or 250 g tobacco. One
bottle of alcohol. Small amounts
of perfume. Personal effects are
admitted duty-free, but large
amounts of equipment may
require a customs bond.

Currency Restrictions
Import and export of local
currency strictly prohibited.
Amounts of foreign currency
brought in are unrestricted but
must be declared on arrival:
the amounts declared may be

re-exported. Hotel bills and business expenses must be paid for in foreign currency.

Health Tips

Drinking water is not purified outside major cities: drink boiled or bottled water and avoid unwashed fruits and vegetables. Take antimalarial tablets a week before arriving, during your stay and for a week after leaving. Good medical services available but must be paid for. Imported pharmaceuticals are expensive and scarce. The altitude in Nairobi (over 5900 ft) can be debilitating, and it will take you one or two days of minimum activity to adapt. Be careful of the sun which can be deceptively strong in Nairobi and the Highlands.

Climate and Clothing

Tropical and hot on the coast; temperate on the plateau and highlands, where light or medium weight clothing is worn most of the year. Sweaters and light raincoats are needed during the rainy seasons: long rains from March to June, short rains from October to December.

Tipping

Generally, 10% tipping is customary for restaurants and nightspots. Although 10% may be included in hotel bills, an additional 10% is appreciated. Give porters 5 shillings for each piece of baggage, taxi drivers, 5 shillings.

Food and Drink

Afternoon tea is customary. European food is the norm in major cities, and Nairobi has familiar fast-food outlets as well as excellent Indian restaurants. The most common Kenyan dishes are made with goat, beef, lamb and chicken. Poshosti is a stiff dough, ugali is a corn-meal porridge and kitumbura is fried bread. Fruits include pineapple, mango and papaya.

Business Brief

GDP
$7.23 billion
(per capita income $355)

Annual Growth Rate
3.9%

Natural Resources
Wildlife, land

Agriculture
Corn, wheat, rice, sugar cane, coffee, tea, sisal, pineapples, pyrethrum, horticultural products, meat and meat products

Industry
Petroleum products, cement, beer, light manufacturing

Imports
Total $1.75 billion
Crude petroleum, machinery, vehicles, iron and steel, paper and paper products, pharmaceuticals, fertilizers, textiles

Exports
Total $961 million
Coffee, petroleum products, tea, hides and skins, meat and meat products, cement, pyrethrum, sisal, soda ash, wattle extract, pineapples

Major Trading Partners
UK, West Germany, US, Canada, Netherlands, Japan, Saudi Arabia, Iran and other African states

Workforce
5.4 million
Agriculture 21.1%, industry and commerce 21.2%, services 10%, public sector 48.2%

Tips For Doing Business
A conservative business suit is recommended for all government and business occasions in Nairobi, although more tropical

clothing, like shorts and open-neck shirts, are often worn in coastal areas. Prior appointments are necessary for all government and business meetings. English is normally used in these circles. Foreign business is usually conducted by British and Indian businessmen, and most of the government officials are black Kenyans. Adopt a friendly but conservative approach: avoid discussing politics and internal troubles with the tribes. Business discussions are often accompanied by endless cups of coffee and tea.

Best Months For Doing Business

June through February are the best months to travel in Kenya. Businessmen generally vacation in April through June, which is the rainy season as well. Avoid the weeks before and after Christmas and Easter.

Business Hours

Government
Mon-Fri 0800/0830-1245, 1400-1630
Sat 0800-1230

Business
Mon-Fri 0800-1230, 1400-1630
Sat 0800-1230

Banks
Mon-Fri 0800/0900-1400
Sat 0900-1100 (first and last Sat of month) On the coast banks open and close 30 min earlier.

Shops
Mon-Fri 0830-1230 & 1400-1630
Sat 0830-1200

English Language Publications

Daily newspapers include The Standard, The Nation, Kenya Times; weekly is The Weekly Review.

Telephone and Communications

Telephone country code: 254
Telphone city code: Nairobi 2, Mombassa 11

Telex country code: 963
International direct dialing and subscriber trunk dialing to all major towns is provided by Kenya Post and Telecommunications Corporation which also supplies telex, facsimile, data communication and other services. You can use public telephones for local and long-distance calls: put required money in the slot and the coins fall automatically. Public telephones cannot be used for international calls unless you call the operator and reverse the charges.
Postage stamps can be obtained at post offices only.
Public telex offices available at central post offices in major cities and main hotels.

Air Travel

International airports at Nairobi (NBO) amd Mombassa (MBA). Kenya Airways regularly offers flights to main commercial centers (Mombassa, Malindi, Kisumu) from Nairobi. Charter companies offer air-taxi service and flights to game reserves and main centers.

Other Transport

Trains have modern first-and second-class service, and travel from Nairobi to Mombassa, Kisumu, Nyeri and Nanyuki. Often late but comfortable, with restaurant cars and sleeping berths. Book sleeping compartments in advance. Fast luxury buses, run by East African Road Services, operate on all major routes.
Car hire is available and nearly all main cities are connected by roads although only about 10% of them are paved and the rest are dirt. This can cause delays in wet weather. Traffic is on the left: international drivers license acceptable.

NAIROBI

Airport Information

Time
GMT +3

Airport
Jomo Kenyatta NBO
Tel: (Embakasi) 822111
17 km (11 mi) SE of city

Airlines
Air France 333305
Alitalia 24361
British Airways 334440
Egyptair 7683
El Al 28123

Iberia 338623
JAL 20591
Kenya Airways 29291
KLM 332673
Lufthansa 335819
Olympic 338026
Pan Am 23581
Sabena 22185
SAS 338347
Swissair 340231

Transport to City
Taxi: takes 15 minutes to
downtown for $11 fare.
Coach: a coach leaves for the city
every 25 minutes with a 24-hour
service.
Transit: local bus leaves every 30

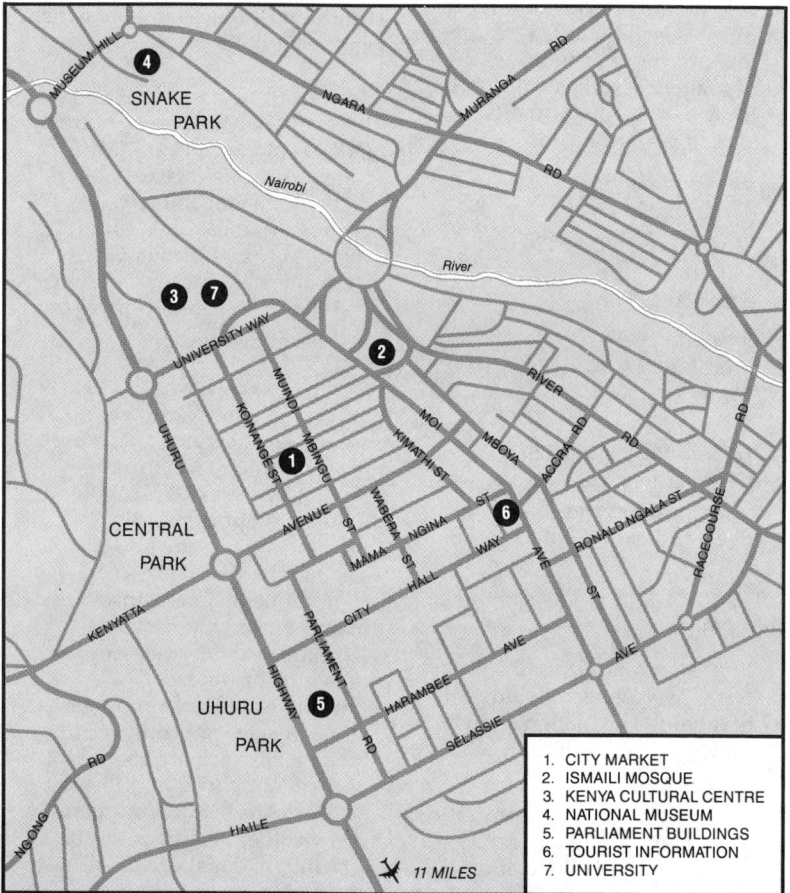

1. CITY MARKET
2. ISMAILI MOSQUE
3. KENYA CULTURAL CENTRE
4. NATIONAL MUSEUM
5. PARLIAMENT BUILDINGS
6. TOURIST INFORMATION
7. UNIVERSITY

Nairobi

minutes from 0630-2000, and takes 30 minutes for fare of 40 cents.

Facilities
Bar, buffet, restaurant, bank with currency exchange, hotel reservations, post office, nursery, vaccination center, shops selling flowers, books and gifts, first aid/medical

Airport Taxes
Per person: International US$10

City Information

Weather
The weather in Nairobi is temperate with rainy seasons March to June, and October to December. June to October is cool and dry with moderate temperatures during the day and cool evenings. Average temps: Jan 24-27c (75-80F) July 27-29c (80-85F)

Transportation
There are three types of taxis available: matatus, shared vans to main bus lines; Peugeot shared taxis on fixed routes; and regular taxis which cannot be hailed on the streets but must be ordered (tel: 557177 or 554486). Agree on fare before starting journey. Tip 10%.
Car hire available at major companies and at hotels and travel companies. An international driving license is required. Drive on the left.

Car Hire
Hertz, Mundi Mbingu St
(tel: 331960 & 822813)
Avis, Union Tower, Moi Ave
(tel: 222383 & 822186)
Car Hire Services Ltd, (tel: 22813)
Europcar, Bruce Hse Standard St
(tel: 332744)
Kenatco (tel: 822356)

Hospitals
Emergency health care for travellers at:

Aga Khan Hospital (tel: 742301)
Nairobi Hospital (tel: 722160)

Trade Fairs
African Health and Lab Exhibition (Aug)
Nairobi International Agricultural Show (Sept-Oct)
International Medical and Lab Equipment Exhibition (Nov)

Hotels
There is a wide range available in main centers, but it is advisable to book and confirm well in advance.
Ambassadeur, Moi Ave
(tel: 336803)
Excelsior, Kenyatta Ave
(tel: 26481)
Fairview, PO Box 40842
(tel: 723211)
Inter-Continental Nairobi, City Hall Way (tel: 335550)
Jacaranda, PO Box 14287
(tel: 742272)
Milimani, PO Box 30715
(tel: 720760)
Hilton International Nairobi, Mama Ngina St, Moi Ave
(tel: 3344000)
Nairobi Serena, PPO Box 46302
(tel: 337978)
New Stanley, Kimathi St. Kenyatta Ave (tel: 333233)
Norfolk, Harry Thuku Rd
(tel: 335422)
Panafric, Kenyatta Ave
(tel: 720822)
Sixeighty, Kenyatta Ave
(tel: 332680)

What To See and Do
Kenya is famous for its safari treks and wildlife. National park sanctuaries have many wild animals including lions, leopards, giraffes and many more. In the city visit the Snake Park, the National Museum, Nairobi National Park (10 minutes drive from the city), Kenyatta Centre, International Casino, Bombas of Kenya with traditional dancing and tribal

villages. Long and short safari journeys can be arranged through local agents: one-day safaris include trips to Lake Naivasha, Nakuru National Park by road, and Mara National Park by air.

Useful Addresses

Embassies and Consulates
American: Haile Selassie Ave (tel: 334141)
Canadian: Comcraft House (tel: 334033)
British: Bruce House, Standard St (tel: 335944)

Business and Commerce
Central Bank of Kenya, Tumbo Rd (tel: 26431)
General Post Office, Kenyatta Av
Nairobi Stock Exchange, Stanbank House, Government Rd (tel: 27803)

National Chamber of Commerce and Industry, Ufansi House, Haile Selassie Av (tel: 20866)
Ministry of Tourism and Wildlife, PO Box 30027
Association of Chambers of Commerce and Industry, PO Box 44365; (tel: 62038)
United Nations Information Office, PO Box 30218 (tel: 332182)

Tourism and Travel
United Touring, Travel House, Mundi Rd (tel: 31960)
Tourist Information Office, (tel: 29751)
American Express Kenya, Consolidated House (tel: 334722)
Automobile Association of Kenya, Nyaku House, Hurlingham (tel: 720882)

KUWAIT

Essential Information

Type of Government
Constitutional Monarchy

Area
17,818 sq km
(6,880 sq mi)

Population
1.9 million

Annual Growth Rate
4.5%

Languages
Arabic (official), English

Religion
Muslim 85%

Ethnic Groups
Arab 84%, South Asian, Iranian, Southeast Asian

Weights and Measures
Metric

Electrical Current
A.C. 50c 240/415V

Major Business Cities
Kuwait City (cap) 700,000
Hawalii 943,000
Ahmadi 304,662
Jahra 279,466
Salmiya 114,000

Currency
Kuwaiti Dinar = 1000 Fils
Notes 250, 500 fils; 1, 5, 10 dinars
Coins 1, 5, 10, 20, 50, 100 fils

Public Holidays
Kuwait is predominately Muslim and since Muslim holidays change yearly with the lunar cycles, it is wise to check current dates with a local consulate (particularly for the time of the month of Ramadan) as business is halted during these periods.

Travellers Information

Entry Requirements
Passport is required by all.
Visa or entry permits required by all. Most travellers require a sponsor for a visa which must then be obtained from an embassy or consulate in your home country since no visas are issued at entry points. Those with a visa from Israel in their passport will be refused entry.

Working Restrictions
Anyone wishing to work in Kuwait needs a contract with a firm in the country before a permit will be issued.

Vaccination Required
International certificates for cholera and smallpox may be required; check for current regulations before travelling. Yellow fever certificate required if travelling from infected area.

Customs and Duty Free
On arrival: 200 cigarets or 50 cigars or 225g/8oz tobacco. You may bring in household goods and personal effects without restriction but there may be a 4% duty on some items. Absolutely prohibited: alcoholic beverages or anything connected with them; pornographic material or suggestive magazines degrading to women; pork and meat products; anything from Israel or South Africa.

Currency Restrictions
There are no currency restrictions.

Health Tips
The drinking water is not purified, but the large hotels filter their own water. Health care is good and efficient; both state and private. Doctors and dentists are Western or trained in the West and most speak English. Imported pharmaceuticals are expensive.

Climate and Clothing
The summers are hot with shade temperatures of up to 38c (100F) and July and August temperatures rising to 49c (120F): can be very humid. Wear tropical weight clothes. Winters (November to March) are cooler especially in December and January when temperatures fall to 7-10c (45-50F) and there are cold winds and rainfalls. Wear medium weight clothes and take a coat or warm raincoat.

Tipping
Taxi drivers are not tipped. Give porter 150 fils per piece of luggage. Hotels, restaurants usually include 10% in the bill. Tip doormen and small services100 fils.

Food and Drink
Most restaurants and hotels serve Western food as well as Middle Eastern. Kuwaiti dishes are known for the subtlety of their spices. Try Khudra, a fish similar to sole, cooked in garlic, tomatoes, tumeric and lemons. Most dishes are served with rice. In October and November, the delicacy fuga (desert truffles) are often available. Desserts include rangina, dates cooked in flour, butter and cardamom; and halawat al-naril, coconut with sugar, saffron and cardamom. Coffee is served in small china cups and alcohol is strictly prohibited.

Business Brief

GDP
$29 billion
(per capita income $13,200)

Annual Growth Rate
5.4%

Natural Resources
Petroleum, fish, shrimp

Agriculture
Most food is imported.

Industry
Petroleum and petroleum products, crude and refined oil, fertilizer, chemicals, construction materials

Imports
Total $5 billion
Manufactured goods, foodstuffs, crude materials, machinery and transport equipment

Exports
Total $7.9 billion
Oil and petroleum products

Major Trading Partners
US, Japan, UK, West Germany, Italy, Netherlands, France, Korea

Workforce
566,000
Social services 45%, construction 20%, trade, hotels and restaurants 12.1%, manufacturing 8.6%, finance and real estate 2.6%, agriculture and fishing 1.9%, power and water 1.7%, mining and quarrying 1.4%

Tips for Doing Business
During the winter months, a conservative business suit should be worn. Prior business appointments are necessary for government visits. Do not plan visits too close together or show signs of impatience if your contact keeps you waiting. Coffee will usually be offered; drink two cups with your right hand, then refuse a third by shaking the cup slightly before returning it to the server. Adopt a low-key approach and be prepared to have group discussions. Business meetings often take place in coffee houses. Most businessmen speak English; still it is wise to get business cards printed in both English and Arabic. Oil has turned Kuwait City from a dusty dessert town into a modern metropolis in a little over 40 years, and there is a great need for automotive and consumer goods. There are no nightclubs and entertaining is done at home. Bring a gift for your business contact but not his wife since women are not included. (Do not ask a man about his wife or take pictures of women in the street.) Avoid the subject of politics. Leave immediately after coffee or tea has been drunk.

Best Months for Doing Business
Go when the weather is cool between November and April. Check carefully for dates of Muslim holidays, particularly the month of Ramadan, when businesses are closed.

Trade Fairs
Modern House Exhibition (Jan)
Perfumes and Cosmetics Exhibition (Mar)
Agricultural Fair (Mar)
International Energy Exhibition (Apr)
Food Exhibition (Apr)
Security Equipment Exhibition (Oct)
Cleaning and Maintenance Exhibition (Nov)
Kuwait Medical Exhibition (Nov)
Arabic Book Exhibition (Nov)
International Children's Books and Toys (Nov/Mar)
Offshore Oil Exhibition (Dec)

Hotels
Most people who visit Kuwait are there on business. In Kuwait City, many internationally recognized hotels have luxurious facilities. Book well in advance.
Carlton Tower, Faahd Al-Salem St, Safat (tel: 2452740)
Holiday Inn, PO Box 18544, Farwaniya (tel: 4742000)
Kuwait Hilton International, PO

Box 5996, Bnaid Al Gar
(tel: 2530000)
Kuwait Hyatt Regency, PO Box
1139, Salmiyah (tel: 562800)
Kuwait Sheraton, Fahd Al-Salem
St, Safat (tel: 2422055)
Meridien Kuwait, Hilali St, Safat
(tel: 2455550)

Business Hours

Government
Winter: Sat-Wed 0730-1300,
Thurs 0730-1130
Summer: Sat-Wed 0700-1300,
Thurs 0700-1100
Ramadan: Sat-Thurs 0900-1300
Friday is the weekly holiday

Business
Sat-Thurs 0830-1230, 1630-2000
(may change during Ramadan)
Friday is the weekly holiday

Banks
Sat-Thurs 0800-1200,
Ramadan: 0900-1230
Friday is the weekly holiday

Shops
Sat-Thurs 0830-1230, 1630-2100
Friday is the weekly holiday

English Language Publications

Local newspapers in English are
the Arab Times and Kuwait
Times.

Telephone and Communications

Telephone country code: 965
Telephone city code: Kuwait
City 0
Telex country code: 959
Local telephone service is good
and direct-dialing is available to
most countries including the US.
Telex facilities available at all
major hotels; a surcharge may be

added. Telegrams may be sent
from the Ministry of Post and
Telegraph Main Offices, Abdulla
Al Salem Square; open 24 hours.

Air Travel

Time
GMT +3

Airport
Kuwait International Airport
KWI
Tel: 734377
16 km (10 mi) S of Kuwait City
There are no internal air
services.

Other Transport
Both private and shared taxis on
set routes; more expensive from
hotel ranks. There is a standard
fare in Kuwait City and drivers
do not expect a tip. If hiring a
taxi for anything other than a
short trip, agree on the fare in
advance.
Car hire is available.
International driving license
(locally approved) and insurance
with Gulf Insurance Company or
Kuwait Insurance Company
essential. Driving is on the right.
Roads are good and at least four
lanes.
Buses, operated by Kuwait
Transport Company, are a good
and economical form of
transport.

Travel and Tourism
The Automobile Association of
Kuwait and the Gulf, Airport
Rd, Khaldiyah Kuwait
Automobile and Touring Club,
Airport Rd, Khaldiyah

MOROCCO

Essential Information

Type of Government
Constitutional Monarchy

Area
409,200 sq km
(171,953 sq mi)

Population
23.4 million

Annual Growth Rate
3.25%

Languages
Arabic (official), French, three
Berber vernaculars

Religion
Sunni Muslim 98.7%, Christian
1.1%, Jewish 0.2%

Ethnic Groups
Arab-Berber 99.1%

Weights and Measures
Metric

Electrical Current
A.C. 50c 115/200V
A.C. 60c 110/125V

Major Business Cities
Rabat (cap) 895,000
Casablanca 2,550,000
Marrakesh 575,000
Fez 595,000
Tangier 350,000

Currency
1 Dirham = 100 Centimes
Notes 5, 10, 50, 100 dirhams
Coins 1, 2, 5, 10, 20,
50 centimes; 1 dirham

Public Holidays
Morocco is a predominantly
Muslim country. The Muslim
holidays change yearly according
to the lunar cycles. It is wise to
check dates before travelling as
government offices and
businesses are closed on both
Muslin and Christian holidays.

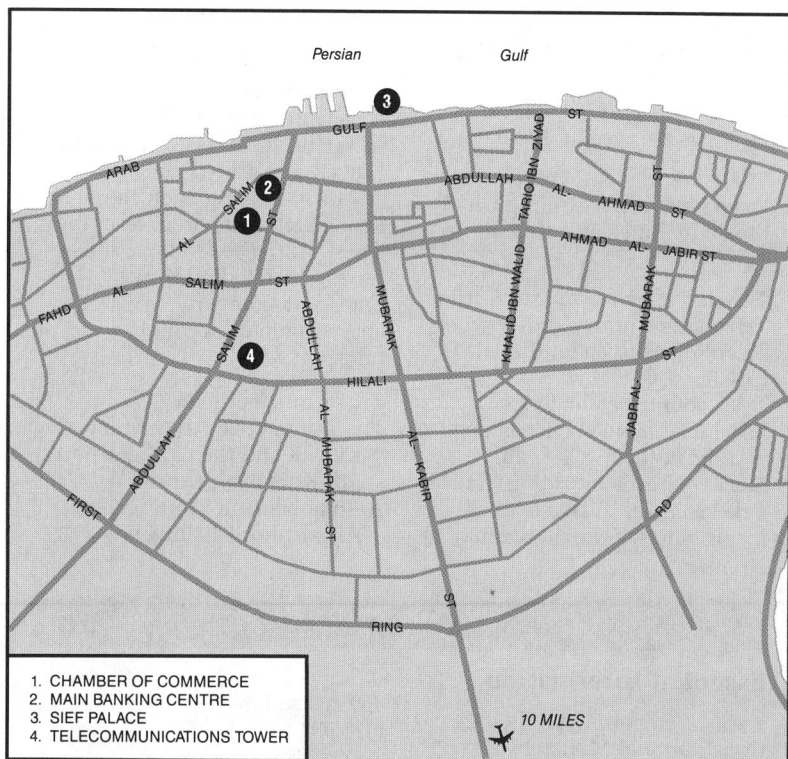

1. CHAMBER OF COMMERCE
2. MAIN BANKING CENTRE
3. SIEF PALACE
4. TELECOMMUNICATIONS TOWER

Kuwait City

Travellers Information

Entry Requirements
Passport is required by all. Visa is not required by nationals of France, West Germany, Japan, UK, US, Australia, New Zealand, Canada and some others for a period of stay not longer than 90 days. Nationals of Israel and South Africa prohibited entry.

Working Restrictions
Work permit is required. Inquire at local embassy or consulate.

Vaccination Required
No vaccinations are required but those against typhoid, polio, cholera and tetanus are strongly recommended. Take antimalarial tablets before and during visit.

Customs and Duty Free
On arrival: 200 cigarets or 50 cigars or 500g/1 lb tobacco; 1 bottle spirits

Currency Restrictions
The import/export of local currency prohibited. There is no restriction on the import of foreign currency and you can take out the amount you declared on arrival. Convert into local currency only the amounts you want to spend. International credit cards accepted.

Health Tips
Drink only bottled water. Avoid fresh fruit and vegetables (unless carefully prepared), and food from street vendors.

Climate and Clothing
The climate varies from Mediterranean on the coast to continental inland. In the summer (May to October) wear lightweight clothes, with a jacket for evenings in mountain areas. In winter, wear medium weight clothes and a raincoat for coastal region (Casablanca, Rabat, Tangier), lightweight inland, warmer clothing for mountains.

Tipping
Tip taxi drivers 10%; porters 5 dirhams per piece of luggage; hotels and restaurants usually include 15% in the bill.

Food and Drink
Morroco is famous for its food and good restaurants. The national dish is couscous, which combines semolina and vegetables with chicken or lamb. Mechoui is roasted lamb, pastilla is a pidgeon pie, and there are a number of delicious stews called tajine. Green mint tea is the national drink, but red wine is available.

Business Brief

GDP
$17.8 billion
(per capita income $800)

Natural Resources
Phosphates, iron, manganese, lead, cobalt, silver, copper, oil shale, fish

Agriculture
Wheat, barley, citrus fruits

Industry
Phosphate mining, sugar refining

Imports
Total $4.03 billion
Machinery, foodstuffs, oil products, cotton, lumber

Exports
Total $2.64 billion
Phosphates, foodstuffs, manufacturing, wine

Major Trading Partners
France, US, West Germany, Italy, UK, Eastern-European countries, Iraq, Spain

Workforce
5.5 million
Agriculture 51%, industry 20%, miscellaneous services 29%

Tips for Doing Business

Wear a conservative business suit at all times and make prior appointments for both business and government visits. Get business cards printed in both English and French. Some businessmen speak English and nearly all speak French or Spanish. Business should be conducted in a formal manner. A large part of foreign trade is done by companies with European connections so Western social customs are common although Muslin ones prevail. Entertaining is extensive and you should be prepared to eat heartily. Foreign resident businessmen will take you out for a meal, but Moroccans will probably invite you home for a meal of numerous courses. Take off your shoes when entering the house. Food should be eaten with the fingers of the right hand. Mint tea follows and after the third cup you should leave.

Best Months for Doing Business

October through May are best months for business visits. Avoid the weeks before and after Christmas and Easter, and the month of Ramadan. Check dates before travelling as they change yearly with the lunar cycles.

Business Hours

Government
Mon-Fri 0830-1200, 1430-1800
Sat 0830-1300
Summer: Mon-Sat 0800-1400
Ramadan: Mon-Sat 1000-1500

Business
Mon-Fri 0830-1200, 1430-1800
Sat 0830-1300
Summer: Mon-Sat 0800-1400
Ramadan: Mon-Sat 1000-1500

Banks
Mon-Fri 0830-1130, 1415-1630
Summer: Mon-Fri 0800-1430
Ramadan: Mon-Fri 0930-1430

English Language Publications

There is no English-language newspaper published in Morocco but British newspapers are available in the large cities.

Telephone and Communication

Telephone country code: 210
Telephone city code: Casablanca 0, Fez 6, Marrakesh 4, Rabat 7, Tangier 9, Tiznit 86
Telex country code: 933
International calls in Casablanca and Rabat can be direct-dialed; in other places you must use Central Post Office. There are public telephones in restaurants and cafes and there is direct dial between cities within the country.
Telex facilities can be found in major hotels. Telegrams must be sent from post offices.

Air Travel

Flights to and from Casablanca are operated by Royal Air Inter; Royal Air Maroc connects most cities within the country.

Other Transport

There is a good cheap bus service between cities and towns. It is advisable to book in advance.

CASABLANCA

Airport Information

Time
GMT +1

Airport
Mohamed V CMN
Tel: 339040 & 339140
35 km (22 mi) S of city

Airlines
Aeroflot 310521
Air France 274242
Alia 311267
Alitalia 222250
Iberia 279600

Iraqi 309111
KLM 272729
Korean 238488
Kuwait Air 313434
Libyan 311500
Lufthansa 312371
Pan Am 314141
Royal Air Maroc 314141
Sabena 326543
SAS 224184
Saudi 313535
Swissair 313280
Syrian 52384

Transport to City
Taxi: to city 95-150 dirhams.
"Grands" taxis seat up to 6
people and operate on set routes
and fares. Tip 10%.

Coach: to city (40 minutes) costs
30 dirhams.

Facilities
Bar, buffet, restaurant, bank
with currency exchange, hotel
reservations, post office, baggage
deposit, first aid/medical,
vaccinations.
Car rental desks: Hertz, Avis,
Budget, Europcar

Airport Taxes
Per person: 10 dirham

City Information

Weather
The climate is dry and hot in
the summer. Winter, from

1. CATHEDRAL
2. C.T.M. BUS TERMINAL
3. EXHIBITION PALACE
4. MAIN POST OFFICE
5. MEDINA
6. MUNICIPAL THEATRE
7. TOURIST BUREAU

Casablanca

November to April, has
moderate temperatures and light
rain.
Average temps: Jun 25c (77F) Jan
21-24c (70-75F)

Transportation
There are two types of taxis:
"grands" taxis which seat up to
six people and operate on set
routes, and "petits" taxis. Make
sure of fare before travelling as
meters rarely work and fares
vary considerable. Tip 10%.

Car Hire
Hertz, 25 Rue de Fouaulds
   (tel: 223220)
Avis, 19 Ave Des F.A.R.
   (tel: 312424)
Budget, 46 Ave L'Armee-Royale
   (tel: 310942)
Europcar, 144 Ave L'Armee-
   Royale (tel: 339517 & 310960)
InterRent, 44 Ave L'Armee-
   Royale (tel: 313737 & 339161)

Hospitals
Good public hospitals and
private doctors are available.

Hotels
Casablanca Hyatt Regency, Place
   Mohammed V (tel: 261234)
El Mansour, 27 Ave L'Armee-
   Royale (tel: 313011)
Marhaba, 63 Ave L'Armee-
   Royale (tel: 224199)
Meridien, Rue de Fes
   (tel: 322021)
Tarik, 41 Blvd de la Corniche-
   Ain-Diab (tel: 367073)

What to See and Do
Visit the Royal Palace, the Old
Medina Quarters, Mohemmedia
Casino. For shopping, the

Medina has higher prices but
better choices than elsewhere. To
ship goods home, shop at the
government-operated Maison de
l'Artisanat which has fixed prices
and guarantees of quality. Go to
the coast road (by public bus)
and visit beaches and excellent
seafood restaurants. The Ain
Diab region has many
nightclubs.

Useful Addresses

Embassies and Consulates
American: 8 Blvd Moulay
   Youssef (tel: 224149)
British: 60 Blvd d'Anfa
   (tel: 221653)

Business and Commerce
Central Bank, 227 Ave
   Mohammed V, Rabat
   (tel: 63009)
Casablanca Stock Exchange,98
   Blvd Mohammed V
   (tel: 279354)
International Chamber of
   Commerce, 4 Rue du Rhone
   (tel: 309716)
American Chamber of
   Commerce, 53 Rue Allal Ben
   Abdallah (tel: 221448)
British Chamber of Commerce,
   Bvld. Mohammed V
   (tel: 303760)

Tourism and Travel
Royal Moroccan Automobile
   Club, Ain Diab, Ave Cote
   d'Emeraude/Rue Mimizan
Touring Club of Morocco,
   3 Ave de l'Armee Royale
Thomas Cook, 60 Rue de
   Foucauld (tel: 261211)

NIGERIA

Essential Information

Type of Government
Military

Area
923,768 sq km
(356,700 sq mi)

Population
87.6 million

Annual Growth Rate
2.5-3%

Languages
English (official), Hausa, Ibo, Yoruba

Religion
Muslim, Christian, indigenous African beliefs

Ethnic Groups
Hausa 21%, Yoruba 20%, Ibo 17%, Fulani 9%, others

Weights and Measures
The British Imperial system is in use. Nigeria is in the process of converting to the metric system.

Electrical Current
A.C. 50c 210/250 V
A.C. 50c 230/415 V

Major Business Cities
Lagos (cap) 3,000,000
Ibadan 2,000,000
Kano 2,000,000
Port Harcourt 600,000

Currency
1 Naira = 100 Kobo
Notes 1, 5, 10, 20 naira; 50 kobo
Coins 1, 5, 10 kobo

Public Holidays
There are Muslim holidays as well as Christian and traditional. These change yearly according to lunar cycles, so it is wise to check with a Nigerian embassy before planning your trip.
Jan 1 New Year
Apr 13-20 Easter Week
May 1 Labor Day
May 27 Childrens Day
Oct 1 National Day
Dec 25-26 Christmas

Travellers Information

Entry Requirements
Passport is required by all except some African nationals and UN document holders.
Business visitors should obtain an entry permit in their own country since they are not issued on arrival. They should also have an onward-going ticket and a letter of introduction. They should write "business visitor" and length of stay on landing cards issued on incoming planes. Carry passport and travel documents at all times. Entry is restricted to nationals of South Africa and those with a South African stamp on their passport.

Vaccination Required
Yellow fever vaccination certificates are required for entry. Check with Nigerian embassy before travelling.
Cholera, maleria and typhoid vaccinations are recommended. Take antimalerial tablets during your visit.

Customs and Duty Free
On arrival: 200 cigarets or 50 cigars or 200g/7oz tobacco; 1 liter alcohol; small amounts of perfume for personal use. No champagne or sparkling wine.

Currency Restrictions
Import of foreign currency is unrestricted and the amount declared upon arrival may be re-exported.
Import and export of more than 20 naira in local currency is prohibited.
Credit cards are not widely used and banks charge heavily for cashing travellers checks.

Health Tips
Take antimalerial pills, preferably for a week before and after as well as during your stay, since there is a risk of maleria even in the cities. Use bottled water exclusively. Imported drugs and toiletries expensive and scarce. There are both public and private hospitals, but prices vary. Most embassies have their own doctors.

Climate and Clothing

Tropical with high humidity on the coast and sub-tropical in the north. Dry season is from November to March; rainy season from April to October. The rainfall is heaviest in the south (Lagos). Take tropical weight clothes and an umbrella. In December and January the harmattan wind blows in from the Sahara. Wear tropical weight clothes with a jacket or sweater for evenings, especially in the north.

Tipping

There is a 10% service charge added to hotel, restaurant and nightclub bills but a further 10% is appreciated. Tip porters 1 Naira for each piece of luggage, and small services 50 kobos. Tip taxi drivers 1 Naira.

Food and Drink

Nigerian food relies heavily on yams, cassava and rice. The dishes are hot and spicy and usually accompanied by a pepper sauce made with fish, meat or chicken. There is also a wide selection of fruits, but visitors should make sure they peel them themselves. European food is available in major cities.

Business Brief

GDP

$62.5 billion
(per capita income $690)

Annual Growth Rate

2.5-3%

Natural Resources

Petroleum, tin, columbite, iron ore, coal, limestone, lead, zinc

Agriculture

Cocoa, palm oil, yams, cassava, sorghum, millet, corn, rice, livestock, groundnuts, cotton

Industry

Textiles, cement, food products, footwear, metal products, lumber, beer, detergents, car assembly

Imports

Total $8.9 billion
Transport equipment, completely knocked down components, foodstuffs, machinery

Exports

Total $12.5 billion
Petroleum, columbite, cocoa, rubber, cotton, tin

Major Trading Partners

UK, US, West Germany, Italy, Japan, Netherlands, France

Workforce

30-38 million
Agriculture 60%, industry, commerce and services 19%, government 15%

Tips for Doing Business

A suit should be worn for government visits, but a suit coat is not expected for business. A tie is always worn. Prior appointments should be made for government visits; it is less necessary for business. Punctuality is a definite asset but sometimes difficult in Lagos due to congested traffic. Allow plenty of time to get where you are going and do not plan appointments too close together.

Best Months for Doing Business

October through May are best months, but check for Muslim holidays. Avoid the week before and after Christmas and Easter. Businessmen take their vacations from June to September.

Business Hours

Government
Mon-Fri 0730-1530
Sat 0800-1300 in some states

Business
Mon-Fri 0800-1230, 1400-1630
Sat 0800-1200 some offices

Banks
Mon 0800-1500
Tue-Fri 0800-1500

Shops
Mon-Fri 0800-1730
Sat 0800-1630

English Language Publications
About 13 dailies and 14 weeklies
published in English. Daily
Times is newspaper for business-
news coverage. Other English-
language newspapers available
in major centers.

Telephone and Communications
Telephone country code: 234
Telephone city code: Lagos 1,
Ibadan 22
Telex country code: 961
Telephone service is improving
and the number of public
telephones is steadily increasing
in Lagos. Direct dialing for major
cities but other long-distance
calls must go through an
operator. International calls to
Europe and North America via
satellite. Telex service operated
by NITEL (Nigerian
Telecommunications Ltd.) Fast
courier service to Europe by
IMNL and DHL.

Air Travel
International airports at Kano
(KAN) and Lagos (LOS).
Nigeria Airways has scheduled
services from Lagos to most
main centers. Seats for all
internal flights should be booked
before arrival in Nigeria. Get to
the airport in plenty of time and
be fairly persistent in getting the
seat you booked. Air charter
flights available in Lagos.

Other Transport
Trains have two classes: some
services have air-conditioning,
some restaurant cars.
Inexpensive but slow. Express
service available between Lagos
and Kano, and Lagos and Jos.
There is bus service available but

roads in the south, apart from an
expressway between Lagos and
Ibadan, are narrow and winding.

LAGOS

Airport Information

Time
GMT +1

Airport
Murtala Mohammed
    International LOS
Tel: 31631
22 km (13.6 mi) N of city

Airlines
Air France 664909
Air India 635281
Alitalia 611559
British Airways 613004
British Caledonian 613004
Eastern 633540
Egyptair 661974
El Al 876046
Iberia 636950
KLM 661463
Lufthansa 664430
Nigerian 900470
Pan Am 610706
Sabena 617738
SAS 630762
Swissair 662299
UTA 664925
Varig 660585

Transport to City
Taxi: there are taxis available but
beware of unsolicited offers of
transport. Be sure to agree on
fare before setting out.
Coach: Nigeria Airways bus/
coach goes to major hotels; 9
nairas.
Transit: local bus to city leaves
every 10 minutes from 0600-2200.

Facilities
Bar, buffet, restaurant, bank,
currency exchange, post office,
baggage deposit, nursery, first
aid/medical, vaccination center,
shops.

Duty-free shop sells cigarets, cigars, tobacco, wines, liquors, lighters and some jewellery. Car rental desks: Hertz, Avis, Europcar, Cross Road

Airport Taxes
Per person: International 5 naira, domestic 2 naira

City Information

Weather
The weather in Lagos is usually tropical with high humidity. It is rainy between March and November (June is the wettest month) and dry and windy in December and January (December is the hottest). Average temps: Jan 27c (81F) July 26c (79F)

Transportation
Taxis are used for transportation in and between towns and are usually yellow Peugeots in Lagos. Fares are set for certain routes and tipping is not expected.
Car rental available (with international driving license) at rental agencies and large hotels, although chauffeur-driven service is highly recommended because of the congested traffic.

Car Hire
Hertz, 35 Simpson St (tel: 655480 & 835920)
Avis, 1155 Apapa (tel: 46336)
Europcar, 2l Broad St (tel: 662892)

Hospitals
Emergency medical help for travellers at:
Nicholas Hospital, Broad St (tel: 631743)
Ajayi Memorial, Apapa Rd (tel: 833361)
Alpha Hospital, Akin Adesola St

Hotels
There is a wide range but rooms are expensive and hard to get in Lagos. Essential to book well in advance through airlines or travel agency. Since confirmation does not guarantee that the room will be available when you arrive, be prepared to persuade politely, persistently, and perhaps monetarily.
Bristol, 6-8 Martins St (tel: 661201)
Eko Holiday Inn, Victoria Island PMB 12714 (tel: 615000)
Excelsior, PMB 1167, Apapa (tel: 803608)
Federal Palace, Victoria Island PO Box 1000 (tel: 610030)
Ikoyi, Kingsway Rd, PO Box 895, Ikoyi (tel: 603200 & 603201/8)
Mainland, PO Box 2158, Ebute Metta (tel: 800300 & 800319)
Sheraton, Airport Rd PMB 21189, Ikeja (tel: 900930 & 900960)

What to See and Do
In Lagos, the Nigerian Museum, Orugea Art Gallery, the National Assembly, Lagos University, the Trade Fair complex and shrines at the Palace of Oba are worth visiting. Badagry Town, 50 km from Lagos, is a former slave post; Ibadan, 135 km from Lagos, is the largest native city; Yankari game reserve is in the northern town of Jos. Tours of Lagos and other areas are easily arranged through travel agents or tour firms. Soccer games on Sundays in the National Stadium. Interesting nightclubs and restaurants with Nigerian meals and performers.

Useful Addresses

Embassies and Consulates
American: 2 Eleke Cres, Victoria (tel: 610097)
Canadian: Niger House, Tinubu (tel: 612382)
British: 11 Eleke Cres, Victoria (tel: 611551)

Business and Commerce
Central Bank of Nigeria, Tinubu Sq (tel: 660100)

Nigerian Stock Exchange, 3/5 Custom St (tel: 660287)
Federal Ministry of Commerce and Industry, Broad St
American Chamber of Commerce, 21/25 Broad St
United Nations Information Office, PO Box 1068 (tel: 51838) .

Tourism and Travel
Nigerian Tourist Board, Tafawa Balewa Sq (tel: 632240)
Nigerian Tourist Association, 47 Marina St (tel: 26129 & 26120)
Lagos Tourist Office, (tel: 22674)
Automobile Club of Nigeria,24 Meray Eneli Surulere (tel: 960514 & 961478)
American Express, Mandilas Travel, 96/102 Broad St (tel: 663339)

SAUDI ARABIA

Essential Information

Type of Government
Monarchy with Council of Ministers

Area
2,331,000 sq km
(830,000 sq mi)

Population
12.5 million

Annual Growth Rate
2.8%

Languages
Arabic, English used widely

Religion
Muslim

Ethnic Groups
Arab 90%, Afro-Asian

Weights and Measures
Metric

Electrical Current
A.C. 60c 110/120V

Major Business Cities
Riyadh (administrative cap) 1,200,000
Jeddah (commercial cap) 750,000
Mecca 405,000
Medina 250,000
Taif 220,000
Damman/Al Khobar 700,000

Currency
1 Riyal = 100 Halalah
Notes 1, 5, 10, 50, 100, 500 riyals
Coins 1, 5, 10, 25, 50 halalah

Public Holidays
Friday is the weekly holiday and government offices are usually closed Thursdays as well. Offices and businesses may also be closed on public and religious holidays. If the holiday falls on a Friday, they will be closed the next day. Since Muslim holidays change yearly according to the lunar cycles, it is wise to consult a Saudi Arabian embassy or consulate for current dates before planning a business trip, particularly in regard to the month-long religious periods of fasting called Hajj and Ramadan.

Travellers Information

Entry Requirements
Passport is required by everyone and must remain valid for up to six months after visit.
Visa required by everyone. A business visa must be obtained in advance. Visa applications must be accompanied by a letter of invitation from a Saudi sponsor. If the Ministry of Foreign Affairs approves the application, the Saudi Arabian Embassy in your country will be

instructed to issue the visa. No visa will be issued if: there is proof you have been to Israel or plan to go there; there is evidence of atheism or the Jewish faith in your passport or application form.

Entry restricted to nationals of Israel or holders of passports with Israeli visas. Keep passport and travel papers with you at all times unless asked to surrender them for a very good reason.

Vaccinations Required

Vaccination certificates are required for yellow fever or cholera if arriving from infected area.

Vaccinations for hepatitis, polio, typhoid, tetanus and malaria are advised. It is a good idea to consult a Saudi embassy before making travel arrangements to check on current regulations.

Customs and Duty Free

On arrival: 600 cigarets or 100 cigars or 500 g/1 pound tobacco; perfume for personal use. Duty may be required on cameras and typewriters but will be refunded if you leave within 90 days. Any alcohols or anything with alcoholic content, food such as pork, and any pornography or material with suggestive photography of women is strictly prohibited. Carry prescription drugs in small amounts and in their original containers with instructions. With the exception of hunting dogs and those used for the blind, dogs are banned.

Currency Restrictions

There are no currency restrictions.

Health Tips

The water is purified in the large hotels in major cities: it is safe but scarce. Take antimalarial tablets as malaria is a minor risk throughout the year. Some doctors and dentists speak English and lists are available from embassies and some hotels. Imported pharmaceuticals and toiletries are expensive. Eating food outside of major hotels and restaurants can be risky.

Climate and Clothing

Jeddah is hot and humid for most of the year with 90% humidity in the summer months. Lightweight clothing, wash-and-wear or easily cleaned, is essential. Riyadh is hotter in summer and cooler winter with heavy rainstorms. Lightweight clothing in summer, medium weight in winter with raincoat and warmer clothing in December and January.

Tipping

In hotels and restaurants, 15% is usually added to the bill. Taxi drivers do not expect a tip.

Food and Drink

When eating finger food, you must always eat it with only the right hand and never the left. Both hands, however, may be used for tearing bread. Saudi dishes are mainly rice with mildly spiced lamb or chicken. Coffee or tea is served before the meal and alcoholic beverages are forbidden by the Koran. However, Western eating and drinking habits are prevalent in large hotels and Western circles.

Business Brief

GDP
$74.2 billion
(per capita income $6,431)

Annual Growth Rate
11.5%

Natural Resources
Hydrocarbons, iron ore, gold, copper

Agriculture
Dates, grains, livestock

Industry
Petroleum production, petrochemicals, cement, fertilizer, light industry

Imports
Total $24.4 billion
Manufactured goods, transportation equipment, construction materials, processed food products

Exports
Total $26.9 billion
Petroleum and petroleum products

Major Trading Partners
Japan, Netherlands, Italy, UK, US, France, Spain, Germany, Bahrain

Workforce
2.7 million
Agriculture 28%, industry 4%, services, commerce and government 44%, construction 21%, oil and mining 3%

Tips For Doing Business
A conservative business suit should be worn during the winter months: women should dress very conservatively and make sure that their arms, legs and shoulders are always covered. Government business appointments can only be made in Riyadh and offices are closed Thursdays and Fridays. Even if you have confirmed an appointment, be prepared to wait and show no overt signs of impatience. Allow plenty of time between appointments. English is widely spoken and understood, but you should still have letters written in Arabic, and business cards and materials printed in both English and Arabic. Saudi Arabia is the strictest of all the Muslim countries: alcohol is illegal, as is smoking in government buildings. Be careful not to insult Saudi women; do not inquire about anyone's wife or approach women in any way. Do not take pictures of Saudi women or of sensitive buildings like the airport or government offices. Remove your shoes if invited into someone's home and avoid talking about politics, especially those of the Middle East.

Best Months For Doing Business
November through March are the best months for the climate and for making appointments. In April through October the temperatures can get up to 55c (130F) with high humidity: this is the time when many businessmen take their vacations. Avoid the months of Hajj and Ramadan as well as the pilgrimage to Mecca when hotel rooms are difficult to get. Check carefully with local embassy for the dates of Muslim holidays.

Business Hours

Government
Offices are closed Thursdays and Fridays.
Sat-Wed 0830-1200, 1300-1500 (summer); 0800-1200, 1300-1500 (winter)

Business
Sat-Thurs 0830-1200, 1600-1930 in Ryadh; 0900-1330, 1630-2000 in Jeddah

Banks
Sat-Wed 0830-1200, 1700-1900; Thurs 0830-1130

English Language Publications
Arab News, Saudi Gazette daily: Saudi Business, Saudi Economic Survey weekly.

Telephone and Communications
Telephone country code: 966
Telephone city code: Jeddah 21, Riyadh 1, Medina 41
Telex country code: 928
Telephone service is improving within the country but is still not

too good for international calls. There is direct dialing between major Saudi centers.

Telex is a better of communicating outside the country, and services are available at all good hotels; telex/telegram offices in Riyadh at the airport, King Faisal Street, in Masiriyah, Deera and Manouha.

Air Travel

There are at least 22 domestic airports, and domestic flights run by Saudia connect all major centers. Economy flights between Riyjadh and Jeddah (75 minutes) and Dhahran (45 minutes) cannot be reserved in advance (unless booked outside the country). Get booking pass at airport the day before travel. First-class reservations can be made for all flights but must be confirmed the day before travelling.

Other Transport

Taxis are orange and metered, although you should still agree on the fare in advance. No tip. Half the main roads are paved. Car hire is available but complicated since a driving test may be required. A valid driving license must be presented to authorities for translation into Arabic, and insurance claims are not legally enforceable. Chauffeur-driven automobiles are strongly recommended. There is a bus service between a few major cities which is operated by the Saudi Arabian Transport Company. Rail service operates daily between Riyadh and Damman: some services offer food and air-conditioning.

RIYADH

Airport Information

Time
GMT +3

Airports
King Khaled International RUH
Tel: 2211000
55 km (34 mi) from city

Riyadh
Tel: 64800 & 61400
7 km (4 mi) N of city

Airlines
Air France 4769666
Alia 4771646
Alitalia 4023933
British Airways 4645550
Canadian International 4652001
Gulf Air 4658222
JAL 4632500
KLM 4774777
Kuwait Air 4631218
Lufthansa 4632040
Pan Am 4652897
Philippine 4788880
PIA 4659608
Sabena 4029727
SAS 4651633
Saudia 4772222
Swissair 4766444
TWA 4760428

Transport to City
Taxis: all taxis are orange and you should agree on fare in advance even though they are metered. Fare from airport is SR35-75 ($10-20), tip not expected.

Coach: Saudi limousines are run by several companies and have fixed fares (about 100 riyals for 4 people) prominently displayed in the airport. Limos are white: either American air-conditioned saloons or London taxis. Pay cashier beforehand. Takes about 35-45 minutes.

Transit: there is a comfortable bus (with facilities) from King Khaled airport to the city every

30 minutes from 0600-0100. Takes about one hour, stops at Al Batha Terminal and major hotels and costs about 10 riyals.

Facilities

Buffet, bank with currency exchange, post office, shops selling candy, gifts, first aid/ medical, vaccinations.
Car rental desks: Avis, InterRent

City Information

Weather

Hot in summer (June to August) and cool to near freezing in winter with heavy rainstorms between November and March. Average temps: Dec-Jan 2c (35F) Jun-Aug 49c (120F)

Transportation

Taxis are orange and metered:

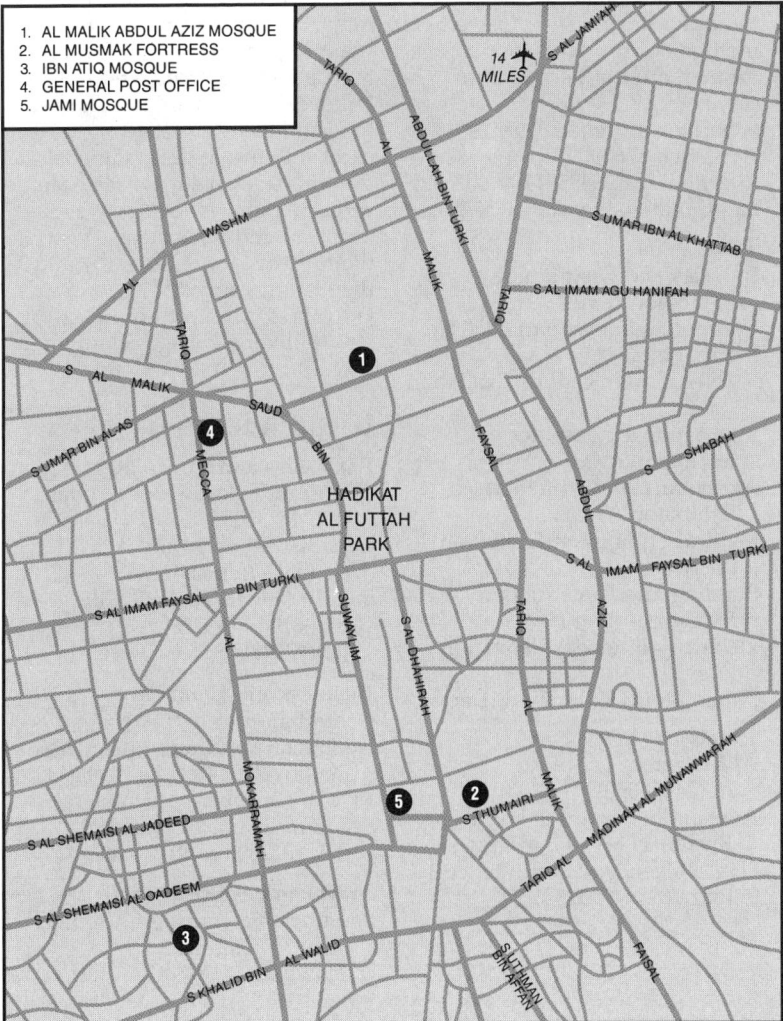

1. AL MALIK ABDUL AZIZ MOSQUE
2. AL MUSMAK FORTRESS
3. IBN ATIQ MOSQUE
4. GENERAL POST OFFICE
5. JAMI MOSQUE

HADIKAT AL FUTTAH PARK

Riyadh

agree on fare in advance but do not tip.

Limos are white and have fixed fares which are posted in the hotels.

Car hire is available, but chauffeur-driven cars are advisable for the newcomer.

Car Hire

Driving test may be necessary to get license. International or foreign license must be presented to authorities for translation into Arabic. Because of difficulties with private motoring most visitors use other methods of transportation. Women are not permitted to drive.

Aber Diyad, (tel: 4762575)
Avis, (tel: 4763909)
InterRent,(tel: 6855541 & 602089)
Saudi Limousine, (tel: 4657224)

Trade Fairs

Vehicles and Distribution Exhibition (Jan)
Computers Show (Jan)
International Telecommunications Exhibition (Jan)
International Computer Exhibition (Mar)
Agriculture and Irrigation Exhibition (Apr)
Medical Equipment Exhibition (Oct)
Building and Construction Exhibition (Nov)
Electricity Engineer Exhibition (Nov)
Public Works Exhibition (Dec)

Hotels

Al Khozama, Oleya Rd (tel: 4654650)
Atallah Sheraton, PO Box 1975, Riyadh 11441 (tel: 4543300)
Hyatt Regency Riyadh, Redec Plaza (tel: 4791234)
Marriott Riyadh, Mathar St (tel: 4779300)
Novotel, Airport St (tel: 4762193 & 4763483)
Riyadh Inter-Continental, Maazar St (tel: 4655000)
Riyadh Palace, Prince Fad bin Abdul Aziz St (tel: 4054444)
Saudi, Nassiriya St (tel: 4024051 & 4035051)
Zahet Alsharq, Airport St (tel: 4028216 & 4038800)

What to See and Do

Because Saudi Arabia is a Muslim country, there are no nightclubs or movie theaters and not many restaurants in Riyadh. Mecca is Mohammed's birthplace but non-Muslims are not allowed to visit. However, there are excellent buys at the traditional Central-Arabian suqs on Persian carpets, antiques, Bedu silver jewellery and other items. Visit the Musmak fortress nearby and the historic capital of Al Saud at Diriyah(20 km north of the city) and traditional villages along the way.

Useful Addresses

Embassies and Consulates

American: Palestine Rd (Jeddah) (tel: 4883800)
Canadian: King Abdul-Aziz St (Jeddah) (tel: 4882288)
British: Jeddah Towers, City Bank Bldg (Jeddah) (tel: 4880077)

Business and Commerce

Central Bank, Saudi Arabian Monetary Authority (SAMA), PO Box 2992 (tel: 4787400/8433)
Riyadh Chamber of Commerce and Industry, PO Box 596 (tel: 4022600 & 4040044)

Travel and Tourism

Saudi Arabia Touring Club, PO Box 276, Damman

SOUTH AFRICA

Essential Information

Type of Government
Republic

Area
1,233,404 sq km
(472,359 sq mi)

Population
33.1 million

Annual Growth Rate
2.5%

Languages
English and Afrikaans (official),
Zulu, Xhosa, North and South
Sotho, Tswana

Religion
Predominantly Christian,
traditional African, Hindu,
Muslim, Jewish

Ethnic Groups
English, Afrikaner, Asian,
African

Weights and Measures
Metric

Electrical Current
A.C. 50c 220/380V

Major Business Cities
Cape Town (legislative cap)
2,000,000
Pretoria (administrative cap)
900,000
Johannesburg 2,300,000
Durban 1,000,000

Currency
1 Rand = 100 cents
Notes 2, 5, 10 rand and higher
Coins 1, 2, 5, 10, 20, 50 cents;
   1 rand

Public Holidays
Jan 1 New Year
Apr 6 Founder's Day
Apr 13-20 Easter Week
May 31 Republic Day
Oct 10 Kruger Day
Dec 16 Day of the Vow
Dec 25 Christmas Day
Dec 26 Boxing Day

Travellers Information

Entry Requirements
Passport is required by all. Visa
is required by all except British
and Irish passport holders,
business travellers from
Switzerland, and certain African
countries. A visa from South
Africa can result in refused entry
to some other countries. Before
travelling, check with embassy
for current entry and transit
regulations.

Working Restrictions
Foreigners are not allowed to
accept employment without
special permission from the
Director General, Internal
Affairs.

Vaccination Required
Yellow fever vaccination
mandatory if travelling from
infected area. Antimalaria shots
(if travelling to lower altitudes)
and cholera shots recommended.

Customs and Duty Free
On arrival: 400 cigarets; 50
cigars; 250 g tobacco; 1 liter wine
or spirits; small amount perfume

Currency Restrictions
Only 100 rand may be imported.
There is no restriction on the
amount of foreign currency you
can bring in and the amount
declared on arrival can be taken
out. Use travellers checks or
bank drafts as foreign cash is not
readily exchangeable.

Health Tips
Drinking water and fresh fruit
and vegetables are safe.
Imported pharmaceuticals and
toiletries are reasonably priced
and readily available. Stay away
from fresh or standing water (no
swimming) to avoid bilharzia.

Because Johannesburg is over five thousand feet above sea level, allow several days to get used to the altitude. Walk slowly, rest, and drink non-alcoholic beverages.

Climate and Clothing

Climate is generally sunny and warm with cool nights. Medium weight clothing is suitable, with a jacket or coat for evenings. Take a raincoat for Johannesburg as there are frequent thunderstorms.

Tipping

Hotels and restaurants often add a service charge. Tipping is not widespread. Tip porters 1 Rand a bag, taxis 10%, barbers and small services 50 cents.

Food and Drink

Afrikaner dishes include babetic (a baked pie of curried meats, bread and eggs), and sosatic (marinated lamb with onions, garlic and chilis). The Boer dish of dry meat called Biltong is a favorite, as is barbecued meat. There is a wide variety of fruit and an excellent selection of sherries, brandies, wines and liqueurs.

Business Brief

GDP

$81.3 billion
(per capita income $2,449)

Annual Growth Rate

12.6%

Natural Resources

Nearly all essential minerals except oil

Agriculture

Corn, wool, dairy products, wheat, sugar cane, tobacco, citrus fruits

Industry

Minerals, automobiles, fabricated material, machinery, textiles, chemicals, fertilizer

Imports

Total $15.3 billion
Machinery, electrical equipment, transportation equipment, office machinery and data processing equipment, metal products

Exports

Total $20.9 billion
Gold, diamonds, corn, wool, sugar, fruit, fish products, metals, metallic ores, metal products, coal

Major Trading Partners

UK, West Germany, Japan, US, France

Workforce

11 million
Agriculture 30%, industry and commerce 29%, services 34%, mining 7%

Tips for Doing Business

Wear a conservative business suit at all times. Make prior appointments. The South African businessman is conservative and appreciates a formal approach. Business is often done in private clubs or in the home. If apartheid is discussed listen, but do not argue.

Best Months for Doing Business

Best months are February through May and September through November. Many businessmen vacation in December and January and in June and July. Avoid the weeks before and after Christmas and Easter, and take major Jewish holidays into consideration when making appointments.

Business Hours

Government
Mon-Fri 0800/0830-1630/1700

Business
Mon-Fri 0800/0830-1630/1700

Banks
Mon Tues Thurs Fri 0900-1530
Wed 0900-1300

Sat 0900-1100

Shops
Mon-Fri 0800-1700

Telephone and Communications
Telephone country code: 27
Telephone city code:
Johannesburg 11, Cape Town 21,
Durban 31, Pretoria 12, East
London 43
Telex country code: 960
Telephones are 90% direct
dialing within the country. Calls
to Europe and North America
can be dialed directly as well.
Telex services extensive.
Automatic exchange at
Johannesburg, Cape Town and
Durban. Public facilities at post
offices in Cape Town, Durban
and Johannesburg (Mon-Fri 0800-
1700, Sat 0830-1200).

Air Travel
There are many domestic flights.
South African Airways (SAS) has
frequent flights which connect all
major centers. Charter flights
available from private
companies.

Other Transport
There is an extensive bus service
run by South African Railways
Road services and private
companies.
Extensive rail service with almost
half electric. Reserve well in
advance for express trains. There
are three classes: choose first
class. Some restaurant and
sleeping compartments in first
and second class.
Car hire readily available and
roads are good.

JOHANNESBURG

Airport Information

Time
GMT +2

Airport
Jan Smuts JNB
Tel: 9751185
24 km (15 mi) E of City

Airlines
Air Canada 4409824
Air France 3315581
Alitalia 285990
American 3313409
British Airways 3310011
Eastern 3310630
El Al 3372525
Iberia 3310621
JAL 291815 KLM 6436671
Korean 213781
Lufthansa 6437332
Olympic 8365951
SAA 281728
Sabena 9753691
SAS 3315201
Singapore 8321701
Swissair 4841980
TAP 3371660
TWA 234028
UTA 3316951
Varig 3312231

Transport to City
Taxi: metered with no hidden
costs: 25 rand for 1-4 people; 30
minutes to city; tip 15%.
Coach: South African Airways
buses go to city terminal; 2.50
rand. Hotels have courtesy
coaches.
Transit: bus to Johannesburg
leaves from front of domestic
arrival hall; 2.20 rand. Every 30
minutes 0615-2300.

Facilities
Bar, buffet, restaurant, bank
with currency exchange, hotel
reservations, post office, baggage
deposit, barber shop, shops
selling flowers, gifts, books.
Duty-free shop has cigarets,
cigars, tobacco, wines, liquors.
Car rental desks: Hertz, Avis,
Budget

Airport Taxes
None

City Information

Weather

The summers are hot with late afternoon thunderstorms. Cool winters, sunny and rainless. Average temps: Jan 20c (69F) July 10C (51F)

Transportation

Taxis are widely available with minimum and standard mileage charges: tip 10%.

Car hire and chauffeur-driven vehicles available.

Car Hire

Hertz, 158 Market St (tel: 3374380 & 9701363)

Avis, 3 Brabazon Rd, Isando (tel: 282555)

Budget, 130 Main St (tel: 3313631 & 9753376)

Europcar, 185 Commission St (tel: 376100)

InterRent, Anderson & Smal Sts (tel: 210431)

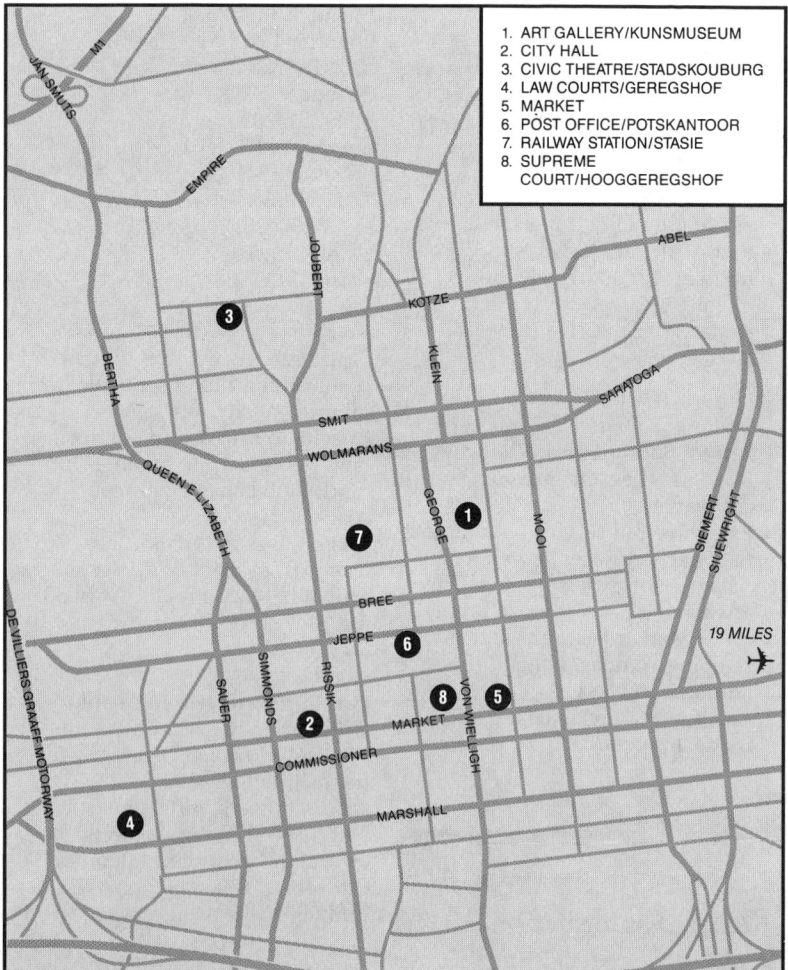

1. ART GALLERY/KUNSMUSEUM
2. CITY HALL
3. CIVIC THEATRE/STADSKOUBURG
4. LAW COURTS/GEREGSHOF
5. MARKET
6. POST OFFICE/POTSKANTOOR
7. RAILWAY STATION/STASIE
8. SUPREME COURT/HOOGGEREGSHOF

19 MILES

Johannesburg

Hospitals
Medical services must be paid for. Care for travellers can be obtained at:
Iamat Center, 501 Medical Towers (tel: 287711)

Trade Fairs
International Machine Tools Exhibition (Feb)
Business to Business Exhibition (Feb)
International Aviation Fair (Mar)
Instruments and Electronics Exhibition (May)
Automotive Exhibition (June)
International Training and Education Exhibition (July)
International Construction Exhibition (Aug)
International Mining Exhibition (Aug)
Star Lifestyle Exhibition (Oct)
International Chemical Process Exhibition (Nov)

Hotels
Carlton, PO Box 7709 (tel: 3318911)
Holiday Inn, Jan Smuts International Airport, PO Box 388 (tel: 011-9751121)
Holiday Inn-Milpark, Empire Rd (tel: 7265100)
Hotel Johannesburger, PO Box 23566 (tel: 7253753)
Landdrost, Twist/Plein Sts (tel: 281770)
President, Eloff St (tel: 281414)
Rand International, 290 Bree St (tel: 292724)
Towers, Kerk St (tel: 372200)

What to See and Do
Go down a gold mine by applying well in advance to the Chamber of Mines (tel: 8388211). By car, visit Lion Park, Krugersdorp, at feeding time; by air to Kruger National Park. Visit South African Railways Museum, Planetarium, Zoological Gardens and African Museum. Many nightspots; good

Indian and Chinese restaurants. Safaris to Mala Mala Game Reserve (500 km north of the city) are conducted in open Land Rovers. Over 200 species of animals. Flights daily from Johannesburg (tel: 3319671) with good local accomodation.

Useful Addresses

Embassies and Consulates
American: Commissioner & Kruis (tel: 3311681)
Canadian: Standard Bank Centre (tel: 8346521)
British: Commissioner St (tel: 3318161)

Business and Commerce
Central Bank, South African Reserve Bank, Pretoria (tel: 213011)
The Johannesburg Stock Exchange, Diagonal St (tel: 8336580)
Johannesburg Chamber of Commerce, Empire Rd, Auckland Park (tel: 7265300)
South African Foreign Trade Organization, Westbank House, 222 Smit St (tel: 7241631)
American Chamber of Commerce, 45 Commissioner St (tel: 8383134)

Tourism and Travel
National Tourist Office, (tel: 215971)
American Express, 123 Commissioner St (tel: 285100)
Springbok Safaris, Monument Rd (tel: 9724121)
Johannesburg Visitors Bureau, Upper Tower Mall, Carlton Center, Commissioner St (tel: 3372727)
Automobile Association of South Africa, 66 de Korte St (tel: 281400)
Thomas Cook, Biccard & Stevens St (tel: 3395171)

TURKEY

Essential Information

Type of Government
Republic

Area
766,640 sq km
(296,000 sq mi)

Population
51.5 million

Annual Growth Rate
2.1%

Languages
Turkish (official), Kurdish,
Arabic

Religion
Muslim (98%), Christian, Jewish

Ethnic Groups
Turkish 85%, Kurdish 12%,
other 3%

Weights and Measures
Metric

Electrical Current
A.C. 50c 110/220V & A.C. 50c
220/380V

Major Business Cities
Ankara (cap) 3,800,000
Istanbul 5,750,000
Izmir 2,700,000
Adana 1,850,000

Currency
1 Turkish Lira = 100 Kurus
Notes 10, 20, 50, 100, 500, 1000,
    5000, 10,000 lira
Coins 5, 10 lira

Public Holidays
There are Muslim holidays
which change yearly according
to the lunar cycle. Check before
travelling.
Jan 1 New Year
Apr 23 Children
May 19 Youth
Aug 30 Victory
Oct 28-30 Republic

Travellers Information

Entry Requirements
Passport required by all foreign
visitors. Visas not required
by nationals of US, Canada,
Australia, New Zealand, Britain
and European member countries
of the Council of Europe
(excepting Sweden) for stays of
less than three months.

Working Restrictions
A working visa is required by
foreigners.

Vaccination Required
Smallpox and cholera certificates
required if coming from affected
area. Antimalerial tablets
recommended.

Customs and Duty Free
On arrival: 200 cigarets or 50
cigars; 1 liter alchohol.
Visitors must register cars, tape
recorders, jewellery and other
valuables on entering the
country. Gifts up to the value of
15,000 lira may be exported.

Currency Restrictions
There are no restrictions on
amounts of foreign currency
brought in by visitors and the
amount declared on arrival may
be reexported. Only 1000 lira
may be brought in. Keep your
exchange slips. Major
international credit cards and
travellers checks accepted widely
in large centers.

Health Tips
Health standards are good in the
large cities. Drink only bottled
water. Turkish law states that
at least one pharmacy in a
neighborhood must stay open all
the time. Some doctors and
dentists speak English. Take
antimalerial tablets.

Climate and Clothing
Extreme variations according to

region. In the north (Ankara, Istanbul, Izmir) it is warm and dry from April to October; wear light to tropical weight clothes. Winter is colder with some rain; medium weight clothes with warm overcoat and footwear.

Tipping
A 10% tip for taxis is optional; drivers are usually quite satisfied with 100 Restaurants and nightspots add 15% to the bill but it is customary to tip the waiter an extra 10%. Hotels usually include 15% service charge in the bill, but tip 100 lira for small services and 500 lira a day for chambermaids. Porters and barbers: 500 lira.

Food and Drink
Turkish food displays Grecian and French influences. Seafood is a popular item, and mullet, swordfish, mackerel, lobster and shrimps are readily available. Yogurts are a staple food and kebabs, especially lamb cooked on a spit and called doner kabab, are popular everywhere. Stuffed vine leaves and vegetables (eggplant, tomatoes, peppers) are popular; rice pilaff comes with meat dishes. For dessert try pastries soaked in honey, or Turkish delight. Fruit is good and abundant. Turkish coffee is very thick and black and traditionally has a large cube of sugar added before drinking. Western food is widely available in all major hotels.

Business Brief

GNP
$73.8 billion
(per capita income $1,498)

Annual Growth Rate
6%

Natural Resources
Coal, chromite, copper, boron, oil

Agriculture
Cotton, tobacco, cereals, sugar beets, fruit, nuts

Industry
Textiles, processed foodstuffs, iron and steel, cement, leather goods

Imports
Total $13.3 billion
Petroleum, pharmaceuticals and dyes, iron and steel, machinery, plastics and rubber, transport vehicles

Exports
Total $10.2 billion
Tobacco, cotton, textiles, cement, raisins, nuts, leather, glass, ceramics, olive oil

Major Trading Partners
West Germany, Belgium and Luxemburg, US, UK, Switzerland, Italy, France, USSR, Libya, Iraq

Workforce
19.2 million
Agriculture 61%, industry 13%, services 25%

Tips for Doing Business
Always wear a conservative business suit and make prior appointments for all business and government visits. Most Turkish businessmen and some government officials speak English, French and German. Turks think of themselves as Europeans, so avoid speaking of Turkey as if it were part of the Middle East. Before a business discussion takes place, there is often a period of polite conversation over a cup of Turkish coffee. Do not discuss politics or Turkey's relations with neighboring countries. The Turks are hospitable and entertain lavishly at both lunch and dinner, so be prepared to eat often and plentifully. They are also approachable and friendly, but you should always

shake hands with everyone you meet formally or informally. If introduced to a businessman's wife, shake hands with her as well. Having been introduced, it is acceptable to invite them both out for a meal if you wish. If you are invited to someone's home, take flowers.

Best Months for Doing Business
September through May. Business vacations are taken in June, July and August and usually last a month.

Business Hours

Government
Mon-Fri 0900-1200, 1300-1700

Business
Mon-Fri 0900-1200, 1300-1700

Banks
Mon-Fri 0830-1200, 1330-1700

Shops
Mon-Sat 0900-1200, 1400-1900

English Language Publications
Daily News, Middle East Review daily; Outlook, weekly.

Telephone and Communications
Telephone country code: 90
Telephone city code: Istanbul 1, Ankara 41, Ismir 51
Telex country code: 821
Local calls can be made from public booths and post offices but you need to buy tokens first. Some long-distance calls can also be made from booths with proper token or operator assistance. Area codes are listed in phonebooks.
Telex is available in major hotels and certain main post offices in Ankara and Istanbul.
Main post office in Istanbul (in the Sirkeci area) is open 24 hours a day. Letter boxes are rare; it is best to use hotel or post office facilities.

Air Travel
Air travel is best method for travel between cities. Turkish Airlines and Bursa Airlines operate regular flights between Izmir, Istanbul, Ankara and other major cities.

Other Transport
Major cities are connected by regular rail and bus service. The train company is state owned (tel: 3360475 Asian side; 5270050 European side) and there are several privately owned bus companies.
There is a steamship service between Istanbul and most major towns.

ISTANBUL

Airport Information

Time
GMT +3

Airport
Yesilkoy IST
Tel: 737964
24 km (15 mi) W of city

Airlines
Aeroflot 1434725
Air Canada 1476775
Air France 1553070
Alia 1423462
Alitalia 1460527
Austrian 1402247
British Airways 1484235
Canadian International 1417366
El Al 1465303
Finnair 1413636
Iberia 1505478
Interflug 1404878
Iran Air 1411916
Iraqi 1454656
JAL 1417366
KLM 5738635
Korean 1444344
Kuwait Air 1404081
Libyan 1464458
Lufthansa 1468441
MEA 1482241
Olympic 1473701

Pan Am 1460230
PIA 1473988
Qantas 1474530
Sabena 1506027
SAS 1466075
Saudia 1564800
Swissair 1312849
Syrian 1461781
THY 5733525
TWA 1460420
UTA 1478200

Transport to City

Taxis: readily available outside terminal at all times. Small cars (Fiats and Renaults) with no air-conditioning. They can charge by the meter or a flat rate of US$6.5 for a shared taxi. Small charge for baggage; takes 30-45 minutes. Coach: airport bus operated by Turkish Airlines is always waiting outside the Domestic Lines terminal and leaves when full. Passengers from any airline can use the service; 40 minutes to airline terminal. Room for luggage.

Transit: a city bus leaves from the front of terminal to Taksim Square stopping several times; every 30 minutes from 0700-2100. Purchase 1150 lira (15 cent) ticket from kiosk; up to 60 minutes. Good, inexpensive ride for passengers with little baggage.

1. ARCHEOLOGICAL MUSEUM
2. FAITH MOSQUE
3. FERRY TERMINALS
4. OPERA
5. ST. SOPHIA/AYASOFYA MUSEUM
6. SULTAN AHMET MOSQUE
7. TOPKAPI PALACE
8. TURKISH & ISLAMIC ART MUSEUM
9. UNIVERSITIES

Istanbul

Facilities

Bar, buffet, restaurant, currency exchange, post office, baggage deposit, hotel reservations, shops, first aid/medical.
Duty-free shop has cigarets, cigars, spirits, liqueurs, cameras, radios, perfume. All convertible currencies accepted.
Car rental desks: Hertz, Avis, Europcar, InterRent

Airport Taxes

Per person: US$8

City Information

Weather

The climate is warm and dry in summer, cool with some rain in the winter.
Average temps: Jan 4c (40F)
Jun 23c (73F)

Transportation

Metered taxis are available but try to negotiate fare before travelling: there are usually set rates for common destinations. Try to get a taxi which is not near a hotel for less conversation about the fare. Shared taxis, called "dolmus", are much less expensive. They have fixed routes and fares, can carry up to eight passengers, and can be picked up anywhere along the route. Car hire is available; international or foreign license accepted. Adequate tram service available.

Car Hire

Hertz, (tel: 5735987 & 1412036)
Avis, Hilton Hotel, (tel: 1467050 & 5736445)
Europcar, Cumhuriyet Cad. (tel: 1508888 & 5737024)
InterRent, (tel: 1416528)

Hospitals

Medical services at municipal or state hospitals are free but private and foreign hospitals offer better service. Medical services for travellers available at:
The American Hospital (tel: 1486030)
The Admiral Bristol Hospital (tel: 486030)

Trade Fairs

International Hospital Equipment Exhibition (Jan)
International Office Equipment Fair (Feb)
Industrial Chemical Products Exhibition (Apr)
Handcraft and Giftware Fair (Nov)
Watch and Jewellery Trade Fair (Nov)
Furniture and Carpet Fair (Dec)

Hotels

Prices vary and many hotels reduce their rates between October and April. Advance reservations and confirmation strongly advised.
Anka, Molla Gurani Cad. 42 (tel: 5256002)
Divan Hotel, Cumhuriyet Cad. 2 (tel: 1314100)
Etap Hotel, Tepebasi (tel: 1514646)
Etap Hotel Marmara, Taksim Meydani (tel: 1514696)
Hilton International, Cumhuriyet Cad., Harbiye (tel: 1314646)
Hotel Instanbul Dedeman, Yildiz Posta Cad. 50, Esentepe (tel: 1728800)
Keban, Siraselviler Cad. 51 Taksim (tel: 1433310)
Macka Hotel, Eytam Cad. 35, Macka (tel: 1401053)
Pera Palas, Mesrutiyet Cad. (tel: 1514560)
Sheraton Hotel, Taksim Park (tel: 1312121)
Yenikoy Carlton Hotel (on shores of Bosphorus) (tel: 1621020)

What to See and Do

In the old city, visit the Blue Mosque; St Sophia famous for its gallery mosaics; the covered bazaar; Topkapi Palace/Museum famous in the film of the same name; Kariye Camii Church for superb fourteenth-century frescoes and mosaics. Also worth visiting are the Archeological Museum and the Suleymaniye Mosque. Take a ferry along the Bosphorus to Tarabya or in summer go to Prince Island, Buyukada from the Sirkeci or Kabatas piers (90 minutes) and tour the Island in a horse-drawn carriage. Nightclubs have local flavor, many feature belly dancing or folk songs and dances.

Useful Addresses

Embassies and Consulates
American: Mesrutiyet Cad. 104
    Tepebasi (tel: 1513602)
British: Mesrutiyet Cad. 34
    Tepebasi (tel: 1447540)

Business and Commerce
Stock Exchange, Borsa
    Komiserligi, Menkul Kiymetler
    ve Kambiyo Borassi, 4 Vakif
    Han, Bahoekapi, Istanbul
    (tel: 5221955)
Istanbul Chamber of Commerce,
    Hal Yolu, Eminonu
    (tel: 5114150)
British Chamber of Commerce,
    Mesrutiyet Cad. 34
    (tel: 1490658)

Tourism and Travel
Ministry of Culture and Tourism,
    Gazi Mustafa Kemal Bulvari
    26, Ankara (tel: 290965)
Touring and Automobile Club of
    Turkey, 364 Sisli Meydani
    (tel: 467090)
American Express, Turk Ekspres,
    Cumhuriyet Cad. 91
    (tel: 10274/5)
Thomas Cook, Cumhuriyet Cad.
    139 (tel: 1460798)

UNITED ARAB EMIRATES

Essential Information

Type of Government
Federation of Emirates

Area
82,880 sq km
(30,000 sq mi)

Population
1.6 million

Annual Growth Rate
0%

Languages
Arabic (official), Farsi and
English widely spoken, Hindi

Ethnic Groups
Arab, Iranian, Pakistani, Indian
(fewer than 20% of population
are UAE citizens)

Weights and Measures
The British Imperial system, the

metric system and local systems
are all used.

Electrical Current
Abu Dhabi A.C. 50c 240/415V
Other Emerites A.C. 50c
220/380V

Major Business Cities
Abu Dhabi (cap) 670,000
Dubai 420,000
Sharjah 270,000

Currency
UAE Dirham = 1000 Fils
Notes 1, 5, 10, 50, 100 dirhams
Coins 1, 5, 10, 25, 50 fils;
    1 dirham

Public Holidays
There are many Muslim holidays
throughout the year which vary
annually according to the lunar
cycles. Check dates before
travelling.

Dec 2 National Day
Muslim holidays (unfixed)

Travellers Information

Entry Requirements

Passport required by all. Visa required by all except holders of British passports (if passport issued after 1/1/83 has "British Citizen" stamped on page 1). Multi-entry visa good for all emirates. Nationals of Israel and South Africa or those with evidence of travel to Israel in their passport are restricted entry.

Working Restrictions

A work permit is needed but you can apply on arrival.

Vaccination Required

No vaccinations required except for cholera and yellow fever if arriving from infected area. Cholera shot recommended; take antimalarial tablets before, during and after visit.

Customs and Duty Free

On arrival: 200 cigarets or 50 cigars or 225g/8oz tobacco. Personal effects are duty-free. Import is refused for pork products, alcoholic beverages, firearms and ammunition although sometimes a special permit may be obtained. Entry prohibited for goods originating in Israel and South Africa.

Currency Restrictions

There are no currency restrictions.

Health Tips

The drinking water in the major cities is good. In Dubai and Sharjah, it is sweet well water piped from inland, and in Abu Dhabi it is purified in distillation plants. Make sure all fruits and vegetables have been washed carefully or peel them yourself. Imported pharmaceuticals are expensive. Take antimalarial tablets before, during and after your stay.

Climate and Clothing

Dress in a conservative manner for a climate which is hot and humid. Between April and November wear tropical weight clothing for temperatures of up to 48c (118F) with 85% humidity. From December to March, temperatures and humidity are more benign calling for light to medium weight clothes and a jacket for evenings. Women should make sure their arms, shoulders and legs are covered at all times.

Tipping

Tip taxi drivers 10% and porters 2 dirhams per piece of baggage. In hotels and restaurants, 10% is usually included in the bill. Small services; 1 dirham.

Food and Drink

Try some of the excellent local fish and many of the dishes which contain dates, one of the staples of the cuisine. Local fruits and vegetables are becoming increasingly available. Hotels serve both Arab and European food, and there are good Indian and Chinese restaurants.

Business Brief

GDP

$23.2 billion
(per capita income $16,700)

Annual Growth Rate

0%

Natural Resources

Oil

Agriculture

Vegetables, dates, limes

Industry

Light manufacturing, petroleum production

Imports
Total $7.2 billion
Machinery, consumer goods,
food, garmets, livestock

Exports
Total $15.8 billion
Petroleum

Major Trading Partners
Japan, US, UK, Switzerland,
West Germany, France,
Lebanon, Italy, India

Workforce
490,000
Oil industry 85%, agriculture
and fishing 5%

Tips for Doing Business
Appropriate conservative
clothing should be worn in
keeping with the time of
year. Prior appointments for
government and large businesses
should be made, but smaller
businesses have a more relaxed
attitude. English is widely
spoken and merchants who do
not speak English have an
interpreter. As in most Arab
countries you may be kept
waiting even with a confirmed
appointment, but do not show
signs of impatience as this is
considered bad manners.
Sheikhs and government
ministers are addressed as "Your
Excellency"; all other men are
addressed as "Sayyed" followed
by their first name. Socializing is
usually done in afterwork coffee
houses or in the home. There are
no nightclubs. Follow the rules
of Muslim social customs: avoid
sitting with the soles of the feet
pointing out at anyone or eating
or passing anything with the left
hand. Take your shoes off when
entering a home or mosque. Do
not photograph official buildings
or women in the street.

Best Months for Doing Business
November through March
is the best time to travel since
the weather is pleasant and
businessmen are not on holiday.
Avoid the summer months,
when the climate is hot and
humid, and the month of
Ramadan. Before travelling,
check the dates of Muslim
holidays with local embassy or
consulate.

Business Hours

Government
Sat-Thurs 0800-1400
Summer: Sat-Thurs 0700-1300

Business
Sat-Thurs 0800-1400
Summer: Sat-Thurs 0700-1300

Banks
Sat-Thurs 0800-1200

Shops
Abu Dhabi Dec-Mar: Sat-Thurs
0800-1300, 1530-1900
Apr-Nov: Sat-Thurs 0800-1300,
1600-1930

English Language Publications
Gulf News; Khaleej Times;
Emirate News; Gulf Mirror;
daily.
Gulf Commercial Magazine;
Recorder; weekly.

Telephone and Communications
Telephone country code: 971
Telephone city code: Abu Dhabi
2, Dubai 4
Telex country code: 944
A modern telephone system
with direct dialing connects the
seven emirates. International
service is good.
Telegrams and telexes can be sent
from major hotels.

Air Travel
International airports: New Abu
Dhabi International (AUH),
Dubai International (DXB),
Sharjah International (SHJ).
Domestic flights between
airports in UAE are regarded as
international although one visa is
good for all emirates. Gulf Air
has frequent flights between Abu

Dhabi and Dubai; there are also services between Abu Dhabi and Sharjah. Arrive at the airport in plenty of time to get a seat. Small light planes and helicopters can usually be chartered.

Other Transport
Taxis are metered, but if going from town to town it is wise to agree on the fare ahead of time. Taxis regularly travel between Abu Dhabi and Dubai.
Car rental is available in Abu Dhabi if you have an international drivers license and two passport photos for a temporary license. It is sometimes easier to travel by taxi.

DUBAI

Airport Information

Time
GMT +4

Airport
Dubai International DXB
Tel: 224222
4 km (2.5 mi) E of city

Airlines
Air France 667775
Alia 232855
Alitalia 284656
British Airways 222158
Canadian International 435800
Egyptair 220074
Gulf Air 285141
Iran Air 222808
JAL 229479
KLM 225281
Korean 221576
Kuwait Air 281106
Lufthansa 221191
Malaysian 432211
MEA 237175
Olympic 214455
Pan Am 436800
Philippine 436800

PIA 220913
Qantas 222151
Sabena 220895
SAS 373440
Saudia 236455
Singapore 232300
Swissair 283151
THY 226038
TWA 222371

Transport to City
Taxi: transportation into the city is handled by owner-operated taxis. You pay a flat fare of $8.00 at taxi desk and 55 cents charge for each bag. Taxis are comfortable and air-conditioned; take 15-20 minutes along an ocean road.
Coach: hotel courtesy coaches to major hotels in the city. Inform hotel of flight number and time of arrival.

Facilities
Bar, buffet, restaurant, bank, hotel reservations, post office, baggage deposit, nursery, first aid/medical, vaccinations, shops selling books, gifts, sweets. Duty-free shop sells cigarets, cigars, tobacco, wines, spirits, liqueurs, cameras, watches, jewellery, radios, electronic goods, handicrafts. All convertible currencies accepted. Car rental desks: Avis, Budget, InterRent, Europcar

Airport Taxes
None

City Information

Weather
Summers are very hot with humidity from July to September reaching 85%. Winters are pleasant with much less humidity.
Average temps: Jan 10-20c (50-60F)
July 48c (118F)

Transportation
Taxis are available, and although

they are metered it is wise to agree on the fare in advance. Chauffeur-driven cars can be booked through major hotels. Car hire is available, but it is necessary to obtain a local license by presenting a valid international license plus two passport photographs. It is generally more convenient to be driven than to drive.

Car Hire
Avis, Al Maktoum St
(tel: 282121)

Budget, Clock Tower, Deira
(tel: 668200)
InterRent, Al Maktoum St
(tel: 370743)
Europcar, Al Rais Center
(tel: 434221)

Hospitals
There is a modern British hospital on Al Maktoum Street with a high standard of medical care. Many doctors practising in the emirates are European or Lebanese who have qualified in Europe or the US.

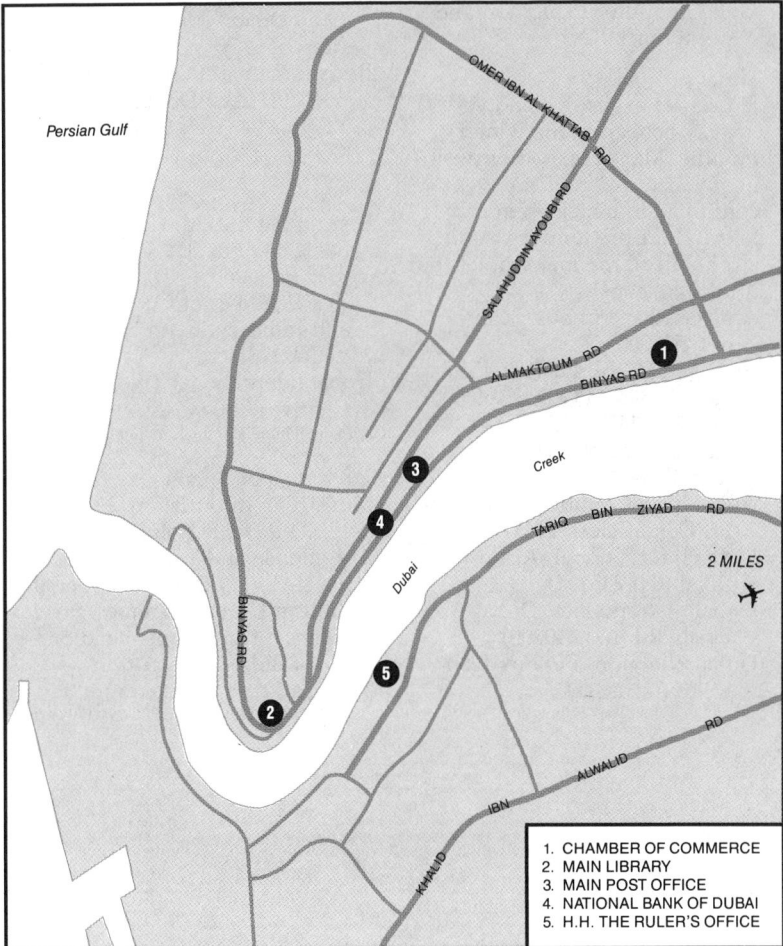

Persian Gulf

OMER IBN AL KHATTAB RD

SALAHUDDIN AYOUBI RD

AL MAKTOUM RD

BINYAS RD

Creek

TARIQ BIN ZIYAD RD

2 MILES

Dubai

BINYAS RD

ALWALID RD

IBN KHALID

1. CHAMBER OF COMMERCE
2. MAIN LIBRARY
3. MAIN POST OFFICE
4. NATIONAL BANK OF DUBAI
5. H.H. THE RULER'S OFFICE

Dubai

The Gulf Sports & Leisure
Exhibition (Jan)
International Consumer Goods
Fair (Jan)
Middle East Electric and
Electronic Exhibition (Jan)
International Jewellery and
Watches Exhibition (Jan)
Arab Air (Feb)
Gulf Communications (Mar)
Arab Gas Technology Exhibition
& Conference (Mar)
Gulf Industrial Plant and Factory
Equipment (Apr)
International Gulf Trade Fair
(May)
Gulf Computer Exhibition and
Conference (Oct)

Hotels
Hotels are expensive and very
heavily booked in the winter
months. Make reservationswell
in advance and get firm
confirmation by telegram or
telex. There are lounges serving
alcohol in all the major hotels but
drinks are expensive.
Ambassador, PO Box 3226
(tel: 531000)
Astoria, PO Box 457 (tel: 434000)
Carlton Tower, PO Box 1955
(tel: 227111)
Claridge, PO Box 1833
(tel: 227141)
Dubai Inter-Continental, Bin Yass
St, Deira (tel:227171)
Dubai International, Airport
Road (tel: 245111)
Dubai Metropolitan, Dubai-Abu
Dhabi Rd (tel: 440000)
Dubai Sheraton, PO Box 4250,
Deira (tel: 281111)

Excelsior, Al Mateena St, Deira
(tel: 665222)
Hilton International Dubai, PO
Box 927 (tel: 370000)
Hyatt Regency Dubai, PO Box
5588, Deira (tel: 221234)
Jebel Ali, PO Box 9255(tel:
084-35252)
Oasis Dubai, PO Box 1566, Deira
(tel: 225252/3/4)
Phoenicia, PO Box 4467, Deira
(tel: 227191)

Useful Addresses

American: (Dubai) Int'l. Trade
Centre (tel: 371115),
(Abu Dhabi) Al-Sudan St.
(tel: 336691)
British: (Dubai) PO Box 65 (tel:
531070), (Abu Dhabi)
PO Box 248 (tel: 326600)

Central Bank, UAE Central
Bank, PO Box 854, Abu Dhabi
(tel: 369200)
Dubai Chamber of Commerce
and Industry, Benn Yass St
(tel: 221181)
Dubai International Trade
Center, PO Box 9292
(tel: 373461)

Ministry of Information, PO Box
17, Abu Dhabi (tel: 825433)
Automobile and Touring Club
for UAE, PO Box 1183, Sharjah
American Express, Kanoo Travel
Agency, Khalid Bin Walid St
(tel: 434614 & 421100)
Thomas Cook, Al Maktoum St
(tel: 222301)

Asia/Pacific

Essential Information

Type of Government
Democratic federal-state system recognizing the British monarch as sovereign

Area
7.7 million sq km
(2.9 million sq mi)

Population
15.5 million

Annual Growth Rate
1.3%

Languages
English (official), aboriginal languages

Religion
Anglican 36%, other Protestant 25%, Roman Catholic 33%

Ethnic Groups
European 97%, aboriginal 1%, Asian .6%

Weights and Measures
Metric (converting from Imperial which is still used)

Electrical Current
A.C. 50c 220/250V

Major Business Cities
Canberra (cap) 290,000
Sydney 3,500,000
Melbourne 3,200,000
Brisbane 1,300,000
Adelaide 1,100,000
Perth 1,150,000

Currency
1 Australian dollar = 100 cents
Notes 2, 5, 10, 20, 50, 100 dollars
Coins 1, 2, 5, 10, 20, 50 cents;
1 dollar

Public Holidays
Jan 1 New Year
Jan 26 (or first Mon after)
   Australia Day
Apr 13-19 Easter week
Apr 25 ANZAC Day
Dec 25-28 Christmas
Queen's Birthday (second Mon in June)

Travellers Information

Entry Requirements
Passport is required by all visitors.
Visa required by all foreigners except those in transit who will only stay 72 hours and those from New Zealand. Six-month visas available to visitors. Business people usually get a 5 year visa good for short visits during that period.

Working Restrictions
People wishing to stay and work must have a work permit which is very difficult to get. Usually arranged through companies.

Vaccination Required
No vaccinations are required for those arriving directly from North America, New Zealand or Europe. However, certificates of vaccination for yellow fever must be presented if coming from an infected area, and for smallpox if you have been in an infected area within 14 days. Restrictions change, so check with tourist or travel agency and local consulate first to be sure.

Customs and Duty Free
On arrival: 200 cigarets; 250g/8oz tobacco products; 1 liter alcohol; gifts to value A$200 may be brought in.
Strict quarantine regulations mean you can't bring in fruits, food or plants without prior arrangement. Pets are strictly prohibited. Visitors must present passport, visa and on-going or return ticket at customs.
Sales and other taxes are included in the price of all items in Australia, but visitors are

exempt if they buy items from the duty-free shop for export.

Currency Restrictions

There are no restrictions on the amount of foreign currency brought in: however keep a record of the amount and transactions so you can take money out again without problems. Regulations govern the amount of Australian currency which can be taken out of the country (no more than A$250 in notes and A$5 in coin). Letters of credit, travellers checks and US currency are freely negotiable.

Health Tips

Australia has no unusual health risks or serious endemic diseases. Hospitals are up-to-date. The visitor is required to pay all costs of medical treatment. Blue Cross, Blue Shield or other medical insurance is recommended because medical costs are high. Some pharmacies are open for 24 hours a day and provide delivery.

Climate and Clothing

Seasons are the reverse of those in the northern hemisphere. Most of southern Australia has warm summers and temperate winters so lightweight clothing can be worn all year. However, it can be cool in the temperate areas in winter and temperatures can change rapidly so its a good idea to bring heavier clothing and an overcoat or warm trenchcoat during these months.

Tipping

Tipping is not generally acceptable except in better hotels and restaurants where 10% is usual for good service. Porters have a set charge for baggage. Although tipping is not expected for taxis, you should give $0.30 or tip up to the nearest dollar. In bars and pubs, it is customary to leave 1 and 2 cent pieces on the bar.

Food and Drink

There is a diversity of cuisine reflecting Australia's immigrant origins: English food, plus Italian, Greek, French, German and Yugoslavian. Delicatessen fare is popular in the cities. Fish, like jogn dory and barramundi, is also popular, and Australians love beef. There is a wide variety of tropical and temperate fruit and vegetables. The Australians are justly famous for their beer (and beer drinking) but wines have been gaining popularity in recent years.

Business Brief

GDP

$193.1 billion
(per capita income $12,091)

Annual Growth Rate

3-4%

Natural Resources

Iron ore, coal, copper, tin, silver, uranium, nickel, tungsten, mineral sands, lead, zinc, diamonds, natural gas, oil

Agriculture

Livestock (cattle and sheep), wheat, wool, sugar, fruit and vegetables. Australia leads the world in wool and beef exports.

Industry

Mining, aircraft maintenance and construction, manufacturing and transportation. About 90% of enterprises are small businesses (less that 100 employees or service enterprises with fewer than 10).

Imports

Total $29.3 million
Industrial supplies, capital goods and parts, consumer goods, transport equipment and parts,

fuel and lubricants, food and beverages

Exports
Total $26.5 billion
Coal, coke and briquettes, non-ferrous ores, wool, wheat and flour, iron ore, meats, sugar, dairy products, animals

Major Trading Partners
Japan, US, UK, West Germany, New Zealand, Taiwan, Singapore

Workforce
7.1 million
Manufacturing 24%, agriculture 6%, miscellaneous and service industry 51%

Tips For Doing Business
Australians are informal and egalitarian. Calling people by their first names on introduction is common practice, and it is generally expected that if a man is travelling alone in a taxi, he will sit up front with the driver. Businessmen usually wear suits and ties in Sydney and Melbourne, although dress is sometimes a little more informal in other places. Business after-hours entertaining is usually done over drinks in a bar or pub with each person taking a turn paying (taking their "shout"). Make business appointments ahead of time and arrive promptly.

Best Months For Doing Business
Best months for business are March through November: summer holidays are taken during December, January and February. Each state has different holidays so check with a travel agency or local Australian consulate before making travel arrangements.

Business Hours

Government
Mon-Fri 0900-1700

Business
Mon-Fri 1900-1700
Sat 0900-1200

Banks
Mon-Thur 1000-1500
Fri 1000-1700

Shops
Mon-Fri 0900-1730
Sat 0900-1200

English Language Publications
There are over 500 newspapers published in Australia. South Pacific editions of Newsweek, Time, and various international newspapers are widely available.

Telephone and Communications
Telephone country code: 61
Telephone city code: Brisbane 7, Melbourne 3, Perth 9, Sydney 2
Telex country code: 790
Reliable domestic and international telephone services available with 99% of the telephones connected to automatic exchanges. Telex facilities are available at General Post Offices in all major cities. The Overseas Telecommunications Commission operates a 24-hour public telex services in Sydney, Melbourne, Brisbane and Canberra. Telegrams can be sent through the telephone operator or at the post office at urgent rate (2-4 hour delivery), ordinary rate (4-6 hour delivery), and letter rate (24-hour delivery).

Air Travel
Because of the great distances to be covered, air transport is the best way of getting around the country and is widely used. Ansett and TAA operate frequent flights between city centers and there are over 400 airfields. Charter flights are easily booked.

Other Transport
Express air-conditioned buses link all the major centers. Long-

distance passenger trains are air-conditioned with sleeping and dining cars. Book well in advance. Car rental available in all cities with a valid international or foreign license: before travelling for long distances, check with the automobile association for weather conditions and other information.

MELBOURNE

Airport Information

Time
GMT +10

Airport
Tullarmarine MEL
Tel: (03) 3382211
24 km (15 mi) S of city

Airlines
Air New Zealand 654311
Alitalia 6700171
British Airways 6023000
Canadian International 6296731
Cathay Pacific 6071111
Continental 6024899
Eastern 635926
El Al 6060111
Garuda 6544311
Gulf Air 3298066
Iberia 3298379
JAL 6542733
KLM 6545111
Korean 635926
Lufthansa 6021155
Malaysian 6543255
Olympic 6025400
Pan Am 6706307
Philippine 621321
Qantas 6026111
Sabena 3298066
SAS 624555
Singapore 6052555
Swissair 679075
Thai 626132
TWA 3291022
UTA 677432

Transport To City
Taxi: about 12-15 dollars, slightly higher at night.
Coach: Frequent airline buses to city about 5 dollars. Skybus Coach Service every 30 minutes from 0630-2330 (Saturday 0630-2030). Leaves from front of domestic terminal and takes 30 minutes to downtown terminal, 5 minutes from hotels.

Facilities
Bank with currency exchange, hotel reservations, post office, baggage deposit, observation deck, information desk, pharmacy, shops, bar, restaurants, first aid/medical Duty-free shop has cigarets, cigars, tobacco, wines, spirits, cameras, watches, radios, jewellery, perfumes, glass and china, handbags and accessories. Local currency accepted plus American Express, Visa and Diners Club credit cards.
Car rental desks: Hertz, Avis, Budget

Airport Taxes
Per person: 20 dollars(cash)

City Information

Weather
Summers are hot and dry, winters, chilly and wet. Average temps: Jan (summer) 26c (78F) July (winter) 13c (56F)

Transportation
Metered taxis can be hailed on the street. Tipping is not expected, but you can give 30 cents or tip up to the nearest dollar. Public transport in Melbourne includes a City Loop underground railway.

Car Hire
Hertz, 97 Franklin (tel: 6982555, 6998899, 3384044)
Avis, 400 Elizabeth St
(tel: 6636366 & 3381800)

Budget, 188 Peel (tel: 3297055,
32063333, 3386955)

Hospitals
Royal Melbourne (tel: 3477111)
St Vincent's (tel: 410221)
Prince Henry's (tel: 620261)
Emergency ambulance 000

Trade Fairs
Clinical & Surgical Exhibition
(Feb)
International Banking & Finance
Exhibition (Feb)
International Motor Exhibition
(Mar)
Giftware Exhibition (Mar)

News Agents Trade Exhibition
(Mar)
Telecommunications Exhibition
(Mar)
Australian Rubber Exhibition
(Apr)
Computer & Communications
Exhibition (May)
International Boat Exhibition
(July)
Giftware Exhibition (Aug)
International Home Exhibition
(Aug)
Food Processing Exhibition
(Sept)
International Computer
Exhibition (Sept)

ASIA/PACIFIC

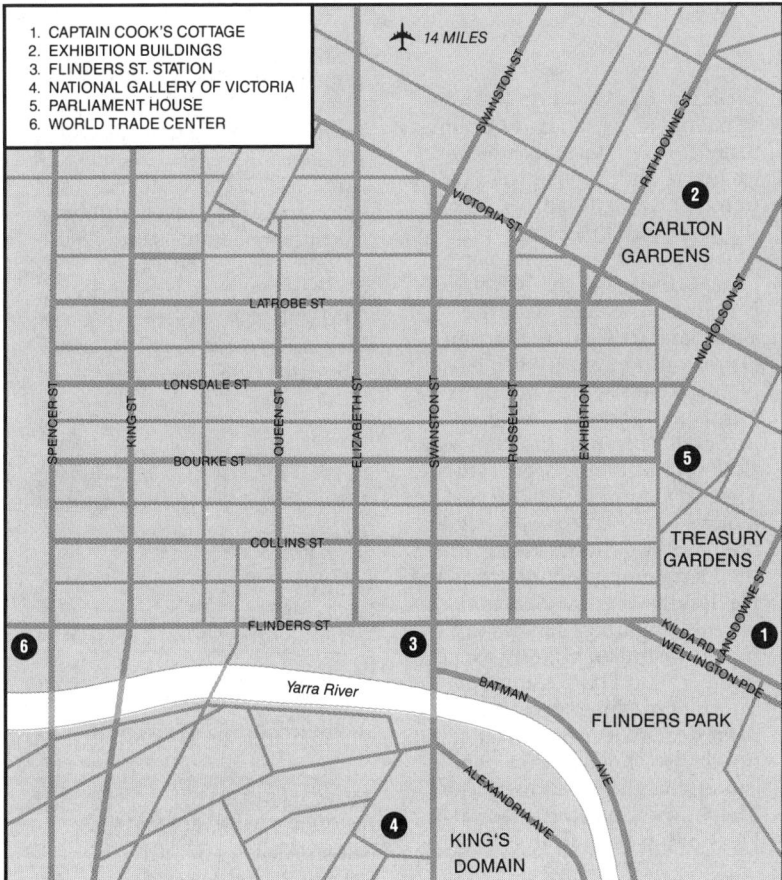

1. CAPTAIN COOK'S COTTAGE
2. EXHIBITION BUILDINGS
3. FLINDERS ST. STATION
4. NATIONAL GALLERY OF VICTORIA
5. PARLIAMENT HOUSE
6. WORLD TRADE CENTER

Melbourne

Hotels

Chateau Melbourne,
131 Lonsdale St (tel: 6631361)
Commodore, 4 Queens Rd
(tel: 2622411)
Hilton International Melbourne,
Corner Wellington Parade &
Clarendon Sts (tel: 4193311)
Hyatt on Collins, 123 Collins St.
(tel: 6571234)
President Melbourne, 63 Queens
Rd (tel: 5294300)
Sheraton, 13-19 Spring St
(tel: 6505000)
Southern Cross, 131 Exhibition
St (tel: 6530221)
Victoria, 215 Little Collins St
(tel: 6530441)
Windsor, 102-115 Spring St
(tel: 630261)

What to See and Do

Melbourne is very European in
atmosphere, particularly Collins
Street, with sidewalk cafes and
exclusive shops. Visit the English
home of Captain James Cook at
the top of Collins Street. Ride
one of the famous trams across
Princes Bridge to the Royal
Britannica Gardens with the
Victorian Art Center. You can
also take the tram to the
picturesque suburbs of South
Yarak and Toorak. Visit the
National Museum, the National
Gallery and the Concert Hall and
Theatre Complex. Cricket test
matches are played regularly at
the Cricket Ground. Nearby in
the Dandenong Mountains is the
Healesville Wildlife Sanctuary,
where kangaroos, koalas and
other Australian wildlife roam
freely. "Cup Day" is the first
Tuesday of November. It has
been designated an official
holiday so thousands of people
can attend the running of The
Melbourne Cup horse race at
Flemington Race Course.

Useful Addresses

Embassies and Consulates

American: 24 Albert Rd
(tel: 6977900)
Canadian: 1 Collins St
(tel: 638431)
British: 330 Collins St
(tel: 6021877)

Business and Commerce

Melbourne Stock Exchange,
351 Collins St (tel: 6178611)
Melbourne Chamber of
Commerce, Flinders & Spencer
(tel: 6112239)
Overseas Trade Dept, 424 St
Kilda Rd (tel: 266901)
American Chamber of
Commerce, 186 Exhibition St
(tel: 6623535)

Tourism and Travel

Gov't Tourist Bureau, 272 Collins
(tel: 630202)
Royal Automobile Club of
Victoria (RACV), 123 Queen St
(tel: 6072211)
Victorian Gov't Travel Authority
(Tourism Commission), 230
Collins St (tel: 6029444)
American Express, 505 St. Kilda
Rd (tel: 2673711)
Deak International, 385 Bourke
St., (tel: 6707065)

PERTH

Airport Information

Time
GMT +8

Airport
Perth International PER
Tel: 4788770/2779200
10 km (6 mi) NE of city

Airlines
Air India 3222511
Air New Zealand 8221111
British Airways 3225011
Cathay Pacific 3227611
El Al 3221267

Garuda 3215213
Gulf Air 3221355
KLM 3250201
Lufthansa 8221020
Malaysian 3254499
Pan Am 3212719
Qantas 3220222
SAA 3212435
Sabena 3221355
SAS 3224799
Singapore 3225833
Swissair 3250201
Thai 3224799

Facilities

Bar, buffet, restaurant, bank with currency exchange, hotel reservations, post office, shops, conference facilities, first aid/medical, vaccinations
Duty free shop sells cigarets, cigars, tobacco, wine, spirits, cameras, perfume, watches, radios, jewellery, glass and china. Local British and American currencies accepted as well as major credit cards.
Car rental desks: Hertz, Avis, Budget

Airport Taxes
Per person: 20 dollars

City Information

Weather
Summer (Nov-Mar) dry and hot
Winter (Jun-Aug) milder
Average temps: July 17c (62F)
Jan 38c (100F)

Transportation
Metered taxis available on the street or in major hotels, shopping areas and taxi ranks. Radio controlled taxis can be booked by phoning numbers listed in the telephone directory. Buses and trams provide good service on the main routes. Car hire is available and current overseas licenses are acceptable but international ones are recommended. Use of seat belts is compulsory. Driving is on the left-hand side.

Car Hire
Hertz, 39 Milligan St (tel: 3217777 & 2779614)
Avis, 46 Hill St (tel: 3257677 & 2771729)
Budget, 33 Milligan St (tel: 322100 & 2779277)

Hotels
Kings Ambassador, 517 Hay Street, (tel: 2356555)
New Freeway, 55 Mill Point Rd., (tel: 367-7811)
Park Towers, 517-519 Hay St. (tel: 3256555)
Parmelia Hilton International, Mill St, (tel: 3223622)
Perth Parkroyal, 54 Terrace Rd, (tel: 3253811)
Riverside, 150 Mounts Bay Rd, (tel: 3214721)
Sheraton-Perth, 207 Adelaide Terrace (tel: 3250501)
Transit Inn, 375 Pier St, (tel: 3257655)

What to See and Do
Perth is the capital of Western Australia and has many parks and gardens. Visit the Court House, the Old Mill (an early nineteenthcentury house which has been turned into a museum) and the Town Hall. South of Perth, the coast has good surfing and fishing; the city of Freemantle has an interesting art gallery and maritime museum. The northern coastline has wrecks of old ships and spectacular scenery. Visitors can visit the many wineries in the Swan Valley.

Useful Addresses

Embassies and Consulates
American: 246 St George's Terrace (tel: 3224466)

British: 95 St George's Terrace
(tel: 3215611)

Business and Commerce
Perth Chamber of Commerce, 14
Parliament Pl (tel: 3222688)
Stock Exchange of Perth, 68 St
George's Terrace (tel: 3225066)
Department of Overseas Trade,
27 St George's Terrace
(tel: 3252322)
American Chamber of
Commerce, 16 St George's
Terrace (tel: 2211177)

Tourism and Travel
Royal Automobile Club of
Western Australia, 228
Adelaide Terrace
American Express, 51 William St
(tel: 3221177)
Government Travel Center, 772
Hay St (tel: 3212471)
Thomas Cook, 51 William St
(tel: 3212896)

SYDNEY

Airport Information

Time
GMT +10

Airport
Kingford Smith International
Airport (Mascot) SYD
Tel: 6670544
11 km (6.8 mi) NW of city

Airlines
Aer Lingus 232742
Air Canada 2325222
Air France 2333277
Air India 2328477
Air New Zealand 9654111
Alitalia 279133
American 2339477
British Airways 2335566
Canadian International 2906972
Cathay Pacific 2315122
Continental 2328222
El Al 2339466
Garuda 2326044
Gulf Air 2903422

Iberia 2903422
JAL 2334500
KLM 2316333
Korean 296832
Lufthansa 2406254
Malaysian 2315066
Northwest 2649715
Olympic 2512044
Pan Am 2351744
Philippine 298475
Qantas 9570111
SAA 2336855
Sabena 2902429
SAS 2511881
Singapore 2360111
Swissair 2321744
Thai 2511722
TWA 298395
UTA 2333277

Transport To City
Taxi: Agree on fare before
travelling; about A$14 dollars to
Kings Cross area. Takes 30-40
minutes.
Coach: Air-conditioned airport
bus offers frequent service to the
city center; comfortable with
plenty of baggage space. Costs
about A$2.20 dollars and takes 40
minutes.

Facilities
Bar, buffet, restaurant, bank,
insurance, hotel reservations,
baggage deposit, post office,
shops, first aid/medical
Duty-free shop sells cigarets,
cigars, wines, spirits, liqueurs,
jewellery, perfume, opals. Local
currencies accepted as well as
Canadian, Dutch, Fijian, French,
Japanese, Malaysian, New
Zealand, Singapore, British, US,
and travellers checks.
Car rental desks: Hertz, Avis,
Budget

Airport Taxes
Per person: 20 dollars (cash)

City Information

Weather
Seasons are the reverse of the

northern hemisphere: climate is warm with rain throughout the year.
Average temps: Jan (summer) 22C (71F) July (winter) 12C (54F)

Transportation
Metered taxis are available and can be hailed on the street. Tip 30 cents or up to the nearest dollar.

Car Hire
Hertz, 51 William (tel: 3576621 & 6690066)

Avis, 222 Botany (tel: 9228161 & 3572000)
Budget, 93 William (tel: 3398822 & 3398888)
Natcar, 318 Willoughby Rd (tel: 3321233)

Hospitals
Emergency ambulance 000
Sydney Hospital (tel: 2300111)

Trade Fairs
Australian Baking Exhibition (Feb)

ASIA/PACIFIC

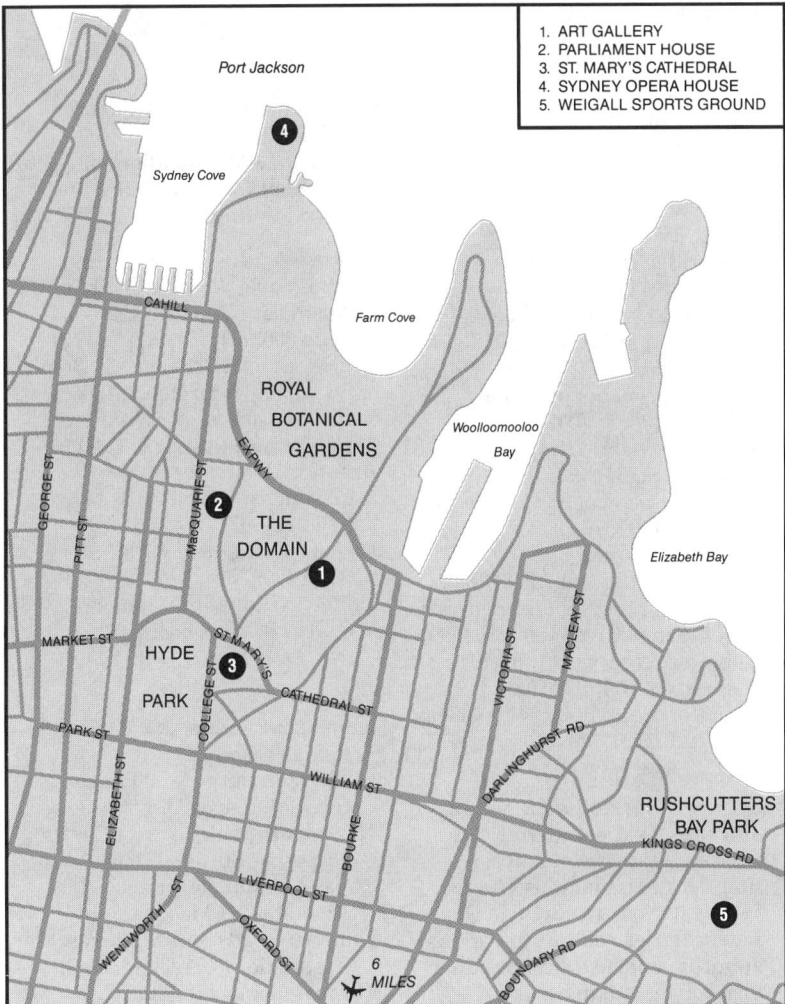

1. ART GALLERY
2. PARLIAMENT HOUSE
3. ST. MARY'S CATHEDRAL
4. SYDNEY OPERA HOUSE
5. WEIGALL SPORTS GROUND

Sydney

International Watch & Jewelry Exhibition (Feb)

International China and Tableware Exhibition (Feb)

International Motorcycle Exhibition (Feb)

International Toy & Hobby Fair (Mar)

Furniture & Bedding Exhibition (Apr)

Fitness & Sports Exhibition (Apr)

Pacific Area Defense Exhibition (May)

Office Products Exhibition (May)

Holiday & Travel Fair (June)

Pool & Spa Exhibition (June)

Int. Catering Trade Fair (June)

Int. Video Exhibition (July)

Building & Construction Exhibition (Aug)

Int. Engineering Exhibition (Sept)

Hotels

Boulevard, 90 William St (tel: 3572277)

Cambridge Inn, 212 Riley St (tel: 2121111)

Camperdown Travelodge, 9-15 Missendon Rd, Camperdown (tel: 5161522)

Hilton International Sydney, 259 Pitt St (tel: 5970122)

Hyatt Kingsgate, Kings Cross (tel: 3561234)

Hyde Park Plaza, 38 College St (tel: 3316933)

Inter-Continental Sydney, 117 Macquire St (tel: 2300200)

Ramada Gazebo, 2 Elizabeth Bay Rd, Kings Cross (tel: 3581999)

Sheraton Wentworth, 61-101 Philip St (tel: 2300700)

Sheraton Potts Point, 40 Macleay St (tel: 3581955)

What to See and Do

Sydney is located on a harbor and there is a wonderful view from Sydney Tower's observation deck. The famous Opera House is close to Circular Quay where ferries sail out to various suburbs. For historical buildings, visit Queen's Square and Macquarie Street. The old maritime center called The Rocks Area has some of the oldest buildings in the city. Visit the Art Gallery of New South Wales; the botanical gardens; Mitchell Library for early Australian documents. Aboriginal artifacts can be found in the Australian Museum. A must for any visitor is a trip around the harbor by ferry, and a trip to one of the many beaches. Kings Cross is the center of entertainment and has many nightclubs and restaurants.

Useful Addresses

Embassies and Consulates

American: Elizabeth & Park Sts (tel: 2647044)

Canadian: AMP Building, 50 Bridge St (tel: 2316522)

British: 1 Alfred St (Tel: 3277521)

Business and Commerce

Central Bank, Reserve Bank of Australia, 65 Martin Place (tel: 2300277)

Sydney Stock Exchange, 20 Bond St, Australia Sq (tel: 2310066)

Sydney Chamber of Commerce, 16 Clarence St (tel: 296001)

American Chamber of Commerce, 50 Pitt St (tel: 2411907)

USA Trade Center, 4 Cliff St (tel: 9290977)

United Nations Information Office, PO Box 4045 (tel: 292151)

Tourism and Travel

American Express, 388 George St (tel: 2390666)

Deak International, 50 Park Street (tel: 4664932)

New South Wales Travel Centre, 16 Spring St (tel: 2314444)

Royal Automobile Club of Australia, 89 Macquarei St

National Roads and Motorists Association, 151 Clarence St

Thomas Cook, 175 Pitt St (tel: 2334733)

CHINA

Essential Information

Type of Government
People's Republic

Area
9.6 million sq km
(3.7 million sq mi)

Population
1,060 billion

Annual Growth Rate
1.5%

Languages
Standard Chinese (Potunghua)
or Mandarin (based on the
Beijing dialect)

Religion
Athiest (official), Muslims,
Buddhists, Lamaists, Christians
and adherents of Chinese folk
religions

Ethnic Groups
Han Chinese 93.3%, Zhuang,
Uygur, Hui, Yi, Tibetan, Miao,
Manchu, Mongol, Buyi, Korean

Weights and Measures
Basically metric but traditional
methods still used widely.

Electrical Current
A.C. 50c 220/380V
A.C. 60c 110/220V

Major Business Cities
Beijing (cap) 9,335,000
Shanghai 12,400,000
Tianjing 6,750,000
Shenyang 5,500,000
Guangzhou (Canton) 4,750,000

Currency
1 Yuan(dollar) = 10 Jiao = 100 Fen
Notes 1, 2, 5, and 10 yuan
Coins 1, 2 and 5 fen

Public Holidays
Dates of the Chinese New Year
change annually. Check before
travelling.
Jan 1 New Year

Jan-Feb Chinese New Year
May 1 Labor Day
Oct 1, 2 National Day

Travellers Information

Entry Requirements
Passport required by all. Visa
required by all; usually arranged
for the business traveller by a
host company in China. Visitor
visas can be obtained through
Chinese embassy or consulate.
Travel permits are also required
for most cities and provinces.

Working Restrictions
Foreigners are not permitted to
work except as a teacher or
technician under contract.

Vaccination Required
Vaccination certificates are
required for cholera and
smallpox if travelling from
infected area. Take antimalarial
precautions.

Customs and Duty Free
On arrival: 400 cigarets; 2 liters/
3.5 pt liquor, 1/2 liter perfume.
You cannot bring firearms,
pornography or materials
considered politically offensive
into the country. Personal effects
like cameras, tape recorders and
typewriters should be listed on
customs declaration form when
entering. Certain items made in
China before 1949 may be
subject to export restrictions.

Currency Restrictions
There is no limit to the amount
of foreign currency you can
bring in but it must be declared.
It is illegal to use foreign
currency within the country so it
must be exchanged for Foreign
Exchange Certificates at the Bank
of China. These must be used to
pay for hotels and travel

ASIA/PACIFIC

expenses. Retain declaration form and all records of exchange transactions which must be presented when you leave.

Health Tips

Take antimalarial tablets during stay. There are no private doctors but the hospitals are excellent and inexpensive. In case of illness, your hotel will direct you to good medical aid. There are all-night pharmacies in most hospitals.

Climate and Clothing

The climate varies from north to south. In the north (Beijing), the temperatures range from very hot in the summer to very cold in the winter. Possible dust storms in April and May and high humidity and rainfall in July and August. Hot and humid summers in the south (Guangzhou and Shanghai) with mild and humid winters. Tropical weight clothes with raincoat for northern summers and the south. Northern winters require heavy winter clothes, boots, hats, gloves.

Tipping

Tipping is banned: it is regarded as an insult.

Food and Drink

Dishes in China vary according to the region. A three course dinner in a restaurant is reasonably priced although the choice of dishes depends on the seasonable ingredients. Business is rarely discussed over a meal.

Business Brief

GNP

$589.9 billion
(per capita income $562)

Annual Growth Rate

7.4%

Natural Resources

Coal, iron, petroleum, mercury, tin, tungsten, antimony, manganese, molybdenum, vanadium, magnetite, aluminum, lead, zinc, uranium, world's largest hydroelectric potential

Agriculture

Rice, wheat, other grains, cotton

Industry

Iron, steel, coal, machinery, light industrial products, armaments, petroleum

Imports

Total $43.4 billion
Grain, chemical fertilizer, industrial raw materials, machinery and equipment

Exports

Total $39.5 billion
Agricultural goods, textiles, light industrial products, nonferrous metals, petroleum, iron, steel, machine tools, and weapons

Major Trading Partners

Japan, Hong Kong, US, West Germany, Canada, Australia, Singapore, Romania, France, Italy

Workforce

476 million
Agriculture 74.4%, industry and commerce 15.1%, other 10.6%

Tips for Doing Business

Foreigners should be as natural as possible with a relaxed manner and style of dress. Do not wear bright colors. A conservative business suit is appropriate for government and business meetings. Prior appointments are essential as is promptness. Business cards are widely used; get them printed with English on one side and Mandarin on the other. Chinese businessmen take a long time making a decision but once made, their word is their bond and as good as a contract. An overly-friendly manner, like gratuitous touching or patting on the back, is considered to be unacceptable behaviour, although friendly smiles go a long way. Be very courteous to older people. Business visitors are often entertained at a restaurant. Arrive a bit early and be prepared to give a return toast to your host. The host will pay; the visitor must make the first move to leave. Expressions of appreciation (small mementoes) and thanks "xiexie", are always appreciated.

Best Months for Doing Business

Best time for travel is when the weather is most temperate; between April and June, and September and November.

Business Hours

Government
Mon-Fri 0800-1230, 1400-1700
Sat 0800-1200
Sunday is weekly holiday

Business
Mon-Fri 0800-1230-1400-1700
Sat 0800-1200
Sunday is weekly holiday

Banks
Banking hours vary from region to region
Mon-Sat 0900-1200, 1345-1630
Sunday is weekly holiday

Shops
Mon-Sat 0800-1200, 1400-1800
Sunday is weekly holiday

English Language Publications

China Daily; Peking Review weekly. Monthly newspapers published in English are China Reconstructs and China Pictorial.

Telephone and Communications

Telex country code: 716
International telephone calls can be put through an International Operator who speaks English and French. Book in advance. These, along with telex and telegraph international calls, can be arranged through your hotel or at the post office. It is cheaper to pay by credit card. Telephone system is automatic for the most part within the country, but it is wise to write down important numbers and codes and keep them with you as directories are not always at hand. Telex facilities available through the offices of the Administration of Telecommunications in both Beijing and Shanghai where telegram service is available as well. Telegrams can also be sent from main post offices. Speedpost allows letters to be sent and received within 48 hours to and from most parts of China and the world.

Air Travel

CAAC provides regular flights between the major cities; some with first class service. There are also independent regional companies. Best to get tickets booked through official guide or travel agent; otherwise book and collect well in advance.

Other Transport

Roads are poor, although a major highway is under construction between Beijing and Tianjin, and this, along with the lack of information available in English, makes bus travel difficult. Rail services operate between main cities; some electric but mostly steam. Deluxe trains have sleeping cars and private dining cars, but distances are so great, train travel is mostly for sightseeing.

BEIJING

Airport Information

Time
GMT +8

ASIA/PACIFIC

Airport
Capital International PEK
Tel: 552515
30 km (18.5 mi) NE of city

Airlines
Aeroflot 523203
Air Canada 2335900
British Airways 523601
CAAC 556720
Canadian International 5001956
JAL 5002221
Lufthansa 5001616
PIA 523274
Pan Am 595261
Philippine 523992
Qantas 5002481
Singapore 5004138
Swissair 5123555
Thai 501978

Transport to City
Taxi: take about 30-40 minutes downtown for fare of RY19-20 (US$5.50).
Coach: bus service by China Travel Service for downtown costs RY 2.7 (75 cents).

Facilities
Snack bar, bank with currency exchange, post office, gift shop Duty-free shop sells cigarets, cigars, liquors. Most convertible currencies accepted.

Airport Taxes
Per person: 10 yuan (cash)

City Information

Weather
Summers (April to October) are hot and dry with rainy season in July and August.
Winters (November to March)

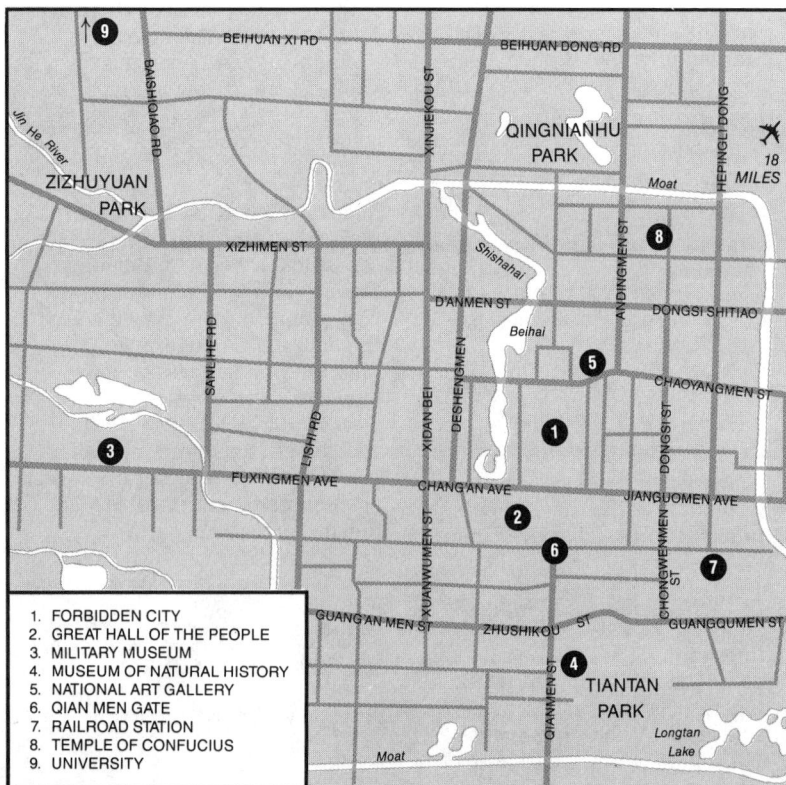

1. FORBIDDEN CITY
2. GREAT HALL OF THE PEOPLE
3. MILITARY MUSEUM
4. MUSEUM OF NATURAL HISTORY
5. NATIONAL ART GALLERY
6. QIAN MEN GATE
7. RAILROAD STATION
8. TEMPLE OF CONFUCIUS
9. UNIVERSITY

Beijing

are very cold and December to February often has sub-zero (-15c) temperatures.
Average temps: Jan 4c (25F) July 40c (104F)

Transportation
Taxis are available but they are hard to find except at hotels. You can hire one by the day, paying for distance travelled and waiting time. Keep the same taxi until you get back to the hotel, paying the waiting time necessary for appointments and meals. Make sure the driver gets fed too. Do not tip. Chauffeur-driven cars may be hired on a daily standard rate. There is a metro transit system in Beijing for the adventurous.

Hospitals
Hospitals are excellent and inexpensive. Emergency medical aid for travellers at:
Capital Hospital (tel: 555678)

Trade Fairs
International Furniture and Woodworking Exhibition (Jan)
International Defense Industries Exhibition (Jan)
International Petroleum Exhibition (Mar)
International Machine Tool Exhibition (Mar)
Electronic Production Exhibition (Apr)
International Garment Equipment Exhibition (May)
International Sports Facilities & Equipment Exhibition (June)
International Educational Equipment Exhibition (June)
International Rubber and Plastics Exhibition (June)
Metallurgical Industry Exhibition (June)
International Automobile Industry Exhibition (July)
Power Systems & Plant Control Exhibition (Aug)
International Mining Equipment Exhibition (Sept)

International Tourism & Hotel Exhibition (Oct)
Defense Technology Exhibition (Nov)

Hotels
There is a shortage of accomodation during peak seasons and it is not unusual for rooms to be shared. You cannot choose your own hotel since this is arranged for you, and the standards are somewhat spartan. New hotels are being built but for the present, inconveniences and a lack of luxury must be borne bravely.

What to See and Do
Visit the Forbidden City and the gate to the ancient Imperial City, Mao Zedong Mausoleum (with China's history from earliest times to the present). Visit the Temple of Heaven and the Imperial Summer Palace. Trips can be arranged to the Ming Imperial Tombs and the Great Wall of China, northwest of the city. Beijing has many museums, parks, and avenues for walking. Tours of the city can be arranged with Luxingshe (the Chinese Tourist office). Tang an Men Ta Chieh is a good street to shop on; best buys are jade, porcelain and scrolls. Antique shops in Liu Li Chang street. Never try to bargain. Ask at travel agencies or hotels for best restaurants and try Peking Duck.

Useful Addresses

Embassies and Consulates
American: Xiu Shui Bei Jie 3 (tel: 523831)
Canadian: 10 Sanlitun (tel: 523536)
British: 11 Guanghua Lu (tel: 521961)

Business and Commerce
If you wish to engage in foreign trade operations in China, initial inquiries should be directed to:

ASIA/PACIFIC

Bank of China, 108 Hsi Chiao
Min Hsiang
China Committee for the
Promotion of International
Trade, Hsi Tan Bldg, Hsi
Chang An Chiah American

Chamber of Commerce, Jian
Guo Men Wai (tel: 522559)

Tourism and Travel
China International Travel
Service, Dong Changan Jie
(tel: 554192)

HONG KONG

Essential Information

Type of Government
British Dependent Territory

Area
1,064 sq km
(411 sq mi)

Population
5.7 million

Annual Growth Rate
1.3%

Languages
Cantonese and English (official)

Religion
Eclectic mixture of local religions
90%, Christian 10%

Ethnic Groups
Chinese 98%, other 2%

Weights and Measures
Metric system, Imperial system
and local units also used.

Electrical Current
A.C. 50c 220V and 200/346V

Major Business Cities
Victoria (cap) 1,250,000
Kowloon 2,500,000
Main business district is Central
on Hong Kong Island.

Currency
1 Hong Kong Dollar = 100 cents
Notes 10, 50, 100, 500, 1000
dollars
Coins 5, 10, 20, 50 cents; 1, 2, 5
dollars

Public Holidays
Many holidays in Hong Kong
are variable (var). Check before
travelling.
Jan 1 New Year
Feb (var) Lunar New Year's
Celebration (3 days)
Apr 5 (var) Ching Ming Festival
Apr 13-20 Easter Week
June (var) Dragon Boat Festival
June (var) Queen's Birthday

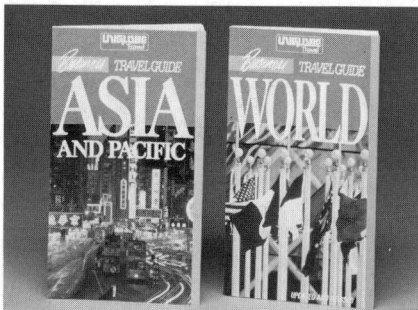

July (var) First Weekend in July
Aug (var) First Monday in
    August
Sept (var) Day after Mid-Autumn
    Festival
Oct (var) Chung Yeung Festival
Dec 25-26 Christmas

Travellers Information

Entry Requirements
Passport required by all. Visa not
required for nationals of most
countries on short visits. Longer
visits allowed for varying lengths
of time depending on
nationality. Nationals of
communist countries must
always have a visa. There are a
number of regulations governing
entry and exit from Hong Kong
and it is a good idea to check
information carefully before
travelling.

Working Restrictions
All nationals must have a work
permit (obtained in advance) if
working in the private sector:
working visa not required for
Hong Kong government
employees.

Vaccination Required
No vaccination certificates
required except one for yellow
fever if travelling from an
infected country.

Customs and Duty Free
On arrival: 200 cigarets or 50
cigars or 250g/8oz tobacco; 1 liter
alcohol; small amount perfume.
Personal effects are allowed in
duty-free.

Currency Restrictions
There are no currency
restrictions.

Health Tips
Drinking water is purified in
Kowloon and Hong Kong Island.
The medical standards are high,
and many doctors and dentists
speak English. It is best to seek
private treatment and pay for it.

Climate and Clothing
Hong Kong is hot and mon-
soonal in the summer (June-
Sept) with particularly heavy
rains in June and July,
temperatures around 30c (86F),
and high humidity. Wear
tropical weight clothes and carry
an umbrella. Winters (Dec-Feb)
are cool and dry, but humidity
can often be as high as 83%.
Wear medium weight clothes
and take a light coat. Other
months call for lightweight
clothes.

Tipping
Hotels and restaurants may
include 10% service charge on
the bill, but you are expected to
tip 10% on top of that. Tip taxi
drivers 10%; porters HK$3 per
piece of luggage; HK$l for small
services.

Food and Drink
There is a wide range of Chinese
food as well as Vietnamese,
Korean, Indonesian and
Japanese. Western food is
available in large hotels and at
fast food outlets. There are
literally hundreds of restaurants,
but travellers are cautioned not
to eat oysters except in the best
restaurants or large hotels. Visit
the open-air night food market
by the Macau Ferry at Hong
Kong Central. Tea and soft
drinks, Western wines and
spirits, and Chinese rice wines
are all popular. Isingtao beer is
imported from China.

Business Brief

GDP
$19.9 billion
(per capita income $3,691)

Annual Growth Rate
9.6%

Agriculture
Vegetables, pigs, chickens, fish

Industry
Apparel, textiles, toys, watches, clocks, and electronics

Imports
Total $48.4 billion
Raw materials and semi-manufactured goods, consumer goods, capital goods, food

Exports
Total $48.5 billion
Clothing and textiles, electronics, toys

Major Trading Partners
US, UK, West Germany, China, Japan

Workforce
2.6 million
Agriculture 1%, industry and commerce 76%, services 23%

Tips for Doing Business
Wear a lightweight suit for all occasions and make prior appointments. Chinese businessmen drive a hard bargain but their word is their bond. Take plenty of sales material and business cards. You may find the Hong Kong businessman particular about packaging: it is wise, for instance, to avoid using blue and white as they are the Chinese colors of mourning. There will be a lot of entertaining, usually in restaurants. Be prepared to answer a toast to your host. Try to eat with chopsticks. Carry your passport at all times.

Best Months for Doing Business
Best months are October and November, and March through April. Avoid the weeks before and after Christmas, Easter, and the 12-day Chinese New Year: check dates before travelling.

Business Hours

Government
Mon-Fri 0900-1300, 1400-1700
Sat 0900-1300

Business
Mon-Fri 0900-1700
Sat 0900-1200

Bank
Mon-Fri 0930-1600
Sat 0930-1200

Shops
Mon-Sat 1000-1800 Central District; 1000-2130 Causeway Bay and Wanchoi; 1000-1930 Tsimshatsui East; 1000-2100 Tsimshatsui, Yamatei and Mong Kok

English Language Publications
English language daily newspapers are South China Morning Post, the Hong Kong Standard, the Star, Asian Wall Street Journal, the International Herald Tribune and China Daily. Hong Kong is the name of a weekly newspaper which lists items of interest to visitors.

Telephone and Communications
Telephone country code: 852
Telephone city code: Hong Kong 5, Kowloon 3, Lantau 5, New Territories 0
Telex country code: 780
There is fully automatic telephone service and overseas calls are efficiently placed. Public telex facilities (24 hours) at Cable and Wireless offices on Connaught Road. Telegrams can be sent at telegram offices or by phone.

Transport
The Kowloon-Canton railway goes to and from China with express trains between Kowloon-Guangzhou and Kowloon-Lowu. You can go to Guangzhou or hire a taxi which costs approximately US$100 for a 3 hour journey. Hovercrafts operate several times a day to and from Guangzhou and Zhuhai. Frequent services to Macau by ferry (2-3 hours), hydrofoil (75 minutes),

hovercraft (45 minutes) and
jetfoil (45 minutes).

Airport Information

Time
GMT +8

Airport
Hong Kong International (Kai
Tak) HKG
Tel: 8297531
7.5 km (4.5 mi) NE of Star Ferry
in Kowloon

Airports
Air Canada 5221001
Air France 5248145
Air India 5221176
Air New Zealand 5640123
Alitalia 5237047
American 5257081
British Airways 5868030

British Caledonian 5260062
CAAC 5216416
Cathay Pacific 5884148
Continental 5221133
Canadian International 5227001
Eastern 5237065
El Al 58420873
Garuda 5235181
JAL 5230081
KLM 5251255
Korean 3686221
Lufthansa 5212311
Malaysian 5218181
Northwest 5217477
Pan Am 5231111
Philippine 3694521
Qantas 5242101
SAA 5775023
Sabena 5252886
SAS 5265978
Singapore 5202233
Swissair 5293670

ASIA/PACIFIC

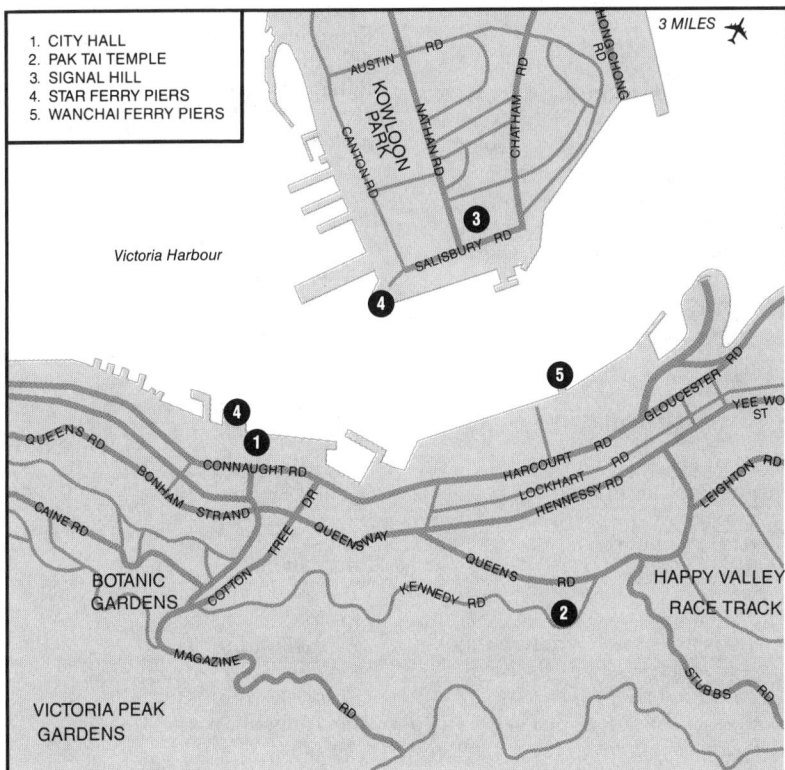

1. CITY HALL
2. PAK TAI TEMPLE
3. SIGNAL HILL
4. STAR FERRY PIERS
5. WANCHAI FERRY PIERS

Hong Kong

Thai 5295601
TWA 5411300
United 5814888
Varig 3690171

Transport to City

Taxi: mostly red-and-grey and available at all times although a bit hard to find between 1600-1800. Average cost to Kowloon HK$20-25 with HK$1 for each large piece of luggage: takes 15-40 minutes. Average cost to Hong Kong HK$25-35 plus tunnel charge: takes 25-60 minutes. Taxi drivers are usually very scrupulous about not overcharging.

Coach: airport coach leaves every 20 minutes (from approximately 0700-2300) for Kowloon (HK$3) and Hong Kong (HK$5): stops at most hotels. Pay driver. Courtesy coaches usually provided by major hotels.

Facilities

Currency exchange, hotel reservations, tourist information, shops selling a variety of items, insurance, post office, telegraph and telephone services
Duty-free shop sells cigarets, cigars, tobacco, wines, spirits, cameras, watches, jewellery, leathers, glass, china.
Car rental desks: Hertz, Avis

Airport Taxes

Per person: HK$120

City Information

Weather

Subtropical with summer monsoons.
Average temps: Jan 21c (70F)
July 30c (86F)

Transportation

Taxis are easy to find and most drivers speak English. Non-metered taxis, called pak api, are double the price. Bus services go nearly everywhere in the colony and are convenient and inexpensive. Trams connect the business districts on Hong Kong Island. They are crowded at rush hour, but an interesting form of transport at other times. The Moss Transit Railway (MTR) runs from 0600-0100. Tickets are only good for 90 minutes from the time they are bought and passengers may not eat, drink or carry bulky packages. There are frequent water services by ferry, hydrofoil, and hovercraft.

Car Hire

Hertz, 9 Connaught Rd
    (tel: 5221013)
Avis, 85 Leighton Rd, Causeway
    Bay (tel: 5719237/9)
Harper Hire, 163 Matauwei
    Road, Kowloon (tel: 37159545)
Toyota Self-Drive, 161 Matauwei
    Road, Kowloon (tel: 57114441)

Hospitals

Emergency medical assistance for travellers at:
Emergency (tel: 999)
Matilda (tel: 596301)
Sing Tao Medical Center, 33
    Queen's Road (tel: 5266505)

Trade Fairs

International Office
    Communications Exhibition
    (Mar)
Personal Computer Fair (Mar)
Clothing Industry Fair (Mar)
Computer Exhibition (Apr)
Business Communications
    Exhibition (May)
International Electronics
    Engineering Exhibition (May)
International Leather Exhibition
    (May)
International Cosmetics &
    Hairdressing Exhibition (May)
Motors & Transformers
    Exhibition (May)
Machinery & Electronics
    Exhibition (June)
International Tourism Exhibiton
    (June)
Plastic Industry Exhibition (Sept)

International Medical Technology
Exhibition (Sept)
International Optics Fair (Sept)
Industrial Machinery Trade Fair
(Oct)
International Office
Communications Exhibition
(Oct)
Consumer Products Trade Fair
(Oct)
International Industrial
Machinery Exhibition (Nov)
International Food & Beverage
Exhibition (Nov)

Hotels

Hong Kong
Furama Inter-Continental,
1 Connaught Rd, Central
(tel: 5255111)
Grand Hyatt Hong Kong, 1
Harbour Rd (tel: 8611234)
Hongkong Hilton, 2 Queens Rd,
Central (tel: 5233111)
Lee Gardens, Hysan Avenue,
Causeway Bay (tel: 5893311)
The Mandarin, 5 Connaught Rd,
Central (tel: 52200111)
The Plaza Tower, 310 Gloucester
Rd, Causeway Bay
(tel: 57901021)

Kowloon
Ambassador, 4 Middle Rd at
Nathan Rd (tel: 3666321)
The Empress, 17-19 Chatham Rd
(tel: 3660211)
Grand, 14 Carnarvon Rd
(tel: 3669331)
Holiday Inn Golden Mile, 50
Nathan Rd (tel: 3693111)
The Hong Kong, 3 Canton Rd
(tel: 3676011)
Hyatt Regency Hong Kong, 67
Nathan Rd (tel: 3111234)
Park, Chatham Rd (tel: 3661371)
The Regent, Salisbury Rd
(tel: 37211211)
Sheraton Hong Kong, 20 Nathan
Rd (tel: 3691111)

What to See and Do

Hong Kong Island is linked to
Kowloon and the mainland by
the Star Ferry and underground
tunnel. Visit Victoria Peak by
electrical railway to see the
harbor view; old "Chinatown" at
the end of Queen's Road for
antiques and Chinese crafts; and
Causeway Bay for good
restaurants. Clearwater and
Repulse Bays are on the south
side of the island. The fishing
village of Aberdeen has a
sampan harbor with floating
seafood restaurants. Visit the
jade market in Kansei Street,
Kowloon. Hong Kong is famous
for its shopping since it is a free
port and prices are competitive.
Stores with the sign of the Hong
Kong Tourist Association (a
black junk) are recommended.
Shop at the Ocean Terminal
Center in Kowloon near the Star
Ferry, and along Nathan Rd,
Harbour City, Causeway Bay
and in Hong Kong central.

Useful Addresses

Embassies and Consulates
American: 26 Garden Rd
(tel: 5239011)
Canadian: Exchange Square
(tel: 5810432)
British: Government House
(tel: 5232031)

Business and Commerce
Central Bank (Hong Kong &
Shanghai Banking Corp)
1 Queens Rd (tel: 8221111)
Hong Kong Stock Exchange,
Edinburgh House (tel: 5221122)
Hong Kong General Chamber of
Commerce, Swire House
(tel: 5299229)
Kowloon Chamber of Commerce,
2 Liberty Avenue
(tel: 37600393)
American Chamber of
Commerce, Swire House 1030
(tel: 5260165)

Tourism and Travel
Hong Kong Tourist Association,
Connaught Centre, Connaught
Rd (tel: 5244191)

Government Information Office, Beaconfield Rd, Queens Rd, Central (tel: 5233191)

American Express, Hong Kong, 16-18 Queens Rd, Central (tel: 58431789)

Deak International, Kai Tak Airport (8 locations)

Deak International, 28 Queen's Road (tel: 252067)

Deak International, 93 Nathan Road, Kowloon (tel: 663341)

Hong Kong Automobile Association, March Rd, Wanchai Reclamation, Wanchai (tel: 5743394)

INDIA

Essential Information

Type of Government
Federal Republic

Area
3,287,263 sq km
(1,268,884 sq mi)

Population
764 million

Annual Growth Rate
2.24%

Lanuages
Hindi, English and 14 other official languages

Religion
Hindu 83%, Muslim 11%, Christian 2.6%, Sikh, Jain, Buddhist, Parsi

Ethnic Groups
Indo-Aryan 72%, Dravidian 25%, Mongoloid 2%, others

Weights and Measures
Metric used in business, but Imperial system and traditional Indian measures still in use.

Electrical Current
A.C. 50c 220/380V and 220V

Major Business Cities
New Delhi (cap) 6,500,000
Calcutta 9,750,000
Bombay 9,950,000
Madras 5,250,000

Currency
1 Rupee = 100 Paisa
Notes 1, 2, 5, 10, 20, 50, 100 rupees

Coins 5, 10, 25, 50 paisa

Public Holidays
There are many public holidays which vary from state to state. They are usually declared at the beginning of the year so it is wise to check with a local travel agent or consulate before travelling.
Jan 1 New Years
Jan 26 Republic Day
May 1 May Day
Aug 15 Independence Day
Oct 2 Ghandi's Birthday
Oct 13-22 Desara (Festival of Ten Nights)
Nov 12 Divali (Festival of Lights)
Dec 25-26 Christmas

Travellers Information

Entry Requirements
Passport required by all. Visas required by most nationals except those with on-going tickets who will leave within 72 hours. Additional visas may be required for re-entry if you visit certain countries in between: Nepal, Sri Lanka, Afghanistan, Burma. Visa regulations are subject to change so it is wise to make enquiries at local consulate or embassy before travelling.

Working Restrictions
You do not need a permit to work in India, but you cannot take earned money out of the country.

Vaccination Required
Vaccination certificates for smallpox, yellow fever and cholera are required if entering the country from infected area. Vaccinations for cholera are recommended as well as antimalerial precautions.

Customs and Duty Free
On arrival: 200 cigarets or 50 cigars or 250g/8oz tobacco; 0.25 liter perfume. Personal goods are duty-free although the import of cameras and film must be a reasonable amount for personal use. High-value items such as cameras, tape recorders, and jewellery should be listed on a tourist baggage re-export form. To buy, carry or consume liquor, obtain a liquor permit on arrival in Delhi, Bombay and Calcutta airports. There are strict regulations on the export of certain goods. Make enquiries on arrival.

Currency Restrictions
Indian currency may not be imported or exported. There is no restriction on the import of foreign currency but the amount must be declared, and all currency transactions then recorded on this declaration form. All money must be exchanged through banks and authorized money changers. There is a careful inspection on departure.

Health Tips
The water is not purified: drink bottled or boiled water at all times, although you need not be quite as cautious in the large luxury hotels. Take antimalarial tablets. Nearly all doctors and dentists speak English and the first-class hotels have doctors on call. Medical services must be paid for but the fees are low. Imported pharmaceuticals are scarce and expensive. In hot weather, stay out of the sun.

Climate and Clothing
Extremes of climate but mainly tropical. Winter (November to March) cold in the north; bright and dry in the south; hot and humid in Bombay, dry and chilly in Delhi with cold nights. Medium weight clothes and a topcoat for Delhi; lightweight in other places. Tropical weight clothes in spring and fall for hot, humid conditions. Summers (June to September) see the monsoon season everywhere but Madras, with heavy rain but little humidity during the dry spells. Tropical weight clothes and umbrella.

Tipping
Most hotels and restaurants include 10% service charge in the bill, but staff still expect a 10% tip. Many people, porters and so on, will crowd around soliciting tips. Generally, give 7 rupees per piece of baggage; taxi drivers about 10%; attendants and small services 5 rupees.

Food and Drink
India is home to one of the great cuisines of the world, based largely on the varied and inventive blending of spices. Curried meats, fish and vegetables can be made to suit the palate of the diner; rice is common in the south and breads (rotis) in the north. A must is Tandoori chicken; chicken marinated and then cooked in a clay oven. In the north, sample the many types of kebabs and biryanis. Try the delicious appetizers made of meats or vegetables fried in pastry triangles and available all over India. Tea is the common beverage in the north and coffee in the south. European food available in all the large hotels.

Business Brief

GDP
$204.8 billion
(per capita income $272)

Annual Growth Rate
4%

Natural Resources
Coal, iron ore, manganese, mica, bauxite, chromite, limestone, barite

Agriculture
Textiles, jute, processed food, steel, machinery, transport equipment, cement, aluminum, fertilizers

Industry
Cement, chemicals, engineering, iron and steel, jute processing, mining, machinery, petroleum refining, sugar refining

Imports
Total $14.7 billion
Crude oil, machinery and transport equipment, edible oils, fertilizers

Exports
Total $9.5 billion
Crude oil, engineering goods, precious stones, cotton apparel and fabrics, handicrafts, tea

Major Trading Partners
UK, US, USSR, Japan, West Germany, Iran, Canada, Belgium, France, Saudi Arabia, United Arab Emirates

Workforce
273 million
Agriculture 70%, industry 11%, trade and services 17%

Tips for Doing Business
Nearly all businessmen speak English and are informal and gracious hosts. Wear a suit coat on the first business visit and for all government visits; then follow your host's lead. Make prior appointments. Do not be surprised if your contact asks you many personal questions since it will be considered good manners to take an interest in your life. Cultivate patience: Indian businessmen like to take their time making decisions. Alcohol is prohibited in most of the country, but is available in luxury hotels in Delhi and Bombay. It is also available in private clubs where most business entertaining is done. Since the majority of the population is Hindu and the cow is sacred, most Indians are vegetarians. Always eat and pass things with the right hand even if you are left-handed. Shake hands with men, with women, put palms together as if in prayer: a gesture called the "namasthe". Do not discuss India's relationship with her neighbors; her poverty; or foreign aid.

Best Months for Doing Business
The cool, dry season is from September to March. October to May is the cool time in Delhi; September and October in Bombay and Calcutta. Businessmen should check for local religious and festive holidays which change from year to year, since all business stops during these times.

Business Hours

Government offices take the second Saturday in each month as a holiday.

Government
Mon-Fri 1000-1700 in Delhi, Calcutta, Madras; 0930-1630 in Bombay

Business
Mon-Fri 1000-1700 in Delhi and Madras; 0930-1700 in Calcutta, 1000-1730 in Bombay usually open half day Saturday

Banks
Mon-Fri 1000-1400, Sat 1000-1200
in Delhi, Calcutta and Madras;
Mon-Fri 1100-1500, Sat 1100-1300
in Bombay

Shops
Mon-Sat 0930-1930 in Delhi;
1000-1830 in Calcutta; 1000-1830
in Bombay; 0900-1930 in Madras

English Language Publications
Numerous local dailies are
published in several languages
including 60 to 70 in English.
The three daily financial
newspapers are the Economic
Times (Delhi, Bombay and
Calcutta), Financial Express
(Delhi, Madras and Bombay),
and Business Standard of
Calcutta.

Telephone and Communications
Telephone country code: 91
Telephone city code: Agra 562,
Bangalore 812, Bombay 22,
Calcutta 33, Delhi 11, Madras 44
Telex country code: 953
Over 86% of telephones have
automatic service. Most
operators speak English. Public
telephones are usually very
busy. Telex facilities available 24
hours at major hotels and from
public telegraph/telex offices in
main cities: in Calcutta at
Dalhousie Square; in New Delhi
at Eastern Court, Janpath.
Telegram service available via
phone or at post offices or public
telegram facilities across the
country.

Air Travel
Because of the vast distances, air
travel is the best form of travel
between main centers. Indian
Airlines operates over 100 flights
a day linking all main cities.

Other Transport
There are many long distance
bus services but local services are
not recommended to visitors
because of the large crowds.

There is an extensive rail service
operated by Indian Railways.
Usually tickets must be bought
in advance: get first-class
accomodation with dining car
and sleeping coaches. Chauffeur-
driven air-conditioned
limousines are readily available;
car rental is not.

BOMBAY

Airport Information

Time
GMT +5.5

Airport
Sahar International BOM
Tel: 535461, 533161
29 km (18 mi) N of city

Airlines
Air Canada 2021111
Air France 2025021
Air India 2023747
Alitalia 222112
British Airways 220888
Canadian International 214224
Cathay Pacific 2029112
Gulf Air 2021626
Iran Air 297070
Iraqi 221399
JAL 233136
KLM 221013
Kuwait Air 2045351
Lufthansa 2020887
Pan Am 2029048
PIA 2021480
Philippine 220676
Qantas 2029288
Sabena 2023817
SAS 214180
Saudia 2020049
Singapore 2023365
Swissair 222402
TWA 223081

Transport to City
Taxi: metered yellow and blue
taxis charge 105 rupees into town
with a small extra charge for
luggage: 50-75 minutes.

ASIA/PACIFIC

Coach: airport bus outside the arrival hall leaves on the hour 24 hours every day. . Costs about 25 rupees and takes 50-75 minutes.

Facilities

Bar, buffet, restaurant, bank with currency exchange, domestic flight insurance, hotel reservations, post office, baggage deposit, shops, conference facilities, first aid/medical Duty-free shop sells cigarets, spirits, liqueurs, cameras, watches, perfume. Accepts most convertible currencies.

Airport Taxes

Per person: 100 rupees

City Information

Weather

Hot and dry in the winter months: during April and May, it is hot and humid. June to September is the monsoon season. October and November, hot and dry.

Transportation

Taxis are available, either by telephone or hailed in the street. Many are metered: if not, negotiate fare (although all rates

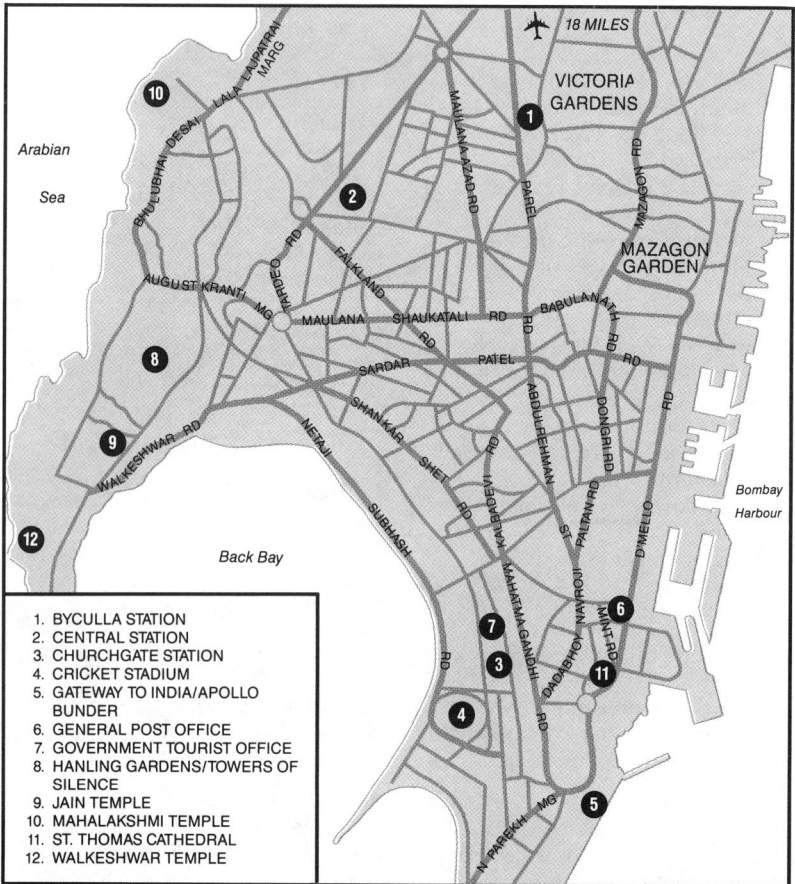

1. BYCULLA STATION
2. CENTRAL STATION
3. CHURCHGATE STATION
4. CRICKET STADIUM
5. GATEWAY TO INDIA/APOLLO BUNDER
6. GENERAL POST OFFICE
7. GOVERNMENT TOURIST OFFICE
8. HANLING GARDENS/TOWERS OF SILENCE
9. JAIN TEMPLE
10. MAHALAKSHMI TEMPLE
11. ST. THOMAS CATHEDRAL
12. WALKESHWAR TEMPLE

Bombay

are reasonable). Tipping is disapproved of but a small tip is expected from visitors. Air-conditioned chauffeured cars are available through agencies and hotels.

Car Hire
Hertz, Shahid Bhagatsingh Road (tel: 230073)
Combard, Advani Chambers, Sir P.M. Road (tel: 361929)
Marson, 78 Nepeansea Road (tel: 381705)

Hospitals
Medical aid for travellers at:
The Breach Candy Hospital (tel: 363651)

Trade Fairs
International Pollution Control Exhibition (Jan)
Communications Technology Exhibition (Oct)
Electronics Technology Exhibition (Oct)

Hotels
International-standard accommodation widely available but heavily booked so reserve well in advance.
Ambassador, Churchgate Extension (tel: 2041131)
Centaur, Santa Cruz Airport (tel: 6126660)
Holiday Inn, Balraj Sahani Rd Juhu Beach (tel: 6204444)
Horizon, 37 Juhu Beach (tel: 6148100)
Nataraj, 135 Netaji Subhash Rd (tel: 2044161)
Oberoi Towers, Marine Drive, Nariman Point (tel: 2024343)
President, 90 Cuffe Parade, Colaba (tel: 4950808)
Ritz, 5 Jamshedji Tata Rd (tel: 220141)
Taj Mahal Inter-Continental, Apollo Bunder (tel: 2023366)
West End, 45 New Marine Lines (tel: 299121)

What to See and Do
Visit the Gateway to India

Monument on the seafront; the Prince of Wales Museum; the Hanging Gardens on Molabar Hill; Chowpathy Beach, at the north end of Marine Drive, with acrobats, sand sculptors and contortionists; Victoria Gardens. Take a motor launch 10 km east of the city to see eighth and ninth-century rock-cut cave temples on Elephanta Island.

Useful Addresses

Embassies and Consulates
American: 78 Bhulabhai Desai Rd (tel: 8223611)
Canadian: Gresham House, Mint Rd
British: Hong Kong Bank Bldg (tel: 274874)

Business and Commerce
Central Bank, Reserve Bank of India, Central Office, New Central Office Bldg (tel: 2861602)
Bombay Stock Exchange, Dallal St (tel: 272720)
Bombay Chamber of Commerce and Industry, Mackinnon Mackenzie Bldg Ballard Estate (tel: 264681)

Tourism and Travel
Tourist Office, 123 M Karve Rd (tel: 293144)
Federation of Indian Automobile Associations, 76 Vir Nariman Rd (tel: 291085)
American Express, 276 DN Naorji Rd (tel: 2048291)
Thomas Cook, DN Naorji Rd (tel: 2045556)

DELHI

Airport Information

Time
GMT +5.5

Airport
Indira Gandhi International DEL

ASIA/PACIFIC

Tel: 391351
14.5 km (9 mi) SE of city

Airlines
Aeroflot 40426
Air Canada 604755
Air France 3310407
Air India 331225
Alitalia 3311019
British Airways 343428
Canadian International 110001
Eastern 344789
Gulf Air 3324293
JAL 3327104
Kuwait 3314221

Lufthansa 3327268
Pan Am 3325222
Philippine 42718
Qantas 353174
Sabena 3312928
SAS 345262
Singapore 3310145
TWA 345118
United 3115013

Transport to City
Taxi: choose Atel taxis which are
yellow and black and metered
but not air-conditioned. They
take up to 4 people and cost

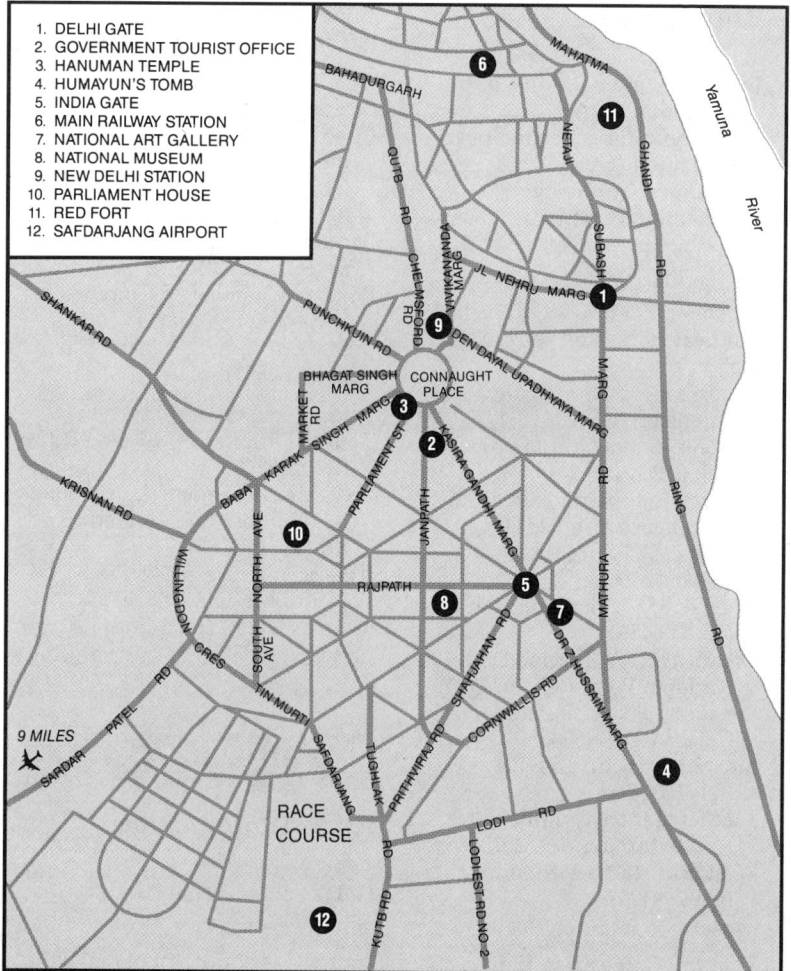

1. DELHI GATE
2. GOVERNMENT TOURIST OFFICE
3. HANUMAN TEMPLE
4. HUMAYUN'S TOMB
5. INDIA GATE
6. MAIN RAILWAY STATION
7. NATIONAL ART GALLERY
8. NATIONAL MUSEUM
9. NEW DELHI STATION
10. PARLIAMENT HOUSE
11. RED FORT
12. SAFDARJANG AIRPORT

Delhi

about 60 rupees with a 5-10 rupee charge for baggage. Tipping is not expected. Don't get too friendly with drivers or they may bother you later for sight-seeing.

Coach: There is an Ex-Servicemen's Air-Link which departs from outside domestic and international arrival halls and meets most flights. Stops at all big hotels and takes 40 minutes: 15 rupees. Chauffeur-driven limosines: air-conditioned — can be reserved at Ashoh Travel and Tour Desk and cost between $11-14.

Transit: Local bus (*780) takes 60 minutes and costs about 8 cents. No room for baggage.

Facilities

Bar, snack bar, bank with currency exchange, domestic flight insurance, post office, hotel reservations, baggage deposit, shops, first aid/medical, vaccinations

Duty-free shop sells cigarets, cigars, tobacco, wines, liqueurs, lighters, silver, batiks, carvings. Most convertible currencies accepted including Canadian, Australian, Japanese, British and US.

There are no car rental facilities.

Airport Taxes

Per person: International 100 rupees; domestic 50 rupees

City Information

Weather

Seasonal extremes in temperature with the winter months cool to cold, and April to July hot, dry and dusty. July to September is the rainy season and humid.

Average temps: 10-13c (50-55F) July 27-33c (80-92F)

Transportation

Taxis are generally available and are usually metered. If not, negotiate fares in advance. Tipping is not customary but a small tip is expected from visitors. Chauffeur-driven cars are also available and preferable to car rental which is almost nonexistent.

Car Hire

Hertz, 23 Kasturba Gandhi Marg (tel: 2727521)

Hospitals

Medical aid for travellers can be obtained from private doctors, (often on call at major hotels) and at:

Holy Family Hospital (tel: 632355/383/444)

Trade Fairs

Electricity, Oil and Gas Exhibition (Sept)

Hotels

Akbar, Chanakyapuri (tel: 604451)

Ambassador, Sujan Singh Park (tel: 690391)

Ashoka, 50-B Chanakyapuri (tel:600121)

Claridges, 12 Aurangzeb Rd (tel: 3010211)

Hyatt Regency, Bhikaiji Cama Pl, Ring Rd (tel: 609911)

Janpath, Janpath (tel: 350070)

Maurya Sheraton, Diplomat Enclave (tel: 3010101)

Oberoi Inter-Continental, Zakir Hussain Rd (tel: 363030)

Oberoi Maidens, 7 Alipur Rd (tel: 2525464)

Taj Mahal, 1 Mansingh Rd (tel: 3016162)

Vikram, Ring Rd (tel: 625639)

What to See and Do

The National Museum on Janpath has a wonderful collection of art and architecture spanning 5000 years of history. Old Delhi is spread out with interesting sights. Qutb Minar is a very high thirteenth-century tower; get good view of Delhi from fourteenthcentury Fort of

Tuqulaquabod; visit the market concourse of Chadni Chowk to barter for bargains. At the eastern end is the famous Red Fort built entirely of red sandstone. Nearby is the Jama Masuid, the largest mosque in India. You can get to and from Agra to see the Taj Mahal in one day by air, train or hired car. Visit Khajuraho to see the famous eleventh-century temples with erotic sculptures. Delhi is accessible to a wealth of interesting and beautiful areas: arrangements are easily made through local hotels and travel agents.

Useful Addresses

Embassies and Consulates
American: Shanti Path, Chanakyapuri 21 (tel: 600651)

Canadian: 7/8 Shanti Path, Chanakyapuri (tel: 608l6l)
British: Shanti Path, Chanakyapuri (tel: 601371)

Business and Commerce
Associated Chambers of Commerce & Trade of India, Allahabad Bank Bldg, 17 Parliament St (tel: 310704)
State Trading Corporation of India, Chandralok, 36 Janpath (tel: 353164)
Stock Exchange Association, 3/4 Asaf Ali Road (tel: 312468)

Tourism and Travel
Government of India Tourist Office, 88 Janpath (tel: 32005)
Automobile Association of Upper India, 14-F Connaught Place
American Express, Connaught Place (tel: 344119)
Thomas Cook, Hotel Imperial, Janpath (tel: 311511)

INDONESIA

Essential Information

Type of Government
Independent Republic

Area
2 million sq km
(736,000 sq mi)

Population
l73 million

Annual Growth Rate
2.1%

Lanuages
Indonesian (official), local languages, the most widely spoken of which is Javanese.

Religion
Muslin 90%, Christian 5% (mostly Roman Catholic), Hindu and Buddhist 3%

Ethnic Groups
Javanese, Sundanese, Batak, Buginese, Minangkabau, Balinese, Chinese, Irianese

Weights and Measures
Metric with local variations

Electrical Current
A.C. 50c 127/220V

Major Business Cities
Jakarta (cap) 8,500,000
Surabaya 3,250,000
Bandung 2,250,000
Medan 2,500,000
Semarang 2,000,000

Currency
1 Rupiah = 100 Sen
Notes 100, 500, 1000, 5000, 10000 rupiahs
Coins 5, 10, 25, 50, 100 rupiahs

Public Holidays
Religious holidays are predominately Muslim. As these change yearly according to lunar

cycles, check carefully before travelling.
Jan 1 New Year
Apr 13-19 Easter
May 28 Ascension
Aug 17 Independence Day
Dec 25 Christmas

Travellers Information

Entry Requirements
Passport, valid for at least the next 6 months after visit, as well as an onward or return ticket is required by all visitors. Visas are not required by tourists or businessmen for a stay of up to 2 months. Anyone with Israeli passport or Israeli visa in passport is restricted entry.

Working Restrictions
Working restrictions are best dealt with in the country.

Vaccination Required
Certificates of vaccinations for smallpox, cholera and yellow fever required if coming from an infected area. Vaccinations for cholera, typhoid and paratyphoid strongly recommended. Take antimalarial precautions.

Customs and Duty Free
On arrival: 200 cigarets or 50 cigars or 100g/3.5 oz tobacco for one week's stay, double for two; 2 liters alcohol; 3 oz perfume. Personal effects allowed in duty-free; electrical equipment subject to duty. Strictly prohibited are: arms and ammunition; pornography; advertising material from Bahasa Indonesia. Photographic equipment and typewriters must be declared on entry and taken out on departure.

Currency Restrictions
There is no restriction on the amount of foreign currency brought in; there is an absolute limit of 50,000 rupiahs in Indonesian currency. Exchange rates for foreign currency are the same at banks and moneychangers.

Health Tips
The general level of sanitation and health is below Western standards but excellent in the large hotels. Drink only bottled or boiled water and take antimalarial tablets. Be careful of the food you eat away from hotels or large centers.

Climate and Clothing
It is hot and humid all year. The summer (May to September) is the dry season: wear tropical weight clothes. October to April is the wet season with short heavy rains: tropical weight clothing and an umbrella.

Tipping Tip
10% in restaurants and hotels if a service charge is not already included in the bill. Give porters and bellhops 800 rupiahs and tip 300 rupiahs for small services. Taxi drivers appreciate a 15% tip although it is not mandatory. Try to give exact change.

Food and Drink
Indonesian cuisine is based on rice, but there is a great variety in the use of spices, fresh vegetables and meats. The national dish is nasi goreng (fried rice with egg, spices and vegetables); also popular are satay (meat cooked in spicy peanut sauce), gado gado (prawn salad) and sato (hot soup). A few hotels still serve the famous rijstafel or rice table with many dishes, fresh fruits and vegetables. Beer is good and so are tropical fruit drinks. Sample the excellent java coffee and, for adventure, try the spicy Balinese wine.

Business Brief

GDP
$92 million
(per capita income $562)

Annual Growth Rate
3%

Natural Resources
Oil, tin, natural gas, nickel, timber, bauxite, copper

Agriculture
Rubber, rice, palm oil, coffee, sugar

Industry
Food and beverages, textiles, cement, fertilizer, light manufacturing, wood processing, minerals and petroleum

Imports
Total $12.5 billion
Food, chemicals, crude petroleum and petroleum products, capital goods, consumer goods

Exports
Total $16.2 billion
Oil, natural gas, plywood, rubber, tin, tea, coffee

Major Trading Partners
US, Japan, West Germany, Netherlands, Singapore, Taiwan, Trinidad and Tobago

Workforce
67 million Agriculture 55%, industry and commerce 29%, services 12%, civil service 4%

Tips for Doing Business
A suit jacket should be worn for government visits but a white tieless shirt and pants are fine for other business appointments. Prior appointments are necessary but do not be offended or show signs of impatience if your contact shows up late. Business is a mixture of state and private trading, but no one comes to a quick decision. Allow plenty of time for your visit (at least a week) and plan your appointments so they are not too close together. It is customary to exchange presents so take small gifts for businessmen, government officials and their wives. A conservative, but courteous and friendly business approach is best. Most of the population is Muslim so social conventions should be observed: you should be particularly careful to eat and pass things with the right hand. Shake hands on arrival and departure. Before business talks, coffee and a sweet is usually served. Do not refuse or reach for it before the host gestures.

Best Months for Doing Business
September to June is the best time although December through February is the rainy period. Check the dates of Muslim holidays carefully before travelling as business stops during these periods. Business vacations are taken in July and August.

Business Hours

Government
Mon-Thurs 0800-1500
Fri 0800-1100
Sat 0800-1400

Business
Mon-Fri 0800/0900-1600/1700
Sat 0800/0830-1230/1400

Banks
Mon-Fri 0800/0830-1200/1300
Sat 0800/0830-1030/1100

Shops
Mon-Sat 0900/1000-2100/2200 (or 1730 for some)

English Language Publications
Local newspapers in English are: Indonesian Observer; The Indonesian Times; The Indonesian Daily News. Local business news coverage in Sinar

Harapan and Indonesian Observer.

Telephone and Communications
Telephone country code: 62
Telephone city code: Bandung 22, Jakarta 21, Medan 61, Surabaya 31
Telex country code: 796
International calls are via satellite, but there are long delays. It is better to have your home office or outside contacts call you, than try to get through from Jakarta. If you call out, it is cheaper to reverse the charges. Cable service is good internationally from Jakarta but not reliable within the country. Telex facilities at major hotels and telegraphic offices. A 24 hour public telex facility in Jakarta is located at the Directorate General for Post and Telecommunications.
Postal services are slow. Businessmen use "kilat khusus" with a 24 hour delivery guarantee on Java and Bali and 48 hour for outer islands. Overseas mail should be sent via Singapore or through Usaha Express.

Air Travel
Most visitors travel by air. Garuda operates daily flights from Jakarta to Surabaya and Medan as well as extensive service to all parts of the country. Since schedules in some places are sometimes changed without notice, do not make your travel plans too rigid.

Other Transport
Express bus services link the major cities. Rail services are mostly on Java, Sumahia and Madura. Java has air-conditioned express trains with sleeping and dining cars between main cities; several trains go from Jakarta to Bandung and Surabaya daily. Take express as ordinary service

is extremely slow. There are many scheduled and unscheduled sailings between the islands.

JAKARTA

Airport Information

Time
GMT +7

Airport
Soekarno-Hatta International
HLP
Tel: 801108
28 km (16 mi) W of city

Airlines
Air France 52731
British Airways 5782460
Canadian International 336573
Cathay Pacific 3806664
China 353195
Garuda 417808
JAL 322207
KLM 320708
Korean 5780236
Lufthansa 710247
Malaysian 320909
Northwest 320558
Pan Am 361707
Philippine 370108
Qantas 327707
Sabena 372039
SAS 584110
Singapore 584041
Swissair 373608
Thai 330816
TWA 326810
United 320038
UTA 323507

Transport to City
Taxi: they come in all colors and should be metered: it costs about 20,000 rupiahs to town with a small additional charge for baggage. Tip 1700 rupiahs. Takes about 60 minutes.
Coach: there may be courtesy coaches or mini-buses from hotels; enquire on arrival.

ASIA/PACIFIC

Facilities
Bar, buffet, restaurant, bank,
currency exchange, insurance,
hotel reservations, post office,
baggage deposit, vaccination
center, shops
Duty-free shop sells cigarets,
cigars, tobacco, wines, spirits,
lighters, cameras, watches,
handicrafts, batiks, jewellery,
silver. Convertible currencies
accepted.

Car rental desks: Hertz, Avis,
Europcar

Airport Taxes
Per person: International 4000
rupiahs, domestic 2500

City Information

Weather
Hot and humid most of the year.
The rainy monsoon season is
from October to April, dry

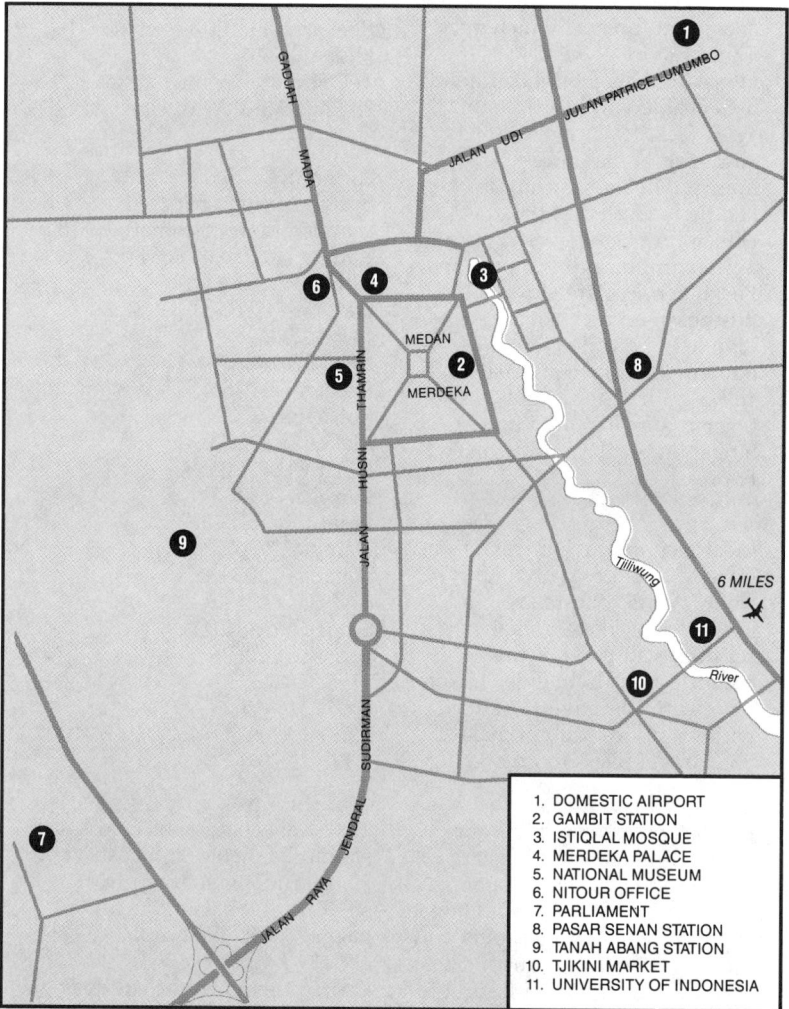

1. DOMESTIC AIRPORT
2. GAMBIT STATION
3. ISTIQLAL MOSQUE
4. MERDEKA PALACE
5. NATIONAL MUSEUM
6. NITOUR OFFICE
7. PARLIAMENT
8. PASAR SENAN STATION
9. TANAH ABANG STATION
10. TJIKINI MARKET
11. UNIVERSITY OF INDONESIA

Jakarta

season from May to September.
Average temps: Jan 26c (79F)
July 27c (80F)

Transportation

Metered taxis are available but make sure the meter is being used: fares are reasonable. It is difficult to hail them so get one at the hotel and keep it until returning. Negotiate an hourly fare plus waiting time. Tip 10%. Taxis can be booked by calling PT Bluebird Taxi (tel: 353556). Bus service is inexpensive, but crowded and complicated. Car hire is available: credit cards accepted. Three-wheel bajajs are available for short journeys.

Car Hire

Hertz, Jalan Maluku (tel: 371208)
Avis, 25 Jalan Dipunegoro
(tel: 371964 & 341964)
Europcar, Kartika Plaza Hotel
(tel: 371479)

Hospitals

Nitron (tel: 40955) will give you the names of English-speaking doctors and dentists. There is a hospital run by Pertamina, the state owned oil company, which has medical standards similar to the West. Other medical aid for travellers at:
Iamat Center, Jalan
Singamangareja (tel: 771445/
744004)

Trade Fairs

Concrete Construction Exhibition
(Mar)
Sugarcane Technology Fair
(April)
International Construction
Exhibition (May)
International Mining Exhibition
(May)
International Trade Fair (July)
International Business Computer
Exhibition (Sept)
International Agriculture & Food
Processing Exhibition (Oct)

International Forestry Exhibition
(Oct)
International Technical Trade
Fair (Nov)

Hotels

Major hotels are air-conditioned and many have business centers with translation and secretarial services. Service charge is added to the bill.
Asoka, Jalan MH Thamrin (tel:
322908)
Hyatt Aryaduta Jakarta, Jalan
Praapatan 44-46 (tel: 376008)
Indonesia, Jalan MH Thamrim
(tel: 320008 & 322008)
Jakarta Hilton International,
Jalan Jen Gatot Subroto,
Senayan (tel: 587981/995 &
589305l/079)
Kartika Chandra, Jalan Jen Gatot
Subroto (tel: 511008 & 582024)
The Mandarin Jakarta, Jalan MH
Thamrin (tel: 325666 & 321307)
President, Jalan MH Thamrin 59,
10350 (tel: 320508)
Sahid Jaya, 86 Jalan Jen
Sudirman (tel: 587031)
Sari Pacific, Jalan MH Thamrin 6
(tel: 323707)

What to See and Do

The National Museum on Merdeka Barat Street has one of the finest collections in Southeast Asia: porcelain; prehistoric-man exhibits; seventh-century statues; and Indonesian arts and crafts. The Dutch influence is still obvious and the Dutch Stadhuis is now a museum. Visit Pasar Ikan, the old Dutch port with Makassar sailing ships which still go between the islands. Visit the zoo and their "Komodo dragons", lizards from Komodo. Visit the Cultural Center for Indonesian dancing and plays, and the Taman Impian Ancal, the recreational park north of Jakarta with golf course, casino, oceanarium, garden of birds, swimming pools, dolphins, movie theater, and art bazaar.

ASIA/PACIFIC

Useful Addresses

Embassies and Consulates
American: 5 Merdeka Selatan
    (tel: 360360)
Canadian: Jalan Jendral
    Sudirman (tel: 510709)
British: 75 Jalan MH Thamrin
    (tel: 330904)

Business and Commerce
Central Bank, Bank Indonesia, 2
    Jalan MH Thamrin (tel: 372408)
The Directorate General of Post
    & Telecommunications, Jalan
    Medan Merdeka Selatan 12 (24
    hours)
The Jakarta Chamber of
    Commerce and Industry,
    Kadin Jaya Graha, Jalan IH
    Juanda 38 (tel: 365609)
Indonesian Chamber of
Commerce and Industry,
    (KADIN) Jalan Medan
    Merdeka Timur 11 (tel: 367096)
American Chamber of
    Commerce, 8F Citibank Bldg,
    55 Jalan HM Thamrin
    (tel: 357703)

Tourism and Travel
Jakarta Visitors Center, Jalan TH
    Thamrin (tel: 54092)
The Directorate General of
    Tourism, Jalan Kramat Raya 81
    (tel: 359001)
Ikatan Motor Indonesia, (IMI),
    Gedun, Koni Pusat (tel:
    5811102)
American Express, Jalan S.
    Wiryopranoto (tel: 652706)

JAPAN

Essential Information

Type of Government
Parliamentary Democracy

Area
377,765 sq km
(145,856 sq mi)

Population
123.8 million

Annual Growth Rate
0.67%

Languages
Japanese

Religion
Shintoism and Buddhism,
Christian 0.8%

Ethnic Groups
Japanese, Korean 0.6%

Weights and Measures
Metric

Electrical Current
A.C. 50 & 60c 100/200V

Major Business Cities
Tokyo (cap) 11,400,000
Osaka 3,250,000
Yokohama 3,250,000
Nagoya 2,500,000
Kyoto 1,750,000
Kobe 1,650,000
Sapporo 1,625,000

Currency
Yen
Notes 500, 1000, 5000, 10000 yen
Coins 1, 5, 10, 50, 100 yen

Public Holidays
Jan l-3 New Year
Jan 15 Coming of Age
Feb 11 National Foundation
Mar 21 Vernal Equinox
Apr 29 Emperors Birthday
May 3 Constitution Day
May 5 Children's Day
Sept 15 Respect for the Aged
Sept 23 Autumnal Equinox
Oct 10 Physical Education Day
Nov 3 Culture Day
Nov 24 Labor Day
Avoid visits during Golden
Week (Apr 29-May 5) and the

Obon festival (late July to third week in August).

Travellers Information

Entry Requirements

Passport is required by all. Visas are not required by nationals of some countries (Britain, Canada, France) for short stays. Nationals of US must have appropriate visa (business or visitor) except for a stay of less than 72 hours as long as their passports are stamped for onward travel and entry and exit are from the same international airport. Specific information can be obtained from a local Japanese consulate and it is always wise to obtain the correct visa in advance in case of a sudden change of plans.

Working Restrictions

A long-term commercial business visa is needed if working for your own company in Japan: others require work permit.

Vaccination Required

No vaccination certificates required unless coming from an infected area. Check with authorities for update just before travelling.

Customs and Duty Free

On arrival: 3 quarts of liquor; 2 cartons cigarets; 2 oz perfume; other gifts to a value of 100,000 yen. Personal effects are allowed in duty-free; souvenir purchases free of tax if they are taken out of the country within 6 months.

Currency Restrictions

There is no restriction on the amount of foreign currency brought in and the amounts declared on entry may be taken out. A certain amount of yen may be taken out: check on arrival.

Health Tips

The drinking water is safe.

Hotels often have English-speaking doctors and dentists on call and there are several health facilities available in each city to assist travellers.

Climate and Clothing

Climate varies from sub-tropical in the south to cooler temperatures in the north. In the winter on the main island (Tokyo, Osaka) it is cold with snow. Appropriate winter clothing including medium to heavy coat and warm footwear. Spring and fall are warm and humid with some rain in spring, and summer is hot and humid: light to tropical weight clothes and umbrella. September to November is monsoon season: take a raincoat and umbrella.

Tipping

Tipping is not the custom so do not be surprised if a proffered tip is refused. At airports and train stations, porters have set fees: about 100 yen per piece of luggage. At hotels and restaurants, 10-15% is usually included in the bill. Do not tip extra.

Food and Drink

Classic Japanese dishes are tempura (deep-fried seafood and vegetables in a batter) and sukiyaki (meat and vegetables cooked at the table in hot oil, then dipped in raw egg). It is all eaten with chopsticks and served with the staple dish, rice. Other popular items include yakitari (charcoal-broiled meats), raw fish (sashumi and sushi), and Kobe beef, which is corn-fed and tender. Meals range wildly in price. Chinese food is very popular everywhere, as is Western food. Sometimes Western food turns up in odd places so don't be surprised to find spaghetti or hot dogs on the breakfast menu. Sake (hot rice wine) is usually served with meals and whiskey (imported and Santory) is also a popular drink. The Japanese beer is excellent.

Business Brief

GNP
$2.79 trillion
(per capita income $22,986)

Annual Growth Rate
5.5%

Natural Resources
Mineral resources, fish

Agriculture
Rice, vegetables, fruits, milk, meat, silk

Industry
Machinery and equipment, metals and metal products, textiles, autos, chemicals, electrical and electronic equipment

Imports
Total $151.1 billion
Fossil fuels, metal ore, raw materials, foodstuffs, machinery and equipment

Exports
Total $231.3 billion
Motor vehicles, machinery and equipment, electrical and electronic products, metals and metal products

Major Trading Partners
US, Australia, Canada, Iran, West Germany, Kuwait, UK, Saudi Arabia, Indonesia, Hong Kong, Taiwan

Workforce
59.6.3 million
Agriculture 9.5%, trade, manufacturing, mining and construction 34.1%, services 48.1%, government 5.9%

Tips For Doing Business
A conservative business suit, tie and white shirt is necessary for all appointments which should be made well in advance. Business cards are very important. Carry a good supply (printed in both Japanese and English) as they are exchanged at every meeting. Hotels can arrange for cards to be printed within days. Usually, Japanese businessmen will entertain you in a restaurant to get to know you; act in a formal but friendly fashion with the good manners of your own country. It is not necessary to get too caught up in the intricacies of bowing: handshakes will do. Add "san" to the last name of everyone when addressing them. It is important to bring small, well-chosen presents (pens, ties) since gift-giving is customary. The Japanese are great whisky drinkers and a bottle of Johnny Walker Black Label is a popular present for your host. Stay at a major hotel so you can return hospitality in good restaurants. If you are invited to a Japanese home, take your shoes off at the door and leave them with the toes pointing toward the outside: bring flowers for your host's wife. Learn a few Japanese phrases phonetically, like "good morning", "please" and "thank you": the Japanese appreciate this. However, get an interpreter when a business deal is being completed and have patience.

Best Months for Doing Business
February to June and September to November. Mid-December to mid-January is a general holiday season and vacations are taken in July and August.

Business Hours

Government
Mon-Fri 1000-1700
Sat 1000-1200

Business
Mon-Fri 0900-1500
Sat 0900-1200

(closed second Saturday of every month)

Banks
Mon-Fri 0900-1500
Sat 0900-1200

Shops
Mon-Fri 1000-1800
Sat 0900-1200
Sat (some stores close on Wednesday or Thursday)

English Language Publications
Main English language dailies are Japan Times, the Mainchi Daily News, the Daily Yomiuri and the Asahi Evening News.

Telephone and Communications
Telephone country code: 81
Telephone city code: Kobe 078, Kyato 075, Nagasaki 0958, Osaka 06, Sapporo 011, Tokoyo 03, Yokohama 045
Telex country code: 781
Telephone directories in English can usually be found in all the major hotels with comprehensive listings of embassies, business companies and chambers of commerce. International calls must be placed through the hotel or main post office: they cannot be placed from public phone booths. These are everywhere. Red booths are for local calls and take a 10 yen piece; red booths with gold bands are for direct long-distance dialing within the country. Blue booths are for emergencies: operator, information, emergency. Telex facilities are available at all the major hotels and at Kokusai Denshin Denwa Co Ltd (KDD) in Tokoyo, Osaka, Yokohama and Nagoya.
Telegrams can be sent from the major hotels, from KDD and main post offices.
Stamps can be obtained at post offices and anywhere with a T on a red background. Use blue mailboxes for express service.

Air Travel
Japan has an extensive domestic air service provided by JAL, All Nippon Airways, Toa Domestic Airlines and Nihon Kinkyori Airways. Most flights from Tokyo to other Japanese cities and towns leave from Haneda Airport although it is possible to get a direct connecting flight to Osaka from Narita, the international airport.

Other Transport
Car hire is available with an international drivers license; driving is on the left. Driving is an excellent way to see the countryside but not always recommended because signs are not easily comprehensible and the roads are often congested. Chauffeur-driven cars are available for trips out of town but are extremely expensive. Rail is the best form of ground inter-city transportation. The Hihari express goes from Tokyo to Osaka in 3 hours and 10 minutes. Many other express services, the famous "bullet" trains with incredible speeds, are available with air-conditioning and restaurant service.
Buses link major cities and are fine if you think you can master the language and direction problems. Otherwise rail or air are the best bets.

ASIA/PACIFIC

OSAKA

Airport Information

Time
GMT +9

Airport
Osaka International (Itami) OSA
Tel: 8566781
20 km (12 mi) SE of city

Airlines

Air Canada 2271180
Air France 2015161
Air India 2641781
Alitalia 3413951
American 2646308
British Airways 3452761
CAAC 9461702
Canadian International 3465591
Cathay Pacific 2456731
Eastern 3617471
Egyptair 3415575
Finnair 3630270
Gulf Air 2821151
JAL 2031212
KLM 3456691
Korean 2621110
Lufthansa 3450231
Northwest 2280747
Pan Am 3647191
Philippine 4442541
Qantas 2621341
Sabena 3418082

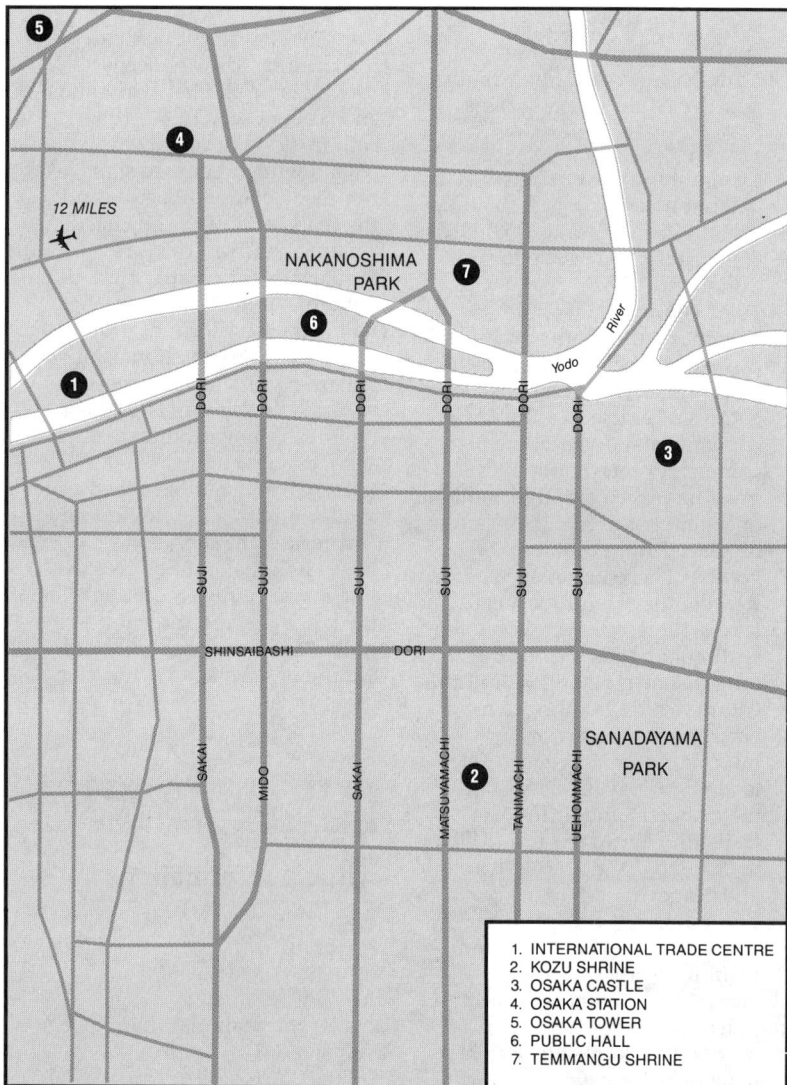

1. INTERNATIONAL TRADE CENTRE
2. KOZU SHRINE
3. OSAKA CASTLE
4. OSAKA STATION
5. OSAKA TOWER
6. PUBLIC HALL
7. TEMMANGU SHRINE

Osaka

SAS 3480211
Singapore 3640881
Swissair 3457851
Thai 2025161
TWA 3417131
United 2715951

Transport to City
Taxi: most taxis are bright yellow, take up to four people, and metered fare to city is between 4500 yen and takes 45 minutes to city.
Coach: Osaka Airport Transport Company has a bus leaving from outside arrival terminal every 15 minutes from 0800-2000. Costs 380 yen and takes 30-45 minutes.

Facilities
Snack bar, bank, currency exchange, hotel reservations, baggage deposit, barber, vaccination center, information desk, shops, conference facilities, first aid/medical
Duty-free shop has cigarets, cigars, tobacco, wines, aperitifs, spirits, liqueurs, lighters, watches, radios, jewellery, pearls, perfume, cameras.

Airport Taxes
Per person: 2000 yen

City Information

Weather
Season temperatures with fairly cold winters and hot, humid summers.
Average temps: Jan 0-9c (32-48F) July 27c (80F)

Transportation
Metered taxis available and easy to get. Have address written down in Japanese and, if possible, marked on a map. Taxi drivers do not accept tips. Chauffeur-driven cars available but expensive.

Car Hire
Hertz (Nippon), Hankyu Umedi
  (tel: 3732652 & 8418175)

Avis, Kyobashi Katamachi 8-22
  (tel: 3560755)
Honda, Ogimachi Office
  (tel: 3120881)
Mitsubishi, Kita-ku (tel: 5382428)
Nissan, 19-22 Chaya-Machi
  (tel: 3720281)

Hospitals
Major hotels provide English-speaking doctors and dentists. Additional medical help available for travellers at:
Yodogawn Christian Hospital
  (tel: 3222250)

Trade Fairs
Hospital Exhibition (Mar)
International Shoe Fair (Mar)
International Trade Fair (Apr)
Robot & Labor Saving Machinery
  Exhibition (May)
Engineering Design Exhibition
  (May)
Woodworking Machinery Fair
  (Sept)
International Food Technology
  Exhibition (Oct)
Plastic Models Trade Exhibition
  (Oct)
International Machine Tools
  Exhibition (Oct)

Hotels
Ana Sheraton Osaka, 1-3-1
  Dojimahama, Kita-ku, 530
  (tel: 3471112)
Holiday Inn Nankai, 28-1
  Kyuzaemon-cho, Minami-ku
  (tel: 2138281)
International Osaka, 58
  Hashizume-cho, Uchihon-machi, Higashi-ku
  (tel: 9412661)
New Hankyu, 1-35 Shibata 1-chome, Kita-ku (tel: 3725101)
Nikko Osaka, 7 Nishino-cho,
  Caihoji-machi, Minami-ku 542
  (tel: 2441111)
Osaka Grand, 2-3-18
  Nakanoshima, Kita-ku 530
  (tel: 2021202)
Osaka Tokyu, 7-20 Chaya-machi,
  Kita-ku (tel: 3732411)
Plaza, 2-49 Oyodo-Minami, 2-

chome, Oyodo-ku
(tel: 4531111)
Toyo, 3-16-19 Toyosaaki Nashi-
dori, Oyodo-ku (tel: 3728181)

What to See and Do

Although the city is a major
industrial center, there are some
interesting things to see,
including Osaka Castle and a
number of temples and shrines.
Visit the Natural Science
Museum, the Botanical Gardens
and the Shin-Kabukiza Theater.
Osaka is convenient to the
ancient capital of Nara, which is
full of sights.

Useful Addresses

Embassies and Consulates

American: 11-15 Nishitenma,
Kita-ku (tel: 3619600)
British: 4-45 Awaji, Higashi-ku
(tel: 2313555)

Business and Commerce

Daiwa Bank, 21
Bingomachi2-chome, Higashi-
ku (tel: 2711221)
Osaka Stock Exchange, Kitahama
2-chome, Higashi-ku
(tel: 2298643)
Osaka International Trade
Center, 2,2-chome, Tamae-
cho, Kita-ku (tel: 4419131)
Osaka Chamber of Commerce
and Industry, 58-7 Uchiho-
machi Hashizume-cho,
Higasahi-ku (tel: 9446412/5)
USA Trade Center, Sankel Bldg,
4-9 Umeda 2-chome, Kita-ku

Tourism and Travel

Travel Center, 1-2 Senba,
Higashi-ku (tel: 2712554)
Tourist Office, Daichi Seimel
Bldg. (tel: 3122189)
American Express, 5-10
Sonezaki, Kita-ku (tel: 3150781)

TOKYO

Airport Information

Time
GMT +9

Airports
Narita International NRT Tel:
322800
66 km (41 mi) SW of city

Haneda (domestic flights)
Tel: 747-8000
17.5 km (11 mi) S of city

Airlines
Air Canada 5863891
Air France 4751511
Air India 2141981
Air New Zealand 2871641
Alitalia 2142111
American 2120861
British Airways 2144161
Canadian International 2125811
Cathay Pacific 5958002
China 4361661
Delta 2138781
Eastern 4792871
Egyptair 2114521
El Al 4791641
Gulf Air 5670230
Iberia 5823631
JAL 4571121
KLM 2160771
Korean 2113311
Lufthansa 5802111
Malaysian 5035961
Pan Am 5082211
Philippine 5932421
Qantas 2121351
Singapore 2133431
Swissair 2121016
Thai 5033311
TWA 2121477
United 8174411
Varig 2116751

Transport to City
Narita
Taxi: airport taxis are cream-
colored with a light blue stripe.
Very expensive ride; about
18,000 yen. Takes about 1-1/2
hours.

Coach: Tokyo Airport Transport Co. have an excellent service with air-conditioned coaches every 5-20 minutes from outside all terminals. Tickets (2,500 yen) should be purchased ahead of time at ticket counter. Last bus, midnight. Room for baggage. About 1 hour and 10 minutes to terminal at Hakazaki-Cho; transportation available by bus or taxi to individual hotels. The company also runs a special bus to major hotels: buy ticket in terminal building for buses which leave hourly. Limos leave every 30 minutes to Haneda Airport (1 hour and 40 minutes) and Yokohama City Air Terminal (2 hours).

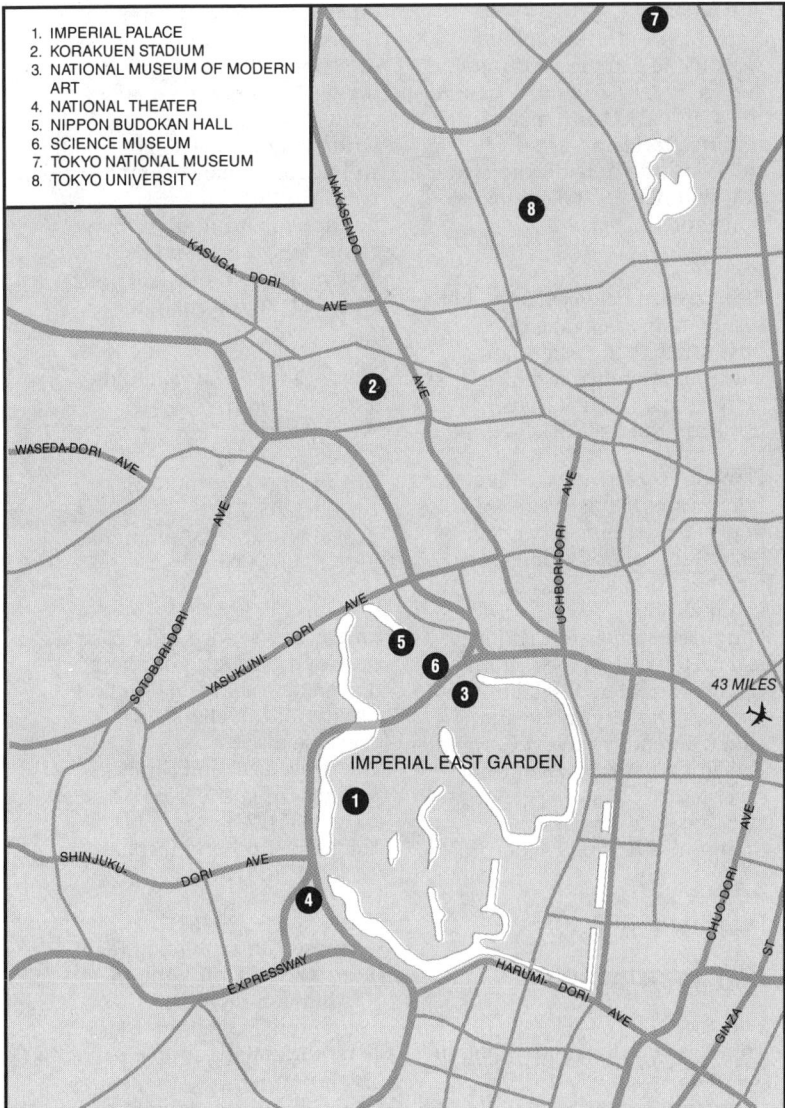

ASIA/PACIFIC

1. IMPERIAL PALACE
2. KORAKUEN STADIUM
3. NATIONAL MUSEUM OF MODERN ART
4. NATIONAL THEATER
5. NIPPON BUDOKAN HALL
6. SCIENCE MUSEUM
7. TOKYO NATIONAL MUSEUM
8. TOKYO UNIVERSITY

NAKASENDO

KASUGA DORI AVE

AVE

WASEDA-DORI AVE

AVE

UCHIBORI-DORI AVE

SOTOBORI-DORI

YASUKUNI DORI AVE

43 MILES

IMPERIAL EAST GARDEN

SHINJUKU DORI AVE

CHUO-DORI AVE

GINZA ST

EXPRESSWAY

HARUMI DORI AVE

Tokyo

Transit: there is a shuttle bus which takes you to Keisei Line Narita Station in 5 or 6 minutes: from there you can catch the Skyliner train: buy ticket (1660 yen) at airport counter.

Haneda
Taxis: yellow taxis have a metered fare to city, about 6000 yen. No extras for baggage and no tipping: about 40 minutes to city center.
Transit: take the monorail for a reasonable 320 yen and frequent service (every 7 minutes). Runs from 0700-2300 and takes 15 minutes to Hamamatsu-Cho. As this is a little outside city center, you will need to take a taxi to your hotel.

Facilities
Narita: currency exchange, hotel reservations, baggage deposit, post office, bar, restaurant, shops, conference facilities, first aid/medical, vaccinations, transport service, ticket counters

Haneda: currency exchange, hotel reservations, baggage deposit, post office, bar, restaurant, shops, conference facilities, first aid/medical, vaccinations
Duty-free shops sell cigarets, cigars, tobacco, wines, spirits, cameras, lighters, watches, radios, jewellery, glass and china. Canadian, West German, British and American currencies accepted.
Car rental desks: Hertz (Nippon), Nissan, Toyota

Airport Taxes
Per person: 2000 yen

City Information

Weather
Tokyo is seasonal and although it avoids extremes of temperature, it can get quite cold in the winter and hot and humid in the summer.
Average temps: Jan 0-9c (32-48F) July 27c (80F)

Transportation
Metered taxis are easy to obtain outside hotels or on the streets. Fares go up late at night and extra is charged for traffic jams. It is essential to have your destination written down in Japanese with the telephone number and some landmarks or directions. It is useful to mark the destination on a map and show it to the driver along with written address. The hotel staff will be more than happy to help you with this. Taxi drivers are not tipped and to do so may give offence. Bus and subway system are fast, efficient and crowded. Avoid rush hour.

Car Hire
Hertz (Nippon) Jinnan Bldg
    (tel: 4688881)
Avis, Akasaka Temekic
    (tel: 5862301)
Mitsubishi, Marunouchi
    (tel: 5635271)
Tokyo Nissan, 52-2 Jingumac
    (tel: 4074431)

Hospitals
Emergency service in English is provided through your hotel's doctors and dentists. Medical service for travellers also available at:
Tokyo Medical and Surgical
    Clinic, opposite Tokyo Tower
    (tel: 4314121)
Tokyo Sanitorium Hospital
    (tel: 3926151)

Trade Fairs
Japanese Gift Exhibition (Feb)
International Golf Equipment
    Exhibition (Feb)
Computers Exhibition (Mar)
Communications Industry Trade
    Fair (Apr)
Health Industry Trade Fair (Apr)

Japanese Technology Trade Fair
  (Apr)
International Food Machinery
  Exhibition (May)
Motion Picture and TV
  Equipment (May)
Medical Instruments Exhibition
  (May)
International Hospital Exhibition
  (June)
International Housewares
  Exhibition (June)
International Welding Exhibition
  (July)
International Gift Exhibition
  (Sept)
International Home Furnishings
  Exhibition (Sept)
International Catering
  Equipment Exhibition (Sept)
International Plastics and Rubber
  Fair (Nov)
International Office Environment
  Exhibition (Nov)
World Travel Fair (Dec)

Hotels

Major hotels are excellent
(although very expensive) with
every conceivable service: they
should be booked weeks in
advance. Service charges and
taxes are added to the bill and
there is no tipping.
Akasaka Tokyu, 14-3, 2-chome,
  Nagata-Cho (tel: 5802311)
Fairmont Tokyo, 2-1-17 Kudan
  Minami (tel: 2621151)
Ginza Dai-Ichi, 8-13-1 Ginza
  (tel: 5425311)
Ginza Tokyu, 15-9 5-chome,
  Ginza (tel: 5412411)
Hill-top, 1 1-chome, Kanda
  Surugadai (tel: 2932311)
Imperial, 1-1-1 Uchiasaiwai-Cho
  (tel: 5041111)
Keio Plaza Inter-Continental, 2-1
  Nishi Shinjuku, 2-chome
  (tel: 3440111)
Palace, 1-1 Marunouchi, 1-chome
  (tel: 2115211)
Shiba Park, 1-5-10 Shiba Koen
  (tel: 4334141)

Takanaya Prince, 13-1-3
  Takanaya (tel: 4471111)
Tokyo Hilton International, 6-2
  Nishi-Shinjuku, 6-chome
  (tel: 3445111)
Tokyo Marunouchi, 1-6-3
  Marunouchi (tel: 2152151)

What to See and Do

Tokyo is the modern capital of
Japan, famous more for its
shopping (Ginza and Akasaka
districts) and nightlife (Shibunyu
and Shinjuku) than its sights.
Guided tours are available
through major hotels. You can
visit the Imperial Palace moat
(the grounds can only be seen in
the company of enormous
crowds, at New Year and the
Emperor's birthday); the Meij
Shrine and Outer Garden; and
the Asakusa Kannon Temple.
There are many theaters. Try to
see some Kabuki; the Takarazuka
all-girl troupe or classical No
theater. Department stores often
sponsor art exhibitions and have
their own museums. If you visit
in the summer, take the bus
most of the way up Mount Fuji
and climb gently up the rest of
the way. If you have 3 extra
days, visit Kyoto, the ancient
capital, to see unforgettable
temples and gardens.

Useful Addresses

Embassies and Consulates

American: 1-10-5 Akasaka,
  Minato-ku (tel: 5837141)
Canadian: 3-8 Akasaka, Minato-
  ku (tel: 4082101)
British: 1 Ichiban-cho
  (tel: 2655511)

Business and Commerce

Central Bank (Bank of Japan),
1-1 Nihonbashi, Chuo-ku
  (tel: 2791111)
Tokyo Stock Exchange, 6,
  1-chome, Nihonbashi-Kayaba-
  cho (tel: 6660141)

ASIA/PACIFIC

Japan Foreign Trade Council,
Sekei Boeki Center Bldg, 4-1
Hamamatsu-cho 2-chome
(tel: 4355950)
Translation Services (Japan
Guide Association), Shin
Kokusai Bldg, 4-1 Marunouchi
3-chome (tel: 2132706)
Tokyo Chamber of Commerce
and Industry, 2-2 Marunouchi
3-chome (tel: 2837500)
Japan Chamber of Commerce
and Industry, Tosho Bldg, 2-2
Marunouchi 3-chome (tel:
2837500)
American Chamber of
Commerce, 2 Fukide Bldg.,
1-21 Toranomon, 4-chome (tel:
4335381)
British Chamber of Commerce, 1

Kowa Bldg., 9-20A Kasaka,
1-chome (tel: 5051734)

Tourism and Travel
Japan National Tourist
Organization, 10-1 Yurakucho
2-chome (tel: 2161901)

Japan Automobile Federation,
Shiba-Koen, 3-5-8 Minato-ku
(tel: 4362811)
Touring Club of Japan, Daini-
Maijma Bldg, Yotsuya 1-9,
Shinjuku-ku
American Express, 4-3 13
Toranomon, 4-chome
(tel: 4596155)

MALAYSIA

Essential Information

Type of Government
Federal Parliamentary
Democracy with a Constitutional
Monarch

Area
329,749 sq km
(127,316 sq mi)

Population
16 million

Annual Growth Rate
2.2%

Languages
Malay, Chinese dialects, English,
Tamil

Religion
Muslim, Hindu, Buddhist,
Confucian, Christian

Ethnic Groups
Malay and other indigenous
59%, Chinese 32%, Indian 9%

Weights and Measures
Metric system with the Imperial
system and some local units still
used.

Electrical Current
A.C. 50c 230V and 240/415V

Major Business Cities
Kuala Lumpur (cap) 1,250,000
Penang 450,000
Ipoh 400,000
George Town 450,000
Malacca 250,000

Currency
1 Ringgit = 100 Cents
Notes 1, 5, 10, 20, 50, 100, 1000
ringgits
Coins 1, 5, 10, 20, 50 cents

Public Holidays
There are a number of religious
and federal holidays in Malaysia
and each State has an additional
3-4 holidays each. Muslim
holidays follow the lunar cycle
and change yearly: it is wise to
check on all holidays before you
travel.
Jan 1 New Year
Feb 1 City Day (Kuala Lumpur)
Apr 17 Good Friday
May 1 Labor Day
Aug 31 Malaysia Day

Dec 25 Christmas

Travellers Information

Entry Requirements

Passport is required by all. Visas are not required by Commonwealth nationals, those with British passports, and citizens of Ireland. Most others (including nationals of US, Europe, Japan and Korea) do not require visas for stays of less than 90 days. All tourists can stay for two weeks without a visa. Visit passes are usually issued at entry but passes issued for Peninsular Malaysia are not good for Sabah and Sarawak. Citizens of Israel are prohibited entry.

Working Requirements

A work permit is required and must be applied for in advance. You need someone in Malaysia to sponsor you.

Vaccination Required

Cholera, smallpox and yellow fever vaccination certificates are required if coming from infected area. Cholera shot recommended. Take antimalerial pills.

Customs and Duty Free

On arrival: 200 cigarets or 50 cigars or 225 g/8 oz tobacco; 1 liter alcohol; reasonable amount of perfume. Firearms must be declared on arrival; failure to do so may result in imprisonment or death. Personal goods imported duty-free. Import of dangerous drugs (including narcotic drugs in medications) strictly prohibited, as is the import of pornography or material degrading to women, knives, and goods from Israel and South Africa. Strict rules against the import of plants and animals.

Currency Restrictions

Any amount of foreign currency may be imported as long as the same amount or less is taken out. To avoid problems on departure, declare large amounts on arrival. You may import 10,000 riggits and export 5,000.

Health Tips

Malaysia is almost entirely free of major infectious diseases. There are local public hospitals but the private care (although it must be paid for) is excellent. The water is safe to drink and imported pharmaceuticals are inexpensive and available. The hotel or embassy will provide you with a list of doctors: most doctors and dentists in Malaysia speak English.

Climate and Clothing

The climate is tropical with little variation: generally high humidity and temperatures about 32-35c (90-95F). Some rainfall from October through March. Wear tropical weight clothes and take an umbrella.

Tipping

Hotels and restaurants often add 10% to the bill: if they have not, add it yourself. Taxi drivers, 1 ringgit; porters 1 ringgit per piece of luggage; small services 50 cents.

Food and Drink

Malaysia is a multicultural community with a diverse cuisine. There are many kinds of Chinese food available as well as well known Malaysian dishes like satay (grilled fish or chicken with a peanut sauce), nasi goreng (chicken and fried rice), and gado gado (a salad with peanut sauce or a spicy seasoning called sambal). Gula mulacca is a popular dessert. Indian and Thai dishes are also popular and European food is available in the larger hotels. A

ASIA/PACIFIC

great choice of fresh tropical fruits is served at each meal and fresh fish is excellent. The water is safe to drink: also popular are fresh fruit drinks, beer (local and imported), and a locally distilled alcohol called Arak.

Business Brief

GNP
$31.6 billion
(per capita income $2,081)

Annual Growth Rate
5.0%

Natural Resources
Petroleum, liquefied natural gas (LNG), tin, minerals

Agriculture
Rubber, palm oil, timber, cocoa, rice, pepper, pineapples, forestry

Industry
Electronics, electrical products, rubber products, automobile assembly, textiles

Imports
Total $12.7 billion
Intermediate goods, machinery, metal products, food products, consumer durables, transport equipment

Exports
Total $17.9 billion
Petroleum, LNG, palm oil, electronic components, natural rubber, timber and logs, electrical products, textiles, tin

Major Trading Partners
UK, Singapore, Japan, US, Australia, China, West Germany, Thailand

Workforce
5.9 million
Agriculture 21%, manufacturing 18%, trade and tourism 14%, government 13%, transportation and communications 8%, finance 8%, utilities 8%, mining and petroleum 5%, construction 5%

Tips for Doing Business
A conservative business suit is necessary for government visits but a white shirt, tie and trousers are acceptable for other business calls. Make prior appointments. You may be dealing with wealthy Chinese businessmen so have cards printed in English and Mandarin. Personal contact is important, and it is not unusual to be asked to dinner so your contact can look you over. Always accept. Call Indian or Chinese businessmen ''Mr'' but Malaysians ''Encik'', pronounced ''ench''. The Malaysian population is Muslim and Muslim social customs prevail. Always use the right hand whether it is to point something out, take or give something, or to eat. Never refuse refreshment. Be very courteous but not overly affectionate with Malaysian women. Bargain everywhere except in department stores when buying goods: check credit rating of contact carefully before signing contract.

Best Months for Doing Business
Almost any month is good for business travel except December, January and February when businessmen vacation. Check carefully for local holidays (Muslim, State and Chinese New Year) before travelling.

Business Hours
The Muslim weekly holiday on Thursday afternoons is observed in some states.

Government
Mon-Fri 0900-1600
Sat 0900-1245

Business
Mon-Fri 0800-1630
Sat 0800-1245

Banks
Mon-Fri 1000-1500,
Sat 0930-1130in Peninsular
Malaysia;
Mon-Fri 0800-1200, 1400-1500,
Sat 0900-1100 in Sabah;
Mon-Fri 1000-1500,
Sat 0930-1130 in Sarawak

Shops
Mon-Fri 0830-1830 in Peninsular
Malaysia;
Mon-Sat 0800-1830 in Sabah;
Mon-Fri 0900-1800,
Sat 0900-1300 in Sarawak

English Language Publications
There are several English
language newspapers in
Malaysia: the main one is The
New Straits Times.

Telephone and Communications
Telephone country code: 60
Telephone city code: Ipoh 5,
Kuala Lumpur 3, Malacca 6,
Penang Hill 4892 Telex country
code: 784
Public telephone booths take 10
cent coin for unlimited use in
Kuala Lumpur: elsewhere cost is
based on distance and time.
When the called party answers,
press black button to connect
call. All 6-digit numbers are
being replaced with 7-digit
numbers. Phone books are
issued yearly with a yellow
pages section.
Telex facilities are available in
the large hotels: public telex
facilities available at Telegraph
Office, Djalon Raja Chulan,
Kuala Lumpur (24 hours).
Telegrams can be sent from any
telegraph office. Post boxes are
painted red and are widely
available.
The post offices at Subong
Airport and the Kuala Lumpur
railway station are open
everyday including holidays.

Air Travel
Malaysian Airlines Service (MAS)
offers comprehensive service
which connects major centers
and even some smaller towns.

Other Transport
The roads in Malaysia are
excellent and 70% of them are
paved. Regular bus service
operates between towns and
cities, and there is car rental
available with a valid national
driving license. Driving is on the
left and seat belts are
mandatory.
Chauffeur-driven cars also
available for hire. Rail service in
Peninsular Malaysia operates day
and night. Regular service
between Kuala Lumpur and Kota
Bharu and Tumpat. Whenever
possible, reserve first-class
accomodation. Some restaurant
cars available.
There is frequent ferry service
between Penang and
Butterworth, and a passenger
service operated by the Straits
Steamship Company which
operates between Port Kelang
and Sabah and Sarawak every
9-10 days.

KUALA LUMPUR

Airport Information

Time
GMT +8

Airport
Subang International KUH
Tel: 7760833
22 km (14 mi) W of city

Airlines
Aeroflot 2423231
Air France 2226952
Air India 2420166
Alitalia 2280366
British Airways 2426177
Canadian International 2425577
Cathay Pacific 2383355
China 2427344
Eastern 420042

ASIA/PACIFIC

Garuda 2420481
JAL 2611722
KLM 2427011
Korean 2428311
Kuwait Air 2201934
Lufthansa 2614666
Malaysian 746300
Northwest 2429633
Pan Am 425044
Philippine 2429140
PIA 2425444
Qantas 2389133
Sabena 2425244
SAS 2426044
Singapore 2923122
Swissair 2426744
Thai 2937133
TWA 2415637
UTA 2427620

Transport to City
Taxis: the city is divided into zones with rates for ordinary, air-conditioned and limousine taxis posted on a board at the airport. Buy coupons at the coupon booth and give to the driver. Tipping is optional. Between midnight and 0800, there is a 50% surcharge.
Coach: air-conditioned luxury bus costs about 5-10 ringgits and takes about 30 minutes.

Facilities
Bar, duty-free shop, restaurant, buffet, bank with currency exchange, post office, shops, baggage deposits, first-aid/ medical
Duty-free shop sells cigarets,

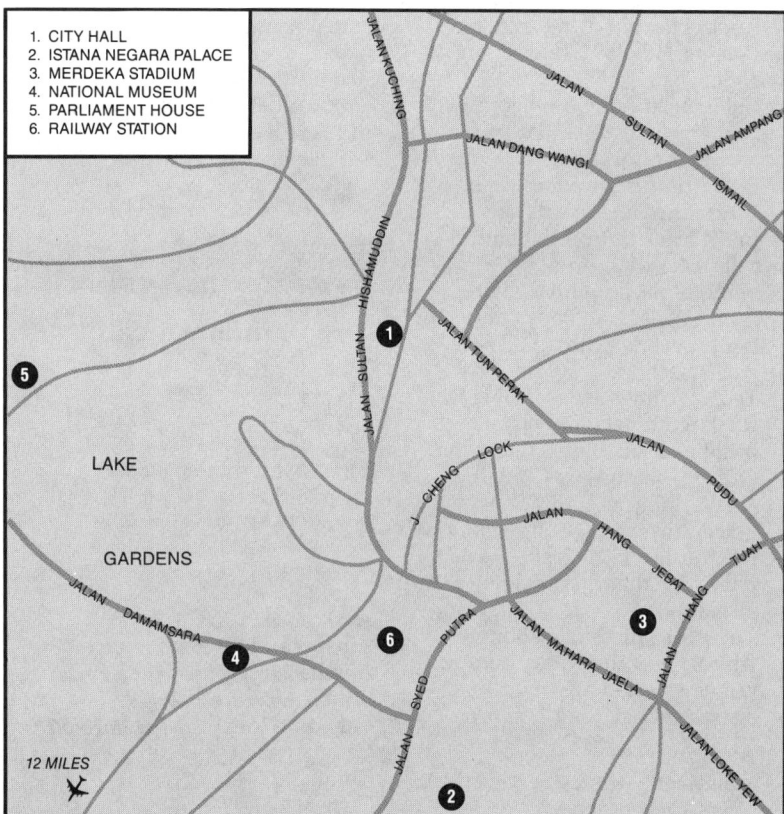

1. CITY HALL
2. ISTANA NEGARA PALACE
3. MERDEKA STADIUM
4. NATIONAL MUSEUM
5. PARLIAMENT HOUSE
6. RAILWAY STATION

LAKE

GARDENS

12 MILES

Kuala Lumpur

cigars, tobacco, wines, spirits, lighters, batik, jewellery
Car rental desks: Hertz, Avis, Europcar, Sintat

Airport Taxes
Per person: International 15 ringgits, domestic 10 ringgits

City Information

Weather
It is tropical with high temperatures and humidity: rainfall throughout the year. Two monsoon seasons: in the north-east between October and February: in the south-west between May and September. Average temps: Jan 27c (81F) July 27c (81F)

Transportation
Taxis are metered and have an extra charge for air-conditioning: easily available at stands, ordered by phone, or hailed. Surcharge of 50% between 0100-0600. You can hire by the hour. Sharing is common for longer journeys. Tipping is optional. Mini-buses run from one end of the city to the other and into the suburbs for a fixed reasonable rate.

Car Hire
Hertz, 52 Jalan Ampang
(tel: 2320202)
Avis, Jalan Raja Chulan
(tel: 2417144)
Europcar, Jalan Raja Chulan
(tel: 7756023)
Sintat, Holiday Inn (tel: 2482388)

Hospitals
Emergency medical service for travellers at:
Asunta Hospital (tel: 563521)
Lady Templar Hospital
(tel: 711751)
Pantar Medical Clinic
(tel: 575077)

Trade Fairs
International Banking Exhibition
(Oct)

International Forrestry Exhibition
(Oct)
International Fashions Fair (Nov)
International Safety & Security
Exhibition (Nov)
For further information contact: Commercial Division, Ministry of Information, Angkasapuri, Kuala Lumpur

Hotels
Equatorial, Jalan Sultan Ismail
(tel: 2612022)
Holiday Inn On-The-Park, Jalan
Pinang (tel: 2481066)
Hyatt Saujana, Subang Airport
Hwy. (tel: 7461188)
Kuala Lumpur Hilton, Jalan
Sultan Ismail (tel: 2422122)
Merlin, Kuala Lumpur, 2 Jalan
Sultan Ismail, (tel: 2480033)
Petaling Jaya Hilton, 2 Jalan
Barat, Petaling Jaya
(tel: 753533)
Regent, Jalan Sultan Ismail
(tel: 2425588)

What to See and Do
Kuala Lumpur is a fairly new city. The old city is in the Chinese quarter down by the river with streetstalls and the Masjid Jame mosque. In the center of town are the Lake Gardens and nearby, the imposing Parliament House. Visit the impressive, modern National Mosque, National Museum and the National Monument. On Sundays, visit the market at Kampung Bahru for bargains. Also plan to visit the limestone Batu Caves 13 km (5 miles) north of the city and see stalagmites, stalactites, batik-printing shops, silversmith shops, the Hindu Shrine, and monkeys in the surrounding trees.

Useful Addresses

Embassies and Consulates
American: 376 Jalan Tun Razak
(tel: 2489011)

Canadian: Ampang Rd, Plaza
MBF (tel: 2612000)
British: 5 Jalan Semantan
(tel: 2541533)

Business and Commerce
Central Bank, (Bank Negara
Malaysia), Jalan Kuching
(tel: 2988044)
Chamber of Commerce, Banguna
Angkasa Raya (tel: 2435004)

Tourism and Travel
Malaysian Tourist Development
Association, Wisma MBI, Jalan
Raja Chulan (tel: 423033)
Tourist Association, Jalan Sultan
Hishamuddin (tel: 81832)
Automobile Association of
Malaysia, 30 Jalan Datuk
Sulaiman, Taman Tun Dr
Ismail
American Express, Mayflower
Acme Tours, 18 Jalan
Segambut Pusat (tel: 486739)
Thomas Cook, 70 Jalan Ampang
(tel: 235034)

NEW ZEALAND

Essential Information

Type of Government
Parliamentary

Area
296,032 sq km
(103,886 sq mi)

Population
3.25 million

Annual Growth Rate
1.4%

Languages
English, Maori

Religion
Anglican 29%, Presbyterian 18%,
Roman Catholic 15%, other 38%

Ethnic Groups
European 85.7%, Maori 8.9%,
other Polynesian 2.7%

Weights and Measures
Metric

Electrical Current
A.C. 50c 230/400V

Major Business Cities
Wellington (cap) 380,000
Auckland 900,000
Christchurch 340,000

Currency
1 dollar = 100 cents
Notes 1, 2, 5, 10, 20, 100 dollars
Coins 1, 2, 5, 10, 20, 50 cents

Public Holidays
As well as national and religious
holidays, provinces have their
own one-day anniversaries.
Jan 1 New Year
Feb 6 National
Apr 13-20 Easter Week
Apr 25 Anzac
June 2 Queen's Official Birthday
Oct 27 Labor Day
Dec 25-26 Christmas

Travellers Information

Entry Requirements
Passport is required by everyone
except Australian citizens and
British subjects permanently
residing in Australia and arriving
directly from Australia. Visas are
not required by citizens of the
British Commonwealth, US and
Japan, with onward going
tickets. There are no special
requirements for business visits.

Working Restrictions
All nationals need a work permit
except those from Australia.

Vaccination Required
Smallpox vaccination certificate
required if travelling from
infected area within 14 days.
Stringent rules for the protection

of plants and animals. Visitors arriving from countries suffering plant or animal diseases may have to be disinfected.

Customs and Duty Free

On arrival: 200 cigarets or 50 cigars or 250 g/8 oz tobacco: 1 liter spirits; 1 liter wine; perfume in moderate amounts. All personal effects may be brought in duty-free. You must declare all animal, vegetable or fruit products.

Currency Restrictions

The amount of foreign currency brought in is unrestricted and the same amount may be taken out. Only NZ$10 allowed for import.

Health Tips

The standard of medical care is high and no special care need be taken with food or drink. Medical services, with the exception of treatment of accidental injuries, must be paid for.

Climate and Clothing

The climate is temperate and can be wet, windy and cool, although the north is warmer. There is a lot of rainfall in the winter months (March to August) and you should wear medium weight clothes and a raincoat for the north; an overcoat for the south. Summer months are drier. Wear lightweight for North Island (Auckland and Wellington) and medium weight for South Island (Christchurch).

Tipping

Neither service charges or taxes are ever added to bills, and tipping is extremely unusual and not expected. Taxi drivers should never be tipped.

Food and Drink

The New Zealand diet is very much like the British with lamb,

beef and pork being common fare. The fish and shellfish are also good and very plentiful and there are excellent oysters. New Zealand lamb is world famous. New Zealanders are very fond of puddings and a meringue dessert called Pavlova. The beer has always been excellent but wine is beginning to catch up, and New Zealand now produces several first-class wines.

Business Brief

GDP

$21.43 billion
(per capita income $7,916)

Annual Growth Rate

2%

Natural Resources

Natural gas, iron sand, coal, timber

Agriculture

Wool, meat, dairy products

Industry

Food processing, textile, machinery, transport equipment, fish, forest products

Imports

Total $7.3 billion
Machinery, manufactured goods, chemicals

Exports

Total $7.2 billion
Meat, wool, manufactured products, forest products, dairy products

Major Trading Partners

UK, Australia, US, France, Italy, Belgium, Japan, Canada, West Germany, China, USSR, Saudi Arabia

Workforce

1.3 million
Agriculture 10.5%, industry and commerce 34.1%, services and government 55%

Tips for Doing Business

New Zealand businessmen are

ASIA/PACIFIC

conservative but friendly. A business suit should be worn at all times and prior appointments made. Shake hands when saying hello or meeting someone and generally follow the tenants of good manners. Do not at any time imply that New Zealanders are the same as Australians.

Best Months for Doing Business

Visit in February, March and April, October and November. Avoid the weeks before and after Christmas and Easter, and January, July and August when most vacations are taken.

Business Hours

Government
Mon-Fri 0800-1630

Business
Mon-Fri 0830-1630

Banks
Mon-Fri 0900-1630

Shops
Mon-Fri 0900-1830
Sat 0900-1300

English Language Publications

There are no national dailies but there are some published morning and evening in individual cities. British papers are also available.

Telephone and Communications

Telephone country code: 64
Telephone city code: Auckland 9, Christchurch 3, Hamilton 71, Rotorua 73, Wellington 4 Telex country code: 791
Local telephone calls are free from hotels, and dials have the numbers in the reverse order to what is customary in Europe and North America. International telex facilities are available at some hotels and at chief post offices in most towns.
Telegrams may be sent from post offices or by telephone.

Air Travel

Domestic air travel is good and Air New Zealand operates most of the flights which connect main centers and over 30 airports. Other airlines include Mount Cook Airlines, Newmans Airways, Eagle Airways. Charter services are readily available.

Other Transport

Taxis are available in all major centers from taxi stands or by telephone (24 hours). Rates vary but usually are higher at night and on weekends.
Roads are well maintained and car rental is available with an Australian, British, Canadian, American or International driving license. Driving is on the left side of the road.
Luxury coaches connect the major centers on both islands. They generally have air-conditioning, sleeping and dining cars.
Car ferries run between Wellington and Picton several times a day and there is a passenger service between Stewart and South Islands. Book ahead.

AUCKLAND

Airport Information

Time
GMT +12

Airport
Auckland International (Mangere) AKL
Tel: 2750789
26 km (15 mi) S of city

Airlines
Aerolineas Argentinas 771579
Air France 31229
Air New Zealand 793510
Alitalia 794455
American 399159

British Airways 771379
Canadian International 390735
Continental 775444
JAL 799906
KLM 391782
Korean 661893
Lufthansa 31528
Pan Am 395982
Qantas 790306
SAS 397749
Singapore 32129
Swissair 794664

TWA 734825
UTA 33521
United 793800
Varig 735728

Transport to City

Taxi: taxis cost about NZ$27 to
city Monday to Friday 0600-2200.
Tipping is not necessary.
Coach: airline buses to city from
international and domestic

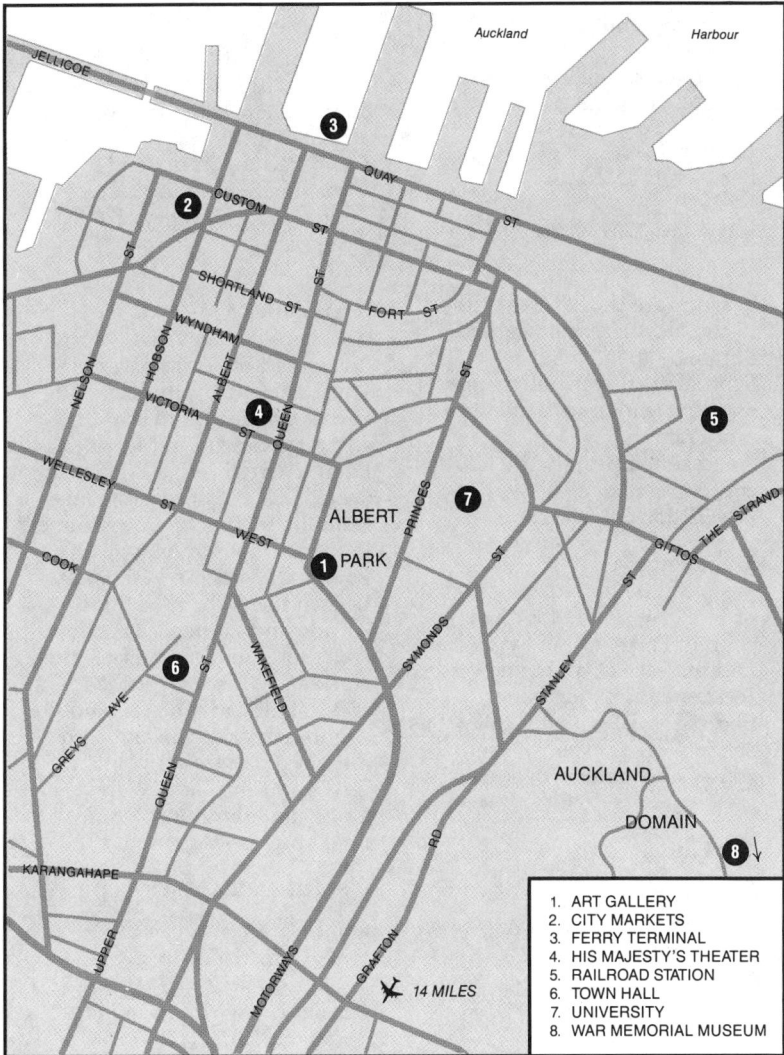

ASIA/PACIFIC

1. ART GALLERY
2. CITY MARKETS
3. FERRY TERMINAL
4. HIS MAJESTY'S THEATER
5. RAILROAD STATION
6. TOWN HALL
7. UNIVERSITY
8. WAR MEMORIAL MUSEUM

14 MILES

Auckland

terminals leave every 30 minutes: cost NZ$7 and take 45 minutes. Hotel coaches go to all the major hotels.

Facilities

Bank with currency exchange, buffet, hotel reservations, baggage deposit, insurance, shops, post office, nursery, first aid/medical, bar, restaurant Duty-free shop sells cigarets, cigars, tobacco, wine, spirits, cameras, lighters, watches, jewellery. All convertible currencies and major credit cards accepted.
Car rental desks: Hertz, Avis, Budget, National

Airport Taxes

Per person: NZ$2

City Information

Weather

Seasons are the reverse of those in the Northern hemisphere. Summers (September to February) are generally sunny and dry: winters are mild but quite rainy.
Average temps: Jan 21-24c (70-75F)
July 10-15c (50-60F)

Transportation

Taxis can be hired from ranks or ordered by phone for an extra charge. Fares are set by distance and increase at night and on weekends. Tipping is not necessary. Diesel and trolley bus services are inexpensive and routes adequately cover the city area.

Car Hire

Hertz, 154 Victoria St. W
    (tel: 34924)
Avis, 22 Wakefield St (tel: 792545
    & 2757239)
Budget, 73 Beach St (tel: 796768)
National, 11 Bowden Rd
    (tel: 572046)

Hospitals

Emergency help for travellers at:
Auckland Hospital, Park Rd,
    Grafton (tel: 797440)
North Shore Hospital,
    Shakespeare Rd, Takapuna
    (tel: 491491)

Trade Fairs

Horticulture Trade Fair (July)
Food Exhibition (Nov)

Hotels

Auckland Gateway, PO Box 53-
    105 (tel: 54079)
Inter-Continental, Princess
    (tel: 797220)
Royal International, Victoria St.
    W (tel: 31359)
Sheraton-Auckland, PO Box 2771
    (tel: 795132)
South Pacific, Queen and
    Custom Sts (tel: 778220)
White Heron Regency, 138 St
    Stephens Ave, Parnell
    (tel: 796860)

What to See and Do

Auckland is a hilly city dominated by its harbor, Waitemata and Manukau, and harbor bridge. There is a stunning view from Mount Eden. Drive through Waitekere Scenic Reserve or take the ferry from the bottom of Queen Street to the previously volcanic Rangitoto Island in Waitemata Bay. In town, visit the Strand Arcade and Parnell Village for craft stores and old houses, the Auckland Museum for Maori and Polynesian artifacts, and the zoo for a look at the kiwi bird. A must is a day trip to Waitomo Caves and the Glow Worm Grotto and on to the famous mud springs at Rotorua.

Useful Addresses

Embassies and Consulates

American: Yorkshire General
    Bldg, Shortland St (tel: 32724)
British: Norwich Union Bldg
    (tel: 32973)

Business and Commerce
Central Bank (Reserve Bank of New Zealand), 2 The Terrace, Wellington (tel: 722029)
Stock Exchange, 82-84 Albert St
Auckland Chamber of Commerce, 2 Courthouse Lane (tel: 31969)
American Chamber of Commerce, 155-161 The Terrace, Wellington (tel: 727549)

Tourism and Travel
Government Tourist Bureau, 99 Queen St (tel: 798180)
American Express, 95 Queen St (tel: 798243)
Automobile Association, PO Box 5 (tel: 774660)
Deak International, 107 Queen Street (tel: 3660052)
Thomas Cook, 9 Commerce St (tel: 491172)

PAKISTAN

Essential Information

Type of Government
Martial Law Regime established in 1977

Area
803,943 sq km
(310,527 sq mi)

Population
98.3 million

Annual Growth Rate
2.8%

Languages
Urdu (official), English, Punjabi, Sindhi, Pushtu, Baluchi

Religion
Muslim 97%, small minorities of Christians, Hindus, and others

Ethnic Groups
Punjabi, Sindhi, Pathan, Baluch

Weights and Measures
Metric (local systems also in use)

Electrical Current
A.C. 50c 220V and 230/400V

Major Business Cities
Islamabad (cap) 375,000
Karachi 5,950,000
Lahore 3,900,000
Faisalabad 1,900,000
Rawalpindi 927,000
Hyderabad 875,000

Currency
1 Pakistani Rupee = 100 Paisa
Notes 1, 5, 10, 50, 100 rupees
Coins 5, 10, 25, 50 piasas

Public Holidays
Pakistan is a Muslim country and since Muslim holidays change yearly according to the lunar cycle, check dates before travelling.
Mar 23 Pakistan Day
May 1 May Day
Aug 14 Independence
Sept 6 Defence of Pakistan
Sept 11 Quaid-e-Azam's death
Dec 25 Christmas

Travellers Information

Entry Requirements
Passport is required by everyone. Visas are not required of most foreign nationals with on-going tickets as long as the stay is shorter than 30 days. Nationals of neighboring countries need visas, and permits are needed for mountain expeditions. Israelis and white South Africans restricted entry.

Vaccination Required
Vaccination certificates for cholera and yellow fever required if coming from infected areas. Take antimalarial precautions. Check carefully for current conditions and

regulations as you might be quarantined otherwise.

Customs and Duty Free
On arrival: 200 cigarets or 50 cigars. Personal effects are allowed in duty-free. No alcohol permitted.

Currency Restrictions
Import of foreign currency is unlimited and the amount declared on entry may be taken out again. Keep all exchange receipts. Domestic currency allowance imported or exported is only 100 Pakistani rupees. Only 500 rupees can be converted to foreign currency on departure.

Health Tips
Use only bottled or boiled water at all times. Eat yoghurt and take antimalarial tablets. There are excellent health facilities with highly trained foreign and national staff. Services must be paid for. Major hotels will recommend doctors and dentists.

Climate and Clothing
The climate varies from sub-tropical in the south to temperate and cool in the mountains and foothills. Generally, the plateau regions and coast (Karachi, Lahore) are hot and dry between April and June calling for tropical weight clothes, and hot and very wet during the monsoon season (July through September) calling for tropical weight clothes and an umbrella. In winter (October to March) it is cool on the plains and coast; wear medium weight clothes and take a light coat.

Tipping
General tipping rule is 10% although most hotels and restaurants include this in the bill. Tip 3 Pakistani rupees per piece of portered luggage.

Food and Drink
Pakistani food is similar to Indian cuisine but since it is a Muslim country, there is a strong Middle Eastern influence. Breads (nan) are eaten more often than rice, and meat is more common than vegetable dishes. Rice is served frequently in pilaus (rice cooked with spicy chicken or lamb). Roasted leg of lamb (sadji), kebabs, and kikkas (barbecued meats) are also popular. In Karachi and along the coast, there are wonderful seafood dishes. The Middle Eastern influence is also seen in the sweet pastries for dessert. Fruit and fruit drinks are plentiful. Western food is widely available as are large British-influenced breakfasts. Alcohol is forbidden but tourists may apply for a liquor permit. At meals, fruit drinks, soft drinks, and tea are generally drunk.

Business Brief

GNP
$36.6 billion
(per capita income $369)

Annual Growth Rate
6.3%

Natural Resources
Land, extensive natural gas, limited petroleum, poor quality coal, iron ore

Agriculture
Wheat, cotton, rice, sugar cane

Industry
Cotton, textiles, fertilizer, steel products, food processing, natural gas

Imports
Total $6 billion
Capital goods, raw materials, crude oil, consumer items

Exports
Total $4.17 billion
Rice, raw cotton, cotton yarn,

textiles, light manufactured products, petroleum products

Major Trading Partners
US, Japan, West Germany, UK, Hong Kong, China, Kuwait, France, Italy

Workforce
28.6 million
Agriculture 55%, industry 20%

Tips for Doing Business
Between the months of November and March, wear a conservative business suit; other times a white shirt, tie and trousers are acceptable. Always wear a suit coat for government visits, however. Make prior appointments. Pakistani businessmen are friendly and interested in foreigners, yet reserved and formal in business. They usually entertain at their clubs and rarely at home. Alcohol is illegal so tea is generally offered at business meetings: it is considered very rude to refuse. Do not take pictures of women without their permission and avoid the subjects of local politics and Pakistan's relations with its neighbors.

Best Months for Doing Business
November through March for the good weather. Find out when the month-long Muslim holiday Ramadan occurs (it is different each year) and avoid it assiduously. During this period, commercial and government offices close half-days and restaurants close until sundown. The heavy monsoon season occurs from May through August when most businessmen go away on vacation.

Business Hours

Government
Sat-Wed 0900-1300
Thurs 0900-1100

Business
Sat-Wed 0900-1300
Thurs 0900-1100

Banks
Sat-Wed 0900-1130
Thurs 0900-1100

Shops
Sat-Thurs 0800/0900-1600/1700

English Language Publications
Many English language newspapers and magazines are available. The main ones published in Karachi are the Morning News, Dawn (local business news information), Daily News, and Leader.

Telephone and Communications
Telephone country code: 92
Telephone city code: Islamabad 51, Karachi 21, Lahore 42, Rawalpindi 51
Telex country code: 952
Telephone satellite links are maintained with many countries. All telephone operators speak English; public phone booths at public telephone offices and post offices. Telex facilities often available in good hotels. In Karachi, the Central Telegraph Office provides 24 hour service for telex and telegrams.

Air Travel
Air travel is the best method of domestic travel. There are daily flights operated by PIA between all main centers. Hotels have good information on flight times and reservation procedures.

Other Transport
About one-third of the roads are considered good and car hire is available, but avoid travelling at night.
Although express coach and mini-bus services are available between main centers, travel by bus is not highly recommended. There is an extensive rail service with 3 classes: book first class. Some services have air-

conditioning, restaurant cars, sleepers, and other advantages. Specify when booking and reserve in advance.

KARACHI

Airport Information

Time
GMT +5

Airport
Karachi International KHI
Tel: 482111
16 km (10 mi) E of city
16 km (10 mi) E of city

Airlines
Aeroflot 529210
Air Canada 511779

Air France 512017
Alia 511232
Alitalia 511097
British Airways 516077
CAAC 435570
Canadian International 510728
Egyptair 511109
Gulf Air 525231
Interflug 512253
Iran Air 515001
JAL 510161
KLM 512031
Korean 528182
Kuwait 510603
Lufthansa 515416
Northwest 551215
Pan Am 510121
Philippine 516535
PIA 511061
Qantas 51106l
Sabena 522621
SAS 516186

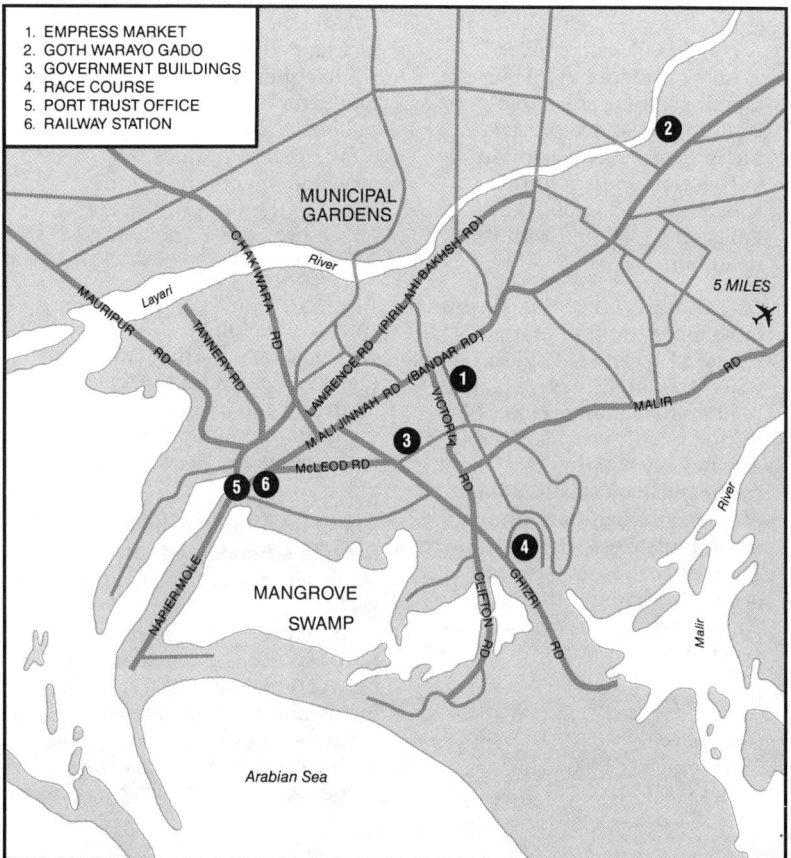

1. EMPRESS MARKET
2. GOTH WARAYO GADO
3. GOVERNMENT BUILDINGS
4. RACE COURSE
5. PORT TRUST OFFICE
6. RAILWAY STATION

MUNICIPAL GARDENS

5 MILES

MANGROVE SWAMP

Arabian Sea

Karachi

Saudia 515804
Singapore 521213
Swissair 512066
Thai 516186
THY 514063
TWA 511779
UTA 512017

Transport to City

Taxis: taxis are available and should cost about 40-55 Pakistani rupees. Agree on fare in advance.
Coach: bus meets all flight arrivals and costs about 20 rupees and takes about 30 minutes to city. Courtesy coaches to major hotels.
Transit: train to city every 30 minutes from 0500-1900; bus leaves every 30 minutes until dark.

Facilities

Bar, buffet, restaurant, bank with currency exchange, insurance, hotel reservations, post office, shops
Duty-free shop sells cigarets, cigars, tobacco, jewellery, glass, china. US, British and Saudi Arabian currencies accepted.

Airport Taxes

Per person: International 100 rupees, domestic 5 rupees

City Information

Weather

Climate is moderate with rainy monsoon season between July and September; hot in the late spring and cooler in winter. Average temps: Jan 13-24c (55-75F)
July 32-35c (90-95F)

Transportation

Taxis can be hailed in the street. Black and yellow ones are metered although meter is not always used. Agree on fare in advance. Tipping is optional. Most hotels have access to car rental; you can hire self-drive,

chauffeur-driven, or minibus. Driving is on left side of road.

Car Hire

Hertz, Central Hotel (tel: 52291)
Akbar Tours, Kutchery Rd
 (tel: 514689)
Avis, Waljis Bldg (tel: 27614)

Hospitals

Medical help for travellers is available through major hotels and at:
Cardiovascular Institute
 (tel: 516716)
Jinnah Hospital (tel: 512551)
Mideast Medical Center
 (tel: 535044)
Seventh Day Adventist
 (tel: 78086)

Trade Fairs

International Leather Fair (Feb)

Hotels

Beach Luxury, Tamizuddin Khan Rd (tel: 551031)
Hilton, Fatima Rd (tel: 511522)
Holiday Inn Karachi, 9 Abdullah Haroon Rd (tel: 520111 & 522011)
Imperial, 2 Moulvi Tamizuddin Rd (tel: 551055)
Inter-Continental Karachi, Dr Ziauddin Ahmed Rd
 (tel: 515021)
Mehran, Shah-reh-E-Faisal
 (tel: 515061)
Metropole, Club Rd (tel: 512051)
Midway House, Karachi Airport, Stargate Rd (tel: 480371)
Sheraton Karachi, Club Rd
 (tel: 521021)
Taj Mahal, Shahrah-e-Faisal
 (tel: 520211)

What to Do and See

Karachi is Pakistan's largest city. Apart from its sights, it has several good beaches for year-round swimming: Clifton, which also has an amusement park and famous aquarium; Sandspit; and Hawkes Bay. Visit Jinnah's tomb; the National Museum; and the Bohri Bazaar for leather goods, brasses and carved screens. Day trips involve a trip to Lahore (by plane) to see the Royal Fort, Shalimar Gardens, and mausoleums. Inquire at your hotel for other day trips.

Useful Addresses

Embassies and Consulates
American: Abdullah Haroon Rd (tel: 515081)
Canadian: Hotel Metropole, Club Rd
British: York Place, Runnymeade (tel: 532041)

Business and Commerce
Central Bank, (State Bank of Pakistan), II Chundrigar Rd (tel: 234141)
Karachi Stock Exchange, Stock Exchange Rd (tel: 229146)
Karachi Chamber of Commerce and Industry, Aiwan-e-Tijarat Rd (tel: 226091/5)

Tourism and Travel
Tourist Information, Club Rd (tel: 510234)
Karachi Automobile Association, Standard Insurance House, 1 Chundrigar Rd (tel: 232173)
American Express, Standard Insurance House, (tel: 224014)

PHILIPPINES

Essential Information

Type of Government
Republic

Area
300,000 sq km
(115,830 sq mi)

Population
55.9 million

Annual Growth Rate
2.4%

Languages
Philipino (based on Tagalog), national language; English, language of government and instruction in higher education.

Religion
Catholic 83%, Protestant 9%, Muslim 5%, other 3%

Ethnic Groups
Malay, Chinese

Weights and Measures
Metric

Electrical Current
A.C. 60C 110/220V
A.C. 50C (110/120V

Major Business Cities
Manila (cap) 6,900,000
Quezon City 1,250,000
Davao 1,750,000
Cebu 1,850,000

Currency
1 Peso = 100 Centavos
Notes 2, 5, 10, 20, 50, 100 pesos
Coins 1, 5, 10, 25, 50 centavos, 1, 2 pesos

Public Holidays
Jan 1 New Year
Apr 9 Bataan Day
Apr 13-20 Easter Week
May 1 Labor Day
May 6 Araw Ng Kagitingan (Hero's Day)
Jun 12 Independence Day
Jul 4 Philippine-American Friendship Day
Sept 21 Thanksgiving
Nov 1 All Saints Day
Nov 30 Bonifacio Day
Dec 25 Christmas
Dec 30 Rizal Day

Travellers Information

Entry Requirements
Passport is required by all.
Visa not required for nationals of

most countries with guaranteed onward passage for stays less than 60 days. Extensions can be granted for a further short period of time. For longer stays, visas should be obtained ahead of time. Some restriction for nationals of South Africa and some communist countries. Regulations can change at short notice so check before travelling.

Vaccination Required
Certificates for yellow fever are required if coming from an infected area, and cholera if arriving by sea. Take antimalaria precautions. Vaccinations for tetanus and typhoid are recommended.

Customs and Duty Free
On arrival: 200 cigarets or 50 cigars or 250g/8oz tobacco. Personal effects are allowed in duty-free. Firearms, explosives, pornography, gambling equipment or games strictly prohibited.

Currency Restrictions
There is no restriction on the amount of foreign currency brought in: amounts over $3,000 must be declared. Amount declared on entry may be exported. Import/export maximum for local currency no more than P500. When changing foreign currency keep receipts since local money can be spent at the duty free shop before leaving as long as receipt is presented.

Health Tips
The drinking water is good and safe in Manila, but drink boiled or bottled water outside of the city and avoid raw fruit and vegetables. Disinfect small cuts immediately and take antimalarial pills. Many doctors and dentists speak English and the medical standards are good.

Climate and Clothing
The climate is tropical with rainfall according to season. From March to October it is hot and humid with possible typhoons occuring during the last four months. Wear tropical weight clothes and take an umbrella plus a light jacket for the occasional cool evening. Between November and February, it is dry and less humid. Wear tropical weight clothes.

Tipping
Although hotels and restaurants generally add 10% to the bill, it is customary to tip 10% for all services except small ones where 2-4 pesos is adequate.

Food and Drink
All kinds of foods are available to the visitor including Chinese, American, Indian, Spanish, Japanese and Korean. Try some of the Filipino delicacies like adobo (pork and chicken cooked in spices, peppers, garlic and onions), mani (noodle soup), pinangat (a spicy vegetable dish), and lechon (roast suckling pig). Local drinks include lemon tea and coconut wine. Filipino San Miguel beer is popular and good, and there is a wide choice of soft drinks and spirits.

Business Brief

GNP
$33.9 billion
(per capita income $617)

Annual Growth Rate
10.4%

Natural Resources
Timber, copper, nickel, iron, cobalt, silver, gold, petroleum

Agriculture
Sugar, coconut products, rice, corn, pineapples, and bananas

ASIA/PACIFIC

Industry
Textiles, pharmaceuticals, chemicals, wood products, food processing, electronics assembly

Imports
Total $7.1 billion
Raw materials, mineral fuels, machinery and transport equipment, consumer goods

Exports
Total $5.6 billion
Logs and lumber, copra, sugar, iron ore, copper, coconut products, pineapple

Major Trading Partners
US, Japan, West Germany, UK, Australia, Netherlands, Indonesia, Saudi Arabia

Workforce
20 million Agriculture 47%, industry and commerce 20%, services 13.5%, government 10%, other 9.5%

Tips for Doing Business
A conservative lightweight business suit should be worn for all government and most business visits. Often, for other occasions, less formal dress is appropriate depending on the weather and the circumstances. Since many industries are American-connected, the Filipino businessman often does business in an American way. However there is a large Chinese business community as well, with the Chinese inclination to ponder decisions. English is widely spoken. The Filipino businessman will entertain at home while the Chinese businessman will take you out to a restaurant with many of his associates.

Best Months for Doing Business
October and November, and January through March. Avoid the weeks before and after Christmas and Easter, and before and after Chinese New Year.

Businessmen take their vacations between June and September.

Business Hours

Government
Mon-Fri 0730-1130, 1230-1630 or 0900-1200, 1300-1800

Business
Mon-Fri 0800-1200/1300, 1300/1400-1700
Sat 0830-1200 (certain business only)

Banks
Mon-Fri 0900-1600 (some banks open half-day on Saturday)

Shops
Mon-Sat 0900-1200, 1400-1930 (many shops in Manila open half-day on Sunday)

English Language Publications
The Bulletin Today

Telephone and Communications
Telephone country code: 63
Telephone city code: Cebu 32, Davao 35, Manila 2, Quezon City 2
Telex country code: 712, 722, 732, 742, 762
Local telephone service is available but not always reliable; 82% of the telephones are in metropolitan Manila with automatic service. Long distance service to the US is excellent. Telex and telegram service available at major hotels, and public telex booths (24 hours) are available.

Air Travel
This is the best form of domestic travel. Philippine Airlines connects Manila and 50 towns throughout the country on a regular basis. One-day round trip flights are possible to some places. Major hotels can arrange bookings in advance.

Other Transport
Bus service is not recommended for travellers because of the

crowds. The Philippine Bureau of Travel and Tourist Industry provides air-conditioned bus service regularly between Manila and Baguio. Some train services have sleeping accomodation and diners.

MANILA

Airport Information

Time
GMT +8

Airport
Manila International MNL

Tel: 8321961
12 km (7.5 mi) SE of city

Airlines
Air France 5217501
Alitalia 503202
American 5219305
British Airways 8170361
CAAC 8179898
Canadian International 8102656
Cathay Pacific 8159417
Continental 8188701

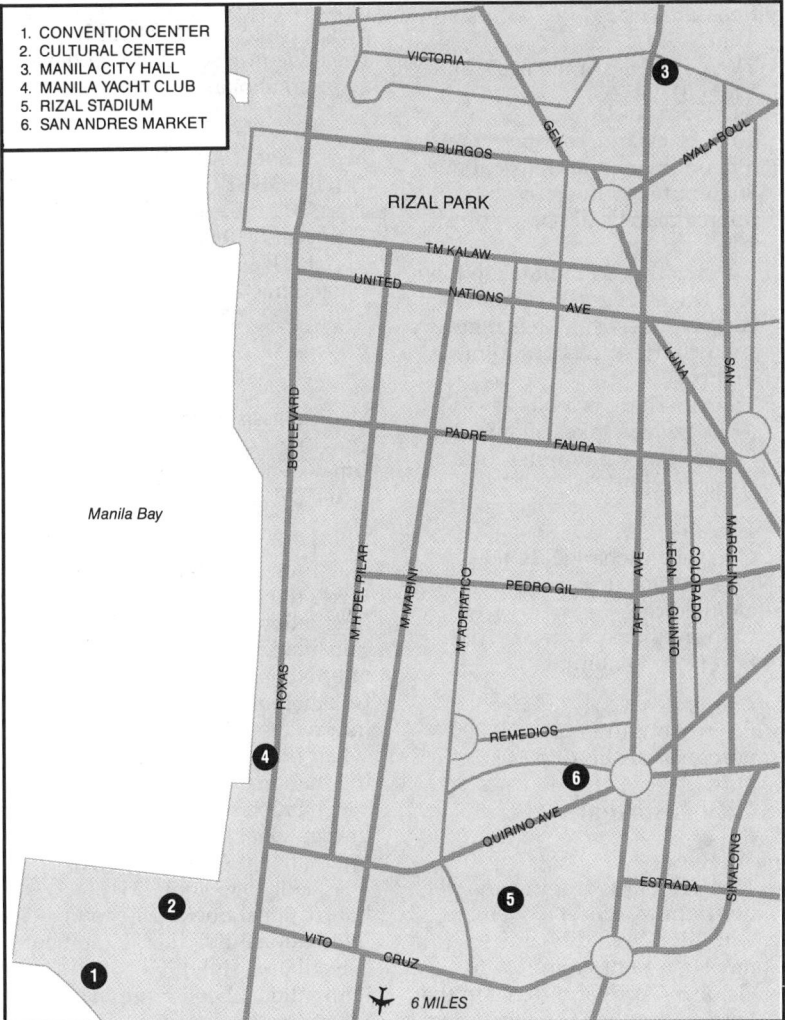

ASIA/PACIFIC

1. CONVENTION CENTER
2. CULTURAL CENTER
3. MANILA CITY HALL
4. MANILA YACHT CLUB
5. RIZAL STADIUM
6. SAN ANDRES MARKET

VICTORIA

GEN

AYALA BOUL

P BURGOS

RIZAL PARK

TM KALAW

UNITED

NATIONS

AVE

LUNA

SAN

PADRE

FAURA

BOULEVARD

Manila Bay

M H DEL PILAR

M MABINI

M ADRIATICO

PEDRO GIL

TAFT AVE

LEON GUINTO

COLORADO

MARCELINO

ROXAS

REMEDIOS

QUIRINO AVE

ESTRADA

SINALONG

VITO

CRUZ

6 MILES

Manila

Egyptair 8310661
Garuda 862458
Gulf Air 8164181
Iberia 584885
JAL 590946, KLM 8154790
Korean 8158911
Kuwait 8172662
Lufthansa 8159271
Northwest 5211911
Pan Am 8190397
Philippine 8323166
PIA 8183711, Qantas 8159491
Sabena 508636
SAS 887218
Saudia 8187866
Singapore 8188341
Swissair 8188351
Thai 8158421
TWA 502656, United 8185421
Varig 8180442

Transport to City

Taxi: black and gold taxis are air-conditioned and take about 30 minutes to town, cost approximately 100 pesos plus 10%.

Coach: takes 30 minutes to town and leaves every 15-30 minutes; costs 8-10 pesos. Hotels regularly send courtesy coaches to meet flights.

Transit: There is a bus to city (#704) which takes 50 minutes. Leaves every 5 minutes and costs very little.

Facilities

Currency exchange, hotel reservations, bar, restaurant, first aid/medical
Car rental desks: Hertz, Avis, Europcar, Qualitrans

Airport Taxes

Per person: International 200 pesos, domestic 40 pesos

City Information

Weather

The weather is tropical and very hot from March to November, with high humidity and monsoon rains from July to October. April and May are the hottest months. The remaining months are dry, slightly cooler and less humid.
Average temps: Jan 29c (85F) July 32c (90F)

Transportation

Metered taxis are the best method of transportation for visitors. They are also very reasonable but make sure that the meter is being used. Tipping is not customary.
Air-conditioned chauffeur-driven car hire is available but expensive. However, due to inner city driving conditions, it is preferable to self-drive car hire. The adventuresome should have an international driving license.

Car Hire

Hertz, Ayala Ave, Makati
   (tel: 8319827)
Avis, 311 P Casal St (tel: 7410907)
Europcar, 810 Pasay Rd
   (tel: 8171613)
Qualitrans, 3 Chapel Rd, Pasay
   (tel: 8323208/3010)

Hospitals

Medical assistance for travellers at:
Iamat Center, 1148 Roxas Blvd
   (tel: 595256 & 501487)

Trade Fairs

Philippine International Trade
   Fair (Jan)
International Office World
   Exhibition (Feb)
International Aerospace
   Exhibition (Feb)
International Livestock & Poultry
   Fair (Feb)
International Travel Exchange
   Exhibition (Mar)
International Fashion Fair (April)
International Agriculture &
   Aquatic Exhibition (May)
International Book Fair (June)
International Building Equipment
   Exhibition (July)
International Food Equipment &
   Services Exhibition (Aug)

International Transport
Equipment Exhibition (Sept)
International Fashions Fair (Nov)
International Safety & Security
Exhibition (Nov)

Hotels
Holiday Inn Manila, 2702 Roxas
Blvd, Pasay City (tel: 597961)
Hyatt Regency Manila, 2702
Roxas Blvd, Pasay City
(tel: 8312611)
Inter-Continental Manila, Hotel
Drive, Ayala Ave, Makati
(tel: 8159711)
The Mandarin, Makati Ave,
Makati (tel: 8163601)
Manila, Rizal Park on Manila Bay
(tel: 470011)
Manila Hilton International,
United Nations Ave. Ermita
(tel: 573711)
The Manila Peninsula, Corner
Ayala and Makati Aves
(tel: 8193456)
Philippine Plaza, Roxas Blvd
(tel: 8320701)
Philippine Village, Mia Ave,
Manila International Airport
(tel: 8317011)
Silahis International, 1990 Roxas
Boulevard (tel: 573811)

What to See and Do
Visit the modern Cultural
Center, the Design Center, the
Folk Art Museum and the
International Convention Center
on Roxas Boulevard. Nayang
Filipino, a permanent exhibition
of Filipino arts and crafts is near
the airport. Visit Rizal Park and
see the remains of old Manila at
the west end. Shop in Santa

Cruz; visit Ermita for clubs and
hotel entertainment, and
Binondo to see Manila's
Chinatown.

Useful Addresses

Embassies and Consulates
American: 1201 Roxas Blvd,
Makati (tel: 5217116)
Canadian: PAL Bldg., Ayala
Makati (tel: 8159536)
British: 115-117 Esteban St,
Makati (tel: 891051)

Business and Commerce
Central Bank, A. Mabina Corner
Vito Cruz, Malate, Metro
Manila (tel: 507051)
Manila Stock Exchange, Muelle
de la Industria & Prensa Sts
(tel: 471125)
Manila Chamber of Commerce,
410 Shurdut Bldg, Intramuros
American Chamber of
Commerce, P.O. Box 1578,
(tel: 865115)
United Nations Information
Office, PO Box 2149,
(tel: 850611)

Tourism and Travel
Ministry of Tourism, Rizal Park
(tel: 599031)
Philippine Motor Association,
683 Aurora Blvd. Quezon City
(tel: 7215761)
American Express, Grd floor,
Philamlife Bldg, UN Ave.
Ermita (tel: 509601/05)
Thomas Cook, 131 Ayala Ave
(tel: 857173)

ASIA/PACIFIC

SINGAPORE

Essential Information

Type of Government
Parliamentary Democracy

Area
618 sq km

(238.6 sq mi)

Population
2.7 million

Annual Growth Rate
1.2%

Languages

English, Mandarin and other Chinese dialects, Malay, Tamil

Religion

Buddhist, Taoist, Muslim, Hindu, Christian

Ethnic Groups

Chinese 77%, Malays 15%, Indians 6%, others 2%

Weights and Measures

Metric system with Imperial system and other units still in use.

Electrical Current

A.C. 50c 230/400V

Major Business Cities

Singapore (cap) 1,950,000

Currency

1 Singapore Dollar = 100 Cents
Notes 1, 5, 10, 20, 50, 100, 500, 1000 dollars
Coins l, 5, 10, 20, 50 cents

Public Holidays

Singapore has holidays which vary (var) according to the lunar cycle. Check before travelling.
Jan 1 New Year
Feb (var) Chinese New Year
Apr (var) Good Friday
May 1 Labor Day
May (var) Vesak Day
June (var) Eid al-Fitr
Aug 9 National Day
Sept (var) Hari Raya Haji
Nov (var) Deepavali
Dec 25 Christmas

Travellers Information

Entry Requirements

Passport required by all. Visas are not required by citizens of the Commonwealth, or other passport holders for short stays of up to 2 weeks. Extensions and permits can be obtained at the Immigration Department, Empress Place.

Working Restrictions

Work permits can be obtained depending on the nationality of applicant. Inquire at local embassy or consulate.

Vaccination Required

Vaccination certificate required for smallpox, yellow fever or cholera if travelling from infected area. Vaccination for cholera recommended.

Customs and Duty Free

On arrival: 200 cigarets or 50 cigars or 250g/8oz tobacco; 1 liter alcohol; perfume for personal use. Personal effects are allowed in duty-free, but goods from South Africa are prohibited entry.

Currency Restrictions

There are no currency restrictions.

Health Tips

The drinking water is purified in major hotels. Singapore is very clean (with a large fine for throwing rubbish, including cigaret butts, on the street) and is nearly free of all infectious diseases. Many doctors and dentists speak English. The medical care must be paid for, but standards are very high.

Climate and Clothing

It is hot and humid throughout the year with heavy rainfalls, especially from November to January. Lightweight to tropical weight clothing, and an umbrella anytime.

Tipping

Hotels and restaurants add a 10% service charge to their bills. Do not tip taxi drivers. Porters usually get 50 cents per piece of luggage.

Food and Drink

Singapore has almost all types of cuisine including seven different kinds of Chinese, as well as Indian, Malaysian and Indonesian. Chinese dim sum,

Cantonese pork, Indian curries and vegetarian dishes, and Malay and Indonesian satay, nasi and mee goreng are all popular. Western food is also available. Food is sold at outdoor markets which are very clean and hygenic. Fruit drinks made from pineapple, mango and papayo are widely drunk; the Tiger beer is good and the water is purified.

Business Brief

GNP
$21.7 billion
(per capita income $6,526)

Annual Growth Rate
7.9%

Natural Resources
None

Agriculture
Hogs, poultry, orchids, vegetables, fruits

Industry
Petroleum products, electrical and electronic products, shipbuilding and ship repair, food and beverages, textiles and garments

Imports
Total $32.6 billion
Rice, machinery, crude oil, manufactured goods

Exports
Total $28.7 billion
Petroleum products, electrical machinery, telecommunications apparatus, rubber, tin, textiles and garments, ships

Major Trading Partners
Malaysia, US, Japan, UK, China, Hong Kong, Australia, West Germany, Saudi Arabia

Workforce
1 million
Agriculture 1%, industry and commerce 59%, services 34%, government 6%

Tips for Doing Business
A business suit should be worn for government visits although the jacket may be left off for all other calls. Prior appointments are necessary. Import/export businessmen are usually Chinese which means you will probably be entertained in a restaurant. Prepare a toast to your host. If you are invited to a Singapore home, take a small gift of candy or flowers, and remove your shoes if your host does. Send a letter of thanks.

Best Months for Doing Business
Best months are March through November. Local businessmen go on vacation during the remaining three months.

Business Hours

Government
Mon-Fri 0800-1300, 1400-1700
Sat 0800-1300

Business
Mon-Fri 0900-1300, 1400-1700
Sat 0900-1200

Banks
Mon-Fri 1000-1500
Sat 0930-1130

Shops
Mon-Sat 0900-1800
Many shops open on Sunday

English Language Publications
The Strait Times is the daily newspaper for local business-news. The Monitor and Business Times are also daily newspapers, and there are many dailies from England, Hong Kong and Australia.

Telephone and Communications
Telephone country code: 65
Telephone city code: 0
Telex country code: 786
Local calls are free except those made from widely available coin operated public telephones. Telephone directories are issued

ASIA/PACIFIC

yearly and in English. Telex facilities available at major hotels. Public facilities at Telecoms Customer Services centers. Telegrams may also be sent from Telecoms Customer Services centers, from post offices, and from major hotels.

Air Travel
There are no domestic flights. Outgoing travel should be reserved well in advance.

Other Transport
Taxis are widely available and metered. There is a 50% surcharge from 2400-0600 and 50 cents for each adult over 2 passengers. Taxis can be hired for about S$25 an hour. There is an extensive bus service and English-language timetables are available at newsstands. Exact fares required. Regular ferry boat services operate to the islands from the World Trade Center. Charter boats also available. Cruise and tour boats at Clifford Pier. Trishaws are bicycles with sidecars. Negotiate fare. Car hire is available with international driving license: driving is on the left-hand side of the road.

SINGAPORE

Airport Information

Time
GMT +8

Airport
Changi SIN
Tel: 5421122 20 km
(12 mi) E of city

Airlines
Aeroflot 96711
Air France 7376355
Air India 2205277
Air New Zealand 5358266
Alia 2921188
Alitalia 7373166

American 2354924
Avianca 2223222
British Airways 2538444
Canadian International 2221977
Cathay Pacific 5305604
Eastern 3387833
El Al 3387833
Garuda 2502888
JAL 2210522
KLM 7377211
Korean 5342111
Kuwait 5330861
Lufthansa 7379222
Malaysian 3366777
Northwest 3367666
Olympic 2258877
Pan Am 5323833
Philippine 3361611
PIA 7373233
Qantas 7373744
Sabena 2216081
SAS 2251333
Saudia 2355660
Singapore 2238888
Swissair 7378133
Thai 2249977
TWA 7370700
United 2200711
UTA 7376355

Transport to City
Taxi: about S$12 to city center. Taxis are metered and there is always a S$3 surcharge over the amount on the meter with S$1 for each piece of luggage. Passengers wishing to ride alone and not share between 0730-1030, may have to pay an extra charge of S$2: takes 30-45 minutes.
Coach: from 0700-2330 there is a coach which leaves every 20 minutes and costs S$4.
Transit: bus (*390) can be hailed outside terminal building about every 15 minutes; costs S$0.80 and runs from 0600-2345. Takes longer (45-50 minutes) but is an interesting ride for people without a lot of baggage.

Facilities
Bar, buffet, insurance, currency exchange, hotel reservations,

post office, nursery, conference facilities, first aid/medical, vaccinations, shops

Duty-free shop sells cigarets, cigars, tobacco, wines, spirits, lighters, watches, radios. Shop open to arrival passengers; convertible currency and major credit cards accepted.

Car rental desks: Hertz, Avis

Airport Taxes

Per person: International S$12, domestic to Malaysia S$4

City Information

Weather

Tropical with rainfall throughout the year and heavy rains from November to January.

Average yearly temps: Day 30c (87F)

Night 24c (75F)

Transportation

Metered taxis are always available. Be sure the meter is running and that the fare reads S$1.60 when starting. Expect to pay S$1 for each piece of luggage, and a 50% surcharge from 2400-0600. Taxis can be hired by the hour for S$25 per hour. There is an extensive bus network and timetables are available at newsstands. Pay exact fares. Automobiles can be hired with an international driving license. Driving is on the left side of the road. All major credit cards accepted.

Car Hire

Hertz, 150 Orchard Rd
　(tel: 7328228)
Avis, Boon Liew Bldg, Bukit
　Timah Rd (tel: 7377870)

ASIA/PACIFIC

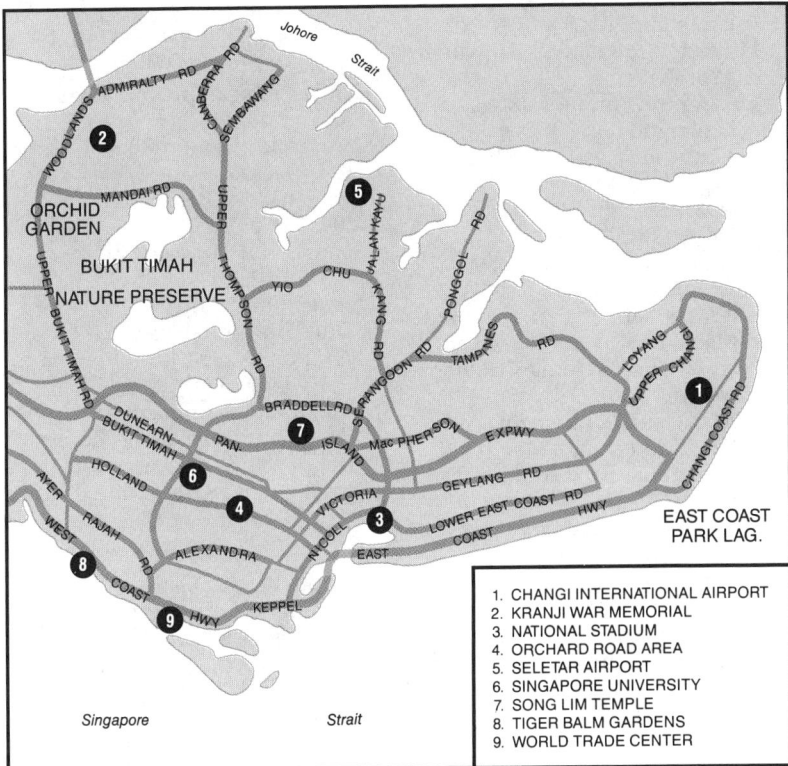

1. CHANGI INTERNATIONAL AIRPORT
2. KRANJI WAR MEMORIAL
3. NATIONAL STADIUM
4. ORCHARD ROAD AREA
5. SELETAR AIRPORT
6. SINGAPORE UNIVERSITY
7. SONG LIM TEMPLE
8. TIGER BALM GARDENS
9. WORLD TRADE CENTER

Singapore

Hospitals

Emergency medical assistance for travellers at:

Gleneagles Hospital (tel: 637222)

Mount Alvernia Hospital (tel: 2538844)

Youngberg Memorial Hospital (tel: 889271)

Trade Fairs

Aerospace Exhibition (Jan)

Petroleum Exhibition (Jan)

Maritime Navigation Exhibition (Feb)

International Construction Exhibition (Feb)

International Water Technology Fair (Feb)

International Glass Manufacture Exhibition (Mar)

International Rubber & Plastics Exhibition (Mar)

Civil Defense Exhibition (Mar)

Singapore Travel Fair (Mar)

Construction Equipment Exhibition (Mar)

Education & Training Exhibition (Apr)

Electronic Communications Exhibition (Apr)

Business Hardware Exhibition (Apr)

International Furniture Exhibition (Apr)

International Food & Hotel Exhibition (May)

International Textile & Garment Machinery Exhibition (May)

International Welding Exhibition (May)

Audio-Visual Equipment Exhibition (June)

International Bank Systems Fair (June)

International Leather Goods Exhibition (June)

International Boats & Equipment Exhibition (June)

Office Automation & Stationary Exhibition (July)

Electronics Production Exhibition (Aug)

Food & Beverage Exhibition (Sept)

International Toy & Gift Fair (Sept)

International Furniture Fair (Oct)

Finance & Investment Exhibition (Oct)

International Transport Equipment Exhibition (Nov)

International Robotics Exhibition (Nov)

International Machine Tool Exhibition (Nov)

Education Exhibition (Dec)

Hotels

Dai-tchi, 81 Anson Rd (tel: 2241133)

Dynasty Singapore, 320 Orchard Rd (tel: 7349900)

Equatorial, 429 Bukit Timah Rd (tel: 7320431)

Goodwood Park, 22 Scotts Rd (tel: 7343706)

Hilton International Singapore, 581 Orchard Rd (tel: 7372233)

Holiday Inn Park View, 11 Cavenagh Rd (tel: 7338333)

Hyatt Regency Singapore, 10-12 Scotts Rd (tel: 7331188)

Mandarin Sngapore, 333 Orchard Rd (tel: 7374411)

Marco Polo, Tanglin Rd (tel: 4747171)

Meridien, 100 Orchard Rd (tel: 7338855)

Miramar, 401 Havelock Rd (tel: 7330222)

Novotel Orchid Inn, 214 Dunearn Rd (tel: 2503322)

Oberoi Imperial, 1 Jalan Rumbia (tel: 7371666)

Pavilion Inter-Continental Singapore, 1 Cuscaden Rd (tel: 7338888)

Sheraton Singapore, Scotts Rd (tel: 7376888)

What to See and Do

Visit the Botanic Gardens, the Zoological Gardens (considered the best in Asia), the Crocodile Farm at 790 Upper Serangoon Road, and Chinatown. The Singapore Handicraft Center in Tanglin has craftsmen from all over Asia; Tiger Balm Gardens on Pasir Pahang Road has displays of China's legends. The Jurong Bird Park is one of the largest in the world. Visit the various Japanese and Chinese gardens for the history of gardening techniques. The National Museum is open daily from 0900-1730. Night-life entertainment is available at the lounges at major hotels.

Useful Addresses

Embassies and Consulates
American: 30 Hill St
(tel: 3380251)
Canadian: Faber House
(tel: 7371322)
British: Tanglin Road
(tel: 4739333)

Business and Commerce
Post Office Information,
(tel: 5330234 & 5324536 & 54493377)
Bank of Singapore, Tong Eng
Bldg, 101 Cecil St 01-02
(tel: 2239266)
Stock Exchange of Singapore,
1603 Hong Leong Bldg, 16
Raffles Quay (tel: 2209455)
Singapore International Chamber
of Commerce, Denmark
House, Raffles Quay
(tel: 2241255)
American Trade Center, 96
Somerset Rd (tel: 373100)
American Chamber of
Commerce, Raffles City Tower
(tel: 3396622)

Tourism and Travel
Singapore Tourist Board, 131
Tudor Court, Tanglin Rd
(tel: 2356611)
Automobile Association of
Singapore, 336 River Valley Rd
(tel: 7372444)
American Express, Holiday Inn
(tel: 375988)
Thomas Cook, 39 Robinson Rd
(tel: 95161)

SOUTH KOREA

Essential Information

Type of Government
Republic

Area
98,500 sq km
(38,000 sq mi)

Population
42 million

Annual Growth Rate
1.6%

Languages
Korean

Religion
Buddhism, Christianity,
Shamanism, Confucianism

Ethnic Groups
Korean, small Chinese minority

Weights and Measures
Metric system is used
commercially but local systems
of measurement are still in use
for some things.

Electrical Current
A.C. 60c 100/220V

Major Business Cities
Seoul (cap) 10,750,000
Pusan 4,250,000
Taegu 2,500,000

Currency
1 Won = 100 Chun
Notes 500, 1000, 5000, 10000 won
Coins 1, 5, 10, 50, 100 won

Public Holidays
Jan 1-3 New Year
Mar 1 Independence Movement
Day
Apr 5 Arbor Day

May 5 Children's Day
Jun 6 Memorial Day
Jul 17 Constitution Day
Aug 15 Liberation Day
Oct 1 Armed Forces Day
Oct 3 National Foundation Day
Oct 9 Alphabet Day
Oct 24 United Nations Day
Dec 25 Christmas

Travellers Information

Entry Requirements

Passport is required by all.
Visa is not always necessary for
visits of less than 5 days
provided onward ticket is
shown. Tourist visas can be
granted for 30 days and then
renewed for another 30 days. For
stays longer than 90 days a visa
is required in advance. Visa
regulations change frequently;
check with travel agent or
consulate before travelling.

Working Restrictions

You need to obtain a work
permit from the Korean embassy
in your own country of
residence.

Vaccination Required

No vaccinations are required but
recommended for cholera,
typhoid, and malaria. A
certificate for cholera may be
required.

Customs and Duty Free

On arrival: 200 cigarets or 50
cigars or 200 g/8oz of tobacco; 2
bottles of alcohol; perfume and
cologne for personal use; gifts of
a value up to 5000 won (more
than 10 of one article subject to
duty). Almost anything
considered to be personal effects
allowed in duty-free. List
valuables, such as cameras,
watches, and typewriters, in
your passport on entry since you
are required to export everything
you bring in. If an item is lost or
stolen during your stay, be
prepared to pay tax and duty on
it.

Currency Restrictions

Import and export of local
currency is illegal. Foreign
currency is unrestricted but must
be declared on arrival and
departure: keep all exchange
receipts.

Health Tips

Outside major hotels, the water
is not safe to drink: be very
careful to use only bottled or
boiled water. It is prudent to
take antimalerial precautions.
Medical personel and hospitals
are of a high standard. Many
hotels have English-speaking
doctors and dentists on call.
Imported pharmaceuticals are
scarce and expensive, and
medical treatment must be paid
for.

Climate and Clothing

The country has four seasons
with a wide range of
temperatures. Winter (December
to February) is dry and very
cold: wear a heavy coat, warm
hat, gloves and appropriate
footwear. Summers (May to
September) are hot and humid:
tropical weight clothing is
necessary, with an umbrella for
July when there are heavy rains.
For the other months, medium
weight clothing with a light coat
is fine.

Tipping

Tipping is not customary: taxi
drivers are never given tips and
waiters, only rarely. Sometimes
500 won is given for small
services, barbers and
hairdressers; bellboys in large
hotels expect 600 won per piece
of luggage. Hotels and
restaurants add 10% service
charge to the bill: do not tip on
top of this. Airport and railway
porters charge a flat rate of 600
won per bag.

Food and Drink

Korean food is usually hot and spicy: kimchi is a spicy pickled dish of chicken, meats, saltfish, cabbage, radish and turnip; bulgogi is marinated and barbecued beef slices; dok is pounded rice cake; kilbichin is steamed beef ribs. Rice is the staple and soups and fish dishes are eaten often. The soups are usually made with garlic and peppers: the fish dishes include abalone and shrimps cooked in chili peppers and mustard, as well as variety of other seafood dishes. Fresh fruit is usually served for dessert. Makkolu is rice wine; junjong a form of saki; and soji a form of vodka. Korean beer is excellent. Western, Chinese and Japanese cuisines are widely available.

Business Brief

GNP
$123 billion

Annual Growth Rate
8%

Natural Resources
Limited coal, tungsten, iron ore, limestone, kaolinite and graphite

Agriculture
Rice, barley, vegetables, fish

Industry
Cement, chemicals, clothing, electronics, footwear, iron and steel, plywood, shipbuilding, textiles, timber

Imports
Total $41 billion
Crude oil, grains, machinery, chemicals and chemical products, base metals and articles, transportation equipment

Exports
Total $47.3 billion
Textiles, transportation equipment, base metals and articles, electrical products, footwear, fish and fish products

Major Trading Partners
US, Japan, Hong Kong, West Germany, UK, Saudi Arabia, Kuwait

Workforce
14.2 million
Agriculture and forestry 53.3%, manufacturing 18%, commerce and other services 28%

Tips for Doing Business
Prior appointments are essential and a conservative business suit should be worn at all times. Shake hands on arrival and departure and have a good supply of business cards with you as these are exchanged and studied at each new meeting. Try to have them printed in both English and Korean: local firms will do this in a couple of days. Korean surnames come first and given names are never used alone in a business situation. Address your contact by his title and surname (i.e. Director Kim). Entertainment is usually done in restaurants with men only. (If invited to a Korean home, take off your shoes). You host will want to get to know you before discussing business. Always pass things and eat with the right hand. Send a note of thanks afterwards. Write it in English since all correspondence, including business, is done in English. Although some of the businessmen may not speak English, there is usually someone in the firm who does; learn a few phrases in Korean anyway. Also, it is greatly appreciated if you familiarize yourself with some of the well-known facts of Korean history and art beforehand. Do not discuss politics, Korea's neighbors or the Korean war.

ASIA/PACIFIC

Best Months for Doing Business

Best months for business travel are February through June, and September, November

Business Hours

Government
Mon-Fri 0900-1200, 1300-1200
Sat 0900-1300
Sunday is the weekly holiday

Business
Mon-Fri 0900-1200, 1300-1800
Sat 0900-1300
Sunday is the weekly holiday

Banks
Mon-Fri 0930-1630
Sat 0930-1300
Sunday is the weekly holiday

Shops
Mon-Fri (department stores) 1030-1930, (small shops) 0800-2200
Half day Saturday
Sunday is the weekly holiday

English Language Publications

Daily: the Korea Herald and the Korea TimesNews are local papers in English. Daily coverage of business is in the China

Telephone and Communications

Telephone country code: 82
Telephone city code: Ichon 32, Pusan 51, Seoul 2, Taegu 53
Telex country code: 787
Telephone service is direct dial. English speaking operators available at major hotels. Public telephone booths are in cafes, stores and restaurants and take a 20 won coin for 3 minutes. Telex facilities available at major hotels: 24 hour service at KTI (Korea National Telegram). Telegrams can be sent from post offices between 0900-1730: there is also an emergency service. Overseas mail should be sent airmail but be aware that it may be opened and censored.

Air Travel

Frequent daily services between Seoul and Pusan, Taegu, Cheju, Ulsan and Kwangju is operated by Korean Air. There are less frequent flights to other centers. For internal flights, no hand baggage is permitted in the cabin and you may be checked for firearms before boarding.

Other Transport

Taxis are plentiful and easy to get at ranks, by telephone or hailing in the street. Between towns, the fare should be negotiated in advance. Chauffeur-driven cars can be hired and, although expensive, preferable for the short-stay visitor than self-drive rental automobiles.
There are several express intercity bus express service linking major centers. Book in advance. Rail service is good. The railway covers the entire length of the country and air-conditioned trains link main centers. Train stations have information clearly marked in English.

SEOUL

Airport Information

Time
GMT +9

Airport
Kimpo International SEL
Tel: 6637185
19 km (12 mi) W of city

Airlines
Air France 75325474
Alitalia 7791676
American 7551345
British Airways 7776871
Canadian International 7538271
Cathay Pacific 7790747

Eastern 7779786
El Al 7783351
Gulf Air 7791676
Iberia 7827461
JAL 7571711
KLM 7531093
Korean 7552221
Kuwait Air 7530041
Lufthansa 7779655
Malaysian 7777761
Northwest 7347800
Pan Am 7578916
Philippine 7251825
Qantas 7776871
Sabena 7780394
SAS 7792621

Saudia 7565621
Singapore 7551226
Swissair 7578901
Thai 7792621
TWA 7774864
United 7571691

Transport to City

Taxi: metered taxis always available. Ride to city takes 30 minutes and costs about $5. After midnight, 20% is added. Have your destination written out in Korean: no tip required. Coach: buses to most major hotels leave every 10 minutes

ASIA/PACIFIC

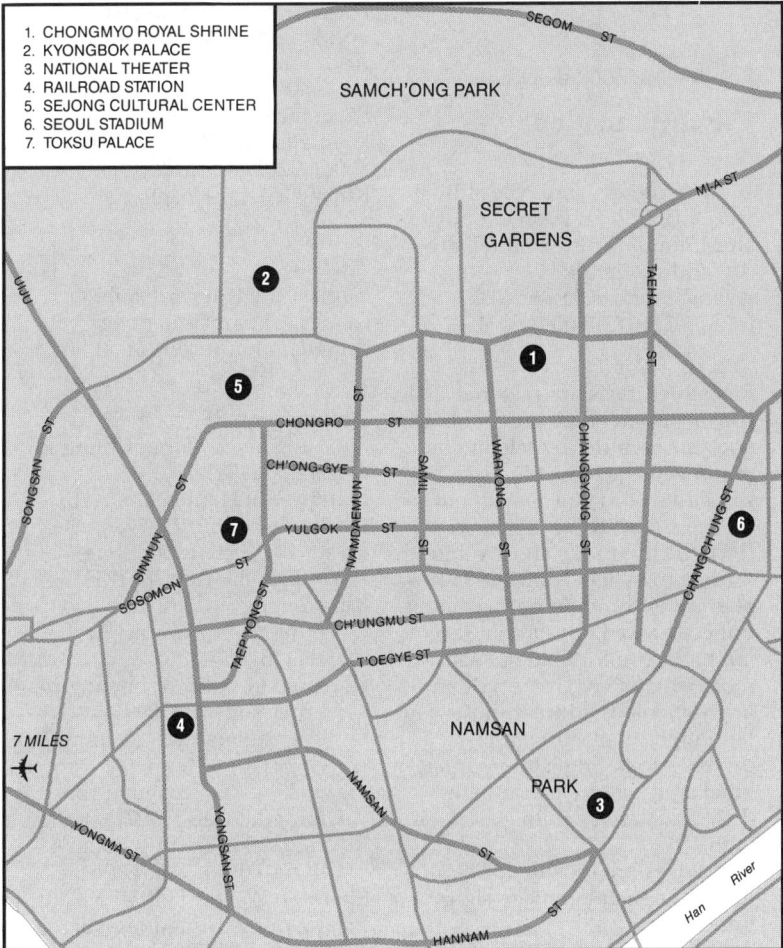

1. CHONGMYO ROYAL SHRINE
2. KYONGBOK PALACE
3. NATIONAL THEATER
4. RAILROAD STATION
5. SEJONG CULTURAL CENTER
6. SEOUL STADIUM
7. TOKSU PALACE

SAMCH'ONG PARK

SEGOM ST

MI-A ST

SECRET GARDENS

TAEHA ST

CHONGRO ST

CH'ONG-GYE ST

WARYONG ST

CHANGGYONG ST

SAMIL ST

NAMDAEMUN ST

YULGOK ST

SONGSAN ST

SINMUN

SOSOMON

TAEPYONG ST

CHANGCH'UNG ST

CH'UNGMU ST

T'OEGYE ST

7 MILES

NAMSAN

NAMSAN

PARK

YONGMA ST

YONGSAN ST

HANNAM

Han River

Seoul

(from 0530-2130) run by Airport Bus Company: approximately $3. Transit: recommended only for those with an adventuresome spirit and little baggage. The #41 bus goes every 5 minutes (0600-2200) from the right of the airport parking lot: costs about $1.

Facilities
Restaurant, bank, hotel reservations, car hire, shops Duty-free shop sells cigarets, cigars, tobacco, liquor, lighters, watches, ginseng, native products, jewellery, perfume Car rental desks: Hertz, Avis, Korean Rent-A-Car

Airport Taxes
Per person: 3000 won

City Information

Weather
Winters are dry and cold, July is wet, and July and August hot and humid. Spring and fall are dry and moderate.
Average temps: Jan 5c (23F) July 25-32c (77-90F)

Transportation
Registered taxis are metered. For the most part, they are plentiful and can be hired by telephone, at ranks or hailed. It is sometimes difficult to get taxis on the street in the center of town. Many ranks are covered to protect travellers from the rain. Sharing is common but tipping is unnecessary. Light-brown taxis are more comfortable but also more expensive. Carry written instructions or address in Korean (although many Korean taxi drivers speak English): your hotel staff will help you with this. Taxis are hard to get late at night.
City buses are crowded. There are no English-language signs or timetables.
An underground system is being built, and a service currently runs from the Seoul Railway Station to Chongnyangni in the northern part of the city.
Car hire is available with an international drivers license, but not recommended for the visitor new to the country.

Car Hire
Hertz, 76-24 Hannam-dong, Yongsan-ku (tel: 7950801)
Avis, 264-2 Hannam-dong (tel: 7981981)
Korean Rent-A-Car, 219 Pyung-dong (tel: 7980801)

Hospitals
Many hotels have English-speaking doctors on call. Additional medical help for the traveller at:
Severance Hospital (English-speaking doctors) (tel: 320171 and 320161)
Korea General Hospital (tel: 758021)

Trade Fairs
Contact the Korean Exhibition Center, 65 Samsung-dong, Gangnam-ku, for information.

Hotels
Ambassador, 186-54 Changchung-dong, Chung-ku (tel: 2751101)
Hilton, 395, Namdaemum-ro, Chung-ku (tel: 7537788)
Hyatt, 747-7 Hannam-dong, Yongsan-ku (tel: 7971234)
King Sejong, 61-3, 2-ka, Chungmu-ro, Chung-ku (tel: 7761811)
Koreana, 61, 1-ka, Taepyung-ro, Chung-ku (tel: 7309911)
Lotte, 1 Sagong-dong, Chung-ku (tel: 77110)
Plaza, 23, 2-ka, Taipyung-ro. Chung-ku (tel: 77122)
Royal, 6, 1-ka, Myung-dong, Chung-ku(tel: 7768171)
Sheraton Walker Hill, 21 Kwang Jang-dong, Sungdong-ku (tel: 4530121)

Shilla, 202, 2-ka, Jangchung-
dong, Chung-ku (tel: 2333131)

What to See and Do

The ruined palace complex in the
center of town contains four
separate palaces: the Changdok
Gung is the most intricate and
best preserved. The National
Museum is also in the complex,
and has art and artifacts from
the Three Kingdom, Silla, Karyo
and Yi Dynasties: the National
Theater and Sejang Cultural
Center have regular
performances of traditional
Korean and Western dance,
drama and music. A one hour
drive along Skyline Drive and
the Nam Sam mountain offers a
spectacular view. A wall once
surrounded Seoul and the eight
gates from that wall still stand.
Visit the Great South Gate and,
nearby, the South Gate Market.
Outside the city, there is a
wooded valley called Upjang,
and gondolas can be hired on
the Hon River.

Useful Addresses

Embassies and Consulates
American: 82 Sejong-ro
(tel: 7322601)

Canadian: 45 Mugyo-dong
(tel: 7764062)
British: 4 Chong-dong
(tel: 7257341)

Business and Commerce
Central Bank (Bank of Korea),
110, 3-ka Namdaemun-ro,
Chung-du (tel: 77107)
Korean Stock Exchange, 1-116,
Yeoudo-dong, Yeongdeungpo-
ku (tel: 7832271)
Korean Exhibition Center, 65
Samsung-dong, Gangnam-ku
(tel: 5622161)
Korean Chamber of Commerce,
111 Sokong-dong, Chung-ku
(tel: 7778031)
American Chamber of
Commerce, Chosun Hotel (tel:
7536471)
American Trade Center, US
Embassy, 82 Sejong-ro
(tel: 7322601)

Tourism and Travel
Korea Tourist Association, 9/F
Kyongwun Bldg, 70
Kyongwun-dong, Chongro-ku
(tel: 7242702)
Korea Automobile Association,
Hanan Bldg 1-150 Yoido-dong
American Express, 57-9
Seosomun Dong (tel: 7779921)

ASIA/PACIFIC

TAIWAN

Essential Information

Type of Government
One-party system

Area
35,981 sq km
(14,000 sq mi)

Population
19.6 million

Annual Growth Rate
1.38%

Languages
Mandarin Chinese (official),
Taiwanese, Hakka

Religion
Confucianism, Buddhism,
Taoism, Christianity

Ethnic Groups
Han Chinese 98%, aborigines
less than 2%

Weights and Measures
Metric system with some Chinese units still in use.

Electrical Current
A.C. 60c 110V

Major Business Cities
Taipei (cap) 2,975,000
Kaohsiung 1,550,000
Taichung 725,000
Tainan 700,000

Currency
New Taiwan Dollar = 100 cents
Notes 10, 50, 100, 500, 1000 dollars
Coins 1, 5, 10 dollars

Public Holidays
The dates of many holidays in Taiwan vary (var) slightly from year to year. Check carefully before travelling.
Jan 1-2 Founding of Republic of China
Feb (var) Chinese New Year
Mar (var) Youth Day
Apr (var) Ching Ming Festival
Jun (var) Dragon Boat Festival
Sept 18 Mid-autumn
Sept (var) Confucious's Birthday
Oct 10 Double Tenth National Day
Oct (var) Taiwan Restoration Day
Oct (var) Veteran's Day
Oct 31 Chiang Kai Shek's Birthday
Nov 12 Dr Sun Yat-Sen's Birthday
Dec 25 Constitution Day

Travellers Information

Entry Requirements
Passport (good for at least 6 more months) is required by all. Visa (tourist, transit or entry) required by all: obtain beforehand at local Republic of China consulate or embassy as visas cannot be given on arrival.

Vaccination Required
Vaccination certificate required for cholera if travelling from infected area.

Customs and Duty Free
On arrival: 200 cigarets or 25 cigars or 250g/8oz tobacco; 1 bottle alcohol. Personal effects are allowed in duty free. Prohibited are any articles made in China, narcotics, gambling aids or games, explosives and firearms. Declare gold and silver ornaments. No more than 2 ounces of additional silver or gold may be taken out.

Currency Restrictions
Import of foreign currency is unrestricted and the amount declared on entry can be taken out. Only NT$1000 dollars may be brought in, and no more than NT$2000 taken out.

Health Tips
Drink only bottled or distilled water. Foreigners must pay for medical services. Some doctors and dentists speak English. Imported pharmaceuticals are scarce and expensive.

Climate and Clothing
Subtropical climate with hot, humid and rainy summers (April through October) calling for tropical weight clothes and umbrella: winters are cool with some rain. Wear medium weight clothes, coat and umbrella.

Tipping
Hotels and restaurants add a service charge of 10%. Tip porters NT$20 per bag; small services NT$10-20. Do not tip taxi drivers.

Food and Drink
Much of the local cuisine is based on Cantonese cooking. Seafood dishes are very popular and large banquets featuring many courses occur frequently in all restaurants. Large hotels have a choice of different styles of cooking, including Western, and

beer and tea are common beverages. Try to eat Chinese food with chopsticks whenever possible.

Business Brief

GNP
$44.3 billion
(per capita income $2,294)

Annual Growth Rate
10.9%

Natural Resources
Small deposits of coal, natural gas, limestone, marble, and asbestos

Agriculture
Sugar cane, lumber, sweet potatoes, rice, asparagus, mushrooms, citrus fruits, pineapples, bananas, peanuts, pears

Industry
Textiles, footwear, electronics, plastics, cement, furniture, other consumer goods, iron, steel, petrochemicals

Imports
Total $19.9 billion
Food raw materials, crude oil, chemicals, pharmaceuticals, capital goods

Exports
Total $30.2 billion
Textiles, machinery, plastics, metal products, plywood, canned food

Major Trading Partners
US, Japan, Hong Kong, West Germany, Australia, Canada, Thailand, Singapore, Saudi Arabia, South Korea, Kuwait

Workforce
7.5 million

Agriculture
20%, industry and commerce 41%, services 32%, civil administration 7%

Tips for Doing Business
A lightweight conservative business suit should be worn on all occasions. Make prior appointments for all visits. Business cards are exchanged at every introduction and should be printed in both Mandarin and English: local firms will do this in several days. Although some English is spoken, it is best to hire a translator for important discussions. Chinese businessmen take time to make decisions but once a verbal contract is agreed upon it is as good as a written one. You may be entertained with a banquet at a Chinese restaurant. Use chopsticks. Eat something of every course and prepare a short speech in case you have to return a toast to the host. Do not discuss Mainland China, and always refer to Taiwan as the Rupublic of China. Gifts are commonly given: Scotch whisky is good for men, French perfume for their wives.

Best Months for Doing Business
The best months are April through September. At other times, avoid the two weeks before and after the Chinese New Year in January or February. Check dates of holidays before visiting as they change yearly according to the lunar cycle.

Business Hours

Government
Mon-Fri 0830-1230, 1330-1730
Sat 0830-1230

Business
Mon-Fri 0830-1230, 1330-1230
Sat 0830-1230

Banks
Mon-Fri 0900-1530
Sat 0900-1200

Shops
Mon-Sat 0900-2100/2200

ASIA/PACIFIC

English Language Publications

China Post and China News are local papers in English. Daily coverage of business is in the China Post.

Telephone and Communications

Telephone country code: 886
Telephone city code: Koohsiung 7, Taichung 42, Taipei 2
Telex country code: 785
The telephone system is 100% automatic and direct overseas telephone call from Taipei can be made to most non-Communist countries. Telex and telegram services are available at major hotels. Telegram service (24 hours) also available at General Post Office, Chung Hsiao Road in Taipei.

Air Travel

China Airlines and Far East Air Transport have a number of flights which connect main centers.

Other Transport

Apart from air, the best forms of domestic travel are by bus or rail. Bus service is extensive with express service linking major centers. Book in advance. Rail service is good. The railway covers the entire length of the country and air-conditioned trains link main centers. Train stations have information clearly marked in English.

TAIPAI

Airport Information

Time
GMT +8

Airport
Chiang Kai Shek International
TPE
Tel: 832001
40 km (25 mi) SW of city

Airlines

Air Canada 5811133
Alitalia 77290206
American 5631200
Avianca 5116341
British Airways 5423111
Canadian International 5033030
Cathay Pacific 7128228
China 7151212
Continental 7152766
El Al 5631200
Eastern 5423111
JAL 5519121
KLM 7171000
Korean 5214242
Lufthansa 5034114
Malaysian 7168384
Northwest 7161555
Olympic 3513302
Pan Am 5615900
Philippine 5214101
Qantas 5212311
SAA 5366445
Sabena 7131900
SAS 7154622
Singapore 5516655
Swissair 5811133
Thai 7154622
TWA 5923911
United 7358868

Transport to City

Taxi: metered taxis service the airport but charge 50% more than the amount shown.
Coach: Air-conditioned cars carry 4 passengers, take 40-50 minutes from outside arrival lounge. Pay before boarding; about US$2-4. There are two routes which run from 0700-2330. There are also a number of hotel courtesy coaches which meet flights.
Transit: a local bus runs from corner outside arrival h all every 15 minutes from 0600-2230 and costs under US$1. Does not run on Sundays or holidays but it is an interesting way to get into town.

Facilities

Currency exchange, hotel reservations, baggage deposit, post office, bar, restaurant, shops, conference facilities, barber shop

Duty-free shop sells cigarets, cigars, tobacco, wines, spirits, lighters, watches, jewellery, glass and china. Most convertible currencies accepted including Australian, Canadian, Japanese, British and US.

Airport Taxes
Per person: International NT$150

City Information

Weather
It is hot and humid with frequent rainfalls between April and October, and cool to chilly between November and March. Average temps: Jan 12c (54F) July 27c (80F)

Transportation
Meter taxis are available but you should have your destination and your return address written

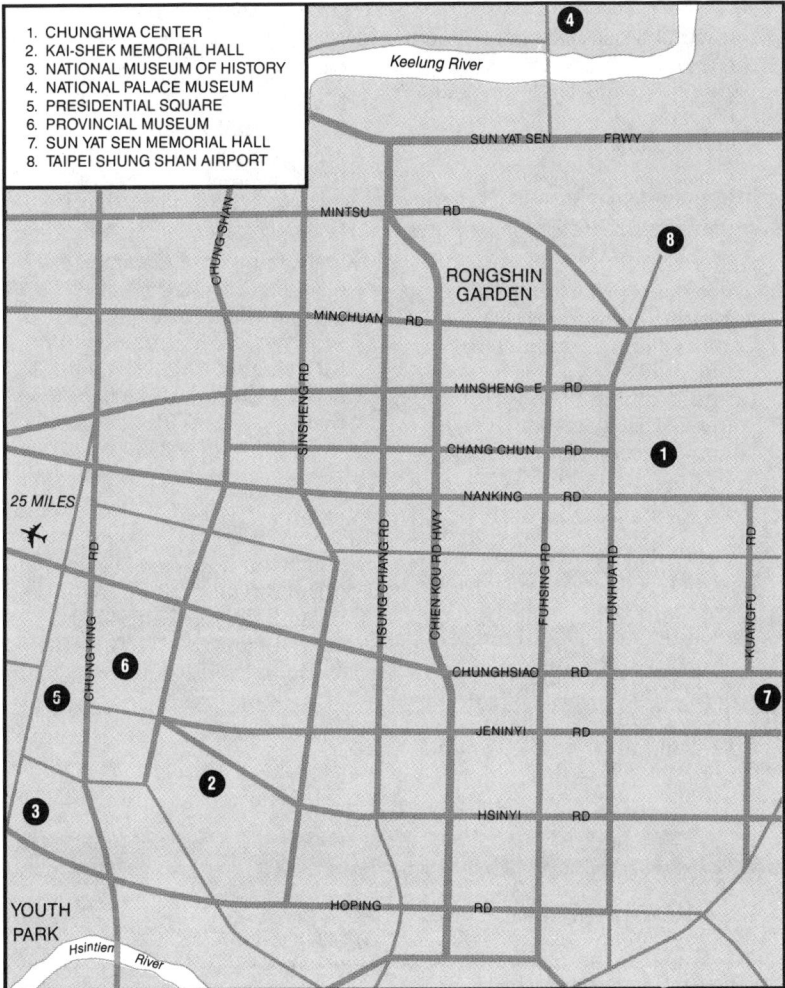

1. CHUNGHWA CENTER
2. KAI-SHEK MEMORIAL HALL
3. NATIONAL MUSEUM OF HISTORY
4. NATIONAL PALACE MUSEUM
5. PRESIDENTIAL SQUARE
6. PROVINCIAL MUSEUM
7. SUN YAT SEN MEMORIAL HALL
8. TAIPEI SHUNG SHAN AIRPORT

Keelung River

SUN YAT SEN FRWY

MINTSU RD

CHUNG SHAN

RONGSHIN GARDEN

MINCHUAN RD

SINSHENG RD

MINSHENG E RD

CHANG CHUN RD

NANKING RD

25 MILES

HSIUNG CHIANG RD

CHIEN KOU RD HWY

FUHSING RD

TUNHUA RD

KUANGFU RD

CHUNGKING RD

CHUNGHSIAO RD

JENINYI RD

HSINYI RD

YOUTH PARK

HOPING RD

Hsintien River

Taipei

out in Chinese to show the driver. Although tipping is not common, small change is appreciated. You can rent cars but the traffic is ferocious and hired chauffeur-driven cars are recommended.

Hospitals
Medical assistance for travellers at:
Mackay Memorial Hospital (tel: 553222)
Taiwan Adventist (tel: 7718151)
Taiwan Chung Hsing hospital (tel: 545641)

Trade Fairs
Industrial Machinery Exhibition (Apr)
Automotive and Cycle Exhibition (May)
Building Materials Exhibition (May)
International Computer Exhibition (June)

Hotels
Ambassador, 63 Chung Shan North Rd, (tel: 5511111)
Century Plaza, 132 Omei St. (tel: 3113131)
Grand, l Chung Shan North Rd (tel: 5965565)
Hilton International Taipei, 38 Chung-Hsiao West Rd. (tel: 3115151)
Hyatt Regency, 420 Keelung Rd (tel: 7542764)
Imperial, 600 Lin Shen North Rd. (tel: 5963333)
Lai Lai Sheraton, 12 Chung Hsiao East Rd. (tel: 3215511)
Mandarin, 166 Tun Hwa North Rd (7121201)
President Hotel, 9 Teh Hwei St. 104, (tel: 5951251)

Taipei Regency, 116 Jen Ai Rd (tel: 7059161)

What to See and Do
The National Palace Museum has more than 300,000 priceless Chinese artifacts: exhibitions change every 3 months and it takes 10 years to show the entire exhibit. Visit the Confucius Shrine, Yangmingshan Park, Botanical Garden, new Pei Tou Hot Spring and Wulai waterfall. At night, go to Lungshan Temple and Snake Alley in the old part of Taipei.

Useful Addresses

Business and Commerce
Central Bank of China, 2 Roosevelt Dr (tel: 3936161)
Taiwan Stock Exchange, 85 Yen-ping South Rd (tel: 3969271)
Taiwan General Chamber of Commerce, 162 Hsin Yi Rd (tel: 7080350)
Taipei Chamber of Commerce, 72 Nanking East (tel: 5318219)
American Chamber of Commerce, 96 Chung Shan N Rd (tel: 5512515)
American Consulate, Hsin Yi Road (tel:7092000)

Tourism and Travel
Taiwan Visitors Association, 111 Minchuan E Rd (tel: 5943261)
Tourism Bureau, 280 Chung Hsiao E Rd (tel: 7218540/1)
American Express, 214 Tun Hwa N. Rd (tel: 7152400)

THAILAND

Essential Information

Type of Government
Constitutional monarchy

Area
514,000 sq km
(198,5000 sq mi)

Population
54.7 million

Annual Growth Rate
2.0%

Languages
Thai, ethnic and regional dialects

Religion
Buddhist 95.5%, Muslim 4%, other 0.5%

Ethnic Groups
Thai 75%, Chinese 14%, other 11%

Weights and Measures
Metric system (local units also in use)

Electrical Current
A.C. 50c 220/380V

Major Business Cities
Bangkok (cap) 5,950,000
Chiengmai 1,250,000
Thonburi 975,000

Currency
1 Baht = 100 Satangs
Notes 10, 20, 100, 500 baht
Coins 25, 50 satang, 1, 5 baht

Public Holidays
Many Buddhist holidays are determined by the lunar cycle and change yearly. Check before travelling.
Jan 1 New Year
Apr 6 Shakri
Apr 13 Songkran
May 5 Coronation
Aug 12 Queen's Birthday
Oct 23 Chulalongkorn
Dec 5 King's Birthday
Dec 10 Constitution
Dec 31 New Year's Eve

Travellers Information

Entry Requirements
A passport is required by all. Visas are not required by nationals of non-Communist countries provided stay is for less than 15 days. Businessmen anticipating a longer stay should apply for a business visa from a local Thai embassy or consulate before travelling.

Vaccination Required
Vaccinations are required for typhoid, yellow fever and cholera if travelling from infected area. Take antimalarial precautions particularly if going to rural areas.

Customs and Duty Free
On arrival: 200 cigarets or 50 cigars or 250g/8 oz of tobacco; 1 liter spirits. Personal effects are allowed in duty free. The import of narcotics or narcotic medicines is strictly prohibited as is pornography, anything from South Africa, and firearms.

Currency Restrictions
There is no limit on amount of foreign currency you can bring in but declare it on arrival and save exchange receipts. Exchange only at authorized banks and dealers. No more than 500 baht can be imported or exported.

Health Tips
Take antimalarial pills. Drink only boiled and filtered water, and avoid any contact with tap water, milk and milk products, and meat which is not well cooked. Avoid raw fruits and vegetables unless they have been washed or peeled.

Climate and Clothing
Wear tropical weight clothes between March and October and carry an umbrella between June and October (monsoon season) as it rains heavily in the afternoons. Lightweight clothes are fine from November to February when it is cooler and dryer.

Tipping
There is usually a 10-15% service charge added to hotel and restaurant bills. Do not tip taxi

ASIA/PACIFIC

drivers. Small services, 5-10 baht.

Food and Drink

Thai food uses chili peppers in varying degrees and can be spicy to very hot. A variety of rices fried with pork, fish or chicken (called khow pat) and tom yam soup (spicy peppered lemon soup) are popular. Local specialties include Thai curries, satay, noodles, and sweet and sour vegetables. Fresh fruit and fruit drinks, coconut milk puddings, and sweet rice with fruit are common desserts. Japanese, Chinese, Korean and Western food are all readily available. Try some Singka (Thai beer) and Mekong whisky, two favorite Thai drinks.

Business Brief

GNP
$46.6 billion
(per capita income $894)

Annual Growth Rate
6%

Natural Resources
Tin, rubber, natural gas, timber, fisheries products, tungsten

Agriculture
Rice, corn, sugarcane, tapioca

Industry
Textiles, agricultural processing, wood products, tin and tungsten mining

Imports
Total $12.9 billion
Petroleum, machinery, food, capital equipment, fertilizer, chemicals

Exports
Total $11.7 billion
Rice, rubber, tin, tapioca, shrimp, corn, sugar

Major Trading Partners
US, Japan, Malaysia, Hong Kong, Singapore, West Germany, Great Britain, Netherlands, Taiwan, Saudi Arabia

Workforce
25 million
Agriculture 73%, industry and commerce 11%, services 10%, government 6%

Tips for Doing Business
For government visits, wear a conservative business suit. For other visits a white shirt, tie and trousers will do. Prior appointments are necessary for government and large company visits. Much of the import/export business is conducted by the Chinese so it is a good idea to get business cards printed in English, Thai and Mandarin. Local printers can do it in a couple of days. Thai businessmen do not like to be rushed and you may need more than one appointment before a deal is set. English is widely spoken and the term "Nai" (pronounced khun) along with the persons first name is how to address a Thai businessman. Never sit with your legs crossed or the soles of your feet showing as this is considered extremely offensive. Dress moderately, speak softly and don't act in a dramatic or effusive manner. Never touch anyone's head as this is considered to be where the soul resides. You will probably not be invited to a Thai home, but if you are, take your shoes off before entering.

Best Months for Doing Business
For good weather, travel from November through March. Check holiday times before visiting, avoid the weeks before and after Christmas, and the months of April and May when most Thai businessmen take their vacations.

Business Hours

Government
Mon-Fri 0830-1630

Business
Mon-Fri 0800-1700

Banks
Mon-Fri 0830-1530

Shops
Mon-Sat 0830-1800/1900

English Language Publications
The Bangkok Post (morning),
The Nation Review (morning),
and the Banghok World
(evening) are main English
language newspapers.

Telephone and Communications
Telephone country code: 66
Telephone city code: Bangkok 2
Telex country code: 788
The telephone system is being
redone, and telephone numbers
are being changed all over
Banghok. If you have difficulty
getting calls to connect properly,
ask hotel staff to help you as
there is a constantly updated
directory assistance service.
Public international telephones
are at Central General Post
Office. Telex facilities available at
General Post Office, and
telegram/cable services at hotels,
GPO, or telegraph offices.

Air Travel
Major centers are connected by
frequent flights operated by Thai
Airways.

Other Transport
There are good roads and
modern highways, but travel by
bus is not highly recommended.
Much better is the extensive rail
service which connects almost all
main centers. There are three
classes: choose first-class.
Express services often include
air-conditioning, sleepers, and
dining cars.

BANGKOK

Airport Information

Time
GMT +7

Airport
Bangkok International (Don
Muang) BKK
Tel: 5237222 and 5236201
22 km
(12 mi) N of city

Airlines
Aeroflot 2336965
Air France 2339477
Air India 2569614
Air New Zealand 2335900
Alitalia 2345253
British Airways 2368655
CAAC 2356510
Cathay Pacific 2336105
China 2521748
Eastern 2511977
Egyptair 2337601
Garuda 2330981
Gulf Air 2355605
Iberia 2526112
Iraqi 2330569
JAL 2349113
KLM 2355150
Korean 2349283
Kuwait Air 2515855
Lufthansa 2341350
Malaysian 2364705
Northwest 2534822
Pan Am 2514521
Philippine 2332350
PIA 2342961
Qantas 2360102
Sabena 2332020
SAS 2538333
Saudia 2357930
Singapore 2360440
Swissair 2332935
Thai 2333810
TWA 2337290
United 2530558
UTA 2360158

Transport to City
Taxi: there are air-conditioned
taxis operated by Thai Airways
International Limousine Service

ASIA/PACIFIC

and bearing their logo which run 24 hours, take 20 minutes to city, cost about $12 and take up to 4 people. Buy ticket at counter outside customs hall. No tipping or extra charges.

Coach: a coach leaves every 20 minutes from 0600-2100 (every 30 minutes from 2100-midnight), and a bus run by Thai Airways International goes from outside main terminal to downtown terminal. Air-conditioned with room for baggage. Buy ticket (about $3-4) at booth outside customs hall. Takes 20 minutes. Do not use unauthorized taxis or guide services.

Transit: train leaves every 40 minutes for Bangkok Railway station from 0300-2000.

Facilities

Currency exchange, hotel reservations, baggage deposit, post office, bar, restaurant, limousine and taxi booking service, barber shop, vaccination center, shops

Duty free shop sells cigarets, cigars, tobacco, wines, spirits, aperitifs, lighters, watches, Thai silk, local crafts. Most convertible currencies accepted. There is also a duty-free shop at city terminal which accepts local currency.

Car rental desks: Hertz, Avis

Airport Taxes

Per person: International 120 baht, domestic 60 baht

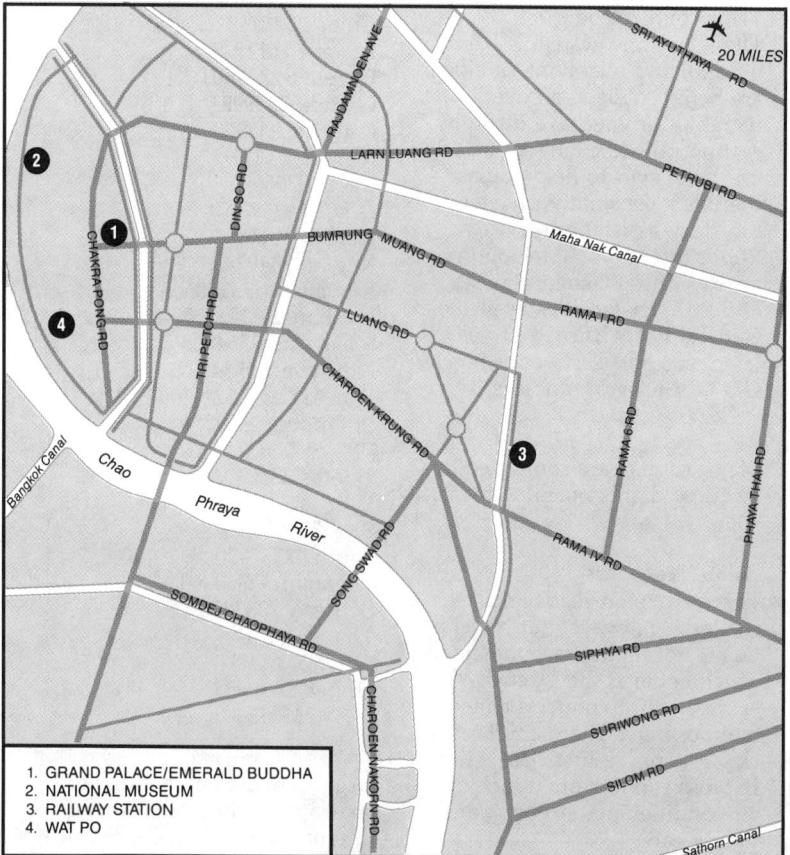

1. GRAND PALACE/EMERALD BUDDHA
2. NATIONAL MUSEUM
3. RAILWAY STATION
4. WAT PO

Bangkok

City Information

Weather

The climate is tropical monsoon with high humidity: hot from March to May; hot and wet from June to October: cool November to February.
Average temps: Jan 18c (65F) July 28c (83F)

Transportation

Taxis have yellow license plates. They are metered but you should still agree on the fare in advance. Have the name and address of your destination written out in Thai: your hotel staff will be glad to do this. Air-conditioned chauffeur-driven limousines are available through the hotels but are more expensive than taxis. Tipping is purely optional and is not commonly done. There is car hire available but driving in Bangkok is crowded, difficult, and on the left.

Car Hire

Hertz, (Lumpini International Rent-a-Car) 1620 New Petchluiri Rd (tel: 2524903)
Avis, 981 Silom Rd (tel: 2354309)
Sintat Rent-a-Car, 16 N Sathorn Rd (tel: 2330397)

Hospitals

Health treatment must be paid for. Emergency medical assistance for travellers at:
Adventist Hospital (tel: 2811026)
Christian Hospital (tel: 2336981)
Ambulance (tel: 2811544)
Emergency (tel: 123191)

Trade Fairs

International Office Equipment Exhibition (Nov)
International Telecommunications Exhibition (Nov)
International Environmental Exhibition (Nov)
International Power Generators Exhibition (Nov)

Hotels

Ambassador, 171 Sukhumvit Rd (tel: 2540444)
Dusit Thani, 946 Rama IV Road (tel: 2331130)
Erawan Hotel, 494 Rajadamri Rd (tel: 2529100)
Hilton International Bangkok, Nai Lert Park, 2 Wireless Rd. (tel: 2530123)
Hyatt Central Plaza Bankok, 1695 Phaholyothin Rd. Bangkhen (tel: 5411234)
Indra Regent, Rajaprarob Rd (tel: 2520111)
Mandarin, 662 Rama IV Rd (tel: 2334980)
Menam Hotel, 2074 New Yannawa (tel: 2891148-9)
Montien Hotel, 54 Suriwongse Rd (tel: 2348060)
Narai Hotel, 222 S Dilom Rd (tel: 2333350)
Oriental, 48 Oriental Ave (tel: 2630400)
Siam Inter-Continental, Srapatum Palace Property, 967 Rama 1 Rd (tel: 2530355)

What to See and Do

There are some fascinating places to visit in Bangkok in spite of its sprawling, Westernized appearance. Go to the Grand Palace and Temple of the Emerald Buddha, a group of temples inside the walls of the old Royal Palace. Nearby in the Wat Po temple is the famous giant reclining buddha; the Golden Buddha (5 tonnes of solid gold) is in Wat Grimir. Other temples worth visiting are Wat Arun and Wat Sraket which have good views of the city. See the canals by boat, and book tours of the countryside by boat at Soi Ekami bridge off Sukhumvit. Visit the National Museum, and Jim Thompson's House for a fascinating display of Asian art. Outside the city is Rose Garden where there are displays of Thai dancing and boxing as well as elephant rides. The main shopping areas are Suriwong and Silom Rd: Thai silks and cottons are famous, bronze items and carved screens are popular and there are any number of shops selling precious and semi-precious stones. You can also attend the Weekend Market in the Promenade Ground near the Grand Palace. Remember that law forbids the export of religious artifacts and antiques.

Useful Addresses

Embassies and Consulates
American: 95 Wireless Rd (tel: 2525040)
Canadian: 138 Silom Rd (tel: 2341561)
British: Wireless Rd (tel: 2527161)

Business and Commerce
General Post Office, New Rd (tel: 2331050)
Central Bank, Bank of Thailand, Sam Sen Rd (tel: 2823322)

Stock Exchange, Securities Exchange of Thailand, Wireless Road (tel: 2500001)
Thai Chamber of Commerce, 150 Rajabornphit Rd, Wat Rajabornphit Phra Nakhom (tel: 2216532)
American Chamber of Commerce, Shell Bldg, 140 Wireless Rd (tel: 2519266)
British Chamber of Commerce, Rm 206, Bangkok Insurance Bldg, 302 Silom Rd (tel: 2341140/69)
United Nations Information Office, Sala Santitham (tel: 818987)

Tourism and Travel
Tourist Organizations of Thailand, Mansion 2 Rajadamnern Ave (tel: 2213351)
Royal Automobile Association of Thailand, 1174 Raholyothin Rd (tel: 5790430)
American Express, S.E.A. Tours, 965 Rama 1 Rd, Siam Center Rm 414 (tel: 2514862/9)

Europe

Essential Information

Type of Government
Federal republic

Area
83,849 sq kms
(32,374 sq mi)

Population
7.6 million

Annual Growth Rate
0.1%

Languages
German 95%

Religion
Roman Catholic 85%

Ethnic Groups
German 98%, Croatian, Slovene

Weights and Measures
Metric

Currency
A.C. 50c 220/380 V

Major Business Cities
Vienna (cap) 1.7 million
Graz 255,000
Linz 210,000
Salzburg 145,000

Currency
1 Austrian Schilling = 100
    Groschen
Coins 1, 2, 5, 10 and 50
    groschen; 1, 5, 10, 25, 50
    schilling
Notes 20, 50, 100, 500 and 1,000
    schilling

Public Holidays
Jan 1 New Year's Day
Jan 6 Epiphany
Apr 13-20 Easter Week
May 1 State Holiday
May 28 Ascension
June 21 Corpus Christi
Aug 15 Maria Ascension
Oct 26 State Holiday
Dec 8 Conception
Dec 25, 26 Christmas

Travellers Information

Entry Requirements
Passport required for everyone
except EEC nationals who only
need a national identity card.
Visa required for visitors from
East Germany, USSR,
Czechoslovakia, and some
African and Asian countires. No
visa is required for others for a
three month stay; for nationals
of Great Britain, a six month
stay.

Working Restrictions
Work permits are needed for all
kinds of employment and are
never issued for part-time jobs.

Vaccination Required
Vaccination certificates required
only if travelling from infected
areas.

Customs and Duty Free
On arrival: 200 cigarettes or 50
cigars or 250 g tobacco; 2 liters
wine; 1 liter spirits; 50 ml
perfume. If arriving from outside
Europe, the cigaret and tobacco
allowance is double.

Currency Restrictions
No restrictions on amount of
Austrian or foreign currency
taken into country. Up to 15,000
schillings in Austrian and 26,000
schillings in foreign currency
may be taken out.

Health Tips
The water is purified everywhere
and in Vienna the water is piped
in from mountain springs. The
standard of medical care is very
high, and pharmacies are well
stocked. Foreigners must pay, so
check out private health
insurance before travelling.

Climate and Clothing
Moderate climate. Wide
variations in temperatures
according to the altitude, with

generally warm summers and cold winters. November to April is cold -1C (30F) with snow and rain. Medium to heavy weight clothes are necessary, as is an overcoat and overshoes or snowboots. May to October is warm and sunny 19C (67F). Wear lightweight clothes, including some sweaters and light woolens at night.

Tipping

Generally tipping of 10-15% is customary. In hotels and restaurants this is usually included in the bill, but an additional 5% for the staff is appreciated. Taxis, 15%. Give porters 5 schillings per piece of luggage, and chambermaids 5 schillings per day. For small services, doormen, room service, ushers, attendants, 5 schillings is also usual.

Food and Drink

The typical Austrian diet is very similar to that of Germany. The breakfast meal is very light with coffee and a roll, and possibly an egg, meat or cheese. Lunch and dinner are large meals which may begin with soup (goulash), and then mainly meat and potatoes.

Specialties include Wiener Schnitzel (veal snitzel in the style of Vienna), cured meats and sausages, and the famous Viennese pastries such as Apple Strudel, Sacher Torte chocolate cake, and pastries of all kinds topped with whipped cream. Austrian beer is a favourite drink, as are the very good white wines from the Grinzing wine region near Vienna.

Business Brief

GDP
$64.90 billion

Annual Growth Rate
0.1%

Natural Resources
Iron ore, petroleum, timber, magnesite, aluminum, coal, lignite, cement, copper

Agriculture
Livestock, forest products, grains, sugar beets, potatoes

Industry
Iron, steel, chemicals, consumer goods

Imports
Total $32.7 billion
Machinery, vehicles, chemicals, iron and steel, fuels

Exports
Total $27.2 billion
Iron and steel products, timber, paper, textiles, construction and industrial machinery, chemical products

Major Trading Partners
West Germany, Switzerland, Italy, Britain, U.S., Sweden, Netherlands, France, Iraq, USSR

Workforce
3.4 million
Industry 49%, agriculture 18%, commerce and service 33%

Tips for Doing Business
Austrians like to be addressed by their titles and familiarity with names is frowned upon. When you are introduced to people, call them Fraulein, Frau or Herr plus their surnames. Find out the rank or degree of business associates and address them accordingly (i.e. Herr or Frau Doktar) which will also do if you speak to an official and do not know his title. It is important to shake hands and exchange a few pleasantries before entering into a meeting; shake hands in order of importance. English is spoken in most business circles. Wear a conservative business suit at all times and make appointments in advance. If invited to a businessman's home, bring

flowers. Avoid the subject of politics and show an appreciation for the wealth of Austrian music, particularly that of Mozart.

Best Months for Doing Business
February to April and September to November are the best months for business travel. Avoid the weeks before and after Christmas and Easter and the summer months when most businessmen take their vacations.

Business Hours

Government
Mon-Fri 0800-1600
Saturday and Sunday are the weekly holidays

Business
Mon-Fri 0800-1600
Saturday and Sunday are the weekly holidays

Banks
Mon-Fri 0800-1230 and 1330-1530 (1730 on Thurs)
Saturday and Sunday are the weekly holidays

Shops
Mon-Fri 0800-1800
Half-day on Sat

English Language Publications
Many English-language newspapers and periodicals are available in the major cities. Die Presse is the daily newspaper for business coverage.

Telephone and Communications
Telephone country code: 43
Telephone city codes: Graz 03-16, Innsbruck 052-22, Salzburg 06-22, Vienna 02-22
Telex country code: 847
Telephone and telegraph services are efficient. It is better to make long distance calls from your hotel or a post office, as most public phone boxes are available only for local calls.
Telex is widely used by Austrian firms. Many hotels have facilities available to guests. Public telex facility available at trade fairs and conferences.
Telegram service is available at any post office.

Air Travel
Austrian Air Services and Tyrolean Airways have regular flights between Vienna and Graz, Linz, Lagenfurt, Innsbruck and Salzburg, as well as between Graz and Innsbruck, Salzburg and Klagenfurt.

Other Transport
Car rental is readily available at airports and in major cities. It is mandatory to wear seatbelts. International driving license, or foreign with German translation. The Austrian Federal Railways system of 6000 km of track is extremely clean, efficient and always on time.

VIENNA

Airport Information

Time
GMT +1
GMT +2 (Apr-Sept)

Airports
Schwechat International VIE
Tel: (0222) 77700
18 km (11 mi) E of city

Airlines
Aer Lingus 318494
Aeroflot 521501
Air Canada 567474
Air France 526655
Alia 723242
Alitalia 651707
Austrian 6800
British Airways 657691
Canadian International 757575
Egyptair 5519143
El Al 524561
Finnair 5875548
Iberia 567636

JAL 655738
KLM 5121604
Korean 568101
Kuwait 561410
Lufthansa 58835
Northwest 528709
Olympic 577623
Pan Am 526646
Philippine 520250
Qantas 577771
Sabena 5873506
SAS 51311050
Singapore 7134656
Swissair 658996

TWA 562200
Varig 5879588

Transport to City
Taxi: Mazur Airport Service
charges a flat rate of about 320
schillings ($25) per passenger
plus S10-20 per bag.
Takes 20-30 minutes to city
center. Other taxis cost about
double, but a fare should be
agreed on before travelling.
Tip 10%.

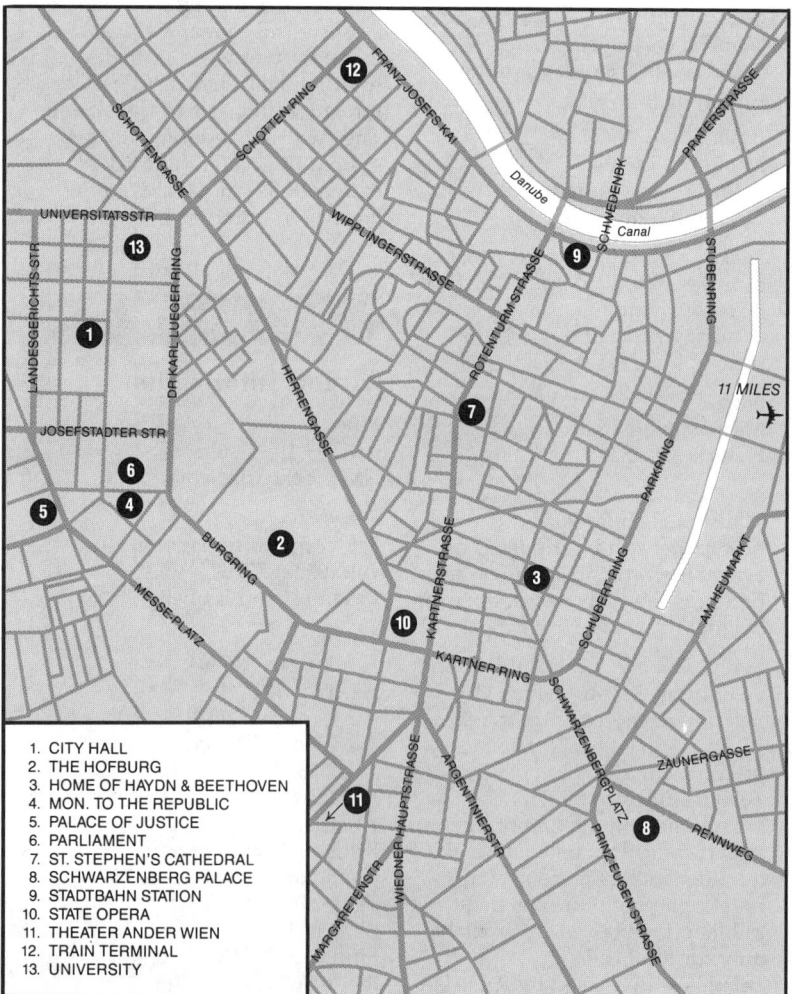

1. CITY HALL
2. THE HOFBURG
3. HOME OF HAYDN & BEETHOVEN
4. MON. TO THE REPUBLIC
5. PALACE OF JUSTICE
6. PARLIAMENT
7. ST. STEPHEN'S CATHEDRAL
8. SCHWARZENBERG PALACE
9. STADTBAHN STATION
10. STATE OPERA
11. THEATER ANDER WIEN
12. TRAIN TERMINAL
13. UNIVERSITY

Vienna

Coach: airport buses cost about 50 schillings ($3.50) and run between the airport and city center or west railway station every thirty minutes or connect with flight arrivals.

Transit: trains between the "Schnallbahn station" Wien Mitte, across from the Hilton Hotel air terminal and the airport departure hall, run every hour and cost only 20 schillings. Buy ticket before boarding train. Depart between 0500-2100 and take 30 minutes; room for luggage. Buses leave every hour from 0700-1800 and cost 50 schillings ($3.50); pay on boarding.

Facilities

Snack bar, restaurant, currency exchange, hotel reservations, baggage lockers, barber shop, tourist information, insurance vending machines, post office, shops.

Duty free shop sells cigarettes, cigars, tobacco, wines, spirits, liqueurs, small clothing items, cosmetics, jewellery and electronic goods. All convertible currencies are accepted.

Car rental desks: Hertz, Ansa, Avis, Budget, InterRent, Kemwel

Airport Taxes

None

City Information

Weather

Warm, sunny and fairly dry summers. Winters can be very cold with with snow.
Average temps: Jan -1 C (30 F)
July 19 C (67 F)

Transportation

Taxis are available 24 hours at stands or by phone. Tip 15%. Public transportation via bus, streetcar and subway is good with one flat fare which is paid on boarding.
The Austrian State Railway provides inexpensive service out of the city, with connections to the rest of the country and Europe.

Car Hire

Hertz, Marxergasse 24, A-1030 (tel: 731596)
Avis, Weyringergasse 33, A-1040 (tel: 6558390)
Europcar, Mollardgasse 15, A-1060 (tel: 571675)
InterRent, Bienengasse 6-8, A-1060 (tel: 565576)

Hospitals

Emergency 144
Many doctors and dentists speak English, and a list can be obtained from your embassy.

Trade Fairs

Interior Design Exhibition (Mar)
International Spring Trade Fair (Mar)
International Toy Fair (Apr)
Paper and Stationery Trade Fair (Apr)
International Solar Heating Exhibition (Apr)
International Office Fair (May)
Electric Installer's Trade Fair (Jun)
International Wine Festival (Jun)
Show of Nations Exhibition (Sept)
Health and Fitness (Sept)
International Machine Tool Fair (Oct)
Hotel and Catering Equipment (Oct)

Hotels

Albatros, liechtensteinstr.89 (tel: 343508)
Ambassador, Neuer Markt 5 (tel: 51466)
Amadeus, Wildpretmarkt 5 (tel: 638738)
Astoria, Karntnerstr. 32 (tel: 51577)
Bristol, Karntnerring 1 (tel: 51516)
Erzherzog Rainer, Wiedner Haupstr. 27-29 (tel: 501110)

EUROPE

Europa, Neuer Markt 3
(tel: 521594)
Hilton Vienna, Am Stadpark
1030 (tel: 7526520)
IBIS Wein, 22-24 Maria
Hilferguertel (tel: 565626)
Imperial, Kaerntnering 16
(tel: 501100)
Intercontinental, Johannesgasse
28 (tel: 75050)
Modul, Peter Jordan Str.
(tel: 471584)
Novotel Wein Airport, A1300
Schwechat (tel: 776666)
Novotel Wein Sud, Nordring 4
(tel: 676506)
Novotel Wein West,
Wientalstrasse (tel: 972542)
Opernring, Operning 11
(tel: 5875518)
Palais Schwarzenberg,
Schwartzenberg 9 (tel: 725125)
Parkhotel Schonbrunn,
Heitzinger Haupstr. 10
(tel: 822676)
President, Wallgasse 23
(tel: 59990)
Prinz Eugen, Wiedner Guertel 14
(tel: 651741)
Roemischer Kaiser, Annagasse 16
(tel: 5127751)
Royal, Singerstrasse (tel: 524631)
Sacher, Philharmonikerstr. 4
(tel: 524631)
Tigra, Tiefer Graben 14
(tel: 5339641)
Westminster,
Harmoniegasstel: tel: 346604)

What to See and Do
Vienna is a city of music,
particularly the waltz music of
the Strauss family. The Vienna
State Opera house is where the
concerts and opera events take
place, and it is one of the most
beautiful in the world. If you
cannot get tickets you can hear
music in the smaller clubs and
halls, or in the summer out in
the Vienna Woods where
summer concerts are held.
Another attraction is the Vienna

Boy's Choir at the
Sangerknaben.
Museums worth a visit include
the Historic Arts Museum, the
Albertina, and the Museum of
Fine Arts. The Hofberg Palace is
magnificent, and while there one
should visit the stables
of the Spanish Riding Academy
to see the world-famous
Lippizaner stallions.
Visit the Belvedere Palace,
Schoenbrunn Castle, St.Stephens
Cathedral, and finally a stop at
one of Vienna's many coffee
houses for Viennese coffee and
some of the best chocolate and
cream pastries made anywhere.

Useful Addresses

Embassies and Consulates
American: Boltzmanngasse 16
(tel: 315511)
British: Reisnerstrasse 40
(tel: 731575)
Canadian: Leuger-Ring 10
(tel: 633691)

Business and Commerce
Central Bank (Osterreichische
Nationalbank), Otto Wagner-
Platz 3 (tel: 243600)
Stock Exchange (Weiner
Borsekammer) 1011 Vienna,
Wipplingerstrasse 34
(tel: 633766)
Trade Fairs
(Wirtschaftsorderungsinstitut)
Horher Markt 3 (tel: 635763)
Austrian Ministry for Commerce,
Trade and Industry,
Stubenring 1 (tel: 5756550)
American Chamber of
Commerce, Turkenstr. 9
(tel: 315751)
British Trade Council,
Johannesgrasse 15
(tel: 5270864)

Tourism and Travel
American Express,
Karntnerstrasse 21/23 (51540)

Austrian National Tourist Office,
  Kinderspitalgasse 5
  (tel: 431608)

Thomas Cook, Kaerntnerring 14
  (tel: 657631)

BELGIUM

Essential Information

Type of Government
Parliamentary democracy under a constitutional monarch

Area
30,500 sq km
(11,776 sq mi)

Population
10.1 million

Annual Growth Rate
0.25%

Languages
Flemish 57%, French 33%, German 0.7%. French is spoken in the south, and Flemish (Dutch) in the north. Brussels is officially bilingual but French predominates.

Religion
Roman Catholic 75%, Protestant 25%

Ethnic Groups
Flemings 58%, Walloons 41%

Weights and Measures
Metric

Electrical Current
A.C. 50c 220/240V, Brussels A.C. 50c 220/380V, Antwerp A.C. 50c 220/380V and A.C. 110/220V

Major Business Cities
Brussels (cap) 2,220,000
Antwerp 1,590,000
Ghent 1,330,000
Liege 995,000

Currency
Belgium Franc (BF) = 100 centimes

Public Holidays
Jan 1 New Year's Day
Apr 13-20 Easter Week
May 28 Labor Day
Jun 9 Whit Monday
Jul 21 Independence Day
Aug 15 Assumption
Nov 11 Remembrance Day
Nov 15 King's Birthday
Dec 25 Christmas
Dec 26 Boxing Day

Travellers Information

Entry Requirements
Either a valid passport or an identity card is required of citizens of EEC, Andora, Austria, Greece, Lichtenstein, Malta, Monaco, San Marino and Switzerland. Citizens of all other countries must have a passport. Visas required by some countries but not by nationals of the US, Australia, Canada, New Zealand, Britain, most Western European countries and Japan for a period of up to three months.

Working Restrictions
Work permits must be obtained by the Belgian employer.

Vaccination Required
None

Customs and Duty Free
On arrival: 300 cigarets to EEC members (400 for non-Europeans); 1 liter spirits; other goods including perfume. Tax is included in the price of most goods but you can avoid it by requesting that the purchased item be delivered outside Belgium or directly to the airport awaiting your departure.

EUROPE

Currency Restrictions
There are no import or export restrictions on currency.

Health Tips
There is no national health service so medical treatment can be expensive. English speaking physicians are listed in the English index telephone directory yellow pages. A list can usually be obtained from your embassy. There will always be one pharmacy open in any given neighborhood at all times; the address is posted on all pharmacy doors. Drinking water is purified.

Climate and Clothing
Temperate climate with rainfall throughout the year: moderate winters with little snow. Temperatures average 5C (42F) in the winter and 23C (73F) in summer. Medium weight clothes, a raincoat and umbrella are necessary in winter, and lightweight clothing other times.

Tipping
In hotels and restaurants a service charge is added to the bill so tipping is unnecessary. However it is considered polite to leave the small change in restaurants. Usherettes in movie theatres are usually tipped 15 to 20 francs. Tip porters 30 francs per piece of luggage, chambermaids 40 francs per day, and doormen and other small services 20 francs. Some barbers and hairdressers add 15-20% to the bill so ask whether service is included. The same applies to taxi drivers.

Food and Drink
The food of Belgium is influenced primarily by the French. Similar ways of cooking fish, meat, poultry and vegetables is found, and wine and the fine Belgium beers normally accompany a meal.

The breakfast meal is usually just a coffee and roll. The main meal is dinner which is taken fairly late in the evening. Some specialties include the excellent Frites (french fries), Belgium chocolates, and the before mentioned beers.

Business Brief

GDP
$159.7 billion

Annual Growth Rate
1.5%

Natural Resources
Coal

Agriculture
Livestock, poultry, grain, sugar beets, flax, tobacco, potatoes, other vegetables, fruits

Industry
Machinery, iron and steel, coal, textiles, chemicals, glass

Imports
Total $83.2 billion
Machinery, fuels, chemical products, food

Exports
Total $84 billion
Machinery, chemicals,, food and livestock, iron and steel

Major Trading Partners
West Germany, France, the Netherlands

Workforce
4 million
Service industry 47%, industry 30%, other services 23%

Tips for Doing Business
Conservative clothing is mandatory and many businessmen prefer to wear suits with a vest. Always make appointments in advance preferably between 1000 and 1700 hours. Punctuality is essential. Shake hands at arrival and departure and do not call

others by their first name unless invited to. Present simple business card with no promotional material on it. Any promotion material should be given separately and printed in both French and Flemish. Luncheon meetings which include good wines are very acceptable. If invited to someone's home, send flowers to the hostess and/or take chocolates along with you.

Best Months for Doing Business

The best months for business are September through November, and January through March, May and June. Avoid the two weeks before and after Christmas, including New Year, the week before and after Easter, and July and August when most businessmen take their vacations. Also avoid "Bourse Days" when businessmen meet at restaurants to discuss trade business. These days are Wednesdays in Brussels and Mondays in Antwerp.

Business Hours

Government
Mon-Fri 0900-1700

Business
Mon-Fri 0830-1730

Banks
Mon-Fri 0900-1630

Shops
Mon-Sat 0900-1830

English Language Publications

International English language publications, including International Herald Tribune, USA Today and some British newspapers available in larger cities. Local publication in English is The Bulletin.

Telephone and Communications

Telephone country code: 32
Telephone city codes: Antwerp 03, Bruges 050, Brussels 02, Ghent 091, Mons 065
Telex country code: 846
Public telephones operate with a 5 franc coin, inserted after hearing the dial tone and giving unlimited time. To make a long distance collect call, dial 987 and request an English-speaking operator.
Telex available in most major hotels. Telegram service available from telegraph offices (open 24 hours) or by telephone.
Incoming mail can be sent "Poste Restante" to main post offices. Present passport when collecting.

Air Travel

There are no internal domestic flights and Brussels is the only large international airport in the country.

Other Transport

There is a very good national railroad system and Brussels has four major train stations. Book "Direct" or "Semi-direct" trains when travelling to major cities. Combined tickets which allow stopovers offer best value. Express trains (TEE) to all French and German cities.
Car rental is readily available and can be paid for by credit card in all towns. There is an excellent and extensive road network and highways run from Brussels to other large cities. Accident level is high so drive carefully. International drivers license is required.

BRUSSELS

Airport Information

Time
GMT +1
GMT +2 (Apr-Sept)

EUROPE

Airport

Brussels National BRU
Tel: (02) 7223111
12 km (7 1/2 mi) NE of city

Airlines

Aeroflot 2186046
Air Canada 5136210
Air France 2193800
British Airways 2176000
British Caledonian 7517870
Canadian International 5115937
KLM 7201750
Pan Am 7518195
Sabena 5119030
TWA 5137916

Transport to City

Taxis: Yellow and black taxis are available at the terminal. Trip to city center is about 20-30 minutes for 1000 fr. plus tip.

Coach: Airline bus to city every 30 minutes, return from Sabena Air Terminus, 37 rue Cardinal Mercier, every 75 minutes before departure. A train runs from terminal to city center every 30 minutes. Both take about 15 minutes.

Transit: Electric trains leave from the lower level in Arrival terminal. Train makes two stops to Brussels North station and Central station. Trains leave every 30 minutes until midnight for 15-20 minute trip to Central station. Fare is 75 fr.

Facilities

Bank with currency exchange, hotel reservations, post office, baggage deposit, tourist

1. BOURSE
2. CENTRAL STATION
3. GRAND-PLACE
4. MUSEUM OF FINE ARTS
5. PALACE OF JUSTICE
6. PALAIS DES CONGRES
7. ROYAL PALACE
8. ST. MICHEL'S CATHEDRAL
9. THEATRE DE LA MONNAIRE

RUE DU MIDI   RUE DES FRIPIERS

10 MILES

MARCHE AUX H-ERBES

BOUL. DES ALEXIENS-CELLEBROESSTR

BOUL. DE L'EMPEREUR

BOUL. DE L'IPERMATRICE-DE BERLAIMONT-IAAN

RUE MIMMIES

RAVENSTEIN

RUE DE LA REGENT

RUE ROYAL

RUE DE LA LOI

AVE LOUISE

BOUL. DE WATERLOO-IAAN
AVE DE LA TOISON D'OR

PLACE DES PALAIS

BRUSSELS PARK

RUE DUCALE

BOUL. DU REGENT
AVE DES ARTS

Brussels

information desk, bar, restaurant, shops, conference facilities, first aid/medical. Duty free shop has cigarets, cigars, tobacco, wines, spirits, cameras, watches, small electronic, jewellery, perfume. Convertible currencies accepted. Car rental desks: Hertz, Avis, Budget, Europcar, InterRent, Transcar, Travelcar.

Airport Taxes
None

City Information

Weather
Climate temperate and rainy throughout the year. Heaviest rainfall October through November. Some snow in December through March. Average temps: Jan 6 C (42 F) July 19 C (68 F)

Transportation
An expanding subway system, streetcars and buses give good local transportation. Fares are transferrable between systems. Taxis are readily available and tipping is not required since there is a standardized fare system which includes service charge.

Car Hire
Hertz, Blvd. Lemonnier 8
(tel: 7206044)
Avis, rue Americaine
(tel: 7518394)
Europcar, Blvd. Brand Whitlock
(tel: 7210592)
InterRent, 235 av. Louise
(tel: 7211178)

Hospitals
Clinique Sainte-Elisabeth
(tel: 3745800)
Clinique Universitaires St Luc
(tel: 7641111)
Hopital Universitaire St-Pierre
(tel: 5380000)
Erasmus Hospital (tel: 5683111)

Trade Fairs
International Leather Goods
Exhibition (Jan)
International Motor &
Motorcycle Exhibition (Jan)
International Agriculture &
Forrestry Exhibition (Feb)
International Building Trades
Fair (Feb)
Florists Materials Exhibition
(Mar)
International Consumer Trade
Fair (Mar)
Medical and Hospital Exhibition
(Apr)
Electronics Trade Show (Apr)
Hotel and Restaurant Equipment
Show (Nov)
Heating, Refrigeration &
Restaurant Equipment Fair
(Nov)

Hotels
Amigo, 1 rue de L'Amigo
(tel: 5115910)
Arcade Stephanie, 91 rue Louise
(tel: 5388060)
Atlanta, 7 Blvd. Adolphe Max
(tel: 2100120)
Brussels Europa, 107 rue de la
Loi (tel: 2301333)
Brussels Hilton, 36 Blvd.
Waterloo (tel: 5138877)
Diplomat, 32 rue Jean Stas
(tel: 5374250)
Holiday Inn, 7 Holiday Straat
(tel: 7205865)
Hyatt Regency, 250 rue Royale
(tel: 2194640)
Novotel Airport, Olmenstraat
(tel: 7205830)
President Centre, 160 rue Royale
(tel: 2190065)
Royal Windsor, 5 rue Duquesnoy
(tel: 5114215)
Sheraton, 3 Place Rogier
(tel: 2193400)
Sofitel, 15 Bessenveldstrratt,
Diegem (tel: 7206050)

What to See and Do
Brussels is a beautiful city with some of the finest architecture in Europe, such as the Grand Palace in the center of the city.

EUROPE

Also St. Michael Cathedral, the Palace Royale and the Palais du Justice. Concerts and opera can be found at the Palais des Beaux Arts, Theatre Royal du Parc and Foret National. The world-famous Bejart Ballet is also located in Brussels.

Museums include the Musee de L'Art Ancien which has one of the finest collections of old Flemish masters. There is also the African Art Museum and the Belleveu museum.

Entertainment can be found along the reu Stassart (near Porte de Namur) for some of Brussels best night life. Near the Grand Palace is rue des Bouchers, a pedestrian street which contains many fine restaurants and boutiques for shoppers.

Useful Addresses

Embassies and Consulates
American: 27 Blvd. du Regent (tel: 5133830)
British: 28 rue Joseph II (tel: 2179000)
Canadian: 6 rue du Loxum (tel: 5137940)

Business and Commerce
Association Belge des Banques, 36 rue Ravenstein(tel: 5125868)
National Bank (Banque de Nationale de Belgique), 5 Boulevard de Berliament (tel: 2194600)
Stock Exchange, 34 Rue de la Montagne (tel: 5113097)
Belgium Chamber of Commerce, rue du Congres 40 (tel: 2173671) American Chamber of Commerce, 50 Avenue des Arts (tel: 5121262)
Canadian Chamber of Commerce (tel: 5115227)
Belgian Foreign Trade Office, 162 Blvd. Emile Jacqmain (tel: 2194450)

Tourism and Travel
American Express, 2 Pl Louise (tel: 5121740)
Belgium National Tourist Office, 61 Rue du Marche Aux Agrves (tel: 5138940)
National Tourist Information Office, Arrival Hall, Brussels International Airport (tel: 7209140)
Royal Auto-Club de Belgique, 53 Rue d'Arlon
Thomas Cook, 52 Blvd. Adolphe Max (tel: 2176240)

CZECHOSLOVAKIA

Essential Information

Type of Government
Socialist Republic

Area
127,870 sq km
(49,371 sq mi)

Population
16 million

Annual Growth Rate
0.6%

Languages
Czech, Slovak, Hungarian

Religion
Roman Catholic, Protestant, Orthodox, Jewish

Ethnic Groups
Czech (65%), Slovak (30%), Hungarian, Polish, Ukrainian, German

Weights and Measure
Metric

Electrical Current
A.C. 50c 220/380 V

Major Business Cities
Prague (cap) 1,700,000

Bratislava 420,000
Brno 390,000
Ostrava 330,000
Kosice 225,000
Pilsen 176,000

Currency
1 Koruna = 100 heller
Notes 10, 20, 50, 100 & 500
  Koruna

Public Holidays
Jan 1 New Year's Day
Apr 13-20 Easter Week
May 1 Labour Day
May 9 Liberation Day
Dec 25,26 Christmas

Travellers Information

Entry Requirements
Passport visas required by U.S.,
U.K., Canadian nationals.
Passports should extend 3
months from issue date of visa.
Business visas valid for 3
months. Currency slips issued
on entry, redeemed at exit.

Working Restrictions
Work permits may be obtained.
See your embassy or consulate.

Vaccination Required
None

Customs and Duty Free
On arrival: Personal belongings,
gifts purchased at TUZEX shops
duty-free. Purchases of less than
300 kcs, excluding glassware,
duty-free 250 cigarettes or
tobacco equivalent. Spirits 1 L,
wine 2 L, perfume 0.5 L.

Currency Restrictions
Import or export of local
currency forbidden. Visitors
must spend a minimum of the
equivalent of L8 per day, unless
hotel bill has been prepaid.
Minimum expenditure rules
exclude credit cards.

Health Tips
Tap water usually safe. Bring
own medications for minor

ailments. Clinic for foreigners at
Karlovo Namesti, Prague.

Climate and Clothing
Warm, dry summers, and cold
winters with possible snowfall.
Raincoat, heavy woolens
recommended Nov-Mar. Light
clothes May-Aug.

Tipping
Officially discouraged, but taxis
5-10%. Tip porters kcs 5 per
piece. Tip waiters, hotels, etc.
10%. Add 3-5% for staff. Tip
barbers, small services 10%.

Food and Drink
Popular dishes include pork
roast, dumplings and sauerkraut.
Goose, ham and sausages are
specialties, with bread and dairy
products available, but fruit only
in season. Breakfast usually
consists of cakes, coffee and
pancakes. Lunch is major meal,
and usually has soup, meat,
dumplings, bread and
vegetables. Wine or beer served.
Supper usually a smaller version
of lunch. Czechs love to snack
between meals. Czech beer
(Pilsner) is reputed to be one of
the world's best.

Business Brief

GDP
$89.2 billion
(per capita income $5,493)

Annual Growth Rate
1%

Natural Resources
Coal, coke, timber, lignite,
uranium, magnesite

Agriculture
Wheat, rye, oats, corn, barley,
potatoes, sugar beets, hogs,
cattle, horses

Industry
Iron and steel, machinery,
cement, sheet glass, motor cars,

EUROPE

armaments, chemicals, ceramics, wood, paper products

Imports
Total $13.87 billion
Machinery, raw materials, food, livestock, manufactured goods

Exports
Total $13.53 billion
Machinery, motor vehicles, iron and steel, chemicals, textiles

Major Trading Partners
U.S.S.R., German Democratic Republic, Poland, Hungary, Romania, West Germany, Austria, Switzerland, Great Britain

Workforce
7.5 million
Agriculture 12%, industry, construction and commerce 66%, government and services 18%

Tips for Doing Business
Since the economy is largely state-owned and operated, business people here are also officials of the state. Prior appointments must always be made and patience and persistence usually rewarded. Conservative business suit the norm. Your main business contacts will be with any of the trade organizations controlled by the Ministry of Foreign Trade. Czech businessmen normally require generous credit terms in major transactions. Frequent business luncheons and dinners.

Best Months for Doing Business
September through May, since business vacations are taken June through August.

Business Hours

Government
Mon-Fri 0800-1600

Business
Mon-Fri 0800-1700

Bank
Mon-Fri 0800-1700

Shops
Mon-Fri 0830-1800
Sat 0900-1200

English Language Publications
American (International Herald Tribune) and some British newspapers are available in hotels and some newsstands in Prague. Local English publications are magazines Welcome to Czechoslovakia and Czechoslovakia Life.

Telephone and Communications
Telephone country code: 42
Telephone city code: Prague 2
Telex country code: 849
Public phones in most public areas. Make foreign calls from Czechoslovakia "collect" if possible due to high rates. Country is 6 time zones in advance of Eastern Standard Time.
Useful numbers in Prague: Operator 128, Directories 120, First Aid 155, Emergencies 373737, Tourist Information 224250.

Air Travel
Czechoslovak Airlines (CSA) operates domestic flights to all major cities. Main airport (Prague) is Ruzyne. One terminal each for domestic and international flights.

Other Transport
Rental cars available at airports from Pragocar, or through Cedok offices. International or foreign driver's licence required and driving not permitted after drinking alcohol.
Buses better than trains for city-to-city transport.
Trains should be booked in advance, with tickets available from railway ticket offices or

Cedok offices. Several major highways link major cities.

PRAGUE

Airport Information

Time
GMT +1
GMT +2 (Apr-Sept)

Airport
Ryzyne International PRG
Tel: (2) 367827
17 (11 mi) W of city

Airlines
Aer Lingus 126055
Aeroflot 260862
Air Canada 121155
Air France 260155
Alia 115858
Alitalia 2310535
Austrian 2312795
British Airways 240847
Egyptair 509111
El Al 146417
Finnair 223012
Gulf Air 595522
Iberia 122222
Interflug 2320954
Iraqi 220950
JAL 113300
KLM 264362

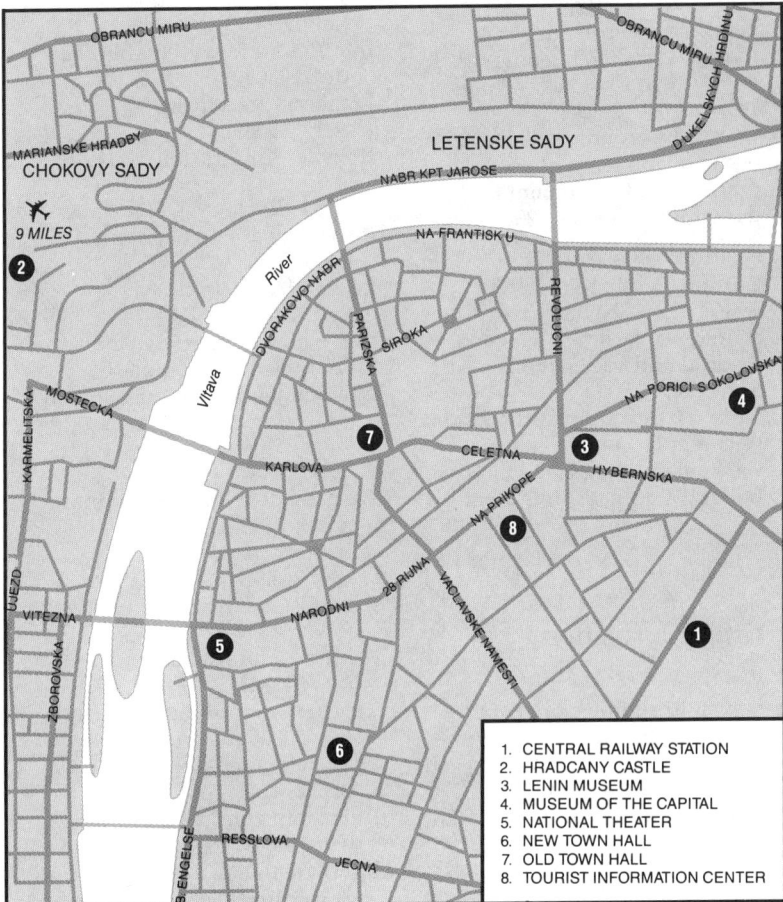

1. CENTRAL RAILWAY STATION
2. HRADCANY CASTLE
3. LENIN MUSEUM
4. MUSEUM OF THE CAPITAL
5. NATIONAL THEATER
6. NEW TOWN HALL
7. OLD TOWN HALL
8. TOURIST INFORMATION CENTER

Prague

EUROPE

Korean 140353
Kuwait Air 150915
Lufthansa 2317551
MEA 114211
Northwest 148899
Olympic 126100
PIA 141833
Qantas 118911
Sabena 367813
SAS 228141
Singapore 143456
Swissair 128090
Syrian 3344480
TAP 116006
Thai 155152
THY 144499
TWA 328088
Varig 119122

Transport to City

Taxis: Leave from airport terminal for 30-60 minute ride to downtown. Cost kcs 480 plus 10% tip.

Coach: Buses are available at the terminal and leave at irregular times. About 30-40 minutes to downtown. Cost kcs 23.

Facilities

Currency exchange, hotel reservations, baggage deposit, conference facilities. First aid/medical and vaccinations also available.

Duty/tax-free shop at the airport sells regular items.

Car rental desks: Hertz, Avis, Budget, Europcar, InterRent.

Airport Taxes

None

City Information

Weather

Spring to summer temperatures average 22 C (73 F) with thunderstorms. Light clothes and raincoat recommended.

Oct to April weather cold, with snow averages 1 C (34 F). Medium weight clothes, boots, hat recommended.

Transportation

Good taxi service in main towns. Basic fare kcs 5 per km plus extra charge daily between 2200 and 0600. Taxi tel: 203941-5 or 202951-5.

Bus tickets in town can be bought for kcs 1 at tobacco shops and others displaying a sign reading "Predprodej Jizdenek". Subway has 3 lines, A, B, and C. Flat fare service from 0500-2400 hrs.

General transportation information tel: 229252.

Car Hire

Hertz, Hotel Intercontinental
  (tel: 3344270)
Europcar, Stepimsku 42
  (tel: 367807)
InterRent, Lidovysch Milici 52
  (tel: 298020)
Pragocar, Stepdhska 42
  (tel: 240089)
Ruzyne, Airport (tel: 3-344270)

Trade Fairs

International Engineering Fair,
  Brno (Sept)
INCHEBA Chemical Fair,
  Brataslava (Sept)
International Fire Prevention
  Equipment Exhibition (Oct)
International Heating Exhibition
  (Nov)

Hotels

Ambassador, Vaclavske namesti
  5 (tel: 221351)
Alcron, Stepanska 40
  (tel: 245741)
Albatros, Nabrezi L. Svobody
  (tel: 2313634)
Admiral, Horejsi nabrezi
  (tel: 547445)
Esplanade, Washingtonova 19
  (tel: 222552)
Flora, Vinohradska 121
  (tel: 274241)
Intercontinental, namesti
  Curieovych (tel: 2311812)
International, namesti Druzby 1
  (tel: 321051)

Jalta, Vaclavske namesti 45
(tel: 265541)
Olympik II-Garni Invalidovna
(tel: 828541)
Splendid, Ovenecka 33
(tel: 375451)
Tri Pstrosi, Drazickeho namesti
12 (tel: 536151)

What to See and Do

Visit Hradcany and Karlstein
castles nearby or St. Jacob's or
St. Nicholas cathedrals. Also
National Gallery, National
Museum and National Theatre
are open to the public. Some
good restaurants include The
Brasserie and The Golden Prague
(Intercontinental Hotel); Opera
Grill (Divadeini 24, tel: 265508);
Pizen (Alcron Hotel); Rotisserie
(Mikulandska 6, tel: 206826); and
Vysocina (Narodni Tr 28,
tel: 225773).
Bars and lounges in most major
hotels. Clothing stores include
Adam (Prikopy 8), Diplomat
(Narodni Trida 15) and Styl
(Narodni Trida 15). Gifts and
craft stores include Moser (Na
Prikope 12), Tuzex (Narodni
Trida 43), and UVA (Na Prikope
25).

Useful Addresses

Embassies and Consulates
American: Trziste 15 (tel: 536641)
British: 1 Thunovska14
(tel: 533347)
Canadian: Mickiewiczova 6

Business and Commerce
State Savings Bank, Vaclavske
namesti 42 (tel: 11398)
Commercial Bank, Na Prikope 14
(tel: 2132)
State Bank, Na Prikope 28
(tel: 2112)
Czechoslovakia Chamber of
Commerce, Argentina 38
(tel: 724111)
Central Automobile Club,
Opletalova 29 (tel: 223544)
Central Post Office, Jindrisska 14
(tel: 264841)
State Railways, namesti Prikope
33 (tel: 11005)
Interpreter/Translation Services,
Cedok, namesti Prikope
(tel: 352000)
Ministry of Foreign Trade, UL
Politickych Veznozo, Legal
Advice Bureau, Advekatini
Poradna Narodni 32
(tel: 224782-7)

Tourism and Travel
Travel Information at Cedok, Na
Pzikope 18 (tel: 224251)
Czechoslovakian Automobile
Club, O Pletalova 29
(tel: 223592 & 220140)
American Express Office,
Foreign Travel Division, Cedok
Na Prikope 18 (tel: 224251 &
224259)

EUROPE

7 WEEKLY FLIGHTS TO STOCKHOLM

+ 7 WEEKLY FLIGHTS TO OSLO

+ 7 WEEKLY FLIGHTS TO COPENHAGEN

= 21 WEEKLY FLIGHTS TO SCANDINAVIA

MONTREAL
DORVAL
dep: 15.50 mon-fri

TORONTO
PEARSON INT'L.
dep: 13.50 daily
dep: 16.30* sun-fri
*connects to SK904 only

ISLAND AIRPORT
dep: 15.00 daily

NEWARK
INTERNATIONAL
AIRPORT

The New
SAS Terminal

● La Guardia Airport

● J.F.K. Airport

SK904 dep: 19.00

SK908 dep: 18.45

SK912 dep: 18.30

STOCKHOLM
arr: 09.00 ARLANDA

OSLO
arr: 08.15 FORNEBU

COPENHAGEN
arr: 08.10

The new easy route to Scandinavia

Welcome to Newark – The new easy way to Scandinavia. Three flights every day to Stockholm, Oslo and Copenhagen.

From Toronto you may choose to depart on convenient flights from either Pearson or Island airports. In Montreal, you can fly direct from Dorval Airport.

Upon arrival in Newark, you'll be welcomed at the new SAS Terminal. You're just a few minutes walk to the SAS departure gates. No changing airports, no taxis, no more crosstown traffic – just one easy connection.

And Newark is one of the most modern customer-friendly airports in the world.

Spacious check-in and security areas, an array of restaurants and lounges, duty-free shopping and more.

The new President's Club Lounge offers a comprehensive selection of services from the business centre. Private conference rooms, work areas and a remarkable world class lounge for relaxation.

Enroute to or from Scandinavia you'll find the new SAS Terminal C at Newark offers a new standard of passenger convenience.

The new SAS route to Scandinavia. **More flights, more often.** Better connections. A new airport terminal – and **twenty-one flights a week**

SAS

SCANDINAVIAN AIRLINES

1075 Bay St., Toronto, Ontario M5S 2B1
(416) 324-8611   Sales Reservations
1-800-387-4799   Sales & Reservations (Ont. & Que.)
1-800-221-2350   Reservations/Information (after business hours)
(416) 324-9183   FAX

DENMARK

Essential Information

Type of Government
Constitutional Monarchy

Area
43,076 sq km
(16,632 sq mi, excluding
Greenland, Faroe Islands)

Population
5.11 million

Annual Growth Rate
3.9%

Languages
Danish, Faroese, Greenlandic,
German

Religion
Evangelical Lutheran

Ethnic Groups
Scandinavian, Eskimo, Faroese,
German

Weights and Measures
Metric

Electrical Current
A.C. 50c 220/380

Major Business Cities
Copenhagen (cap) 1,500,000
Aarhus 260,000
Odense 175,000
Aalborg 160,000

Currency
Danish Krone (kr) = 100 ore

Public Holidays
Jan 1 New Year
Apr 13-20 Easter Week
Apr 25 Prayer Day
May 28 Ascension
June 5 Constitution
Dec. 24,26 Christmas

Travellers Information

Entry Requirements
Most visitors need passports.
U.S. tourists need visas for stays
of more than 90 days. South
African, Arab, and East
European visitors require visas.

Working Restrictions
Canadian, British, American
nationals need permits, but none
being issued at present time.
EEC nationals do not need
permits.

Vaccination Required
Smallpox, only if travelling from
an infected area. No others
required.

Customs and Duty Free
Personal effects duty free plus
allowance.
On Arrival: 300 cigarettes or 75
cagars or 400 g of tobacco plus 1
L of spirits.

Currency Restrictions
No restrictions on foreign
currency taken in or out. No
restrictions on Danish currency
in. Up to Kr. 25,000 only may be
taken out.

Health Tips
Drinking water is safe, and has
been purified.

Climate and Clothing
Temperature range from 22 C to
-3 C. Westerly winds make
climate temperate year-round,
but changeable. Coats always
advisable.

Tipping
Taxi fares already include tips.
Tip porters 4 kr per piece. 15%
tip always included in hotel,
restaurant, and club bills. Tip
doormen, small services 2 kr,
barbers and beauticians 4 kr.

Food and Drink
The Danes are very fond of fish,
and prepare herring pickled or
in sour cream. Danish ham and
bacon are popular and are
favorite ingredients in the
popular open-faced sandwich

EUROPE

which is consumed at lunchtime. Danish beers, Tuborg and Carlsberg are excellent.

Business Brief

GDP
$66.2 billion
(per capita income $12,944)

Annual Growth Rate
2%

Natural Resources
Oil, iron ore, coal, lead, uranium

Agriculture
Barley, oats, potatoes, rye, sugar beets, wheat

Industry
Beverages, chemicals, electronics, engineering, fishing, food processing, furniture, metal manufacture, paper and printing, shipbuilding, textiles.

Imports
Total $25.5 million
Fuel, chemicals, yarn, clothing, paper, iron and steel, machinery, vehicles, petroleum

Exports
Total $25.6 million
Meat products, dairy products, fish, eggs, machinery, transport equipment, furs, textiles, furniture, beverages

Major Trading Partners
Sweden, West Germany, Great Britain, U.S., Norway, Netherlands, France, Italy

Workforce
2.6 million
Manufacturing employs about 24%, trade 16%, building and construction 8%, and agriculture 9%

Tips for Doing Business
A conservative business suit advised for most occasions, and a raincoat. Prior appointments must be made. Shake hands upon greeting or leaving your contact. Soft-sell, low-key approach. Be punctual, bring flowers to social occasions.

Best Months for Doing Business
September through May. Avoid the two weeks before and after Christmas and Easter, and between June 15 and July 30.

Business Hours

Government
Mon-Fri 0900-1630

Business
Mon-Fri 0800-1630
Sat 0800-1300 (check first)

Banks
Mon-Fri 0930-1600
Thu 0930-1800
Sat closed

Shops
Mon-Thu 0900-1730
Fri 0900-1900
Sat 0900-1300

English Language Publications
British daily newspapers as well as the International Herald Tribune and USA Today are available at newsstands in Copenhagen and some major cities. Danish Radio 3 provides English news broadcast Mon-Fri 0815

Telephone and Communications
Telephone country code: 45
Telephone city area codes:
Aalborg 08, Aarhus 06, Allerod 02, Ansager 05, Assens 09, Borup 03, Copenhagen 01 or 02, Esbjerg 05, Gedsted 08, Haderslav 04, Holstebro 07.
Telex country code: 392
For assistance with local calls dial 0030, for outside Denmark dial 009.
Telegrams and telexes may be sent daily from 0900-2200 at Kobmagergade 37.
For coin boxes in restaurants, bars, etc. insert two 25-ore coins or 1 kr.-coin, dial digits or letters

Air Travel

Kastrup-Copenhagen airport Good domestic service provided by Scandinavian Airlines and Danair. For weekend flights or stays of three nights a 50% discount is available on some routes.

Other Transport

Taxis can be hailed, by telephone, or at ranks. A green sign marked FRI means they are available. Cost is kr. 12 plus kr. 1 per km. Fare includes a tip. Buses offer frequent service. All major cities and provinces linked by modern highways or ferries.
Danish Railways telephone 141701

COPENHAGEN

Airport Information

Time
GMT +1
GMT +2 (Mar 28 - Sept 18)

Airport
Kastrup International CPH
Tel: 509333
10 km (6 mi) SE of city

Airlines
Aer Lingus 126055
Aeroflot 126338
Air Canada 121155
Air France 127676
Alia 115858
Alitalia 128850
Austrian 117725
British Airways 146000
Canadian International 129523
El Al 146417
Finnair 120855
Gulf Air 595522
Iberia 122222
Interflug 522503
Iraqi 111119
JAL (Japan) 113300
KLM 113334

Korean (KAL) 140353
Kuwait 150915
Lufthansa 126511
MEA 114211
Northwest 148899
Olympic 126100
Qantas 118911
Sabena 123027
SAS 147555
Singapore 143456
Swissair 128090
Syrian 144425
TAP 232455
Thai 155152
THY 144499
TWA 328088
Varig 119122

Transport to City
Taxis: Airport to city costs about kr 85 ($12). Tip is included. 20-min ride.
Coach: SAS bus to Hotel Scandinavia and Central Railway Station. Hrs 0545-1110. Costs kr 20 ($3).
Transit: Yellow buses run every 10-15 min. from arrivals hall. First bus 0435, last bus 1150.

Facilities
International terminal has bar, buffet, currency exchange, baggage deposit, post office, candy, gifts, etc.
Domestic terminal has bar, snacks, baggage lockers.
Duty-free shop sells tobacco products, wines, spirits, liqueurs. Convertible currencies accepted.
Car rental desks: Hertz, Europcar, InterRent, Pitzner, Auto.

Airport Taxes
None

City Information

Weather
Generally mild throughout the year with very damp conditions. Average temps: Jan 2 C (35 F) July 28 C (69 F). Wear light to

EUROPE

medium weight clothing and have a raincoat or umbrella handy.

Transportation

Taxis hailed in street at stands, or by phone. Costs are kr 12 plus kr 1 per km, tip included. Buses are frequent and fare is kr 6 for use on any bus within 1 hr of purchase.
No subway.

Car Hire

Hertz, Royal Hotel (tel: 127700 & 144222 & 509300)
Ansa, Trommesalen 4
   (tel: 111234)
Avis, Vester Sogade 10
   (tel: 141331)

Budget, V. Farimagsgade 3
   (tel: 133900)
InterRent, Jernbanegade 6
   (tel: 116200 & 503090)
Pitzner Auto (tel: 111234)

Hospitals

Emergency tel: 000. Doctor on call 24 hrs per day. Emergency dental Oslo Plas 14 tel: 380251

Trade Fairs

International Crafts and Trades Exhibition (Jan)
Microcomputers Exhibition (Jan)
International Boat Exhibition (Feb)
Men's and Ladies' Wear Exhibition (Mar)
Shoe Trade Exhibition (Mar)
Scandinavian Dental Fair (April)

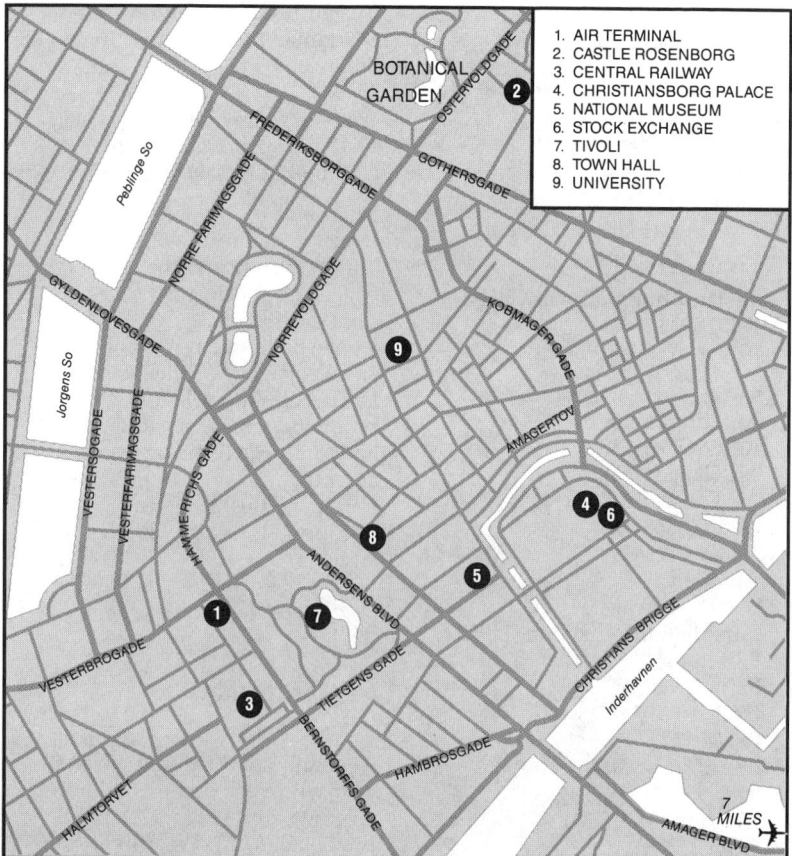

1. AIR TERMINAL
2. CASTLE ROSENBORG
3. CENTRAL RAILWAY
4. CHRISTIANSBORG PALACE
5. NATIONAL MUSEUM
6. STOCK EXCHANGE
7. TIVOLI
8. TOWN HALL
9. UNIVERSITY

Copenhagen

Scandinavian Furniture Fair
(May)
Home Textiles and Carpeting
Fair (Aug)
Clothing Trade Exhibition (Aug)
Development Projects Fair (Sept)
Scandinavian Shoe Fair (Sept)
International Business & Data
Exhibition (Oct)
Hydraulics & Pneumatics
Exhibition (Oct)

Hotels
Alexandria, H.C. Andersens
Blvd. 8 (tel: 142200)
D'Angleterre, Kongens Nytorv
34 (120095)
Amager, Amagerbrogade 29
(tel: 544008)
Ascot, Studiestrade 57 (126000)
Astoria, Banegardspladsen 4
(141419)
Bel Air, Lojtegardsvej 99
(tel: 513033)
Carlton, Halmforvet 14
(tel: 212551)
City, Peder Skrams Gade 24
(130666)
Comfort, Longangsstraede 27
(126570)
Codan, Skt. Annae Plads 21
(tel: 133400)
Danhotel, Kastrup Airport
(tel: 511400)
Grand Hotel, Vesterbrogade 9
(tel: 313600)
Kong Frederick, Voldgade 25-27
(tel: 125902)
Mercure, 17 Vester Farimagsgade
(tel: 125711)
Park Hotel, 5 Jarmers Plads
(tel: 133000)
Plaza Sheraton, Bernstoffsgate 4
(tel: 149262)
Royal Hotel, Hammerichsgade 1,
(tel: 14142)
SAS Globetrotter, Rasmussen
Engrei 171 (tel: 551433)
Savoy Hotel, Vesterbrogade 34
(tel: 112324)
Scandinavia, Amager Blvd. 70
(tel: 112324)
Sheraton Copenhagen, 6 Vester
Sogade 1601 (tel: 143535)

What to See and Do
Night visits to Tivoli pleasure
gardens in the center of town
offers fountains, restaurants and
pavilions. Attend the Royal
Danish Ballet (reservations
144665) or watch the Changing
of the Guard at Amalienborg
Palace. Bars stay open to 0500.
Nyhara contains quaint sailors'
quarters, nightlife, between
Kongens Nytorv Sq. and the
harbor. Stroget, the pedestrian
mall, features fashionable shops,
stores, sex cinemas, Georg
Jensen silver, and Royal
Copenhagen porcelain.

Useful Addresses

Embassies and Consulates
American: D. Hammarskjolds
Alle 25 (tel: 423144)
Canadian: Kr. Bernikowsgade 1
(tel: 122299)
British: Kastelsvej 38-40
(tel: 264600)

Business and Commerce
Central Bank, 5 Havnegade
(tel: 141411)
Company Information, Nygade 4
(tel: 124280)
Shipping, Amaliegade 33
(tel: 114088)
Statistics, Sejrogade 11
(tel: 298222)
Stock Exchange, Nikolas Plads 2
(tel: 933366)
Chamber of Commerce, Borsen
(tel: 155320)
United Nations Information
Office, H.C. Andersens Blvd.
37 (tel: 122120)
Commercial Bank Holmens Kanal
2 (tel: 950061)
Central Telegraph Office,
Kobmayergade 37 (tel: 120903)

Tourism and Travel
Tourist Board, H.C. Andersens
Blvd. 22 (tel: 111325)
Danish National Tourist Office,
Banegard spl. 2 (tel: 111415)

EUROPE

Automobile Club of Denmark,
  Blegdamsvej 124 (tel: 382112)
American Express, Amagertorv
  101818 (Stroget) (tel:122301)

Thomas Cook/Wagons-Lits,
  Vesterbrogade 2 (tel: 142747)

FINLAND

Essential Information

Type of Government
Constitutional Republic

Area
338,000 sq km
(130,160 sg mi)

Population
5 million

Annual Growth Rate
5%

Languages
Finnish (93.5%). Finland is
officially bilingual. Swedish 6.3%

Religion
Lutheran 97%, Orthodox 1.2%

Ethnic Groups
Finns, Swedes, Lapps, Gypsies,
Tartars

Weights and Measures
Metric

Electrical Current
A.C. 50c 220/380 V

Major Business Cities
Helsinki (cap) 535,000
Turku 175,000
Tampere 175,000
Espoo 156,000
Vantaa 144,000

Currency
1 markka (Finnmark) = 100
  pennia
Notes 5, 10, 50, 100 and 500
  markka
Coins 5, 10, 20, 50 pennia, 1
  markka

Public Holidays
Jan 1 New Year
Jan 6 Epiphany
Apr 13-20 Easter Week
May 1 Labour Day
May 28 Ascension
Jun 9 Whitsun
Jun 21 Flag Day
Nov 1 All Saints' Day
Dec 6 Independence Day
Dec 25,26 Christmas

Travellers Information

Entry Requirements
Visas not required for Canadian,
British, American visitors, nor
for most European countries.

Working Restrictions
Work permit required of all
visitors

Vaccination Required
No vaccinations required

Customs and Duty Free
On arrival: 400 cigarettes or 500
gm (1 lb) of tobacco; spirits 2 L,
wine 2 L plus beer 4 L; perfume
and eau du cologne for personal
use.

Currency Restrictions
Foreign currency may be
imported but must be declared.
An equal amount of foreign
currency may also be exported,
but also declared. Local
currency, if imported, may also
be exported (up to fmk 10,000).

Health Tips
Tap water is drinkable, medical
facilities very good but also
expensive. Travel health
insurance coverage advisable.
Emergency first aid, Meilahti
Hospital, Haartmaninkatu 4, tel:
4711.

Climate and Clothing
Jun-Sept average 19 C (66 F) but July can be very hot. Light to medium-weight clothes and light jacket recommended. Summers quite temperate.
Oct-May average -4 C (25 F) to 8 C (46 F) but much colder, more snow in the north. Heavy clothes, boots, hats highly advisable.

Tipping
Taxis require no tips, but tip porters 5 markka. A 15% tip is usually included in all hotel, restaurant and nightspot bills. Tip 3 markka for newspapers, services, etc.

Food and Drink
Finnish food much like North American, except Finns enjoy more fish and fewer vegetables. Eating snacks on the street is not advisable. Avoid political or religious discussions and loud talking or laughing in restaurants and social occasions.

Business Brief

GDP
$53.2 billion
(per capita income $10,500)

Annual Growth Rate
4.9%

Natural Resources
Forestry, copper, zinc, iron, farmland, nickel, chromium, cobalt

Agriculture
Pigs and beef cattle, wheat, rye, barley, oats, potatoes, dairy products, sugar beets

Industry
Iron and steel, forestry products, foodstuffs, textiles, clothing, chemicals, electronics, furniture

Imports
Total $19.8 billion
Vehicles, food, fuels, petroleum, minerals, consumer finished goods, machinery, chemicals

Exports
Total $20,1 billion
Paper and paperboard, machinery, lumber chemicals, glass manufactured goods, engineering products

Major Trading Partners
Sweden, U.S.S.R., Great Britain, West Germany, U.S., Norway, Denmark, Saudi Arabia

Workforce
2.6million
Services 38%, industry 34%, agriculture 14%

Tips for Doing Business
Most Finnish businesspeople speak English. Business suit recommended for all business and social occasions. If invited to dinner, be prompt and bring flowers. Refrain from drinking until host gives first toast. For business visits always make an appointment first, and Finns like to be addressed by their title. Business deals not negotiated on social occasions, which are reserved for after the deal is made. Invitation to join host for a sauna should always be carefully considered. This is a compliment to you and should usually not be refused. Always shake hands with both men and women.

Best Months for Doing Business
February through May and October through December. Business vacations are taken June through August. Also avoid weeks of Christmas and Easter

Business Hours

Government
Mon-Fri 0800-1615

Business
Mon-Fri 0800-1615

EUROPE

Banks
Mon-Fri 0915-1615

Shops
Mon-Fri 0900-1700 or later
Sat 0900-1600 (close 1400 in
summer months)

English Language Publications
International Herald Tribune,
USA Today and British daily
newspapers are widely available
in Helsinki. English language
publication in Finland is called
Helsinki This Week.

Telephone and Communications
Telephone country code: 358
Telephone city code: Helsinki 90
Telex country code: 857
Local calls in public booths, etc.
cost 1 markka. Useful numbers
in Helsinki: Emergencies, 000,
003; Directory, 92020; Bus and
trams, 4722-252; Railways,
659411; Ambulance, 0066;
Medical service, 008; News in
English, 040 or 018; Telegrams,
021. Direct dialling to most
western and some Eastern
European countries possible.

Air Travel
Helsinki-Vantaa major airport.
Finnair provides excellent and
cheap inter-city service
throughout the country.

Other Transport
Efficient coach service the
hallmark of public transport,
particularly in Lapland.
Wide network of cheap railways,
but passengers must book
express trains in advance. Passes
available allowing continuous
travel. Phone 659411.
Distance from Helsinki to Turku:
165 km (102 mi); Tampere 176
km (109 mi).

HELSINKI

Airport Information

Time
GMT +2
GMT +3 (Mar 28-Sept 25)

Airport
Helsinki-Vantaa International
  HEL
Tel: (90) 82921
19 km (12 mi) N of the city

Airlines
Aeroflot 659655
Air France 625862
Austrian 171311
British Airways 650677
Eastern 822124
El Al 146246
Finnair 818800
Iberia 640944
Interflug 170833
KLM 646645
Lufthansa 6949900
Pan Am 6942422
Qantas 410411
Sabena 647421
SAS 175611
Swissair 175300
THY 240120

Transport to City
Taxis: charge by the kilometer,
with ride to Helsinki costing
about fmk 90 ($18-20). Surcharge
for more than two passengers,
and up to four may ride
together.
Finnair Coach: run every 30 min
to Hotel Intercontinental, central
railway station, and other stops
as required. First bus 0645. Last
bus meets last flight arriving.
Fare: fmk 11 ($2.25).
Transit: public buses #614 to bus
station, #615 to railway station,
leave from arrival hall. Fare: fmk
9 ($1.95). Ride takes 30-40 min to
downtown.

Facilities
Currency exchange, bank, post office, information desk, duty-free shop sells cigarettes, cigars, wine, liqueurs.
Car rental desks: Hertz, Avis, Carop, InterRent.

Airport Taxes
None

City Information

Weather
Summer: long, bright sunny days
Winter: dark, bitterly cold
Average temps: Jan -5 C (23 F)
July 17 C (62 F)

Transportation
Taxis with "Taksi" sign on roof can be hailed in the street, by phone or at stands. Fare is fmk 10 plus fmk 3 per km. Tipping not expected, but added charges at night and on weekends.
Trams (streetcars) available on major streets.
Buses provide good service. Flat fare in Helsinki is fmk 4.60.

Car Hire
Hertz, Intercontinental Hotel
  (tel:446910 & 821699)
Avis, Fredrikinkatu 36
  (tel: 6944400 & 822833)
Europcar, Mariankatu 24
  (tel: 717211 & 821052)
InterRent, Hesperia Hotel
  (tel: 408443 & 826677)

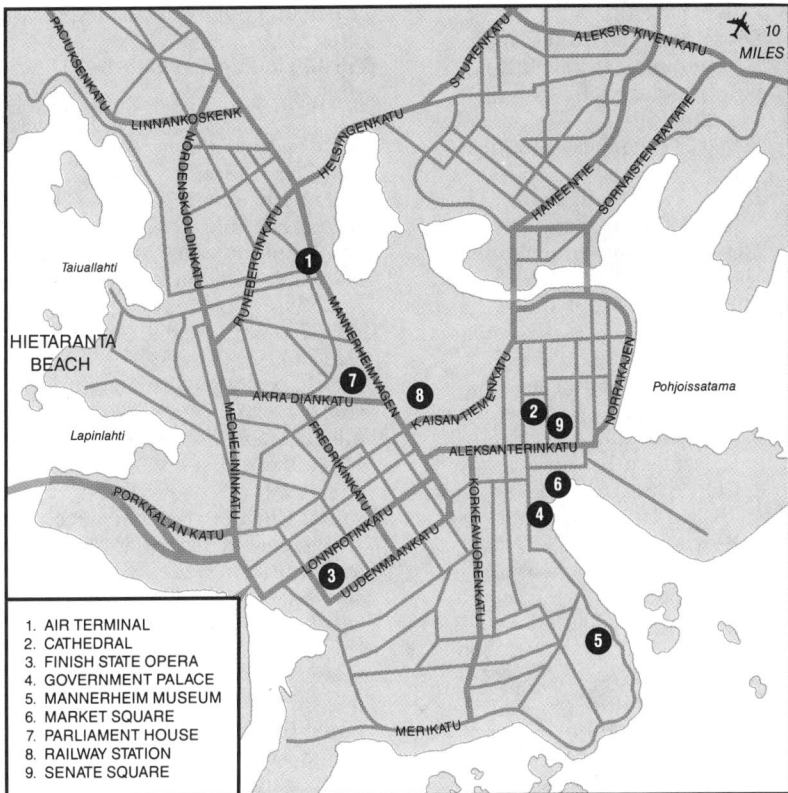

1. AIR TERMINAL
2. CATHEDRAL
3. FINISH STATE OPERA
4. GOVERNMENT PALACE
5. MANNERHEIM MUSEUM
6. MARKET SQUARE
7. PARLIAMENT HOUSE
8. RAILWAY STATION
9. SENATE SQUARE

Helsinki

EUROPE

Hospitals
Toolo Hospital (tel: 40261)
All-night pharmacy (tel: 179092)

Trade Fairs
Medicine and Health Care (Jan)
Finnish Fashion Fair (Jan)
International Boat Exhibition
(Feb)
Finnish Shoe and Boot Fair (Mar)
Sports Trade Fair (Mar)
International Building Fair
(April)
International Business Machines
Exhibition (Aug)
International Technical Fair (Oct)
International Consumer Goods
Trade Fair (Nov)
Education and Teaching
Materials Fair (Nov)

Hotels
Aurora, Helsingkinatu 50
(tel: 717400)
Dipoli Summer Hotel,
Jamerantaival (tel: 461811)
Finn, Kalevankatu 3B
(tel: 640904)
Haaga, Nuijamiestentie 10
(tel: 578311)
Helka, P. Rautatienkatu 23
(tel: 440581)
Hesperia, Mannerheimintie 50
(tel: 441311)
Hospiz, Vuorikatu 17B
(tel: 170481)
Intercontinental,
Mannerheimintie 46
(tel: 441331)
Kalastajatorppa,
Kalastajatorpantie 2
(tel: 488011)
Marski, Mannerheimintie 10
(tel: 641717)
Olympia, L. Brahenkatu 2
(tel: 750801)
Presidentti, E. Rautatiekatu 4
(tel: 6911)

What to See and Do
Visit the colorful marketplaces
along the waterfront of Helsinki,
or the presidential palace or

Uspenski Cathedral. In summer
take the ferry to the fortress at
Sveaborg, or visit the
Mannecheim Military Museum.
Nightclubs and supper clubs are
expensive, among them the 'M'
club at the Marski Hotel,
Hesperia at the Hesperia Hotel,
and the Red Room at the
Kalastajatorppa Hotel. Opera
and ballet at The National
Opera. Also visit the Tapiola
Garden City, Sibelius
Monument, or the Korkeasaari
Island Zoo. Many of Helsinki's
better restaurants may be found
in the hotels listed above.

Useful Addresses

Embassies and Consulates
American: Itainen Puistotie 14A
(tel: 171931)
Canadian: Pohjoisesplanadi 25
(tel: 171141)
British: Uudenmaankatu 16-20
(tel: 647922)

Business and Commerce
Main Post Office,
Mannerheimintie 11
Bank of Helsinki,
Aleksanterinkatu 17 (tel: 17521)
State Bank, Unioninkatu 20
(tel: 35801641)
Central Bank, Box 160, 00101,
Helsinki 10 (tel: 1831)
Stock Exchange, Fabianinkatu 14
(tel: 611623)
Foreign Trade Association,
Arkadiankatu 4-6B
(tel: 6971122)
Central Chamber of Commerce,
Fabianinkatu 14 (tel: 650133)
Finnish-British Trade
Association, Etela Esplanaoi 2
Helsinki Chamber of Commerce,
Kalevankatu 12 (tel: 644601)

Tourism and Travel
Tourist Board, Kluuvikatu 8
Finland Travel Bureau,
Kaivokatu 10A (tel: 170515)

Helsinki Tourist Office,
  Pohjoisesplanadi 19
  (tel: 1693757)
Automobile and Touring Club of
  Finland, 10 Kansakoulukatu
  (tel: 6940022)
American Express, Travek

Travelbureau Ltd. (R),
  Etelaranta 16, Helsinki (tel: 90
  171900)
American Express, Travek
  Travelbureau Ltd. (R),
  Humalistonkatu 3, Turku (921
  337111)

EUROPE

FRANCE

Essential Information

Type of Government
Republic

Area
551,110 sq km
(212,783 sq mi)

Population
55.2 million

Annual Growth Rate
1.75%

Languages
French

Religion
Catholic

Ethnic Groups
Almost entirely French, but with large Arab and African populations in large cities.

Weights and Measures
Metric

Electrical Current
A.C. 50c 220/380 V

Major Business Cities
Paris (cap) 9,300,00
Marseilles 1,300,000
Lyon 1,250,000
Bordeaux 650,000
Toulouse 550,000
Nantes 350,000

Currency
1 franc (fr) = 100 centimes
Notes 50, 100, 200, and 500 francs
Coins 5, 10, 20, 50 centimes. 1, 5, and 10 fr

Public Holidays
Jan 1 New Year
Apr 13-20 Easter Week
May 1 Labour Day
May 28 Ascension
May 19 Pentecost
July 14 Bastille Day
Aug 15 Assumption
Nov 1 All Saints' Day
Nov 11 Armistice
Dec 25 Christmas

Travellers Information

Entry Requirements
Passport required, but no visa required by Canadian, U.S. or British nationals if staying less than 3 months.

Working Restrictions
North Americans need work permits, nationals of EEC countries do not.

Vaccination Required
Typhoid vaccination recommended only.

Customs and Duty Free
On arrival: 200 cigarettes, or 50 cigars, or 250 gr (8 oz) of tobacco; spirits 1 L (1.7 pt.); wine 2 L (3.5 pt.); perfume 50 gr (1.7 oz.); eau de cologne 25 cl. (8 oz.). Other gifts to a value of fr 140.

Currency Restrictions
Foreign currency may be exported by non-residents up to 5,000 fr, unless you declared a higher amount on entry. All foreign currency must be declared on arrival, and reconverted from fr upon exit.

Health Tips
No public health service. Health services are good but expensive. Travel health coverage strongly advised. American Hospital in Paris accepts insurance plans. Tel: 7475300. Drinking water is purified.

Climate and Clothing

Northern France
May-Sept average 15-24 C (60-75 F) and are generally sunny and warm. Oct-April average 7 C (45 F) and are cool and wet.

EUROPE

Lightweight to medium weight clothes.

Southern France
Mediterranean climate characterized by hot May-Sept averaging 27-32 C (80-90 F), and mild, dry Oct-April averaging 10-15 C (50-60 F). Lightweight clothes all year round.

Tipping
Tip taxi drivers 15%, porters 8 francs per bag, and waiters 5% only for very good service, since all restaurants add 15% for service to the bill. In small cafes, ask the waiter if a service charge has been added. Tip approximately 3-5 francs for small services.

Food and Drink
French food is world-renowned for delicate sauces, soups, crusty breads, and pastries among others. Breakfast usually consists of coffee and croissants or pastries, with eggs available on request only. Lunch or dinner is usually the main meal and can be a lengthy affair. Long business lunches are traditional, and late night dinners standard. Meals begin with an aparatif, then an appetizer followed by a main course, and either dessert or cheese. Wine is a source of national pride to Frenchmen and so it is consumed with most meals. French beer is also very good.
Some French regional specialties include Camenbert cheese and Apple Brandy in Normandy, fish and seafood of all kinds throughout France, but especially in Brittany and along the Cote d'Azur in the south. The beef from the Camargue region is excellent, as is the lamb anywhere, but especially in Provence cooked with the pungent herbs from that area. The red wines from Burgundy and Bordeaux are world-class, as are the whites from Burgundy, Chablis and the Loire. Paris is the gourmet capital of France, with many excellent restaurants serving specialties from everywhere in France.

Business Brief

GDP
$988.4 billion
(per capita income $17,845)

Natural Resources
Iron ore, potash, bauxite coal, natural gas, sulphur. Also deposits of zinc, lead, pyrite, phosphates, uranium.

Agriculture
Barley, fodder crops, fruits, grapes, potatoes, sugarbeets, vegetables, wheat

Industry
Chemicals, clothing, food, iron and steel, machinery, metal-working, textiles, tourism, transport equipment, and wine

Imports
Total $158.5 billion
Electronic and communications equipment, petroleum, minerals, ores, machine tools, paper and wood pulp, non-ferrous metals

Exports
Total $148.4 billion
Machinery and transport equipment, iron and steel products, foodstuffs, chemicals, manufactured goods of all kinds, perfume and haute couture, spirits, textiles and fabrics

Major Trading Partners
West Germany, Belgium, Luxembourg, Italy, U.S., Switzerland, Great Britain, Netherlands, Algeria, Japan, Saudi Arabia

Workforce
23.6 million
Manufacturing 38%, trades and

services 47%, agriculture, fishing, forestry, etc. 10%

Tips for Doing Business

Wear conservative business suits, and always make appointments. Knowing a few words or phrases in French is a major advantage, since French businesspeople take their culture very seriously. Business meetings tend to be lengthy, protracted and sombre. Address your contacts simply as, "Monsieur," or "Madame," and entertaining is usually carried on in restaurants. Shake hands at every opportunity, but do not discuss a man's business affairs generally, and be discreet on all other matters. It will be appreciated, and possibly rewarded.

The long business lunch is a tradition and you should take advantage of both its gourmet and profit potential.

Best Months for Doing Business

February through May and September through November will find most businesspeople at work. Month-long vacations in July through September are the norm. Also avoid the two weeks before and after Christmas.

Business Hours

Government
Mon-Fri 0830-1200, 1400-1800

Business
Mon-Fri 0900-1200, 1400-1800

Banks (in Paris)
Mon-Fri 0900-1630
(Banks close for a half-day before a legal holiday and on the Monday before a Tuesday holiday.)

Shops
Mon-Sat variable hours

English Language Publications

International Herald-Tribune is available in Paris and other major cities. Also some British and American (USA Today) newspapers on sale in hotels and at kiosks.

Telephone and Communications

Telephone country code: 33
Telephone city code: Paris 1, Lyon 78
Telex country code: 42F
Public phones require either a 1-fr coin or a "jeton" which may be purchased in shops or cafes. Local calls cost 80 centimes. Insert the coin or jeton and dial. Fast beeping sound means phone is ringing. When answered, push button on the phone to complete the call. If call is interrupted by a signal more coins are required. To dial direct long distance (while in France) to Lyon, Marseilles, Nantes, Nice, and Toulouse first dial 15 then the number. To Lille and Strasbourg first dial 16 then the number. Useful numbers in Paris: Operator 10, International calls 24 and 30, Police 17, Emergency Dental Care 2537653. Telex facilities available in post offices of major cities and in 2 public telex offices in Paris.

Air Travel

Air France is the national airline for international flights, while Air Inter and Touraine Air Transport operate most domestic flights. All major commercial cities well served. Major Paris airports are Charles de Gaulle (23 km NE of the city), Orly (14 km S of Paris). Other international airports at Bordeaux, Lyon, Marseilles, Nice, and Toulouse.

Other Transport

Bus and coaches, operated by the railways, offer good long-distance services. Flat fare is normal. Excellent but narrow

EUROPE

roads, high-speed motorways are the norm.

Modern high-speed trains operated by Societe Nationale des Chemins de Fer Francaise (SNCF) connect major cities in the north and south and offer an attractive alternative to air travel. In cities, taxis may be hailed or called by phone or at stands. Basic fare is 8-10 fr plus charge per km. Tip 10-15% is normal. Very extensive Metro (subway) in Paris. Tickets or tokens may be used on subways or on buses.

LYON

Airport Information

Time
GMT +1
GMT +2 (Mar-Sept)

Airport
Lyon-Satolas International LYS
Tel: (78) 19221
26 km (16 mi) E of city
Domestic and international flights

Airlines
Air Algerie 78426495
Air Canada 78424317
Air France 78427900
Alitalia 78377738
British Airways 78377461
Iberia 78427691
KLM 78381769
Lufthansa 72226666
Olympic 78374497
Sabena 78376684
SAS 8636456
Swissair 7807015
TAP 78376307
TWA 78422162
UTA 78420730
Varig 78373200

Transport to City
Taxis: Taxis are available at the terminal for half-hour ride to downtown for fare of about

fr 140.
Coaches: depart from the airport every 20 minutes for the 40-minute ride to Lyon. Fare is approximately fr 35, and bus to the airport may be boarded at Gare de Perrache, av. Bertholot and av. J. Mermoz from 0500-2100.
Some hotel courtesy coaches also available.

Facilities
The Central Terminal Building, with a domestic and international wing, provide bank with currency exchange, hotel reservations, post office, baggage deposit, shops.
Duty-free shop sells cigarettes, cigars, wines, spirits, watches, etc.
Car rental desks: Hertz, Avis, Europcar, InterRent, Citer, Budget

Airport Taxes
None

City Information

Weather
More temperate than Paris although it can get very cold during the winter season with the possibility of snow. Temperatures from 5-15C (40-60F) from Oct-Apr, and 18-27C (65-80F) from May-Sept.

Transportation
Taxis available at taxi stands and hotels. Intercity bus system runs frequently and covers the entire city and outlying areas. Roads are very good and car rental is a good means of getting around.

Car Hire
Hertz, Airport (tel: 78719451)
Ansa, Airport (tel: 78719474)
Avis, route de Vienne 8
    (tel: 78719525)
Europcar, 7 rue Duhamel
    (tel: 78719527)

InterRent, rue de l'Abondance
(tel: 8602528)

International Furniture and
Furnishings Exhibition (Sept)
International Contracting Show
(Oct)

Hotels

Axotel, near cours Verdun
(tel: 78375655)
Bristol, 28 cours Verdun
(tel: 8375655)
Frantel, 129 rue Servient
(tel: 8629412)
Grand Hotel Concorde, 11 rue
Grolee (tel: 78425621)

IBIS Lyon Gerland, 68 ave
Leclerc (tel: 8583070)
IBIS Lyon Part Dieu Sud, Place
Renaudel (tel: 8583070)
Mercure La Part-Dieu, 47 Blvd.
Vivier-merle (tel: 2341812)
Mercure Nord, A & Dardilly
(78352805)
Mercure Pont Pasteur, 70 ave
Leclerc-Gerland (tel: 78586853)
Meridien, Satolas airport (tel:
78719161)
Novotel Airport, Rue Lionel-
Terrey (tel: 78269748)
Novotel Nord, A & Porte de
Lyon (tel: 78351341)

1. CATHEDRAL
2. CITY HALL
3. THE MAIN STATION
4. NOTRE DAME
5. POST OFFICE

QUAI ST V INCENT

COURS LAFAYETTE

AVE MAR FOCH

RUE GARIBALDI

PLACE
BELLECOUR

QUAI FULCHIRON

QUAI TILSIT

QUAI DOCTEUR GAILLETON

QUAI C BERNARD

AVE MAR DE SAME

COURS GAMBETTA

COURS DE VERDUN

QUAI DES ETROITS

Saone

QUAI PRAMBAUD

Rhone

RUE DE L'UNIVERSITE

19 MILES

QUAI JEAN J ROUSSEAU

QUAI PERRACHE

AVE LECLERC

AVE JEAN JAURES

AVE BERTHELOT

EUROPE

Lyon

Piolat et Lutetia, 114 blvd. des
   Belges
Royal, 20 pl. Bellecour
   (tel: 78375731)
Simplon, 11 rue Duhamel
Sofitel, 20 quai Gailleton
   (tel: 78427250)

What to See and Do

Visit old Lyon, with many
ancient Renaissance and
medieval buildings still intact.
Also the cathedral of Notre-
Dame-de-Fourviere and the parc
de la Tete d'Or. Beaux-Arts
Museum and Automobile
Museum are close to the center
of town. An interesting side trip
for lunch and sightseeing should
be arranged to the medieval
village of Perouges. Sampling
fine restaurants and just visiting
some of the smaller towns
around Lyon, like Nyons, can be
fun, while the Ardeche, on the
other side of the Rhone river is
more isolated and rugged.

Useful Addresses

Embassies and Consulates

American: 7 quai General Sarrail
   (tel: 78246849)
British: 24 rue Childebert
   (tel: 78375967)

Business and Commerce

British Chamber of Commerce,
   20 rue de la Bourse
   (tel: 78381010)
Lyon Chamber of Commerce,
   Palais du Commerce
   (tel: 78381010)

Tourism and Travel

Tourist Office, Place Bellecour
   (tel: 422575)
American Express, 6 rue
   Childeberte (tel: 78734069)
Wagons-Lits/Cook, 105 rue E.
   Herriot (tel: 78425326)

PARIS

Airport Information

Time
GMT +1
GMT +2 (April-Oct)

Airports
Charles de Gaulle International
CDG
Tel: 48621212
23 km (14 mi) from city
Orly Airport ORL
Tel: 48843210
14 km (9 mi) from city

Le Bourget Airport
Tel: 48621212
13 km (8 mi) from city

Airlines
Aer Lingus 47421250
Aeroflot 42254381
Aerolineas Argentinas 42563116
Aeromexico 47424050
Air Afrique 45625199
Air Algerie 42603062
Air Canada 47422121
Air France 45356161
Air India 42661372
Alia 42615745
Alitalia 42566500
American 42890522
Austrian 42663466
Avensa 47422007
Avianca 42603522
British Airways 47781414
British Caledonia 46370101
Canadian International 42617234
CAAC 45001994
Delta 43354080
Egyptair 42665559
El Al 47424129
Finnair 47423333
Garuda 45623866
Gulf Air 47237070
Iberia 47230023
Iran Air 43590120
JAL 42258505
KLM 42665719
Korean 42615174
Kuwait Air 42603060
Lufthansa 42653735
Malaysian 47422600

MEA 4669393
Northwest 42257436
Olympic 42659242
Pan Am 42664545
Philippine 42270693
PIA 45629241
Qantas 42665200
SAA 42615787
Sabena 47424747
SAS 47420614
Saudia 47237272
Singapore 42615309
Swissair 45811101
Syrian 47421197
TAP 42961609
Thai 47206450
THY 47426085
TWA 47206211
UTA 47764152
United 42651965
Varig 47200333

Transport to City

Charles de Gaulle
Taxis: Fare from airport to city start at 150 fr with 50% surcharge after 2200 and on Sundays. Tips are 15%.
Coach: Buses will take passengers to the Invalides city terminal or the Porte Maillot city terminal. Fare is 45-55 fr.
Transit: Express train runs to the Gare du Nord railway station and Chatelet subway station. Fare is 18-40 fr.
Orly
Taxis: Fare is about 100-120 fr + 15% tip.
Coach: Bus service between Orly and Charles de Gaulle airports. Airport bus or coach fare city is 25-45 fr.

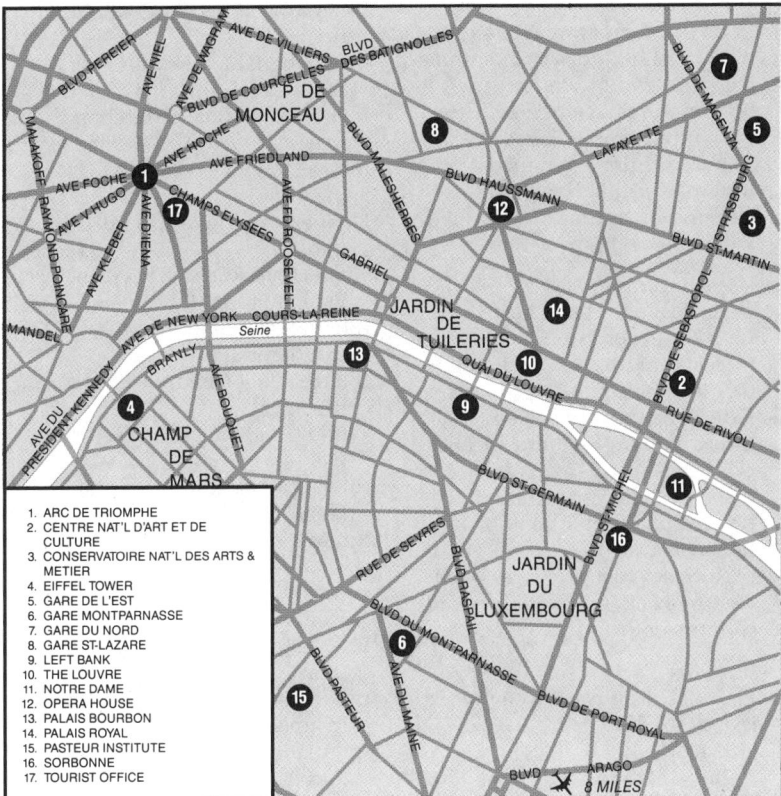

1. ARC DE TRIOMPHE
2. CENTRE NAT'L D'ART ET DE CULTURE
3. CONSERVATOIRE NAT'L DES ARTS & METIER
4. EIFFEL TOWER
5. GARE DE L'EST
6. GARE MONTPARNASSE
7. GARE DU NORD
8. GARE ST-LAZARE
9. LEFT BANK
10. THE LOUVRE
11. NOTRE DAME
12. OPERA HOUSE
13. PALAIS BOURBON
14. PALAIS ROYAL
15. PASTEUR INSTITUTE
16. SORBONNE
17. TOURIST OFFICE

EUROPE

Paris

Transit: Express train from airport to station. Fare is 18-40 fr.
Le Bourget
Taxis: Available at stands.
Coach: Airport bus or coach service costs 25-45 fr.
No train service.

Facilities
Duty-free shops available at all 3 airports. Also currency exchange, retaurants, bars, baggage deposit, hotel reservations, information desk. Car rental desks: (de Gaulle & Orly) Hertz, Alfa, Avis, Europcar, InterRent.

Airport Taxes
None

City Information

Weather
Paris has temperate climate, warm to hot and wet in summer, cold and wet in winter. July temperatures average 20 C (68 F), winter temperatures average 3 C (38 F). Bring a raincoat or umbrella and lightweight clothing in summer, medium weight clothing in winter.

Transportation
Taxis cost about 8 fr basic fare plus 2.5 fr per km. Double these prices at night, and add 10% for day or night trips.
Extensive subway system (Metro) offers first and second-class cars, with some cars reserved only for veterans, the handicapped, etc. Book of 10 tickets is called a "carnet" and each ticket costs 2.5 fr in book. Metro tickets may also be used to transfer onto bus system.

Car Hire
Hertz, 27 Rue St. Ferdinand
    (tel: 47885151)
Ansa, 159 Rue Blomet
    (tel: 43418220)
Avis, 99 Av. Charles de Gaulle

(tel: 46099212 & 455032
Budget (tel: 05100001)
Europcar, 42 Av. de Saxe
    (tel: 43451882)
InterRent, 26 Gouvion Saint-Cyr
    (tel: 45678217)
Kemwel (tel: 48623333)

Hospitals
American Hospital (tel: 47475300) for emergency service
Emergency doctor's service
    (tel: 47077777)
Emergency dental service
    (tel: 43375100)
Drugstores usually open to 0200, except in July and August, when most are closed for the holidays.

Trade Fairs
International Furniture Exhibition (Jan)
International Lighting Exhibition (Jan)
International Jewelry and Gifts Exhibition (Jan)
International Boat Exhibition (Jan)
International Games and Toys (Jan)
Leather and Travel Goods Fair (Jan)
Confectionary and Chocolate Exhibition (Jan)
International Stationery Exhibition (Jan)
International Children's Fashion Fair (Feb)
World Tourism and Travel Fair (Feb)
International Knitwear Exhibition (Feb)
International Bakery and Pastry Exhibition (Feb)
Agricultural Machinery Exhibition (Mar)
International Fur Industries Fair (Mar)
International Plastics and Rubber Exhibition (April)
International Wallcovering and Furnishings Exhibition (May)
International Carpet and

Floorcoverings Exhibition (May)

International Biomedical & Hospital Equipment Exhibition (May)

International Dairy Equipment Exhibition (June)

Commercial Arts & Gifts Exhibition (June)

International Gold & Silver Fair (Sept)

International Sporting Goods Exhibition (Sept)

International Leather Exhibition (Sept)

International Office Products Exhibition (Sept)

International Ladieswear Fashion Exhibition (Sept)

International Hotel and Catering Exhibition (Oct)

International Automobile Show (Oct)

International Food Products Exhibition (Oct)

International Electronic Equipment Exhibition (Nov)

International Food Industry Equipment Exhibition (Nov)

International Packaging Exhibition (Nov)

International Laboratory Exhibition (Dec)

International Chemical Engineering Exhibition (Dec)

Hotels

Abbaye Saint-Germain, 10 rue Cassette, 6e (tel: 45443811)

Angleterre-Champs-Elysees, 91 rue La Boetie, 8e (tel: 43593545)

Burgundy, 8 rue Duphot, 1er (tel: 42609432)

Bristol, 112 fbg St-Honore, 8e (tel: 42669145)

Champs-Elysees, 2 rue d'Artois, 8e (tel: 43591142)

Crillon, 10 pl. de la Concorde, 8e (tel: 42652424)

Cusset, 95 rue de Richelieu, 2e (tel: 42974890)

Esmeralda, 4 rue St-Julien-le-Pauvre, 5e (tel: 43541920)

Excelsior-Opera, 5 rue La Fayette, 9e (tel: 48749930)

Ferrandi, 92 rue du Cherche-Midi, 6e (tel: 42229740)

George V, 31 av. George V, 8e (tel: 47235400)

IBIS Bagnolet, rue jean-Jaures, Bagnolet (tel: 43600276)

IBIS La Defense, 4 Blvd. de Neuilly, Courbevoie (tel: 47781560)

IBIS Monmartre, 5 rue Caulaincourt (tel: 42941818)

Intercontinental-Paris, 3 rue de Castiglione, 1er (tel: 42603780)

Lotti, rue de Castiglione, 1er (tel: 42603734)

Mayfair, 3 rue Rouget-de-l'Isle, 1er (tel: 42603814)

Mercure Etoile, 27 av. des Ternes (tel: 47664918)

Mercure Monmartre, 1-3 rue Caulaincourt (tel: 42941717)

Mercure Montrouge, 13 rue Francois Ory (tel: 46571126)

Mercure Nord, rue J. Moulin-St. Witz, Fosse Survilliers (tel: 4682828)

Mercure Porte de Pantin, 25 rue Scandicci (tel: 48467066)

Mercure Porte de Versailles, rue du Moulin, Vanves (tel: 46429322)

Meridien, 81 Boulevard Gouvion St. Cyr (tel: 47581230)

Nantes, 55 rue St-Roch, 1er (tel: 42616778)

Napoleon, 40. av. de Friedland, 8e (tel: 47660202)

Nikko Hotel, 61 quai de Grenelle (tel: 45756262)

Normandie, 7 rue de l'Echelle, 1er (tel: 42603021)

Novotel Paris Evry, Parc du Bois Briard (tel: 40778270)

Novotel Bagnolet, 1 av. de la Republique (tel: 43600210)

Novotel La Defense, 2 Blvd. de Neuilly (tel: 47781668)

Plaza Athenee, 25 av. Montaigne (tel: 47237833)

Quai Voltaire, 19 qu. Voltaire, 7e (tel: 42615091)

EUROPE

Ritz, 15 pl. Vendome, 1er
  (tel: 42603830)
Sofitel Boubon, 32 rue Saint
  Dominique (tel: 45559180)
Sofitel Paris, 8 rue Louis Armand
  (tel: 40603030)
Sorbonne, 6 rue Victor-Cousin,
  5e (tel: 43545808)
Windsor, 14 rue Beaujon, 8e
  (tel: 45630404)

What to See and Do

Major tourist attractions include
the Eiffel Tower, Arc de
Triomphe, the Opera, Place des
Invalides, Notre Dame Cathedral
and the church of Sacre Coeur.
The museum of the Louvre
houses one of the world's
largest, most complete
collections of art both modern
and classical and from all over
the world. National museums
are free on Sundays and
Wednesdays. Visit the Museum
of Modern Art at the Centre
Beauborg or the Rodin Museum
across the Seine. Take a boat
ride along the Seine for 25 fr.
Boats leave every half hour from
Bateaux Mouches, quai de la
Conference and Pont de l'Alma.
Take in a cabaret show at the
Lido on the Champs-Elysees or
the Crazy Horse on av. George
V. Jazz clubs include Caveau de
la Montagne on the rue
Descartes and New Morning at
7-9 rue des Petits Ecuries.
There is almost an unlimited
choice of good restaurants, and
cafes and basseries offer good
light meals, wine, beer and
beverages at reasonable prices.
Some good bars include Bar du
Fouquet's, 99 av. des Champs-
Elysees; Harry's Bar, 5 rue
Daunou; Bar de la Closerie, 171
bd. du Montparnasse; and Le
Furstenburg, 27 rue de Buci.
For nightlife, clubs, and discos,
try Castels, 15 rue Princesse;
Elysees Matignon, 2 av.
Matignon; Le Privelege, 1 ter

Cite Bergere; and of course,
Regine's, 49 rue de Ponthieu.

Useful Addresses

Embassies and Consolates

American: 2 av. Gabriel
  (tel: 42961202)
British: 35 rue de Faubourg
  (tel: 42669142)
Canadian: 35 av. Montaigne
  (tel: 47230101)

Business and Commerce:

Central Bank, 39 rue Croix des
  Petits Champs (tel: 42924292)
Company Information, 1 Quai
  Corse (tel: 43291260)
Stock Exchange, 4 Place de la
  Bourse (tel: 42618590)
Translators, 24 rue Aumale
  (tel: 48784332)
American Chamber of
  Commerce, 8 rue Gmarose
  (tel: 45051308)
British Chamber of Commerce, 6
  rue Halevy (tel: 40734921)
International Chamber of
  Commerce, 38 Cours Albert
  (tel: 45623456)
International Monetary Fund, 64
  av. d'Iena (tel: 47235421)
Ministry of External Trade, 41
  Quai Branly (tel: 45507111)
Ministry of Industry, 101 rue de
  la Grenelle (tel: 45563636)
Paris Chamber of Commerce, 27
  av. de Friedland (tel: 42897000)
Paris Stock Exchange, Palais de
  la Bourse (tel: 45089655)
U.N. Information Office, rue
  Miollis (tel: 43069125)
U.S.A. Trade center, 123 av.
  Charles de Gaulle
  (tel: 46243313)

Tourism and Travel

National Bureau of Tourist
  Information (tel: 47204306)
FRAM, 38 av. Georges V
  (tel: 42561300)
French Automobile Association,
  9 rue Alltole-de-la-Forge
  (tel: 42278200)

Touring Club of France, 6-8 rue
  Firmin-Gillet (tel: 45322215)
American Express, 11 rue Scribe
  (tel: 42660999)

American Express, 83 bis, rue de
  Courcelles (tel: 47660300)
Thomas Cook, 92 rue St. Lazaire
  (tel: 42603320)

GERMANY (WEST) FRG

Essential Information

Type of Government
Federal Republic

Area
249,535 sq km
(95,975 sq mi)

Population
61.6 million

Annual Growth Rate
2.6%

Languages
German

Religion
Protestant 44%, Roman Catholic
45%

Ethnic Groups
German with a small Danish
minority

Weights and Measures
Metric

Electrical Current
A.C. 50c 220/380 V

Major Business Cities
Bonn (cap) 350,000
West Berlin 2,250,000
Hamburg 2,000,000
Munich 1,300,000
Cologne 1,100,000
Dusseldorf 700,000
Frankfurt 690,000

Currency
1 Deutsche Mark (dm) = 100
  pfennig (pf)
Notes 5, 10, 20, 50, 100, 500 and
  1,000 dm
Coins 1, 2, 5, 10,, and 50 pf & 1,
  2, 5, 10 dm

Public Holidays
Jan 1 New Year

Apr 13-20 Easter Week
May 1 Labour Day
May 28 Ascension
Jun 9 Whitsun
Jun 17 German Unity
Jun 21 Corpus Christi
Nov 1 All Saints' Day
Dec 25, 26 Christmas

Travellers Information

Entry Requirements
Passports but no visas required
for American, British or
Canadian nationals. Visa may be
required for visit to West Berlin.
Nationals of most European
countries do not need a visa.

Working Restrictions
Nationals of EEC countries need
no work permit. For others a
permit will be issued after work
has been found.

Vaccination Required
None

Customs and Duty Free
On arrival: 400 cigarettes, 100
cigars or 500 gr (1 lb.) of tobacco;
spirits 2 L (2 qts.), wine 2 L;
perfume and eau de cologne for
personal use allowed, as well as
gifts totalling no more than dm
100.

Currency Restrictions
No restrictions on local or
foreign currency

Health Tips
Drinking water, dairy products
and food generally meet or
exceed North American
standards.
Emergency medical service in
Berlin at Arzlicher Notdienst (tel:

EUROPE

310321), in Frankfurt at Arzlicher (tel: 7920200), or in Hamburg at Arzlicher Notdienst (tel: 248181). An Englishspeaking physician in Bonn is Dr. Uwe Olschowka (tel: 633680). In Hamburg, Dr. Hinnaui Khaled (tel: 243504 or 242052). In Berlin, Dr. Wolf Damus (tel: 8811833). In Frankfurt, Dr. Heinrich Hain (tel: 6963645) or Dr. Helmut Baark (tel: 5092081).

Climate and Clothing
West Germany has a temperate climate with warm summers and cold winters. Average temperature May-Sept is 20 C (68 F) but hotter in the south and east of the country. Oct-April average 5 C (38 F) but can get much colder, especially in the south and east. Wear light to medium weight clothes in summer, medium to heavy clothes, boots, hat, etc. in winter.

Tipping
Tip taxis 10-15%, porters 2 DMper piece of baggage. A 10-15% tip is usually included in larger bills, but add5-10% for the staff, especially if service is good. Tip chambermaids, barbers, ushers, etc. 2 DM.

Food and Drink
German breakfasts are light, continental style, while the main meal, lunch, usually consists of soup, a main dish and a dessert. Smoked meats, cheese, sausage and sauerkraut are very popular, and beer and wine are usually served with meals. Heavier foods like potatoes, dumplings, noodles and pastries are the norm. Some American-style fast-food restaurants are also available in the large cities.

Business Brief

GDP
$1,272.6 billion
(per capita income $20,845)

Annual Growth Rate
2.6%

Natural Resources
Iron, coal, potash, lead, zinc, salt, barites, petroleum and natural gas. Coal is the most important mineral.

Agriculture
Barley, oats, wheat, sugarbeets, potatoes, grapes, rye

Industry
Chemicals, clothing, electrical engineering, electronics, food processing, iron and steel, mining, transportation equipment, mechanical engineering

Imports
Total $228 billion
Fuels, petroleum, non-ferrous metals, agricultural foodstuffs, lubricants, textiles

Exports
Total $294 billion
Machinery and transport equipment, iron and steel, metal products, chemicals, electrical equipment, precision instruments, machine tools, manufactured goods

Major Trading Partners
U.S., France, Netherlands, Great Britain, Belgium, Italy, Switzerland, Austria

Workforce
27 million
Industry in general 36%, services 37%, trade 18%, agriculture 6%

Tips for Doing Business
A conservative business suit and (in the north) a felt fedora are recommended. Be prepared to shake hands often during the business meeting, and address

your contact formally by "Herr" plus his title and name. It is best to know your subject and get straight to the point. Make prior appointments and always be punctual. Try to bring an interpreter if you speak no German, and have business cards in German and English. If invited to a businessman's home, bring flowers, but not red roses. Bring scotch whiskey as a gift for your host, not wine, and never smoke until after dinner.

Best Months for Doing Business
Best months are January through June and September through November. Avoid the weeks around Christmas and Easter.

Business Hours

Government
Mon-Fri 0900-1230 & 1400-1700

Business
Mon-Fri 0830-1700

Banks
Mon-Fri 0900-1300 & 1500-1600
Thu 0900-1300 & 1500-1730

Shops
Mon-Fri 0800 or 0900-1830
Sat 0830-1400

English Language Publications
International Herald Tribune, USA Today and some British daily newspapers available in major cities. American and British Forces Broadcasting Services broadcast popular programs and local news on the radio.

Telephone and Communications
Telephone country code: 49
Telephone city code: Bonn 228, Frankfurt 69
There are public telex offices in Berlin at 21 Fermeldeamt 1, and Winterfeldstr 21, in Bonn at Presshaus 1 and Heussallee 2-10, and at major hotels. Telegrams are available through most post offices. Local phone calls from public booths cost 20 pf. Use of postal code in all mailings obligatory.

Air Travel
DLT and Lufthansa operate as domestic and international airlines, respectively. West Berlin airport in Berlin served on domestic routes only by British Airways and Pan Am. Most direct flights are early-morning to major business centres.

Other Transport
Nationwide and excellent coach services run by German Federal Railways and others. 6,500 km total of autobahns with no speed limit enforced. German Federal Railways operates a trans-European express service as well as inter-city trains. Book tickets in advance, and trains always run on time.

DUSSELDORF

Airport Information

Time
GMT +1
GMT +2 (Mar 28 - Sept 18)

Airport
Dusseldorf International DUS
Tel: (0211) 421223
7.4 km (4.5 mi) N of city
International and domestic flights

Airlines
Aer Lingus 80232
Aeroflot 320491
Air Canada 80453
Air France 3879411
Alitalia 388631
Austrian 84423
British Airways 162161
Canadian International 371017
Finnair 353373
Iberia 01306363
JAL 1679111

EUROPE

KLM 325066
Korean 370491
Lufthansa 2118885
Olympic 84941
Qantas 326076
Sabena 328048
SAS 890731
Singapore 132002
Swissair 87977
TWA 84814
Varig 847469

Transport to City

Taxis: the 15-minute trip to the city will cost about 20 dm for up to 4 passengers, with a 10% tip. Coach: take bus #727 to the main central railway station. The fare will be 3 dm for the

25-minute trip.
Transit: the air terminal connects with trains beneath the terminal building. Self-serve ticket machines dispense farecards, two zones of which will get you by train (Train #37) to the central railway station in Dusseldorf. The 13-minute ride costs about 3 dm, and there is lots of room for luggage.

Facilities

Currency exchange, hotel reservations, baggage deposit, post office, conference facilities, first aid/medical.
Duty-free shop sells tobacco products, wines, spirits,

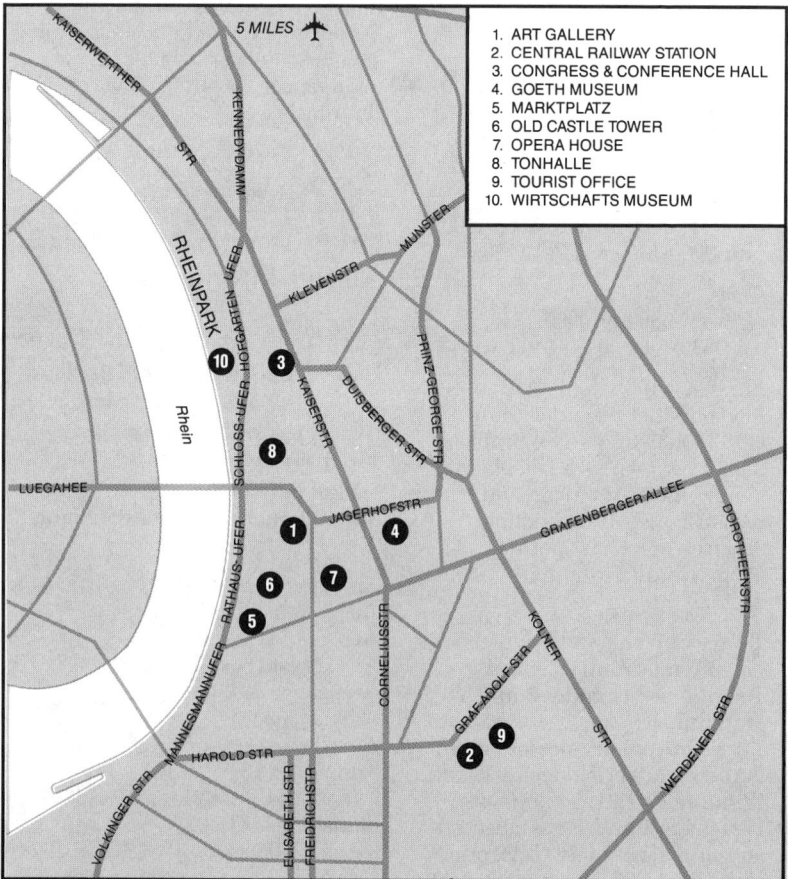

5 MILES

1. ART GALLERY
2. CENTRAL RAILWAY STATION
3. CONGRESS & CONFERENCE HALL
4. GOETH MUSEUM
5. MARKTPLATZ
6. OLD CASTLE TOWER
7. OPERA HOUSE
8. TONHALLE
9. TOURIST OFFICE
10. WIRTSCHAFTS MUSEUM

Dusseldorf

liqueurs, coffee, tea, perfume. North American and British currencies accepted, as well as Swedish, Danish, Belgian, Italian, and French.
Car rental desks: Hertz, Avis, InterRent, Autohansa, Sixt, Europcar, Ansa, Budget, Kemwel.

Airport Taxes
None

City Information

Weather
Dusseldorf is generally mild with the average summer (July) temperature about 17 C (63 F) and the winter (Jan) being about -1 C (31 F). Some winter days can be very cold, but in general winters are cool and dry, summers warm and dry.

Transportation
Good taxi service in Dusseldorf, with fares of 3.20 dm plus 1.60 dm for each km.
Buses and (in some areas) trams also run frequently with a flat fare starting at about 2.50 dm.

Car Hire
Ansa, Berliner Allee 26, (tel: 325040)
Avis, Berliner Allee 32 (tel: 329050 & 4216748)
Budget, Karlstr 72 (tel: 360401)
Europcar, Corneliusstr. 5 (tel: 374058 & 4216496)
Kemwel (tel: 4216499)
InterRent, Charlottenstr. 50 (tel: 350033)

Trade Fairs
International Boat Exhibition (Jan)
Environmental Pollution Control Exhibition (Feb)
International Fashion Trade Fair (Mar)
International Preventive Medicine Exhibition (Mar)
International Footwear Exhibition (Mar)
International Fashion Trade Fair (April)
International Wine & Cable Exhibition (April)
International Printing and Paper Fair (May)
International Gas Turbine Exhibition (June)
International Powder & Metallurgy Exhibition (July)
International Trade Fair (Aug)
International Fashion Trade Fair (Sept)
International Instrumentation & Automation Exhibition (Oct)
International Plastics and Rubber Fair (Nov)
International Hotel & Restaurant Fair (Nov)
International Medical & Technical Exhibition (Nov)
International Swimming Pool & Sauna Exhibition (Nov)

Hotels
Astor, Kurfurstenstr. 23
Berger, Worringer Str. 6
Breidenbacher Hof, Heinrich-Heine-Allee 36 (tel: 8601)
Central, Luisenstr. 42-44 (tel: 379001)
Dusseldorf Hilton, Georg Glock Str. 20 (tel: 434963)
Eden, Adersstr. 29-31 (tel: 381060)
Excelsior, Kapell & Kaiserstr. (tel: 486006)
Germania, Freiligrathstr. 21
Intercontinental, K. Arnold Pl.. 5 (tel: 45530)
Nikko, Immermannstrasse 41 (tel: 8661)
Novotel Breitscheider Kreuz, Lintorfer Weg 75 (tel: 17621)
Novotel Sud, Am Schoenkamp 9 (tel: 741092)
Savoy Hotel, Oststrasse 128 (tel: 360336)
Steigenberger Park Hotel, Corneliusplatz 1 (tel: 8651)

What to See and Do
Dusseldorf is an administrative and cultural center, containing the Goethe Museum of Music

EUROPE

and the Municipal Art Museum. Above all, it caters to the prosperous of every nationality, so for shopping the super-rich can be found in any of the stores of the Konigsallee, popularly known as the Ko. The shops carry fine porcelain and crystal, antiques, cameras and photo equipment, steel carving sets. For toys and novelties, visit Lutgenau at Graf Adolph Strasse 15.

Fine dining exists in restaurants in the better hotels, but spicier, more common dishes can be had in roadside eating places. The light local beer is called Kolsch, and many excellent German white wines are available to accompany meals.

For sightseeing, visit Jagerhof Castle, St. Lambert's Church, Benrath Castle, Hofgarten, Fine Arts Museum, and the Opera.

Useful Addresses

Embassies and Consulates
American: Cecilienallee 5
(tel: 490081)
British: Georg-Glock Str. 14
(tel: 434281)
Canadian: Immermanstr. 3
(tel: 353471)

Business and Commerce
American Chamber of
Commerce, Geibelstr. 45
(tel: 683343)
Dusseldorf Chamber of
Commerce, Ernst Schreider
Platz (tel: 35571)
Duffeldorf Stock Exchange,
Ernst-Schreider-Platz 1
(tel: 8621)
Tourism and Travel
Tourist Information Office,
Konrad-Adenauer Platz 12
(tel: 350505)
Hapag-Lloyd, Elberfelder Str. 2
(tel: 00771)
American Express, Heinrich
Heine-Allee 14 (tel: 80222)

Wagons-Lits/Cook, Wehrhan 33
(tel: 353403)

FRANKFURT

Airport Information

Time
GMT +1
GMT +2 (Mar 28 - Sept 18)

Airport
Frankfurt/Main (Rhein Main)
  FRA
Tel: (0611) 6901
12 km (7 mi) SW of city
International and domestic
flights

Airlines
Aer Lingus 292054
Aeroflot 230771
Air Algerie 233281
Air Canada 250131
Air France 230501
Air India 230241
Air New Zealand 291987
Alia 231853
Alitalia 633431
American 230591
Austrian 25600233
Avensa 717327
Avianca 236251
British Airways 250121
British Caledonian 290371
CAAC 233038
Canadian International Cathay
720900
Delta 668041
Egyptair 235509
El Al 20326
Finnair 236241
Garuda 2380688
Gulf Air 7911211
Iberia 728254
Iran Air 25600693
Iraqi 235227
JAL 13600
KLM 290401
Korean 239201
Kuwait Air 236028
Lufthansa 25701
Malaysian 230621

MEA 239166
Northwest 234344
Olympic 75345
Pan Am 25650
Philippine 60900231
PIA 2385300
Qantas 230041
SAA 2998030
Sabena 29900692
SAS 26461
Saudia 2733111
Singapore 7240204
Swissair 26026
TAP 724956
Thai 7560972
THY 253031
TWA 770601
United 230223
Varig 2710213

Transport to City
Taxis: Taxis are available outside the Arrivals hall, with a fare of 25-30 dm ($12-15) to points in the city. Extra charge of 2 dm per bag also required plus a 10% tip.

Transit: The best form of public transit to Frankfurt and surrounding cities is by train (S-Bahn) from the airport but tickets must be purchased from machines at the baggage claim level in advance. No tickets are sold on the train. The 12-minute trip to Frankfurt's main railway station will cost about 4 dm ($2.25). Trains also run to Mainz, Wiesbaden, Dusseldorf, Cologne, Dortmund, Amsterdam and Munich. Also, buses #61 and #62 run every 20 minutes to the main railway station.

Facilities
Airport has 3 zones for

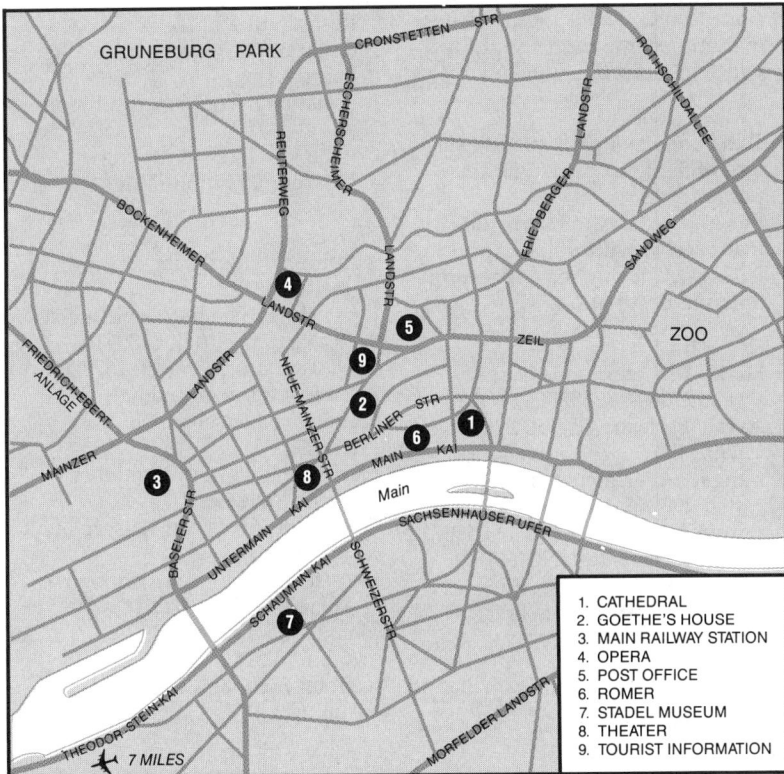

1. CATHEDRAL
2. GOETHE'S HOUSE
3. MAIN RAILWAY STATION
4. OPERA
5. POST OFFICE
6. ROMER
7. STADEL MUSEUM
8. THEATER
9. TOURIST INFORMATION

EUROPE

Frankfurt

Lufthansa and East European airlines, Berlin and international destinations and charter flights.
Hotel reservations, nursery, travel agency, bank with deposit, barber shop, first-aid, information, pharmacy.
Duty-free shop sells tobacco products, wines, spirits, lighters, perfume, watches, radio, jewellery, glass.
Car rental desks: Hertz, Avis, Europcar, InterRent, Autohansa, Auto Sixt, Auto-Alig, Eurorent, Schuldt.

Airport Taxes
None

City Information

Weather
Frankfurt has generally a mild climate year-round with average July temperature about 25 C (77 F) and average Jan temperature close to 0 C (32 F). Light clothes in summer, medium weight in winter should be sufficient.

Transportation
Taxis are available with a basic fare of 3.20 dm plus 1.60 dm per km.
Bus and streetcars run through main areas, with a flat fare from 2.50 dm. and higher depending on zone destination.

Car Hire
Hertz, Mainzer Landstr. 139 (tel: 730404 & 6905011)
Avis, Niddastr. 46 (tel: 230101 & 6902777)
Budget, Allerheiligenstr. 52 (tel: 290066)
Europcar (tel: 318960 & 6905107)
Godfrey-Davis (tel 290066)
InterRent, Stephanstr. 15 (tel: 291028)

Hospitals
Emergency hospital (Arztlicher Notdienst) (tel: 7920200)

Trade Fairs
International Home Furnishings & Textiles Exhibition (Jan)
International Amusement & Vending Trade Fair (Jan)
International Microcomputers Fair (Jan)
International Musical Instruments Fair (Feb)
International Consumer Goods Fair (Mar)
International Fur Fair (April)
International Clothing & Textile Fair (April)
International Databank Exhibition (May)
International Meat Industries Fair(May)
International Textile Trade Fair (June)
International Consumer Goods Trade Fair (Aug)
Automobile Equipment & Parts Exhibition (Sept)
Frankfurt Book Fair (Oct)
Culinary Art, Hotels & Restaurant Fair (Oct)
International Clothing & Textiles Fair (Oct)
International Tourism Exhibition (Nov)
Consumer Goods & Building Market Exhibition (Nov)

Hotels
Admiral, Holderlinstr. 25 (tel: 448021)
Crest Hotel, Isenburger Schneise 40, Niederrad (tel: 678051)
Ebel, Taunusstr. 26 (tel: 252736)
Frankfurt Intercontinental, Wilhelm-Leuschner-Str. 43 (tel:230561)
Frankfurt Sheraton, Frankfurt airport (tel: 69811)
Frankfurter Hof, Am Kaiserplatz (tel: 20251)
Hessischer Hof, Freidrich-Ebert-Anlage 40 (tel: 740251)
Maingau, Schifferstr.38 (tel: 617001)
Novotel Eschbom, Philipp Helfman 10 (tel: 42812)

Novotel Airport, Am Weiher 20
   (tel: 75050)
Parkhotel, Wiesenhuttenplatz 28-
   38 (tel: 230571)
Rex, Berlinerstr. 31 (tel: 287290)
Vera, Mainzer Landstr. 118
   (tel: 745023)
Westfalinger Hof, Dusseldorfer
   Str. 10 (tel:234748)
Wur Hemberger Hof, Karlstr. 14
   (tel: 233106)

What to See and Do
There are several pedestrian
shopping areas, notably the
Hauptwache Zeil (department
and furniture stores),
Kleinmarkthalle (indoor fruit and
vegetable market), and the main
fur trade is centered on
Dusseldorf Strasse, Niddastrasse,
and Moselstrasse.
Nightspots are elegant in the
major hotels, a little more seedy
but still lively around the main
railway station on Kaiserstr. and
Moselstr. There's an organized
tour of local cabarets run from
the south side of the main
railway station (price = 90 dm,
including drinks and a show).
Chief sightseeing stops should
include the Old Town (Altstadt)
with many medieval and
restored buildings, including
Goethe's house. Also visit the
Saalhof, the old palace of
Frederick Barbarossa. The
Romerberg is a must-see, the
medieval square dominated by
Gothic buildings, a square which
was the scene of rejoicing after
the coronation of Holy Roman
Emperors. Try to see the
emperors' coronation hall which
is open to the public.
The main entertainment area is
south of the river in old
Sachenhausen where the
traditional drink Affelshaft
(Apple Wine) in consumed in
great quantities accompanied by
singing and frivolity.
For museums, try the Industrial

Art Museum, Seckenberg
National History Museum,
Stadel Art Institute or the Kunst
Verein Art Gallery.

Useful Addresses

Embassies and Consulates
American: Siesmayerstr. 21
   (tel: 753040)
British: Bockenheimer 51
   (tel: 720406)

Business and Commerce
American Chamber of
   Commerce, Rossmarkt 12
   (tel: 283401)
Central Bank, Wilhelm-
   Epsteinstr. 14 (tel: 6111581)
Frankfurt Chamber of
   Commerce, Borenstr. 8
   (tel: 21971)
Frankfurt Stock Exchange,
   Borsenplatz 6 (tel: 717361 &
   2197377)
U.S.A. Trade Center,
   Bockenheimer Landstr. 2-4
   (tel: 7208011)

Tourism and Travel
Tourist Board, Beethovenstrasse
   69 (tel: 6117572)
Tourist Information Office,
   Untermainanlage 6
   (tel: 236351)
German Automobile Club,
   Lyoner Strasse 16
American Express, Steinweg 5
   (tel: 21051)
Thomas Cook, Kaiserstr. 11
   (tel: 295263)

HAMBURG

Airport Information

Time
GMT +1
GMT +2 (Mar. 28 - Sept 18)

Airport
Hamburg-Fuhlsbuttel
   International HAM
Tel: (040) 5081

EUROPE

12 km (7.5 mi) N of the city

Airlines
Aeroflot 335972
Air Canada 341296
Air France 32877
Alitalia 5082984
Austrian 327578
British Airways 33397
Canadian International 339344
El Al 449262
Finnair 342056
Iberia 306363
JAL 3280010
KLM 341501
Korean 343843
Lufthansa 35951
Northwest 351541
Pan Am 5009281
Qantas 330155
Sabena 321819

SAS 5071080
Singapore 373154
Swissair 32895
THY 240120
TWA 372491

Transport to City
Taxis: charge about 22 dm, while
Hotel courtesy coaches serve the
Reichshof, Atlantic and Plaza
hotels. There is also an expensive
taxi service (250 dm) to Hanover
Airport, 90 min away.
Coach: fare for the 20-min ride to
the city is 8 dm and buses leave
every 20 min from 0600 — 2300.
They return from stops at the
Atlantic and Plaza hotels.
Transit: Local buses nos. 31 and
109 charge 2.3 dm for the 35-min
ride to town. They return from

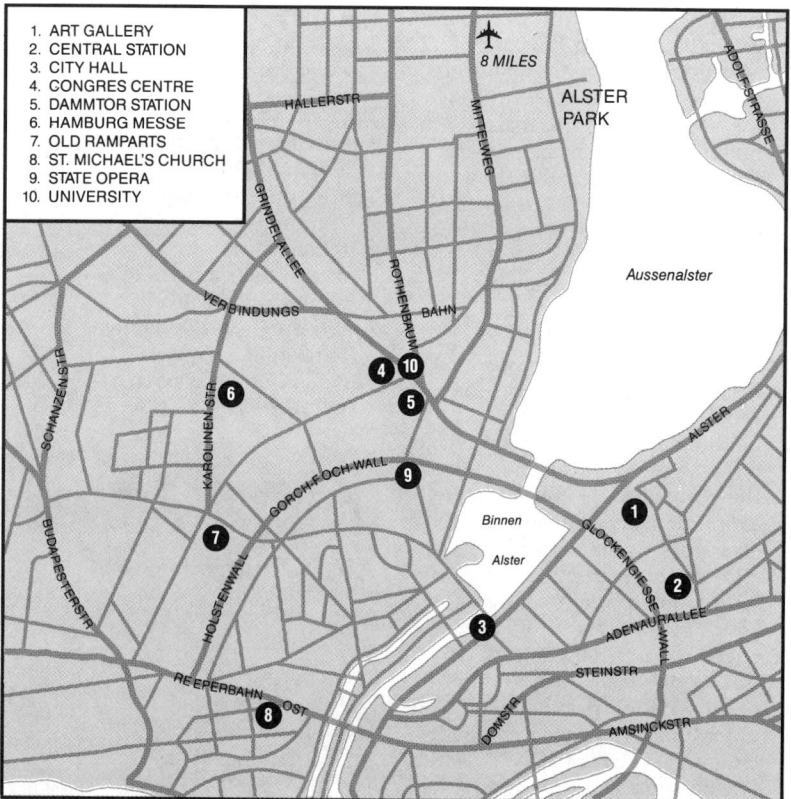

1. ART GALLERY
2. CENTRAL STATION
3. CITY HALL
4. CONGRES CENTRE
5. DAMMTOR STATION
6. HAMBURG MESSE
7. OLD RAMPARTS
8. ST. MICHAEL'S CHURCH
9. STATE OPERA
10. UNIVERSITY

Hamburg

the main railway station on
Rathausmarkt, Stephansplatz.

Facilities
Bank, currency exchange, hotel
reservations, post office, baggage
deposit, flowers, gifts, toys,
restaurants.
Duty-free shop sells tobacco
products, wines, spirits, etc.
Local and many foreign
currencies accepted, and most
credit cards.
Car rental desks: Hertz, Avis,
Europcar, InterRent.

Airport Taxes
None

City Information

Weather
Generally mild weather, colder
in winter, with average winter
temperatures about -1 C (31 F)
and average summer
temperatures 17 C (63 F). Very
wet climate so be prepared for
rain, or possibly snow. Carry
umbrella or raincoat.

Transportation
Taxis available at hotels and on
the streets. Excellent public
transit, bus and tram, system
serves Hamburg and one fare
will get you anywhere in the
area.

Car Hire
Hertz, Kirchenallee 34
   (tel: 2801201 & 5082302)
Ansa, Hoheluftchausse 117
   (tel: 5082301)
Avis, Drehbahn 15 (tel: 341651 &
   5082314)
Budget, Ellmenreichstr. 26
   (tel: 241466)
Europcar, Spalding Str. 77
   (tel: 244455 & 5082809)
Godfrey-Davis (tel: 508305)
InterRent, Rodingsmarkt 14
   (tel: 520181)
Kemwel, Hoheluftchausse 117
   (tel: 5082809)

Hospitals
Hospital (Arztlicher Notdienst)
   (tel: 228022)

Trade Fairs
International Hotel and Catering
   Exhibition (Mar)
International Baking Trades
   Exhibition (April)
International European
   Computer Exhibition (May)
International Shipping and
   Machine Technology
   Exhibition (Sept)
European Marine Trade
   Exhibition (Oct)
International Boat Exhibition
   (Oct)
Sanitation, Heating and Air-
   Conditioning Exhibition (Nov)

Hotels
Ambassador, Heidenkampsweg
   34 (tel: 234041)
Atlantic, An der Alster 72
   (tel: 28880)
Auto-Hotel Am Hafen,
   Spielbudenplatz 11
   (tel: 316631)
Baseler Hospiz, Esplanade 11
   (tel: 341921)
Berlin, Borgfelderstr. 1
   (tel: 251640)
Falck, Kielerstr. 333
   (tel: 5402061)
Forsthaus, Reinbekerweg 77
   (tel: 7213084)
Gasthaus zum Wattkorn,
   Tangstedter Landstr. 230
   (tel: 5203797)
Graf Moltke, Steindamm 1
   (tel: 5402061)
Hamburg-Plaza, Marseillerstr. 2
   (tel: 35020)
Novotel, Oldesloerstr. 166
   (tel: 5502073)
Ramada Renaissance, Gross
   Belichen (tel: 349180)
Wappen von Hamburg, St. Pauli
   Landungsbrucken
Wedina, Gurlittstr.23
   (tel: 243011)

What to See and Do
Hamburg has the raciest nightlife
of all Germany, and is centered

EUROPE

in the St. Pauli Reeperbahn and Ankerplatz der Freude quarters. Nightclubs, strip joints, call girl bars, male companions and nude male revues are everywhere, so stay up late and sleep in if possible.

Tours of the harbor are also available, leaving from the St. Pauli Wharf, and sightseeing tours are also available. Try walking tours also, particularly of the Fleete, a labyrinth of narrow canals and small streets. Take a walk through the fine Municipal Park or take in a gallery display at the Kunsthalle. Museums include the Altonaer and the Hamburg Historial Museum. For music and opera, take in a show at the Musikhalle or a performance at the State Opera house. For animal lovers there is the Hagenbeck Zoo.

American Chamber of
   Commerce, Alsterkamp 23
   (tel: 447784)
Hamburg Chamber of
   Commerce, Borse, Adolph
   Platz (tel: 366382)
Hamburg Stock Exchange, Borse,
   Adolph Platz (tel: 367444)
Ministry of Trade, Alter
   Steinweg 4 (tel: 34912427)

Business and Commerce
American Chamber of
   Commerce, Alsterkamp 23
   (tel: 447784)
Hamburg Chamber of
   Commerce, Borse, Adolph
   Platz (tel: 36117)
Hamburg Stock Exchange, Borse,
   Adolph Platz
Ministry of Trade, Alter
   Steinweg 4

Tourism and Travel
Tourist Information at the airport
   (tel: 508557)
Tourist Information Center,
   Nordkanalstrabe 36
   (tel: 241234)
American Express, Rathaus

Markt 5 (tel: 331141)
Wagons-Lits/Cook, Ballindamm
   39 (tel: 321831)

MUNICH

Airport Information

Time
GMT +1
GMT +2 (Mar 28-Sept 18)

Airport
Munchen-Reim Airport MUC
Tel: 92111
10 km (6 mi) E of city

Airlines
Aer Lingus 51138
Aeroflot 288261
Air Canada 288451
Air France 21067
Alitalia 2380031
Austrian 226666
British Airways 292121
Canadian International 2609004
Egyptair 592618
El Al 296888
Finnair 281023
Iberia 01306363
JAL 225255
KLM 268026
Korean 292921
Lufthansa 51138
MEA 592521
Olympic 224148
Pan Am 181091
Philippine 2607018
Qantas 292071
Sabena 555845
SAS 908021
Singapore 596654
Swissair 23633
Syrian 222067
THY 539417
TWA 597643
UTA 297979

Transport to City
Taxis: The 30-min. by metered taxi costs about 22 dm, with tip at your discretion.

Coach: "Munich Airport City Service" bus leaves the arrivals area every 20 minutes for the main railway station. From there, taxis or trains are available for the inner city. Coach service is 8 dm. Main station is on Arnulfstrasse.

Transit: "S-Bahn" trains and streetcars (or trams) serve the city, but if you have baggage, taxis are a better value. If travelling to Riem, catch the #37 bus to the S6 train at the main station.

Facilities
Bank with currency exchange, hotel reservations, information desk, first-aid, flowers, candies, insurance, post office, baggage deposit, barber shop, nursery. The duty-free shop sells tobacco products, spirits, wines, liqueurs, lighters, watches, jewellery, perfume.
Car rental desks: Hertz, Avis, Europcar, InterRent, Autohansa, Scheer Sixt, Budget, Mages

Airport Taxes
None

City Information

Weather
Munich has a continental climate, with average January temperatures about -5 C (23 F), and summer temperatures about

1. CATHEDRAL
2. CONGRESS CENTRE
3. DEUTSCHES MUSEUM
4. HOUSE OF PARLIAMENT & SENATE
5. MAIN RAILWAY STATION
6. MARIENPLATZ
7. OLD CITY HALL
8. OLYMPIA STADIUM
9. OPERA
10. PRINZ-CARL PALAIS
11. UNIVERSITY

8 MILES

EUROPE

Munich

25 C (77 F). Heavy winter clothing is advisable for winter, light clothing for summer.

Transportation

Public transit in the city is a combination of trains, streetcars (trams), subways and buses, but tickets are all the same. They must be cancelled at large blue machines bearing a black letter E against a yellow background before starting your ride. Tickets are checked regularly. A ticket good for 24 hours of travel costs 6 dm.

Car Hire

Hertz, Nymphenberger str. 1 (tel: 1295001 & 908744)
Ansa, Schiesstatt str. 10 (tel:907448)
Avis, Nymphenberger str. 6 (tel: 92118250)
Budget, Seitzstr. 9 (tel: 79107225)
Europcar, Schwanthaler str. 10 (tel: 594723 & 318960)
InterRent, Hirtenstrasse 14 (tel: 557145 or 908734)
Kemwel, Schiesstatt str. 10 (tel: 908401)

Hospitals

Artzlicher Notdienst (tel: 558661)

Trade Fairs

International Watches & Jewelry Fair (Feb)
International Sports Equipment (Feb)
International Lighting Equipment (Mar)
International Fashion Fair (Mar)
International Construction Equipment Exhibition (April)
International Cosmetics & Health Care Exhibition (May)
Biochemical & Instrumental Analysis Exhibition (May)
International Transportation Systems Trade Fair (June)
Wood & Timber Technology Exhibition (June)
Electrical Technology Exhibition (July)

International Sports Equipment Exhibition (Sept)
International Food Industry Trade Fair (Sept)
International Fashion Fair (Oct)
International Electronics Trade Fair (Nov)

Hotels

Arabella Muenchen, Arabellastrasse 5 (tel: 92320)
Bayerischer Hof, Promenade pl. 2 (tel: 21200)
Bundesbahnhotel, Im Haupbahnhof (tel: 558571)
Der Konigshof, Karlsplatz 25 (tel: 551360)
Deutscher Kaiser, Arnulfstrasse 2 (tel: 558321)
Eden Wolff, Arnulfstrasse 4-8 (tel: 551150)
Excelsior, Schutzenstr. 11 (tel: 551370)
Holiday Inn, Leopoldstrasse 188 (tel: 340971)
Mercure Hotel, Senefelder Str. 9 (tel: 551320)
Munich Penta, Hochstrasse 3 (tel: 4485555)
Novotel, Rudolf Vogel Bogen 3 (tel: 638000)
Sheraton, Arabellastrasse 6 (tel: 92640)
Vier Jahreszeiten Maximilianstr. 17 (tel: 230390)

What to See and Do

Sightseers can take in a variety of outdoor settings and places including the Theresian Meadows, Botanical Gardens, English Gardens and the Hellabrun Zoo. Munich is near fine skiing facilities in the Alps, and a short drive will take you to King Ludwig (of Bavaria's) Castle. Nightclubs and dancing can be found in the Schwabing district of the city, while you might want to take in a show at the Bavarian State Opera, the Currillies Theatre or the Prince Regent Theatre. For singing and drinking, the Hofbrauhas is a must, and museums like the Deutsches and Bavarian National are also noteworthy.

Useful Addresses

Embassies and Consulates
American: Koeniginstr. 5 (tel: 23011)
British: Amalienstr. 6 (tel: 394015)

Business and Commerce
American Chamber of Commerce, Zweibruekenstr. 6 (tel: 295953)
Munich Chamber of Commerce, Max-Josefstrasse 2 (tel: 951161)
Munich Stock Exchange, Lenbackplatz 2 (tel: 554631)
Ministry of Trade, Prinzregenten 28

Tourism and Travel
Tourist Information Office, Rindermarkt 5 (tel: 23911)
Tourish Information Office, Railway Station (tel: 2391256)
German Automobile Club, '8 Am Westpark 8000 (tel: 8976761)
American Express, Promenadeplatz 6 (tel: 08921990)
Wagons-Lits/Cook, Lenbachpl. 3 (tel: 591167)

WEST BERLIN

Airport Information

Time
GMT +1
GMT +2 (Mar 28 - Sept 18)

Airport
Berlin-Tegel International TXL
Tel: (030) 41012307
8 km (5 mi) NW of city
International and domestic flights

Airlines
Air Canada 8818077
Air France 261051
Alitalia 2110129
Austrian 245024
British Airways 691021
Canadian International 294044
Finnair 2618055
Iberia 2617001
JAL 2611374
KLM 8811081
Lufthansa 88755
Pan Am 881011
Sabena 8834048
SAS 8817011
Swissair 8839001

Transport to City
Taxis: Metered cab fare is from 15-18 dm, with a 10% tip and 1 dm per bag surcharge.
Coach: Airport city bus #9 leaves from Gate 8 and Main Hall every 10 min from 0500-1100. Fare to city centre is 2.2 dm ($1.10). 35-min ride in comfortable coach with baggage racks to Central Train Station in city center. Buses return from Bahnhof Zoo or Budapester strasse.

Facilities
Currency exchange, hotel reservations, baggage deposit, restaurants, flowers, books, tobacco, perfumes, radios, photographic film, etc. Also a bank and post office in the Gallery.
Duty-free shop sells cigarettes, cigars, tobacco, wines, spirits, liqueurs, lighters. Local currencies accepted.
Car rental desks: Hertz, Avis, InterRent, Europcar, Engler, Both Autohansa

Airport Taxes
6 dm per passenger for international flights

City Information

Weather
Climate for West Berlin is generally dry, with cold winters and hot summers. Medium weight clothes, sweaters, boots,

EUROPE

etc. for winter, lightweight clothes, light sweaters for summer recommended. Summers average 20 C (68 F), winters average -5 C (23 F).

Transportation
Good taxi service in all main cities, with fares about 3.20 dm plus 1.60 dm per kilometre.
Bus and streetcars charge a flat fare of 2.50 dm for any local distance. Unlimited travel tickets, good for all public transportation are available and recommended.

Car Hire
Hertz, Palace Hotel (tel: 4101331)
Ansa, Kurfurstendamm 160
    (tel: 41013384)
Avis, Europacenter (tel: 2611881
    & 41013148)
Europcar, Kurfursten 101
    (tel:2137097)
Godfrey Davis (tel: 41103308)

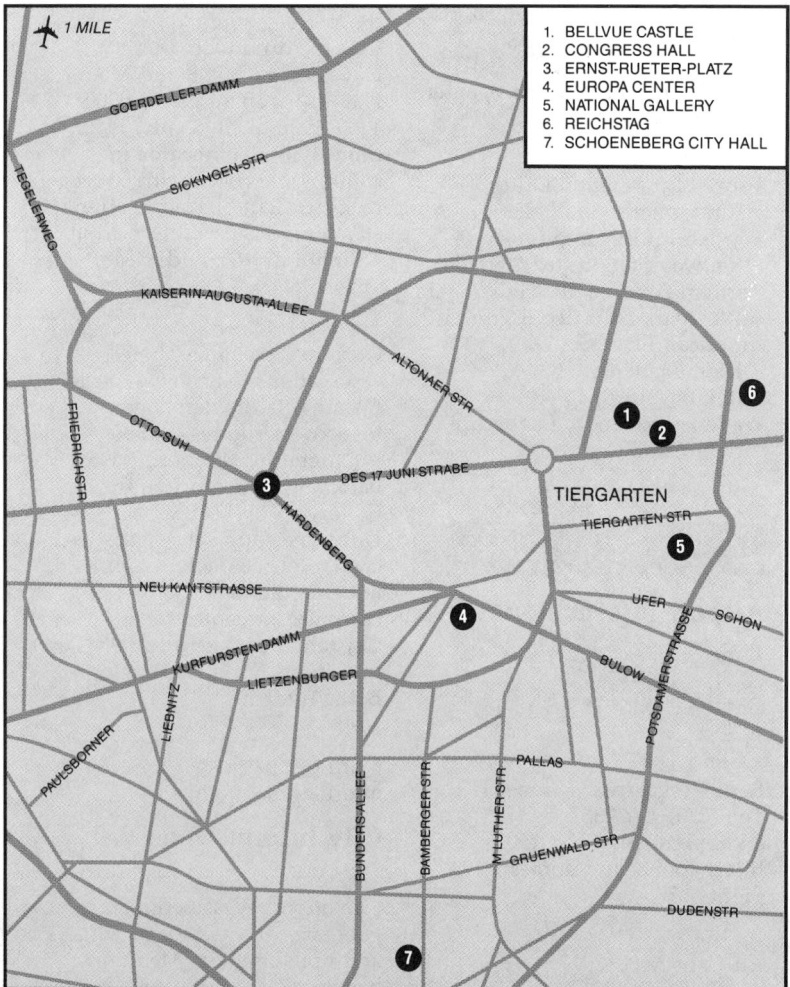

1 MILE

1. BELLVUE CASTLE
2. CONGRESS HALL
3. ERNST-RUETER-PLATZ
4. EUROPA CENTER
5. NATIONAL GALLERY
6. REICHSTAG
7. SCHOENEBERG CITY HALL

Berlin

InterRent, Kurfurstendamm 178
(tel: 8818093)

Hospitals
American Hospital (tel: 7475300)

Trade Fairs
International Tourism Exchange
(Feb)
International Pharmaceuticals
Exhibition (May)
Overseas Import Fair (Sept)

Hotels
Ambassador, Bayreutherstr. 42
(tel: 219020)
Astoria, Fasanenstr. 2
(tel: 3124067)
Atlas, Uhlandstrasse 171/2
(tel: 8837919)
Berlin, Lutzowplatz 17
(tel: 26050)
Borse, Kurfurstendamm 34
(tel: 883021)
Bremen, Bleibtreustr. 25
(tel: 8814076)
Bristol-Hotel-Kempinski,
Kurfurstendamm 27
(tel: 881091)
Central, Kurfurstendamm 66
(tel: 8816343)
Engelberger, Mommsenstr. 6
(tel: 8815536)
Hamburg, Landgrafenstr. 4
(tel: 269161)
Intercontinental, Budapester Str.
2 (tel: 26020)
Novotel Airport, Kurt
Schumacher Damm 220
(tel: 41060)
Novotel Siemenstadt,
Ohmstrasse 4-6 (tel: 381061)
Palace Europacenter, Budapester
Str. (tel: 269111)
President, An der Urania 16
(tel: 219030)

What to See and Do
Visit the large Aquarium at
Wannsee Zoo or the
Brandenburg Gates,
Charlottenburg Palace, Europa
Center, Museum Dahlem. Also
visit the National Gallery's art
collection or take in a symphony
performance at Philharmonic
Hall. For spicier fare try the
transvestite bar Chez Nous, on
Marburger Str. 14 or the
nightclub/supper club, Red Rose,
in the Europa Center. Also to be
seen are the House of Parliament
(Reichstag) and Checkpoint
Charlie at the Berlin Wall.

Useful Addresses

Embassies and Consulates
American: Clay Alee 170
British: Uhlandstr. 7
(tel: 3095292)

Business and Commerce
American Chamber of
Commerce, Kurfurstenstr. 114
(tel: 2442646)
Berlin Chamber of Commerce,
Hardenberg Str. 16-18 (tel:
31801)
Berlin Stock Exchange,
Hardenbergstr. 16/18 (tel:
31800)
Ministry of Trade, Martin-Luther
Str. 105 (tel: 7838100)

Tourism and Travel
German Auto Club, Bundesallee
29-30
Tourist Information Office,
Fasanenstr. 7/8 (tel: 240111)
American Express,
Kurfurstendamm 11 (tel: (030)
8827575 & 8814333)
Wagons-Lits/Cook, Ku-Damm 42
(tel: 818030)

EUROPE

GREECE

Essential Information

Type of Government
Presidential Parliamentary
Republic

Area
131,957 sq km
(51,146 sq mi)

Population
10 million

Annual Growth Rate
2.2%

Languages
Greek, English, French

Religion
Greek Orthodox 97%, Muslim
2%

Ethnic Groups
Greek 98%, others 2%

Weights and Measures
Metric

Electrical Current
A.C. 50c V varies

Major Business Cities
Athens (cap) 2,500,00
Thessaloniki 725,000
Piraeus 425,000
Patras 250,000
Iraklion 111,000

Currency
1 drachma = 100 leptae
Notes 50, 100, 500, 1,000 and
  5,000 drachmas
Coins 1/2, 1, 2, 5, 10, 20 and 50
  drachmas

Public Holidays
Jan 1 New Year
Jan 6 Epiphany
Mar 17 Ash Monday
Mar 25 Independence Day
Apr 13-20 Easter Week
Aug 15 Assumption
Oct 28 National Holiday
Dec 25, 26 Christmas

Travellers Information

Entry Requirements
Passport is required by all
visitors. No visa required for
most travellers, but subject to
change at short notice.

Working Restrictions
Most nationals need a work
permit from the Greek Ministry
of Labour.

Vaccination Required
A typhoid vaccination is
recommended by the Greek
medical authorities. No other
vaccination required.

Customs and Duty Free
Most personal effects are duty-
free, plus an additional
allowance.
On arrival: 200 cigarettes or 50
cigars or 200 gr. of tobacco
(7 oz.); 1 bottle of alcohol; 60 gr.
of perfume (2 oz.), 1 L of eau de
cologne and gifts to a value of
$150.

Currency Restrictions
No restrictions on import or
export of foreign currency, but a
limit of dr 1,500 is in effect for
import or export. Foreign
currency must be declared on
arrival.

Health Tips
Do not drink local water outside
the main cities. The International
Association of Medical
Assistance to Travellers has a list
of English-speaking doctors who
can be contacted while travelling
in Greece, and hospitals charge a
nominal fee.

Climate and Clothing
A Mediterranean climate, with
the rainy season in Nov-Mar,
and hot, sunny weather from
April-Nov. Winter temperatures
can occasionally fall to 0 C
(32 F), but in general wear

mediumweight clothes, including a raincoat in winter, light weight clothes in summer. Summer temperatures can reach 38 C (100 F) in the shade.

Tipping
Your restaurant and hotel bill will already include a tip, but tip 8-10% above that for good restaurant service. Leave the bus boy's tip separate from the bill. Small services usually require tips from dr 50-300, depending on level of difficulty. Tip taxis 10-15%, porters, dr 40, barbers and beauticians 10%.

Food and Drink
Lamb dishes and seafood are the main attractions of Greek cuisine with cheese and olives basic to many meals. Lunch is the main meal, taken between 1200 and 1400 hrs. Meals are a social occasion, with many diners often joining together to order a variety of dishes. Dinners can be as early as 1800 or 1900 hrs. Greek wine is very good,d with the exception of Retsina which takes some getting used to. Popular spirit is Ouzo, an anise based alcohol.

Business Brief

GDP
$41.6 billion
(per capita income $3,800)

Annual Growth Rate
2.2%

Natural Resources
Bauxite, lignite, magnesite, oil, iron and chromite

Agriculture
Citrus fruits, cotton, currants, grapes, olives, potatoes, sugarbeets, tobacco, wheat, wine, dairy products

Industry
Processed food, textiles, metals, chemicals, electrical equipment, cement, glass, transport, equipment, petroleum products, construction, aluminum, tourism.

Imports
Total $11.4 billion
Fuel petroleum, lumber, iron and steel, machinery, transport and electrical equipment, chemicals, finished goods, meat

Exports
Total $5.7 billion
Textiles, metal products, cement, chemicals, pharmaceuticals, fruits and vegetables, olive oil, wine, cotton, petroleum products, ships, currants, raisins

Major Trading Partners
West Germany, Italy, United States, U.K., France, Netherlands, Japan, Saudi Arabia

Workforce
3.9 million
Services 42%, industry 29%, agriculture 28%

Tips for Doing Business
Dark-coloured conservative business suits are the norm for doing business and prior appointments are necessary only for governmental visits. Business discussions are usually sociable and decisions made over strong Greek coffee and Ouzo. Refusing an invitation to dine or drink with a business contact is an insult, so think before you decline even the smallest invitations. If invited ahead of time, bring flowers or chocolate for your hostess and avoid business contacts from 1430-1700. English is spoken widely.

Best Months for Doing Business
Best months are Sept through May. Avoid the week before and two weeks after Christmas and the week before and after Greek Orthodox Easter.

EUROPE

Business Hours

Government
Mon-Sat 0800-1430

Business
Mon-Fri 0830-1330 & 1600-1930
Sat 0800-1330

Banks
Mon-Sat 0800-1300

Shops
Mon, Wed, Sat 0800-1500
Tu, Thur, Fri 0800-1400 & 1730-2030

English Language Publications

English-language newspapers include the Athens Daily Post and Athens News Daily. Foreign English papers are available at newstand kiosks in Athens and Salonika. Television news in English on Ch.5 at 1815 and on Ch.11 at 1915.

Telephone and Communications

Telephone country code: 30
Telephone city code: Athens 01, Corfu 661
Telex country code: 863
Public phones are widely available at shops, kiosks and in hotels. Charge for local calls is dr 5.

Air Travel

Olympic Airways offers excellent domestic service to 25 airports throughout the islands, with international airports at Athens, Iraklion (Crete), Salonika, Corfu and Rhodes.

Other Transport

Main roads are paved, but smaller roads can be rough, narrow and dangerous to drive. Exercise caution when driving outside built-up areas, and you must carry an International Driver's License. Self-drive cars are not recommended, especially in major cities, where (unless you speak Greek) you will not be able to read road signs.
Railways link major towns and cities, while ferries connect the larger islands in the chain. Most towns and cities can also be reached from Athens by bus.

ATHENS

Airport Information

Time
GMT +2
GMT +3 (Apr 4-Sept 25)

Airport
Athinai International (Hellinikon ATH
Tel: (01) 97991
11 km (6 mi) S of the city
Domestic and international flights (west and east terminal respectively).

Airlines
Aeroflot 3221022
Air Canada 3230347
Air France 3238507
Alia 3241377
Alitalia 3244315
Austrian 3230844
British Airways 3250601
Canadian International 3230347
Egyptair 3233575
El Al 3230116
Finnair 3255235
Gulf Air 32220506
Iberia 3237524
Interflug 3624807
Iran Air 3607611
Iraqi 9229573
JAL 3248211
KLM 3251310
Kuwait Air 3234147
Libyan 3248816
Lufthansa 3294411
MEA 3226911
Northwest 3607936
Olympic 9616161
Pan Am 3235242
Philippine 3241116
PIA 3225383
Qantas 3250520
SAA 3247108
Sabena 3236821

SAS 3634444
Saudia 3228211
Singapore 3239111
Swissair 3237581
Syrian 3238711
Thai 671087
THY 3220561
TWA 3226451
UTA 3230501
Varig 3226743

Transport to City

Taxi: The 30-minute ride downtown by metered taxi should cost about dr 800, but add a tip of 10% plus dr 25 for each suitcase. The fare doubles between 0100 and 0500. Taxi to the port of Piraeus costs dr 210.

Coach: Olympic Airways bus leaves every 30 minutes for the Athens city terminal. Fare is about dr 90.

Facilities

Currency exchange, hotel reservations, baggage deposit, post office, restaurants, bank, vaccination center, books, gifts, flowers, toys.
Duty-free shop sells tobacco products, wines, spirits, liqueurs, cameras, jewellery.
Car rental desks: Hertz, Avis, Budget

Airport Taxes

None

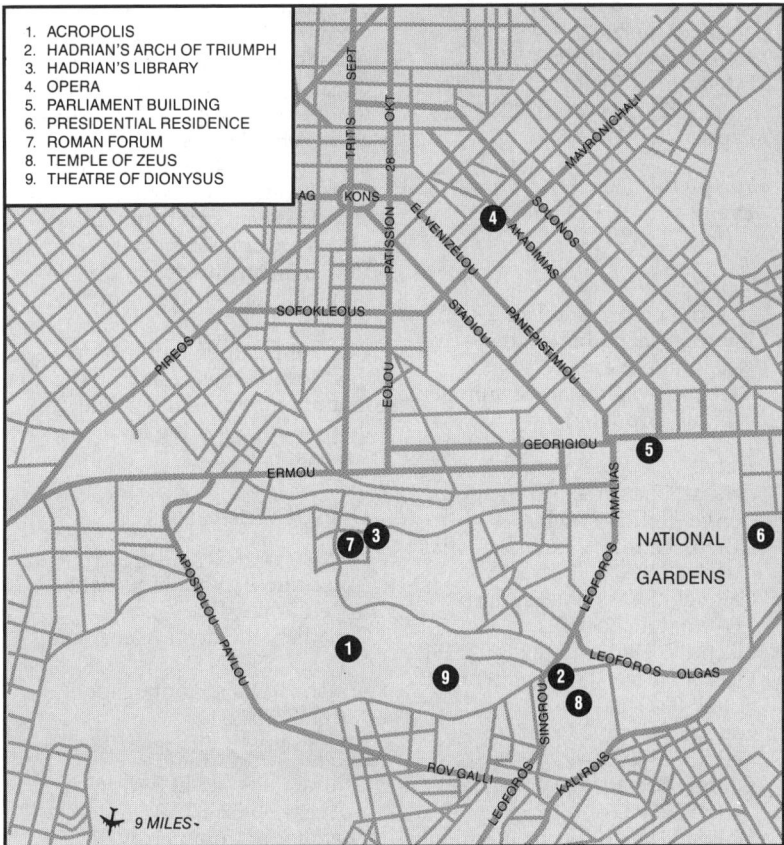

1. ACROPOLIS
2. HADRIAN'S ARCH OF TRIUMPH
3. HADRIAN'S LIBRARY
4. OPERA
5. PARLIAMENT BUILDING
6. PRESIDENTIAL RESIDENCE
7. ROMAN FORUM
8. TEMPLE OF ZEUS
9. THEATRE OF DIONYSUS

EUROPE

Athens

City Information

Weather
Mild, wet climate in both seasons. Average temperature for winter is about 11 C (52 F) and for summer 30 C (88 F).

Transportation
Athens taxis charge dr 20 plus dr 17 per km. Many other extra charges.
Buses charge dr 30 within city limits.

Car Hire
Hertz, 12 Syngrou (tel: 9510921)
Ansa, 31 Syngrou (tel: 9225718)
Avis, 48 Amalias Ave.
    (tel: 3224951)
Budget, 90 Syngrou (tel: 9214771)
Europcar, 148 Syngrou
    (tel: 9235352)
Hellas Cars (tel: 3233487)
InterRent, 4 Syngrou
    (tel: 9215788 & 9613424)
Pappas (tel: 3220087)

Hospitals
Evang.   Hospital
    (tel: 7220001)

Trade Fairs
International Trade Fair (Sept)
International Film Festival,
    Salonika (Sept)
Defense Systems and Equipment
    Exhibition (Oct)

Hotels
Athens Chandris, 385 Syngrou
    Ave. (tel: 9414824)
Athens Hilton, Vassilissis Sofias
    (tel: 7220201)
Caravel, 2 Vass, Alexandrou
    Ave. (tel: 7290721)
Electra, 5 Hermou (tel: 3223223)
Electra Palace, 18 Nicodimon St.
    (tel: 3241401)
Esperia Palace, 22 Stadiou
    (tel: 3238001)
Grande Bretagne, Syntagma Sq.
    (tel: 3230251)
Holiday Inn, 50 Michalacopoulou
    (tel: 7248322)

King, Minos, 1 Piraeus
    (tel: 5231-111)
Royal Olympic, 28-32 Diakou
    (tel: 9226411)
St. George Lycabettus, 2
    Kleomenous (tel: 7290-711)

What to See and Do
Visiting the ancient ruins of Greece's Classical Age is still the best value for the sightseer. The Acropolis in particular, but also the Agora and the Temple of Zeus and the Parthenon. Most can be explored through informative and fascinating tours. Visit the National Archaeological Museum where many of the country's historical treasures are kept, while museums and art galleries of every kind abound in this teeming city. In summer, the Athens festival presents ballet, music and the Tragedies at the foot of the Acropolis, while the ancient Epidaurus Theatre presents the Tragedies in June. More lively nightspot entertainment can be found at discos on Ergostasio and Vouliagmenis Blvds., and in nightclubs and cabarets on Athinea and Syngrou Blvd. Gambling can be indulged in at the Mont Parnes casino on the mountain of the same name, less than an hour's drive from Athens.

Useful Addresses

Embassies and Consulates
American: 91 Vassilissis Sofias
    (tel: 7212951)
Canadian: 4 Odos I. Genadiou
    (tel: 7239511)
British: 1 Odos Ploutarchou
    (tel: 7236211)

Business and Commerce
Central Bank, 21 El Venizelou
    Ave. (tel: 3233278)
Chamber of Commerce, 7
    Akadimias St. (tel: 3604815)

Athens Stock Exchange, Sophocleus 10 (tel: 3211301)

American Chamber of Commerce, 17 Valaoritou St. (tel: 3636407)

Athens Chamber of Commerce, 7 Akadimias St (tel: 3604815)

British Chamber of Commerce, 4 Odos Valaoritou St. (tel: 362168)

Ministry of Commerce, Palaia Kaningos (tel: 3616251)

Ministry of Industry, Zalokosta 10 (tel: 3630911)

Heraklion-Crete Chamber of Commerce and Industry, P.O. Box 154, Heraklion, Crete (tel: 282420)

Tourism and Travel

Automobile Touring Club of Greece, 2-4 Mesogion St.

Tourist Organization, Odos Amerikis 2 (tel: 3223111125)

American Express, Constitution Square (tel: 981980)

Wagons-Lits/Cook, 3 Odos Stadiou (tel: 3232546)

HUNGARY

Essential Information

Type of Government
Communist Republic

Area
93,030 sq km
(35,919 sq mi)

Population
10.9 million

Annual Growth Rate
0.2%

Languages
Hungarian (official)

Religion
Roman Catholic 67.5%, Calvinist 20%, Lutheran 5%

Ethnic Groups
Magyar 92.4%, Gypsy 3.3%, German 2.5%, Jewish 0.7%, other 1.1%

Weights and Measures
Metric

Electrical Current
A.C. 50c 220/380 V

Major Business Cities
Budapest (cap) 2,250,000
Miskolc 220,000
Debrecen 215,000
Szeged 190,000

Currency
1 forint = 100 filler
Notes 20, 50, 100 and 500 forints
Coins 10, 20, and 50 filler, and 1, 2, 5, and 10 forints

Public Holidays
Jan 1 New Year's Day
Apr 4 Liberation Day
Apr 13-20 Easter Week
May 1 Labour Day
Aug 20 Constitution Day
Nov 7 October Revolution Day
Dec 25, 26 Christmas

Travellers Information

Entry Requirements
All visitors need passports. Travellers from North America and Britain need visas and they should be obtained beforehand or may be obtained on entry (except at railway border stations).

Working Restrictions
A work permit is needed by anyone seeking employment in Hungary.

Vaccination Required
None

Customs and Duty Free
On arrival: 250 cigarettes or 40 cigars or 200 gr. of tobacco; 1 L

EUROPE

of spirits or 2 L of wine; 250 gr. of perfume. Most personal goods are duty-free.

Currency Restrictions
Foreign currency should be declared but no restrictions in force. However, no more than ft 200 may be imported or exported.

Health Tips
Health services are very good, and tap water is generally potable. Fruits and vegetables should be washed when eaten raw, but avoid products without preservatives added. Bring your own pharmaceuticals.

Climate and Clothing
Winters are generally cold and dry, summers hot and dry, and spring and fall wet and mild. Heavy winter clothes recommended from Nov-Mar and lightweight clothes, together with a raincoat from June-Oct.

Tipping
Taxis are usually tipped 5-10%, porters 20 ft per piece of luggage and barbers and beauticians 10% of the bill. Tip hotels, restaurants and nightspots 10-15%, small services fr 10-15.

Food and Drink
Hungarian food consists of a wide variety of ethnic dishes, reflecting its central location in Eastern Europe. Goulash is a popular dish, pork the main meat, and side dishes of noodles, potatoes, onions and dumplings are popular. Fruits and vegetables are widely available for most of the year. Lunch is the main meal of the day, taken between 1200 and 1400, and dinner may be served well after 1900.

Business Brief

GDP
$46 billion

(per capita income $4,123)

Annual Growth Rate
2.6%

Natural Resources
Coal, bauxite, iron ore, lignite

Agriculture
Barley, grapes, corn, oats, potatoes, rice, rye, sugar beets, vegetables, wheat, fruits

Industry
Aluminum, bus manufacture, chemicals, engineering, food processing, machinery, metallurgy, petrochemicals, textiles

Imports
Total $10.8 billion
Crude oil, raw cotton, automobiles, rolled steel, livestock, machinery, manufactured goods

Exports
Total $10.5 billion
Transport equipment, medicine, machinery, shoes, foodstuffs, electronics

Major Trading Partners
U.S.S.R., East Germany, Czechoslovakia, Poland, Italy, West Germany, Austria

Workforce
5 million
Agriculture 20%, industry and commerce 40%, services 32%, government 5%

Tips for Doing Business
Wear a conservative business suit for business and social contacts. Prior appointments must be made for government visits, and remember that the economy is state-owned and operated, making businessmen also officials. Exercise courtesy and patience and be prepared to offer generous credits to a price-conscious economic system. Business is frequently conducted over lunch or dinner in a restaurant, and knowing a few

phrases in German or Hungarian will go a long way in smoothing a path to your goals.

Best Months for Doing Business
September to May are the best months, since business vacations are taken June through August.

Business Hours

Government
Mon-Fri 0800-1630
Sat 0800-1300

Business
Mon-Fri 1000-1800

Banks
Mon-Fri 0900-1300
Sat 0900-1100

Shops
Mon-Fri 0830-1700
Sat 0830-1330

English Language Publications
The Daily News and Hungarian Week publish in English and are available at kiosks and hotels, as well as the International Herald Tribune.

Telephone and Communications
Telephone country code: 36
Telephone city code: Budapest 1
Telex country code: 86
Public phones are available widely as are telegram and telex services. 3-minute local calls can be made with small forint coins. Telexes are available at hotels and central post office, as are telegrams.

Air Travel
There is no internal or domestic air service in Hungary but international flights are handled from Budapest by Malev Hungarian Airlines, the national carrier.

Other Transport
A country-wide bus service is run by Volan-Mavaut, with the main terminal at Engels Ter. Express train service operate

from Keleti and Nyugati railway stations, and tickets should be booked in advance from the central office of MAV.
By water, there is a hydrofoil service from Belgrade to Vienna, Austria, and an extensive inland waterway system.

BUDAPEST

Airport Information

Time
GMT +1
GMT +2 (April 4 - Sept 5)

Airport
Ferihegy International BUD
Tel: 140400
16 km (10 mi) SE of city

Airlines
Aeroflot 185892
Air Canada 754615
Air France 185238
Alitalia 186898
Austrian 171550
British Airways 183299
Canadian International 184333
Finnair 174022
Interflug 186016
Iraqi 169476
KLM 174742
Lufthansa 184511
Malev 189033
Pan Am 187922
Sabena 184111
SAS 185675
Swissair 172500
Syrian 515197
TWA 189033

Transport to City
Taxis: Hire a taxi at car rental counters (Volan Taxi) for the 20-minute ride to Pest or Buda. The fare will be about 150 fr but add a small tip.
Coach: Volan Bus #1 will take you from the airport to Vorosmarty Terminal in Pest. The bus leaves the terminal

EUROPE

every 30 minutes, and the fare is about 20 fr. The bus has an airplane symbol on it.
Transit: For Bus #93, purchase ticket inside the air terminal from self-serve machines for 3 fr. Once on board you must validate the ticket in a machine. There is little or no baggage space, and you may have to stand for the half-hour ride to the main train station. From there, take any train for Budapest. Total trip takes 1 hour and costs a total of 3 fr.

Facilities
Buffet, restaurant, post office, bank, gift shop, currency exchange, baggage deposit. Duty-free shop sells tobacco products, wines, spirits, liqueurs, records, watches, radios, tape recorders, porcelain and food.
Car rental desks: Avis, Europcar, InterRent

Airport Taxes
None

City Information

Weather
Winters are cold with snow. Average temperatures from 1-

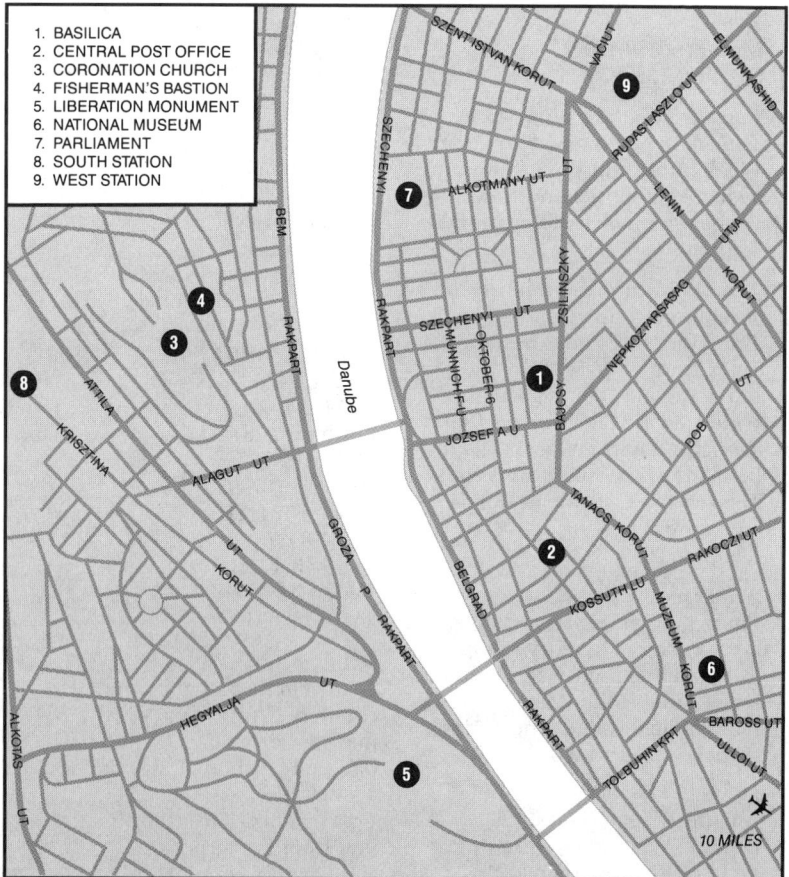

1. BASILICA
2. CENTRAL POST OFFICE
3. CORONATION CHURCH
4. FISHERMAN'S BASTION
5. LIBERATION MONUMENT
6. NATIONAL MUSEUM
7. PARLIAMENT
8. SOUTH STATION
9. WEST STATION

10 MILES

Budapest

15C (34-60F). Wear medium clothing with overcoat and hat. Summers are warm and sunny. Temperatures 15-27C (60-80F). Some rainfall in Spring, Umbrellas or raincoat recommended.

Transportation

There are both public and private taxis available, and all are identified by a stripe of red and white squares running along the side of the taxi. They can be ordered by phone (tel: 222222) or for advance booking (tel: 888888).

For streetcars (trams) the care is 1 ft. flat fare. Use yellow-line tickets.

Intercity buses operate from Engels Terminal with a blue-line ticket of 1.5 ft. flat fare.

Subway lines are identified by a large M, and a coin- operated yellow-line ticket may be purchased. Fare is 1 ft. for any of the 3 lines. All tickets for buses, trams or subways are self-cancelled on machines.

Car Hire

Hertz, V. Kossuth Ter 13-15
(tel: 221471 & 576592)
Avis, Martineli 8 (tel: 475754 & 184158)
Budget, Vaskapu 16 (tel: 142819)
Europcar, Vaskapu 16
(tel: 334783 & 342540)
InterRent, Kertes 24
(tel: 221471)
Volantourist, Vaskapu 16
(tel: 334783)

Hospitals

Some doctors and dentists speak English, and some emergency hospital services are free.

Trade Fairs

International Tourism Exhibition (Mar)
International Aeronautics Exhibition (April)
International Building Industry Exhibition (April)
International Technical Fair Exhibition (May)
International Consumer Goods Fair (Sept)
International Water & Environmental Pollution Exhibition (Sept)
International Packing & Handling Exhibition (Oct)
International Food Processing (Oct)

Hotels

Astoria, Kassuth Lajos Utca 19
(tel: 173411)
Atrium Hyatt, Box H-1366
(tel: 383000)
Beke, Lenin Korut 97 (tel: 323300)
Buda Penta, Krisztina Krt.
(tel: 566333)
Budapest Hilton, Hess Andras Ter 1-3 (tel: 751000)
Budapest Szilagyi, Erzsebet 47
(tel: 153230)
Duna Intercontinental, Apaczai Czere 4 (tel: 175122)
Forum, 1368 Apaczai Czere Janos u. (tel: 179111)
Gellert, Gellert Ter.1111
(tel: 852200)
Grand Royal, Lenin Korut 43-49
(tel: 533133)
Novotel, Alkotas u.63
(tel: 869588)

What to See and Do

Visit the neo-gothic Houses of Parliament or stroll along Budapest's grandest street, the Nepkoztarsasagutja. It runs 2 miles from the center of the city to the entrance of the city park. You can rent a boat in summer on the lake in Varosliget Park, or skate there in winter. In the north corner of the park is a zoo. Next to the city park is the Vidam Park, a sort of amusement park complete with roller coaster and circus. Other places of interest are the Citadel Magdalen and St. Nicholas Towers, and the National Museum. Finally, there are over 2,000 restaurants and taverns, many of which should be sampled for their inexpensive, ethnic dishes.

Useful Addresses

Embassies and Consulates
American: V. Szabadsag ter. 12 (tel: 126450)
British: Harmincad u.6 (tel: 182888)
Candian: Budakeszi U.32 (tel: 767312)

Business and Commerce
Ministry of Foreign Trade, Honved Utca 13 (tel: 530000)
Chamber of Commerce, Kossuth L. Ter.6 (tel: 314155)

National Bank, Szabadsag Ter.8 (tel: 532600))
State Development Bank, Deak Ferenc utca 5 (tel: 225672)

Tourism and Travel
Budapest Main Railway Station, Lenin Korut 111 (tel: 227860)
Volantourist, Oktober 6 utca 11-13 (tel: 123410)
Hungarian Travel Agency (IBUSZ) Felszabadulas Ter.5 (tel: 186888)
Hungarian Automobile Club, Remer Floris Utca 4/a (tel: 152040)
American Express, Petrofi Ter.3 (tel: 184848 & 185070 & 184865)
Wagons-Lits/Cook, 1,3 Pilvax Koz (tel: 182788)

IRELAND

Essential Information

Type of Government
Parliamentary Republic

Area
70,282 sq km (27,136 sq mi)

Population
3.4 million

Annual Growth Rate
1.1%

Languages
English, Irish (Gaelic)

Religion
Roman Catholic 94%, Anglican 4%

Ethnic Groups
Celtic, English

Weights and Measures
Metric, plus some British Imperial

Electrical Current
A.C. 50c 220/380 V

Major Business Cities
Dublin (cap) 1,100,000

Cork 210,000
Limerick 60,000

Currency
1 Irish pound = 100 pence
Notes 1, 5, 10, 50, and 100 pounds
Coins 1/2, 1, 2, 5, 10, and 50 pence

Public Holidays
Jan 1 New Year
Mar 17 St. Patrick's Day
Apr 13-20 Easter Week
Jun 2 Spring
Aug 4 Summer
Oct 27 Autumn
Dec 25, 26 Christmas

Travellers Information

Entry Requirements
All visitors must have a valid passport, except those from the United Kingdom. Canadian and American visitors need passports only.

Working Restrictions
No work permit needed for

Commonwealth citizens, but one required for all others.

Vaccination Required
None

Customs and Duty Free
On arrival: Personal effects are duty-free. Passengers from EEC countries are allowed 300 cigarettes, or 150 cigarillos or 75 cigars or 400 gr. of tobacco; 1.5 L of spirits or 3 L of liqueurs and 3 L of wine; 75 gr. of perfume and other personal goods to a value of L52 per traveller.

North American may bring in 200 cigarettes or 100 cigarillos or 50 cigars or 250 gr. of tobacco; 1 L of spirits or 2 L of liqueur plus 2 L of wine; 50 gr. of perfume. No imports of meat are allowed.

Currency Restrictions
No limit on currency, foreign or domestic, brought in. However, a total of only L100 in Irish currency and Ir.L 500 in foreign currency may be exported.

Health Tips
Drinking water is excellent and pharmaceuticals and toiletries are available. There are many physicians should you need one, and all speak English.

Climate and Clothing
Ireland's climate is usually mild and wet in summer and spring, cool and wet in fall and winter. Light clothes and a raincoat should be worn in spring and summer, mediumweight clothes and a raincoat at other times.

Tipping
In restaurants a tip of 12 1/2% is included in the bill. Tip taxis 15%, porters 50 pence per piece of baggage, chambermaids 50 pence. Barbers and beauticians 15%. Small services 40 pence.

Food and Drink
Irish food is not fancy but wholesome and plentiful. Local produce predominates, including fish, meat, potatoes, fresh vegetables and bread. Tea, coffee and beer are the most popular beverages. In the cities restaurants catering to every taste can be found, and meals are generally sumptious. After meals are usually spent in the pub where the favorite drinks are the dark. rich Irish beer Guinness, and Irish whiskey.

Business Brief

GDP
$19.7 billion
(per capita income $5,556)

Annual Growth Rate
0%

Natural Resources
Zinc, lead, natural gas, barite, copper, gypsum, limestone, dolomite, peat, silver

Agriculture
Barley, oats, potatoes, sugarbeets, wheat, cattle and dairy products

Industry
Beverages, chemicals, clothing, food processing, footwear, metal and engineering products, textiles, tobacco, pharmaceuticals, construction

Imports
Total $13.6 billion
Petroleum, non-electric machinery, fuel, iron & steel electrical equipment, paper, finished consumer goods, capital equipment, grains, textile yarns

Exports
Total $16 billion
Cattle and dairy products, eggs, fish, textiles, ores, chemicals and concentrates, transport equipment, computers

Major Trading Partners
Great Britain, U.S., West

EUROPE

Germany, France, Netherlands, Japan, Italy, Belgium, Luxemburg

Workforce
1.2 million
Industry 30%, agriculture 23%, services 40%

Tips for Doing Business
Wear a conservative business suit for most occasions, and make prior appointments. Irish businesspeople are easy-going, hospitable and friendly so be casual rather than formal whenever possible. Traffic drives on the left-hand side, as in Britain, so you may want to take a taxi first before you try a rental car.

Best Months for Doing Business
Avoid travelling to Ireland for business in early May, July and August, and the weeks around Christmas and New Year. Also avoid January.

Business Hours

Government
Mon-Fri 0900-1730

Business
Mon-Fri 0900-1300, 1400-1730

Banks
Mon-Fri 1000-1230, 1330-1500
Thu 1000-1700

Shops
Mon-Fri 0930-1730

English Language Publications
Most publications are in English, some in Gaelic. American papers such as the International Herald Tribune and USA Today are available in Dublin.

Telephone and Communications
Telephone country code: 353
Telephone city code: Dublin 01
Telex country code: 852
Public phones can be found in restaurants, pubs, and booths and require 5 or 10-pence coins for local calls. To phone, lift the receive, insert the coin, dial, press button A and speak. If there is no answer, press button B to get your coin back. To get the operator, simply lift the receiver.
There is a public telex office at the Dept. of Posts and Telegraph, Marlborough St., Dublin.

Air Travel
Aer Lingus operates domestic flights between Dublin and Shannon and Dublin and Cork. Dublin is principal international airport.

Other Transport
Although roads are fair to good in most of Ireland, bus services, including express coaches are the most relaxing and fastest way to get to the main cities.
By train, express service is provided between Dublin and most major towns.
There are also 400 km of navigable inland waterways.

DUBLIN

Airport Information

Time
GMT
GMT +1 (Mar 28 - Sept 18)

Airport
Dublin International DUB
Tel: (01) 379900
8.8 km (5.5 mi) N of the city

Airlines
Aer Lingus 377747
Air Canada 771488
Air France 778899
Alitalia 775171
British Airways 686666
Eastern 370011
Gulf Air 377747
Iberia 779846
KLM 778241

Korean 370011
Lufthansa 761595
Northwest 717766
Qantas 770747
Sabena 716677
SAS 421922
Swissair 712197
TWA 859900

Transport to City

Taxis: The metered cabs to Buswell's Hotel, a 30-minute ride, will cost about L 9. Drivers are friendly and helpful, and a tip of 15% is common.

Coach: The Irish Transport Service operates coaches to the main bus terminal on Store St. Buses are boarded outside the Arrivals terminal and the fare paid the driver is L 2.20 L 3.00. The trip takes 45 min.

Transit: Dublin City Services run several double-decker buses into the city, chiefly #41, #41A and #41C, and they can be boarded at a top a short distance from the Arrivals terminal. It leaves every half hour for Eden Quay, with stops in between, and the fare is 75p.

Facilities

Bars, banks, currency exchange, hotel reservations, post office, flowers, candy, books, gifts, barber shop, first aid. Duty-free shop sells tobacco products, wines, spirits, liqueurs, cameras, lighters, watches, radios.

Car rental desks: Hertz, Avis, Dan Ryan, TM Nationwide, Johnson & Perrot, Murray's.

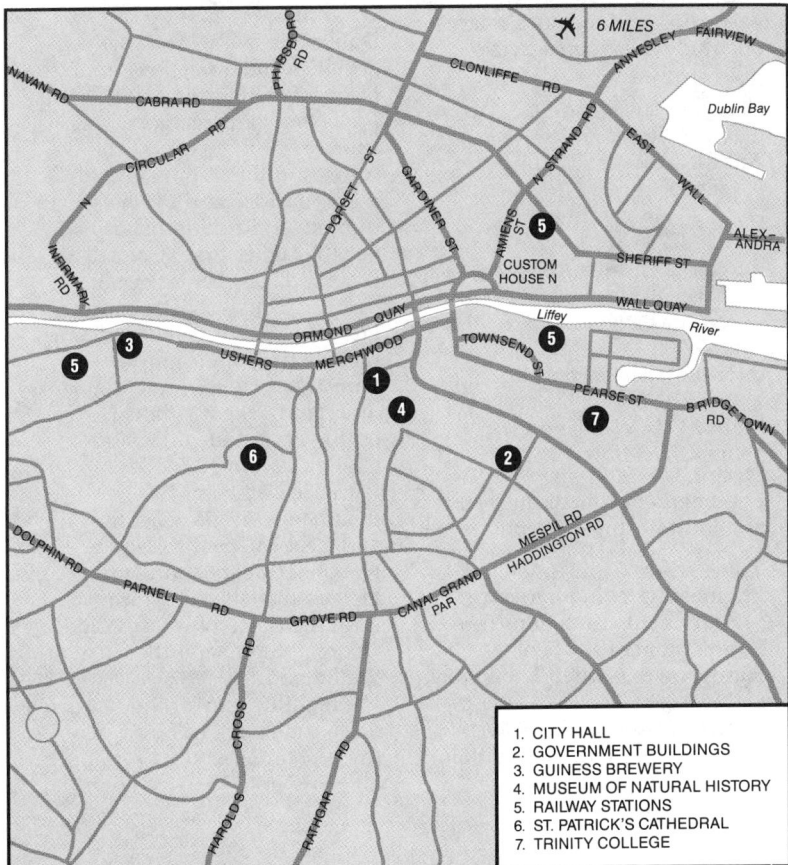

1. CITY HALL
2. GOVERNMENT BUILDINGS
3. GUINESS BREWERY
4. MUSEUM OF NATURAL HISTORY
5. RAILWAY STATIONS
6. ST. PATRICK'S CATHEDRAL
7. TRINITY COLLEGE

EUROPE

Dublin

Airport Taxes
None

City Information

Weather

Dublin has mild winters and cool summers, and many days of rain. Winter temperatures average 5 C (42 F), summer temperatures 15 C (60 F). Be prepared with umbrella or raincoat at any time.

Transportation

Metered taxis can be hired at cab stands, hailed in the street, or booked by telephone.

For self-drive rental cars, prior booking should be arranged and a national or international driver's license obtained. Driving is on the left.

Local public transport system is very good and includes inter-city bus route and train service.

Car Hire

Hertz, 19-20 Hogan Place
(tel: 371693 & 765594)
Ansa, 42 Westland Row
(tel: 767213)
Avis, 1 Hanover St.
(tel: 372369)
Budget, 29 Lower Abbey St.
(9034668)
Europcar, Baggot St. (378179 & 681777)
InterRent, 313 Airport Rd.
(tel: 770704)
Kemwel, 42 Westland Row
(tel: 376348)

Hospitals

For emergency medical treatment at a local hospital, telephone 999.

Trade Fairs

Engineering & Industrial Equipment Exhibition (Feb)
Futura Home Fair (Feb)
Hardware & Garden Exhibition (Mar)
Sports & Fashion Fair (Mar)
Amusement Trades Exhibition (Mar)
International Computer Exhibition (April)
Spring Industrial Fair (May)
Sports & Fashion Fair (Sept)

Hotels

Berkeley Court, Lansdowne Rd.
(tel: 601711)
Burlington, Upper Leeson St.
(tel: 605222)
Fitzpatrick's Castle, Southern Suburb (851533)
Gresham, O'Connell St.
(tel: 746881)
Jury's Dublin, Pembroke Rd.
(605000)
Royal Dublin, 40 Upper O'Connell St. (733666)
Sachs, 2125 Morehampton Rd.
(tel: 680995)
Shelbourne, St. Stephen's Green
(tel: 766471)

What to See and Do

Dublin offers a wide variety of activities and attractions from its blend of architectural styles to its parks and gardens. For sportsmen, there are 30 golf courses in the vicinity and the Irish Tourist Board can help with hunting and fishing holidays. For the sightseer, O'Connell St. is a good start before heading over to Trinity College and the Library. Notable public buildings include the 18th-century Parliament House (now the Bank of Ireland), the Customs House on the River Liffey, Dublin Castle (built in 1208), St. Patrick's Cathedral (where Jonathan Swift preached in 1715) and Christ Church. Also the National Gallery and Leinster House, the latter of which was once the home of Oscar Wilde, George Moore, and the Duke of Wellington.

For nightlife, any of the boisterous pubs will do where the Irish are friendly to strangers and sing until the wee hours.

Useful Addresses

American: 42 Elgin Rd.,
  Ballsbridge (tel: 688777)
British: 33 Merrion Rd.
  (tel: 695211)
Canadian: 65 St. Stephen's
  Green (tel: 781988)

Central Bank of Ireland, Dame
  St. (tel: 716666)
The Stock Exchange, 24-28
  Angelsea St. (tel: 778808)
American Chamber of
  Commerce, 20 College Green
  (tel: 712733)
Confederation of Irish Industries,
  Kildare St. (tel: 779801)

Dept. of Industry & Commerce,
  Kildare St. (tel: 779801)
Dublin Chamber of Commerce, 7
  Clare St. (tel: 764291)
Irish Export Board, Strand Rd.
  (tel: 695011)

Automobile Association, 23
  Suffolk St.
Tourist Information Office, 14 U.
  O'Connell (tel: 765871)
Royal Irish Auto Club, 34
  Dawson St.
American Express, 116 Grafton
  St. (tel: 772874)
Thomas Cook, 118 Grafton St.
  (tel: 771721)

ITALY

Essential Information

Republic

301,225 sq km
(116,303 sq mi)

58.9 million

0.7%

Italian

Roman Catholic

Italian

Metric

A.C. 50c 220/380 V, 127/220 V

Rome (cap) 3,250,000
Milan 1,950,000
Naples 1,500,000

Turin 1,200,000
Genoa 875,000

Lire
Notes 500, 1,000, 2,000, 5,000,
  10,000, 20,000, 50,000 and
  100,000 lira
Coins 5, 10, 20, 50, 100, 200 and
  500 lira

Jan 1 New Year
Apr 13-20 Easter Week
Apr 25 Liberation Day
May 1 Labour Day
May 28 Ascension
Aug 15 Assumption
Nov 1 All Saints' Day
Dec 8 Immaculate Conception
Dec 25, 26 Christmas

Travellers Information

Passport required of British and
North American travellers. No
visa required.

Visitors from EEC countries do

EUROPE

not need work permits, others do.

Vaccination Required
Typhoid vaccinations are recommended.

Customs and Duty-Free
On arrival: 200 cigarettes or 50 cigars or 250 gr. of tobacco; 3 L of spirits or 2 L of wine; also 50 gr. of perfume, .25 L of eau de cologne, and gifts to a value of L 15,000.

Currency Restrictions
No restrictions on foreign currencies, although large amounts should be declared on entry. A limit of L200,000 may be imported or exported.

Health Tips
Drinking water is purified in large towns and cities but mineral water is more popular with Italians. Medical facilities are very good and fees are high, but hospitals are a little unsanitary. Wash or peel all fruit and drink only pasteurized or sterilized milk. For emergency medical assistance at Rome's Day Hospital, tel: 595184.

Climate and Clothing
Climate is generally sunny and warm in summer (May-Sept) in the north and central regions (including Rome). In the south, summer days can reach 30 C (90 F). Northern and central winter months are cold with some rain and snow. Southern winters are warmer, reaching 10-15 C (50-60 F).

Tipping
A service charge of 15% is already included in most restaurant bills, but add 10% of the bill for waiters. Tip porters L700 per piece of luggage. Tip taxi drivers 10-15%. L200-500.

Food and Drink
Italian food is among the richest, flavorful and varied cuisines in the world, and is typified by the large number of courses at lunch and dinner. It is considered impolite to refuse a course, even though there may be twelve courses for dinner (the trick is to eat only a little of each course). In contrast to lunch and dinner, breakfast consists only of bread and coffee. Dinners are lengthy amd are served late in the evening. They usually begin with a pasta course, a meat, fish or poultry main course, and a dessert or dark coffee (espresso). Italian wines are excellent, especially the red wines from Peimonte or Tuscany.

Business Brief

GDP
$653.7 billion
(per capita income $11,080)

Natural Resources
FIsh, gas, mercury, iron ore, lignite, pyrite, coal, sulphur, natural gas

Agriculture
Cereals, fruits, grapes, nuts, olives, rice, vegetables, wheat

Industry
Automobiles, chemicals, engineering, food processing, footwear, machinery, petroleum refining, tourism

Imports
Total $125 billion
Fuel, petroleum, chemicals, meat, feed grains, lumber products, crude materials, steel products, minerals, and machinery

Exports
Total $116 billion
Machinery & transport equipment, manufactured goods,

food, knitwear, textiles, iron &
steel, vegetable oils, spirits

Major Trading Partners
West Germany, France, Great
Britain, U.S., U.S.S.R., Canada,
Saudi Arabia and Libya

Workforce
20 million
Industry 43%, agriculture 15%,
services and government 40%

Tips for Doing Business
A conservative business suit is
recommended, and prior
appointments are a must for
business and government
contacts. Lunch tends to be the
focus of weekdays, so
appointments should not intrude
on this meal. Few Italian
businessmen speak English but
many speak French, so phone
ahead to see what difficulties
may arise. Milan and Rome
businessmen are open and
friendly, whereas their
counterparts in Turin and Genoa
are more formal and taciturn. Do
not discuss politics, women, or
taxes and try not to include your
contact's wife in the business
affairs or social occasions arising
therefrom.

Best Months for Doing Business
Best months are February
through May and September
through November. Most
businesspeople take their
vacations in July and August.

Business Hours

Government
Mon-Fri 0830-1345

Business
Mon-Fri 0830-1245, 1700-2000
Sat 0830-1245

Banks
Mon-Fri 0830-1330

Shops
Mon-Sat 0900-1300, 1530-1930

English Language Publications
The Daily American and
International Daily News are
published in Rome, and you can
purchase the International
Herald-Tribune and British
papers in kiosks and hotels in
major cities.

Telephone and Communications
Telephone country code: 39
Telephone city code: Milan 02,
Rome 06, Turin 11, Naples 81
Telex country code: 843
Telephone tokens, called gettoni
can be purchased in shops,
restaurants, post office, and
many other places. There are
English-speaking operators to
handle your international calls.
Telex service available at larger
post offices.
Telegrams may be sent from any
post office or by phone.
Telephone ITALCABLE.

Air Travel
Alitalia and Aero Transporti
Italiani provide excellent
domestic air service to major
cities in Italy. In addition,
Alisarda operates flights linking
Rome, Milan and Turin with
Sardinia.

Other Transport
Network of roads makes for
good driving and there is a good
bus service available between
cities and towns.
Italian State Railways provide an
extensive network of passenger
services, but express tickets
should always be booked in
advance.

EUROPE

MILAN

Airport Information

Time
GMT +1
GMT +2 (May-Sept)

Airports

Enrico Forlanini/Linate LIN
Tel: (02) 74851
7 km (4.5 mi) E of the city
International and domestic
flights
Milano Malpensa MXP
Tel: (02) 868032
46 km (29 mi) NW of the city
International and domestic
flights

Airlines

Aer Lingus 700080
Aeroflot 669985
Air Canada 270829
Air France 773821
Alitalia 2836
Austrian 807794
Avensa 875792
Avianca 802440
British Airways 809041
Canadian International 879121

Egyptair 865777
El Al 806500
Finnair 864265
Iberia 8899
Interflug 8052873
JAL 8690251
KLM 807846
Korean 8693320
Kuwait Air 878190
Libyan 878137
Lufthansa 85581
MEA 5456486
Northwest 865932
Olympic 878692
Pan Am 877241
Philippine 872153
Qantas 807551
Sabena 876787
SAS 867541
Singapore 797651
Swissair 6598341
TAP 809691
THY 866350

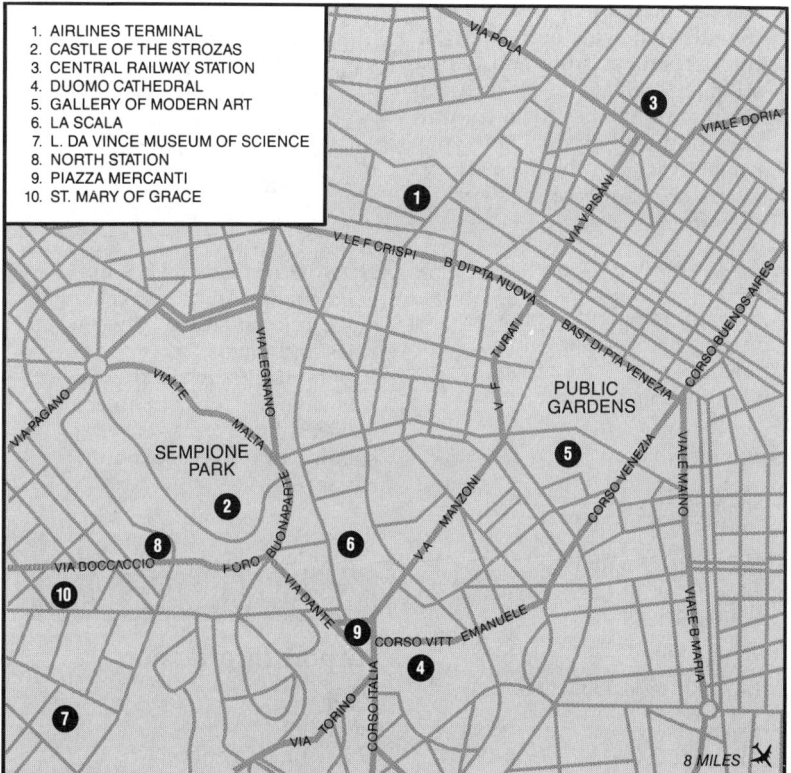

1. AIRLINES TERMINAL
2. CASTLE OF THE STROZAS
3. CENTRAL RAILWAY STATION
4. DUOMO CATHEDRAL
5. GALLERY OF MODERN ART
6. LA SCALA
7. L. DA VINCE MUSEUM OF SCIENCE
8. NORTH STATION
9. PIAZZA MERCANTI
10. ST. MARY OF GRACE

Milan

TWA 77961
United 5468730
Varig 3452151

Transport to City

Linate

Taxis: Avoid gypsy cabs and take a metered yellow taxi for the 20-minute trip. Fare of L15,000 includes tip.

Coach: A 20-minute coach ride to the city returns from the Alitalia Terminal, Viale Don Luigi Sturzo 37. SEAV operates a coach service to the Central Milan train station. Also stops at Garibaldi Station.

Transit: ATM bus *73 departs from near the SEAV office every 15 minutes. Ticket can be purchased ahead of time from a machine at the bus stop. Bus connects with Plaza San Babila and the subway system.

Malpensa

Taxis: A 60-minute trip to the city. Fare L60,000

Coach: Coaches marked "Airpullman" meet all international flights between 0800 and 2400, and take an hour to get downtown.

Facilities

Linate: Currency exchange, hotel reservations, baggage deposit, post office, restaurant, shops, first-aid, vaccinations

Malpensa: Currency exchange, hotel reservations, baggage deposit, post office, bar, restaurant, shops, first-aid, vaccinations.

Duty-free shops at both airports sell tobacco products, wines, aperitifs, spirits, cameras, watches, lighters, radios (Linate only), jewellery, glass and china. Car rental desks: (Linate) Hertz, Avis, Europcar, Maggiore (Malpensa) Hertz, Avis, Europcar, Maggiore, Eurotrans, Autoravel, InterRent

Airport Taxes

None at either airport

City Information

Weather

Milan is one of Italy's northernmost cities, and as such has hot summers but usually cold, wet winters with lots of snow. Spring and fall can also bring frequent heavy showers. Summers average 24 C (76 F) and winters 8 C (46 F).

Transportation

Taxis without meters should be avoided, and even those with meters may want to charge a flat fee. Try to agree on the fare or the meter.

Bus trips in Milan must be the best bargain in Italy. Monthly passes are available, but single tickets are valid for only 70 minutes and can be used on either buses or the subway.

Car Hire

Hertz, Via Larga 20 (tel: 7384580)
Ansa, Linate airport
  (tel: 6559464)
Avis, Via Fabio Fiezi 43
  (tel: 7561020)
Budget, Via Moscati 11
  (tel: 3453831)
Europcar, Via Galvani 12
  (tel: 5011116 & 7387278)
Godfrey-Davis (tel: 717210)
InterRent, Corso Como 4
  (tel: 6570477)
Kemwel, Corso Como 4
  (tel: 868221)

Trade Fairs

International Furniture
  Exhibition (Nov)
International Industrial &
  Mechanical Exhibition (Nov)
International Power Equipment
  Exhibition (Nov)
New Trends in Medicine (Nov)
International Research
  Equipment Exhibition (Nov)

EUROPE

International Sanitation
Exhibition (Nov)
European Knitwear Exhibition
(Dec)

Hotels
Ambasciatori, Galleria del Corso
(tel: 790241)
Cavalieri, Piazza Missori 1
(tel: 8857)
Excelsior-Gallia, Duca d'Aosta 9
(tel: 6277)
Jolly President, Largo Augusto
10 (tel: 7746)
Marino, P.della Scala 5
(tel: 867831)
Michelangelo, Via Scarlatti 23
(tel: 6755)
Milano Hilton, Via Galvani 12
(tel: 6983)
Palace, Piaza Repubblica
(tel: 6236)
Principe & Savoia, Piaza
Repubblica (tel: 6230)
Windsor, Via Galilei 2 (tel: 6346)

What to See and Do
Some of Milan's more beautiful
sights include the Gothic
Cathedral, the Castello
Sfrozesco, the Brera Palace and
the Church of Santa Maria delle
Grazie (containing da Vinci's
"The Last Supper"). An
interesting side visit to the
Leonardo da Vinci Museum of
Science and Technology holds
may curiosities for business
people. Also, no trip to Milan is
complete without taking in an
opera at La Scala. Even if you
are not an opera fan, La Scala is
one of the greatest opera and
concert venues in the world and
simply must be visited.

Useful Addresses
Embassies and Consulates
American: Piazza Repubblica 32
(tel: 652841)
British: Via San Paolo 7
(tel: 803442)
Canadian: Via Vittor Pisani 19
(tel: 652600)

Business and Commerce
American Chamber of
Commerce, Via Agnello 12
(tel: 8690661)
Stock Exchange, Piazza Affari 6
(tel: 85341)
British Chamber of Commerce,
Via Tarchetti 1-3 (tel: 635860)
Intl. Chamber of Commerce, Via
Cordusio 2 (tel: 802517)
Milan Chamber of Commerce,
Via Meravigli 9-11 (tel: 85151)
U.S.A. Trade Center, Palazzo
Agricoltura Via Gattamelata 5
(tel: 4696451)

Tourism and Travel
Tourist Information Office, Via
Marconi 1 (tel: 870016)
C.I.T. (Tourist board), Gal.
Vittorio Emanuele (tel: 866661)
Italian Touring Club, Corso Italia
10 (tel: 2809871)
American Express, Via Vittor
Pisani 19 (tel: 02670960 &
02670969)
Wagons-Lits/Cook, Via Fabio
Filzi 8 (tel: 654632)

ROME

Airport Information

Time
GMT +1
GMT +2 (May-Sept)

Airport
Leonardo da Vinci FCO
(Fiumicino)
Tel: (06) 6012
32 km (20 mi) W of the city
International and domestic
flights

Airlines
Aer Lingus 4758518
Aeroflot 4757704
Aerolineas Argentinas 4750971
Air Afrique 4743041
Air Algerie 484866
Air India 475851
Air New Zealand 460761

Alia 460809
Alitalia 5455
American 4750542
Austrian 463303
Avensa 4741231
Avianca 4741750
British Airways 479991
Canadian International 463517
Egyptair 4742641
El Al 4742301
Finnair 4745817
Garuda 4755815
Iberia 841041
Interflug 4743629
Iran Air 4741141
Iraqi 6799712
JAL 4755141
KLM 4747012
Kuwait Air 483654
Libyan 4757941
Lufthansa 4660210
MEA 486734
Olympic 4742201
Pan Am 4773

Philippine 483486
PIA 486713
Qantas 486451
SAA 4742141
Sabena 4750241
SAS 4745947
Saudia 4759931
Singapore 4758943
Swissair 8470555
Syrian 4759902
TAP 4755341
Thai 4756669
THY 4751149
TWA 47211
UTA 479519
United 5403641
Varig 4758556

Transport to City

Taxis: Metered taxis should be hired with the proviso that the fare will be determined by the meter or by a flat fee. If you prefer the former, a tip of 5-10%

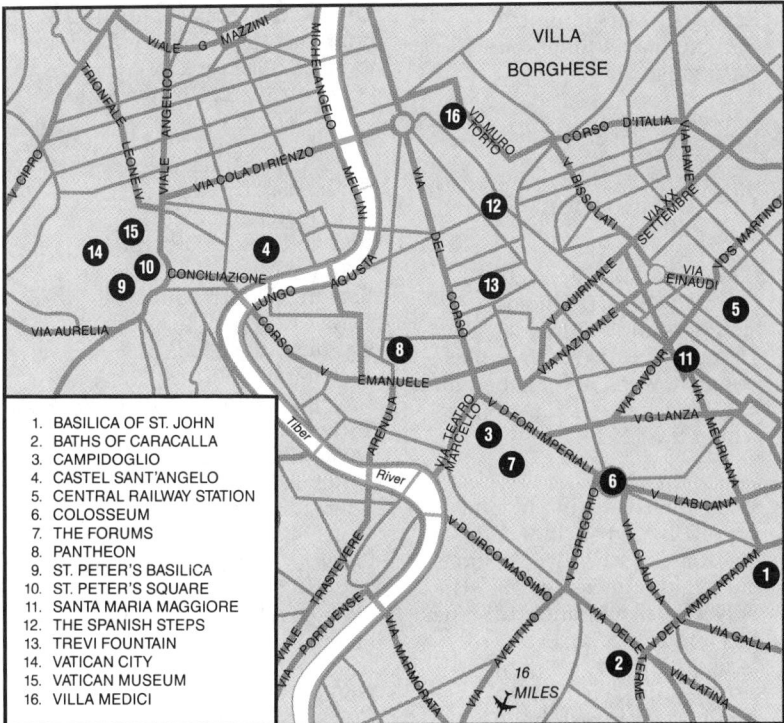

1. BASILICA OF ST. JOHN
2. BATHS OF CARACALLA
3. CAMPIDOGLIO
4. CASTEL SANT'ANGELO
5. CENTRAL RAILWAY STATION
6. COLOSSEUM
7. THE FORUMS
8. PANTHEON
9. ST. PETER'S BASILICA
10. ST. PETER'S SQUARE
11. SANTA MARIA MAGGIORE
12. THE SPANISH STEPS
13. TREVI FOUNTAIN
14. VATICAN CITY
15. VATICAN MUSEUM
16. VILLA MEDICI

EUROPE

Rome

should be added to the 45-minute trip to Rome. Avoid any misunderstanding before your trip starts.

Coach: The Acotral coach departs every 15-30 minutes from outside the arrival terminal where you can also purchase the ticket. The hour-long trip by bus is a small tour in itself. There are also hotel coaches to some of the better hotels, including Cavalieri, Holiday Inn, Grand, Excelsior, and Satellite.

Facilities

Bank, currency exchange, hotel reservations, baggage deposit, vaccinations, chapel, meeting point, insurance, post office, pharmacy, nursery.

Duty-free shop sells tobacco products, aperitifs, spirits, liqueurs, lighters, watches, scarves, records, leather goods, cameras, tape recorders.

Car rental desks: Hertz, Avis, Europcar, Maggiore, Italy by Car, Autoravel, InterRent, Eurotrans

Airport Taxes

None

City Information

Weather

Rome has a Mediterranean climate with hot, humid summers and mild winters. Late spring and early summer may bring showers, and temperatures in July average 24 C (76 F), in winter 8 C (46 F).

Transportation

Taxis are usually in plentiful supply in towns, cities and resort areas, at railway stations, but avoid unmetered cabs. Tip only a small amount at all times. Bus and subway facilities are very good, if crowded in Rome, but try to avoid travel at rush hour. Bus

fare is L400 in Rome and L1600 for use on any service for one day. Some tickets may have a time-limit for travel so ask when you purchase. Monthly tickets are also available. Rome has a very extensive subway system where exact change is required.

Car Hire

Hertz, Gelsomino 42 (tel: 601448)
Ansa, Da Vinci Airport (tel: 866956)
Avis, Via Sardegna 38 (tel: 601531)
Europcar, Via Lombardia 7 (tel: 465802 & 601879)
Godfrey-Davis (866956)
InterRent, Via Nizza 154 (tel: 859342)
Kemwel, Via Nizza 154 (tel: 6011237)
Maggiore, della Republica 57 (tel: 851620)

Hospitals

The larger hospitals provide 24-hour emergency service. Look in the telephone directory unde "Guardia Medica permanente."

Hotels

Albani, Via Adda 45 (tel: 84991)
Ambasciatori Palace, 70 Via Veneto (tel: 473831)
Bernini-Bristol, Barberini 23 (tel: 463051)
Boston, Via Lombardia 47 (tel: 473951)
Cardinal, Via Giulia 62 (tel: 6542719)
Cavalieri Hilton, Cardiolo 101 (tel: 3151)
De la Ville, Via Sistina 69 (tel: 6733)
Eden, Via Ludovisi 49 (tel: 4743551)
Excelsior, Vittorio Veneto 125 (tel: 4708)
Flora, Via Veneto (tel: 497821)
Hassler Medici, Trinita dei Monti 6 (tel: 6782651)
Holiday Inn, Via Aurelia Antica 415 (tel: 5872)

Inghilterra, Via Bocca di Leone 14
(tel: 672161)
Jolly, Corso d'Italia 1 (tel: 8495)
Oxford, via Boncompagni 89
(tel: 4756852)

What to See and Do

Rome is a veritable feast for the eye and the mind, being one of the world's most ancient and varied cities. Its Roman and Christian-era monuments and architecture are unsurpassed. No visit to Rome would be complete without trips to the Colisseum, the Forum, the Palatine Hill and the Theater of Marcellus. A ride down the old Appian Way furnishes a wonderful idea of the ancient Roman lifestyle, as does a trip to the Baths of Caracalla. Any tour of religious places must begin with St. Peter's Square and the Vatican Museum in Vatican City, and include the medieval castle fortress of the Popes, Castel Sant Angela. Beautiful churches from nearly every period in Roman history abound, and the art galleries contain rich treasures of the city's heritage. Take in an opera in summer at the Baths of Caracalla or visit the famous seventeenth-century gardens of Tivoli with their landmark fountains. A trip outside Rome to Hadrian's Villa can be a very relaxing break for the business traveller. Also of interest are the Etruscan tombs of Tarquinia. Among other noteworthy places are Hadrian's

Tomb, the Catacombs, the Pantheon, Circus Maximus, Borghese Gallery and the Gallery of Modern Art.

Useful Addresses

Embassies and Consulates

American: Via Vittorio Veneta
119 (tel: 4674)
British: Via XX Settembre 80
(tel: 475541)
Canadian: Via G.B. de Rossi 27
(tel: 855341)

Business and Commerce

Rome Stock Exchange, Via del
Burro 147 (tel: 6794541)
Italian Government Agency for
Promotion of Foreign Trade,
Via Liszt 21 (tel: 5992)
Ministry of Foreign Trade, Viale
Boston (tel: 5993)
Office of the President, Palazzo
di Quininale (tel: 4699)
Central Bank, Via Nazionale 91
(tel: 4672)
Rome Chamber of Commerce,
Piazza Sallustio 21 (tel: 462565)
United Nations Information
Office, Piazzi San Marco

Tourism and Travel

ENIT, Via Marconi 1 (tel: 461851)
Ministry of Tourism, Via della
Ferratella in Laterano 51
(tel: 7732)
Automobile Club of Italy, 8 Via
Marsala (tel: 4998)
American Express, Piazza di
Spagna 38 (tel: 0667641)
Thomas Cook, Via Veneto 9
(tel: 462327)

EUROPE

NETHERLANDS

Essential Information

Type of Government
Parliamentary Democracy

Area
41,160 sq km
(16,464 sq mi)

Population
14.2 million

Annual Growth Rate
0.4%

Languages
Dutch

Religion
Roman Catholic, Protestant,
others

Ethnic Groups
Dutch, some Indonesian,
Surinamese

Weights and Measures
Metric

Electrical Current
A.C. 50c 220/380 V

Major Business Cities
Amsterdam (cap) 945,000
Rotterdam 1,000,000
The Hague 670,000

Currency
1 guilder (or florin) = 100 cents
Notes 5,10, 25, 50, 100 and 1,000
    guilders

Public Holidays
Jan 1 New Year
Apr 13-20 Easter Week
Apr 30 Princess Juliana's
Birthday
May 5 Liberation Day
May 28 Ascension
Jun 9 Whitsun
Dec 25, 26 Christmas

Travellers Information

Entry Requirements
A passport is required of North
American and British travellers.
No visa is required by most
nationals, but only up to three
months' stay.

Working Restrictions
All nationals except for those
from EEC countries need work
permits.

Vaccination Required
None

Customs and Duty Free
On arrival: 200 cigarette or 50
cigars or 250 gr. of tobacco;
spirits 1 L or wine 2 L; perfume
50 gr. or gifts to a value of fl 110.

Currency Restrictions
There are generally no
restrictions on currency of any
kind or amount, but it may save
problems and delays later if you
declared abnormally large
amounts going in or coming out.

Health Tips
Most doctors and dentists speak
English, but pharmaceuticals,
while available, can be
expensive. Bring your own. For
the Central Doctors' Service, tel:
425277. Tap water is excellent
although the Dutch like mineral
water as well.

Climate and Clothing
Weather is temperate in general
with rainfall occurring frequently
and in any season. Temperatures
seldom go above 18 C (65 F) in
summer or below 7 C (45 F) in
winter, but bring light to
medium weight clothes in
summer, mediumweight in
winter. Always take a raincoat.

Tipping
Large bills, like those for dinner,
hotel, etc. include a tip already,
as do taxis. It is customary to tip
a few florins after restaurant
meals or drinks, or for services
of various kinds in your room.

Food and Drink
The staple food of Dutch cuisine
are bread, potatoes, fish, meat
and vegetables. Coffee is the
usual beverage for most meals,
and dinner eaten about 1800 is
the main meal of the day.
Herring, smoked eels, oysters,
and hotchpotch (mashed
potatoes mixed with vegetables)
are popular dishes, but there is
also a wide variety of restaurants
serving Indonesian cuisine.
National specialties include the
very good Dutch cheeses, and
also world-famous beers such as
Heiniken and Amstel.

Business Brief

GDP
$244.2 billion
(per capita income $16,775)

Annual Growth Rate
0.5%

Natural Resources
Natural gas, salt, crude oil

Agriculture
Wheat, barley, oats, sugar beets, fruits, potatoes, poultry, vegetables, flowers and bulbs

Industry
Petroleum refining, steel, metal products, electronics, bulk chemicals, natural gas, construction, ship-building

Imports
Total $91.3 billion
Fuel, petroleum, iron and steel, scientific and precision instruments, optical goods, tobacco, sugar, foodstuffs, lumber, cars, textiles, grains

Exports
Total $92.4 billion
Livestock, meat, fish, dairy products, eggs, machinery and transport equipment, manufactured goods, chemicals, lubricants, fabrics, textiles, electrical and communication equipment, natural gas

Major Trading Partners
West Germany, Belgium, Luxumbourg, France, Great Britain, U.S.

Workforce
4.6 million
Industry and commerce 36%, services 34%, government 15%, agriculture 6%

Tips for Doing Business
Wear a conservative business suit on all occasions, and prior appointments are always necessary. Dutch business people are formal, so try to be businesslike and avoid personal references. The Dutch like to entertain for business (or be entertained) so be prepared for a large number of meals or snacks during the business day. Business people do not shake hands as often as those in Italy, for example. If invited to someone's home for dinner, a half-dozen flowers for the hostess and a short thank you note the next day will be appreciated.

Best Months for Doing Business
March through May and mid-September through November. Avoid the two weeks before and four weeks after Christmas, as well as the week before and after Easter. Businesspeople take their vacations from June through August.

Business Hours

Government
Mon-Fri 0830-1730

Business
Mon-Fri 0830-1730

Banks
Mon-Fri 0900-1600

Shops
Mon-Fri 0900-1730 (or 20000 Wed-Thurs)
Sat 0900-1700 or 1730

English Language Publications
Most Dutch speak English and read foreign papers themselves. The International Herald Tribune, USA Today and some British daily newspapers are available at shops and in some hotels in Amsterdam and major cities.

Telephone and Communications
Telephone country code: 31
Telephone city codes:
Amsterdam 020, Rotterdam 010
Telex country code: 844
Postal system is fast, with next-

EUROPE

day service throughout the country. In Amsterdam, letters can be mailed all night and there is a telephone office open at Spuistraat. Telephone information available in English or French.
Telex facilities available in main hotels.
Telegrams can be sent from large post offices.

Air Travel
Domestic air services are handled by NLM City-Hopper, with flights to all the Netherlands' major cities, including Groningen, Eindhoven, and Maastricht.

Other Transport
There is frequent bus service between major towns on the country's excellent highways. Fast regular rail services are operated by the Netherlands Railways. Most trackage has been electrified.
There are also extensive inland waterways and regular ferry services are frequent and inexpensive.

AMSTERDAM

Airport Information

Time
GMT +1
GMT +2 (Mar 28 - Sept 25)

Airport
Amsterdam-Schiphol AMS
Tel: (020) 5179111
15 km (9.3 mi) SW of the city
International and domestic flights

Airlines
Aer Lingus 239589
Aeroflot 245715
Air France 5731585
Alia 226566
ALitalia 5576333

American 648686
Austrian 234980
British Airways 229333
British Caledonian 262440
Canadian International 851721
El Al 220191
Finnair 244799
Garuda 246397
Iberia 850401
Interflug 715209
Iraqi 220330
JAL 264011
KLM 747747
Korean 248787
Kuwait Air 262555
Lufthansa 263511
Malaysian 262420
Northwest 220022
Olympic 233614
Pan Am 262021
Philippine 464346
Qantas 255015
SAA 164444
Sabena 262966
SAS 763015
Singapore 464545
Swissair 624141
TAP 246268
Thai 2218770
THY 227984
TWA 262277
United 434125
Varig 227671

Transport to City
Taxis: Taxis are metered and ride automatically includes a tip. The 25-minute ride costs about fl 35.
Coach: You can catch a KLM Coach Company bus outside the Arrivals hall. The 30-minute ride to Center Station costs about fl 10 and leaves every 15-20 minutes during regular hours. These coaches are comfortable and have baggage space.
Transit: Trains connect the airport with Amsterdam's South Station and RAI Centel. The 20-minute trip costs about fl 3, and trains leave every 18 minutes. Tickets may be purchased at the station outside the Arrivals hall. Buses of the Centraal Nederland

go to Amsterdam Centraal Station and the 35-minute trip costs about fl 7. There is little or no baggage space available.

Facilities
Bank, currency exchange, hotel reservations, tourist information desk, bar, buffet restaurant, insurance, post office, baggage deposit, barber shop, information desk, flowers. Duty-free shop sells tobacco products, wines, spirits, cameras, watches, lighters, radios, jewellery, bicycles, glass and china, diamonds, caviar. Car rental desks: Hertz, Avis, Europcar, InterRent, Budget, Van Wyk

Airport Taxes
None

City Information

Weather
Climate in Amsterdam is generally moderate with few extremes of heat, cold or humidity, and rain is frequent and often unexpected. Temperatures range from 4 C (40 F) in winter to 18 C (64 F) in summer. A raincoat is always an advisable companion.

Transportation
The nationwide fare zoning system also applies to all cities. Taxis can be boarded wherever found or called and hired by phone.
Amsterdam has an excellent subway system and there is an interlinking bus and streetcar system.

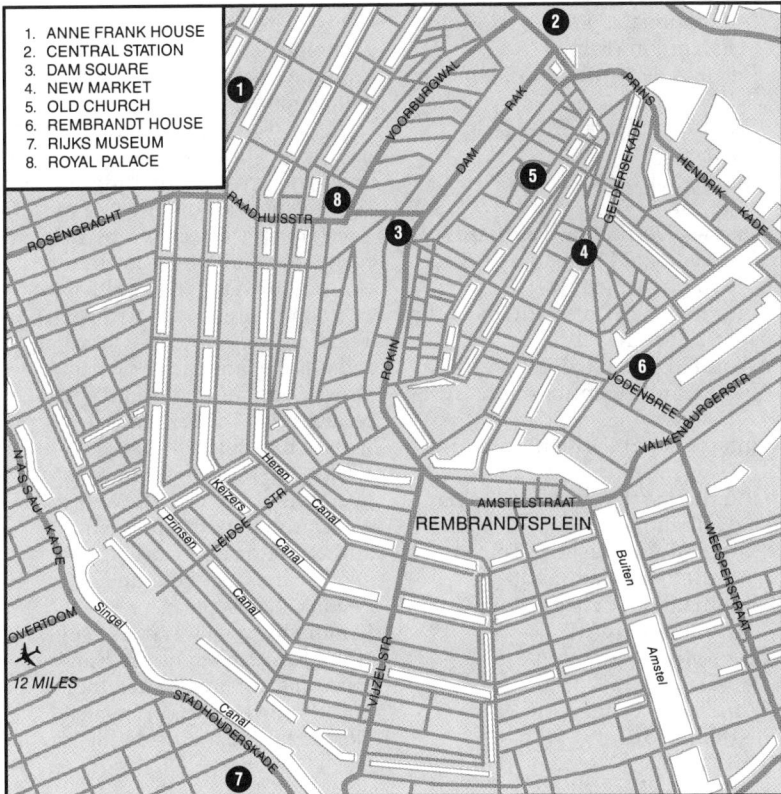

1. ANNE FRANK HOUSE
2. CENTRAL STATION
3. DAM SQUARE
4. NEW MARKET
5. OLD CHURCH
6. REMBRANDT HOUSE
7. RIJKS MUSEUM
8. ROYAL PALACE

EUROPE

REMBRANDTSPLEIN

12 MILES

Amsterdam

Car Hire

Hertz, Overtoom 333 (tel: 122414
& 170866)
Avis, Keizergracht 485
(tel: 262201 & 176754)
Europcar, Overtoom 51
(tel: 184595 & 175447)
Godfrey-Davis, Overtoom 51
(tel: 832123)
InterRent, 232 van Ostadestraat
(tel: 177666)
Kemwel, 98 Argonautenstraat
(tel: 172405)

Hospitals

For emergency help telephone
police at 222222 or 425277.

Trade Fairs

International Garden Trade Fair
(Jan)
International Hotel & Catering
Exhibition (Jan)
International Agriculture
Machinery Exhibition (Jan)
International Commercial Motor
Exhibition (Feb)
Retail and Distribution Exhibition
(Mar)
Electronics Trade Exhibition
(Mar)
International Households Fair
(April)
Interior Decoration Fair (April)
International Petroleum
Exhibition (April)
International Traffic Engineering
Fair (April)
World Tobacco Exhibition (May)
European Communications Week
(May)
International Fashion Trade Fair
(Aug)
International Water Technology
Exhibition (Sept)
International Buses & Touring
Cars Exhibition (Sept)
International Office Equipment
Exhibition (Oct)

Hotels

American, Leidsekade 97
(tel: 245322)
Amstel, Prof. Tulpplein 1
(tel: 226060)
Amsterdam Hilton, Apollolaan
138 (tel: 780780)
Amsterdam Marriott,
Stadhouderskade 21
(tel: 835151)
De L'Europe, Nieurve Doelenstr
2 (tel: 234836)
Esterea, Singel 305-307
(tel: 245146)
IBIS Hotel, Schipolweg 181
(tel: 681234)
Novotel, Europa Blvd. 10
(tel: 5411123)
Okura, Ferd. Bolstr. 175
(tel: 787111)
Pulitzer, Prinsegracht 315-331
(tel: 228333)
Schiphol Airport Hilton, P.O.
Box 7685 (tel: 5115911)
Sonesta, Kattengat 1 (tel:212223)
Trianon, J.W. Brouwesstraat 3
(tel: 733918)

What to See and Do

Monuments, museums, statues
and fine examples of architecture
can be found everywhere in this
700-year-old center of European
culture. A stroll down practically
any major avenue, or a trip in a
sightseeing boat on any one of
Amsterdam's canals can be richly
rewarding and a treat for the
eye. Try to visit the Royal Palace
on Damsquare and the Tower of
Tears, or walk down tje Joordan,
a charming labyrinth of narrow
streets, antique shops and
restaurants. The Rijksmuseum
houses most of Rembrandt's
works; the Van Gogh museum
nearby is also worth the short
walk. Anne Frank's home (now
a museum) is also closeby. Clubs
and cabarets can be found at
Zeedijk, Leidseplein, or
Rembrandtsplein. Try the Blue
Note, King's Club or the Run-
inn. Amsterdammers call their
pubs "brown cafes." A
worthwhile visit outside the city

is the 14th-century castle Muiderslot with its magnificent view overlooking the Ijsellake (the Zuyderzee).

Useful Addresses

Embassies and Consulates
American: Museumplein 19
  (tel: 654661)
British: J. Vermeerstraat 7
  (tel: 764343)

Business and Commerce
Central Bank, Westeinde 1
  (tel: 524911)
Chamber of Commerce, Prinses Beatrixlaan 5, The Hague
  (tel: 836646)
Stock Exchange, Beursplein 5
  (tel: 239711)
American Chamber of Commerce, Carnegieplein 5
  (tel: 659808)
Chamber of Commerce and Industry for Amsterdam, Koningin Wilhelminaplein 13
  (tel: 17288882)

Tourism and Travel
ANWB Auto Club, Musemplein 5
National Tourist Office, Avenue den Haag 2594 (tel: 814191)
American Express, Damrak 66
  (tel: 020 262042)
Thomas Cook Centraal Station
  (tel: 244011)
VVV Tourist Office, Rokin 5
  (tel: 266444)

ROTTERDAM

Airport Information

Time
GMT + 1
GMT + 2 (Mar 28 - Sept 25)

Airport
Rotterdam International RTM (Zestienhoven)
Tel: (010) 4371144
9 km (5.5 mi) NW of the city

International and domestic flights

Airlines
Air France 5731585
Alitalia 134807
British Airways 262440
Iberia 148955
KLM 4747747
SAS 132351

Transport to City
Taxis: The far from the airport to Rotterdam is about fl 22-30, with tip included in the metered fare. Also taxi service to Amsterdam airport.
Coach: KLM provides a regular coach service to downtown and the fare is variable, depending on the stop.
Transit: Bus #33 runs between the airport and Central Station, and the 30-minute trip will cost about fl 3-6.

Facilities
Bar, buffet, restaurant, bank with currency exchange, hotel reservations, post office, baggage deposit, books, gifts, flowers, information desk.
Duty-free shop sells tobacco products, wines, aperitifs, spirits, cameras, lighters, watches, radios, jewellery, leather goods.
Car rental desks: Hertz, Avis, Europcar

Airport Taxes
Per person: International fl 12.50

City Information

Weather
Climate is very similar to Amsterdam, and typical of the Netherlands. Temperatures are moderate but weather is very changeable, so carry a raincoat at all times.

Transportation
Taxis can usually be boarded at

EUROPE

taxi stands or booked ahead by phone.

Streetcars, buses and subway are available for short local routes.

Car Hire

Hertz, Municipal Airport
  (tel: 4371185)
Avis, Kruisplein 21 (tel: 4332233
  & 4158842)
Budget, Conradstr. 63
  (tel: 113022)

Europcar, Rodezand 23
  (tel: 4143006 & 4371826)
InterRent, Geysendorfferweg 15
  (tel: 297171)

Trade Fairs

International Maintenance &
  Renovations Trade Fair (Jan)
International Harbours &
  Transport Exhibition (April)
International Energy
  Conservation Fair (May)

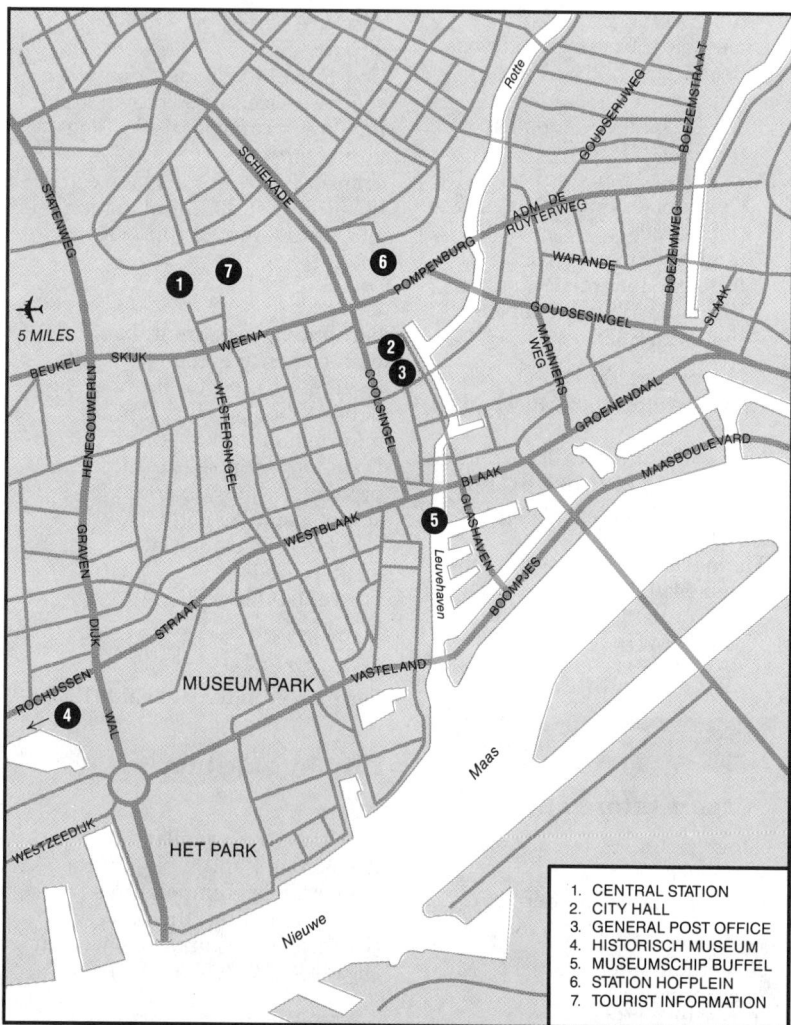

1. CENTRAL STATION
2. CITY HALL
3. GENERAL POST OFFICE
4. HISTORISCH MUSEUM
5. MUSEUMSCHIP BUFFEL
6. STATION HOFPLEIN
7. TOURIST INFORMATION

Rotterdam

International Trade Fair (Sept)
International Timber &
    Woodworking Exhibition (Oct)
International Shipping & Fishery
    Trade Fair (Nov)

Hotels

Atlanta, Aert van Nesstraat
    (tel: 4110420)
Central, Kruiskade 12
    (tel: 4140744)
Delta, Massboulevard 15
    (tel: 4345477)
Hilton Rotterdam, Weena
    10   (tel: 4144044)
Novotel Schiedam, Hargalaan 2
    (tel: 4713322)
Parkhotel, Westersingel 70
    (tel: 4363611)
Rijnhotel, Schouwburgplein 1
    (tel: 4333800)
Savoy, Hoogstraat 81
    (tel: 4139280)

What to See and Do

A rather unique attraction in
Rotterdam, a 600-year-old fishing
port, is the Visserijmuseum, a
sea-fishing museum complete
with pictures and models of
Dutch fishing vessels and species
of fish. There is constant activity
along the quays, and the
incessant shipping traffic can be
watched from the comfort of the
glass-walled restaurant in the
Delta Hotel. Sightseeing flights
over Rotterdam can be booked at
the airport, and an interesting
view provided for this city, so
heavily rebuilt after the Second
World War.

For shopping, visit the Linjbaan
Shopping Center. Also try and
visit the International Building
Center, Crane House, the
Pilgrim Fathers' Church, the
Blijdrop Zoo or the Rotterdam
Town Hall. For the masochists at
heart, a trip to the Taxation
Museum is a must.

Useful Addresses

Embassies and Consulates

American: Vlasmarkt 1
    (tel: 4117560)

Business and Commerce

Rotterdam Chamber of
    Commerce & Industry,
    Coolsingel 58 (tel: 4145022)
Singapore ASEAN Trade
    Promotion Center, Coolsingel
    58 (tel: 4130787)
World Trade Center, Meent 134
    (tel: 333611)

Tourism and Travel

ANWB Auto Club, Westblaak
    210
Tourist Information Office,
    Stadhuisplein 19 (tel: 4136000)
American Express, Meent 92
    (tel: 4330300)
Wagons-Lits/Cook, 56
    Schiedamsevest (tel: 4116200)

EUROPE

POLAND

Essential Information

Type of Government
Communist Republic

Area
312,612 sq km
(120,700 sq mi)

Population
41.6 million

Annual Growth Rate
0.9%

Languages
Polish

Religion
Roman Catholic 95%, Eastern
Orthodox 5%

Ethnic Groups
Polish 98%, Ukrainian 0.6%,
Byelorussian 0.5%

Weights and Measures
Metric

Electrical Current
A.C. 50c 220/380 V

Major Business Cities
Warsaw 1,800,000
Lodz 950,000
Krakow 775,000
Wroclaw 675,000
Poznan 600,000
Gdansk 500,000

Currency
1 Zloty (zl) = 100 groszy
Notes 50, 100, 200, 500, 1,000
    and 2,000 zl
Coins 10, 20, 50 groszy; 1, 2, 5,
    10, 20 zl

Public Holidays
Jan 1 New Year's
Apr 13-20 Easter Week
May 1 Labour Day
May 9 Victory Day
July 2 National Day
Nov 1 All Saints' Day
Dec 25 Christmas

Travellers Information

Entry Requirements
Passport is required of most
visitors. Visas valid for 90 days
at a time are required for North
American and British travellers.
Exit visa is required for Polish
nationals.

Working Restrictions
Foreigners cannot work in
Poland.

Vaccination Required
None

Customs and Duty Free
On arrival: 250 cigarettes or 50
cigars or 250 gr. of tobacco;
spirits 1 L; wine 1 L; perfume for
personal use. Also gifts to a
value of zl 6,000. On departure,
goods for export must not
exceed 50% of the value of the
currency that you changed into

zlotys (maximum zl 2,000). Keep
all receipts for customs.

Currency Restrictions
A daily minimum of $15 (U.S.)
must be spent for food and
accomodation. Vouchers are
obtainable from all Polish
National Tourist offices, and
though there are no limits on
foreign currency, it must be
declared and the amount
exported must be less than that
imported. The black market in
currency is strictly illegal, and
the law is enforced on visitors.

Health Tips
Drinking water is purified in
cities and resorts. Medical
services are generally good and
prices are not excessive. Bring
your own pharmaceuticals and
toiletries, since they are both
scarce and expensive in Poland.
Pharmaceuticals available only
by prescription.

Climate and Clothing
Winters are very cold, with snow
and ice from Nov to Mar.
Medium to heavy weight clothes
should be brought, together with
boots, hat, and fur-lined gloves.
From Apr to June, temperatures
average 10-13 C (50-55 F) so
carry medium weight clothing.
June to Aug are the hottest and
driest months, and lightweight
clothes are recommended.

Tipping
Tipping is frowned upon by
Polish authorities, but privately
your tip will be appreciated. Tip
taxis 10%, porters zl 30 per piece
of luggage, barbers and
beauticians 10%, small
services zl 10. A tip of 10% is
already included in bar,
restaurant, and nightspot bills.

Food and Drink
Breakfasts are light, often
consisting only of a beverage,
while a light sandwich or snack

is taken at 1000. The main meal, taken after 1500 usually consists of soup, meat or fish, salad, potatoes and tea. A light snack of pastries or ice cream may be taken later, and a light supper is eaten at home. Bread, dairy products and canned fish used to be popular -- today they are scarce, and Poles must stand in long lines waiting for a chance to purchase them.

Business Brief

GDP
$130.7 billion

Annual Growth Rate
3%

Natural Resources
Coal, sulphur, copper, natural gas, silver, salt, zinc

Agriculture
Barley, oats, potatoes, rye, sugar beets, hogs, livestock

Industry
Machine building, iron and steel, chemicals, shipbuilding, food processing, cement, electrical engineering, motor vehicles, power production

Imports
Total $11.2 billion
Oil, iron ore, fertilizers, wheat, leather footwear, cotton

Exports
Total $12.2 billion
Copper, sulphur, coal, ships, textiles, steel, cement, chemicals, foodstuffs, engineering products

Major Trading Partners
U.S.S.R., East Germany, Czechoslovakia, West Germany, Great Britain, U.S., Iran, Italy, France, Austria, Hungary

Workforce
17.2 million
Agriculture 30%, industry amd commerce 44%, government 8%, services 11%

Tips for Doing Business
Wear a conservative business suit for all occasions and prior appointments are always necessary. Many state-run industries employ people who can speak English, but knowing German is an advantage. Poland, like Czechoslovakia, is very price conscious, so generous credit terms will be necessary. Business visitors may be required to work from early morning until about 1600 without a meal, a gruelling Polish custom.

Best Months for Doing Business
September through May. Avoid June, July and August, when businesspeople take their vacations.

Business Hours

Government
Mon-Fri 0800-1500

Business
Mon-Fri 0830-1530

Banks
Mon-Sat 0900-1330

Shops
Mon-Sat 1100-1900

English Language Publications
Few English-language publications are available in Poland, but some radio stations occasionally carry broadcasts in English.

Telephone and Communications
Telephone country code: 48
Telephone city code: Warsaw 22
Telex country code: 867
Public telephones are available in public places and in street booths. Local calls cost zl 1. There is a cheaper rate on long-distance calls between 1600 and 0600.
Telegrams are available in post offices and by phone, and telex facilities are in main ORBIS hotels, Foreign Trade

EUROPE

Enterprises, and at URZAD POCZTOWY in Warsaw.

Air Travel

All internal domestic flights are operated by LOT, or Polish Airlines, a network linking all major towns and cities. Flights connect Warsaw, Gdansk, Kracow, Poznan, Wroclaw, Szczecin, Rzeszow, Katowice, Koszalin, Bydgoszcz, Zielona, Gova and Stupsk.

Other Transport

Extensive bus and coach services are run by PKS (Polish Motor Communications).
Train services connect major towns, and 30% of Poland's rail network has been electrified. There are also over 5,000 km of inland waterways, one-fifth of which are canals.

WARSAW

Airport Information

Time
GMT +1
GMT +2 (Mar 28 - Sept 25)

Airport
Okecie Airport WAW
Tel: 469670
10 km (6 mi) SW of the city
International and domestic flights

Airlines
Aeroflot 211611
Air Canada 512222
British Airways 289431
British Caledonia 460411
Canadian International 460411
KLM 217041
LOT 217021
Lufthansa 275436
Pan Am 260257
SAS 469505
Swissair 275016

Transport to City
Taxis: To Warsaw, the taxi fare is zl 100 and 200, depending on time of day. Night fares can be double that of the daytime. Add a tip of 10%.
Coach: Coaches run to the city every 30 minutes from 0500-2300. They return from the LOT office, at Warynskiego 9. Fare is about zl 5-10.
Transit: Bus #175 leaves every 15 minutes for Warsaw. Tickets for zl 1.50 can be bought at the "RUCH" sign of a newspaper stand in the Arrivals hall. Buses return from Plac Zwyciestwa.

Facilities
Restaurants, bank, currency exchange, post office, baggage deposit.
Duty-free shop sells spirits, crystals, clothing, perfume, folk art in wood, amber and silver, local and foreign food.
Car rental desks: Hertz, Avis, Europcar

Airport Taxes
None

City Information

Weather
Warsaw can be quite warm and sunny in summer but bitterly cold in winter. Precipitation is evenly distributed through every season, with possible heavy snowfall in winter. Average temperatures: Jan (winter) -1 C (30 F).
July (summer) 16 C (61 F)

Transportation
Taxis are available in Warsaw and rates generally increase from 2300-0500 and for out-of-town journeys. An international driver's license is required for all self-drive cars.
Streetcars and buses provide good interconnecting service and

tickets for either can be purchased at newspaper kiosks. There is also a partly completed subway system, parts of which are open for transit use.

Car Hire

Hertz, Victoria Inter-Continental Hotel, Krolewska 11 (tel: 274185 & 469896)
Avis, Victoria Inter-Continental Hotel (tel: 293875 & 469896)
Europcar, Victoria Inter-Continental Hotel (tel: 260271 & 469896)
ORBIS, Forum Hotel (tel: 211360)

Hospitals

For ambulance services to local hospitals, telephone 999. Staff are available in most hospitals who can speak English.

Trade Fairs

International Book Fair (May)

Hotels

Europejski, Krakowskie Przedmiescie 13 (tel: 265051)
Forum Inter-Continental, Nowogrodzka 24 (tel: 210272)
Grand, Krucza 28 (tel: 294051)
Metropol, Ul. Marszalkowska 99A (tel: 294001)
Novotel, Pierwszego Sierpnia 1 (tel: 464051)
Solec, Zagorna 1 (tel: 259241)

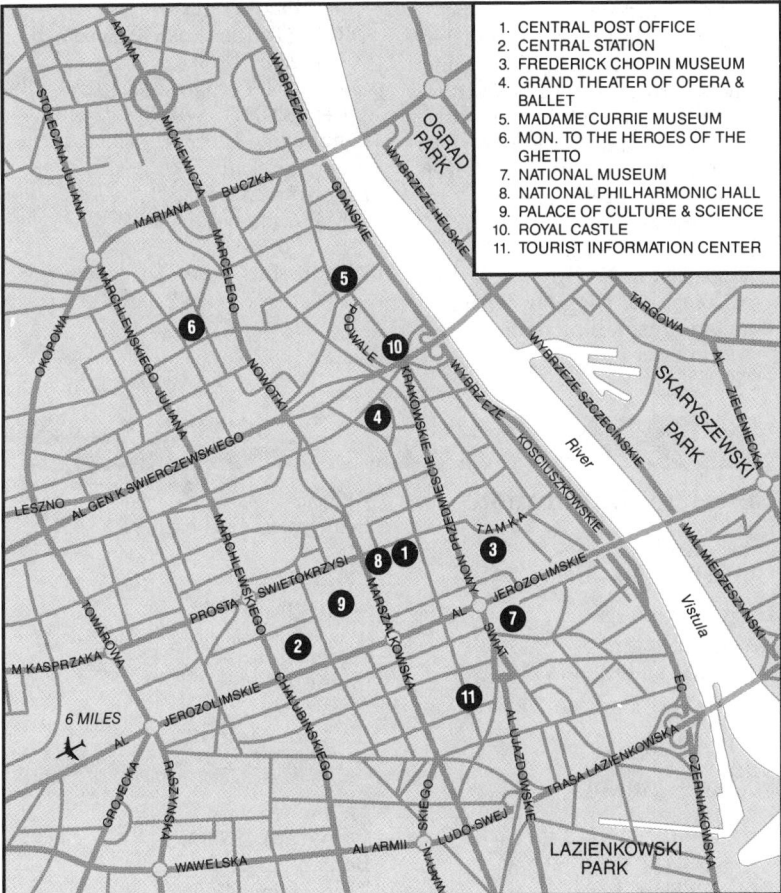

1. CENTRAL POST OFFICE
2. CENTRAL STATION
3. FREDERICK CHOPIN MUSEUM
4. GRAND THEATER OF OPERA & BALLET
5. MADAME CURRIE MUSEUM
6. MON. TO THE HEROES OF THE GHETTO
7. NATIONAL MUSEUM
8. NATIONAL PHILHARMONIC HALL
9. PALACE OF CULTURE & SCIENCE
10. ROYAL CASTLE
11. TOURIST INFORMATION CENTER

EUROPE

Warsaw

Victoria Inter-Continental,
Krolewska 11 (tel: 278011)

What to See and Do
Much of Warsaw today has been
restored to its former beauty
after its destruction during the
Second World War. Its charming
Old Town section is now closed
to vehicles, and its old
marketplace beautifully
revitalized. Here churches,
palaces, and prominent
residences have been
magnificently restored, and
open-air art exhibits are held
every summer.
The leisure centerpiece of
Warsaw is Lazienki Park, where
former kings built their summer
palaces, and near there is the
Chopin monument beside which
concerts are held in the summer.
The 37-storey Palace of Culture
and Science, a gift to Poland
from Josef Stalin, offers the best
vantage point of the city. Seven
miles north of Warsaw is
Mlociny with its
Ethonographic Museum.
Southeast of Warsaw, visit the
old palace of King Jan Sobieski,
now a museum of art treasures
and antiques.

Useful Addresses

Embassies and Consulates
American: Aleje Ujazdowskie 29/
31 (tel: 283041)
British: Al. Rozi (tel: 281001)
Canadian: Matejki 1/5
(tel: 298051)

Business and Commerce
Polish Chamber of Foreign
Trade, Trebacka 4 (tel: 260221)
Ministry of Foreign Trade,
Wiejska 10
Chamber of Commerce, Ul.
Trebacka 4 (tel: 260221)
U.S.A. Trade Center, Ulica
Wieljska 20 (tel: 214515)
National Bank, Ul. Swietokrzy
11/21 (tel: 200321)

Tourism and Travel
ORBIS (Tourist Board), Bracka 16
(tel: 260271)
ORBIS, Marszalkowska 142
(tel: 278031)
Automobile Club of Poland, Ul.
Senatorskall
American Express,
Marszalkowska 142
(tel: 267501)
Wagons-Lits/Cook, Ul. Nowy
Swiat 64 (tel: 263867)

NORWAY

Essential Information

Type of Government
Constitutional Monarchy

Area
324,220 sg km
(125,050 sq mi)

Population
4.1 million

Annual Growth Rate
0.4%

Languages
Norwegian, Lappish

Religion
Evangelical Lutheran 94%

Ethnic Groups
Germanic, Lapps

Weights and Measures
Metric

Electrical Current
A.C. 50c 220/230 V

Major Business Cities
Oslo (cap) 485,000
Bergen 225,000
Trondheim 140,000

Currency

1 Norwegian Krone (kr) = 100 ore

Notes 10, 50, 100, 500 and 1,000 kroner

Coins 5, 10, 25 and 50 ore. 1 and 5 kroner

Public Holidays

Jan 1 New Year
Apr 13-20 Easter Week
May 1 Labour Day
May 17 Constitution Day
May 28 Ascension
Dec 25, 26 Christmas

Travellers Information

Entry Requirements

Passport is required by all visitors. No visa required by North American or European visitors.

Working Restrictions

A work permit is required of all visitors seeking employment in Norway.

Vaccination Required

None

Customs and Duty Free

On arrival: 200 cigarettes or 250 gr. of cigars or tobacco; 200 leaves of cigarette paper; spirits .75 L, wine 1 L, beer 2 L; perfume and eau de cologne for personal use, and gifts to a value of kr 700. Importing alcoholic beverages over 120 proof is prohibited.

Currency Restrictions

Foreign currency may be imported but must be declared. Foreign currency may be exported, but the amount must not be greater than that brought in. A maximum of kr 2,000 in cash may be exported.

Health Tips

Drinking water is purified and safe to drink. English is spoken widely in medical facilities and services are good, if expensive.

Bring your own pharmaceuticals and toiletries.

Climate and Clothing

Coastal areas can be mild most of the time, while inland, weather shows more extremes. Winter months are cold with rain or snow, with heavy rainfall in the west. Coastal temperatures in winter average 4-10 C (40-50 F), inland -18 - 1 C (0-35 F). Summer months on the coast average 13-15 C (55-60 F), inland 18-21 C (65-70 F). Generally wear lighter clothing on the coast, whatever the season, but take a raincoat. Inland, wear heavy sweaters in summer, heavy coat and boots in winter.

Tipping

Tip taxis 5-10%, porters kr 6 per piece of luggage. A tip of15% is included in hotel, restaurant and nightspot bills. Tip 3 kr for small services.

Food and Drink

Meat, fish, potatoes, vegetables and soup are common Norwegian fare, with dinner being the main meal. Breakfasts, lunches and evening snacks are light. Fish is particularly abundant, since Norway is one of the world's great fishing nations.

Specialties include open-faced sandwiches (smorbrod), pickled herring, smoked fish and lamb. Norweigen beer is very good, and the favorite national spirit is Aquavit.

Business Brief

GDP

$70.7 billion
(per capita income $16,830)

Annual Growth Rate

0.6%

Natural Resources

Fish, timber, electrical power,

EUROPE

ores (including iron and molybdenite), and oil and gas

Agriculture
Dairy products, livestock, grain, potatoes, vegetables, fruits, berries, furs, wool

Industry
Oil and gas, fish and food products, pulp and paper, fertilizers, petrochemicals, electronics, printing and publishing, transport equipment

Imports
Total $22.7 billion
Fuel, petroleum, chemicals, transport equipment, foodstuffs, grains, fruits, vegetables, textiles, ores, mineral oil, iron and steel

Exports
Total $21.7 billion
Crude oil, natural gas, pulp and paper, metals, chemicals, fish products, ships, iron and steel, machinery, fertilizers

Major Trading Partners
Great Britain, Sweden, West Germany, U.S., Denmark, Japan, France, Netherlands

Workforce
2 million
Industry 20%, building & construction 8%, natural resources 8%, commodity trade 15%, government 7%, banking & insurance 5%, education and research 7%, health & social services 12%

Tips for Doing Business
Conservative business dress and punctuality are key business traits. Norwegians tend to be a bit formal in their business approach, so avoid unnecessary pleasantries. Hospitality is great tradition, so you will likely be entertained at home. If so, be on time and send flowers or a thank-you note to your hostess the next day.

Best Months for Doing Business
February through May, October and November. Avoid the two weeks before and three after Christmas, as well as Easter week. Business people vacation in July and August.

Business Hours

Government
Mon-Fri 0800-1545

Business
Mon-Fri 0800-1600
Sat 0900-1300

Banks (in Oslo)
Mon-Wed, Fri 0845-1545
Thu 0815-1800

Shops
Mon-Fri 0830-1800
Sat 0830-1400

English Language Publications
International Herald Tribune and some British newspapers are available in kiosks and hotels in Oslo and Bergen.

Telephone and Communications
Telephone country code: 47
Telephone city codes: Oslo 02, Bergen 05, Trondheim 07
Telex country code: 856
Public telephones can be found in cafes, shops, stations and booths. Local calls cost about kr 1. There is limited direct dialing to European cities, but no cheap off-peak-hours rate.
Telex information can be obtained by phoning 488990 in Oslo.
Telegrams can be dictated over the phone and sent from post offices.

Air Travel
Braathens and SAS operate extensive domestic services between major towns and cities. Air taxi services in more northerly regions are also good, using small planes, seaplanes, and helicopters. Major airports

are at Oslo, Stovanger, and Bergen.

Other Transport

Roads are generally narrower and rougher than in other European countries, and Norway has few highways.
Main railway lines branch out from Oslo, but make your train reservations well in advance at travel agencies.
Extensive coastal waterway services, including hydrofoils and ferries.

OSLO

Airport Information

Times
GMT +1
GMT +2 (Mar 28 - Sept 25)

Airport
Oslo International (Fornebu) OSL
Tel: (02) 593340
10 km (6 mi) SW of the city
International and domestic flights

Airlines
Aeroflot 413362
Air France 421045
Alitalia 425905
Austrian 413770
Avianca 420802
British Airways 418750
Finnair 425856
Gulf Air 410300
Iberia 413543
JAL 426100
KLM 426530
Korean 412441
Lufthansa 200836
Northwest 417710
Pan Am 415600
Sabena 334100
SAS 427550
Swissair 412118
TWA 110202
Varig 428630

Transport to City
Taxis: "Barum" taxis are available into Oslo for kr 80. The ride will take about 25 minutes. Tip 10%.
Coach: SAS runs coaches from the Arrivals hall to Central Railway Station every 15 minutes during normal hours. Also stops at Hotel Scandinavia and Haakon 7 St. Baggage facilities on board. Pay the driver.
Transit: Bus *31 leaves from the Arrivals hall every 30 minutes. Pay the driver about kr 20. No baggage room. The bus stops often during its 25-minute ride to the center of town.
Some flights may now be transferred to the new Gordermoen airport, but coaches and taxis connect the two airports.

Facilities
Snack bar, currency exchange, post office, baggage deposit, information desk, meeting point, bank, insurance, barber shop, nursery, restaurants, bars.
Duty-free shop sells tobacco products, wines, spirits, liqueurs, lighters.
Car rental desks: Hertz, Avis, Budget, InterRent, Scandinavia, Kjoles, Kemwel

Airport Taxes
None

City Information

Weather
Summers are generally cool in Oslo, winters quite cold. Summer temperatures range from 4-17 C (39-63 F), in winter, -4 to -5 C (25-41 F) is usual. Bring light or medium weight clothes in summer, plus sweaters and a raincoat. Heavy waterproof clothing and boots are needed in winter, which can also be very icy, especially on the roads.

EUROPE

Transportation

Taxis are widely available at stands or by dialing 348. Oslo rates are about kr 12.50 plus kr 4 per km. Add a tip of 10-15%. Rental cars are available at the airport and in towns and cities. Check with your hotel. A car will cost you about kr 2650, and public transportation is almost as good and is much cheaper. Oslo has a subway system radiating from the National Theater station and the Sentrum station.

Car Hire

Hertz, G. Brichsgate 16
  (tel: 545410 & 533647)
Avis, Munkedamsveien 27
  (tel: 410060 & 530557)
Budget, Forenebu airport
  (tel: 537924)
Europcar, Friedensborgvn 33
  (tel: 426920& 530535)
Godfrey-Davis (tel: 676818)
InterRent, Drammensveien 145
  (tel: 236685)
Kemwel, Drammensveien 126
  (tel: 530936)

Trade Fairs

International Furniture
  Exhibition (Jan)
Caravan Exhibition (Jan)
Lighting Fair (Feb)
International Fashion Exhibition
  (Feb)
International Boat Exhibition
  (Mar)
Microcomputer Exhibition (April)
Forestry Exhibition (June)

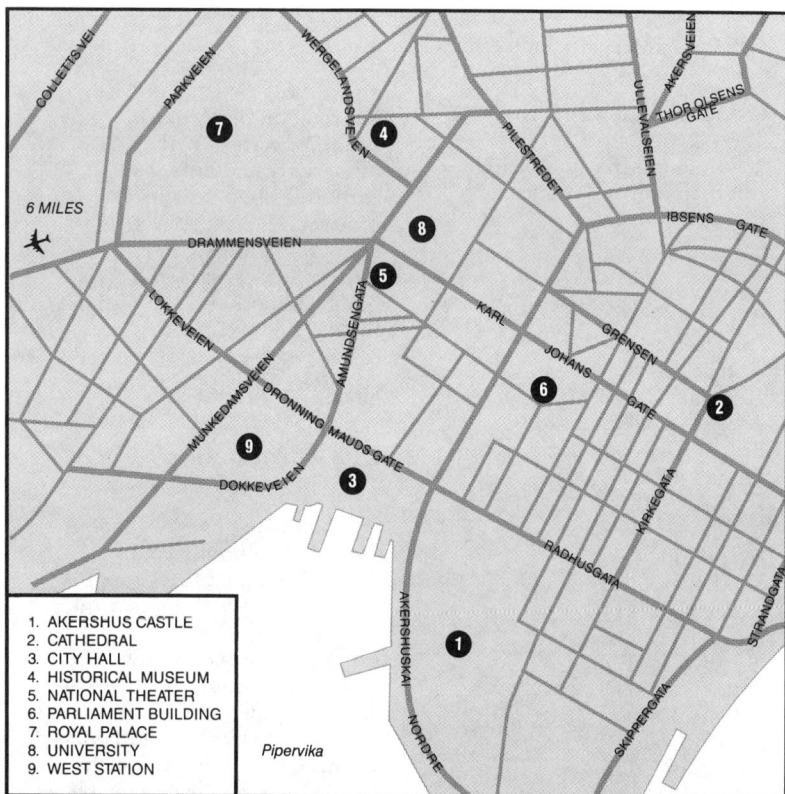

1. AKERSHUS CASTLE
2. CATHEDRAL
3. CITY HALL
4. HISTORICAL MUSEUM
5. NATIONAL THEATER
6. PARLIAMENT BUILDING
7. ROYAL PALACE
8. UNIVERSITY
9. WEST STATION

Pipervika

Oslo

International Fisheries Fair (Aug)
Gift & Decoration Exhibition
(Aug)
Chemical & Hydraulics
Equipment Exhibition (Sept)
International Furniture
Exhibition (Oct)
Hardware & Kitchen Exhibition
(Oct)
Home & Hobbies Exhibiton
(Nov)

Hotels
Ambassadeur, Camilla Colletsvei
15 (tel: 441835)
Astoria, Akersgate 21 (426900)
Bristol, Kristian IV Gate 7
(tel: 415840)
Carlton, Parkveien 78
(tel: 696170)
Continental, Stortingsgate 24
(tel: 419060)
Grand, Karl Johansgate 31
(tel: 429390)
Holmenkollen, Kongevien 26
(tel: 146090)
Kna-Hotellet, Parkvn. 68
(tel: 446970)
Nobel, Karl Johansgate 33
(tel: 427480)
SAS Park Royal, Lysake 1324
(tel: 120220)
Scandinavia, Holbergsgate 30
(tel: 113000)
Stefan, Rosenkrantzgate 1
(tel: 429250)

What to See and Do
Visit the shops and boutiques
along Oslo's main thoroughfare,
Karl Johansgate, and end up at
the Royal Palace. Below the
palace, on the harbor side, is the
National Theater, center of
Oslo's cultural life. The City Hall
is replete with murals of many of
Norway's best know painters,
and Akershus Fortress, occupied
by the Nazis, contains a
fascinating Resistance Museum
dedicated to the Norwegian
patriots executed by them. For
the best view of Oslo, take the
streetcar to Sjomannsskolen,
from the terrace of which you
can see most of the harbor,
fjords and the old and new
town.
The best excursion is to Bygdoy.
Take the boat from the Pipervika
or wharfs behind City Hall to see
Roald Amundsen's polar ship
the Fram. The nearby museum
houses Thor Heyerdahl's Kon
Tiki balsa raft, and the Maritime
Museum features three fine
Viking vessels.
Some other noteworthy places to
visit are the Nobel Institute, Oslo
Cathedral, Frogner Park, and the
National Art Gallery.

Useful Addresses

Embassies and Consulates
American: Drammensveien 18
(tel: 448550)
British: T. Heftyesgate 8 (tel:
563890)
Canadian: Oscar's Gate 20 (tel:
466955)

Business and Commerce
Central Bank, Bankplassen 2
(tel: 316000)
Company Information
(tel: 468900)
Oslo Stock Exchange,
Tollbugaten 2 (tel: 423880)
Export Council of Norway,
Drammensveien 40
(tel: 114030)
Oslo Chamber of Commerce,
Drammensveien 30
(tel: 557400)

Tourism and Travel
Norwegian Tourist Board, H.
Heyerdahlsgate 1 (tel: 427044)
Norwegian Automobile Club,
Stopgt. 2 (tel: 429400)
American Express, Karl
Johansgate 33 (tel: 429150)
Thomas Cook, Soreng Kaia (tel:
297000)

EUROPE

PORTUGAL

Essential Information

Type of Government
Republic

Area
94,276 sq km
(36,390 sq mi)

Population
10.6 million

Annual Growth Rate
0.7%

Languages
Portuguese

Religion
Roman Catholic 97%

Ethnic Groups
Portuguese

Weights and Measures
Metric

Electrical Current
A.C. 50c 220/380 V, 110/190 V

Major Business Cities
Lisbon (cap) 1,900,000
Oporto 850,000
Coimbra 410,00

Currency
1 Escudo = 100 centavos
Notes 20, 50, 100, 500, 1,000 and
    5,000 escudos
Coins 1, 2 1/2, 5, 25 and 50
    centavos

Public Holidays
Jan 1 New Year
Apr 13-20 Easter Week
April 25 Portugal Day
May 1 Labour Day
Jun 10 Camoes
Jun 21 Corpus Christi
Aug 15 Assumption
Oct 5 Republic Day
Nov 1 All Saints' Day
Dec 1 Independence
Dec 8 Immaculate Conception
Dec 25 Christmas

Travellers Information

Entry Requirements
Passports required of most visitors. No visa needed by Canadians for up to 3 months' stay. No visa required of British nationals up to 2 months' stay. No visa required of American visitors, except if travelling to the Azores. Allowances are subject to change so consult your Portuguese embassy or consulate.

Working Restrictions
Work permits are required of all non-Portuguese.

Vaccination Required
Typhoid vaccinations are recommended to all visitors by the government.

Customs and Duty Free
On arrival: 200 cigarettes, 100 cigarillos, 50 cigars or 250 gr. of tobacco; spirits 1 L; wine, 2 L; perfume 50 gr. and eau de cologne .25 L. Also gifts to a value of 3,000 escudos, except for jewellery, which must be declared.

Currency Restrictions
Up to 5,000 escudos in Portuguese currency may be brought in, and there is no limit on the import of foreign currency. The latter, however, should be declared on arrival.

Health Tips
Tap water is generally drinkable in built-up areas, but bottled water is recommended to be safe. Sanitation and health standards are high.

Climate and Clothing
Winters in Portugal (Nov-April) tend to be cool, with rain in the north, milder in the south. Lisbon is wet and windy from

Jan-Mar. Medium weight clothes and a raincoat would be advisable. In summer (May-Oct) climate is warm and dry with temps reaching 27 C (80 F). Lightweight clothes, with possibly a jacket at night is recommended.

Tipping
Tip taxis 15%, porters 40-50 escudos per piece of baggage. A 10-15% tip is automatically included in the bills of hotels, restaurants and nightspots. Tip chambermaids 40-50 escudos per day, barbers and beauticians 15%, small services 40 escudos.

Food and Drink
Fish, vegetables and fruits are staples in the Portuguese diet. Bacalhau, or dried codfish, is a specialty and wine is plentiful and cheap. Sweets and pastries are also very popular. Light breakfast and lunch is normal, with the largest meal being dinner in the late evening. Dinner consists of soup, main course (usually fish) and vegetable. The wines of Portugal can be very good, and the fortified wines of Oporto and Madiera are very popular, and are exported throughout the world.

Business Brief

GDP
$24.1 billion

Annual Growth Rate
0.7%

Natural Resources
Fish, cork, tungsten, iron and uranium ores, copper, pyrites

Agriculture
Grapes, maize, olives, potatoes, rice, rye, sugar, beets, tomatoes, wheat, almonds

Industry
Textiles, footwear, wood and pulp products, cork, metalworking, ore processing, chemicals, canning, wine, cement, fertilizers, glassware, ship-building

Imports
Total $13.4 billion
Machinery, appliances, fuel, petroleum, chemicals, coal, iron, steel, transport equipment

Exports
Total $9.1 billion
Clothing fabric, pulp, cork manufactures, canned vegetables, wines, fish products, diamonds

Major Trading Partners
West Germany, U.S., Great Britain, France, Italy, Spain, Iraq, Sweden

Workforce
4.1 million
Agriculture 25%, industry & commerce 32%, government and services 44%

Tips for Doing Business
Portuguese are informal socially, but conservative on business occasions. Shaking hands before and after business is a good habit to get into. Be sure to either write or phone in advance to make business appointments, and avoid high-pressure sales tactics. Be prepared to be entertained on business occasions in any one of many local coffee houses, but do not ask or expect women to be present.

Best Months for Doing Business
October through June. Avoid the two weeks before and after Christmas as well as the two weeks bracketing Easter. Business people take their vacations July through September.

Business Hours

EUROPE

Government
Mon-Fri 0930-1230, 1430-1730

Business
Mon-Fri 1000-1200, 1400-1800

Banks
Mon-Fri 0900-1200, 1400-1530

Shops
Mon-Fri 0900-1300, 1500-1900
Sat half day

English Language Publications
The International Herald
Tribune, USA Today and some
British dailies may be purchased
in shops and hotels in Lisbon.

Telephone and Communications
Telephone country code: 351
Telephone city code: Lisbon 01
Telex country code: 832
Telephone system offers direct-
dialing services to the rest of the
country and to many European
countries. International pay
phones take 5 ot 25 escudo
pieces, and there is a night-
service operator available for
calls at the Post Office, Praca do
Restauradores in Lisbon.

Air Travel
Air Portugal (TAP) operates daily
domestic service between Lisbon
Oporto and Faro. Also, flights to
Madeira and the Azores by air
taxi can be arranged.

Other Transport
Regular coach services link major
towns.
There are good express trains
operated by the nationalized rail
company, to Oporto, Lisbon and
Faro. Book seats in advance for
these express trains, but avoid
shorter train trips.
Car rentals are available and
travel is good if you stick to the
main highways. Secondary roads
are subject to poor conditions
and frequent roadblocks in the
form of livestock.

LISBON

Airport Information

Time
GMT
GMT +1 (Mar 28 - Sept 25)

Airport
Lisboa International LIS
(Portela de Sacavem)
Tel: 881101
7 km (4.5 mi) N of the city

Airlines
Aeroflot 561243
Air France 562171
Alitalia 536141
Avensa 561742
British Airways 360931
Canadian International 539511
Eastern 537610
El Al 576593
Finnair 531076
Gulf Air 899121
Iberia 539571
Iraqi 540231
KLM 579110
Korean 556644
Lufthansa 573852
Pan Am 537610
Qantas 575020
SAA 536102
Sabena 579110
SAS 557116
Swissair 371111
TAP 575020
TWA 527141
Varig 539181

Transport to City
Taxis: The black taxis with the
green tops will take you to the
Ritz Hotel for 400 escudos. Extra
bags incur an additional charge.
Tip is about 10% extra.
Coach: They run between the
airport and Praca D Pedroiv-
Rossio and stop at the
Intercontinental, Mundial, Penta
and Avenida Palace hotels.
Transit: A Green Line bus
outside the Arrivals hall can take
you to the Santa Apolonia

Railroad Station with 8 stops enroute. Pay the driver about 200 escudos. One stop, Marques de Pombal Plaza, is near several major hotels. Bus also connects with the subway at Entrecampos.

Facilities

Currency exchange, hotel reservations, baggage deposit, information desk, meeting point, bar, restaurant, insurance, post office.
Duty-free shop sells tobacco products, wines, spirits, liqueurs, lighters, perfume, scarves, jewellery.
Car rental desks: Hertz, Avis, Budget, Europcar, InterRent, Contauto, Guerin, Travelcar.

Airport Taxes

None

City Information

Weather

Lisbon usually has dry summers and damp, mild winters. Summers can occasionally get very hot but winters reply by getting very wet. Mean summer temps 28 C (82 F), mean winter temps 14 C (57 F).

Transportation

Taxis, green and black, are cheap, costing about 60 escudos plus 20 escudos per km. Taxis can be hard to come by at rush hour, however.
Bus, streetcars, and a subway

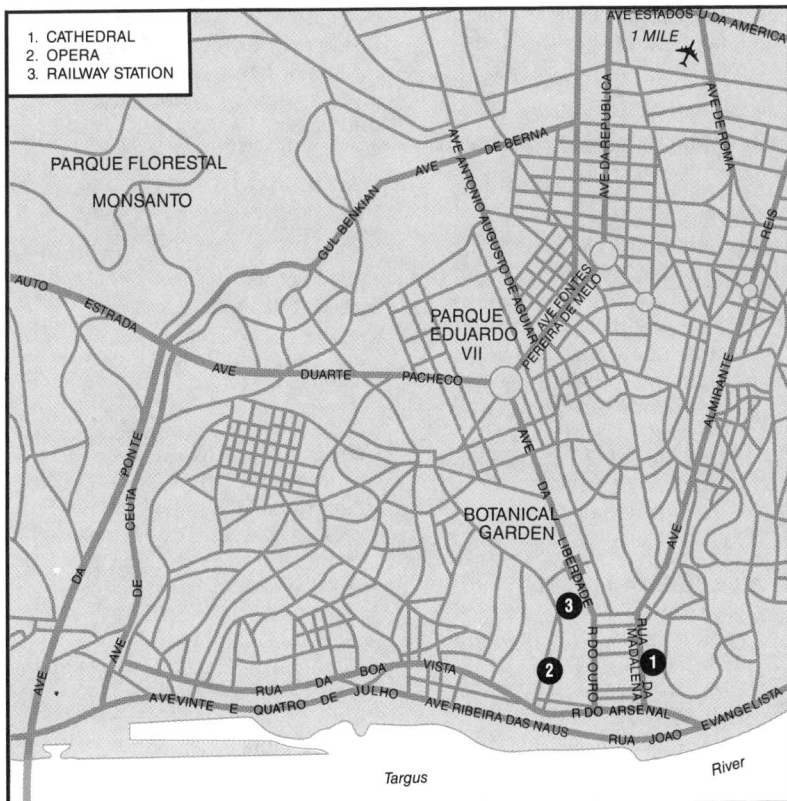

1. CATHEDRAL
2. OPERA
3. RAILWAY STATION

EUROPE

Lisbon

system are reasonably efficient in Lisbon, but allow time to get to your destination, especially if you have an appointment.

Car Hire
Hertz, Ave. 5 de Octubre 10 (tel: 892722 & 539817)
Ansa, Rua L. Cordeiro 4-A (tel: 689174)
Avis, Ave. P. de Victoria 12 (tel: 894836)
Budget, Ave. Fontes Pereira 6 (tel: 801785)
Europcar, Ave. A. de Aguiar 24 (tel: 801176)
InterRent, Ave. A. Cabral 45-B (tel: 573624)
Kemwel, Ave. Antonio Augusto 24 (tel: 886191)

Hospitals
For the British Hospital, tel: 602020; the CUF Hospital, tel: 609111; and for the Red Cross Hospital, tel: 783003.

Trade Fairs
International Office Equipment Exhibition (Jan)
International Sports & Leisure Exhibition (Mar)
International Pharmaceuticals Exhibition (April)
International Fish Industries Fair (May)
European Graphics Show (Aug)
International Furniture & Light Exhibition (Oct)
International Electrical Appliances Exhibition (Oct)
International Cattle & Agriculture Fair (Nov)

Hotels
Altis, Rua Castilho 11 (tel: 522496)
Avenida Palace, Rua Dezembro 123 (tel: 360151)
Diplomatico, Castilho 74 (tel: 562041)
Embaixador, Duque de Loule 73 (tel: 530171)
Fenix, Marques de Pombal 8 (tel: 535121)
Florida, Duque Palmela 32 (tel: 576145)
Lisboa Penta, Ave. does Combatentes 4 (tel: 740141)
Mundial, R.D. Duarte 4 (tel: 863101)
Novotel, Ave. Elias Garcia 49-60 (tel: 735751)
Rex, Castilho 169 (tel: 682161)
Tivoli, Ave.. da Liberdade 185 (530181)

What to See and Do
Visit the old Moorish section, the Alfama, St. George Castle, or the Presidential Palace. Also, the Manueline Monastery, Coach Museum and gardens at Belem are worth the trip. For sportsmen, there is golf at Estoril and fishing at Cascias, or in summer you can take in a bullfight at the Campo Pequeno bullring. There are good fish restaurants at the Cacilhas, and for singing and drinking visit any Portuguesa Fado house after dinner.

Useful Addresses

Embassies and Consulates
American: Ave. das F. Armadas (tel: 266600)
British: Domingos Lapa 35 (tel: 661191)
Canadian: Rue Rosa Araujo (tel: 563821)

Business and Commerce
Central Bank, Rua do Commercio (tel: 362931)
International Chamber of Commerce, Rua das Portas de Santo Antao 89 (tel: 363304)
Stock Exchange, Praca do Comercia (tel: 365417)
American Chamber of Commerce, Ruada D. Estefania 155 (tel: 572561)
British Chamber of Commerce, Rua Estrela 8 (tel: 661586)
Dept. of Foreign Trade: Rua Nova S. Mamede 76
Lisbon Chamber of Commerce,

Rua does Portas de Santo
Antao 89 (tel: 327179)

Tourism and Travel
Tourist Board, Antonio Augusto
de Aguiar 86 (tel: 575162)
Tourist Information, P.
Restauradores (tel: 325231)

Automobile Club of Portugal,
Rua Rosa Araujo 24/26
(tel: 563931 & 775475)
American Express, Avenida
Sidonio Pais 4-A (tel: 599871 &
539871)

SPAIN

Essential Information

Type of Government
Constitutional Monarchy

Area
507,606 sq km
(195,988 sq mi)

Population
40.2 million

Annual Growth Rate
0.5%

Languages
Spanish (official), Catalan,
Galician, Basque

Religion
Roman Catholic 98%

Ethnic Group
Mediterranean and Germanic
composite

Weights and Measures
Metric

Electrical Current
A.C. 50c 110/130 V, 220/380 V

Major Business Cities
Madrid (cap) 3,700,000
Barcelona 2,250,000
Valencia 790,000
Seville 750,000

Currency
1 peseta = 100 centimos
Notes 100, 200, 500, 1,000, 2,000
and 5,000 pesetas
Coins 1, 5, 25, 50 and 100
pesetas

Public Holidays
Jan 1 New Year

Jan 6 Epiphany
Mar 1 St. Joseph
Apr 13-20 Easter Week
May 1 Labour Day
Jun 21 Corpus Christi
Jun 24 King's Saints' Day
Jul 25 St. James
Aug 15 Assumption
Oct 12 Day of the race
Nov 1 All Saints' Day
Dec 8 Immaculate Conception
Dec 25, 26 Christmas

Travellers Information

Entry Requirements
Most visitors need passports, but
British and North American
travellers do not need a visa for
stays up to 90 days.

Working Restrictions
A work permit is needed for all
visitors. Nationals of EEC
countries may soon be exempt, if
they are not already.

Vaccination Required
No specific vaccination is
required, but a typhoid
immunization is recommended.

Customs and Duty Free
On arrival: 200 cigarettes or 50
cigars or 250 gr. of tobacco;
spirtis 1 L; wine 2 L; perfume 50
gr.; also eau de cologne up to .25
L and gifts to a value of 1,700
ptas.

Currency Restrictions
You may not import more than
100,000 pesetas in local currency

EUROPE

or export more than 20,000. You may export, however, up to a value of 50,000 pesetas in foreign currency, 100,000 if you are a business person.

Healthy Tips

Sanitary conditions are generally good, but the drinking water may not be purified outside the larger cities. Bottled mineral water is a safer bet. Fees for health care are in medium price range, but health insurance coverage is advised.

Climate and Clothing

Summers in Spain are very hot and dry in the north, and hot with frequent thunderstorms in the south. Mediterranean climate predominates in the south, and lightweight clothes are recommended. Winters (Nov-April) are cool, with rain in the north and central areas, colder with snow in the mountains. Winters are generally warmer and drier in the south but bring medium weight clothes and a raincoat.

Tipping

Hotel, restaurant and nightspot bills normally include a service charge, but an additional 10% is welcomed. Tip hotel staff 500 ptas each per week of stay, and tip taxi drivers 10-15%, porters 50 ptas per piece of luggage, barbers and beauticians 15%, and 75 ptas for small services.

Food and Drink

Typical Spanish fare includes fresh vegetables, meat, eggs, chicken and fish. Breakfasts are light, lunches heavier and a large meal is eaten about 2100. In between meals, Spaniards like to snack. Some of their favorite food includes "churros," a breakfast snack, "bocadillo," or special sandwich, and "tortilla espanola," an omelette with potatoes and onions, or evening snacks called "Tapas". Spanish wines are excellent, especially the red wines from the Rioja region, and the excellent fortified wine Sherry which is exported all over the world.

Business Brief

GDP

$224.9 billion
(per capita income $4,180)

Annual Growth Rate

2.5%

Natural Resources

Coal, lignite, iron ore, uranium, mercury, pyrites, fluorspar, gypsum, zinc, lead, tungsten, copper, kaolen, hydroelectric power

Agriculture

Cereals, feedgrains, vegetables, citrus fruits, wine, olives, olive oil, livestock, grapes, potatoes

Industry

Processed foods, textiles, footwear, petrochemicals, steel, automobiles, consumer goods, ships, furniture

Imports

Total $49.1 billion
Oilseeds, grains, oil, machinery, transportation equipment, fuel, petroleum, lubricants, iron and steel, electrical equipment, tobacco

Exports

Total $34.2 billion
Fresh and canned fruits, automobiles, iron and steel products, footwear, textiles, ships, transport equipment

Major Trading Partners

U.S., West Germany, France, Great Britain, Saudi Arabia, Italy, Netherlands,
U.S., West Germany, France, Great Britain, Saudi Arabia, Italy, Netherlands, Japan

Workforce
13.2 million
Services 49%, industry and
commerce 34%, agriculture 17%

Tips for Doing Business
Book all appointments ahead of
time and wear conservative
business dress with white shirts,
black shoes if possible. Spanish
businesspeople tend to be polite,
formal and conservative, and
shaking hands on meeting and
on departing is the custom. A
few phrases of Spanish, as well
as business cards in Spanish and
English, will aid your
introduction to strangers. Many
businesspeople begin their day
at 1100 and leave for a long
lunch at 1430. However they
return by 1700 and often work
until 2100 (the old custom of
stopping work for a siesta has
been superseded by the long
leisurely business lunch).
Spaniards are addressed "Senor"
or "Senorita," together with the
first of their two surnames, and
"Don" or "Dona" are added
terms of respect for husband and
wife.

Best Months for Doing Business
October through June. Avoid the
weeks before and after
Christmas and Easter.
Businesspeople take their
vacation in July and August.

Business Hours

Government
Mon-Sat 0900-1300 & 1600-1900

Business
Mon-Fri 0900-1845 (winter)
Mon-Fri 0900-1400 & 1630-1900
(summer)

Banks
Mon-Sat 0900-1330

Shops
Variable hours depending
entirely on city and region

English Language Publications
The Iberian Sun is the English
language publication. The
International Herald Tribune,
USA Today, and some British
dailies are available in larger
cities. Also some radio
broadcasts are made in English.

Telephone and Communications
Telephone country code: 34
Telephone city codes: Barcelona
93, Madrid 91
Telex country code: 831
Public telephones will take 25 or
50 ptas in coins and are fully
automatic, with charge based on
time used. Call boxes carry
instructions in English.
Telegrams can be sent from post
offices, which also have telex
facilities.

Air Travel
Iberia and Aviaca provide
frequent domestic service on
flights radiating outwards from
Madrid. Book flights well in
advance during the holiday
periods. Most major cities have
international airport and internal
flights.

Other Transport
Spanish roads are generally
paved and well maintained,
especially coastal roads. There is
also a regular bus and coach
service between built-up areas.
Two railroad companies offer
train service throughout the
country. Book in advance either
with Red. Nacional de los
Ferrocarriles Espanoles (RENFE)
or Ferrocarriles Espanoles de Via
Estrecha (FEVE).

EUROPE

BARCELONA

Airport Information

Time
GMT +1

GMT +2 (Mar 28 - Sept 25)

Airport

Barcelona International
(Muntadas) BCN
Tel: (93) 3170008 & 3170012
15 km (9 mi) SW of the city
International and domestic
flights

Airlines

Air Algerie 2160008
Air France 2152870
Alitalia 2380424
Austrian 2152173
British Airways 2152112
Finnair 3186372
Iberia 3027656
KLM 2092288
Lufthansa 2150300
PanAm 3017249
Qantas 3180031
Sabena 2154732
SAS 2153900

Swissair 2159100
TAP 3182333
TWA 2158486
Varig 3016070

Transport to the City

Taxis: The 15 to 20-minute taxi
ride to the city costs about 1,300
ptas and includes baggage. Tip
10%.
Coach: An express train operated
by RENFE, will whisk you
comfortably to Sants Station, if
you can find the train station at
the airport. Buy a ticket before
boarding. Train departs every 20
minutes.
Transit: A local bus marked
"EH" stops at both ends of the
Arrivals hall. The 28-minute ride
to Plaza Espana costs 70 ptas,
and the bus departs every 40

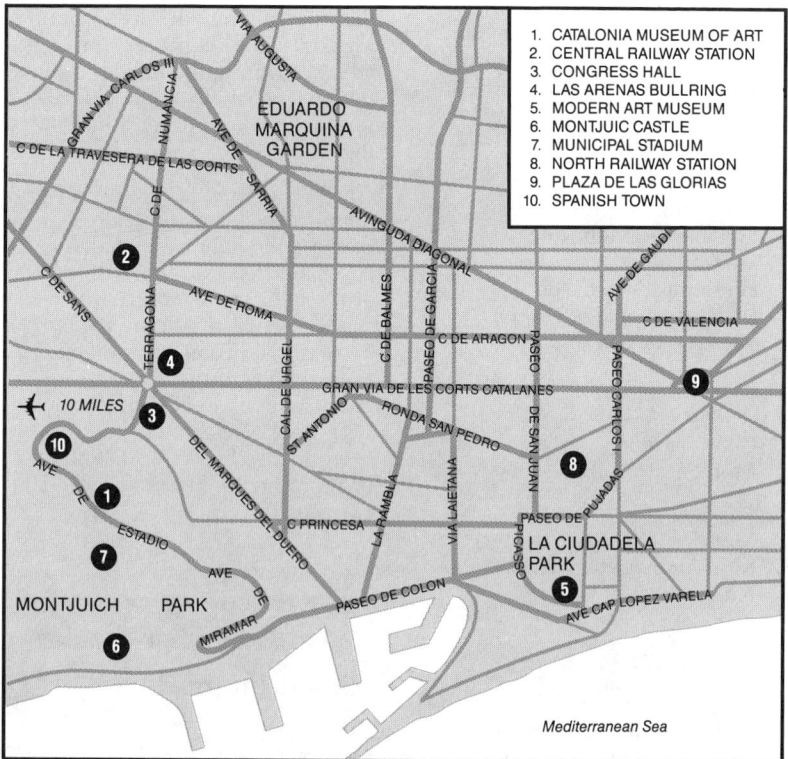

1. CATALONIA MUSEUM OF ART
2. CENTRAL RAILWAY STATION
3. CONGRESS HALL
4. LAS ARENAS BULLRING
5. MODERN ART MUSEUM
6. MONTJUIC CASTLE
7. MUNICIPAL STADIUM
8. NORTH RAILWAY STATION
9. PLAZA DE LAS GLORIAS
10. SPANISH TOWN

EDUARDO MARQUINA GARDEN

VIA AUGUSTA
GRAN VIA DE CARLOS III
C DE LA TRAVESERA DE LAS CORTS
NUMANCIA
AVE DE SARRIA
AVINGUDA DIAGONAL
C DE SANS
TERRAGONA
AVE DE ROMA
C DE BALMES
PASEO DE GARCIA
AVE DE GAUDI
C DE VALENCIA
C DE ARAGON
CAL DE URGEL
GRAN VIA DE LES CORTS CATALANES
PASEO CARLOS I
10 MILES
ST ANTONIO
RONDA SAN PEDRO
DE SAN JUAN
DEL MARQUES DEL DUERO
LA RAMBLA
VIA LAIETANA
PASEO DE
C PRINCESA
PASEO DE PUJADAS
PICASSO
LA CIUDADELA PARK
ESTADIO
AVE
PASEO DE COLON
AVE CAP LOPEZ VARELA
MONTJUICH   PARK
MIRAMAR

Mediterranean Sea

Barcelona

minutes. It connects with the subway system.

Facilities
Bar, buffet, restaurant, bank, currency exchange, hotel reservations, post office, baggage deposit, barber shop, vaccination center, flowers, candy, books. Duty-free shop sells tobacco products, alcohol, perfumes, cosmetics and liqueurs. Car rental desks: Hertz, Avis, Europcar, Atesa, Budget, InterRent.

Airport Taxes
None

City Information

Weather
Mediterranean climate and is mild in winter 10-20C (50-70F) with some rain, and hot and dry in the summer (20-35C (70-95F). Light clothing should be worn the year around.

Transportation
An average taxi ride in Barcelona should not cost much more than 400 ptas.
The subway system is cheap and extensive, with a small flat fare in operation.
A kiosk in Plaza Cataluna opposite Calle Vergara can sell you maps of the bus and subway routes, as well as a ticket which can be used on both systems.

Car Hire
Hertz, Tuset 10 (tel: 2178076 & 2411381)
Ansa (tel: 2452402)
Atesa (tel: 3022832)
Auto Europa (tel: 2378140)
Avis, Casanova 209 (tel: 3794026)
Budget, Sofia Hotel (tel: 3306358)
Europcar, Consejo Ciento 363 (tel: 3176980)
InterRent, Balmes 141 (tel: 2378140)

Kemwel, Batalla Belchite 15 (tel: 3215141)

Hospitals
Emergency medical treatment can be obtained at the Red Cross, by phoning 2359300. Few doctors or nurses speak English.

Trade Fairs
Leather and Suede Exhibition (Jan)
International Boat and Caravan Exhibition (Feb)
International Food Fair (Mar)
International Clothing Machine Exhibition (April)
International Tourism Exhibition (April)
International Aerospace & Defense Exhibition (April)
International Automotive Components Exhibition (April
International Trade Fair (June)
International Veterinary Exhibition (July)
International Image, Sound, & Electronics Exhibition (Sept)
International Gift Fair (Sept)
International Book Exhibition (Sept)
Sports & Camping Exhibition (Oct)
Jewellery & Clock Fair (Oct)
International Hospital Equipment Exhibition (Oct)

Hotels
Avenida Palace, J. Antonio 605-607 (tel: 3019600)
Colon, Av. Catedral 7 (tel: 3011404)
Cristal, Diputacion 257 (tel: 3016600)
Diplomatic, Pau Claris 122 (3173100)
Gran Sarria, Av. de Sarria 50 (tel: 2391109)
Presidente, Diagonal 570 (tel: 2002111)
Princess Sofia, Plaza Pio XII 28 (tel: 3307111)
Ritz, Catalanes 668 (tel: 3185200)

What to See and Do
Go to the Ramblas, the wide

EUROPE

promenades which replaced the old city walls in 1860. The whole area teems with life until the early morning hours and reminds you of Picadilly Circus in London or Place Pigalle in Paris. It is the center of nightlife in this Catalonian capital. Barcelona is the jumping off point for visits to the world-famous monastery of Montserrat, seat of the Holy Grail (as legend would have it). The monastery is over 1,000 years old, but is still inhabited by nearly 300 Benedictine monks. A funicular will carry you to the Grotto of San Juan Garin and you can get a sweeping vista from the Hermitage of San Jeronimo. The seaside resort of Sitges is nearby to the south, as is Tarragona, with many of the ancient ruins of Roman times still standing. Other noteworthy places of interest in Barcelona are the Palacio de la Generalidad, Montjuich Park, Pueblo Espanol, the Santa Maria (Columbus' ship), Municipal Museum of Archeology and the Picasso Museum.

Useful Addresses

Embassies and Consulates
American: Via Layetana 33 (tel: 3199550)
British: Diagonal 477 (tel: 3222151)

Business and Commerce
American Chamber of Commerce, Diagonal 477 (tel: 3218195)
Barcelona Chamber of Commerce, Ample 11 (tel: 3023366)
Barcelona Stock Exchange, Paseo Isabel II, Apartado 115 (tel: 3196200)
British Chamber of Commerce, Paseo de Garcia II (tel: 3173220)

Central Bank, Alcala 50 (tel: 4469055)

Tourism and Travel
Tourist Board, Velazquez 47 (tel: 2755603)
Real Auto Club of Spain, Santalo 8
American Express, Paseo de Gracia 101 (tel: 2170070)
Wagons-Lits/Cook, Ronda General Mitre 126 (tel: 2123742)

MADRID

Airport Information

Time
GMT +1
GMT +2 (April-Oct)

Airport
Madrid-Barajas International
MAD
Tel: (91) 2221165
12 km (7.5 mi) E of the city
International and domestic flights

Airlines
Aer Lingus 2414216
Aeroflot 2419934
Aerolineas Argentina 2483206
Aeromexico 2475800
Air Algerie 2420801
Air Canada 2618500
Air France 2424900
Alia 2475201
Alitalia 2418900
Austrian 2471607
Avensa 2420300
Avianca 2487303
British Airways 2475300
Eastern 2481305
Egyptair 2213406
El Al 2412005
Finnair 2653400
Iberia 4112011
Iraqi 4457866
JAL 2421108
KLM 2418805
Kuwait Air 2480805
Libyan 2470206

Lufthansa 2757540
MEA 2425305
Olympic 2419941
Pan Am 2414200
Qantas 2474200
SAA 2418306
Sabena 2418903
SAS 4796611
Saudia 2414901
Swissair 2477100
TAP 2412000
THY 4632312
TWA 4106012
United 4193069
Varig 2486204

Transport to City

Taxis: The fare in the black taxis to Plaza Colon is about 1,300 pts, plus 15 ptas for night or holiday service and 50 ptas per bag.

Check the meter before setting off.
Coach: There is a special airport coach outside the Arrivals hall. The bus runs every 30 minutes and the fare (pay the driver) is 150 ptas. There is room for luggage, and the short ride with stops at Avenida America, Francisco Silvela, Maria de Molina, Velasquez, Serrano, Ortega y Gasset and Plaza Colon, takes about half an hour.

Facilities

Snack bar, bank with currency exchange, hotel reservations, post office, information desk, bar, buffet, baggage deposit, barber shop, nursery.
Duty-free shop sells cigarettes,

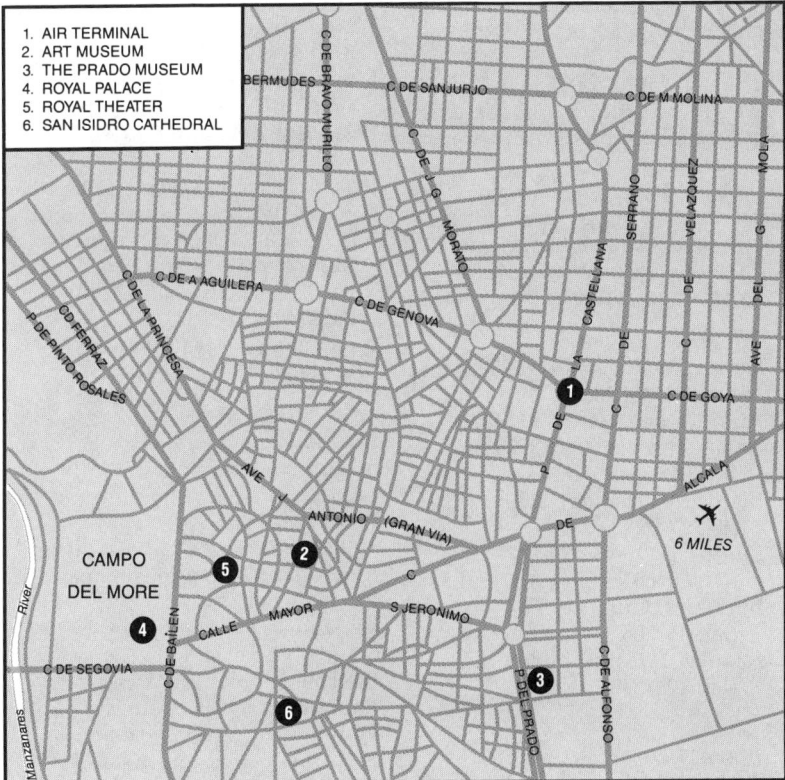

1. AIR TERMINAL
2. ART MUSEUM
3. THE PRADO MUSEUM
4. ROYAL PALACE
5. ROYAL THEATER
6. SAN ISIDRO CATHEDRAL

EUROPE

Madrid

cigars, tobacco, wines, spirits, liqueurs.
Car rental desks: Hertz, Avis, Europcar, Atesa, Budget, InterRent

Airport Taxes
None

City Information

Weather
Madrid is generally mild all year round, and dry, although thunderstorms can occur unexpectedly and often in summer. Average temps: Jan (winter) 5 C (41 F)
July (summer) 24 C (76 F)

Transportation
Taxis are black in Madrid and most are metered. Avoid them if they are not, and if they are, check the meter before heading out.
The subway is a quick and easy way to get around. There are 10 separate lines and it runs from 0600-0100.
By bus, it is cheaper to buy a collective ticket good for 10 rides at a time, called a "bono-bus." Take one of the smaller, less-crowded microbuses if possible.

Car Hire
Hertz, Fleming 44 (tel: 2419585)
Atesa (tel: 4502062)
Auto-Europe (tel: 2479117)
Avis, Gran Via 60 (4579706 & 2472048)
Budget, Estebanez Calderon *5 (tel: 2701213)
Europcar, Orense 29 (tel: 4566546)
InterRent, Gran Via 59 (tel: 4502062
Kemwel, 3 Garcia Morato 175 (tel: 4017510)

Hospitals
For emergency treatment in Madrid, call 2616199, or the

Anglo American Hospital at 2333100.

Trade Fairs
Maintenance Equipment & Services Exhibition (Feb)
International Security & Safety Exhibition (Feb)
International Art Fair (Sept)
International Office Equipment Trade Fair (Nov)

Hotels
Arosa, Salud 21 (tel: 2321600)
Castellana, Castellana 49 (tel: 4100200)
Emperador, Gran Via 53 (2472800)
Eurobuilding, Padre Damian 23 (tel: 2422100)
Luz Palacio, Castellana 57 (tel: 4425100)
Melia-Madrid, Princesa 27 (tel: 2418200)
Miguel Angel, Miguel Angel 29-31 (tel: 4420022)
Monte Real, Arroyo Fresno 17 (tel: 2162140)
Palace, Pl. Las Cortes 7 (tel: 4297551)
Plaza, Plaza de Espana 8 (tel: 2471200)
Suecia, Marques de Casa Riera 4 (tel: 2316900)
Villa Magna, Castellana 22 (tel: 2614900)
Wellington, Velasquez 8 (tel: 2754400)

What to See and Do
Madrid is a modern city of 4 million built up around a 17th century core. Near the Ritz and Plaza hotel stands the Prado, one of the world's greatest art museums. The Prado is home to the works of El Greco, Velazquez, Goya and Murillo, among others, and also houses the Flemish masters Titian, Raphael, Botticelli, Veronese and Tintoretto. Nearby is the Retiro Park, where you can rest and relax after your stunning experience at the Prado. Don't

miss the Goya Pantheon in the Hermitage of San Antonion de la Florida. For a relaxing afternoon try a sherry or two in any of the central city's cosy little cafes, followed by dinner at 1900 and a flamenco show in a club. Try to visit the Royal Palace and Old Madrid, where the Spanish Inquisition had its headquarters.

Useful Addresses

Embassies and Consulates
American: Calle Serrano 75 (tel: 2763400)
British: Fern el Santo 16 (tel: 4190220)
Canadian: Nunez de Balboa 35 (tel: 4314300)

Business and Commerce
Central Bank, Alcala 50 (tel: 4469055)
Chamber of Commerce, Claudio Coello 19 (tel: 2753400)

Stock Exchange, Plaza de la Lealtad 1 (tel: 2214790)
American Chamber of Commerce, Padre Damian 23 (tel: 4586520)
British Chamber of Commerce, Marques de Valdeiglesias 3 (tel: 2219622)
Madrid Chamber of Commerce, Huertas 13 (tel: 4293193)
Madrid Stock Exchange, Plaza de la Lealtad (tel: 2214790)
Ministry of Foreign Trade, Paseo la Castellana 14 (tel: 2257980)

Tourism and Travel
Ministry of Tourism, Ave. Generalisimo 39 (tel: 2796000)
Tourist Board, Velazquez 47 (tel: 2755603)
Automobile Club of Spain, 3 Jose Abascalio (tel: 4473200)
American Express, Plaza de las Cortes 2 (tel: 2221180 & 4295775)
Wagons-Lits/Cook, Calle Alcala 23 (tel: 2621900)

SWEDEN

Essential Information

Type of Government
Constitutional Monarchy

Area
449,964 sq km
(179,986 sq mi)

Population
8.3 million

Annual Growth Rate
0.2%

Languages
Swedish

Religion
Lutheran 95%, others 5%

Ethnic Groups
Swedes, Finns, Lapps, Yugoslavs, Danes, Norwegians, Greeks

Weights and Measures
Metric

Electrical Current
A.C. 50c 220/380 V

Major Business Cities
Stockholm (cap) 1,650,000
Gothenburg 750,000
Malmo 525,000

Currency
1 Krona (kr) = 100 ore
Notes 10, 50, 100, 1,000 and 10,000 krona
Coins 1, 5 krona

Public Holidays
Jan 1 New Year
Jan 5, 6 Twelfth Night
Apr 13-20 Easter Week
May 1 Labour Day
May 28 Ascension
May 18 Whitsun

EUROPE

Jun 20 Midsummer
Aug 14 Anniversary Day
Nov 2 All Saints' Day
Dec 24, 25 Christmas

Travellers Information

Entry Requirements
Passport is required by most
visitors, except Scandinavian
nationals. Visas are not required
for most visitors.

Working Restrictions
Work permit is required by all
visitors to Sweden if they wish
to work in the country.

Vaccination Required
None

Customs and Duty Free
On arrival: 200 cigarettes or 50
cigars or 250 gr. of tobacco;
spirits, wine 1 L; beer 2 L;
perfume for personal use and
gifts to a value of kr 600. Visitors
from outside Europe may import
400 cigarettes.

Currency Restrictions
A maximum limit of kr 6,000 can
be exported, but no limit on
imports of krona or other
currencies.

Health Tips
Sweden has a national health
plan but foreigners must pay
their own bills. Tap water is
generally drinkable and public
health standards are high.
Doctors can be reached by
dialing 90000.

Climate and Clothing
Winters (Nov-April) are very
cold, with snow and ice similar
to North American winters.
Temps hover around freezing,
and heavy clothes with boots
and a fur hat would be wise.
The rest of the year is mainly
dry and sunny, but usually
cooler in the north. Temps
average between 17-21 C (63-70
F).

Tipping
Tip taxi drivers at least 10%,
since they are taxed that amount
anyway. Tip about kr 3 per
person for various small hotel
services, but hotel and restaurant
bills normally include a service
charge of about 13.5%. It is
customary, however, to tip a
further 10%.

Food and Drink
Meat, fish and cheese are some
of the major staples of the
Swedish diet. The smorgasbord
is a typical dinner arrangement,
and is a whole table full of
breads, cheese, fish, meats and
vegetables which may serve as
the appetizer or may be dinner
itself. Swedish beer usually
accompanies a meal.

Business Brief

GDP
$169.6 billion)
(per capita income $20,268)

Annual Growth Rate
1.40%

Natural Resources
Iron ore, gold, silver, lead,
copper, zinc, pyrites, tungsten,
manganese, granite, quartz,
marble, forestry, hydroelectric
power

Agriculture
Dairy products, grains, sugar
beets, potatoes, barley, fodder
crops

Industry
Cement, chemicals, electronics,
iron and steel, machinery, motor
vehicles, paper products, ship-
building

Imports
Total $40.7 billion
Fuel, petroleum, chemicals,
lubricants, machinery, ores, raw
materials, textiles, foodstuffs,
grains

Exports
Total $44.5 billion
Machinery, transport equipment, manufactured goods, paper, wood pulp, timber, non-electric machinery

Major Trading Partners
EEC nations, U.S., Canada, Norway, Finland, Denmark

Workforce
4.3 million
Government 34.9%, industry & commerce 39.2%, services 20.3%, agriculture 5.6%

Tips for Doing Business
A business suit is recommended for all occasions, and prior appointments are advisable. Punctuality is vital. Business dinners may be formal, and sometimes black-tie. If dinner is formal, bring the hostess flowers and toast her first in appreciation. A follow-up thank you note next day is also appreciated. Some business is usually done at lunch, but you are more likely to be invited to the businessman's home. Use titles whenever possible, such as "Engineer," or "Director." Also be sure to shake hands with everyone upon first meeting, and introduce yourself.

Best Months for Doing Business
February through May and September through November. Avoid the two weeks before and after Christmas and the week before and after Easter. June, July and August are business vacation months.

Business Hours

Government
Mon-Fri 0900-1300, 1400-1700

Business
Mon-Fri 0900-1700 (summer closings 1530)

Banks
Mon-Fri 0930-1500

Shops
Mon-Fri 0900-1800
Sat 0900-1400 or 1600

English Language Publications
International Herald Tribune, USA Today and some British dailies are available in Stockholm in hotels or at kiosks.

Telephone and Communications
Telephone country code: 46
Telephone city codes: Stockholm 08, Gothenburg 031
Telex country codes: 854
Phones are widely available, and direct dialing is possible to anywhere in Europe or North America. Shops with a sign reading "Tele" or "Telebutik" offer cheap international service. Telex facilities are located in large hotels and at telegraph offices.
Telegrams can be sent from only a few post offices, telegraph offices or by phone.

Air Travel
Sweden has excellent inter-city flights operated by both SAS from Arlanda airport in Stockholm and by Linjeflyg from Bromma airport.

Other Transport
Sweden has a good network of motorways and secondary roads, so hiring a car will present few driving difficulties.
The State Railways run an efficient coach service between major cities, which links up with the railway system. Book express trips by train in advance.
State Railways also operate the ferry services along the coast, and some inland waterway transportation.

EUROPE

STOCKHOLM

Airport Information

Time
GMT +1
GMT +2 (Apr-Sept)

Airport
Arlanda International ARN
Tel: (08) 244000
41 km (25 mi) N of the city
International and domestic
flights

Airlines
Aer Lingus 249325
Aeroflot 215376
Air Canada 240350
Air France 234200
Alitalia 245845
American 246145
Austrian 142850
British Airways 233900
Canadian International 2221977
El Al 248130
Finnair 244330
Gulf Air 248315
Iberia 237875
Interflug 207128
JAL 233430
KLM 231350
Korean 100962
Lufthansa 230505
Northwest 143880
Pan Am 231920
Philippines 245325
Qantas 231635
Sabena 230980
SAS 240080
Singapore 243680
Swissair 143040
TWA 232245
United 246755

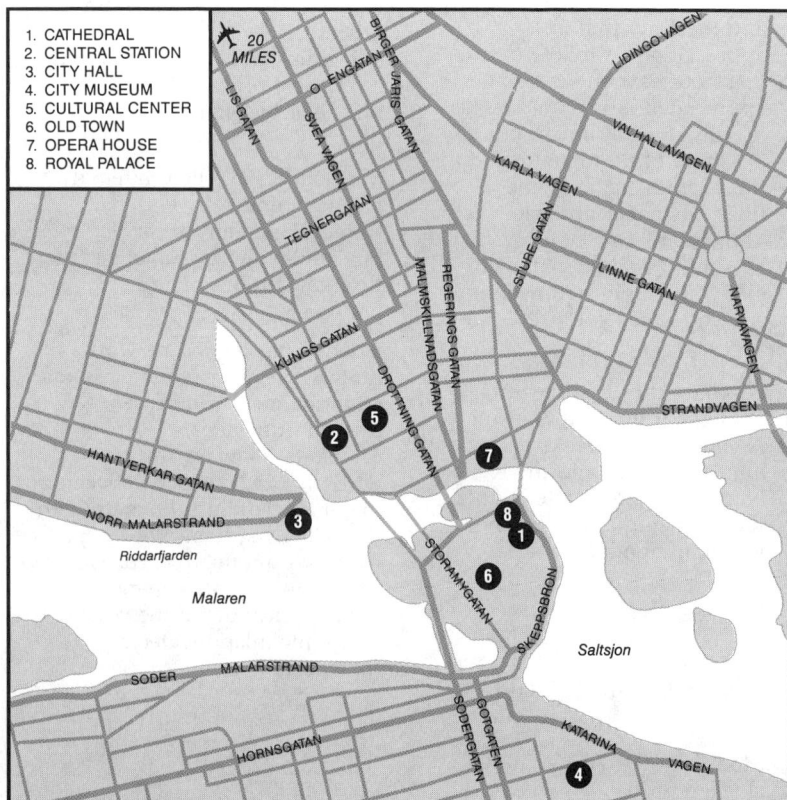

1. CATHEDRAL
2. CENTRAL STATION
3. CITY HALL
4. CITY MUSEUM
5. CULTURAL CENTER
6. OLD TOWN
7. OPERA HOUSE
8. ROYAL PALACE

Stockholm

Varig 140910

Transport to City

Taxis: Take any of several taxis for the 40-minute ride into Stockholm. The fare will be about kr 200 plus a 10% tip. Taxis accept credit cards for payment.

Coach: A special airport bus, operated by Stockholm Transport, runs to Central Station at Vasagatan 6-14. It can be boarded outside the Arrivals hall, and has room for luggage. Fare is about kr 28 for the 40-minute trip. Bus stops at Haga Park Air Terminal and Ulriksdal Air Terminal. A luxury limousine run by S.A.S. may also be hired for kr 145, but the return trip to the airport must be booked in advance.

Facilities

Baggage deposit, barber shop, buffet, bank with currency exchange, insurance, post office, information desk, nursery, snack bars, restaurants, bar.

Duty-free shop sells tobacco products, wines, spirits, liqueurs, watches, radios, jewellery.

Car rental desks: Hertz, Avis, Europcar, Budget, InterRent

Airport Taxes

None

City Information

Weather

Winters tend to be long, dark and gloomy in Stockholm, but with little snow or ice. In contrast summer days can have as many as 18 hours of daylight. Average (winter) temps: -1 C (31 F)

Average (summer) temps: 17.8 C (64 F)

Transportation

City taxis are available for a cost of about kr 10 plus kr 3 per km.

They can be called by phone but waiting time is extra.

Buses, streetcars and the subway have a flat fare of kr 6, or two coupons, and books of coupons may be purchased at Press Agency newstands. Cost: kr 35.

Car Hire

Hertz, Odengatan 32
 (tel: 76061118 & 181315)
Ansa, Brigarengatan 12
 (tel: 242655)
Avis, Linnengt. 9 (tel: 349910 & 76061885)
Budget, Brantingsgatan
 (tel: 7371737)
Europcar, B. Jarlsgatan 59
 (tel: 231070 & 76046013)
Frey Limousine (tel: 670360)
InterRent, Lindhagensgatan 72
 (tel: 240280)
Kemwel, Birger Jarlsgatan 59
 (tel: 61013)

Hospitals

For emergency medical services, police, fire or ambulance, dial 90000. Karolinska Sjukhuset hospital can be reached at tel: 7361000, Sophiahemmet at tel: 222800.

Trade Fairs

International Electronics Trade Fair (April)
International Sports Suppliers Exhibition (April)
International Scientific Exhibition (May)
International Book Trade Fair (May)
International Control Technology Exhibition (May)
Pharmacology & Therapeutic Exhibition (July)
International Medical Laboratory Exhibition (Aug)
International Perfume Trade Fair (Aug)
International Stamp Exhibition (Aug)
International Fashion Fair (Sept)
International Show Fair (Sept)
International Technical Fair (Oct)

EUROPE

Hotels

Anglais, Humlegardsgatan 23
(tel: 249900)
Birger Jarl, Tulegatan 8
(tel: 151020)
Continental, Vasagatan
(tel: 244020)
Diplomat, Strandvagen 7
(tel: 635800)
Esplanade, Strandvagen 7A
(tel: 630740)
Flamingo, Hotelgattan 11
(tel: 830800)
Grand, S. Blasieholmshamnen 8
(tel: 221020)
Lady Hamilton,
Storkyrkobrinken 5
(tel: 234680)
Lord Nelson, Vasterlanggatan 22
(tel: 232390)
Malmen, Gotgatan 49-51
(tel: 226080)
Sheraton, Tegelbacken 6
(tel: 142600)
Strand, Nybrokajen 9
(tel: 222900)

What to See and Do

The Old Town, site of the Royal Palace, is a good place to start your sightseeing of Stockholm, one of the world's most beautiful cities. Stockholm is a city made up of islands and the mainland, each providing a compact but different look at what the city has to offer. The Royal Palace is magnificent and fully open to the public with the exception of the Royal apartments. Nearby is Stockholm Cathedral, built in 1250. Take the bridge across the adjacent canal and railroad tracks to Riddarholm Church, once part of a Franciscan monastery. Here is buried Gerstavas Adolphus, the great Swedish general of the Thirty Years' War, as well as the astoundingly-skilled warrior Carolus Rex. Until 1950, this church held the remains of all Swedish kings.

Go to Skansen, a unique, exhilarating open-air area of handicrafts, museums, dancing halls and a zoo. It also contains coffeeshops, restaurants and workshops and offers a kind of overview of Swedish cultural heritage. Try to see the Wasa, the 17th-century flagship sunk in the harbor but raised and restored.

Other noteworthy places to visit are Drottningholm Palace, Saltsjobaden, the Haga Pavilion, National Museum, and Nordic and Maritime Museums. Some of the finer nightclubs are Berns Salonger, Hamburger Bors, and the Chat Noir.

Useful Addresses

Embassies and Consulates

American: Strandvogen 101
(tel: 7835300)
British: Skarpogatan 8
(tel: 670140)
Canadian: Togelbacksen 4
(tel: 237920)

Business and Commerce

Central Bank, P.O. Box 16283
(tel: 787000)
British Chamber of Commerce,
Grevgatan 34 (tel: 653425)
Ministry of Industry, Fredsgatan
8 (tel: 7631000)
Ministry of Trade, Tegelbacken 2
(tel: 7631000)
Stockholm Chamber of
Commerce, V. Tradgardsgatan
9 (tel: 231200)
Stockholm Stock Exchange,
Kallargrand 2 (tel: 143160)
U.S.A. Trade Center,
Skeppargatan 37 (tel: 7838000)

Tourism and Travel

Central Train Station, Vasagatan
6-14
Kungl Auto Club,
Wahrendorfsgatan 1
Tourist Board, Hamngatan 27
(tel: 2263280)

S.J. Tourist Service, Vasagatan 22
  (tel: 234450)
Swedish Automobile

Association, Sturegatan 32
  (tel: 670580)
American Express, Birger
  Jarlsgatan 1 (tel: 235330)

SWITZERLAND

Essential Information

Type of Government
Federal State (Federation)

Area
41,288 sq km
(15,941 sq mi)

Population
6.5 million

Annual Growth Rate
0.1%

Languages
German, French, Italian,
Romansch

Religion
Roman Catholic 49%, Protestant
48%, Jewish 0.3%

Ethnic Groups
Mixed European stock, primarily
German, French and Italian

Weights and Measures
A.C. 50c 110/220 V, 220/380 V

Major Business Cities
Bern (cap) 300,000
Zurich 850,000
Basel 380,000
Geneva 385,000
Lausanne 265,000

Currency
1 Swiss franc = 100 centimes
Notes 10, 20, 50, 100 and 1,000 fr
Coins 1, 2, 5, 10, 20 and 50
  centimes; 1, 2 and 5 fr

Public Holidays
Jan 1 New Year
Apr 13-20 Easter Week
May 28 Ascension
Jun 9 Whit Monday
Aug 1 National Day
Dec 25, 26 Christmas

Travellers Information

Entry Requirements
Passport required by most
visitors. Visas are not required
by British or North American
nationals, but check with local
Swiss consulate before leaving
your country.

Working Restrictions
A work permit is required for all
visitors seeking employment.

Vaccination Required
None

Customs and Duty Free
On arrival: 200 cigarettes or 50
cigars or 250 gr. of tobacco;
spirits 1 L, wine 2 L.

Currency Restrictions
None

Health Tips
Drinking water is safe. Doctors
and dentists speak English and
many hotels have their own
resident doctors. Pharmaceuticals
are reasonably priced and widely
available.

Climate and Clothing
The weather can vary,
depending on the altitude.
Generally, summer months (Apr-
Oct) are sunny and dry, but
colder higher up. Winters (Nov-
Mar) are cold, with snow, but
temperatures seldom drop below
0 C (32 F). Wear mediumweight
clothes most of the year, with
boots, scarf, gloves, etc. in
winter.

Tipping
Restaurant and hotel bills
already include a service charge

EUROPE

of 10-15%. Tip taxi drivers, barbers, and beauticians 15%. Tip chambermaids, doormen, porters 2 fr per day or per piece carried.

Food and Drink

Breakfasts usually consist of bread and butter, cheese, hot chocolate, or coffee. Lunch is the main meal, and meat, potatoes, vegetables, pasta and salad are staples. A light dinner is served from 1800-1900, usually the same food as what was served for lunch. Swiss beer and white wines are excellent. Specialties include Emmenthal and Gruyere cheeses, chocolates and pastries. Swiss cuisine varies considerably depending on the region. In most areas the cuisine is similar to that of Germany, but in the French-speaking areas (Geneva) the cooking shifts toward French-style. Near the Italian border pastas are common.

Business Brief

GDP
$159.4 billion
(per capita income $24,531)

Annual Growth Rate
0.1%

Natural Resources
Forestry, hydroelectric power, salt

Agriculture
Dairy products, livestock, grains, fruit and vegetables, potatoes, grapes

Industry
Chocolate, chemicals, electrical equipment, engineering, pharmaceuticals, textiles, watchmaking, banking, insurance, precision instruments

Imports
Total $50.7 billion
Fuel, petroleum, raw materials, chemicals, transport equipment, foostuffs, grains, metal, clothing

Exports
Total $45.5 billion
Precision and optical instruments, watches, machinery, chemicals, pharmaceuticals, textiles, glass, binding materials and foodstuffs

Major Trading Partners
West Germany, France, U.S., Italy, Great Britain, Austria

Workforce
3.1 million
Service industry 50%, industry & commerce 39%, agriculture 7%, government 4%

Tips for Doing Business
A conservative business suit and prior appointments are absolutely necessary at all times. Swiss businesspeople demand punctuality and patience with their contacts, and work hard for long days. Patience is an absolute virtue when dealing with the Swiss, but once a contract has been signed, it will always be lived up to. The Swiss have great reverence for firms that have a history, so play up your company's history when possible. Business is not normally conducted in restaurants, and often a dinner invitation may come only at the conclusion of your business dealings — or not at all. This is no reflection on the success of your visit, since Swiss businesspeople do not like to mix business and social occasions.

Business Hours

Government
Mon-Fri 0800-1800

Business
Mon-Fri 0800-1800

Banks
Mon-Fri 0830-1230, 1330-1630
Fri 0830-1230, 1330-1830

Shops
Mon-Sat 0800-1215, 1330-1800

English Language Publications

International Herald-Tribune, USA Today and some major British dailies are available in larger towns and cities.

Telephone and Communications

Telephone country code: 41
Telephone city codes: Basel 61, Geneva 22, Zurich 01, Berne 31
Telex country code: 845
Public telephones are located in shops, etc., and in post offices. Directories are published in several languages.
Telex facilities are widely available at hotels and at main post offices in larger towns. Telegrams can be sent from loca post offices, but are seldom used within the country.

Air Travel

Local air service, operated by Swissair is efficient, punctual and expensive. Only the Zurich to Geneva route is widely used; business people prefer the train.

Other Transport

Switzerland has excellent roads and motorways, so a rental car is a good way to travel.
Swiss trains may be the best-run in Europe. They are fast, comfortable, punctual, and the scenery can be spectacular. Journeys between major cities rarely take more than two hours.

GENEVA

Airport Information

Time

GMT +1
GMT +2 (Mar 28-Sept 25)

Airport

Geneva - Cointrin International
GVA
Tel: (022) 981122
4 km (2.5 mi) NW of the city
International and domestic flights

Airlines

Aer Lingus 321656
Aeroflot 311643
Air Algerie 311120
Air Canada 314980
Air France 310400
Air India 283335
Alia 323524
Alitalia 316650
Austrian 315730
British Airways 314050
British Caledonian 320803
Delta 317510
Egyptair 313836
El Al 320550
Finnair 312530
Gulf Air 982121
Iberia 317650
Iran Air 310130
Iraqi 313180
JAL 317160
KLM 983777
Korean 322320
Kuwait Air 319560
Lufthansa 319550
MEA 212322
Olympic 219621
Pan Am 323834
Qantas 320450
Sabena 326620
SAS 216522
Saudia 319150
Singapore 322203
Swissair 982121
TAP 317350
THY 316120
TWA 450350
Varig 317730

Transport to City

Taxis: Taxis are plentiful and clearly marked. Most are metered and the tip is usually included in the fr 25 fare. The short trip downtown takes about 20 minutes.
Coach: A Swissair coach operates

EUROPE

from the Arrivals hall exit every 20 minutes, with stops at the Air Terminal and Cornavin Station (railway station). The 15-minute trip costs about fr 5 and returns from Cornavin and Place de Montbrillant with pickups at the Penta Hotel.

Transit: Bus #33 of the TPG runs every 15 minutes to Cornavin railway station. It can be boarded opposite the World Trade Center building. The 13-minute trip costs about fr 2, but there is no baggage space. Also, the airport will soon be linked to Geneva by train.

Facilities

Snack bar, bank with currency exchange, post office, hotel reservations, baggage deposit, barber shop, information desk, first-aid, nursery, bath, and shower rooms.

Duty-free shop sells tobacco products, wines, spirits, aperitifs, liqueurs, lighters, watches, perfume.

Car rental desks: Hertz, Avis, Budget, Europcar, InterRent.

Airport Taxes
None

City Information

Weather
Climate is hot and dry in summer, cold and snowy in winter. Winter temps average -1

1. BRUNSWICK MONUMENT
2. CATHEDRAL ST. PIERRE
3. GARE DE CORNAVIN
4. GRAND THEATRE
5. PALAIS DE JUSTICE
6. RATH MUSEUM
7. UNIVERSITY

Geneva

C (31 F), while summers average about 16 C (60 F).

Transportation
Taxis are in plentiful supply and may or may not be metered. Fare is generally about fr 4 plus fr 2 per km. Fare usually includes a tip.
Tickets for streetcars and buses should be purchased in advance from vending machines, and ticket is good for up to 5 stops.

Car Hire
Hertz, Rue Berne 60 (tel: 328328 & 982202)
Auto-Europe (tel: 321758)
Avis, Rue de Lausanne 44 (322606 & 983321)
Budget, Rue de Zurich 36 (tel: 984491)
Europcar, Rue de Lausanne 63 (tel: 981110)
Foremost-Euro (tel: 321758)
Godfrey-Davis (tel: 320407)
InterRent, Rue de Lausanne 20 (tel: 319160)
Kemwel, Rue de Zurich 36 (tel: 982253)

Hospitals
Hospital Cantonal (tel: 469211). Many hotels have house physicians who can help in an emergency, and most hospital personnel speak very good English.

Trade Fairs
International Commercial Vehicles Exhibition (Jan)
International Cycle & Motorcycle Exhibition (Feb)
International Ready-to-Wear Fashion Exhibition (Feb)
International Motor Exhibition (Mar)
International Exhibition of Inventions & New Technology (April)
International Biotechnology Exhibition (May)
International Vehicle Industry Suppliers Exhibition (May)
European Nuclear Exhibition (June)
International Banking Services Exhibition (June)
International Energy & Environmental Technology Exhibition (June)
International Minerals Fair (Sept)
International Wine Exhibition (Oct)
Home Furnishings & Decoration Fair (Nov)

Hotels
Bristol, eue du Mont Blanc 10 (tel: 324400)
B.W. Beau-Rivage, Quai du Mont Blance 13 (tel: 310221)
B.W. California, Rue Gevray 1 (tel: 315550)
Cornavin, Blvd. James Fazy 33 (tel: 322100)
D'Angleterre, Quai du Mont Blanc 17 (tel: 328180)
De la Paix, Quai du Mont Blanc 11 (tel: 326150)
Hilton Geneva, Quai du Mont Blanc 19 (tel: 319811)
InterContinental, Petit Saconnex 9 (tel: 346091)
Metropol, Quai General Guisan 34 (tel: 211344)
Novotel Airport, Route de Meyrin (tel: 408523)
Penta, Av. Louis-Casai 75 (tel: 984700)
President, Quai Wilson 47 (tel: 311000)
Reserve, On the Lake (Geneva) (tel: 741741)
Savoy, Place Cornavin 8 (tel: 311255)

What to See and Do
Nightclubs, dance halls and discotheques populate the old-town section of Geneva, although antique shops remain more typical of the area. There is a large flea market in which to browse, on the Plainpalais, a large central park. Try to take a steamer trip on Lake Geneva, or a bus trip to Chamonix in France. Either trip offers

EUROPE

breathtaking panoramas of this city.

Lake Geneva forms the center of this beautiful and ancient city, but some of its best sights can still be taken in by walking from the railway station along rue du Mont Blanc. Follow this promenade to the Place Neuve with its Grand Theater and Conservatory of Music. Try to visit St. Peter's Church, where John Calvin preached, or visit No. 40 Grand-Rue, where Jean-Jacques Rousseau was born. Another noteworthy visit would be to Ariana Park, where you can tour the Palais des Nations, former home of the League of Nations. Also visit the Botanical Gardens, History and Art Museum and the Voltaire and Rosseau Museums.

Useful Addresses

Embassies and Consulates
American: Rte de Pregny 11 (tel: 335537)
British: Rue Vermont 37 (tel: 343800)
Canadian: Av. de Bude 8 (tel: 341950)

Business and Commerce
Geneva Chamber of Commerce & Industry, Blvd. du Theatre 4 (tel: 215333)
Geneva Stock Exchange, Rue de Petitot 10 (tel: 280684)
European Communities Commission, Rue de Vermont 37-39 (tel: 349750)
GATT, Rue de Lausanne 154 (tel: 310231)
UN Information Office, Palais des Nations (tel: 331000)

Tourism and Travel
Tourism Office, Rue des Moulins 2 (tel: 287233)
Swiss Touring Club, Rue Pierro Fatio 9 (tel: 371212)
American Express, Rue du Mont Blanc 7 (tel: 317600)

Wagon Lits, Mont Blanc 4 (tel: 312130)

ZURICH

Airport Information

Time
GMT +1
GMT +2 (Mar 28-Sept 25)

Airport
Zurich International ZRH
Tel: (01) 8162211
12 km (7.5 mi) N of the city
International and domestic flights

Airlines
Aer Lingus 2112850
Aeroflot 2114633
Aerolineas Argentinas 2119740
Air Algerie 8163548
Air Canada 2110777
Air France 2111377
Alitalia 3023333
American 2213110
Austrian 2115890
Avianca 8141727
British Airways 2114090
CAAC 2111617
Canadian International 2113794
Delta 2513434
Egyptair 2212592
El Al 2110491
Finnair 2211460
Garuda 3636444
Iberia 2211425
JAL 2111557
KLM 2110161
Korean 2114031
Kuwait Air 2117330
Lufthansa 2297220
MEA 2111010
Northwest 2512000
Olympic 2113737
Pan Am 2028022
Qantas 2114411
SAA 2115130
Sabena 2112171
SAS 8164080
Singapore 2113094

Swissair 2513434
TAP 2112733
Thai 2524300
THY 2111071
TWA 3614111
UTA 230591
Varig 2210011

Transport to City

Taxis: Taxis are not metered, so agree on a fare before leaving the airport. Fr 30 is a good bargaining amount for the 15-minute trip to town. Fare may or may not include a 10% tip, so ask first.

Coach: Hotel courtesy coaches are provided to the Hilton, Movenpick Holiday Inn, Welcome, and International hotels.

Transit: Rail service to the city leaves every half hour for a fare of fr 4.40 to fr 5.20, depending on class of seat. Baggage check-in and tickets purchased in the Arrivals hall of either Terminals A & B. Trains return from the main railway station (Hauptbahnhof). Trains are located beneath the airport.

Facilities

Snack bar, lounge, restaurant, bank with currency exchange, hotel reservations, baggage lockers, nursery, first-aid, flowers, tobacco, souvenirs.

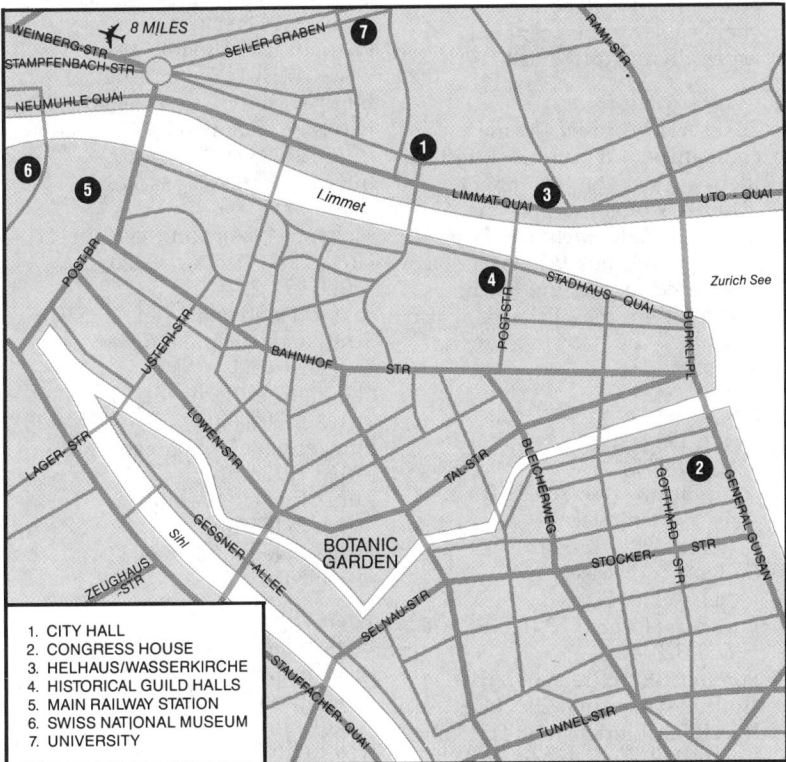

1. CITY HALL
2. CONGRESS HOUSE
3. HELHAUS/WASSERKIRCHE
4. HISTORICAL GUILD HALLS
5. MAIN RAILWAY STATION
6. SWISS NATIONAL MUSEUM
7. UNIVERSITY

EUROPE

Zurich

Duty-free shop sells tobacco products, wines, aperitifs, spirits, liqueurs, perfume. Car rental desks: Hertz, Avis, Europcar, InterRent, Budget

Airport Taxes
None

City Information

Weather
Generally the weather in Zurich is sunny, dry and warm in summer but quite cold in winter. Spring and fall are mild. Winter temperatures are in the -1 C (31 F) range, summer in the 16 C (60 F) range. Temperatures are lower and precipitation higher the further up in the mountains. The weather can also be very changeable, so be prepared, especially in April and May.

Transportation
Taxi service run by several companies, but you must find them at their stands. Fare is about fr 4 plus fr 2 per km. Charge usually includes a tip. Streetcar and bus tickets can be purchased in vending machines, and multi-journey tickets are also available. The flat fee covers up to 5 stops.

Car Hire
Hertz, Lagerstr. 33 (tel: 2414760 & 2418077)
Auto-Europe (tel: 3632164)
Avis, Gartenhofstr 17 (tel: 8130084 & 8102020)
Budget, Todistrasse 9 (tel: 4911011)
Europcar, Josefstr 53 (tel: 642820 & 8132044)
Foremost-Euro (tel: 3632164)
Godfrey-Davis (tel: 2021144)
InterRent, Lindenstr 33 (471747)
Kemwel, Todistrasse 9 (tel: 8133131)

Hospitals
Kantonspital (tel: 2551111)

Trade Fairs
International Radio, TV and Electronics Fair (Aug)
International Ladies' Fashion Fair (Sept)
International Hairstyling Exhibition (Oct)
Swiss Wine Exhibition (Oct)

Hotels
Ascot, Lavaterstr 15 (tel: 2011800)
Baur au Lac, Talstrasse 1 (tel: 7211650)
Bellerive au Lac, Utoquai 47 (tel: 2517010)
B.W. Glarnischhof, Clairdenstr 30 (tel: 2024747)
Carlton Elite, Bahnhofstr 41 (tel: 2116560)
Continental, Stampfenbackstr (tel: 3633363)
Dolder Grand, Kurhausstrasse (tel: 2516231)
Eden au Lac, Utoquai 45 (tel: 479404)
Europe, Dufourstr. 4 (tel: 471030)
Excelsior, Dufourstr. 24 (tel: 2522500)
International, Am Markplatz (tel: 3114341)
Movenpick, Airport (tel: 8101111)
Nova Park, Badenstr. 420 (tel: 4912222)
Savoy, Paradeplatz (tel: 2115360)
Schifflande, Schifflande 18 (tel: 694050)
Sheraton, Doltschiweg 234 (tel: 4630000)
Splugenschloss, Spluegenstr 2 (tel: 2010800)
Zum Storchen, Weinplatz 2 (tel: 2115510)
Zurich, Neumuhlequai 42 (tel: 3636363)

What to See and Do
English-language films can be seen frequently and nightspots usually combine drinking with singing and dancing. For the well-to-do Zurich offers fabulous shopping opportunities, particularly along the Bahnhofstrasse. Chez Max is one of the best restaurants, where

you might like to try the local favourite, "Zurcher Geschnetzelte," or veal in wine and a cream sauce, with "rosti," or fried potatoes.

The liveliest quarter of Zurich is the Niederdorf, but you may find it rather tame compared to the exotic quarters of Paris, London or Istanbul. Some interesting things to visit are the Congress Hall, St. Peter's Church, the Botanical Gardens, the Observatory, Landesmuseum and the Town Hall.

Useful Addresses

Embassies and Consulates
American: Zollikerstrasse 141 (tel: 552566)
British: Dufourstr 101 (tel: 47152026)

Business and Commerce
Central Bank, Borenstrasse 15 (tel: 2213750)

Union of Swiss Banks, Bahnhofstrasse 45 (tel: 2341111)
Stock Exchange, Bahnhofquai 7 (tel: 2112870)
American Chamber of Commerce, Bellariastrasse 38 (tel: 2023737)
British Chamber of Commerce, Dufourstrasse 51 (tel: 2513060)
Swiss Trade Development Office, Stamfenbachstr 85 (3632250)
Zurich Stock Exchange, Bleicherweg 5 (tel: 2111470)

Tourism and Travel
Swiss Travel Agency Federation, Hardstrasse 316 (tel: 426442)
Swiss National Tourist Office, Bellariastrasse 38 (tel: 2023737)
American Express, Bahnhofstrasse 20 (tel: 2118370)
Wagon Lits, Talacker 42 (tel: 2118710)

USSR

Essential Information

Type of Government
Federal Union

Area
22,402,076 sq km
(8,650,000 sq mi)

Population
274 million

Annual Growth Rate
0.9%

Language
Russian, plus 18 other languages which are spoken by 1 million or more persons.

Religion
Russian Orthodox, Muslim, Georgian Orthodox, Roman Catholic, Armenian, Apostolic, Protestant, and Jewish, although religious activity is officially discouraged by the Communist Party.

Ethnic Groups
White Russian 52%, Ukrainian 16%, Uzbek 5%, Belorussian 4%

Weights and Measures
Metric

Electrical Current
A.C. 50c 127/220 V and 220 V

Major Business Cities
Moscow (cap) 8,950,000
Leningrad 5,250,000
Kiev 3,200,00
Tashkent 2,250,000

Currency
1 rouble = 100 kopeks
Notes 1, 3, 5, 10, 25, 50 and 100 roubles

EUROPE

Coins 1, 2, 3, 5, 20 and 50
kopeks, 1 rouble

Public Holidays
Jan 1 New Year
Mar 8 Women's Day
May 1, 2 May Day
May 9 V E Day
Oct 7 Constitution Day
Nov 7, 8 Anniversary of
Revolution

Travellers Information

Entry Requirements
Passport required of all visitors.
Visas required of British and
North American visitors and
most others, except CMEA
nationals. Visa must be obtained
in advance, and ask your
embassy to make your visa as
specific and comprehensive as
possible.

Working Restrictions
A work permit is required to
work in the Soviet Union.

Vaccination Required
An immunization against
typhoid is recommended by the
government, as is one against
cholera.

Customs and Duty Free
On arrival: 250 cigarettes or 250
gr. of tobacco; spirits 1 L, wine 2
L; perfume for personal use.
There is a ban on bringing in
what authorities may consider
anti-Soviet propaganda,
including any printed matter or
videotape. Antiquities or works
of art may not be exported
without permission from the
Ministry of Culture. Also
imports of fruits, seeds, meat or
fowl products are prohibited.
Weapons must be declared and
all gifts to other people.

Currency Restrictions
Import and export of roubles is
prohibited. Foreign currency
must be declared on entry, and

may be exported only up to the
amount declared on entry.
Foreign Trade Bank certificates
must be obtained to allow the
export of foreign currency in an
amount greater than that
brought in.

Health Tips
Drinking water is purified in
Moscow only. Medical care can
be arranged through the
Intourist service bureau of most
hotels. If booked through the
plan medical services may be
free. The Poliklinika can provide
free medical assistance, and can
be reached at tel: 2290382.

Climate and Clothing
From June-August (summer)
temperature are warm with some
rain in Moscow, Leningrad and
Kiev. It is generally cool and dry
in Arkhangel, Tomsk and
Irkutsk, warm and dry on the
Black Sea coasts. Light to
medium weight clothes are
recommended, together with a
raincoat. From Sept-May (winter)
most of the Soviet Union is
bitterly cold, except the Black
Sea area, which is cold and wet.
Warmest clothes,
hat, boots, fur-lined gloves, etc.
highly recommended for winter
in most of the country.

Tipping
Add 10% to your restaurant bills,
a 5-rouble note to your
headwaiter and 20-30 kopeks to
cloakroom attendants or for
other small services. Tip taxis
10%, barbers and beauticians
10%. Tip porters 50 kopeks per
piece of luggage.

Food and Drink
Soviet food tends to concentrate
on vegetables like potatoes, beets
and cabbage, because meat is not
plentiful. Sausage, bread and
coffee and tea make up
breakfast, but a large meal is
taken in mid-afternoon. Suppers

are light, but tourist meals in hotels and restaurants are large and quite good. Evening meal is usually accompanied by eigher beer, wine or Vodka, which is also consumed in great quantities unaccompanied. After 2000, most restaurants in the Soviet Union have an orchestra play and dance music is very popular.

Business Brief

GDP
$1.46 trillion
(per capita income $5,292)

Annual Growth Rate
2.8%

Natural Resources
Fossil fuels, hydroelectric power, timber, manganese, lead, zink, nickel, mercury, potash, phosphate, iron, petroleum

Agriculture
Wheat, rye, oats, potatoes, sugar beets, linseed, sunflower seed, cotton, flax, cattle, pigs, sheep, tobacco

Industry
Mining, ferrous and non-ferrous metallurgy, fuels and power, building materials, chemicals, machines, building cement, electronics, textiles and electricity

Imports
Total $92.2 billion
Machinery and equipment, foodstuffs, raw materials, grains, cement, cotton, wool, meat, sugar, rubber, transport equipment

Exports
Total $100.7 billion
Iron and steel, potassic salts, chemicals, ores, machinery and equipment, raw materials, optical instruments, petroleum products, textiles, paper products

Major Trading Partners
East Germany, Czechoslovakia, Bulgaria, Poland, Hungary, West Germany, Cuba, Finland, Yugoslavia, Italy, France, Romania, Japan, U.S., India, Great Britain

Workforce
130 million
Industry 29%, services 26%, agriculture 19%, transportation & communications 10%, government 2%

Tips for Doing Business
Try to have your firm contact the people you want to see before leaving for the U.S.S.R. State what topics you wish to discuss, where you will be travelling, and your ports of entry and exit. A letter from the host company is invaluable when dealing with customs officials. Do not discuss politics nor make any negative comments about the Soviet Union. Vast quantities of patience are required when dealing with many aspects of Soviet life and business affairs. Be friendly and courteous, but do not seek out conversations with strangers, since Soviet citizens are not encouraged to talk with foreigners. Refer to the country as "the Soviet Union," not Russia, and be prepared to offer generous credit terms on your firm's behalf. Keep in mind that in most consumer goods, demand far outstrips supply in the Soviet Union. Most visitors will require the services of a translator.

Best Months for Doing Business
October through June. Business vacations are taken June through August.

Business Hours

Government
Mon-Fri 0900-1800

EUROPE

Business
Mon-Fri 0900-1800
Check with your trade
organization in advance.

Banks
Mon-Fri 0900-1300

Shops
Mon 0800-1900
Tues-Sat 0800-2100

English Language Publications
Some British and American
papers, such as the International
Herald Tribune, can be
purchased in Moscow and
Leningrad.

Telephone and Communications
Telephone country code: 7
Telephone city code: Moscow 95
Telex country code: 871
Public phones are located in
hotels, restaurants and booths,
the latter coin-operated. For an
English-speaking operator, say
"Po-Angliski." Telephone
directories are never available,
but important numbers may be
obtained from a hotel service.
Book international calls through
your hotel. Telephone calls and
telegrams may be sent from the
Central Post Office on 7 Gorky
Street.
For telex service, use your
embassy's facility if possible.

Air Travel
Aeroflot, the national airline,
operates frequent flights to every
major city in the huge country.
In fact, it is the only practical
national mode of transportation,
given the size of the country.

Other Transport
Rail network provides electrified
service for all 140,000 km of track
but great distances make train
travel impractical for anyone in a
hurry. Sleepers should be
booked well in advance.
Rental cars are available for self-
drive, but roadsigns are
confusing, and distances vast.

MOSCOW

Airport Information

Time
GMT +3

Airport
Sheremetyevo International SVO
Tel: 1555005 & 1569435
26 km (16 mi) NW of the city
International and domestic
flights

Airlines
Aeroflot 1568002
Air Algerie 2212523
Air France 2373344
Air India 2373293
Alitalia 9239840
Austrian 2531670
British Airways 2532482
CAAC 1431560
Finnair 2928798
Interflug 2807233
Iraqi 2313838
JAL 2216448
KLM 2532151
Libyan 1352437
Lufthansa 9230488
Pan Am 2532659
Sabena 2481691
SAS 9254747
Swissair 2538988
Syrian 2373628

Transport to City
Taxis: Available from the
Arrivals hall, but be prepared to
wait. The 40-minute ride to the
Kremlin costs about 5 roubles.
Coach: Intourist provides
chauffeured limousines for their
clients only, and between
railway stations and the airport.
Other coaches make the 50-
minute run downtown for a fare
of 1 rouble, and return via the
Central Air Terminal.
Transit: A shuttle bus that runs
every 60 minutes connects the
airport with the city air terminal
and the subway system. There is
little or no room for luggage on
the subway system.

Facilities
Buffet, bank with currency
exchange, baggage deposit,
Intourist information desk, post
office, nursery shops.
Duty-free shop sells cigarettes,
wine, spirits, liqueurs, cameras,
records, jewellery, caviar.
Car rental desks: Hertz
(Intourist)

Airport Taxes
None

City Information

Weather
Winter in Moscow (Oct-Apr) can
be colder than anything you

have experienced. Warm boots,
hat, scarf, gloves and heavy
waterproof coat are advisable,
and with proper clothing, winter
need not be debilitating.
Summer months (July-Sept) can
be quite hot and sticky, but
temperatures average about 19 C
(66 F). A light raincoat or cape is
advisable for the summer period.

Transportation
Taxis are easily identifiable by
the checkerboard markings on
their side, and are for hire if
they display a green in the top
corner of the windshield. Write
down (or have someone write it
for you) your destination and

EUROPE

1. BOLSHOI THEATER
2. BYELORUSSIA STATION
3. INTERNATIONAL POST OFFICE
4. THE KREMLIN & RED SQUARE
5. LENIN CENTRAL STADIUM
6. LENINGRAD STATION
7. LENIN MAUSOLEUM
8. MOSCOW STATE UNIVESITY
9. POKROVSKY MUSEUM (ST. BASIL'S)
10. PUSHKIN MUSEUM
11. SAVELOVSKY STATION
12. TRETYAKOV GALLERY

Moscow

hand it to the driver. A 10% tip will sometimes be handed back to you, since tipping is discouraged.

Cars are available to be rented, but are not advisable unless you speak Russian.

Buses are cheap, though crowded, and run on a flat fare of about 5 kopeks.

Subway is fast, clean and efficient, the best way to get around Moscow quickly. There are 120 stations which you can access for a flat fare.

Car Hire
Avis, Ukrania Hotel
    (tel: 2294206)
Intourist, Prospekt Karla Marxa 1
    (tel: 2036962)

Hospitals
Free medical and dental service is available to Soviet citizens and to foreigners. In an emergency, call Intourist or your hotel receptionist.

Trade Fairs
International Sporting Goods
    Exhibition (Jan)
Watch, Clock and Jewellery
    Exhibition (Jan)
Physics Research Exhibition (Jan)
International Aviation Exhibition
    (Jan)
International Technical and
    Commerce Exhibition (Mar)
Metorological Engineering
    Exhibition (Apr)
International Communications
    Exhibition (May)
Aluminium Production
    Exhibition (Jul)
Railway Transport Exhibition
    (Jul)
Catering Equipment Exhibition
    (Sept)
Electronic Engineering Exhibition
    (Oct)
International Packaging
    Technology Exhibition (Nov)
Pollution Control Equipment
    Exhibition (Nov)

Hotels
Belgrade, Smolenskaya Square 5
    (tel: 2486692)
Intourist, Ulitsa Gorki 3
    (tel: 2034007)
Leningradskaya, Kalanchevskaya
    21 (tel: 2255730)
Metropole, Marx Prospekt 1
    (tel: 2256677)
Minsk, Ulistsa Gorki 22
    (tel: 2991214)
National, Marx Prospekt 14
    (tel: 2036539)
Ostankino, Ulitsa Botanicheskaya
    (tel: 2195411)
Rossiya, Ulitsa Razin 6
    (tel: 2981442)
Ukraina, Prospekt Kutzovsky 10
    (tel: 2433021)

What to See and Do
The principal sight in which to immerse yourself in Moscow is the Kremlin, city within a city. Explore any one of the four cathedrals, the Church of the Deposition of the Robe, or the Ivan the Great Bell Tower. Also, the Palace of Facets, Grand Kremlin Palace, the Armory, the Arsenal and the Palace of Congresses. Nearby is Lenin's apartment, which is also open to the public.

Outside the Kremlin, but in Red Square lies Lenin's mausoleum, the Cathedral of the Intercession, the History Museum, and the GUM Department store.

Other noteworthy landmarks include the Rublyev Museum, Botanical Gardens, Moscow University, and the Donskoi Monastery. A relaxing visit to Gorky Park or Izmailovo Park may help to settle you down after this architectural panorama, and Gorky Park is quite close to the Park Kultury subway station. There are also 16 drama theatres in Moscow and of course you can buy tickets to either the Bolshoi or the Stanislovsky Musical Theatre. Or you may just want to do some shopping on Gorky Street, Arbat Kuznetsky Most, Petrovka, Stoleshnikov, and Kalinin Prospekt.

Useful Addresses

Embassies and Consulates
American: Ulitsa Chaykovskogo 19 (tel: 2522451)
British: Morisa Toreza 14 (tel: 2318511)
Canadian: Starolonyushenny Per 33 (tel: 2419155)

Business and Commerce
U.S.S.R. Chamber of Commerce, Ulitsa Kuibysheva 6 (tel: 9234323)
Foreign Trade Corporation, Krasnopresnenskaya 12 (tel: 2537729)

State Bank, Ulitsa Neglinnaya 12 (tel: 2231870)
Ministry of Foreign Trade, Smolenskaya Sq. 32 (tel: 2441947)
Novosti News Agency, Zubovsky bul 4 (tel: 2012424)
U.S.A. Trade Center, 15 Chaykovskovo

Tourism and Travel
Intourist, Prospekt Marksa 16 (tel: 2036962)
Moscow Excursion Bureau, Karla Marxa 1
Balkantourist, Metropole Hotel (tel: 218575)
Auto. Federation of the U.S.S.R., Marx Prospect 16 (tel: 4918661)
American Express, Sadovo-Kudrinskaya St. 21A (tel: 2544495 & 2544305 & 2544505)

UNITED KINGDOM

Essential Information

Type of Government
Constitutional Monarchy

Area
244,013 sq km
(94,400 sq mi)

Population
56.5 million

Languages
English, Welsh and some Gaelic

Religion
Church of England (Protestant), Roman Catholic

Ethnic Group
Mostly English (Anglo-Saxon) with Irish (Celtic) and Scottish (Gaelic). Large cities have significant populations of East and West Indians, African and Arabic peoples.

Weights and Measures
Metric & Imperial

Electrical Current
A.C. 50c 240 V, 240/415 V

Major Business Cities
London (cap) 8,100,000
Birmingham, 1,200,000
Glasgow 1,000,000
Leeds 800,000
Liverpool 700,000
Manchester 595,000

Currency
1 pound (L) = 100 pence (p)
Notes 5, 10, 20, 50
Coins 1, 2, 5, 10, 20 pence and L1

Public Holidays
Jan 1 New Year
Apr 13-20 Easter Week
May 1 May Day
May 26 Spring
Aug 25 Late Summer
Dec 25 Christmas
Dec 26 Boxing Day

EUROPE

Travellers Information

Entry Requirements

All visitors must have a valid passport good for a minimum of two months after departure date. No visa is required by Canadian or American nationals.

Working Restrictions

Commonwealth country nationals aged 17-27 can work for up to two years on a holiday visa. All others need a work permit.

Vaccination Required

None

Customs and Duty Free

On arrival: 200 cigarettes or 50 cigars or 250 gr. of tobacco; alcohol 1 L, wine 2 L; perfume 50 gr., eau de cologne for personal use. Also gifts to a value of L28. Personal effects are duty-free.

Currency Restrictions

None

Health Tips

Tap water is purified throughout England, and medical service through the National Health plan, may be free to visitors, depending on agreement between U.K. and government of country of origin.

Climate and Clothing

The U.K.'s climate is temperate, with rainfall distributed almost evenly across the seasons. Spring (Mar-May) can be cool and wet, with sunny periods, summer (June-Sept) gets quite warm, and winter is cold and wet most of the time. Medium weight clothes are recommended for all but summer and a raincoat or umbrella would be wise all year round.

Tipping

Tip taxis 25%, hotels, restaurants and nightspots 10-15%, barbers and beauticians 15%. Tip porters 50p per piece of luggage, chambermaids 50p per day, and small services 50p. Tip L2-3 for special services, like a waiter who provides good service to you over a matter of days.

Food and Drink

English food is plain, dominated by meat, potatoes and few zesty sauces or accompaniments. Tea and biscuits are eaten about 1600, and dinner (the main meal) is eaten about 3 hours later. Beer and tea are the most popular beverages, though coffee has gained popularity over the years. Fish and chips remains the main British fast food. Other regional specialties include Cornish Pasties, Shepard's Pie, Steak & Kidney Pudding, Sausages, and a Joint (Roast Beef) with Yorkshire Pudding.

In Northern Ireland fried foods and potatoes are common at lunch and dinner, as are tea, bread and pastries. In Scotland, "mince and tatties" (ground meat and potatoes), fish and chips, lamb and beef stew, and simple cooked vegetables are the main fare. Try the Scottish favorite Haggis.

Breakfasts are usually light, consisting of toast and tea, and perhaps an egg. Desserts can be sweet and sticky. Welsh food is plain, solid, but not elaborate. Breakfast and lunch are large meals, a snack is served mid-afternoon and dinner (called "tea") is served about 1830-1900. The pub is a good place to lunch before 1500, and it reopens about 1800 for evening meals, or just plain drinking of the fine English beers and ales.

Business Brief

GDP

$775 billion

(per capita income $10,200)

Annual Growth Rate
2.3%

Natural Resources
Natural gas and oil, coal, iron, limestone, tin, gravel, oil shale

Agriculture
Barley, potatoes, sugar beets, vegetables, wheat

Industry
Chemicals, consumer goods, electrical engineering, food processing, iron and steel, motor vehicles, transport equipment, petroleum refining, textiles

Imports
Total $154 billion
Fuel, petroleum, timber, paper, wool, cotton, foodstuffs, meat, vegetables, fruit, crude materials, finished goods, grains

Exports
Total $131 billion
Machinery and transport equipment, manufactured goods, vehicles and aircraft, iron and steel, electrical equipment, textiles, chemicals, spirits, petroleum products

Major Trading Partners
U.S., West Germany, Australia, South Africa, Ireland, Canada, France, Netherlands, Italy, Belgium, Luxembourg, Japan, Saudi Arabia

Workforce
26.1 million
Manufacturing 28%, agriculture 2%, other 70%

Tips for Doing Business
A conservative suit with a vest, and single-colour tie are highly recommended at all times. Never wear a striped tie since it could be confused with the cherished "school" tie. Make prior appointments and be punctual. Refer to everyone as British, not English, Welsh, Irish, etc., and maintain a proper respect for royalty and the royal family. Conduct business in a relaxed but formal way. Most if not all business entertaining is done in pubs or restaurants, but breakfast conferences are unheard of in Britain. When being entertained, sherry or gin-and-tonic are the preferred pre-meal drinks, tea or beer with dinner, coffee afterward. Smoking during meals is considered offensive. If in a pub, take your turn buying beer.

Best Months for Doing Business
February through June and September through November. Avoid the two weeks before and after Christmas and the two weeks around Easter. Business people usually vacation in July and August.

Business Hours

Government
Mon-Fri 0900-1300, 1400-1730

Business
Mon-Fri 0900-1730

Banks
England & Wales
Mon-Fri 0930-1530
Scotland
Mon-Thu 0930-1230, 1330-1530
Fri 0930-1530

Shops
Mon-Sat 0900-1730

Telephone and Communications
Telephone country code: 44
Telephone city codes:
Birmingham 21, Edinburgh 31, Glasgow 41, London 01, Manchester 61
Telex country code: 851
Public phones are located in booths, pubs, restaurants and post offices. Calls are based on a time limit, and additional coins will have to be added if you continue a long conversation. Long-distance calls are called

EUROPE

"trunk calls" and collect calls are known as "reverse charge" calls. Calls to emergency services are free. Dial 999 and ask for assistance.

Telex facilities can be found in major hotels and at Electra House, Victoria Embankment, London.

Telegrams can be sent by phone or from a post office.

Excellent postal service available, including other highspeed delivery service.

Air Travel

Seven domestic airlines provide frequent service to 21 major airports in the country. Service is expensive, however, and train travel preferred by most British business people.

Other Transport

British Rail competes directly and well with the airlines for inter-city services, because trains are cheaper and distances are relatively short, except the London to Scotland route.

Buses are also good value, since roads and motorways are in good shape and provide an extensive network.

There are also 3,000 km of navigable inland waterways, and an extensive sea-ferry service to the continent.

The roads, especially the highways (M routes), are very good and car rentals are a preferred method of business travel as long as the distances are not great, and as long as North Americans rememeber that driving is on the left side of the road.

BIRMINGHAM

Airport Information

Time
GMT

GMT +1 (Mar 21 - Oct 23)

Airport
Birmingham International (Elmdon) BHX
Tel: (021) 7436227
10.5 km (6.5 mi) E of the city
International and domestic flights

Airlines
Aer Lingus 0345010101
Air Canada 6439807
Air France 4999511
British Airways 2367000
Gulf Air 6325931
JAL 6431368
KLM 6430991
Lufthansa 6438568
Qantas 2363824
Sabena 4376950
SAS 6434778
Swissair 7827882

Transport to City
Taxis: The fare for the 30-minute trip from the airport to Birmingham is about L6, with an extra charge of 25% for destinations more than 16 km from the centre of the city.
Coach: Hotel courtesy coach available for the Excelsior Hotel.
Transit: Buses #58 and 159 leave every 10 minutes for the 50-minute trip to the city. The fare is 75p, and the bus returns from High St. or New St. Railway Station. There is also a regular train service from a terminal 1 km from the airport. Follow signs marked "Transit Link," and ride the magnetic levitation vehicle to the railway station. Trains depart every 20 minutes for the 15-minute ride and the fare is 70p. Trains return from New St. Station.

Facilities
Bar, buffet, restaurant, bank with currency exchange, post office, baggage deposit, hotel reservations, information desk. Duty-free shop sells tobacco products, wines, spirits,

liqueurs, cameras, lighters, watches, radios and jewellery. Car rental desks: Hertz, Avis, Europcar.

Airport Taxes
None

City Information

Weather
Weather in Birmingham is generally clear, sunny and warm during the summer months but days can be changeable with showers. Winters are cool and wet but it rarely snows. When it does the city is in chaos. Heavy rubber boots, umbrellas, and raincoats should be carried during the winter months; medium weight clothes and an umbrella during the summer months.

Transportation
Birmingham taxis can be hailed in the street, at cab stands, or can be reached by phone. Taxi drivers can be a wealth of information. Basic fare is about 80p plus 20p per half km. There may be extra charges.
Bus system is extensive and efficient, though crowded at rush hour. Bus service comes rapidly to a halt after 2300. Taxis are in order after midnight.

Car Hire
Hertz, 7 Suffolk St. (tel: 7825158)
Ansa, 23 Erdington (tel: 3730456)
Avis, Park St. (tel: 7826183)
Budget, Prestige House,
    Holloway Head (tel: 6430493)
Europcar, Monaco House
    (tel: 9505050)
InterRent, Dudley Rd., Spring
    Hill (tel: 4547671)

EUROPE

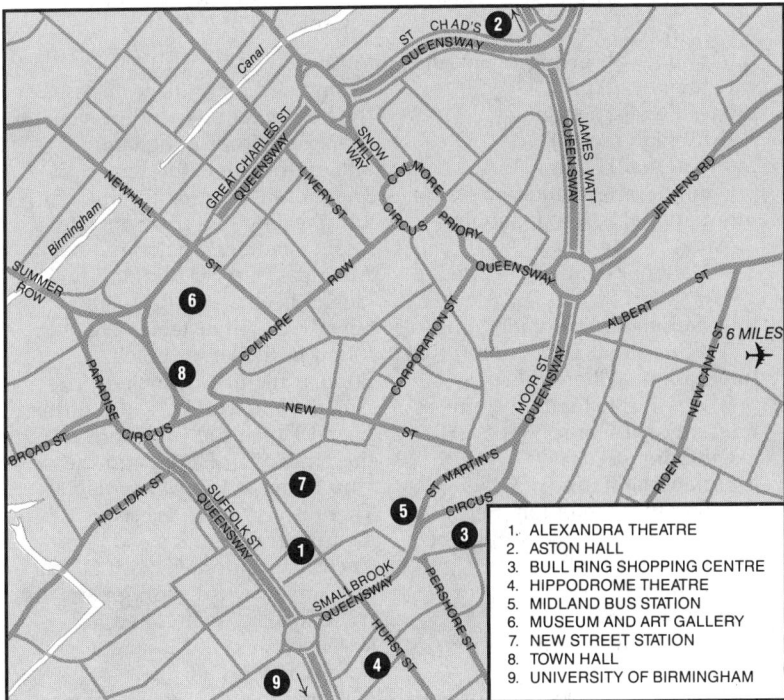

1. ALEXANDRA THEATRE
2. ASTON HALL
3. BULL RING SHOPPING CENTRE
4. HIPPODROME THEATRE
5. MIDLAND BUS STATION
6. MUSEUM AND ART GALLERY
7. NEW STREET STATION
8. TOWN HALL
9. UNIVERSITY OF BIRMINGHAM

Birmingham

InterRent, Dudley Rd., Spring
Hill (tel: 4547671)

Hospitals
Medical care in Birmingham, like
the rest of the U.K., is free to
British and some foreign citizens.

Trade Fairs
International Holiday and Trade
Fair (Jan)
International Giftware Fair (Feb)
Marketing & Promotion Services
Exhibition (Feb)
International Electro-Technical
Exhibition (Feb)
Glass & Glass Technology
Exhibition (Mar)
International Food Processing
Exhibition (Mar)
International Handling & Storage
Exhibition (Mar)
International Motor Trade
Exhibition (Mar)
International Antiques Fair
(April)
International Confectionary Fair
(April)
International Brewing & Bottling
Exhibition (April)
International Packaging
Exhibition (April)
International Heating & Air
Conditioning Exhibition (May)
International Safety Exhibition
(May)
The National Home & Garden
Fair (May)
International Refrigeration and
Air Condition Exhibition (June)
International Chemical &
Processing Exhibition (June)
International Home Video & TV
Exhibition (Aug)
International Foundry Castings
& Forging Exhibition (Sept)
International Metal-Cutting Tools
Exhibition (Sept)
International Metallurgical
Exhibition (Sept)
Water Pollution Control
Exhibition (Sept)
International Semiconductor Fair
(Sept)

The Design Engineering Fair
(Sept)
Factory Efficiency Fair (Sept)
Exotic & Fine Wine Fair (Sept)
Household Textiles Fair (Sept)
The British Motor Exhibition
(Oct)

Hotels
Albany, Smallbrook, Queensway
(tel: 6438171)
Grand, Colmore Row
(tel: 2367951)
Imperial Centre, Temple St.
(tel: 6436751)
Metropole, National Exhibition
Centre (tel: 7804242)
Midland, New St. (tel: 6432601)
Plough & Harrow, Hagley Rd.
(tel: 4544111)
Post House, Chapel Lane
(tel: 3577444)
The Royal Angus, St. Chad's,
Queensway (tel: 3464211)
Strathallan, 225 Hagley Rd.
(tel: 4559777)
Warwick, National Exhibition
Centre (7804242)

What to See and Do
Dining and nightlife seem to be
the best ways of spending your
spare time in Birmingham,
although there is the Repertory
Theatre, Birmingham Cathedral,
and the City Library. Some good
local restaurants include
Amandas, Carver's Table, Iron
Horse, Peels, and the
Silverbirch, all of which are
found in the larger hotels.
Popular nightspots include The
American or The Backyard at the
Grand Hotel, the Claymore at
the Strathallan Hotel, and the
Gun Room at the Albany Hotel.
There is also some excellent
shopping. For radios and
electronic equipment visit Global
on Conventry Rd.; for apparel
try Mates or Austin Reed; for
jewellery shop at Montague or
Perry Graves; and for
department stores try Rochams
or Binibeca.

Useful Addresses

Embassies and Consulates
Canadian: 2 St. Philip's Pl.
(tel: 2332127)

Business and Commerce
Birmingham Chamber of
Industry and Commerce,
Harborne Rd. (tel: 4546171)

Tourism and Travel
Automobile Assoc., 1134 New
Street
Tourist Information Office,
Council House, Victoria
Square (tel: 2353411)
American Express, 17-19
Martineau Sq. (tel: 2332141)
Thomas Cook, 99 New St.
(tel: 6435142)

EDINBURGH

Airport Information

Time
GMT
GMT +1 (Mar 21 - Oct 23)

Airport
Edinburgh International EDI
Tel: (031) 3331000
11 km (7 mi) W of the city
International and domestic
flights

Airlines
Aer Lingus 2257392
British Airways 2252525
British Caledonian 600700
Iberia 2259257
KLM 2253978

Transport to City
Taxis: Airport taxis are metered
and can take four people. Fare is
between L6-8 but no extras. The
trip to Edinburgh takes 20
minutes. Taxi stands located
near Door D, between Gates 3 &
4. Tip driver 15%.
Coach: Hotel courtesy coaches to
Royal Scot and Edinburgh Crest
Hotels.

Transit: Bus marked "Airlink
#100" leaves from outside Door
D. Half-hourly service to the city
costs L1.65, with stops at
Ingliston, Maybury, Drum Brae,
Zoo, Murray Field, Haymarket,
West End, Waverley Station.
Ride takes 30 minutes. Bus
returns from Waverley Bridge
Bus Station off Princess St.

Facilities
Bar, buffet, restaurant, bank
with currency exchange, hotel
reservations, baggage deposit,
nursery, information desk.
Duty-free shop sells tobacco
products, aperitifs, spirits, and
liqueurs. Major credit cards
accepted.
Car rental desks: Hertz, Avis,
Europcar, Swan National

Airport Taxes
None

City Information

Weather
Climate is generally temperate
and wet, with heavier rains in
winter than in summer.
Summers can be cool and windy,
but
the weather is changeable on
any given day. In winter, storms
regularly lash the North Sea off
Edinburgh. In summer
lightweight clothing with a
raincoat is sufficient; in winter
medium weight clothing together
with a raincoat or umbrella is
advisable.

Transportation
Taxis, buses and inter-city trains
are available. Check for local
fares based on distance.

Car Hire
Hertz, 10 Picardy Pl.
(tel: 5568311 & 3331019)
Ansa-Kenning, 40 Duff St.
(tel: 3378145)
Auto-Europe (tel: 3378145)

EUROPE

Avis, 100 Dairy Rd. (tel: 3376363
& 3331866)
Budget, Comley Bank
(tel: 3325054)
Europcar, 24 East London St.
(tel: 5573456 & 3332588)
InterRent, St. Andrew Sq.
(tel: 5565515)
Kemwel, 136 Glasgow Rd.
(tel: 3342214)

Hospitals
The National Health Service
provides free emergency medical
services to visitors in local
hospitals. For local hospitals,
contact your hotel receptionist.

Trade Fairs
Golf Trade Exhibition (Feb)
Royal Highland Exhibition (June)

Hotels
Barnton, Queen's Ferry Rd.
(tel: 3391144)
Caledonian, Prince's St.
(tel: 2252433)
Carlton, North Bridge
(tel: 5567277)

Edinburgh Crest, Queen's Ferry
Rd. (tel: 3322442)
Ellersly House, Ellersly Rd.
(tel: 3376888)
George, 19 George St.
(tel: 2251251)
King James, St. James Ctr.
(tel: 5560111)
North British, 53 Prince's St.
(tel: 5562414)
Oratava, Craigmillar P.
(tel: 6679484)
Post House, Corstorphine Rd.
(tel: 3348221)
Roxburghe, Charlotte Sq.
(tel: 2253921)
Royal Scot, 111 Glasgow Rd.
(tel: 3349191)
Sheraton, 1 Festival Square
(tel: 2299131)
Stakis Grosvenor, Grosvenor St.
(tel: 2266001)

What to See and Do
Noteworthy sightseeing trips
must include Edinburgh Castle,
the Palace of Holy Rood House,
St. Giles Cathedral, Chapel of

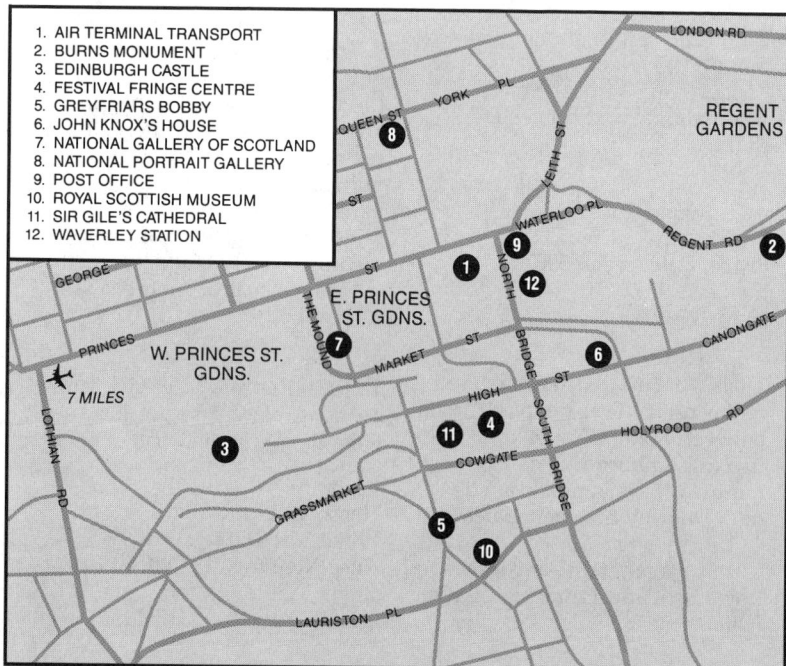

1. AIR TERMINAL TRANSPORT
2. BURNS MONUMENT
3. EDINBURGH CASTLE
4. FESTIVAL FRINGE CENTRE
5. GREYFRIARS BOBBY
6. JOHN KNOX'S HOUSE
7. NATIONAL GALLERY OF SCOTLAND
8. NATIONAL PORTRAIT GALLERY
9. POST OFFICE
10. ROYAL SCOTTISH MUSEUM
11. SIR GILE'S CATHEDRAL
12. WAVERLEY STATION

Edinburgh

the Most Ancient and Most Noble Order of the Thistle, Parliament House, Cannonball House, Scot Monument, the Museum of Childhood, Royal Scottish Academy, and the National Museum of Antiquities. Some of the better restaurants include the Consort in the Roxburghe Hotel, Cousteau's, Denzler's, the Garden Room at the Ellersly House Hotel, and Le Figaro at the Barnton Hotel. Popular nightspots include Happy Sam's at North British Hotel, Cocktail at the Carlton Hotel, Edinburgh at the Royal Scot Hotel, and the Lothian Lounge at the Caledonian Hotel. Popular shopping trips should include Binns Department Store on Prince's St., James Grant & Company on Northbridge St. and Mappin & Webb on George St.

Useful Addresses

Embassies and Consulates

American: 3 Regent Terrace
   (tel: 5568315)

Business and Commerce

Institute of Bankers in Scotland,
   20 Rutland Sq.
   (tel: 2299869)
Bank of Scotland, The Mound
   (tel: 2292555)
Royal Bank of Scotland PLC,
   Box 31, 42 St. Andrews Sq.
   (tel: 5568555)
Edinburgh Chamber of
   Commerce & Manufacturers,
   3 Randolph Crescent
   (tel: 2255851)

Tourism and Travel

Royal Auto Club, 17 Rutand
   Square
Scottish Tourist Board, Ravelston
   Terrace (tel: 3322433)
Tourist Information Office, 5
   Waverley Bridge (tel: 3322433)
American Express, 139 Prince's
   St. (tel: 2257881)
Thomas Cook, 9-11 Castle St.
   (tel: 2257125)

EUROPE

IT'S THE WAY WE MAKE YOU FEEL.

On British Airways business class, CLUB, it's not simply the exceptional service, the attention to detail or even the high comfort level that makes the difference. It's the way we make you feel.

British Airways understands the pressures facing today's business people and that's why we've created CLUB, a truly unique stress-free environment. Which allows you to perform to your potential.

CLUB

BRITISH AIRWAYS
The world's favourite airline.

LONDON

Airport Information

Time
GMT
GMT +1 (Mar - Oct)

Airports
Gatwick International LGW
Tel: (0293) 28822
43 km (27 mi) S of the city
International and domestic
flights

Heathrow International LHR
Tel: (01) 7594321
24 km (15 mi) W of the city
International and domestic
flights

Airlines
Aer Lingus 7341212
Aeroflot 4921764
Air Algerie 4875709
Air Canada 7592636
Air France 4999511
Air India 4917979
Air New Zealand 9303434
Alia 7342557
Alitalia 6027111
American 8345151
Austrian 4390741
Avensa 5689144
Avianca 4081889
British Airways 3705411
British Caledonian 6684222
CAAC 7114052
Canadian International 9305664
Cathay Pacific 9307878
Delta 6680935
Eastern 517622
Egyptair 7342395
El Al 4379255
Finnair 4081222
Garuda 4372918
Gulf Air 4081717

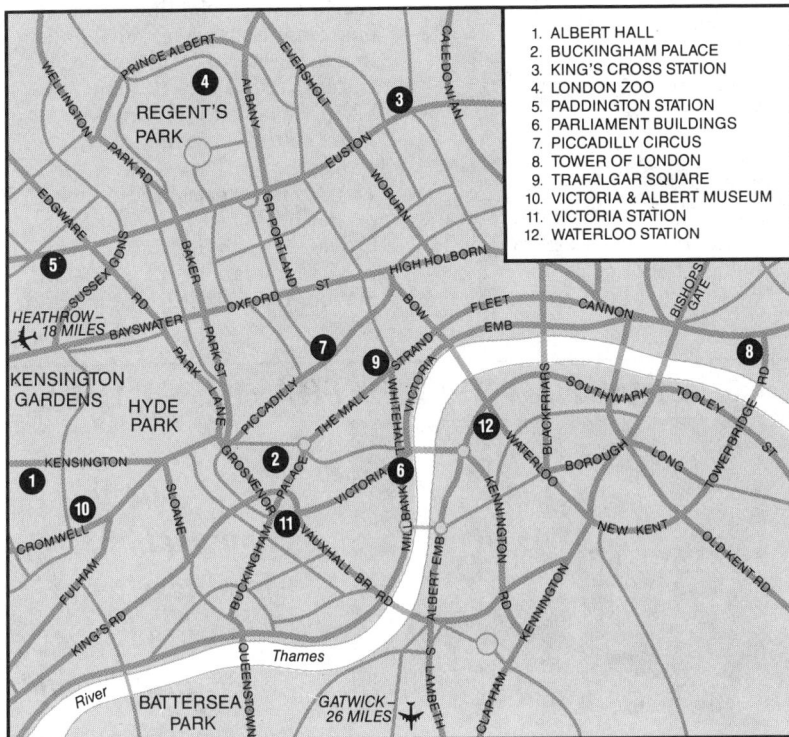

1. ALBERT HALL
2. BUCKINGHAM PALACE
3. KING'S CROSS STATION
4. LONDON ZOO
5. PADDINGTON STATION
6. PARLIAMENT BUILDINGS
7. PICCADILLY CIRCUS
8. TOWER OF LONDON
9. TRAFALGAR SQUARE
10. VICTORIA & ALBERT MUSEUM
11. VICTORIA STATION
12. WATERLOO STATION

EUROPE

London

Iberia 4375622
Iran Air 4913656
Iraqi 9301155
JAL 4081000
KLM 5689144
Korean 9306513
Kuwait Air 4866666
Lufthansa 4080442
Malaysian 4914542
MEA 4935681
Northwest 6295353
Olympic 8469080
Pan Am 4090688
Philippine 6296767
PIA 7419374
Qantas 0345747767
SAA 4379621
Sabena 4376960
SAS 7344020
Saudia 9957777
Singapore 7470007
Swissair 4394144
Syrian 4932853
TAP 8280262
Thai 4999113
THY 4999247
TWA 4390707
UTA 4934881
United 9970179
Varig 6295824

Transport to City
Gatwick
Taxis: Taxis are metered and the 45-minute trip to central London will cost about L30.
Coach: Flightline bus #777 leaves every half hour to Victoria Coach Station. The 70-minute trip will cost about L3 and there is room for luggage. Driver loads and unloads baggage. Hotel courtesy coaches also available.
Transit: There is rail service provided by Railair Link to London leaving every 15 minutes. Trains take 30-minutes and cost between L5-7. They are supplementary to regular British Rail Service which makes more stops and is generally slower to Victoria Railway Station.

Heathrow
Taxis: Black cabs are metered, with a fare about L20 to Piccadilly Circus downtown. There is an extra charge of 20p per passenger, plus 5p tip for each piece of luggage. Tip drivers 15%.
Coach: There is half-hourly coach service (Flightline #767 bus) from each air terminal and the bus terminal to Victoria Coach Station. Fare is about L2.50, payable to the driver. Hotel courtesy coaches also available.
Transit: Two special red double-decker buses, A1 and A2, provide bus service. Bus A1 goes to Victoria Station, A2 to Euston Station, the former providing

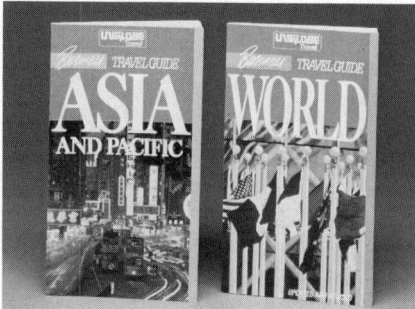

more frequent service. Both trips take about an hour, with other stops enroute, and the fare is L3.00, payable to the driver. Subway: (Underground) line runs to Central London, with trains leaving every 4 minutes at peak times, every 10 minutes at other times. The L1.60 ticket (to Piccadilly) can be purchased at a counter or machines for the 45-minute trip to the city. Little room for luggage.

Inter-Airport Transit: There are two services operating between Heathrow and Gatwick airports. Green Line Bus #747 operates from all terminals and the Central Bus Station every half-hour for L4.50. Speedlink runs buses every 20 minutes between airports, and the trip takes about 50 minutes.

Facilities
Gatwick (1 terminal)
Bar, buffet, coffeeshop, restaurants, bank with currency exchange, insurance, hotel reservations, post office, baggage deposit, information desk, nurseries, medical center. Duty-free shop sells tobacco products, wines, aperitifs, spirits, liqueurs, cameras, lighters. Most foreign currencies accepted.
Car rental desks: Hertz, Avis, Europcar

Heathrow (3 terminals)
Bar, buffet, restaurant, bank with currency exchange, insurance, hotel reservations, post office, baggage deposit, nursery, information desk, barber shop.
Duty-free shops sell tobacco products, wine, aperitifs, spirits, liqueurs, lighters, watches, perfumes, gifts. Major currencies and credit cards accepted.

Car rental desks: Hertz, Avis, Europcar, Swan National

Airport Taxes
None

City Information

Weather
London can be quite mild year-round but also quickly changeable. Rain is frequent and unpredictable, especially in winter, but summers are usually bright and warm. Temperatures average 4 C (40 F) in January, 18 C (64 F) in July.

Transportation
The distinctive black taxis with their fold-down reverse back seats are numerous, and can be hailed in the street, at stands, or booked by phone. London cabbies must complete a two-year course in taxi training, so they know the streets well. Basic fare is 80p to L1, plus 20p per half-km. There are also extra charges for passengers, unusual luggage, and night or weekend journeys.
Bus and subway systems are extensive though not always interlinked. Many surface routes still worked by those distinctive red double-deckers, though they are gradually disappearing, except on tourist routes. Subway system is very old, with some stations far underground, but still the fastest way to get between two points. Fares vary per distance travelled, and tickets are purchased based on where you wish to exit the system.

Car Hire
Hertz, 200 Buckingham (tel: 6791799 & 8973347)
Ansa, Heathrow Airport (tel: 9495241)
Auto-Europe (tel: 9683388)

EUROPE

Avis, 68 North Row (tel: 8488733
& 8979321)
Budget, 50 Curzon St.
(tel: 7592216)
Europcar, Victoria Station
(tel: 9505050 & 8970811)
Foremost-Euro (tel: 7270123)
Godfrey-Davis, Davis House
SW1 (8346701)
InterRent, Horseferry Road,
Westminster (tel: 9959242)
Kemwel, Heathrow Airport (tel:
8973232)

Hospitals
Emergency hospital services as
well as most medical care in
general is provided free to
Britons and some foreigners. The
emergency number is 999 for
hospital and ambulance services.

Trade Fairs
International Boat Exhibition
   (Jan)
International Lighting Exhibition
   (Jan)
Amusement Trades Exhibition
   (Jan)
Stationery Industry Exhibition
   (Jan)
The International Flooring
   Exhibition (Jan)
International Toy & Hobby Fair
   (Jan)
International Hotel & Catering
   Exhibition (Jan)
Electronics, Oil & Gas Exhibition
   (Feb)
International Golf Exhibition
   (Feb)
International Frozen Foods
   Exhibition (Feb)
International Automotive Parts
   Exhibition (Feb)
International Computer Graphics
   Fair (Feb)
Sound & Communications
   Exhibition (Feb)
The Fashion Fair (Feb)
Swimming Pool & Leisure Fair
   (Feb)
International Men's & Boys'
   Wear Exhibition (Feb)

International Power Supply
   Exhibition (Mar)
Plastics Market Exhibition (Mar)
International Electronics
   Exhibition (Mar)
Designer Shoes Exhibition (Mar)
Business Travel Exhibition (Mar)
Information Technology
   Exhibition (Mar)
Fashion Fabrics Exhibition (Mar)
International Book Fair (April)
Leather Trades Fair (April)
International Health & Safety
   Exhibition (April)
Electronics Retailing Exhibition
   (April)
Marine Electronics Exhibition
   (April)
The Audio Visual Fair (April)
The International Cleaning &
   Maintenance Exhibition (April)
Electronics Components Fair
   (April)
Jewellery & Sterling Silver
   Exhibition (May)
International Interior Design
   Exhibition (May)
International Furniture
   Exhibition (May)
Biotech Europe Exhibition (May)
Wine Trade Fair (May)
International Contemporary Art
   Fair (May)
Chemical & Industrial Trade Fair
   (June)
Advanced Manufacturing
   Technology Exhibition (June)
Advertising Industry Exhibition
   (June)
International Water Exhibition
   (July)
International Watch & Jewellery
   Exhibition (Aug)
International Women's Wear
   Exhibition (Sept)
International Bus & Coach
   Exhibition (Sept)
International Hair & Beauty
   Exhibition (Sept)
International Fashion Shoe
   Exhibition (Sept)
International Flower Trades
   Exhibition (Oct)

National Graphic Design
Exhibition (Oct)
International Design &
Technology Exhibition (Oct)
International Concrete Exhibition
(Oct)
The Caravan & Camping
Exhibition (Nov)
The Mid-Season Fashion
Exhibition (Nov)
World Travel Market (Nov)
International Crafts Exhibition
(Nov)

Hotels

The Athenaeum Court,116
Piccadilly (tel: 4993464)
Basil, Basil St. (tel: 5813311)
The Berkeley, Wilton Pl.
(tel: 2356000)
Bloomsbury Crest, Coram St.
(tel: 8371200)
The Bristol, 3 Berkeley St.
(tel: 4938282)
Britannia, Grosvenor Sq.
(tel: 6299400)
Browns, Dover & Albemarie Sts.
(tel: 4936020)
Cavendish, Jermyn St.
(tel: 9302111)
Charing Cross, The Strand
(tel: 8397282)
Claridges, Brook St.
(tel: 6298860)
Clifton-Ford, Welbeck St.
(tel: 4866600)
Connaught, Carlos Pl.
(tel: 4997070)
Cunard International,1
Shortlands Way (tel: 7411555)
Dorchester, Park Lane
(tel: 6298888)
Grosvenor House, Park Lane
(tel: 4996363)
Holiday Inn, 1 Berkeley St.
(tel: 4938282)
Hyatt Carleton Tower, Cadogan
Pl. (tel:2456570)
The Hyde Park, 66 Knightsbridge
(tel: 2352000)
Inn on the Park, Hamilton Place
(tel: 4990888)
InterContinental, 1 Hamilton
Place (tel: 4093131)

Kensington Hilton, Holland Park
Ave. (tel: 6033355)
London Hilton, 22 Park Lawn
(tel: 4938000)
The Mayfair, Stratton St.
(tel: 6297777)
Novotel London, 1 Shortlands
(tel: 7411555)
Park Lane, Piccadilly
(tel: 4996321)
Royal Garden, Kensington High
St. (tel: 9378000)
Savoy, The Strand (tel: 8364343)
Sheraton Belgravia, 20 Chesham
Pl. (tel: 2356040)
Sheraton Park, 101 Knightsbridge
(tel: 2358050)
Stafford, 16 St. James Pl.
(tel: 4930111)
The Waldorf, Aldwych
(tel: 8362400)
Westbury, New Bond St.
(tel: 6297755)

What to See and Do

Sightseeing: The Tower of
London, Westminster Abbey, St.
Paul's Cathedral, Houses of
Parliament, Buckingham Palace
(changing of the Guard 1130),
the British Museum, the
National Gallery, the National
Portrait Gallery, Tate Gallery,
Victoria and Albert Museum,
Hyde Park, Regent's Park,
National Army Museum, Mme.
Tussaud's Wax Museum, Marble
Arch, and Speaker's Corner,
Palace of St. James, Oxford
Circus, Piccadilly Circus,
Trafalgar Square.
Activities: For the culture-
minded, performances at the
Royal Opera House (Covent
Garden), Festival Hall, Albert
Hall, and by the National Opera
Company and by the Royal
Shakespeare Company are a
must on any trip to London.
Nightlife: Popular nighttime
haunts are many, but should
include clubs and cabarets like
Quaglino's, the Latin Quarter,

EUROPE

Tramp, or the Rock Garden (Covent Garden).

Sports: London has 9 football teams, several of which are bound to be playing at home on any given Saturday between Sept and May. There are also several rugby and cricket grounds, golf courses, and horse-racing tracks in and around the city. Tennis can be played with a minimal fee in local parks.

Pubs: As a quiet relaxing alternative to any of the above, go on a pub crawl in the neighborhood of your hotel. Pub life is still the most important, even crucial form of socializing in Great Britain. North American has nothing like it for conversation and camaraderie.

Useful Addresses

Embassies and Consulates

American: 24 Grosvenor Sq. W1 (tel: 4999000)
Australia: 10 Maltravers St. WC2 (tel: 4388000)
Canadian: 1 Grosvenor Sq. W1 (tel: 6299492)
French: 58 Knightsbridge SW1 (tel: 2358080)
German (West), 23 Belgrave Sq. (tel: 2355033)
Indian: India House Aldwych WC2 (tel: 8368484)
Japanese: 43 Grovesnor St. W1 (tel: 4936030)

Business and Commerce

Bank of England, Threadneedle St. (tel: 6014444)
ECC, 20 Densington Palace Gdns. (tel: 7278090)
Stock Exchange, Old Broad St. (tel: 5882355)
American Chamber of Commerce, 75 Brook St. (tel: 4930381)
The Canada-U.K. Chamber of Commerce, 3 Regent St. (tel: 9302794)

London Chamber of Commerce, 69 Cannon St. (tel: 2484444)
United Kingdom Chamber of Commerce, 1 Lower Regent St. (tel: 9302794)
U.S.A. Trade Center, 24 Grosvenor Sq. (tel: 6730581)
Central Government Office of Information, Hercules Rd. (tel: 9282345)

Tourism and Travel

British Tourist Authority, 64 St. James (tel: 8469000)
Automobile Association, Farnum House, Basingstoke Hants. (tel: 20123)
Royal Automobile Club, P.O. Box 100, Lansdowne Rd., Croydon (tel: 6862525)
American Express, 6 Haymarket (tel: 9304411)
American Express, 78 Brompton Rd. (tel: 5846182)
American Express, 85 High St., Wimbledon Village (tel: 9476281 & 9466813)
Deak International, 22 Leinater Terrace W2 (tel: 4025128)
Deak International, 15 Shaftsbury Ave. W1
Deak International, 4-8 Victoria Bldgs., Terminus Pl. SW1
Deak International, 237 Oxford Street W1
Deak International, 4-5 Tower Place EC3
Deak International, 2 London Street W2
Deak International, Liverpool St., Mainline Station
Deak International, 177 Portobello Road W11
Deak International, 3-5 coventry Street W1
Deak International, Kings Cross Main Station NW1
Thomas Cook, 45 Berkeley St. (tel: 4994000)

MANCHESTER

Airport Information

Time
GMT
GMT +1 (Mar 21-Oct 23)

Airport
Manchester International
(Ringway) MAN
Tel: (061) 4375233
16 km (10 mi) S of the city
International and domestic
flights

Airlines
Aer Lingus 8328611
Air Canada 4893000
Air France 4363800
Air New Zealand 8323266
Alitalia 2281653
British Airways 2286311
British Caledonian 600700
El Al 8324208
Finnair 4362400
Gulf Air 8329677
Iberia 4366444
JAL 8322807
KLM 5689144
Kuwait Air 8344161
Lufthansa 4363018
Northwest 4992471
Olympic 8325236
Qantas 747767
Sabena 4992326
SAS 4991335
Swissair 8328161

Transport to City
Taxis: Traditional black taxis to
central locations charge about
L6, plus 10p for each additional
passenger and per bag. For

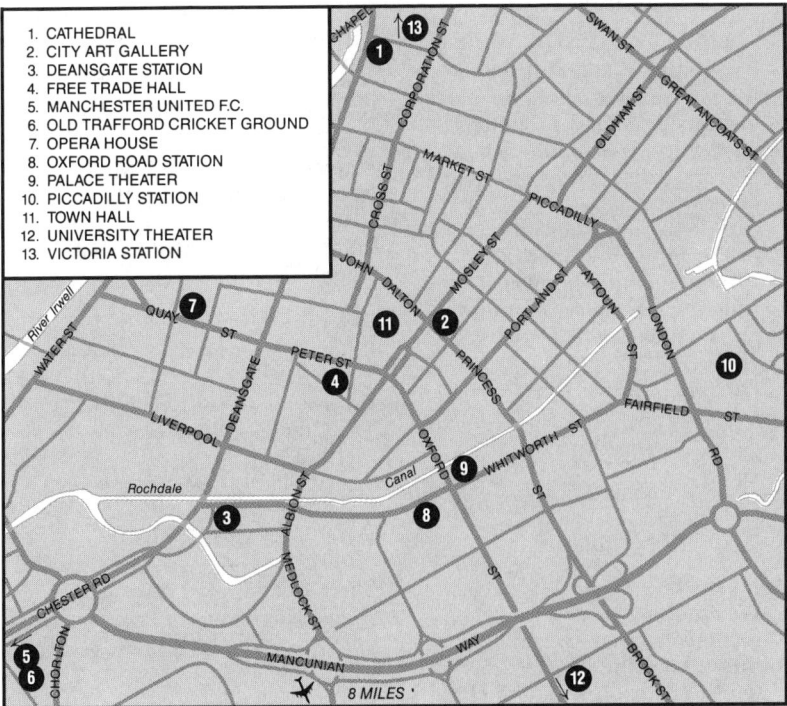

1. CATHEDRAL
2. CITY ART GALLERY
3. DEANSGATE STATION
4. FREE TRADE HALL
5. MANCHESTER UNITED F.C.
6. OLD TRAFFORD CRICKET GROUND
7. OPERA HOUSE
8. OXFORD ROAD STATION
9. PALACE THEATER
10. PICCADILLY STATION
11. TOWN HALL
12. UNIVERSITY THEATER
13. VICTORIA STATION

Manchester

EUROPE

destinations outside the city, settle on a fee with the driver first.

Coach: City-operated coaches outside the Arrivals hall have 3 destinations: Chorlton St. Coach Station, Piccadilly Station, and Victoria Station. Buses leave every half hour, and luggage space is available. The fare is L1. Transit: Buses outside domestic or international terminals depart every 20 minutes or 30 minutes depending on time of day. The L1-trip takes 1 hour with frequent stops. Buses stop at Chorlton St., Portland St., Piccadilly Gardens, Oxford Rd., Arndale Centre, and Albert Sq. Baggage racks are available. Train service runs from Heald Green Station, 3 km from the airport. Buy ticket at the station for L1.20 for the 15-minute ride to Piccadilly Station.

Facilities

Bar, buffet, restaurant, bank with currency exchange, insurance, hotel reservations, post office, barber shop, nursery, flowers, gifts, candy, meeting point.

Duty-free shop sells tobacco products, wines, aperitifs, spirits, liqueurs, lighters, watches, jewellery, perfume, glass, china, leather goods, toys and pens.

Car rental desks: Hertz, Avis, Europcar

Airport Taxes

None

City Information

Weather

Weather is very changeable. Rainfalls spread evenly throughout the year. Winters tend to be cool, wet, and cloudy, while summers are warm and wet. Coastal area very windy. Light clothes in summer,

including raincoat or umbrella are recommended. Medium weight clothes, rubber boots, and raincoat are a must in winter.

Transportation

Taxis can be hailed in the street, at taxi stands, or called by phone. Cabs normally charge 80p-L1 plus 20-30p for each half-km driven. Extra charges for large number of passengers or extra pieces of luggage. Tip taxi drivers 10%.

Bus service offers the best way of seeing the city cheaply. Fares based on distance travelled.

Car Hire

Hertz, Ringway Airport
  (tel: 4378208 & 4893215)
Ansa-Kenning, Valley Lodge
  Hotel (tel: 6432240)
Avis, Piccadilly Station
  (tel: 4362020)
Budget, Ringway Airport
  (tel: 9981711)
Europcar, Piccadilly Plaza
  (4376161 & 9505050)
Foremost-Euro (tel: 8348151)
InterRent, 615 Oldham Rd.
  (tel: 2056221)
Kemwel, 615 Oldham Rd.
  (tel: 4363290)

Hotels

Britannia, Portland St.
  (tel: 2282288)
Excelsior, Airport (tel: 4375811)
The Grand, Aytoun St.
  (tel: 2369559)
The Midland, Peter St.
  (tel: 2363333)
Piccadilly, Piccadilly Plaza
  (tel: 2368414)
The Portland, 3-5 Portland St.
  (tel: 2283400)
Post House, Palantine Rd.
  (tel: 9987090)
Stanney Lands, Airport
  (tel: 525225)
Willow Bank, 340 Wilmslow Rd.
  (tel: 2240461)

What to See and Do

Visit John Ryland's Library, the Free Trade Hall, Platt Hall, the Atheneum, Belle Vue Zoological Gardens, the City Art Gallery, Halle Orchestra or Royal Exchange Theatre. Some good restaurants include Angelique's at the Portland Hotel, Casa Espana, La Marmite on Faulkner St., La Terrazza, and Templars in the Grand Hotel. Nightspots include Highlander in the Portland Hotel, and Astro in the Excelsior Hotel. Major department stores include Kendal Mine in Deansgate, and Liberty & Co. Ltd., 16 King St.

Useful Addresses

Embassies and Consulates
Canadian: Barlow House
(tel: 2360682)

Business and Commerce
Manchester Chamber of Commerce & Industry, 56 Oxford St. (tel: 2363210)
Cooperative Bank, Box 101, Balloon St. (tel: 8323456)

Tourism and Travel
Royal Auto Club, 135 Dickenson Rd.
Tourist Information Office, Town Hall, Albert Square (tel: 2363377)
American Express, 1 Cross St. (tel: 8330121)
Thomas Cook, 2 Oxford St. (tel: 2360754)

YUGOSLAVIA

Essential Information

Type of Government
Federal Republic

Area
255,804 sq km
(99,000 sq mi)

Population
23.1 million

Annual Growth Rate
0.7%

Languages
Macedonian (official), Serbo-Croatian, Slovenian, Albanian, Hungarian, Italian

Religion
Eastern Orthodox 41%, Roman Catholic 32%, Islamic 12%, atheist 12%, other 3%

Ethnic Groups
Serbs 36%, Croats 19.7%, Bosnian Moslems 8.9%, Slovenes 7.8%, Albanian 7.7%, Macedonians 5.9%, Yugoslavs 5.4%, Montenegrins 2.5%, Hungarians 1.9%, Gypsies, Turks, Slovaks, Romanians and others

Weights and Measures
Metric

Electrical Current
AC 50c 220/380 V

Major Business Cities
Belgrade (cap) 1,750,000
Zagreb 975,000
Ljubljana 350,000
Sarajevo 495,000
Skopje 575,000
Novi Sad 260,000
Pristina 210,000
Titograd 132,000

Currency
1 Dinar = 100 para
Notes 10, 20, 50, 100, 500 and 1,000 dinar
Coins 10, 20 and 50 para. 1, 2, 5 and 10 dinar

Public Holidays
Jan 1 New Year's Day
May 1-2 May Day
July 4 War Veterans' Day

EUROPE

Nov 29-30 National (Day of the Republic)

Travellers Information

Entry Requirements

Passport is required by all visitors. Visas not required by nationals of most European countries. For others, visas for up to 3 months can be obtained at frontier posts or a Yugoslavian embassies and consulates. All visitors must register with officials 48 hours after arrival.

Working Restrictions

All foreigners must obtain a work permit.

Vaccination Required

Vaccination only against Typhoid is recommended. Cholera and smallpox vaccinations required only if travelling from an infected area.

Customs and Duty-Free

On arrival: 200 cigarets or 50 cigars or 250 gr of tobacco; 1 L spirits, 1 L wine; perfume for personal use. Pets need a vaccination certificate.

Currency Restrictions

Maximum of 1500 dinars per calendar year may be imported or exported. Import of foreign currencies has no restrictions.

Health Tips

Tap water is purified and safe to drink in major cities. Good medical service is available to travellers, and at a reasonable cost.

Climate and Clothing

Yugoslavia is a fairly large country, with a Mediterranean climate (hot and dry) along the Adriatic Coast, an Alpine climate (cold and wet) in the mountain areas, and a temperate climate (warm and dry) throughout the rest of the country.

Winters on the coast are mild. Temperatures average 18C (65F). Wear light to medium weight clothing. In the mountains it is cold. Temperatures 5C (40F) require heavy clothing with hat and boots.

In summer it is hot along the coast and in the central region. Temperatures average 30C (85F). Wear tropical weight clothing. In the mountains it is cool, especially at night. Medium weight clothing with a jacket for the evenings.

Tipping

Restaurants, hotels and nightclubs usually include a tip of 10% in the bill, but 5-10% additional is the custom for staff. Tip taxis 10%. Barbers, porters, and other service persons will require a tip of 50 to 100 dinars depending on the service.

Food and Drink

An extensive variety of many ethnic dishes make Yugoslavia a real treat for the gastronomic traveller. Specialties made from lamb, mutton, chicken, and (on the coast) fish, mainly spiced with paprika and other exotic spices are widely available, and only dishes containing beef are expensive.

Pastries, ice cream, fruits and chocolate are widely available as are huge bunches of figs, dates and grapes which can be eaten with the excellent local yoghurt. Breakfasts are continental-style with bread and coffee. Lunch (served around 1400) is the main meal of the day, when all activity ceases for the repast. Dinners are light and consumed in the late evening.

Yugoslavian beer is very good as are some of the wines which are available throughout the country and are extremely cheap.

Business Brief

GDP
$80.2 billion
(per capita income $3,466)

Annual Growth Rate
1.7%

Natural Resources
Coal, copper, bauxite, timber, iron, antimony, chromium, lead, zinc, asbestos, mercury

Agriculture
Corn, wheat, tobacco, sugar beets, livestock

Industry
Wood, food processing, non-ferrous metals, machines, textiles, leather goods, construction

Imports
Total $12 billion
Machinery and metal products, chemicals, iron, petroleum, coking coal, steel, agricultural products, transport equipment

Exports
Total $10.2 billion
Tobacco, metal products, ships, minerals, textiles, leather goods and shoes, furniture, agricultural products

Major Trading Partners
USSR, West Germany, Iraq, Italy, Czechoslovakia, US, France, Austria

Workforce
8.9 million
Agriculture employs 32%, all others (industry and government) 65%

Tips for Doing Business
A conservative business suit is appropriate for most occasions, and prior appointments for government visits must be made. The economy is controlled to varying degrees by the State. The numerous workers' trade companies will be your contacts for transactions, and Yugoslavia as a whole demands generous credit terms for repayment. Yugoslavs are very hospitable, so try not to refuse anything offered to you during business. You may need an interpreter since few businessmen speak English well enough for complicated negotiations. If invited to a private home for dinner, bring the wife flowers or chocolates, and be prepared to eat huge meals and consume large amounts of red wine - both are customs for business entertaining.

Best Months for Doing Business
September through May. Yugoslavs, like most other Europeans, vacation in the hottest months - June through August. Some also vacation in January to go skiing in Sarajevo.

Business Hours

Government
Mon-Fri 0700-1430
Wed 0700-1700

Business
Mon-Fri 0700-1430

Banks
Mon-Fri 0800-1200 1700-2000

Shops
Mon-Fri 0800-1200 1700-2000
Sat 0800-1500

English Language Publications
The Internatinal Herald Tribune, USA Today, British newspapers and western magazines are available in large cities.

Telephone and Communications
Telephone country code: 38
Telephone city code: Belgrade 011, Zagreb 41
Telex country code: 862
Public telephones can be found in many public places. A local call costs 2 dinar. Direct-dial long distance service is available

EUROPE

within the country, as well as to US, Canada, Australia and most European countries.

Telex facilities are available in hotels and larger post offices. Telegrams may be sent ordinary rate or express rate from main post offices.

Air Travel

JAT operates regular and charter domestic flights with frequent service to all major towns and cities. Additional services to tourist destinations are offered from June to September. Flight departure times fluctuate however, so check by phone ahead of time and often before boarding your flight. Contact the local JAT office for fares.

Other Transport

Although there are nearly 120,000 km of roads, many are of substandard quality. Avoid driving off the main highways if possible.

The State railway service (Zajednica Jugoslovenskih Zeleznica) operates international express trains with sleepers. Reduced fares are available for foreign travellers, but sleepers must be booked in advance. Very colorful ferry boat service plys the Adriatic coast, stopping at major port cities of Split, Dubrovnic, Rijeka, and even across to Italy.

BELGRADE

Airport Information

Time
GMT +1

Airport
Belgrade International BEG
Tel: 011 601555
20 km (12 mi) W of city
International and domestic

Airlines
Aeroflot 325814
Air Algerie 342161
Air Canada 330310
Air France 638811
Alitalia 687799
Austrian 337056
British Airways 333160
CAAC 410213
Gulf Air 413168
Interflug 338180
Iraqi 325442
JAT 131392
KLM 639266
Lufthansa 324976
Olympic 683164
Pan Am 441484
Qantas 639166
Sabena 435483
SAS 331385
Swissair 688266
TWA 138360
Varig 330008

Transport to City
Taxis: Taxis operate on a meter basis from the airport. Cost is about 2000 dinar, plus 10% tip, for the 20 minute trip.
Coach: There is a JAT airways bus to the city that leaves every 10 minutes to the downtown terminal. The 30-minute ride costs 500 dinar.

Facilities
Reservations, baggage deposit, post office, bar, restaurant, shops, first-aid/medical, vaccinations, bank with currency exchange, nursery, shops
Duty-free shop sells tobacco products, wine, aperitifs, spirits, cameras, lighters, watches, perfume, jewellery, technical goods, cloths, paintings
Car rental desks: hertz, Avis, Putnik, Unis

Airport Taxes
European and International flights: per passenger 650 dinar. Domestic flights: per passenger 180 dinar.

City Information

Weather
Belgrade's weather can have extremes of heat and cold, particularly in mid-summer and winter. Average temperatures are -10 C (14 F) in winter; 30 C (80 F) in summer. Rainy season is in the spring.

Transportation
Taxis are numerous and offer good value in Belgrade. They are usually metered, with a 10% tip the normal extra charge.

There is also a good bus service which serves the entire city area and is very reasonably priced.

Car Hire
Hertz-Kompas, Obiljcev Venac 25
  (tel: 605555)
Avis, Revolucije 94
  (tel: 433323)
Inex, Cryene Armije 40
  (tel: 451467)
InterRent, Makedonska 22
  (tel: 213947)
Putnik, Knez Milosa 82
  (tel: 605555)
Unis Turist, Cara Urosa 10
  (tel: 634766)

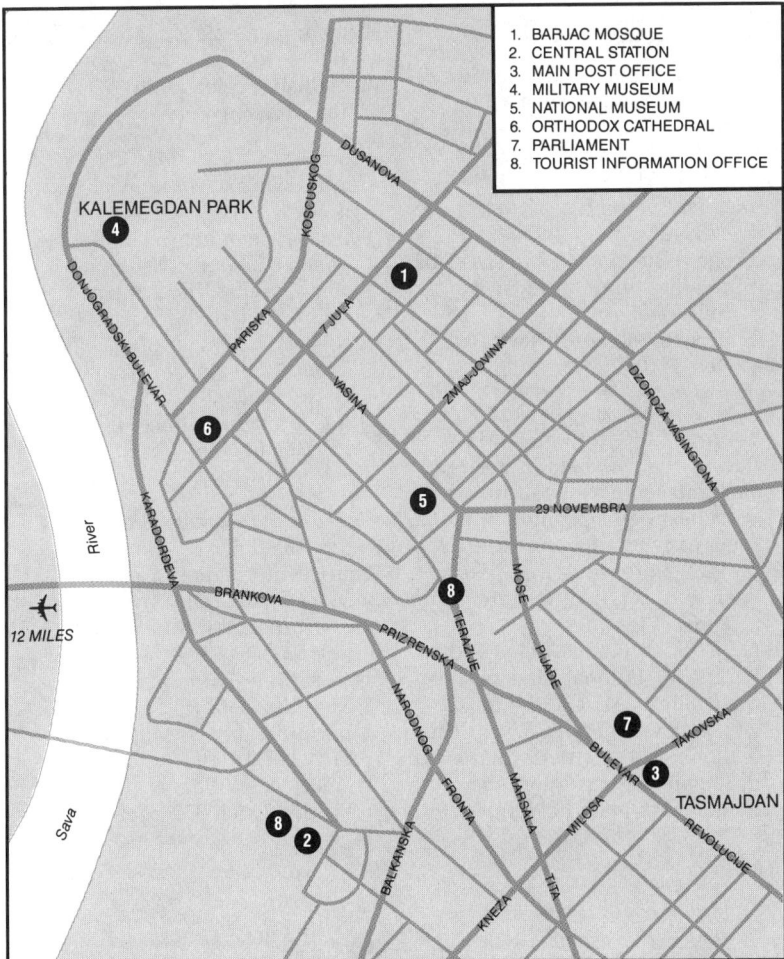

1. BARJAC MOSQUE
2. CENTRAL STATION
3. MAIN POST OFFICE
4. MILITARY MUSEUM
5. NATIONAL MUSEUM
6. ORTHODOX CATHEDRAL
7. PARLIAMENT
8. TOURIST INFORMATION OFFICE

KALEMEGDAN PARK

TASMAJDAN

12 MILES

EUROPE

Belgrade

Hospitals
Some doctors and dentists speak English, and medical care and facilities are generally very good, and moderately priced. Traveller's health insurance is recommended, however.

Hotels
Balkan, Prizenska 2 (tel: 687466)
Excelsior, Kneza Milosa 5 (tel: 331381)
InterContinental, Vladimira Popovica 10 (tel: 138708)
Jugoslavija, Bvl. E. Kardlja 3 (tel: 600222)
Majestic, Obilicev Venac 28 (tel: 636022)
Metropol, revolucije 69 (tel: 330911)
Moskva, Balkanskai (tel: 686255)
Park Hotel, Njegoseva 4 (tel: 334722)
Prag Hotel, Narodnog fronta 27 (tel: 663443)
Slavija, Svetog Save 9 (tel: 450842)
Srbija, Ustanicka 127 (tel: 413255)
Sumadija, Sumadijski trg 8 (tel: 554255)
Union Hotel, Kosovska 11 (tel: 341055)

What to See and Do
There is little nightlife and few decent clubs or bars in Belgrade, so sightseeing and culture are your best bets for entertainment. Most of Belgrade's public buildings are more than 150 years old, while others are very modern. Visit the old Turkish Fort at Kalemegdan Park, the National Museum, or the Modern Art Gallery (on the left bank of the Sava River. The National Theater performs opera in Italian, and an international theater festival is held annually in the city in September-October. Belgrade has many excellent restaurants, featuring ethnic dishes from all over the country. Souvenirs, such as hand-carved wood figures, may be purchased in Narodna Radinost shops. Other places of interest include Archangel Michael Cathedral, Ex-Royal Palace, Bariak Mosque, Frescoes Museum and the Ethnographic Museum.

Useful Addresses

Embassies and Consulates
American: Kneza Milosa 50 (tel: 645655)
British: Generala Zdanova 46 (tel: 645055)
Canadian: Proleterskih 69 (tel: 644666)

Business and Commerce
Central Bank of Jugoslavia, Bulevar Revolicije 15
Belgrade Chamber of Commerce, Terazije 23 (tel: 339461)
Foreign Trade Office, Kneza Milosa 24 (tel: 682555)
Jugoslavia Chamber of Commerce, Kneza Mihailova 10 (tel: 624666)
UN Information Office, PO Box 157 (tel: 642655)

Tourism and Travel
Centroturist, revolucije 64 (tel: 465925)
Tourist Information Center, Mosa Pijade (tel: 345918)
Inex Tourist, Trg Republike 5 (tel: 622368)
Yugoslavian Automobile Club, Ruzveltova 18 (tel: 401699)
American Express, Mose Pijade 11 (tel: 341471)
Thomas Cook/Wagon Lits, Mosa Pijade 21 (tel: 335331)

North/South America

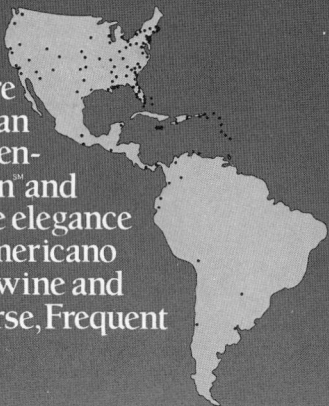

More flights to more cities in Latin America from more cities in North America than any other airline. The convenience of One-Time Check-In℠ and advance seat selection. The elegance of our exclusive El Inter Americano inflight service including wine and gourmet food. And, of course, Frequent Traveler Bonus Points.

Eastern Airlines: The businessman's airline to Latin America.

Business is always a pleasure when you fly Eastern to Latin America. For reservations and more information call your Travel Agent, or Eastern Airlines at 1-800-E-A-S-T-E-R-N.

✈ EASTERN

© 1987 Eastern Air Lines, Inc.

ARGENTINA

Essential Information

Type of Government
Republic

Area
2,777,815 sq km
(1,072,514 sq mi)

Population
29.5 million

Annual Growth Rate
1.6%

Language
Spanish (official)
English, Italian, German, French

Religion
Roman Catholic 92%,
Prostestant, Jewish and other 6%

Ethnic Groups
97% European, primarily
Spanish and Italian

Weights and Measures
Metric

Electrical Current
A.C. 50c 220V

Major Business Cities
Buenos Aires (cap) 10,750,000
Rosario 960,000
Cordoba 995,000
La Plata 565,000

Currency
1 Austral = 1000 Argentine Pesos

Public Holidays
Jan 1 New Year
Apr 13-20 Easter Week
May 1 Labor Day
May 25 National Day
June 30 Flag Day
July 9 Independence
Aug 17 San Martin's
Dec 8 Immaculate Conception
Dec 25 Christmas

Travellers Information

Entry Requirements
A passport is required by all except those from neighboring countries.
Visa required by everyone except visitors from some South American and European countries and Canada.

Working Restrictions
Work permits required.

Vaccination Required
No vaccination certificates required, but antimalarial precautions are advised if going on to tropical areas.

Customs and Duty Free
On arrival: 400 cigarets or 50 cigars or 250g/8oz tobacco; 2 liters alcohol; 5 kilos of food with the total value not exceeding US$400.

Currency Restrictions
There are no currency restrictions.

Health Tips
Good medical services are available, especially in the larger cities, but all medical services must be paid for. Drinking water is purified in large cities. Wash fruit and vegetables.

Climate and Clothing
Sub-tropical in north to sub-antarctic in south. In central zone December through March is hot season (80-95F) June to August cool season (40-60F). Light to medium weight clothing with dark business suits preferable.

Tipping
A service charge of 19-24% is usually added to the bill in hotels and restaurants. If so, leave 5-10% to waiter, otherwise 15%. Tip taxi drivers 10-15%.

Food and Drink
Beef is the main dish and the asado (barbecue) is a weekly

NORTH/SOUTH AMERICA

custom. Popular dishes are puchero (meat, corn, potatoes and squash), carbonada (ground beef with onions and tomatoes), and locra (thick soup of corn, pumpkin, white beans and herbs). Desserts are often thick jellies with cheese, and/or excellent fruits. Argentine red wine is the usual drink, often mixed with soda water. National drink is yerba mate, a strong herbal tea.

Business Brief

GDP
$110.9 billion

Annual Growth Rate
3%

Natural Resources
Lead, zinc, oil, tin, copper, iron, sulphur, silver, gold

Agriculture
Grains, corn, grapes, sugar, tobacco, rice, soybeans, citrus fruits

Industry
Meat packing, motor vehicles, textiles, printing chemicals

Imports
Total $6 million
Machinery, fuel, iron and steel products, wood, lumber, automotive equipment and parts

Exports
Total $6.5 million
Grains, meats, oilseeds

Major Trading Partners
Europe, Brazil, Chile, USSR, Japan, US, Netherlands

Workforce
10 million
Manufacturing 25%, agriculture 19%, services

Tips For Doing Business
When greeting someone, it is customary to shake hands and address them with a title(Mr or Mrs, or Senor or Senora). Wear conservative clothing, especially when doing business. Always make prior appointments. If a businessman invites you to his home for dinner, bring a gift and/or send flowers the next day.

Best Months For Doing Business
May through November. Avoid the weeks before and after Christmas and Easter. Business vacations are taken in January, February and March.

Business Hours

Government
Mon-Fri 0730-1300
(1230-1930 in winter)

Business
Mon-Fri 0730-1300

Banks
Mon-Fri 1000 to 1600

Shops
Mon-Sat 0900-1900
(some close at 1200 on Sat)

English Language Publications
Buenos Aires Herald is the daily newspaper.

Telephone and Communications
Telephone country code: 54
Telephone city code: Buenos Aires 1
Telex country code: 390
Automatic telephone system throughout the country, but it is not too good and local systems can get bogged down. Outside Buenos Aires or for international or long-distance calls, go to the telephone office. There are usually English-speaking operators at most exchanges. Telex and telegrams: available at main telephone offices in Buenos Aires 24 hours a day and in large hotels.

Air Travel
Argentina's main international airport is Ezeiza in Buenos Aires, and domestic and regional

services go from Jorge Newberry, the city airport known as Aeroparque. Air transport is the best form of travel in the country. Extensive services offered by Aerolineas Argentinas and Austral. LADE serves smaller centers.

Other Transport

Roads linking major centers are in good condition. Car hire is available, and the ACA (Automovil Club Argentino) is useful for detailed information. Long distance buses operated by different companies. Train service is good and operates on a comprehensive rail system. Choose Pullman services with air-conditioning and restaurants and book well in advance. In Buenos Aires good booking and information services are available.

BUENOS AIRES

Airport Information

Time
GMT -3

Airport
Ezeiza EZE
tel: 6200043
35 km (20 mi) SW of city

Airlines
Aerolineas Argentinas 3625008
Air France 3110388
Air New Zealand 3121438
Alitalia 3128421
Avensa 314192
Avianca 3123693
British Airways 3924854
Canadian International 3223662
Eastern 340031
El Al 3928840
Iberia 359421
KLM 3118921
Luthansa 3128171
Pan Am 450111

Sabena 3929160
SAS 3128161
Swissair 3120901
TWA 3119237
United 3120664
Varig 355431

Transport to City
Taxis: usually air-conditioned, cost about US$22-25 and take 20-30 minutes to downtown. Tip by rounding up to nearest peso. Coach: there are special bus stops outside both terminals for airconditioned buses with baggage room. Stops at several hotels and goes to downtown bus terminal. Costs about US$5 and you pay before boarding, 35-45 minutes to downtown; meets both flights.
Limousine-type cars, comfortable and air-conditioned, run by Manuel Tienda Lean; available at both terminals. Will drop off passengers at any destination and cost about US$18 to downtown.

Facilities
Currency exchange, hotel reservations, baggage deposit, bar, restaurant, first aid/medical Duty-free shop sells cigarets, cigars, tobacco, wines, spirits, liqueurs.
Car rental desks: Hertz, Avis, National

Airport Taxes
Per person: International 3 australs, (2 australs to neighboring countries) domestic 1 austral

City Information

Weather
The climate is generally temperate but December through February can be very hot with rainstorms. Winters are cold and rainy. Average temps: Jan 26c 89F) July 10c (50F)

Transportation

Taxis have yellow roofs and can be hailed on the street or found in taxi stands. They are metered and tips are not necessary but 510% expected from tourists. Extra charge for each piece of luggage.

There is a good "pay as you board" bus service which operates 24 hours a day although buses are often crowded. Metro is known as "Subte" and operates from early morning to late at night. Fixed-fare system; tokens can be bought at booking offices.

Car Hire

Avis, Av Corrientes 1302, piso 6 (tel: 4529286 & 6200362)

Europcar, Esmeralda 1084 (tel: 319303 & 313583)
National, Esmeralda 1084 (tel: 3111885)

Hospitals

Medical help for travellers available at:
Hospital Britanico de Buenas Aires (tel: 2310819)

Trade Fairs

International Book Fair (Apr)
International Modern Living Exhibition (Oct)
Commercial and Computer Exhibition (Dec)

Hotels

Buenos Aires Sheraton, San Martin 1225 (tel: 3116311/6511)

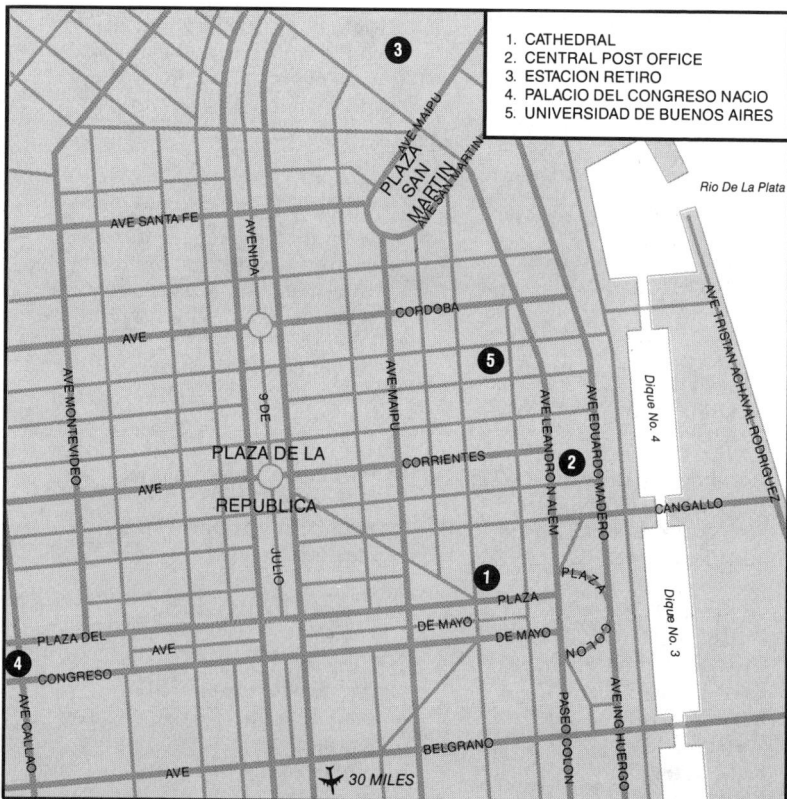

1. CATHEDRAL
2. CENTRAL POST OFFICE
3. ESTACION RETIRO
4. PALACIO DEL CONGRESO NACIO
5. UNIVERSIDAD DE BUENOS AIRES

Buenos Aires

Claridge, Tucuman 535
(tel: 3937212/4107)
Elevage, Maipu 960 (tel: 3132082)
Gran Hotel Buenos Aires,
Marcelo T de Alvear 767
(tel: 323001)
Libertador, Av Cordoba y Maipu
1054 (tel: 3922095)
Plaza, Calle Florida 1005
(tel: 3115011)

What to See and Do
In the Plaza de Mayo you can
see many buildings of interest
including Government House
(called Casa Rosada because it is
painted pink) and the Cabildo,
the center of government during
the Spanish viceroys. Both have
museums open from 1400-1700.
Visit the old quarter of the city
on the south side of the square
for bohemian atmosphere. A
little south is La Boca, a colorful
Italian neighborhood. Farther
north, in the elegant "Barrio
norte" is the beautiful square
called Plaza San Martin. Teatro
Colon is one of the world's
greatest opera houses and there
are many theaters. Visit the
racetrack in San Isidro.

Useful Addresses

Embassies and Consulates
American: 4300 Colombia
(tel: 7747611)

Canadian: Calle Suipacha 1111
(tel: 3129081)
British: Luis Agote 2412
(tel: 8247071)

Business and Commerce
National Bank, San Martin 275
(tel: 495411)
Stock Exchange, Leandro N
Alem 356 (tel: 2214125)
Buenos Aires Stock Exchange,
Esq 25 de Mayo y Sarmiento
Buenos Aires Chamber of
Commerce, Bartolome Mitre
519 (tel: 348252)
Argentine Chamber of
Commerce, Av Leandro N
Alem 36 (tel: 338051)
American Chamber of
Commerce, Av Rs Pena 567
(tel: 335591)
British Chamber of Commerce,
25 de Mayo No 444
(tel: 326673)
Ministry of Foreign Trade, Av Pr
Julio A Roca 651
United Nations Office, Marcel T
de Alvear 684 (tel: 314239)

Tourism and Travel
American Express, City Service
Travel Agency, Florida 890,
4th floor (tel: 3128416)
Automovil Club Argentino, Av
del Libertador 1850
(tel: 8026061 & 8027061)
Thomas Cook, Cordoba 746
(tel: 3921988)

BOLIVIA

Essential Information

Type of Government
Republic

Area
1.1 million sq km
(424,162 sq mi)

Population
7 million

Annual Growth Rate
2.7%

Languages
Spanish (official) Aymara,
Quechua

Religion
Roman Catholic 95%

Ethnic Groups
Aymara 25%, Quecha 30%,
European 5-15%, mixed 25-30%

Weights and Measures
Metric and some old Spanish
measures

NORTH/SOUTH AMERICA

Electrical Current
A.C. 50c 111/220V

Major Business Cities
Sucre (cap legal) 90,000
La Paz (cap de facto) 1,100,000
Santa Cruz 470,000
Cochabamba 350,000

Currency
1 Bolivian peso = 100 Centavos

Public Holidays
Jan 1 New Year Mar Carnival
Apr 13- 19 Easter Week
May 1 Labor Day
Jun 21 Corpus Christi
July 16 La Paz Day (La Paz only)
Aug 6 Independence Day
Dec 25 Christmas Day

Travellers Information

Entry Requirements
Passport is required by all visitors except a few UN document holders.
Visas are required by all except nationals of US, Britian, Canada, Denmark, West Germany and Spain. With a valid passport, a 90 day visa can be obtained at the airport. Check carefully before travelling, as visitors may be required to prove they have the equivalent of US$500 before being allowed into the country.

Working Restrictions
Only residents of Boliva are allowed employment.

Vaccination Required
Yellow fever vaccination is recommended and required if going to Santa Sierra de la Cruz.

Customs and Duty Free
On arrival: 200 cigarets or 50 cigars or 450g/1lb tobacco; 2 bottles of spirits. Cameras must be declared and receipt obtained.

Currency Restrictions
There are no restrictions on the amount of local and foreign currency you can import, and the amounts declared on entry may be re-exported.

Health Tips
Antimalarial tablets are recommended if travelling outside La Paz. The altitude is debilitating and anyone with heart or lung problems should get medical advice before visiting. Rest for the first few days, avoid alcohol and eat lightly. Humidity is low in La Paz so drink plenty of non-alcoholic beverages. The drinking water is unpurified so use only bottled water. Avoid unwashed fruit and vegetables and undercooked fish and meat.

Climate and Clothing
The climate depends on the altitude. The rainy season is December through March throughout the country. The rains are particularly heavy in the eastern region (Santa Cruz), but La Paz can have several hours of sunshine a day during this period. Santa Cruz and Cochabamba tend to be hot and humid so wear tropical weight clothing and carry a large umbrella during the rainy season. La Paz is cool to cold at night: a warm coat and sweaters are recommended.

Tipping
There is no tipping for taxi drivers. Tip porters 1000 pesos for each piece of luggage, chambermaids 1000 pesos, and barbers and beauticians 10%. Restaurants and nightspots 10-25%, attendants and small services 500 pesos.

Food and Drink
Avoid salads and fresh fruit and eat the excellent lake and river fish instead. Food is highly seasoned and hot chilis (locati) are used in many meat and vegetable dishes. Soups are very filling and spicy. A meat stew

wrapped in dough is popular as the first meal of the day, and beef from the area around Santa Cruz is excellent. Tropical fruit juices and mineral waters are available. The beer is thought to be the best in South America: wine and spirits are available in the larger cities but are expensive.

Business Brief

GDP
$1.9 billion
(per capita income $296)

Annual Growth Rate
-10%

Natural Resources
Tin, natural gas, petroleum, zinc, tungsten, antimony, silver, iron, rubber. cinchona bark

Agriculture
Potatoes, sugar cane, coffee, corn, rice, barley, bananas, wheat

Industry
Textiles, food processing, mining, chemicals, plastics

Imports
Total $761 million
Machinery and transportation equipment, consumer products, construction and mining equipment

Exports
Total $566 million
Tin, natural gas, sugar, silver. timber, coffee

Major Trading Partners
US, Brazil, Argentina, Japan, UK, Peru, Chile

Workforce
1.7 million
Workers in agriculture have declined from 25% to 15%, industry and commerce 20%, service and government 37%

Tips for Doing Business
A conservative business suit should be worn at all times. A knowledge of Spanish helps, and business cards should be printed in both English and Spanish: they can be printed locally in several days. Promotional material should also be printed in Spanish and be low-key rather than forceful. Shake hands on arrival and departure. Make prior appointments and don't be too boisterous. Bolivian businessmen are sensitive, so hang back a bit; do not praise Chile or talk about politics. Watch out for the altitude in La Paz and do not schedule anything requiring energy for the first several days. Take taxis instead of walking, eat lightly and rest. Business meetings are usually conducted in restaurants. Delicately refuse fresh fruit and vegetables.

Best Months for Business
April, May, September and October. The rainy summer months are between December and March. Very little business is done during Carnival time which begins the Saturday before Ash Wednesday and continues for five days. Check dates. Avoid the two weeks before and after Christmas, and the week before and after Easter as well as the first week in August. Businessmen usually take vacations during January, February, and March.

Business Hours

Government
Mon-Fri 0900-1200 and 1400-1800
Sat 0900-1200

Business
Mon-Fri 0900-1200 and 1400-1800
Sat 0900-1200

Banks
Mon-Fri 0900-1200 and 1400-1630

Shops
Mon-Fri 0900-1200 and 1400-1800
Sat 0900-1200

Telephone and Communications
Telephone country code: 591
Telephone city code: La Paz 2
Telex country code: 356
Efficient automatic telephone
and telex services. Public
telephones in restaurants and
cafes. You can reverse the
charges when calling US, Brazil
and Chile. Postage stamps must
be purchased at the post office.

Air Travel
International Airport in La Paz is
John F. Kennedy/El Alto (LPB).
Lloyd Aereo Boliviano (LAB),
TAB (army airline), and Linea
Aerea Imperial (LA) operate
domestic services to main
centers. Because of the country's
mountainous terrain, air
transport is recommended.

Other Transport
Rail car (Ferrobus) to all main
cities with sleeper and firstclass
services. Booking first-class is
advisable and booking in
advance is essential.

LA PAZ

Airport Information

Time
GMT -4

Airport
Internacional John F. Kennedy
  (El Alto) LPB
Tel: 810122
15 km (9 mi) SE of city

Airlines
Air France 358094
British Airways 355541
British Caledonia 343641
Eastern Airlines 351362
Iberia 320270
JAL 375251

Lufthansa 372170
Pan Am 341863
Swissair 375057
TWA 322047

Transport to City
Taxi: always available to city.
Coach: LAB bus to city
(20 minutes) every 5 minutes:
24 hour service.

Facilities
Currency exchange, hotel
reservations, post office, bar,
restaurant, barbershop,
conference facilities, first aid/
medical, shops.
Duty-free shop sells cigarets,
wines, liquor, jewellery,
souvenirs, woven goods. All
currencies accepted.

Airport Taxes
Per person: International 250
pesos, domestic 18 pesos

City Information

Weather
Temperatures in La Paz range
from cool to cold; a coat or
sweater is useful year round.
The rainy season lasts December
through March.

Transportation
Yellow cabs with green flags
are called "trufis". They are
frequently shared with fixed
rates per passenger and must be
hailed from the street.
The bus service is extensive but
crowded so avoid it if possible.
Trucks are also used for travel
around town but reserve a seat
in advance. Inquire at your
hotel.

Car Hire
International license issued
by member of Federacion
InterAmericana de Touring y
Automovil Clubs. Drivers must
buy a hoya de ruta, a form
which notes your itinerary. Drive
on the right side of the road.

Hertz, Sheraton Hotel
(tel: 322654 and 24549)
Kolla Motors, Calle R. Gutierrez
(tel: 341660)
Oscar Crespo, Calle M. Carranza
492 (tel: 372782)

Hospitals
Boston Clinic (tel: 322410 &
388778)

Hotels
Crillon Hotel, Plaza Isabel
Catolica (tel: 25212)
Hotel La Paz, Av Camacho 1277
(tel: 355292)
Hotel Plaza La Paz, Paseo del
Prado (tel: 378311)
Sucre Hotel, Av 16 de Julio 1636
(tel: 355081)
Hotel Sheraton, Av Acre-
Guachalla, Casilla 8689
(tel: 356950)

What To See and Do
Museo Nacional del Arte,
Central Market, Palacio
Quemado, Congreso Nacional,
the Cathedral, Plaza Murillo.

Useful Addresses

Embassies and Consulates
American: Banco Popular Del
Peru Bldg (tel: 350251)
Canadian: Alborada Bldg. Office
508, 1420 J. De La Riva St
(tel: 3705224)
British: Avenida Acre 2732-2754
(tel: 329401)

Business and Commerce
Central Bank, Ayacucho esq.
Mercado, Cajon Postal 3118
Central Post Office, Ayacucho
esq. Potosi
American Chamber of
Commerce, Avda Arce 2071
(tel: 342523)

Tourism and Travel
Bolivian Tourism Institute, Plaza
Venezuela (tel: 367463/4)
American Express, Magri
Tourismo Ltda (R) Av 16 de
Julio 1490, 5th floor
(tel: 341201)
Automobile Club Bolivian,
Avenida 6 de Agosto, 2993 San
Jorge, Casilla 602
(tel: 351/667/325/325 136)

BRAZIL

Essential Information

Type of Government
Federal Republic

Area
8.5 million sq km
(3.3 million sq mi)

Population
141 million

Annual Growth Rate
2.3%

Languages
Portuguese (official), English

Religion
Roman Catholic 90%, Macumba
and other 10%

Ethnic Groups
Portuguese, Italian, German,
Japanese, African, American
Indian.

Weights and Measures
Metric

Electrical Current
Rio de Janiero A.C. 60c 127/220V
Sao Paulo A.C. 60c 115/230V
Brasilia A.C. 60c 220/240V

Major Business Cities
Brasilia (cap) 1,975,000
Sao Paulo 11,000,000
Rio de Janiero 6,750,000
Belo Horizonte 2,500,000
Salvador 2,000,000
Porto Alegre 1,450,000

NORTH/SOUTH AMERICA

Currency
1 Cruziero = 100 Centavos
Notes 100, 200, 500, 1000, 5000
   cruziero
Coins 1, 2, 5, 10, 20, 50 centavos;
   1 cruziero

Public Holidays
Jan 1 New Year
Feb 9-11 Carnival
Apr 12-19 Easter Week
May 1 Labor Day
Sept 7 Independence Day
Nov 2 All Souls Day
Nov 15 Proclamation of the
Republic
Dec 25 Christmas

Travellers Information

Entry Requirements
Passport is required by all except
citizens of Argentina, Chile,
Paraguay, Uruguay.
Visa not required by most
citizens of Latin America,
Western Europe or Canada for
short visits of less than 3
months. Visa required by
citizens of US, Australia and
New Zealand.

Working Restrictions
Working visas and permits are
only issued in conjunction with a
work contract certified by the
Brazilian Ministry of Labor.

Vaccination Required
No vaccinations required,
although recommended for
yellow fever, typhoid and
malaria.

Customs and Duty Free
On arrival: 200 cigarets or
25 cigars or 250g/8oz tobacco; 2
liters of alchohol.

Currency Restrictions
There are no restrictions on the
amount of currency brought in.
International credit cards widely
used although cash advances can
be given in cruzieros.

Health Tips
Public health service is not good
and private doctors expensive,
but medical services are available
in large cities. Drinking water is
not purified outside major cities.
Take antimalarial tablets.

Climate and Clothing
Climate varies from tropical in
the north to temperate in the
south. In most parts of the
country, days range from warm
to hot except during rainy
season from November to
February. Driest month is July.
Wear medium weight or
lightweight clothing.

Tipping
Most hotels add 10-20% service
charge and most restaurants add
10%, but 5% is usually given to
the staff. Tip airport porters the
equivalent of 50 cents per piece
of luggage and taxi drivers
15-20%.

Business Brief

GDP
$252 billion
(per capita income $1,861)

Annual Growth Rate
3-4%

Natural Resources
Iron ore, manganese, bauxite,
nickel, uranium, gemstones

Agriculture
Coffee, soybeans, sugar cane,
cocoa, rice, beef, corn, oranges

Industry
Steel, chemicals, petrochemicals,
machinery, motor vehicles,
consumer goods, cement,
lumber, ship building

Imports
Total $16.5 billion
Crude oil, chemicals, raw
materials, machinery and
electrical equipment, transport
equipment, wheat, weapons and
ammunition

Exports
Total $27 billion
Manganese, iron ore, sugar, nuts, coffee, cocoa, cotton, corn, lumber, tobacco, soybeans

Major Trading Partners
US, West Germany, Argentina, Italy, The Netherlands, UK, France, Japan

Workforce
50 million
Agriculture 35%, industry 25%, services 40%

Tips for Doing Business
Conservative clothing should be worn for business and government meetings. Brazilian businessmen are friendly and informal, and many speak English. Prior appointments are usually necessary and punctuality is an asset. Always address your contacts formally by their surnames when discussing business.

Best Months for Doing Business
Best months for travel are March through November. Avoid December through January, when Brazilians take their holidays, and Carnival in February.

Business Hours

Government
Mon-Fri 0900-1100, 1400-1800

Business
Mon-Fri 0900-1130, 1400-1800

Banks
Mon-Fri 1000-1630

Shops
Mon-Fri 0900-1800 Sat 0900-1300

English Language Publications
The Brazil Herald. Foreign English-language papers available in large cities.

Telephone and Communications
Telephone country code: 55
Telephone city code: Rio de Janiero 021, Sao Paulo 011
Telex country code: 391
Long-distance telephone calls can be made from state telephone company offices, post offices and hotels. Local calls can be made from public telephone boxes found in bars, cafes and sidewalk booths. They are operated with tokens called Fichas which can be purchased in retail shops. Telegrams can be sent over the phone, and telegrams and telexes from post offices and hotels. There is a 40% tax on all international communications.

Air Travel
Regular air travel available between all major cities. Air charters also available at domestic airports. Reservations required, except for air shuttle between Rio de Janiero and Sao Paulo.

Other Transport
Major cities connected by good surfaced highways: the condition of local roads is not quite as good.
There is frequent bus services available between main centers, some with sleeping berths.
Rail travel available throughout the country, but not as good or frequent as bus service.

RIO DE JANEIRO

Airport Information

Time
GMT -3

Airports
Galeao Airport GIG
Tel: (021)3986060
20 km (12.5 mi) NW of city

Airlines
Air Canada 2974440

Air France 2203666
Alitalia 2625088
Avensa 2245345
British Airways 2200914
Canadian International 2205343
Cruzeiro 2974400
El Al 2206098
Iberia 2102415
JAL 2219663
KLM 2101342
Lufthansa 2821283
Pan Am 2103214
Sabena 2086033
SAS 2101222
Singapore 2407749
Swiss Air 2032144
Transbrasil 2974422
TWA 8008086
United 2203397
Varig 2926600
Vasp 2922080

Transport to City
Taxi: there are regular metered taxis but it·is best to take one from either Cotramo or Transcopas. These companies provide luxury cabs, English-speaking drivers and a VIP waiting room. You can buy a ticket at counter. Trip to town 25-40 minutes.
Coach: special airport bus decorated with flowers, known as The Daisy Bus (Frescao), is provided by the city and leaves every 30 minutes. It makes several stops at all beaches and major hotels, ending at Hotel Nacional, and can take up to 60 minutes.

Facilities
Currency exchange, hotel

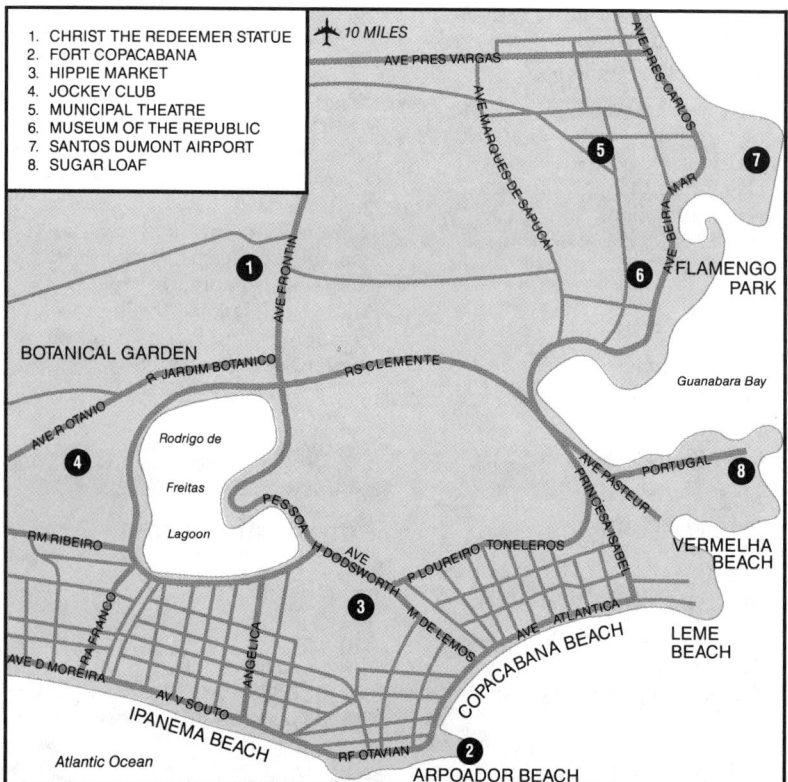

1. CHRIST THE REDEEMER STATUE
2. FORT COPACABANA
3. HIPPIE MARKET
4. JOCKEY CLUB
5. MUNICIPAL THEATRE
6. MUSEUM OF THE REPUBLIC
7. SANTOS DUMONT AIRPORT
8. SUGAR LOAF

Rio De Janeiro

reservations, baggage deposit, post office, bar, restaurant, conference facilities, first aid/ medical, vaccinations, barber shop, shops selling books, candy, toys.
Duty-free shop has cigarets, cigars, tobacco, wines, spirits, cameras, lighters, watches, jewellery, Brazilian-Indian crafts. Local currency not accepted but major convertible currencies are. Open to arrival and departure passengers.
Car rental desks: Hertz, Avis, Localiza, Locabras, Nobre

Airport Taxes
Per person: International 240 cruziero, domestic 54 cruziero

City Information

Weather
Hot and tropical Average temps: Jan (summer) 26c (79F) July (winter) 21c (70F)

Transportation
Two subway networks in the city, closed on Sunday.
Taxis have red number plates with white digits. Most are metered and can be hailed. Tipping optional.
Cars may be rented and an international driving license is required validated by Automobile Club of Brazil. Gas is expensive and the traffic congested. All service stations closed on Sundays.
Buses are cheap and efficient. Many, with blue and white symbol in window, connect with subway lines.

Car Hire
Hertz, Praia do Flamengo 194, (tel: 2754996 & 2851249)
Avis, Praia do Flamengo 244 (tel: 5424249 & 3983083)
Europcar, Av Pres Wilson 210 (tel: 3984455)

Nobre, Rua Gustavo Sampaio 826 (tel: 2755297)

Hospitals
Call your consulate for a list of English-speaking doctors or inquire at hotel. Public health system is poor and doctors are expensive. There are several all night pharmacies. Medical assistance for travellers at:
Iamat Center, Av Princesa Isabel (tel: 2253443)

Trade Fairs
International Maritime Exhibition (Oct)

Hotels
Rio-Sheraton, Av Neimeyer 121 (tel: 2741122)
Inter-Continental Rio, Praia da Gavea 222 (tel: 3222200)
Nacional-Rio, Av Neimeyer 769 (tel: 3221000)
Rio Palace, Av Atlantica 4240 (tel: 5213232)
Rio Othon Palace, Av Atlantica 3264 (tel: 2558812)
Meridien-Rio, Av Atlantica 1020 (tel: 2759922)
Copacabana Palace, Av Atlantica 1702 (tel: 2557070)
Ceasar Park Ipanema, Av Vieira Souto 460 (tel: 0212873122)
Everest Rio, Rua Prudente de Morais 1117 (tel: 2878282)
Gloria, Praia do Russel 632 (tel: 2057272)
Leme Palace, Av Atlantica 656 (tel: 2758080)
Ouro Verde, Av Atlantica 1456 (tel: 5421887)
Excelsior, Av Atlantica 1800 (tel: 2571950)
Lancaster, Av Atlantica 1470 (tel: 5411887)
Miramar, Av Atlantica 3tel: tel: 2476070)
Trocadero, Av Atlantica 2064 (tel: 2571834)

What to See and Do
Take the cable car to the top of Sugar Loaf Mountain; taxi or train to Corcovado Mountain

with the illuminated statue of Christ the Redeemer; Flamingo Park has tropical gardens and sports facilities. Famous beaches include Copacabana, Ipanema and Leblon. On Sunday afternoons there are soccer games at Maracana Stadium or arts and crafts displays in General Osorio Square.

Useful Addresses

Embassies and Consulates
American: Av Pres Wilson 147 (tel: 2927117)
Canadian: Av Pres Wilson 165 (tel: 2409912)
British: Praia do Flamengo 284 (tel: 5521422)

Business and Commerce
Central Post Office, Rua Primerio de March 64
Central Bank, Av Pres Vargas 84 (tel: 2237773)
Stock Exchange, Praca 15 de Novembro 20 (tel: 2315854)
Rio de Janiero Chamber of Commerce, Rua da Candelaria 9 (tel: 2445255)
American Chamber of Commerce, Av Rio Branco 123 (tel: 2221983)
United Nations Office, Rua Cruz Lima 19 (tel: 2453000)
Foreign Trade Office, Av Rio Bronco 91 (tel: 2211901)

Tourism and Travel
Tourist Information Center, Barata Ribeiro 272
American Express, Av Atlantica 2316 Copacabana (tel: 2351396)
Automobile Club of Brazil, Rua do Passeto 90 (tel: 2524055)
Touring Club of Brazil, Praca Maua (tel: 2635583)
Thomas Cook, Rio Branco 156 (tel: 2217756)

SAO PAULO

Airport Information

Time
GMT -3

Airports
Campinas-Viracopos VCP
Tel: (0192)80925
97 km (60 mi) SW of city
International terminal

Congonhas CGH
Tel: (011)5317444
14 km (8 mi) S of city
International and domestic

Airlines
Air France 2552211
Air New Zealand 2599824
Alitalia 2575758
Avianca 2598455
British Airways 2558413
Iberia 2585333
JAL 2595244
KLM 2574011
Korean 2596719
Lufthansa 2583555
Pan Am 2576655
Philippine 2599824
Singapore 8008818
SAS 2594300
Swiss Air 2586211
Transbrasil 2282022
TWA 2558086
United 2312988
Varig 2230100
Vasp 5332211

Transport to City
Campinas-Viracopos
Taxi: the great distance between this airport and the city makes travel by taxi an expensive method of transportation. It could cost as much as US$70 and take two hours. Better to travel on the bus which leaves every couple of hours and costs much less, although it will also take two hours to get into the city.

Congonhas
Taxi: metered taxis are available

but decide on fare with driver beforehand. Tip 15-20%.
Coach: there is a bus which leaves every 25 minutes and costs the equivalent of US$3-6.

Facilities
Viracopos
Bank with foreign exchange, baggage deposit, shops.
Car rental desks: Hertz, Avis
Congonhas
Foreign exchange, post office, bar, restaurant, shops, first aid/medical, baggage deposit
Car rental desks: Hertz, Avis, Locarauto

Airport Taxes
Per person: International 180 cruziero, domestic 45 cruziero

City Information

Weather
Summers (Dec-Mar) are warm in daytime but cool at night.
Winters (June-Aug) can be chilly.
Average temps: Jan 17c (63F)
July 9c (49F)

Transportation
Metered taxis have red number plates with white digits and can be hailed. Radio taxis available.
Price goes up after 2200. Tipping (10-15%) optional.
Two subway lines connect with good bus system. Integrated bus/metro system available.
International driving license required for rental cars.

1. ANHEMBI CONVENTION CENTER
2. ART MUSEUM
3. BONIFACIO MUSEUM
4. MARCO ZERO
5. SAO PAULO BUSINESS CENTER
6. SAO PAULO FORUM
7. TOURIST OFFICE

Sao Paulo

NORTH/SOUTH AMERICA

Car Hire
Hertz, Rua da Consolacao 307
(tel: 2569722 & 2558055)
Avis, Rua da Consolacao 347
(tel: 2560873 & 2411817)
National, Av Paulista 535
(tel: 2207611)

Hospitals
Private doctors expensive and
public health care poor. Medical
assistance for travellers at:
Hospital Samaritano (tel: 512154)

Trade Fairs
Shoe and Leather Fair (Jan)
International Textile Fair (Feb-
Mar)
International Fair of Office
Equipment (Sept)

Hotels
Brasilton Sao Paulo, Rua Martins
Fontes 330 (tel: 2585811)
Caesar Park, Rua Augusta 1508
(tel: 2856622)
Eldorado Boulevard, Av Sao Luiz
234 (tel: 2570222/2568833)
Eldorado Higienopolis, Rua
Marques de Itu 836
(tel: 2223422)
Grand Hotel Ca D'Oro, Rua
Augusta 129 (tel: 2568011)
Holiday Inn Crowne, Froi
Caneca 1360 (tel: 2310888)
Maksoud Plaza, Alameda
Campinas 150 (tel: 2512233)
Novotel, Rua Ministro Nelson
Hungria 450 (tel: 5421244)
Othon Palace Hotel, Rua Libero
Badaro 196 (tel: 2393277)
Sao Paulo Hilton, Av Ipiranga
165 (tel: 2560033)

What to See and Do
Excellent restaurants and Art
Museum. Classical music and
dance at the Municipal Theater.
Sunday morning craft fair at

Praca de Republica. Simba Safari,
the largest animal park on the
continent, is less than an hour
away. Samba shows at night at
Jogral, Av Rui Barbosa 333,
Telecoteco na Paraquia, Rua
Santo Antonio 1015, Oba Oba,
Av Paulista 412. Ceasa Market is
the huge produce market on
outskirts of town.

Useful Addresses

Embassies and Consulates
American: Rua Joao Manoel 933
(tel: 8816511)
Canadian: Av Paulista 854
(tel: 2872122)
British: Av Paulista 1938
(tel: 2877722)

Business and Commerce
Central Post Office, Praca do
Correio
Sao Paulo Chamber of
Commerce, Viaduto Boa Vista
51 (tel: 2391333)
Stock Exchange, Rua Alvares
Penteado 151 (tel: 2587222)
American Chamber of
Commerce, Rua Formosa 367
(tel: 2226377)
British Chamber of Commerce,
Rua Baraode Itapetininga 275

Tourism and Travel
American Express, Rua Marconi
71 (tel: 2594211)
National Tourist Office, Av
Brigadeiro Faria Lima 1323
(tel: 2124266)
City Tourist Office, Av Praca da
Republica (tel: 2593144)
Thomas Cook, Av Sao Luis 258
(tel: 2566491)

CANADA

Essential Information

Type of Government
Parliamentary Democracy

Area
9.92 million sq km
(3.8 million sq mi)

Population
25.6 million

Annual Growth Rate
1.2%

Language
English and French are official
languages

Religion
Roman Catholic 46%, United
Church 18%, Anglican 12%

Ethnic Groups
British-Canadian 45%, French
29%, other European 23%,
Indian and Eskimo 1.5%

Weights and Measures
Metric is official, but the British
Imperial system is still used
widely

Electrical Current
A.C. 60c 110/220V

Major Business Cities
Ottawa (cap) 825,000
Toronto 3,700,000
Montreal 3,200,000
Vancouver 1,500,000
Edmonton 800,000
Calgary 690,000
Winnipeg 635,000

Currency
1 Dollar = 100 Cents
Notes 1, 2, 5, 10, 20, 50, 100
  dollars
Coins 1, 5, 10, 25, 50 cents

Public Holidays
Jan 1 New Year
Apr 13-20 Easter Week
May 18 Victoria Day
Aug 3 Civic Holiday
Jul 1 Canada Day
Sept 7 Labour Day
Oct 12 Thanksgiving Day
Nov 11 Remembrance Day
Dec 25 Christmas Day
Dec 26 Boxing Day

Travellers Information

Entry Requirements
Passport is required for all
travellers entering Canada,
except for US citizens who must
have valid identification. No
visas are required from citizens
of the US or Commonwealth
countries. For other countries,
check with the Canadian
Consulate.

Working Restrictions
Work permit required.

Vaccination Required
No vaccinations are required.

Customs and Duty Free
On arrival: 200 cigarets, 50 cigars
or 2 lbs/900 gr of tobacco and
40 oz/1.1 liter of wine or spirits.
Visitors may bring in goods for
personal use and commercial
samples duty free.

Currency Restrictions
There are no import or export
restrictions on currency

Health Tips
Health care in Canada is
excellent. Emergency medical
treatment is available at all
hospitals. Canadian citizens are
eligible for free government-
administered health programs,
but visitors must pay when
treated. Traveller's health
insurance is advised.

Climate and Clothing
The climate in Canada varies
greatly since it is the world's
second largest country in area.
Following is a brief description
of four major climate areas.

NORTH/SOUTH AMERICA

Atlantic Canada
November-April. Very cold with heavy snow and wind. Temperatures vary from -10 to 4C (15-40F). Wear medium to heavy clothing with overcoat, boots and hat.
May-October. Hot and humid in interior areas, milder on the coast. Rainshowers frequent. Light clothing with raincoat.

Central Canada
November-April. Cold, with heavy snow at times. More temperate in Southern Ontario. Temperatures -10 to 10C (15-50F). Medium clothing, heavy in Northern regions, with overcoat, boots and hat.
May-October. Hot and humid with frequent thunderstorms in summer. Temperature 18-32C (65-85F). Light clothing with raincoat.

Western Canada
November-April. Very cold in Rocky Mountain region and on the Praries, temperate on the West Coast. Heavy snowfalls in mountains and snow or rain in coastal regions. Temperatures -18 to 18C (0-65F). Light clothing on coast, heavy clothing in mountains.
May-October. Hot and dry on the Praries, warm to cool in the mountains, and warm with frequent rain on the coast. Temperatures 18-35C (65-95F). Light clothing with raincoat or umbrella on the coast.

Northern Canada
November-April. Extremely cold, with snow and ice, sub-artic conditions. Temperatures from -22 to 0C (-30-32F). Heavy clothing with overcoat, gloves, boots and hat.
May-October. Warm to cool, and dry with little rain. Temperature

4-24C (40-75F). Light to medium clothing with jacket at night.

Tipping

Tipping is very similar to the United States. Tip 15% for good service in restaurants and bars. Taxi drivers, hotel door attendants, airport porters, maids should all be tipped from 50 cents to $2.00. Other small services, barber, hat check etc., can be rewarded with a small tip.

Food and Drink

The cuisine of Canada can be described as North American, with various European influences in selected regions. The dishes of Quebec and French Canada are heavily derived from the original French settlers. French restaurants in Montreal and Quebec City are among the best in North America. Specialties include Tortiere (pork pie), recipes with maple syrup and French-style cheeses, breads and pastries. Central Canada, inhabited primarily by descendents from Great Britain and Scotland, favor British-style foods such as steak and kidney pie, sausages, etc. For the most part, the diet of Canadians is not that much different from that of Americans. As well, large European immigrant populations, such as Italians, Portuguese and Ukranians, have added spice to the traditional Canadian diet. Regional specialties include seafood (especially lobster) from Atlantic Canada, potatoes and potato dishes from Prince Edward Island, maple syrup from Quebec, lamb, pork and cheddar cheese from Ontario, beef from the Praries, and King Crab and salmon from British Columbia.

Business Brief

GDP
$338 billion
(per capita income $13,400)

Annual Growth Rate
4.5%

Natural Resources
Petroleum and natural gas, copper, nickle, zinc, iron ore, gold, fish, forests, wildlife

Agriculture
Barley, wheat, corn, Potatoes, Tobacco, feed grains, oilseeds, dairy products, fruits and vegetables

Industry
Motor vehicles and parts, chemicals, food processing, fish and forest products, petroleum refining, mineral processing, paper and wood products, dairy products, and machinery manufacturing

Imports
Total $92.7 billion
Motor vehicles and parts, machinery, communication and electrical equipment, textiles, petroleum, agricultural machinery

Exports
Total $98.1 billion
Motor vehicles and parts, Newsprint, paper, lumber, wheat, petroleum, natural gas, nickel, copper, chemicles, livestock

Major Trading Partners
US, Japan, Britain, France, Netherlands, Germany, Italy

Workforce
12.2 million
Agriculture 4%, industry and commerce 52%, services 28%, government 6%

Tips for Doing Business
Business customs are similar to those of the United States.

Business suits are worn during meetings, and appointments are usually made. The business lunch, and more now, the business breakfast, are popular times for discussing business. Relaxed and informal meetings are the rule.
In Quebec, most businessmen speak fluent English, but occasionally some prefer French. Check prior to making appointments.

Best Months for Doing Business
Normally the Spring and Fall. Canadians take their vacations between June and September, or in January-February when the weather is cold.

Business Hours

Government
Mon-Fri 0900-1630

Business
Mon-Fri 0900-1700

Banks
Mon-Fri 1000-1500
Occasionally Saturday

Shops
Mon-Fri 0930-1900
Some nights until 2100
Sat 0930-1800

Telephone and Communications
The telephone and communications system in Canada, like that in the United States, is probably the finest in the world. You can direct dial anywhere within Canada, or the rest of the world. Dial 0 for the operator, 411 for information and 911 for emergency (not in all cities). For long-distance dialing in Canada and the US begin with 1 followed by the city area code. For dialing overseas, begin with 011. Public pay phones are available everywhere and require 25 cents for a local call. Many new credit card phones are now

available, especially at the airports.

Telephone country code: 1
Telephone city codes:
Calgary 403
Edmonton 403
Halifax 902
Hamilton 416
London 519
Montreal 514
Ottawa 613
Quebec City 418
Regina 306
St. Johns (NB) 506
St. John's (NF) 709
Toronto 416
Vancouver 604
Victoria 604
Windsor 519
Winnipeg 204

Air Travel

Canada has an extensive regional carrier system which provides good service, even into the far northern regions such as the Yukon and Northwest Territories. Major international carriers are Air Canada, Canadian International (formerly CP Air and Pacific Western), and Wardair.

Because of the great distances between major Canadian cities, air travel is usually the fastest means of travel.

Other Transport

Taxis are plentiful in the major cities, but a rental car is probably the easiest way to get around most metropolitan areas.

If you have the time, VIA Rail operates a transcontinental train service from Montreal to Vancouver. It is the most efficient train service in North America and travels through spectacular scenery in the Rocky Mountains.

Long-distance bus services are provided by Greyhound, Voyageur, and Grey Line.

CALGARY

Airport Information

Time
GMT -7
GMT -6 (Apr-Oct)

Airport
Calgary International (McCall) YYC
Tel: 276-0254
19 km (12 mi) NE of city

Airlines
Air Canada 265-9555
British Airways 1-800 268-8090
Canadian International 265-2760
Lufthansa 294-0354
SAS 1-800 221-2350
United 1-800 265-4873
Wardair 261-0600

Transport to City
Taxis: From airport terminal to downtown takes about 30 minutes for $15, plus tip.
Coach: Airporter bus departs every 30 minutes between 0530-2330 to downtown hotel locations. Fare $5. Some hotels offer courtesy van service.

Facilities
Duty-free shop, currency exchange, hotel reservations, baggage deposit, post office, bar, restaurant, shops
Car rental desks: Hertz, Avis, Budget, Holiday, Tilden

Airport Taxes
None

City Information

Weather
November-April. Very cold, windy, with snow and occasional blizzard conditions. Temperature -9-5C (15-40F). Medium to heavy weight clothing with overcoat, hat and boots.

May-October. Warm, sunny and dry with occasional hot summer days. Temperature 10-27C (50-80F). Light clothing with jacket or sweater in evenings.

Transportation

Calgary is a wide-open city and the best and easiest way to get around is by automobile. Rental cars are available at the airport and in the city. Taxis are difficult to find on the streets, but can be caught at hotel stands or call Yellow Cab (276-8311). The city bus system is good and covers a wide portion of the city. Fares are $1, exact change required. There is also a short rapid-transit line running through the center of the city.

Car Hire

Hertz, The Bay, 227 6th Ave. SW 263-8400

Budget, 407 Centre St. 1-800 268-8900

Tilden, 114 5th Ave. SE 263-6386

Hospitals

Calgary General, 841 Centre Ave. East 268-9111

Trade Shows

Sportsman's Exhibition (Mar)

Hotels

BW Hospitality Inn, 135 Southland Dr SE, 278-5050

BW Village Park Inn, 1804 Crowchild, 289-0241

Delta Bow Valley, 209 4th Ave. SE 266-1980

Four Seasons, 110 9th Ave. SE 266-7331

Glenbow Inn, 708 8th Ave SW, 263-7600

Holiday Inn, 4206 MacLeod Trail SE 287-2700

Marlborough Inn, 1316 33rd St NE, 248-8888

Palliser Hotel, 133 9th Ave. SW 262-1234

Prince Royal Inn, 618 5th Ave SW, 263-0520

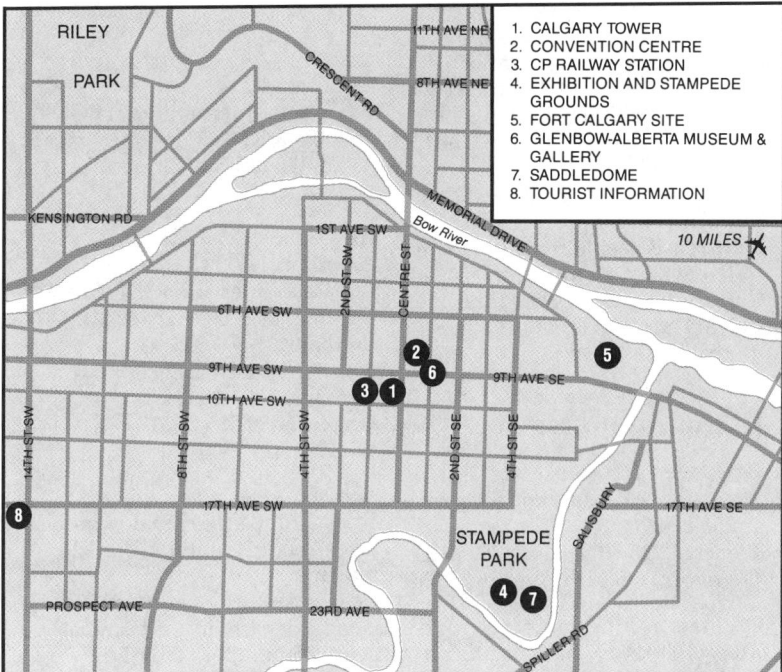

1. CALGARY TOWER
2. CONVENTION CENTRE
3. CP RAILWAY STATION
4. EXHIBITION AND STAMPEDE GROUNDS
5. FORT CALGARY SITE
6. GLENBOW-ALBERTA MUSEUM & GALLERY
7. SADDLEDOME
8. TOURIST INFORMATION

Calgary

NORTH/SOUTH AMERICA

Relax Airport Inn, 2750
Sunridge, 291-1260
Relax Inn South, 9206 Macleod
Trail, 253-7070
Sandman Inn, 888 7th Ave SW,
663-6900
Sheraton, 2620 32nd Ave. NE
291-0107
Westin Hotel Calgary, 320 4th
Ave. SW 266 -1611
Westward Inn, 119 12th Ave. SW
266-4611

What to See and Do

The biggest annual event in
Calgary is normally the Calgary
Stampede, which is held in July.
This spectacle is the largest
rodeo in North America and it
attracts thousands of visitors
from all over the world.
However, the event that will
supersede this will be the 1988
Winter Olympics. The many fine
ski areas, some of which will be
used for Olympic events, are
easily accessible from Calgary.
Even in the summer, the Rockies
are a premier attraction and just
a short drive from Calgary.
In Calgary proper, there are
many fine parks, the Glenbow/
Alberta Institute museum of
Eskimo art and Indian artifacts,
Heritage Park, Fort Calgary
and the Military Museum. The
Calgary Philharmonic and
Alberta Ballet Company are both
popular companies. For sports
enthusiasts, aside from the many
rodeo events, there are the
Calgary Flames (hockey) and the
Calgary Stampeders (Canadian
football).

Useful Addresses

Embassies and Consulates
American: 615 MacLeod Trail SE
266-8962
French: 3223 Utah Place 289-8123
German: 1115 11th Ave. 269-5900

Business and Commerce
Alberta Stock Exchange, 300 5th
Ave. 262-7791

Calgary Chamber of Commerce,
517 Centre St. 263-7435
Calgary Tourist and Convention
Bureau, 1300 6th Ave. SW
263-8510
Calgary Convention Centre, 110
9th Ave. 261-8800

Tourism and Travel
Alberta Motor Assoc., 435 36th
St. NE 235-3503
Deak International, 401 9th Ave
SW, 292-1000
Uniglobe Advance Travel Centre,
800736 6th Ave S, 237-7040
Uniglobe McGowan Travel,
209-5940 MacLeod Trail,
259-8747
Uniglobe Prestige Travel, 220-932
17th Ave SW, 244-7887
Uniglobe Swift Travel, 321 10th
St., 270-8111

EDMONTON

Airport Information

Time
GMT -7
GMT -6 (Apr-Oct)

Airport
Edmonton International YEG
Tel: 955-8382
28 km (18 mi) S of city

Airlines
Air Canada 423-1222
American 1-800 433-7300
Canadian International 422-6438
Continental 1-800 525-0280
Lufthansa 1-800 387-9210
Northwest 422-6458
SAS 1-800 221-2350
United 1-800 265-4873
Wardair 423-5500

Transport to City
Taxis: From airport to downtown
takes about 30 minutes for $24,
plus tip.
Coach: Airport buses (Grey
Goose) depart airport terminal
every 45 minutes, Mon-Fri,
hourly on weekends. Fare $7.

Facilities
Duty-free shop, currency exchange, hotel reservations, post office, bar, restaurant, shops
Car rental desks: Hertz, Avis, Budget, Holiday, Tilden

Airport Taxes
None

City Information

Weather
November-April. Very cold, dry with snow and occasional blizzard conditions. Temperature -15-5C (10-40F), but it can fall to below 0 F during winter. Wear medium to heavy clothing with overcoat, hat and boots.
May-October. Warm, sunny and dry with infrequent rainfall. Some hot days during summer. Temperature 10-27C (50-80F). Light to medium clothing with jacket at nights.

Transportation
A rental car is the best way to get around the Edmonton area. Bus service is good if time is not a factor. Exact fare of $1.00 is required. Taxis are hard to find on the streets but can be found at hotels, or you can call Yellow Cab (426-3456).

Car Hire
Hertz, Bay Parkade, 10042 103rd St. 423-3431
Hertz, 11830 Kingsway Ave. 451-6707

Hospitals
Edmonton General, 11111 Jasper Ave. 482-8111

Hotels
BW Ambassador, 10041 106th St, 423-1925
Continental Inn, 16625 Stony Plain Rd., 484-7751
Fantasyland Hotel, 17700 87th Ave., 444-3000
Four Seasons, 10235 101st St. 428-7111
Hilton Edmonton, 10235 101st St., 428-7111
Ramada Renaissance, 10155 105th St., 423-4811
Relax Inn, 18320 Stony Plain Rd., 483-6031
Sandman Hotel, 17635 Stony Plain, 483-1385
Sheraton Caravan, 10010 104th St. 423-2450
Westin Edmonton, 10135 100th St. 426-3636

What to See and Do
The downtown center of Edmonton is the Civic Centre, site of City Hall, the Centennial Library, Citadel Theatre, and the Edmonton Art Gallery. Other attractions include the Provincial Museum of Alberta, the Alberta Legislative Building, Fort Edmonton Park, St. Albert Museum, and the Jubilee Auditorium, home of the Edmonton Symphony Orchestra and the Edmonton Opera Society. Outside of Edmonton is the Alberta Game Farm 14 km (9 mi) and the Ukrainian Cultural Heritage Village.
The biggest pride and joy of Edmonton is Wayne Gretzky and the Edmonton Oilers, champions of the National Hockey League. Other sports include the Canadian football (Edmonton Eskimos), and rodeos, of which the Klondike Days in July is Edmonton's extravaganza event of the year.

Useful Addresses

Embassies and Consulates
British: 10025 Jasper Ave.428-0375
French: 10240 124th St. 428-0232
German: 10004 104th Ave.422-6175
Japanese: 10020 100th St.422-3752

Business and Commerce

Edmonton Chamber of
Commerce, 10123 99th St.
426-4620

Edmonton Convention Bureau,
10123 99th St. 426-4715

Tourism and Travel

Alberta Motor Assoc., 11230
110th St. 474-8660

Deak International, Edmonton
Airport 955-6655

Deak International, 10405 Jasper
Ave., 421-4442

Edmonton Visitor's Information
Bureau, 5068 103rd St.434-5322

Travel Alberta, 10065 Jasper Ave.
427-4321

Uniglobe Achievers Travel, 9330
49th St, 466-1222

Uniglobe Alamo Travel, 171
Northtown Mall, 478-6677

Uniglobe Geo Travel, 580-10250
101st St, 424-8310

OTTAWA

Airport Information

Time

GMT -5
GMT -4 (Apr-Oct)

Airport

Ottawa International (Uplands)
YOW
Tel: 998-3151
18 km (11 mi) SW of city

Airlines

Air Canada 237-5000
Air France 1-800 361-7240
Alitalia 521-2694
British Airways 236-0881
Canadian International 237-6175
Eastern 1-800 361-3020
Iberia 227-1882
Lufthansa 1-800 645-3880
Sabena 1-800 361-2600
SAS 1-800 221-2350
Wardair 1-800 387-0514

Transport to City

Taxis: Takes about 20-30 minutes
to downtown for $15, plus tip.
Coach: Airport bus (Blue Line)
departs outside of baggage area
every 30 minutes from 0700-2300
Mon-Fri, every hour otherwise,
for downtown hotels. Fare $4.50.
Transit: City bus #83 leaves
every half hour from 0600-0300
for downtown.

Facilities

Duty-free shop, currency
exchange, hotel reservations,
baggage deposit, post office, bar,
restaurant, shops
Car rental desks: Hertz, Avis,
Budget, Tilden

Airport Taxes

None

City Information

Weather

November-April. Cold, dry with
heavy snowfall. Temperatures
-3-7C (20-45F). Wear medium to
heavy clothing with overcoat,
hat and boots.
May-October. Warm (hot and
humid in summer), with
frequent rain and thunderstorms. Temperatures 16-27C
(60-80F). Light clothing with
light raincoat and umbrella.

Transportation

Ottawa has good taxi service.
They can be hailed on the street
or at hotel taxi stands. Main taxi
companies are Blue Line (238-
1111) and Capital (746-2233).
There are two bus systems in
Ottawa which give excellent
coverage of the city. Fares are
transferable.

Car Hire

Hertz, 881 St. Laurent Blvd.
746-6683
Hertz, 2 Granton St. 225-8503
Avis, 320 Queen St. 1-800
268-2310

Budget, 441 Somerset St. W.
  1-800 268-8900
Tilden, 199 Slater St. 361-5334

Hospitals
Civic Hospital, 1053 Carling Ave.
  729-2511
General Hospital, 501 Smyth Rd.
  737-7777

Hotels
Chateau Laurier, 1 Rideau St.
  232-6411
Delta Inn, 361 Queen St.238-6000
Four Seasons, 150 Albert
  St.238-1500
Howard Johnson, 140 Slater St.,
  238-2888

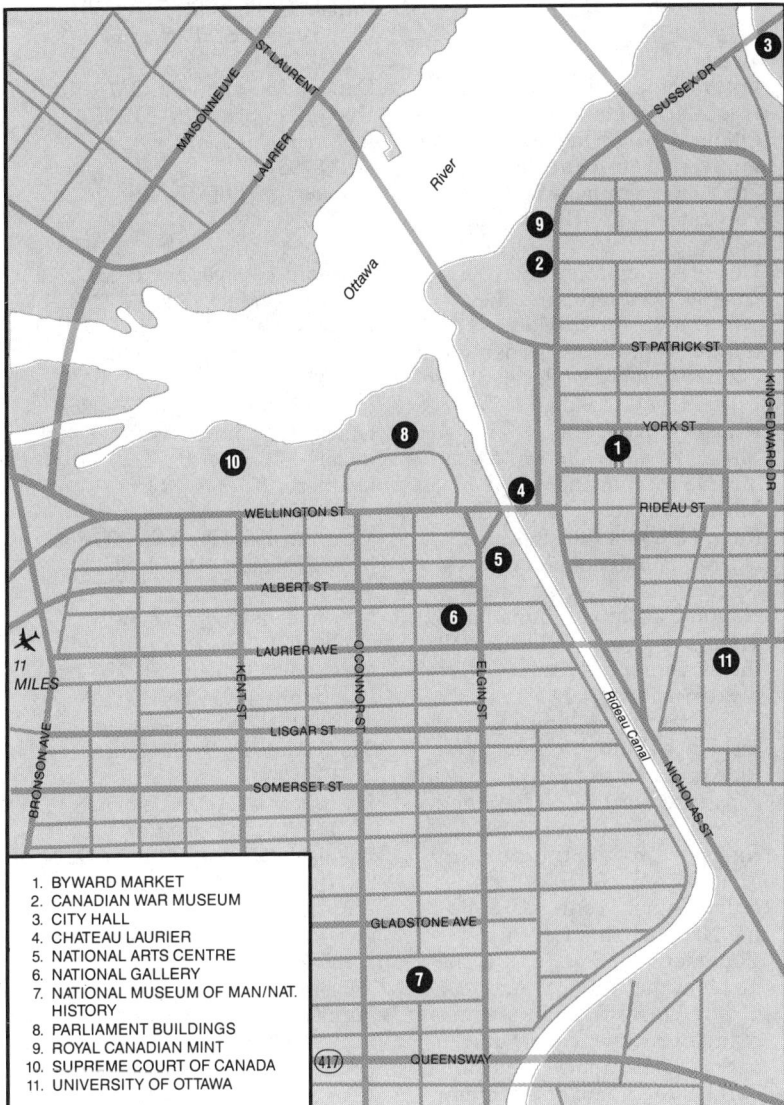

1. BYWARD MARKET
2. CANADIAN WAR MUSEUM
3. CITY HALL
4. CHATEAU LAURIER
5. NATIONAL ARTS CENTRE
6. NATIONAL GALLERY
7. NATIONAL MUSEUM OF MAN/NAT.
   HISTORY
8. PARLIAMENT BUILDINGS
9. ROYAL CANADIAN MINT
10. SUPREME COURT OF CANADA
11. UNIVERSITY OF OTTAWA

Ottawa

NORTH/SOUTH AMERICA

Lord Elgin Hotel, 100 Elgin St.,
235-3333
Novotel Hotel, 33 Nicholas St.,
230-3033
Radisson Hotel, 100 Kent St.,
238-1222
Relax Plaza, 402 Queen St.,
236-1133
Venture Inn, 480 Metcalfe St.,
237-5500
Westin Hotel, 11 Colonel By Dr.
560-7000

What to See and Do

Ottawa, the nation's capital,
is located in Ontario along the
Ottawa River. The most
impressive structures in Ottawa
are the government buildings on
Parliament Hill. The Parliament
buildings, consisting of the
House of Commons, Senate
Chamber, Library, and the
Supreme Court, are located on a
hill, majestically overlooking the
Ottawa River. Also located here
is the Royal Canadian Mint
which allows tours.
Museums and galleries to visit
include the Canadian War
Museum, National Museum of
Man, National Museum of
Science and Technology,
National Archives, and the
National Gallery of Canada.
Tours are given at Rideau Hall,
the Governor General's
residence, and at 24 Sussex
Drive, the Prime Minister's
residence. Both are near the
Rideau Canal and Locks,
constucted in 1832 to link the
Ottawa with Montreal and
Kingston on the St. Lawrence
River.
Entertainment centers around
the National Arts Centre on
Confederation Square. It is the
home of the National Arts
Centre Orchestra, and features
regular concerts, ballets and
operas. Civic Centre (Lansdowne
Park) is the home of the Ottawa
Roughriders (Canadian football).

Useful Addresses

Embassies and Consulates

American: 100 Wellington St.
238-5335
Australian: 130 Slater St.
236-0841
Austrian: 445 Wilbrod St.
563-1444
Belgian: 85 Range Rd. 236-7267
Brazilian: 255 Albert St. 237-1090
British: 80 Elgin St. 237-1530
Chinese: 515 St. Patrick St.
234-2706
Danish: 85 Range Rd. 234-1016
Dutch: 275 Slater St. 235-5030
Egyptian: 454 Laurier Ave.
234-4931
Finnish: 222 Somerset St.
236-2389
French: 42 Sussex Dr. 232-1795
German: 1 Waverley St. 232-1101
Greece, 80 MacLaren St. 238-6271
Hong Kong: 80 Elgin St. 237-1530
Indian: 10 Springfield Rd.
744-3751
Irish: 170 Metcalfe St. 233-6281
Israeli: 410 Laurier Ave. 237-6450
Italian: 275 Slater St. 232-2401
Japanese: 255 Sussex Dr.
236-8541
Mexican: 130 Albert St. 233-6665
New Zealand: 99 Bank St.
238-5991
Norwegian: 90 Sparks St.
238-6571
Pakistani: 151 Slater St. 238-7881
Philippine: 130 Albert St.
233-1121
Saudi Arabian: 99 Bank St.
237-4100
South Korean: 85 Albert St.
232-1715
Spanish: 350 Sparks St. 237-2194
Swedish: 441 MacLaren St.
236-8553
Swiss: 5 Marlborough Ave.
235-1837
Thailand: 85 Range Rd. 237-1517
Turkish: 197 Wurtemberg St.
232-1577
USSR: 52 Range Rd. 236-7220
Venezuelan: 924 Albert St.
235-5151

Yugoslavian: 17 Blackburn Ave. 233-6289

Business and Commerce

Bank of Canada, 24 Wellington St. 563-8111

Canadian Business Centre, 235 Queen St. 995-5771

Canadian Chamber of Commerce, 200 Elgin St. 238-4000

Eastern Ontario Devel. Corp., 56 Sparks St. 566-3707

Federal Business Devel. Bank, 151 Sparks St. 237-8430

Ottawa Board of Trade, Press Club Bldg. 236-3631

World Trade Centre of Canada, 90 Sparks St. 233-5666

Tourism and Travel

American Express, 220 Laurier St. 563-0231

CAA Ottawa, 2525 Carling Ave. 820-1890

Canadian Office of Tourism,235 Queen St. 996-4610

Capital Visitor's and Convention Bureau, 55 Elgin St. 237-5158

Deak International, 320 Queen St., 235-3325

Deak International, 109 Bank St., 232-2691

Ottawa Central Train Station, Alta Vista & Queensway

Uniglobe Premiere Travel,130 Slater St. 230 7411
130 Slater St. 230 7411

MONTREAL

Airport Information

Time
GMT -5
GMT -4 (Apr-Oct)

Airports
Montreal International (Mirabel) YMX
Tel: 476-3010
55 km (34 m1) NW of city
International

Montreal International (Dorval) YUL
Tel: 636-3223
21 km (13 mi) SE of city
Domestic and to U.S.

Airlines
Aeroflot 288-2125
Aerolineas Argentinas 1-800 361-8159
Air Canada 931-4411
Air France 284-2825
Alitalia 842-5201
American 397-9635
Avensa 866-2451
British Airways 287-9282
Canadian International 286-0303
Delta 337-5520
Eastern 483-6363
El Al 875-8900
Finnair 879-1752
Iberia 861-9531
KLM 844-2011
Korean 874-4560
Lufthansa 39709121
Olympic 878-3891
Pan Am 288-4204
Sabena 845-0215
SAS 1-800 221-2350
Swissair 879-9154
TAP 849-4217
US Air 871-0017
Wardair 288-9231

Transport to City
Mirabel Airport
Taxis: Very expensive (about $50) to downtown Montreal for a 40-60 minute ride.
Coach: Airport bus departs every 90 minutes until 1200, then every 30-40 minutes until 2000. About 50-60 minutes downtown for $9.00. Some hotels offer courtesy buses to their hotels.
Transit: City bus to downtown metro station (Bourassa) leaves terminal every hour from 0600-2400. $3.50

Dorval Airport
Taxis: Taxi to city center is $20, plus tip for 20-30 minute ride.
Coach: Airport bus (Aerocar)

leaves the terminal every 20 minutes from 0700-1000, then every 30 minutes. Fare is $6 for 25 minute run to several downtown hotel locations. Several hotels also offer free courtesy rides.

Inter-Airport: Coach to Mirabel Airport leaves Dorval every hour in the morning, and 40-minute intervals afternoon and evenings. Takes 45 minutes, $9.

Facilities
Duty-free shop (both airports), currency exchange, baggage deposit, hotel reservations, conference rooms, bar, restaurant, post office, shops Car rental desks: Hertz, Avis, Budget, Holiday, Tilden

Airport Taxes
None

City Information

Weather
November-April. Cold, dry, with snow (heavy at times). Temperature -5-7C (2--45F). Medium clothing with overcoat, hat and boots.
May-October. Warm, but can be hot and humid in summer, with frequent thunderstorms. Temperature 16-27C (60-85F). Light clothing with light raincoat.

Transportation
The transit system in Montreal is one of the best in North America. Bus service (MUCTC) covers the metro area extensively, and a fare of $1 (exact change required) will get you anywhere you wish to go. The bus system is transferable

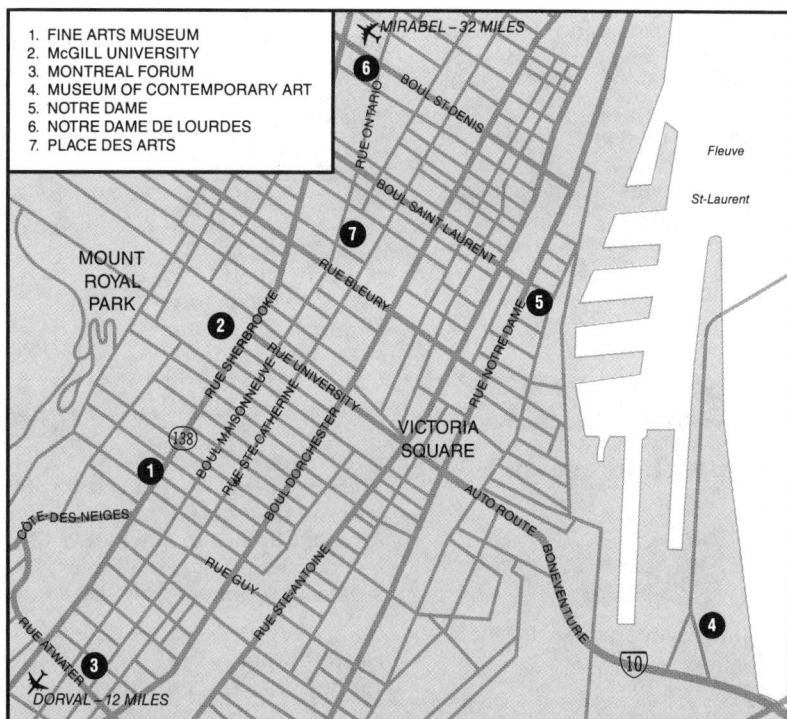

1. FINE ARTS MUSEUM
2. McGILL UNIVERSITY
3. MONTREAL FORUM
4. MUSEUM OF CONTEMPORARY ART
5. NOTRE DAME
6. NOTRE DAME DE LOURDES
7. PLACE DES ARTS

MIRABEL – 32 MILES
RUE ONTARIO
BOUL ST-DENIS
Fleuve
St-Laurent
BOUL SAINT LAURENT
MOUNT ROYAL PARK
RUE BLEURY
RUE SHERBROOKE
RUE UNIVERSITY
RUE NOTRE DAME
BOUL MAISONNEUVE
RUE STE-CATHERINE
BOUL DORCHESTER
VICTORIA SQUARE
AUTO ROUTE
CÔTE-DES-NEIGES
RUE GUY
RUE STE-ANTOINE
BONAVENTURE
RUE ATWATER
DORVAL – 12 MILES

Montreal

onto the subway lines. Taxis are plentiful on downtown streets. They can be hailed on streets or found at hotel taxi stands.

Car Hire

Hertz, The Bay, 1475 Aylmer St. 636-9530

Hertz, 960 Taschereau Blvd.679-1110

Avis, 750 Laurentian Blvd.1-800 268-0303

Budget, 1460 Guy St. 1-800 268-8970

Tilden, 1200 Stanley St. 842-9445

Hospitals

Montreal General Hospital, 1650, avenue Cedar 937-6011

Centre Hospitalier Douglas, 6875 boul. LaSalle 761-6131

Trade Fairs

International Sporting Goods Exhibition (Feb)

Outdoor and Camping Exhibition (Mar)

Plant and Industrial Equip. Exhibition (May)

Hotels

Bonaventure Hilton, Place Bonaventure 878-2332

Chateau Champlain, Place du Canada 878-9000

Constellation, 3407 Peel St.845-1234

Delta Hotel, 450 Sherbrooke St. W, 286-1986

Four Seasons, 1050 Sherbrooke St. 284-1110

Holiday Inn Downtown, 420 Rue Sherbrooke 842-6111

Holiday Inn Richelieu, 505 Sherbrooke St. 842-8581

Hotel des Gouverneurs, 1415 Hubert St., 842-4881

Hyatt Regency, 777 University St. 879-1370

La Citadelle, 410 Sherbrooke St. W, 844-8857

Meridien-Montreal, 4 Complexe Dejardins 285-1450

Queen Elizabeth, 900 Dorchester W. 861-3511

Ramada Inn, 1005 Guy St., 866-4611

Ramada Olympic Park, 5500 Sherbrooke, 256-9011

Ramada Renaissance, 3625 Ave du Parc, 288-6666

Ramada Vaudreuil, 21700 Trans-Canada, 455-0955

Ritz Carlton, 1228 Sherbrooke St. 842-4212

Sheraton Le Centre, 1201 Rene Levesque, 878-2000

Sheraton Mt. Royal, 1455 Peel St. 842-7777

What to See and Do

Montreal, the most European of North America's great cities, has the advantages of both - the charm of France, and the conveniences of Canada. Head first to old Montreal (le Vieux Montreal) an area of narrow

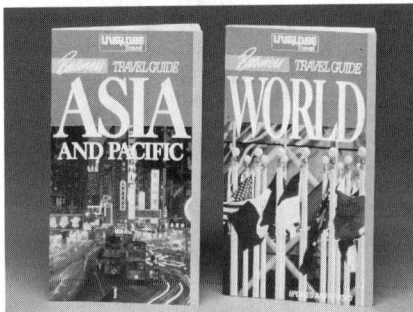

cobblestone streets, old stone buildings and charming outdoor restaurants. Also in old Montreal is City Hall, Chateau Ramezay museum, and the Bonsecours Market. Here also is Notre Dame de Bonsecours church, built in 1777. Just a little further west at the Place d'Armes is Notre Dame, the equal of the great cathedrals of Europe.

A unique feature of Montreal is its underground city, a vast complex of below-ground shops, restaurants and theaters where many residents spend their winters.

Other sites include Mount Royal, Olympic Village, the chic French-speaking Rue St-Denis, Man and His World on Ile St. Helene, and the world-famous Montreal Botanical Gardens.

Sporting events are centered around Olympic Stadium, which features the Montreal Expos (baseball) and Concordes (Canadian football), and the Forum where the Canadiens hockey team plays.

Useful Addresses

Embassies and Consulates
American: 1155 University St., 281-1886
British: 635 Rene Levesque Blvd.866-5863
French: 2 Elysee, Place Bonaventure 878-4381
German: 3455 Mountain St.286-1820
Israeli: 2085 Union St. W.268-9277
Japanese: 1155 Rene Levesque, 393-9372866-3429
USSR: 3655 ave. de Musee843-5901

Business and Commerce
Canadian Chamber of Commerce, 1080 Beaver Hall Hill 866-4334
Federal Business Development Bank, 800 Place Victoria 878-9571
German Chamber of Commerce, 2015 Peel St. 844-3051
Ministry of Industry, Commerce & Tourism, 1 Place Ville-Marie 873-3530
Montreal Chamber of Commerce, 1080 Beaver Hall Hill 866-2861
Montreal Convention and Visitors Bureau, Place Bonaventure 871-1129
Montreal Stock Exchange, 800 Victoria Square 871-2424
Montreal World Trade Center, 1191 rue de la Montagne 866-1352
Quebec Chamber of Commerce, 1010 ouest, rue St. Catherine 879-1717

Tourism and Travel
American Express, 1141 Maisonneuve 284-3300
CAA Quebec, 1425 Mountain St. 288-7111
Central Station (Amtrack and VIA Rail) 1-800 361-6142
Deak International, Dorval Airport (4 locations) 636-3582
Deak International, 1155 Sherbrooke, 285-1307
Thomas Cook, 2020 University Rd. 842-1161
Uniglobe Voyages Avat, 5870 Sherbrooke E, 255-9117
Uniglobe Voyages Centre-Ville, 1253 McGill College 397-9221
Uniglobe Voyages Chad, 2015 Peel St., 843-5710
Uniglobe Voyages Gelgoot, 500 Sherbrooke W, 845-6400
Uniglobe Voyages GesMa, 1015 Beaver Hall Hill 397-1155

TORONTO

Airport Information

Time
GMT -5
GMT -4 (Apr-Oct)

Airport
Lester B. Pearson International
  YYZ
Tel: 676-3506
28 km (17 mi) NW of city
Terminals 1 and 2

Airlines
Aer Lingus 362-6565
Aeromexico 363-9017
Air Canada 925-2311
Air China 968-3300

Air France 364-0101
Air India 865-1030
Alitalia 363-2001
American 283-2243
Avianca 482-1617
British Airways 595-2500
Canadian International 675-2211
Canadian Partner 675-2211
City Express 360-4444
Delta 868-1717
Eastern 362-3461
El Al 864-9779
Finnair 927-7400
Iberia 964-6625
Japan Airlines 364-7226
KLM 366-9041
Kuwait Air 364-8444
Lufthansa 869-0505
Northwest 1-800 225-2525
Olympic 964-7137

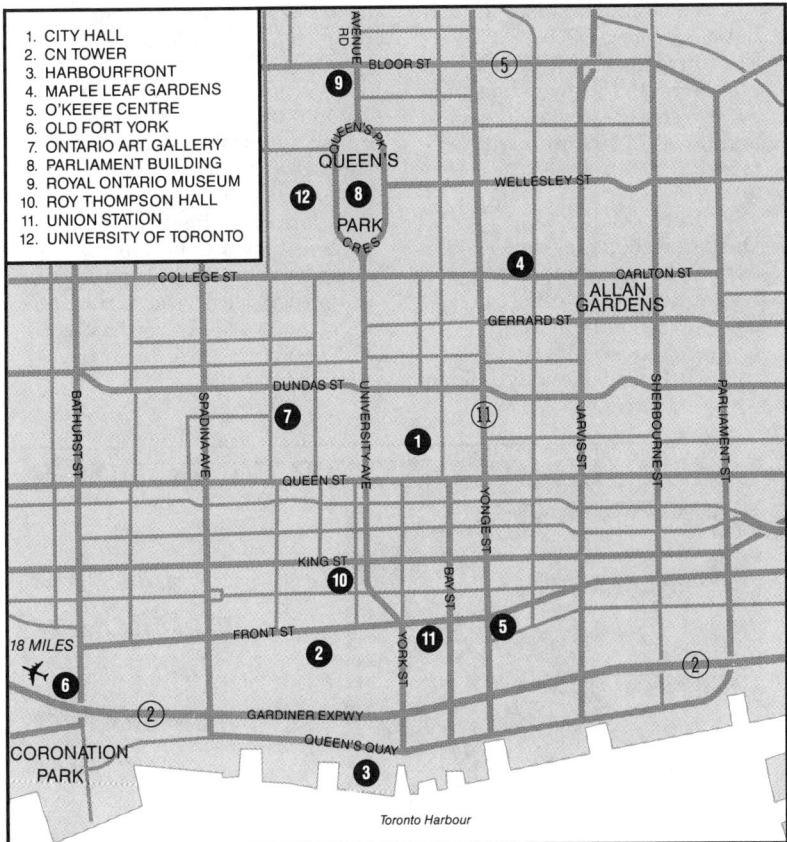

1. CITY HALL
2. CN TOWER
3. HARBOURFRONT
4. MAPLE LEAF GARDENS
5. O'KEEFE CENTRE
6. OLD FORT YORK
7. ONTARIO ART GALLERY
8. PARLIAMENT BUILDING
9. ROYAL ONTARIO MUSEUM
10. ROY THOMPSON HALL
11. UNION STATION
12. UNIVERSITY OF TORONTO

Toronto Harbour

Toronto

Pan Am 964-1150
Philippine 1-800 435-9725
Qantas 1-800 663-3423
Sabena 961-2075
SAS 1-800 221-2350
Singapore 366-7555
Swissair 960-5203
TWA 1-800 221-2000
United 362-5000
US Air 361-1560
Varig 362-7504
Wardair 620-9800

Transport to City

Taxis: Taxis available at both terminals departure levels for 30-45 minute ride to downtown for about $25, plus tip.
Coach: Airport bus (Grey Coach) departs every 20 minutes from 0630-2400 for downtown hotels. About 30 minutes, more in rush hour, for fare of $7.50.
Transit: Grey Coach to Islington Station on the subway line costs $4. transfer to subway line for additional $1.10 for downtown stops.

Facilities

Duty-free shops, currency exchange, baggage deposit, hotel reservations, post office, first-aid, bar, restaurant, shops
Car rental desks: Hertz, Avis, Budget, Dollar, Holiday, Tilden

Airport Taxes

None

City Information

Weather

November-April. Cold with frequent snow. Temperature -1-10C (30-50F), dropping to below freezing during winter months. Medium weight clothing with overcoat, hat and boots.
May-October. Warm and sunny. Hot and humid with frequent thunderstorms during summer months. Light to medium weight clothing with raincoat and umbrella.

Transportation

Taxis are plentiful and can be hailed in the streets or found at hotel stands. Call Metro Cab (363-5611), Diamond Cab (366-6868) or Co-op Cab (364-8161). Toronto has one of the best transit systems in North America. The bus and streetcar system (TTC) is excellent, and for a fare of $1 you can ride to almost any location in downtown or metro Toronto. As well, it will allow you to transfer to the subway (TTC), which is also one of the best in North America.

If your business takes you out to suburban areas you are probably best having a car rental.

Car Hire
Hertz, Airport, 676-3241
Hertz, Yonge & Bloor, 961-3320
Hertz, Simpsons, 35 Richmond St. 363-9022
Avis, 211 Adelaide, 598-5007
Budget, Bay & Scollard, 964-6383
Tilden, 930 Yonge St. 925-4551

Hospitals
North York General, 4001 Leslie St. 492-4500
St. Michael's Hospital, 30 Bond St. 360-4000
Toronto General Hospital, 101 College St. 595-3111

Trade Fairs
National Gift Show (Jan)
International Automobile Exhibition (Feb)
Construction Exhibition (Feb)
Luggage & Leather Goods Exhibition (Apr)
Gift and Tableware Exhibition (Aug)

Hotels
Bond Place, 65 Dundas St. E, 362-6061
Bradgate Arms, Avenue Rd. & St. Clair 967-1331
Carlton Inn, 30 Carlton St.977-6655
Delta Chelsea Inn, 33 Gerrard St. 595-1975
Four Seasons, 21 Avenue Rd. 964-0411
Hampton Court, 415 Jarvis St. 924-6631
Hilton Harbour Castle, 1 Harbour Square 869-1600
Ibis Hotel, 240 Jarvis St., 593-9400
Journeys End Hotel, 111 Lombard, 367-5555
King Edward Hotel, 37 King St. E. 863-9700
L'Hotel, 225 Front St. 567-1400

Novotel Toronto, 45 Esplanade, 367-8900
Park Plaza, 4 Avenue Road924-5471
Plaza II, 90 Bloor St. W. 961-8000
Primrose Hotel, 111 Carlton St., 977-8000
Roehampton Hotel, 808 Mt. Pleasant Rd. 487-5101
Royal York, 100 Front St. W. 368-2511
Sheraton Centre, 123 Queen St. W. 361-1000
Strathcona Hotel, 60 York St., 363-3321
Sutton Place, 955 Bay St.924-9221
Venture Inn, 89 Avenue Rd., 964-1220
Westbury Hotel, 475 Yonge St., 924-0611

What to See and Do
Toronto has transformed itself in a short time from a conservative, Victorian city to one of North America's most modern and dynamic centers. From the top of the CN Tower, the world's tallest free-standing structure, you can survey the growth of the downtown financial and business core. At the foot of the tower is the Metropolitan Toronto Convention Centre, and just west is the site of the future domed stadium. At the waterfront is Harbourfront, where you can take the ferry to Toronto Island, a picnic and recreation area.

Uptown is chic Yorkville, a street filled with boutiques, galleries and restaurants. See Queen's Park, the seat of government for Ontario.

The Toronto Symphony Orchestra performs at Roy Thompson Hall, which also hosts other concert events.

The Canadian Opera Company and the world-famous National Ballet of Canada perform at the O'Keefe Centre.

Historic sites worth visiting are Fort York, Casa Loma, and Black Creek Pioneer Village. The Royal Ontario Museum is one of the world's finest. Also there is the Art Gallery of Ontario and the Ontario Science Centre.

Ontario Place, located just west of downtown and on the waterfront, is a futuristic park with science exhibits, picnic grounds, children's activities, restaurants, and an outdoor amphitheater which presents a fine series of big-name concerts during the summer months. Adjacent is the Canadian National Exhibition grounds, where the CNE, Canada's largest fair, is held during the summer. In the CNE grounds is Exhibition Stadium, home of the Toronto Blue Jays (baseball) and the Toronto Argonauts (Canadian football). Maple Leaf Gardens, in downtown Toronto, is the home of the Toronto Maple Leafs (hockey). Racing fans should head to Greenwood and Woodbine racetracks.

Useful Addresses

Embassies and Consulates
American: 360 University Ave. 595-1700
British: 777 Bay St. 593-1290
French: 40 University Ave. 977-3131
German: 77 Admiral Rd. 925-2813
Japanese: TD Centre, King & Bay Sts. 363-7038

Business and Commerce
Federal Business Development Bank, 240 Richmond St. W. 598-0341
Metropolitan Board of Trade, 3 First Canadian Place 366-6811
Ontario Chamber of Commerce, 2323 Yonge St. 482-5222
Ontario Ministry of Industry and Tourism, 900 Bay St. 965-4008

Toronto Chamber of Commerce, 11 Adelaide St. 368-6811
Toronto Convention and Visitors Bureau, Eaton Centre 979-3133
Toronto Stock Exchange, 2 First Canadian Place 927-4700
World Trade Center, 60 Harbour St. 863-2000

Tourism and Travel
American Express, 12 Richmond St. E. 868-1044
CAA Toronto, 2 Carlton St.964-3111
CAA Toronto, 451A Yonge St. 964-3002
Deak International, 10 King St. East 863-1611
Deak International, 60 Bloor St. West 923-6549
Deak International, 55 Bloor St. West 961-9822
Deak International, 123 Queen St. West 363-4867
Deak International, 1 Yorkdale Rd. 789-1827
Deak International, 948 St. Clair Ave West 654-4255
Toronto Bus Terminal (Greyhound & Grey Line)610 Bay St.
Toronto Island Airport, Toronto Island 863-2212
Uniglobe Deer Park, 60 St. Clair Ave., 924-4083
Uniglobe Express Travel,121 Richmond St. W. 364-7376
Uniglobe Normark Travel,33 Harbour Sq. 364-4888
Uniglobe Vector Travel, 10 St. Mary St., 925-8888
Uniglobe Yonge-Eglinton Travel, 2221 Yonge St. 488-8500
Uniglobe Yorkville Travel,113 Yorkville Ave. 923-9939
Union Station (VIA Rail), Front Street 367-4300

VANCOUVER

Airport Information

Time
GMT -8
GMT -7 (Apr-Oct)

Airport
Vancouver International YVR
Tel: 276-6101
15 km (9 mi) SW of city

Airlines
Air BC 278-3800
Air Canada 688-5515
Air France 1-800 361-7257
Air New Zealand 1-800 663-9881
American 1-800 433-7300
British Airways 1-800 268-8090
Cathay Pacific 1-800 663-9393
Canadian International 683-7171
Finnair 687-7582
Japan Airlines 688-6611
KLM 682-4606
Korean 689-8431
Lufthansa 683-1313
Philippine 1-800 435-9725
Qantas 684-8231
SAS 1-800 221-2350
United 683-7111
Wardair 688-2222

Transport to City
Taxis: Taxis take 30-40 minutes
from airport to downtown,
longer during rush hours. Fare
about $15, plus tip.
Coach: Airport bus (Hustle Bus)
departs terminal every 15

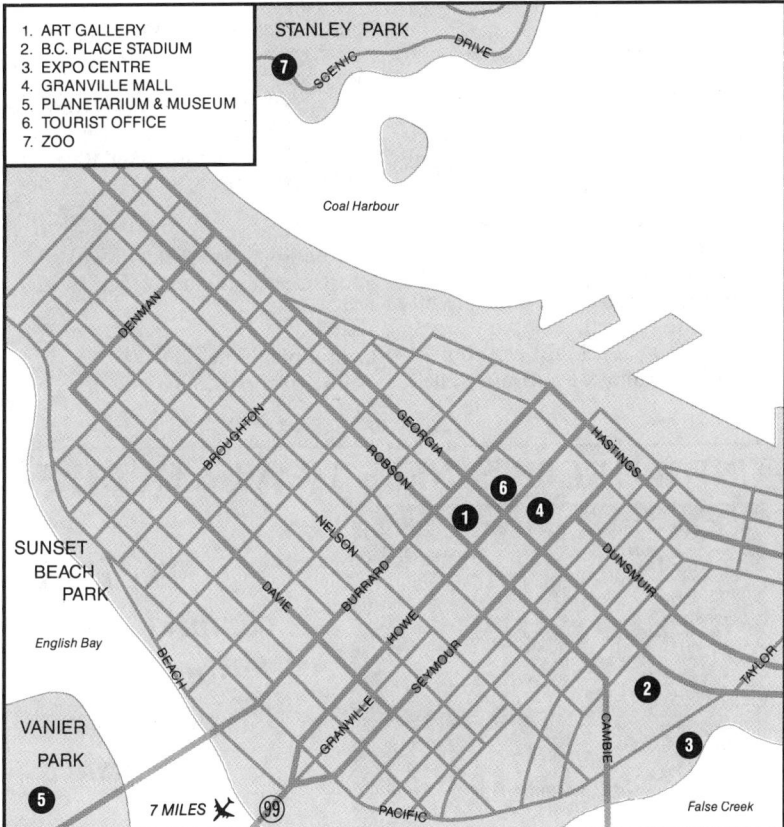

1. ART GALLERY
2. B.C. PLACE STADIUM
3. EXPO CENTRE
4. GRANVILLE MALL
5. PLANETARIUM & MUSEUM
6. TOURIST OFFICE
7. ZOO

STANLEY PARK

SCENIC DRIVE

Coal Harbour

DENMAN

BROUGHTON

GEORGIA

ROBSON

HASTINGS

NELSON

SUNSET
BEACH
PARK

English Bay

DAVIE

BURRARD

DUNSMUIR

HOWE

SEYMOUR

TAYLOR

VANIER
PARK

GRANVILLE

CAMBIE

BEACH

7 MILES ✈ (99)

PACIFIC

False Creek

Vancouver

minutes from 0600-0300 to downtown hotels and main bus station. Fare $5.75. Several hotels offer free courtesy van service. Transit: City buses leave from departure level every 30 minutes from 0600-1530, then hourly until 0300. Transfer at Granville & 70th to #21 Victoria bus for downtown. Total time takes about 40 minutes. Fare is $1.15, or during rush hours $1.55.

Facilities
Duty-free shop, currency exchange, hotel reservations, baggage deposit, post office, first-aid, bar, restaurant, shops Car rental desks: Hertz, Avis, Budget, Dollar, Holiday, Tilden

Airport Taxes
None

City Information

Weather
November-April. Cool, cloudy with frequent rain and sometimes snow during winter. Temperatures 2-10C (35-50F), seldom dropping below freezing during winter. Medium clothing with raincoat and overcoat. May-October. Warm, sunny with moderate rainfall. Temperatures 16-27C (60-80F). Light clothing with light raincoat and umbrella.

Transportation
Travelling by automobile is the easiest form of transportation. The roads and highways are excellent in the Vancouver area. Taxis are difficult to find on the streets, but you can find them at hotels or call Yellow Cab (681-3311) or Black Top Cab (681-2181). The municipal bus system is very good for downtown destinations. Fare is $1.15 and is transferable throughout the system.

Car Hire
Hertz, The Bay, 666 Seymour St. 1-800 263-0600
Hertz, Westin Bayshore, 1601 W. Georgia 682-7117
Avis, 757 Hornby St. 682-1621
Budget, 450 W. Georgia St.685-0536
Tilden, 1140 Alberni St. 1-800 387-4747

Hospitals
St. Paul's Hospital, 1081 Burrard St. 682-2344
Vancouver General Hospital, 855 12th Ave. 876-3211

Trade Fairs
International Boat Show (Feb)
Sportsman Exhibition (Mar)

Hotels
Centennial Hotel, 898 W. Broadway, 872-8661

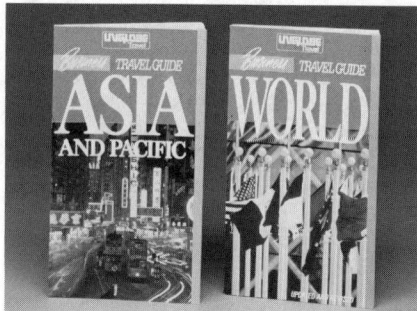

Century Plaza, 1015 Burrard St. 687-0575

Delta Place Hotel, 645 Howe St., 687-1122

Four Seasons, 791 W. Georgia 689-9333

Holiday Inn Harbourside,1133 W. Hastings St. 689-9211

Hyatt Regency, 655 Burrard St. 687-6544

International Plaza, 1999 Marine Dr. 984-0611

Meridien, 845 Burrard St.682-5511

Palisades, 1277 Robson St.688-0461

Pan Pacific, 999 Canada Place 662-8111

Quality Inn, 1335 Howe St., 882-0229

Ramada Renaissance, 1733 Comox, 699-7711

Sandman Hotel, 180 W. Georgia, 1-800 663-6900

Sheraton Landmark, 1400 Robson St. 687-0511

Sheraton Plaza, 500 W. 12th Ave. 873-1811

Sylvia Hotel, 1154 Gilford, 681-9321

Travelodge, 3475 East Hastings, 294-4751

Wedgewood Hotel, 845 Hornby St. 689-7777

Westin Bayshore, W. Georgia & Cardero 682-3377

What to See and Do

Vancouver occupies a beautiful natural setting on a peninsula on the coast of British Columbia. It has a deep natural harbour, a string of beautiful beaches, parks and gardens, and sits below the beautiful mountains of the Coast Range. All of this means that Vancouver is an outdoor city. Sunbathing, skiing, water sports, and strolling in the beautiful parks and gardens are favorite activities of both visitors and residents.

Stanley Park, Vancouver's largest, contains a zoo, aquarium, gardens, walking trails and a summer theater. There is also Vanier Park, where the Maritime Museum, Centennial Museum, and MacMillan Planetarium are located. Other parks are the Nitobe Memorial Japanese Gardens and Queen Elizabeth Park.

The main entertainment district is known as Gastown, a renovated area of old brick factories which is now a collection of boutiques, restaurants, clubs, galleries and antique shops. Adjacent is Chinatown, North America's second largest.

Just two hours across the Strait of Georgia by ferry lies Vancouver Island. Here you will find Victoria, the beautiful, quaint and very British capital of British Columbia.

The Expo 86 fairgrounds, site of the recent World's Fair, is located on False Creek near downtown Vancouver. Many of the exhibits and attractions can still be enjoyed.

The spectacular new domed stadium, B.C. Place, is home to the Vancouver Canucks (hockey) and B.C. Lions (Canadian football).

Useful Addresses

Embassies and Consulates

American: 1075 W. Georgia, St. 685-4311

British: 1111 Melville St. 683-4421

French: 736 Granville 681-2301

German: 325 Howe St. 684-8377

Japanese: 1177 W. Hastings St. 684-5868

Business and Commerce

B.C. Development Corp., 200 Granville St. 689-8411

Canadian Chamber of Commerce, 626 W. Pender St. 681-5541

Dept. of Industry, Trade &
Commerce, 595 Burrard St.
666-1434

Federal Business Development
Bank, 885 Dunsmuir St.
681-7484

Vancouver Board of Trade,
1177 W. Hastings St. 681-2111

Vancouver Convention and
Visitors Bureau, Burrard &
Georgia Sts. 682-2222

Vancouver Stock Exchange,
609 Granville St. 689-3334

World Trade Centre, 700 W.
Georgia St. 688-0811

Tourism and Travel

American Express, 701 W.
Georgia St. 689-2813

British Columbia Auto Assoc.,
999 W. Broadway 733-6660

British Columbia Auto Assoc.,
2307 W. 41st St. 263-7799

British Columbia Ferries,
Tsawassen 669-1211

Deak International, Pacific
Centre, 617 Granville St.
687-6111

Deak International, 999 Canada
Place 641-1222

Deak International, 1111 Guilford
Centre, Surrey 583-3338

Deak International, 1055
Dunsmuir, 688-9444

Tourism British Columbia
Information Centre,800
Robson St. 668-2300

Uniglobe Advance Travel, 700
1199 West Pender, 688-3551

Uniglobe Master Travel, 2423
Granville St, 737-0220

Uniglobe One-Stop Travel, 3405
Kingsway, 437-5565

Uniglobe Universal Travel, 601 W
Cordova, 669-0110

Uniglobe Vista Travel, 50-475
West Georgia, 687-5141

Uniglobe Willoughby Travel,
1003-1166 Alberni, 688-8816

Uniglobe Quayside Travel, 221
W. Esplanade, N. Vancouver
980-0531

Uniglobe Accent Travel, 8980 No.
Three Rd., Richmond277-6623

VIA Rail, Vancouver Station
682-5552

Winnipeg

Airport Information

Time
GMT -6
GMT -5 (April-October)

Airport
Winnipeg International
(Stevenson) YWG
Tel: 786-4111
4 mi (7 km) NW of city

Airlines
Air Canada 943-9361
Alitalia 256-8373
British Airways 1-800 268-8090
Canadian International 947-1221
Northwest 475-2730
SAS 1-800 221-2350
Wardair 1-800 661-9989

Transport to City
Taxi: From airport terminal to
downtown takes about 15
minutes. Fare $7.00 plus tip.
Coach: Airport buses (Kidd)
leave every 30 minutes from
0600-0100 for 15 minute ride to
downtown hotels. Some hotels
offer courtesy van service.
Transit: City bus (Mountain)
departs at 20 minute intervals
from terminal from 0630-0300 for
downtown at Portage & Main
Sts. Exact fare of $0.80 required.

Facilities
Duty free shop, currency
exchange, hotel reservations,
post office, bar, restaurant,
shops.
Car rental desks: Hertz, Avis,
Budget, Tilden.

Airport Taxes
None

City Information

Weather
November-April. Extremely cold in winter months with heavy snow. Temperature -5-40F (-21-4C), and frequently falls below 0F. Wear heavy clothing with overcoat, hat and boots. May-October. Warm, sunny and occassional rain. Temperature 50-80F (10-27C). Light clothing with sweater or jacket at nights.

Transportation
The best way to get around Winnipeg is by car rental. Taxis are hard to find on streets. City bus service runs from 0600-0130. Fare for adults is $0.80.

Car Hire
Hertz, The Bay, Portage & Memorial Sts. 786-8551
Hertz, 1577 Erin St. 786-8551
Hertz, 2405 Pembina Hwy. 261-6320

Hospitals
Health Sciences Centre, William Ave. 787-3661
St. Boniface Hospital, Tache Ave. 237-2193
Victoria General Hospital, Pembina Hwy. 269-3570

Hotels
Charter House, 330 York Ave. 942-0101
Delta Winnipeg, 288 Portage Ave. 956-0410
Holiday Inn, 350 St. Mary Ave. 942-0551
Holiday Inn South, 1330 Pembina Hwy., 452-4747
Journey's End Airport, 1770 Sargent, 783-5627
Norlander Inn, 1792 Pembina Hwy., 269-6955
Ramada Inn, 1824 Pembina Hwy. 269-7700
Relax Plaza, 360 Colony St., 786-7011
Viscount Hotel, 1670 Portage Ave., 775-0451

Westin Hotel, 2 Lombard Place 957-1350

Useful Addresses

Embassies and Consulates
American, 6 Donald St., 475-3344
France, 185 Provencher, 233-4359
Germany, 310 Donald, 947-0958
Japanese, 215 Garry St. 943-5554

Business and Commerce
British Government Trade Office, York Centre, 185 Hargrave St. 942-3151
Federal Business Development Bank, 386 Broadway Ave. 944-9991
St. Boniface Chamber of Commerce, St. Mary & Eugenie Sts. 247-6991
Winnipeg Chamber of Commerce, 177 Lombard St. 944-8484
Winnipeg Convention Bureau, 375 York Ave. 943-1970
Winnipeg Stock Exchange, 360 Main St. 942-8431

Tourism and Travel
American Express, 285 Garry St. 949-0388
Government Tourist Reception Office, Legislative Bldg., Broadway & Osborne 944-3777
Greyhound/Grey Goose Bus Terminal, 487 Portage Ave.
Manitoba Government Travel, 200 Vaughn St. 944-3796
Thomas Cook, 424 Portage942-0246
Uniglobe Renaissance Travel, 330 St. Mary Ave. 942-0738
Uniglobe Regent Travel, 11-850 Keewatin, 694-2200
VIA Rail, CNR Station, Broadway & Main Sts.944-8785

CHILE

Essential Information

Type of Government
Republic

Area
756,946 sq km
(292,257 sq mi)

Population
12.4 million

Annual Growth Rate
1.7%

Language
Spanish

Religion
Roman Catholic 89%, Protestant
11%, small Jewish population

Ethnic Groups
Spanish-Indian (mestizo) 66%,
Spanish 25%, Indian 5%

Weights and Measures
Metric

Electrical Current
A.C. 50c 220/380V

Major Business Cities
Santiago (cap) 4,650,000
Vina del Mar 360,000
Valpariso 295,000

Currency
1 Peso = 100 Centavos
Notes 50, 100, 500, 1000 pesos
Coins 1, 5, 50, 100 pesos

Public Holidays
Jan 1 New Year
Apr 12-19 Easter Week
May 21 Navy Day
Aug 15 Assumption
Sept 18 National Day
Sept 19 Army Day
Oct 12 Discovery Day
Nov 1 All Saints
Dec 8 Immaculate Conception
Dec 25 Christmas

Travellers Information

Entry Requirements
Passport is required by most
nationals with the exception of
those from Argentina, Bolivia,
Brazil, Ecquador, Uruguay, who
only require a national identity
card.
Visas not required for short-term
visits by citizens of countries that
have diplomatic relations with
Chile. This includes US, Canada,
Britain, Australia and New
Zealand.

Working Restrictions
Work permits required.
Applications must be sponsored
by a company.

Vaccination Required
No immunizations are required,
but inoculation for typhoid
recommended.

Customs and Duty Free
On arrival: 500 cigarets or 100
cigars or 1 gallon alcohol; camera
and articles for personal use

Currency Restrictions
No restriction on the import or
export of foreign or Chilean
currencies.

Health Tips
Health service conditions are
good in Chile. Drinking water is
safe in the cities but not in the
countryside. Do not eat
unwashed fruit or vegetables.
English speaking doctors
available in cities.

Climate and Clothing
Seasons are the reverse of those
in northern hemisphere. The
summer (Dec-Mar) is dry and
warm in the north, dry and hot
in central region (Santiago), and
cool and wet in the south.
Lightweight clothes
recommended. April through
September is dry and cool in the

north, dry and cold in the central regions, and cold and wet in the south. Warm clothing recommended.

Tipping
Tip 10-15% in restaurants and bars. Tip porters, chambermaids, doormen small amount for each service and a token amount above the fare for taxi drivers.

Food and Drink
Chile has 4200 km of coastline, so seafood is a major part of the cuisine. Ceviche, raw fish marinated in lime juice, is popular as is chupe de mariscas, a delicious thick shellfish soup. Try caldillo de congrio (conger eel soup), and cazuela, a casserole with a meat base and vegetables. Empanadas are pastry shells with various fillings eaten as snacks.
Chilean wines are excellent. Free wine tasting in Santiago's Enoteca. Other local drinks include pisco (sugar cane brandy) and chicha (fermented fruit juice).

Business Brief

GDP
$27.35 billion
(per capita income $2,265)

Annual Growth Rate
6.2%

Natural Resources
Copper, timber, fish, iron ore, nitrate, precious metals, molybdenun

Agriculture
Wheat, potatoes, corn, sugar beets, onions, beans, fruits, livestock

Industry
Mineral refining, metal manufacturing, food processing, fish processing, pulp, paper and wood products

Imports
Total $3.8 billion
Petroleum, sugar, wheat, capital goods, vehicles, electronic equipment, consumer durables

Exports
Total $5.1 million
Copper, molybdenum, iron ore, paper products, fish, fruits, wood products

Major Trading Partners
US, West Germany, Argentina, UK, Japan, Brazil, Saudi Arabia

Workforce
3.8 million Industry and commerce 38%, agriculture, forestry and fishing industries 16%

Tips for Doing Business
Conservative business suit (not light colored) should be worn at all times. Manners are formal and it is customary to shake hands upon arrival and departure. Make prior appointments. Business cards should be printed in English and Spanish and can be done locally in several days. Keep sales approach low-key. English is widely spoken and businessmen work long hours. Business entertaining often takes place in major hotels and restaurants (lunch 1400 and dinner 2200). Praise Chilean wines and fruits and avoid the subject of politics.

Best Months for Doing Business
The good weather months (Mar-Nov) are the best months for doing business. Avoid times around Christmas and Easter, and Independence Day in September. Vacations are usually in January and February.

Business Hours

Government
Mon-Fri 1000-1230

Business
Mon-Fri 0830-1230, 1400-1800

Banks
Mon-Fri 0900-1400

Shops
Mon-Fri 1030-1930 Sat 0930-1330

English Language Publications
Foreign publications available in hotels and news shops.

Telephone and Communications
Telephone country code: 56
Telephone city codes: Santiago 2, Vina del Mar 31, Valparaiso 31
Telex country code: 392
Public telephones are found in all restaurants, hotels and shops. Long-distance calls can be made at Central Telephone Office or through the operators, many of whom speak English.
Telex and telegrams available in main towns through Telex Chile, Transradio Chilena and ITT Comunicaciones Mundiales.
Good postal service.

Air Travel
Lan-Chile Airlines and Ladeco Air operate domestic flights to most major cities. Reservations recommended.

Other Transport
Self-drive cars can be rented in major cities. Excellent Pan American highway runs 3600 km north and south as far as Punta Arenas.
Express bus and train service is good between major cities. Taxis cheap and widely available. Initial charge displayed in front window.

SANTIAGO

Airport Information

Time
GMT -4
GMT-3 (Oct-Mar)

Airport
Arturo Merino Benitez SCL
Tel: 719709
16 km (10 mi) NW of city
International and domestic terminals

Airlines
Air France 725333
Alitalia 6983336
Avianca 81919
British Airways 726339
Canadian International 393058Eastern 716266
Iberia 6988487
JAL 6990264
Korean (KAL) 723956
Lan-Chile 6990505
Lufthansa 330173
Pan Am 710919
SAS 391105
Swissair 6692324
TWA 2253780
Varig 395976

Transport to City
Taxi: there are taxis available to the city center. Fare $10 plus tip.
Coach: an air-conditioned bus leaves from front of airport and goes to Plaza de la Constitution in the center of town in about 30 minutes. Leaves every half hour from 0600-2400. Fare $.060.

Facilities
Currency exchange, hotel reservations, post office, bar, restaurant, shops, baggage deposit, first aid/medical.
Car rental desks: Hertz, Avis, Budget

Airport Taxes
Per person: International 875 pesos

City Information

Weather
Warm and sunny Oct-Apr with cool nights.
May-Sept, cool and wet.
Average temps: Jan (summer)

29c (84F)
July (winter) 10c (50F)

Transportation
Taxis are black and yellow. They are metered but have extra charges on nights and Sundays. Check price per destination before hiring. Tipping not necessary.
Efficient subway system consisting of 2 lines runs between 07002300.
Good city bus service.

Car Hire
Hertz, Avenida Andres Bello 1469 (tel: 2259328)
Avis, Dardignac 129 (tel: 770546)
Budget, San Francisco 280 (tel: 383427)

Hospitals
Medical help for travellers at:

Iamat Center, Eliodero Yanez 1049 (tel: 494001)
Asistencia Publica, Avenida Portugal 125 (tel: 394871)

Trade Fairs
FISA Trade Fair (Oct-Nov)

Hotels
El Conquistador, Miquel Cruchaga 920 (tel: 396231)
Gran Palace, Heurfonos 1171 (tel: 712551)
Holiday Inn-Crowne Plaza, Avenida B O'Higgins 136 (tel: 381042)
Holiday Inn-Galerias, 65 San Antonio (tel: 384011)
Panamericano, Teatinos (tel: 723060)
Sheraton San Cristobal Hotel, Avenida Santa Maria 1742 (tel: 745000)
Tupahue, San Antonio 477 (tel: 35891)

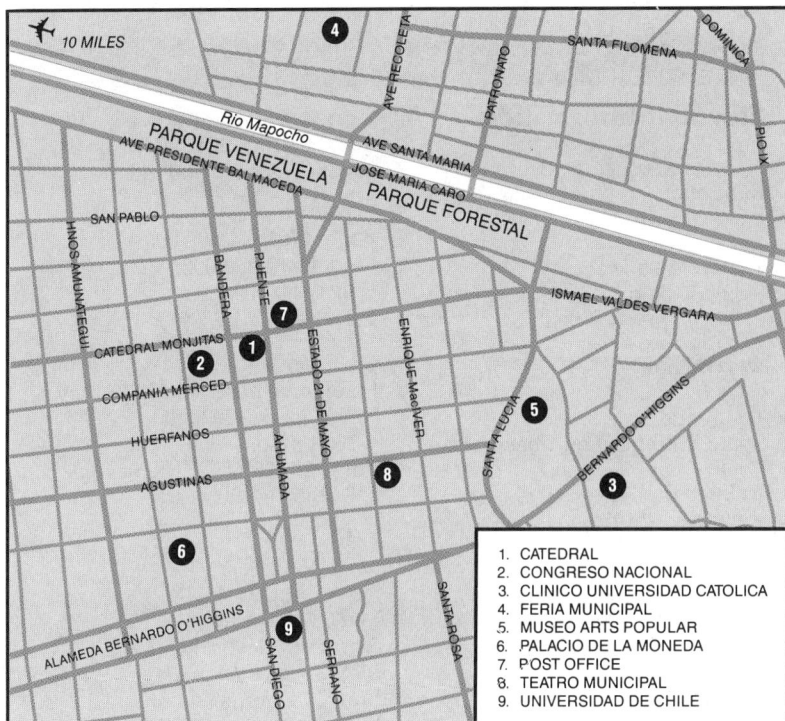

1. CATEDRAL
2. CONGRESO NACIONAL
3. CLINICO UNIVERSIDAD CATOLICA
4. FERIA MUNICIPAL
5. MUSEO ARTS POPULAR
6. PALACIO DE LA MONEDA
7. POST OFFICE
8. TEATRO MUNICIPAL
9. UNIVERSIDAD DE CHILE

Santiago

NORTH/SOUTH AMERICA

What to See and Do

Shop in Providencia, easily reached by subway for good buys in lapis lazuli and copper goods. The Parque Forestal east of downtown contains the Palace of Fine Arts. San Cristobol Hill park has a restaurant and wine museum as well as a good view of the city. Skiing in the Andes is popular in the winter (JuneSept). Farellones and Lagunillas, about 50 km east of the city, are two popular resorts In the summer, visit the seaside resort of Vina del Mar.

Useful Addresses

Embassies and Consulates

American: Agustinas 1343 (tel: 710133)
Canadian: Ahumada 11 (tel: 6962256)
British: La Concepcione 177 (tel: 2239166)

Business and Commerce

Central Bank, Agustinas 1180
State Post and Telegraph Office, Plaza de Armas
Stock Exchange, La Bolsa 64
Chile Chamber of Commerce, Santa Lucia 302 (tel: 397694)
American Chamber of Commerce, Casilla 4131 (tel: 747167)
British Chamber of Commerce, Agustinas 972 (tel: 85266)

Tourism and Travel

National Tourist Office, Cathedral 1159 (tel: 8215)
American Express, Agustinas 1173 (tel: 6982164)
Automobile Club of Chile, Avenida Pedro de Valdivia195 (tel: 749516)
Railway Information Center,B O'Higgins 853 (tel: 382577)
Thomas Cook, Agustinas 1058 (tel: 6986254)

COLOMBIA

Essential Information

Type of Government
Republic

Area
1,138,914 sq km
(439,536 sq mi)

Population
29.5 million

Languages
Spanish (official and business)

Religion
Roman Catholic

Ethnic Groups
Mestizo 58%, Caucasian 20%, Mulatto 14%, Negro 4%, Indian 1%

Weights and Measures
Metric

Electrical Current
A.C. 60c 150/240V
Bogota A.C. 60c 150/240

Major Business Cities
Bogota (cap) 4,500,000
Medellin 2,250,000
Cali 1,500,000
Barranquilla 1,250,000

Currency
1 Colombian Peso = 100 Centavos
Notes 20, 50, 200, 500, 1000 pesos
Coins 10, 20, 25, 50 centavos, 1, 2, 5, 10, 20 pesos

Public Holidays
Jan 1 New Year
Jan 6 Epiphany
Mar 19 St. Joseph
Apr 13-19 Easter Week
May 28 Ascension Day
June 21 Corpus Christi
June 29 Sts Peter & Paul

July 20 Independence
Aug 7 Battle of Boyaca
Aug 15 Assumption
Oct 12 Columbus
Nov 1 All Saints
Dec 8 Immaculate Conception
Dec 25 Christmas

Travellers Information

Entry Requirements
Passport is required by all except citizens of Ecuador and certain tourist visitors from Trinidad and Tobago. US nationals require an entry card, others do not unless staying longer than three months.
Visa not required by nationals of Britian, West Germany, and Japan, under certain circumstances: valid passport, return ticket and a stay of under 90 days.

Working Restrictions
Work visa is required and must be obtained from a Colombian consulate.

Vaccination Required
Yellow fever, malaria, and typhoid shots recommended. Yellow fever certificates strongly advised if travelling from infected area.

Customs and Duty Free
On arrival: 200 cigarets or 50 cigars or 250g/8oz of tobacco; 2 bottles of alhohol. Unrestricted entry on personal effects (camera, typewriter, radio) as long as they are not new. Permits are required to bring in guns and ammunition: apply in advance to the Ministry of Defense or the Colombian National Tourist Board.

Currency Restrictions
There are no restrictions on the amount of foreign currency you may bring in, and the amounts declared on entry may be reexported. Only 550 pesos may be imported or exported.

Health Tips
Drink only boiled or bottled water, except in large hotels, and peel all fruit and vegetables before eating. It is wise to take malaria tablets. Many doctors and dentists speak English. Medicines and toiletries are expensive. Foreign nationals must pay for all medical services.

Climate and Clothing
Temperatures vary considerably with the altitude (tropical in coastal regions, temperate on the plateau and cold in the Andes) but there are no seasons as such. Rainy most of the year. Coastal regions (Cali, Medellin,) are hot and damp, 21-33c(70-90F). Bogota is cooler 10-20c(50-70F). Tropical weight clothing for coast and medium weight for Bogota. Light raincoat essential.

Tipping
It is not required to tip taxi drivers, although in some cases 10% is appreciated. Porters: 50 pesos per piece of luggage. Hotels, restaurants and night spots, 10-15%.

Food and Drink
Columbian cooking varies according to the region. Coastal areas serve fish and shellfish, paella is a popular dish, and meals are often served with tropical fruit and rice. Food is often cooked in coconut milk. In the higher country, rice, potatoes and corn predominate in soups and meat dishes. International cuisine is available in many good hotels and restaurants. All spirits are imported. Tropical fruit drinks are very popular and available everywhere. Some local wine and many good brands of beer. Columbian coffee is justly famous. Avoid tap water.

Business Brief

GDP
$35 billion
(per capita income $1,258)

Annual Growth Rate
0.8%

Natural Resources
Petroleum, gold, limestone, sand
and gravel, platinum, emeralds
marine salt

Agriculture
Coffee, bananas, cotton, rice,
sugar, tobacco

Industry
Cement, chemicals, consumer
goods, food processing, metal
manufacturering, petroleum,
pulp and paper, textiles

Imports
Total $4.5 billion
Mechanical and electrical
equipment, petroleum products,
manufactured goods, consumer
products, grains, vehicles, metals

Exports
Total $4.6billion
Coffee (50%), emeralds, cut
flowers, tobacco, cattle, cotton,
bananas

Major Trading Partners
US, West Germany, Spain,
Japan, Netherlands, UK,
Sweden, The Andean Group

Workforce
9 million
Agriculture 27%, industry 21%,
other services 14%

Tips For Doing Business
A conservative business suit is
necessary for business in Bogota,
Medellin and Cali. A little less
formal in Barranquilla: no jacket
but a tie. Prior appointments
are necessary. Colombian
businessmen are polite and
helpful. They appreciate visitors
who speak Spanish and, if
possible, sales literature and
business cards should be printed
in both Spanish and English.
Much business will be done
slowly over many cups of
Colombian coffee called "tintos".
Avoid the subject of local
politics. If you are invited out for
dinner there will probably be a
long cocktail party ahead of time
with the meal starting at 2300. If
you are invited to a Colombian
home for dinner, take the
hostess a gift of candy or
flowers.

Best Months for Doing Business
March through November.
Avoid the weeks before and after
Christmas and Easter. Avoid
June and July in Barranquilla
(holiday time) as well as the five
days before Ash Wednesday
which is Carnival time. Business
vacations are usually taken in
December and January.

Business Hours

Government
Mon-Fri 0800-1500

Business
Mon-Sat 0700-1200, 1500-1730

Banks
Mon-Thurs 0900-1500
Fri 0900-1530

Shops
Mon-Sat 0900-1230, 1430-1930

English Language Publications
There is no English-language
newspaper published, but the
Miami Herald, Newsweek and
the New York Times are
available in the larger cities.

Telephone and Communications
Telephone country code: 57
Telephone city code: Bogota 0,
Cali 3, Medellin 4
Telex country code: 396 Public
telephone booths available in
street, hotels, restaurants and
cafes. Direct dialing possible
between most Colombian cities.

Major hotels can handle long distance telephone calls, telegrams and telex messages. Send all post by air.

Air Travel
Major international airport El Dorado in Bogota.
Air services between Bogota and other main centers is frequent and inexpensive. Internal flights are operated by Avianca, SAM, Aces Aires and Intercontinental. Book in advance.

Other Transport
Taxis can be hailed and are often shared. Tipping is not usual. Green and white taxis have English-speaking drivers.
Cars may be rented with an international driving license for up to three months. Traffic in the city is dense during the day and driving is on the right.
Bus service is for the adventuresome. Taking the train is not recommended as the rail service has greatly deteriorated.

BOGOTA

Airport Information

Time
GMT -5

Airport
El Dorado BOG
Tel: 2669200
12 km (7.5 mi) NW of city

Airlines
Air Canada 2639511
Air France 2339166
Alitalia 2857305
Avensa 2341981
Avianca 2669700
British Airways 2412100
Canadian International 841800
El Al 2841637
Iberia 2866100
JAL 2579853
Lufthansa 2819573
Olympic 2454314
Pan Am 2968436
Swiss Air 2186300
TWA 2184630
Varig 2853340

Transport to City
Taxis: always available during the day cost about 400 pesos and take 30 to 40 minutes to center of town.
Coach: hotels often arrange their own transportation to and from the airport for a minimal fee.
Transit: bus (Consul) to city takes 30 minutes; every 20 minutes from 0600 to 2000.

Facilities
Bar, buffet, restaurant, bank with currency exchange, insurance, hotel reservations, post office, conference facilities, first aid/medical, vaccinations, shops selling flowers, candy, books and toys.
Duty-free shop sells cigarets, cigars, tobacco, wines, spirits, liqueurs, lighters, cameras, radios, watches, glass and china. US currency accepted.
Car rental desks: Hertz, Avis

Airport Taxes
Per person: International 505 pesos, domestic 150 pesos

City Information

Weather
The climate is mild with plenty of rain but no changeable seasons.
Average temps: Jan 17c (64F) July 14c (58F)

Transportation
Taxis are the most convenient form of transportation in Bogota. They are usually metered with a minimum charge and cost extra at night, holidays and Sundays. They can be hailed, are often shared, and tipping is not usual. Green-and-white taxis have Englishspeaking drivers and can

be rented by the hour or the day. City buses tend to be crowded but have reasonable fares.

Car Hire
National or international driving licence for rental up to three months.
Hertz, Tequendama Hotel
(tel: 2842696 & 2841123)
Arrendautos El Dorado
(tel: 2837910)
Avis, Carrera 10 No 27-29
(tel: 2662147 & 459122)
Dollar, Avenida 13 No 78-78
(tel: 2687670 & 2574550)

National, Avenida 19 No 100-10
(tel: 457111)

Hospitals
Emergency medical assistance at:
Red Cross (tel: 2506611)
Clinica Marly (tel: 2320872)
Clinica Samper (tel: 2570100)

Trade Fairs
International Industrial Fair (Jul)

Hotels
Bacata, Calle 19 No 5-20
(tel: 2432210/838111)
Bogota Plaza Hotel, Calle 100 No
18A-30 (tel: 2572200)

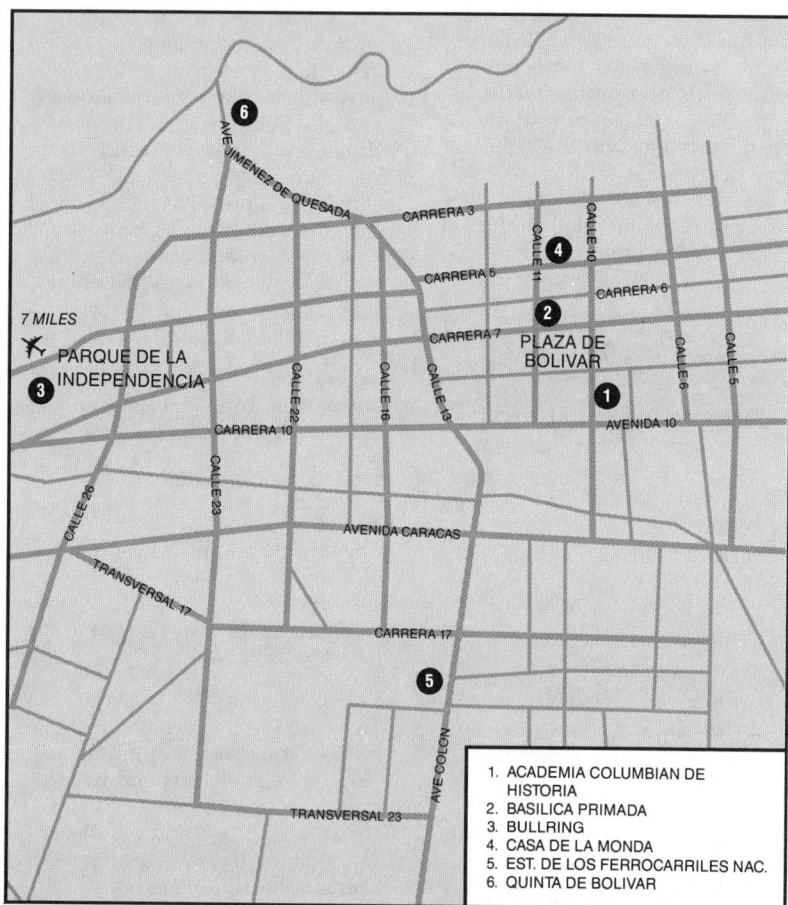

1. ACADEMIA COLUMBIAN DE HISTORIA
2. BASILICA PRIMADA
3. BULLRING
4. CASA DE LA MONDA
5. EST. DE LOS FERROCARRILES NAC.
6. QUINTA DE BOLIVAR

Bogota

Continental, Avenida Jimenez
(tel: 821100)
Dann, Calle 19 No 5-72
(tel: 840100)
El Presidente, Calle 23 No 9-45
(tel: 2841100)
Hilton International Bogota,
Carrera 7 No 32-16
(tel: 2870788)
Inter-Continental Hotel
Tequendama, Carrera 10 No
26-21 (tel: 2861111)
La Fontana, Diagonal, 127A No
21-10 (tel: 2740200)

What To See and Do

The city has a reputation for
mugging: nevertheless there are
interesting places to see. Not
to be missed is the Gold
Museum with thousands of pre-
Colombian gold pieces and two
films daily explaining the legend
of El Dorado. The National
Museum near the Hilton has
pleasant gardens as does the
Quinta de Bolivar--the liberators
villa at the edge of town. Visit
the Teatro de Colon and the
Colonial Art Museum, San
Carlos Palace where Simon
Bolivar once lived, the churches
of San Francisco, La Tercera and
Veracruz. For a spectacular
view, take the cable car to the
Monserrate Peak. A little over an
hour away at Zipaquira is the
outstanding Salt Cathedral,
carved out of salt half-a-mile
beneath the surface of the earth
and inhabited by 10,000 people.

Useful Addresses

Embassies and Consulates
American: Calle 38 No 8-61
(tel: 2851300)
Canadian: Calle 76 No 11-52
British: Calle 98 N0 9-03
(tel: 2185111)

Business and Commerce
Central Bank, Banco de la
Republica, Carrera 7 No 14-78
(tel: 2831111)
Bogota Stock Exchange, Carrera
8A No 13-82 (tel: 2436501)
Bogota Chamber of Commerce,
Carrera 9 No 16-21
(tel: 2342540)
American Chamber of
Commerce, Bogota Hilton
Hotel, Ste. 701, Apartado
Aereo 8008 (tel: 329701)
Colombia-American Chamber of
Commerce, Bogota Hilton
Hotel (tel: 329701)
United Nations Information
Office, Apartado Postal 6567
(tel: 432205)
Merchants National Federation,
Jimenez 10-58

Tourism and Travel
National Tourist Board, Calle 28
No 13-15 (tel: 2839466)
American Express, Calle 92 No
15-63 (tel: 2573542)
Thomas Cook, Carrera 5 No
15-89 (tel: 2869700)
Touring Automobile Club of
Columbia, Avida CaracasNo
46-64/72 (tel: 2327580)

MEXICO

Essential Information

Type of Government
Republic

Area
1,972,545 sq km
(761,599 sq mi)

Population
81.4 million

Annual Growth Rate
2.5%

Languages
Spanish (official)

Religion
Roman Catholic

Ethnic Groups
Mestizo (Indian-Spanish) 60%,

American Indian 30%, Caucasian 9%, other 1%

Weights and Measures
Metric

Electrical Current
A.C. 60c V varies

Major Business Cities
Mexico City (cap) 18,500,000
Guadalajara 3,000,000
Monterrey 2,500,000
Puebla 1,100,000
Acapulco 1,000,000

Currency
1 Peso = 100 Centavos
Notes 50, 100, 500, 1000, 2000, 5000, and 10,000 pesos

Public Holidays
Jan 1 New Year
Feb 5 Constitution Day
Mar 21 Birth of Benito Juarez
Apr 13-20 Easter Week
May 1 Labor Day
May 5 Victory against French Occupation
Sept 16 Independence
Oct 12 Colombus Day
Nov 2 All Souls
Nov 20 Anniversary of the 1910 Revolution
Dec 25 Christmas

Travellers Information

Entry Requirements
Passport is not required by citizens of US and Canada: only a tourist card and proof of identity. Tourist card essential to leave the country. Citizens of almost all other countries need a valid passport and visa obtained from a Mexican consulate. Check on visa as renewal can take several weeks. To transact business inside the country, it is important that business travellers also show cards/permits stating the nature of their business and the firms to be visited. Apply to a Mexican embassy in advance.

Working Restrictions
No work permits available unless specifically requested by a Mexican company.

Vaccination Required
No vaccinations required but recommended for typhoid, malaria and polio.

Customs and Duty Free
On arrival: 400 cigarets or 50 cigars; 2 bottles of alcohol (any size); perfume for personal use. You are allowed unrestricted amount of goods for personal use as long as they are not new. Pets require a vaccination certificate.

Currency Restrictions
There are no import restrictions on currency.

Health Tips
Avoid drinking tap water especially outside main cities as it is not purified. Cooked food is safe but avoid raw vegetables and fruits. Take malaria tablets. Medical facilities in larger cities are good. Public hospitals are inexpensive but not recommended: be prepared to pay for medical and dental treatment and ask your embassy to recommend a list of English-speaking doctors. Mexico City has a very high altitude so spend the first few days at a slow pace with light meals and no alcohol.

Climate and Clothing
The climate varies with the altitude. Tropical in the lowlands. The higher areas around Guadalajara and Mexico City are moderate year round. Lightweight business suits are worn in the cities, more informal clothing worn for social occasions in the coastal zones. Light raincoat for Mexico City.

Tipping
Hotel and airport taxi drivers are usually tipped 15% although

other taxi drivers are not. Waiters in bars, restaurants or hotels usually receive 15% of the bill. It is customary to tip for all small services.

Food and Drink

Mexican food is usually highly spiced and served with a rich sauces. Famous dishes throughout the country are mole negro con pollo (chicken in a chocolate based sauce), chiles rellenos (stuffed hot peppers), enchiladas and tortillas (corn pancakes with various fillings). Fresh fish is excellent, and the tropical fruit varied and delicious. Be sure to peel it yourself. Tequila and mescal are national drinks. Fruit juice is popular and Mexican beer is excellent.

Business Brief

GDP
$176.9 billion
(per capita income $2,350)

Annual Growth Rate
3-7%

Natural Resources
Petroleum, silver, copper, gold, lead, zinc, natural gas, timber

Agriculture
Corn, beans, oilseeds, fruit, grains, cotton, sugar cane, coffee, vegetables

Industry
Manufacturing, services, commerce, transportation and communications, petroleum and mining

Imports
Total $12.7 billion
Grains, machinery, equipment, industrial vehicles, intermediate goods

Exports
Total $21.1 billion
Petroleum and petroleum products, coffee, cotton, fruit, vegetables, semi-manufactured products

Major Trading Partners
US, West Germany, UK, France, Canada, Switzerland, Italy, Israel, Brazil

Workforce
20 million
Agriculture 41%, industry and mining 34%, service industry 25%

Tips for Doing Business
A conservative business suit is required for all occasions. Prior appointments are necessary, and since businessmen in Mexico travel frequently, you should write well in advance. Courtesy is extremely important. Always address people by their correct and formal title and give a firm handshakes. Although many Mexican businessmen speak English, they prefer that you make an attempt at Spanish. Do not answer a letter written in Spanish with one written in English. In business the direct approach is considered rude. Do not hurry. The midday meal is taken between 1430 and 1630, and the evening meal after 2100. Inviting anyone to eat before those times is considered gauche. Most entertaining takes place in restaurants.

Best Months for Doing Business
Avoid July, August and December as this is when most business vacations are taken. Also avoid the two weeks before and after Christmas and the week before and after Easter.

Business Hours

Government
Mon-Fri 0800-1400

Business
Mon-Fri 0900-1330, 1430-1900 (Mexico City has no lunch-time closing)

NORTH/SOUTH AMERICA

Banks
Mon-Fri 0900-1330
(Certain banking services
available in large cities 1600-1800)

Shops
Mon Tues Thurs Fri 1000-1900
Wed Sat 1100-2000

English Language Publications
The News. Foreign English
publications available in major
cities.

Telephone and Communications
Telephone country code: 52
Telephone city code: Mexico City
905
Telex country code: 383
There is an automatic telephone
system in Mexico city. Telephone
services between major cities is
good, although foreign
longdistance calls are heavily
taxed. Telegrams in Mexico City
may be sent from Telegrafas
Nacionales y Colon. Public telex
offices in all major cities: in
Mexico City at Ejercito Nacional
132 and Bolderas 7.

Air Travel
Domestic air travel is excellent
and there are a number of daily
scheduled flights between major
cities operated by Aeromexico
and Mexicana. From Mexico City
to Guadalajara is about an hour,
and to Monterrey about
75 minutes.

Other Transport
The bus service in Mexico is
good. There are three classes:
first, second and local. Choose
first-class. Rail service is slower
than bus. There are three classes:
special first, regular first, and
second class. Between Mexico
City and other major cities there
is a sleeper service available.
Book well in advance. The
highway system is extensive,
and over one-third of the roads
are paved. Cars can be rented

and a foreign license is
acceptable.

MEXICO CITY

Airport Information

Time
GMT -6

Airport
Internacional Benito Juarez MEX
Tel: (905)5713600
13 km (8 mi) E of city

Airlines
Aeroflot 5665388
Aeromexico 5531517
Air Canada 5112094
Air France 5660066
Alitalia 5335590
American 3999222
Avensa 5464655
Avianca 5668570
British Airways 5259133
Canadian International 5285520
Continental 2031148
Eastern 5926011
El Al 5663599
Iberia 5922988
JAL 5335515
KLM 5968088
Lufthansa 5922755
Mexicana 6604444
Northwest 2501855
Pan Am 3950077
Philippine 5161274
Sabena 2867109
SAS 5330177
Singapore 5668388
Swissair 5336363
TWA 5668388
United 5319002
Varig 5359700

Transport To City
Taxis: use only authorized taxi
services and pay fare in advance
at booth. Costs about 700 pesos
to hotels Inzona Rosa and takes
30-45 minutes.
Coach: mini-buses (Settas) hold

six people and cost very little. Pay at counter before boarding. Baggage is handled quickly and air-conditioned ride is comfortable and reasonably priced.

Facilities

Bar, buffet, restaurant, bank, currency exchange, insurance, hotel reservations, baggage check, post office, barber shop, first aid/medical, vaccinations, shops selling flowers, candy, books, gifts, toys
Car rental desks: Hertz, Avis, Dollar, Budget, Europcar

Airport Taxes

Per person: International US$13, domestic US$5

City Information

Weather

Summer (June-Sept) has moderate to warm days with the evenings cool to chilly. Rainy almost every afternoon or evening. Winter (Dec-Feb) can have occasional frosts.
Average temps: Jan 12c (54F) July 17c (63F)

Transportation

Taxis are metered, but sometimes the meter is not used so agree on the fare in advance. Fixed-route taxis are green: no-fixed route taxis are yellow. They are often shared. Green-and-

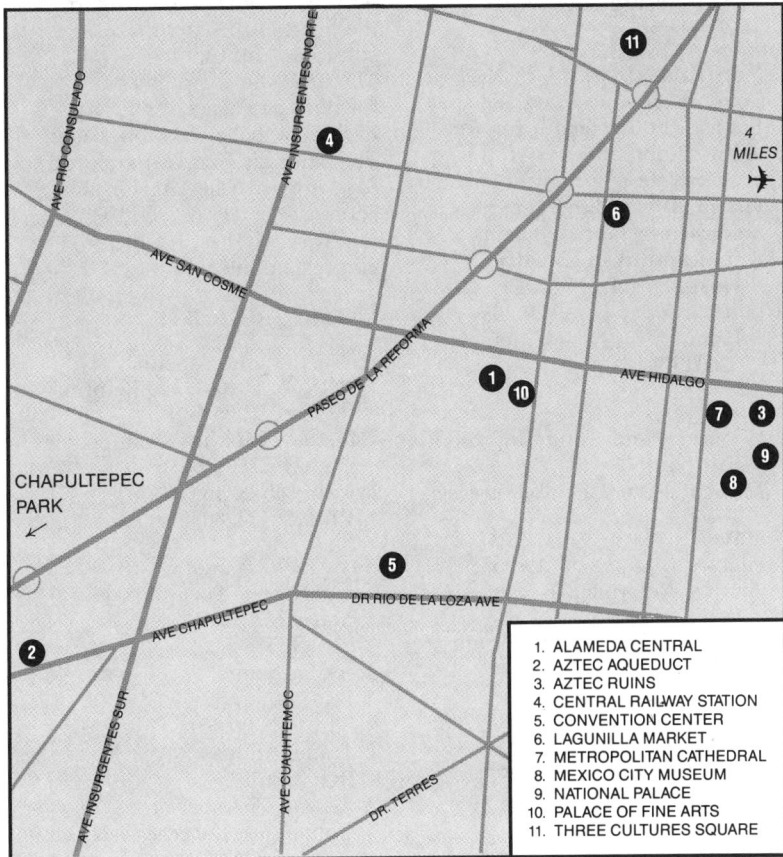

1. ALAMEDA CENTRAL
2. AZTEC AQUEDUCT
3. AZTEC RUINS
4. CENTRAL RAILWAY STATION
5. CONVENTION CENTER
6. LAGUNILLA MARKET
7. METROPOLITAN CATHEDRAL
8. MEXICO CITY MUSEUM
9. NATIONAL PALACE
10. PALACE OF FINE ARTS
11. THREE CULTURES SQUARE

CHAPULTEPEC PARK

AVE RIO CONSULADO
AVE INSURGENTES NORTE
AVE SAN COSME
PASEO DE LA REFORMA
AVE HIDALGO
DR RIO DE LA LOZA AVE
AVE CHAPULTEPEC
AVE INSURGENTES SUR
AVE CUAUHTEMOC
DR. TERRES

4 MILES

Mexico City

NORTH/SOUTH AMERICA

white vehicles are special tourist taxis and have English-speaking drivers. Bus service is inexpensive but crowded. Peribus service circulates the city. Seven-line subway system. Maps available at Insurgentes Station on Pink line. Often crowded. Car hire available but expensive. Foreign driving licence accepted.

Car Hire
Hertz, Versailles 6 (tel: 5666902 & 7847547)
Avis, Dr Velasco 138(tel: 7623688 & 7613300)
Budget, Reforna 60 (tel: 7620900 & 5666800)
National, Marsella 48(tel: 5330375 & 5718710)
Thrifty, Insurgentes Sur 26(tel: 5465116)

Hospitals
Many doctors and dentists speak English. Public health services are not good and it is wise to seek private treatment for which you must pay. Emergency medical assistance available at:
American-British Cowdry Hospital (tel: 277500)
Iamat Center, Paseo de las Palmas 745, No 402 (tel: 5203132)

Trade Fairs
Computer and Communication Fair (Jan)
Mexico Defence Exhibition (Feb)

Hotels
Alameda, Juarez 50 (tel: 5180620)
Aristos, Reforma 276 (tel: 2110122)
Camino Real, Mariano Escobedo 700 (tel: 5456960)
El Presidente Chaputepec, Campos Eliseos (tel: 2507700)
Fiesta Palace, Paseo de la Reforma 80 (tel: 5667777)
Galeria Plaza, Hamburgo 195 (tel: 2110014)
Holiday Inn Crowne Plaza, 80 Paseo de la Reforma Blvd (tel: 5667777)
Hotel Continental Mexico City, Paseo de la Reforma 166 (tel: 5180700)
Maria Isabel Sheraton, Paseo de la Reforma 325 (tel: 2110001)
Plaza Florencia, Florencia 61 (tel: 5254800)
Reforma, Reforma y Paris (tel: 5469685)

What to See and Do
National Palace with Diego Rivera murals; Guadalupe Shrine; the Cathedral and beside it the remains of the Aztec temple on which it was built. Teotihuacan Pyramids; San Francisco and Santo Domingo churches; Museum of Modern Art; the Aztec pyramid dig in the heart of the city; the stunning Anthropological Museum; the Chapultepec Castle. The Palace of Fine Arts has opera, ballet and folk ballet. The Saturday bazaar (Bazaar de Sabado) is at San Angel in the south of the city: good quality jewellery, clothes, handicrafts and restaurants.

Useful Addresses

Embassies and Consulates
American: Paseo de la Reforma 305 (tel: 2110042)
Canadian: Melchor Ocampo 463 (tel: 2543288)
British: Rio Lerma 71(tel: 5114880)

Business and Commerce
Central Bank, Avenida 5 de Mayo 2, Apdo 98 bis(tel: 5180500)
Stock Exchange, A.C., Juares-4 Piso 10 (tel: 5850983)
Mexican Institute of Foreign Trade, Alfonso Reyes 30 (tel: 2536191)
American Chamber of Commerce, Lucerna 78(tel: 5660866)

British Chamber of Commerce, Tiber 103 (tel: 5332454)
United Nations Information Office, Presidente Mazaryk No 29 (tel: 2501364)

Tourism and Travel
National Tourist Office, Avenida Juarez 92 (tel: 5123781)

AMA, Orizaba 7, Colonia Roma 24-486 (tel: 5111084)
American Express, Hamburgo 75 (tel: 5533599)
Thomas Cook, Insurgentes 1310 (tel: 5245969)

PERU

Essential Information

Type of Government
Constitutional Republic

Area
1.28 million sq km
(496,222 sq mi)

Population
20.2 million

Annual Growth Rate
2.6%

Languages
Spanish and Quechua (both official)

Religion
Roman Catholic

Ethnic Groups
Indian 45%, Mestizo 37%, Caucasian 15%, black, Asian and other 3%

Weights and Measures
Metric

Electrical Current
A.C. 60c 220V

Major Business Cities
Lima (cap) 5,500,000

Currency
1 Sol = 100 Centavos
Notes 5, 10, 50, 100, 500, 1000, 5000, 10000 sol
Coins 50 centavos; 1, 5, 10, 50, 100 sol

Public Holidays
Jan 1 New Year
Apr 13-19 Easter Week

May 1 Labor Day
Jun 24 Countryman's Day
Jun 29 Sts Peter & Paul
Jul 28-29 Independence Days
Aug 30 St Rose of Lima
Oct 8 Combat of Angamos
Nov 1 All Saints Day
Dec 8 Immaculate Conception
Dec 25 Christmas

Travellers Information

Entry Requirements
Passport is required by all. Visa not required for tourist visits of up to 90 days by nationals of Austria, Canada, Britain, EEC, Finland, Japan, Portugal, Spain, Sweden, Switzerland, US and other countries. Required by nationals of Australia and New Zealand. Onward passage must be assured. If you apply for a business visa, you must fill out a tax declaration before leaving; apply for a tourist visa instead.

Working Restrictions
Work permits are obtainable but everything must be arranged within the country.

Vaccination Required
There are no vaccinations required except for yellow fever if you are arriving from an infected area. Vaccinations for malaria and typhoid are recommended.

Customs and Duty Free
On arrival: 200 cigarets or 25

cigars or 250g/8oz tobacco; 2 liters alcohol; reasonable amount of perfume and gifts for personal use. Visitors must declare all money they bring into the country.

Currency Restrictions
There are no currency restrictions on under US$l000 in foreign exchange, and Peruvian money can be changed back when you leave. In main cities, most international credit cards accepted.

Health Tips
Avoid drinking tap water and use only bottled water except in large hotels. Wash and peel all fruits and vegetables. Imported pharmaceuticals are expensive. Some doctors and dentists speak English. Medical attention is expensive but can be obtained in Lima at British-American Hospital (tel: 23000 & 403570).

Climate and Clothing
Climate has great variations according to the region. In the coastal area it is dry and mild; the Andes are temperate to frigid; and the eastern lowlands, tropically warm and humid. Winters (Jun-Sept) are cool and damp in Lima with up to 98% humidity.
Cool in mountains (Cuzco) with very cold nights. Medium weight clothes with overcoat for Lima and Cuzco.
Summers (Nov-May) are dry, sunny and warm in Lima; hot with a good deal of rain in northeast (Iquitos).
Wear lightweight clothes in Lima; tropical weights and umbrella inIquitos; and medium weight and raincoat for Cuzco.

Tipping
Do not tip taxis. Hotels, restaurants and nightspots usually include 10% in the bill but an additional 5-10% to the staff is usual. Tip porters the equivalent of 25 cents per piece of baggage and the same amount for each small service.

Food and Drink
Peruvian food concentrates on potatoes, corn and peppers as well as fish dishes along the coast. The soups are excellent and often a meal in themselves. Ceviche is a popular dish made of raw fish marinated in lime juice and ceviche stands are on the streets of major cities. Meat stews with vegetables are very good and Peruvian beer is wonderful.

Business Brief

GDP
$20.1 billion
(per capita income $1,015)

Annual Growth Rate
11.9%

Natural Resources
Minerals, metals, petroleum, forests, fish

Agriculture
Coffee, cotton, cocoa, sugar, wool, corn

Industry
Mineral processing, oil refining, fish meal, textiles, food processing, light manufacturing, automobile assembly

Imports
Total $3.4 billion
Machinery, cereals, chemicals, pharmaceuticals, petroleum and mining equipment

Exports
Total $2.6 billion
Petroleum, copper, silver, zinc, lead, fish meal, coffee, cotton, canned and frozen fish

Major Trading Partners
US, West Germany, Argentina, UK, Japan, Netherlands, Ecuador, Chile

Workforce
5.6 million Agriculture 40%, industry and mining 19%, government and services 41%

Tips for Doing Business
A conservative business suit is essential for all business and government visits. Prior appointments necessary. Never be late although Peruvian businessmen often are. Try to get business cards printed in both English and Spanish. Local printers will get them done in 2 to 3 days. Peruvian businessmen are conservative and proud of their Spanish and Inca heritage. Conduct business in a conservative and mannerly fashion and do not discuss local politics.

Best Months for Doing Business
Best months for travel are August through October. April is also good although you should avoid the week before and after Easter as well as the two weeks before and after Christmas. January, February, and March are the months when businessmen take their vacations.

Business Hours

Government
Apr-Dec: Mon-Fri 0900-1200, 1300-1600
Jan-Mar: Mon-Fri 0800-1300

Business
Apr-Dec: Mon-Fri 0900-1700
Jan-Mar: Mon-Fri 0800-1400/1500

Banks
Apr-Dec: Mon-Fri 0830-1130
Jan-Mar: Mon-Fri 0915-1245 Most banks open for several hours after 1630 but close for balances Jun 30 and Dec 31.

Shops
Mon-Sat 1100-1900 (small shops close for an hour at lunch)

English Language Publications
The Lima Times

Telephone and Communications
Telephone country code: 51
Telephone city code: Lima 14
Telex country code: 394 & 334
Direct international and long-distance dialing available from all major hotels. Public telephones in restaurants, cafes and street booths. Telex: Empresa National de Telecommunications (ENTEL) operate about 90 public telex booths in Lima and other cities. Closed evenings and holidays. Permanent telex service at Av Bolivia 347 in Lima. Telegrams slow.

Air Travel
AeroPeru and Faucett operate regular domestic flights between Lima and other cities. Often overbooked so reconfirm bookings and arrive in plenty of time. Weather conditions often delay or cancel flights so phone first to check.

Other Transport
The Pan-American Highway, paved for the most part, runs north and south along the coast. Highways between the coast and mountain regions are sometimes blocked by landslides in rainy season (DecMay). Cars can be hired easily, but payment with credit cards is necessary. International driving license preferred.

LIMA

Airport Information

Time
GMT -5

Airport
Jorge Chavez Internacional LIM
Tel: 529570
16 km (10 mi) NW of city

Airlines
Aeroperu 287825
Air France 704702
Air New Zealand 316324
Alitalia 428505

Avensa 242119
Avianca 704232
British Airways 477219
Eastern 428555
Iberia 283831

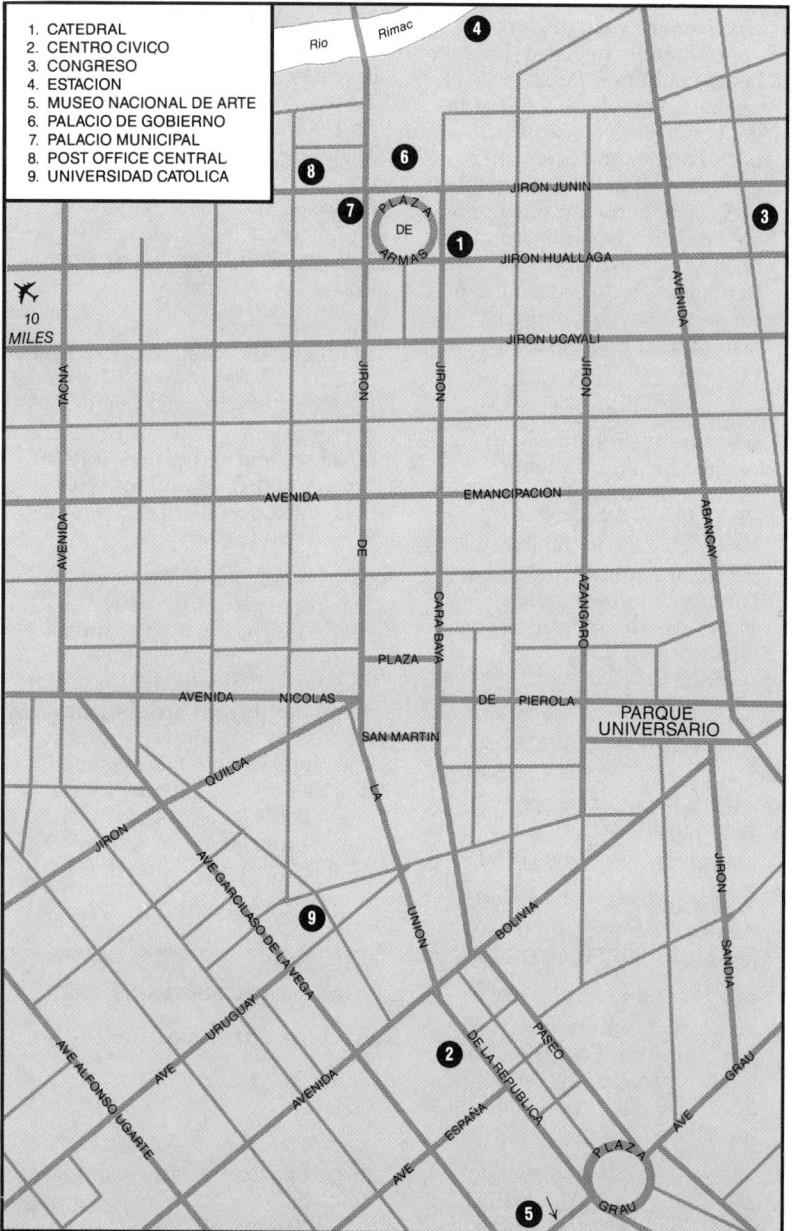

1. CATEDRAL
2. CENTRO CIVICO
3. CONGRESO
4. ESTACION
5. MUSEO NACIONAL DE ARTE
6. PALACIO DE GOBIERNO
7. PALACIO MUNICIPAL
8. POST OFFICE CENTRAL
9. UNIVERSIDAD CATOLICA

Lima

JAL 704433
KLM 471394
Korean 314552
Lufthansa 424466
Olympic 409582
Pan Am 417421
Sabena 403901
Singapore 431919
Swissair 312271
TWA 239181
Varig 246060

Transport to City

Taxi: there are two types of taxis: regular and colectivos. Regular taxis are unmetered and charge a fixed rate of the equivalent of US$12 to town with no extra charges or tipping; 3540 minutes. Colectivos take five passengers and do not leave until taxi is full; cost the equivalent of about US$ 4-5 with an additional charge for baggage. Ask drivers before engaging which type of taxi it is. Coach: coach leaves every 20 minutes and takes about 1 hour to the city center; costs about US$5 and operates for 24 hours. Hotels often provide reasonably-priced courtesy coaches. Inform your hotel of your flight number and arrival time.
Transit: airport bus leaves from Enatru Bus Station ourside the airport, costs about US$1.50, and provides luggage space. Leaves every 60 minutes and takes 1-2 hours.

Facilities

Bar, buffet, restaurant, bank with currency exchange, insurance, hotel reservations, first aid/medical, vaccinations, post office, baggage deposit, barber shop, nursery, shops selling flowers, candy , books, gifts.
Duty-free shop sells cigarets, cigars, tobacco, wines, aperitifs, spirits, liqueurs, watches, lighters, cameras, radios, jewellery, electrical goods, glass, china. US currency and

American Express credit cards accepted.
Car rental desks: Hertz, Avis, Budget, Europcar, Nova, Safari

Airport Taxes
Per person: International US$10

City Information

Weather
It is cool and damp in Lima from June to October and there are frequent mists from the sea. From November to May it is sunny and warm.

Transportation
Taxis are the best way of getting around town and can be hailed or found in ranks. Taxis from ranks (estaciones) usually cost as much as 50% more. Shared taxis (colectivos) carry up to six people on set routes. They leave from La Colmena on both sides of the Plaza San Martin and the rates are officially set. With other taxis, agree on the fare for the journey before setting off. After 2200 all fares are 50% more. Yellow city buses and mini-buses run from the city to suburbs and around town. Cars are available for hire although the traffic is frequently congested around rush hour. International license preferred and payment by credit card mandatory. Basic insurance is covered in the cost.

Car Hire
Hertz, Jr Ocona 262 (tel: 288477)
Avis, Av Republica 170
   (tel: 524774 & 327245)
Budget, Centro Civico de Lima
   (tel: 314735)
National, Av Espana 449
   (tel: 523426 & 232526)

Hospitals
Medical help for travellers can be found at:
British American Hospital
   (tel: 403570-409100)

International Trade Fair (Nov)

Alcazar, Jiron Camana
  (tel: 276290)
Country Club, Los Eucaliptos,
  San Isidro (tel: 404060)
Crillon, PO Box 2981 (tel: 283290)
El Pueblo Hotel, PO Box 2585
  (tel: 350777)
Gran Hotel Bolivar, Plaza San
  Martin, (tel: 276400)
Lima Sheraton Hotel, Paseo de la
  Republica 170 (tel: 329050/8676)
Miraflores Cesar's, PO Box 5172
  (tel: 441212)

Lima, founded by the conqueror
Francisco Pizarro in 1535 and
once the capital of the Spanish
South American Empire, is now
a modern metropolis and the
capital of Peru. It has many
colonial buildings in the center:
the cathedral and Torre Tagle
Palace are worth visiting. The
Church and Convent of San
Francisco have catacombs and
what purports to be the remains
of Pizarro. The Museum of
Anthropology and Archaeology
in the suburb of Pueblo Libre
has pre-Inca artifacts and a scale
model of Macchu Picchu. Visit
the Gold Museum in Monterrico;
the National Inca Museum; the
Museum of the Inquisition.
Jiron Union is the center for
entertainment and shopping,
and there are many good
restaurants and nightclubs in the
suburbs of Miraflores and San
Isidro.

Useful Addresses

American: Av I.G. de laVega y
  Espana (tel: 338000)
Canadian: 132 Calle Libertad
  (tel: 444015)
British: Plaza Washington
  (tel: 334738)

Central Bank, Jiron Miro
  Quesada cuadra 4 (tel: 276350)
Lima Stock Exchange, Jiron Miro
  Quesada 265 (tel: 286280)
Lima Chamber of Commerce,
  Av Ortiz de Zevallos 398
  (tel: 240071)
American Chamber of
  Commerce, Av Ricardo Palma
  836 (tel: 479349)
United Nations Information,
  Av Arenales 815 (tel: 326534)
International Translation Service,
  Av Arequipa 3200, San Isidro
  (tel: 41396)

Touring and Automobile Club of
  Peru, Av Cesar Vallejo 699
  (tel: 403270/225957)
American Express, SA, Belen
  1040 (tel: 276624)
Thomas Cook, Jiron Ocona 174
  (tel: 278353)

UNITED STATES

Essential Information

Type of Government
Federal Republic

Area
9,371,839 sq kms
(3.6 million sq miles)

Population
244 million

Annual Growth Rate
4%

Language
Predominantly English, with
some Spanish

Religion
Primarily Christian. Protestant
30%, Roman Catholic 20%, with
numerous other demoninations.

Ethnic Groups
Primarily European. English
13%, German 10%, Irish 6%,
Italian 3%. Major non-white
groups are Black 12%, Hispanic,
Chinese and Japanese.

Weights and Measures
Americanized version of British
Imperial system. Some metric is
used.

Electrical Current
AC 60c 110/220V

Major Business Cities
Washington D.C. (Cap)
    3.1 million
New York 11.5 million
Los Angeles 7.2 million
Chicago 7.0 million
Philadelphia 4.9 million
Detroit 4.5 million
Boston 3.4 million
San Francisco 3.2 million
Dallas 2.5 million
Pittsburgh 2.4 million
Cleveland 2.1 million
Houston 2.1 million
Minneapolis-St. Paul 2 million
Atlanta 1.7 million
Seattle 1.5 million
Miami 1.4 million
Denver 1.4 million

Currency
$1 (Dollar) = 100 cents
Notes: $1, 5, 10, 20, 50, 100
Coins: 1, 5, 10, 25, 50 cents,
    1 dollar

Public Holidays
Jan 1 New Years Day
Jan 19 Martin Luther King Day
Feb 12 Lincoln's Birthday
Feb 16 Washington's Birthday
Apr 13-20 Easter Week
May 25 Memorial Day
Jul 4 Independence Day
Sept 4 Labor Day
Oct 12 Columbus Day
Nov 12 Veterans Day
Nov 26 Thanksgiving Day
Dec 25 Christmas Day

Travellers Information

Entry Requirements
Passport and visa required by all
travellers except for Canadian
citizens, who must have
identification.

Working Restrictions
Work permit (Green Card)
required.

Vaccination Required
None required

Customs and Duty Free
On arrival: 200 cigarettes or 50
cigars (non-Cuban) or 3 lbs. of
tobacco, and 1 quart of alcohol.
Total duty free limited to $300
each month. No meat, plants,
fresh fruit or vegetables may be
brought in.

Currency Restrictions
No currency restrictions.
Amounts over $5000 must be
declared when entering or
leaving.

Health Tips
No major health risks.

Drinking water from tap is safe throughout the country. Medical care and facilities are excellent but expensive. Foreign travellers should have medical insurance.

Climate and Clothing

Northeast
November-April: Cold with heavy snow and winds. Temperatures from 25-45F (-2-4C), colder in New England states. Wear winter clothes with heavy overcoat, boots and hat.
May-October: Hot and humid with frequent thunderstorms. Temperatures 75-90F (24-32C). Lightweight clothes with light raincoat.

South
November-April: Mild with light rain and occasional frost. Temperatures 60-75F (15-24C). Light to mediumweight clothes and light raincoat.
May-October: Hot and humid, cooler along the coastlines. Frequent thunderstorms. Temperatures 85-95F (31-35C). Light tropical clothes and umbrella.

Midwest
November-April: Very cold with snow and blizzards. Temperatures 10-20F (-7 -11C), but may fall below 0F. Wear warm clothing with overcoat, hat and boots.
May-October: Hot and humid, moderate rainfall with occasional thunderstorms. Temperatures 70-95F (21-35C). Light clothing with raincoat or umbrella.

Southwest
November-April: Sunny and mild with some light rain. Temperatures 55-75F (13-24C), colder in higher elevations. Light to medium weight clothing.
May-October: Dry, sunny and hot. Temperatures 75-100F (24-38C), and can go over 100F in desert areas. Light clothing with light jacket.

West Coast
November-April: Mild with occasional rain. Much more rainfall in Pacific Northwest. Temperatures 45-60F (7-13C). Medium weight clothing with raincoat.
May-October: Warm and mainly dry, although frequent rain in Pacific Northwest. Temperatures 70-80F (21-27C). Light clothing with jacket or sweaters in evenings.

Tipping

Normally 15% of the bill for good service in restaurants and nightclubs. Service charge is rarely included in the bill. Others who expect tips are taxi drivers, doormen and airport porters who should be tipped from 50 cents to $1.00, more if warranted.

Food and Drink

The cuisine of the United States is much too varied to cover in this short description. Basically, the majority of good restaurants offer the cuisine of other countries - French, Italian, Mexican, etc. Usually, the more expensive restaurants in larger cities offer a French or hybrid-Continental menu. Lately there has been an awakening of the new "American" cuisine.
This rediscovery of indigenous foods has spawned many fine restaurants in larger cities offering dishes which compete with the finest foods in the world.
Some of the specialties in the United States are the fine beef steaks (especially Iowa corn-fed beef), New England lobster and soup chowders, the Cajun and Creole-style cooking of Louisiana, Texas BBQ's, the Mexican-style foods in the

Southwest, creative California cooking featuring local produce, and the traditional fried chicken, hamburgers, corn and apple pie. The fine wines from California's Napá and Sonoma regions are some of the best in the world, especially the Cabernet Sauvignon, Chardonnay, and Zinfandel.

Business Brief

GDP
$4.5 trillion

Annual Growth Rate
3%

Natural Resources
Coal, copper, iron ore, oil and natural gas, lumber, hydroelectric power, gold and other minerals

Agriculture
Wheat, corn, barley and other grain crops, soybeans, tobacco, cotton and livestock

Industry
Chemicals, steel, machinery, automobiles have been under attack from imports in recent years. Other main industries are electronics, paper products, food and beverages, apparel, printing and publishing

Imports
Total $424 billion
Petroleum, metals and ores, machinery, automobiles, meat, fish, textiles, apparel, steel, electronics, fruit and coffee

Exports
Total $250 billion
Agricultural and industrial machinery, chemicals, pharmaceuticals, livestock, grains, paper, fertilizers, iron, communication and electronic equipment, military hardware, computers and electrical equipment

Major Trading Partners
Canada, Japan, Britain, West Germany, Netherlands, Mexico, Italy, France, Australia and Brazil

Workforce
120 million
Manufacturing and service industries 95%

Tips for Doing Business
Business people should wear a suit and tie (for men) for all business meetings. Advance appointments are necessary since most business people have busy daily schedules. Business meetings are usually not as formal in other parts of the world. Casual talk, humor and politics are not out of place. Best months for travel are September through June. Avoid the Christmas holiday season. The business lunch is an established tradition, and the business breakfast is becoming popular.

Business Hours

Government
Mon-Fri 0900-1200, 1300-1630

Business
Mon-Fri 0900-1200, 1300-1700

Banks
Mon-Fri 1000-1500

Shops
Mon-Sat 0900-1800 (occasionally Sunday)

Telephone and Communications
The United States has the most advanced telephone system in the world. You can dial directly anywhere from public and hotel telephones. Dial 0 for operator, 411 for information, and in most large cities, 911 for police or emergency.
For dialing long distance, the city area code is listed in the

NORTH/SOUTH AMERICA

telephone book, or you can call information.

Telephone Country Code: 1
Telephone City Codes:
Atlanta 404
Boston 617
Chicago 312
Cleveland 216
Dallas 214
Denver 303
Detroit 313
Honolulu 808
Houston 713
Kansas City 816
Los Angeles 213
Miami 305
Minneapolis 612
New Orleans 504
New York 212
Philadelphia 215
Pittsburgh 412
St. Louis 314
San Francisco 415
Seattle 206
Washington D.C. 202
Country Telex Codes: 327, 347, 367

Air Travel

A large, frequent and well-organized system of air travel exists between most cities in the U.S. Major carriers, shuttle services and smaller regional airlines provide air service to almost any destination. For airline and airport services see the Airport section under the specific city of your choice.

Other Transport

Taxis: Cab service is available in every major city and can be hailed from the curb or ordered by telephone. Hotels will call a taxi for guests.
Roads: The most extensive road and highway system in the world. Roads are for the most part excellent, especially the interstate highway system. Toll highways exist in the eastern states. However, because of the distances involved driving is not a practical method of travel for the average businessman. Only in large, sprawling cities such as Los Angeles is an automobile the preferred method of travel.
Bus and Rail: Bus service is a good and inexpensive method of travel. Greyhound and Trailways provide cross-country service, and most large cities have intercity bus service. Amtrak, although experiencing difficulties in recent years, provides excellent service throughout its passenger rail network.

ATLANTA

Airport Information

Time
GMT -5 (Eastern)
GMT -4 (April-October)

Airport
William B. Hartsfield
   International ATL
Tel: 530-6600
10 miles (16 km) S of city

Airlines
Alitalia 1-800 233-5730
American 521-2655
Avensa 237-6358
Avianca 1-800 284-2622
British Airways 1-800 247-9297
Canadian International 1-800 426-7000
Continental 1-800 525-0280
Delta 765-5000
Eastern 435-1111
Korean 522-7461
Lufthansa 1-800 421-8200
Northwest 1-800 225-2525
Ozark 68-9565
Pan Am 1-800 221-1111
Piedmont 681-3100
Republic 762-5561
Sabena 1-800 645-3790
SAS 1-800 221-2350
Swissair 1-800 221-4750
TWA 522-5738
United 394-2234
Varig 1-800 468-2744

Transport to City

Taxis: $16-20 plus tip. Fifteen to 20 minute ride to downtown locations.

Coach: Airport bus $7 to downtown. Leaves airport approximately every 20 minutes from 5 AM to midnight. Airport limousines available, about $10.

Transit: City bus service to rail/subway leaves every 18 minutes from 0500-0030.

Facilities

Duty-free shop, currency exchange, bar, restaurant, coffee shop, baggage deposit, shops, hotel reservations, flight insurance and post office

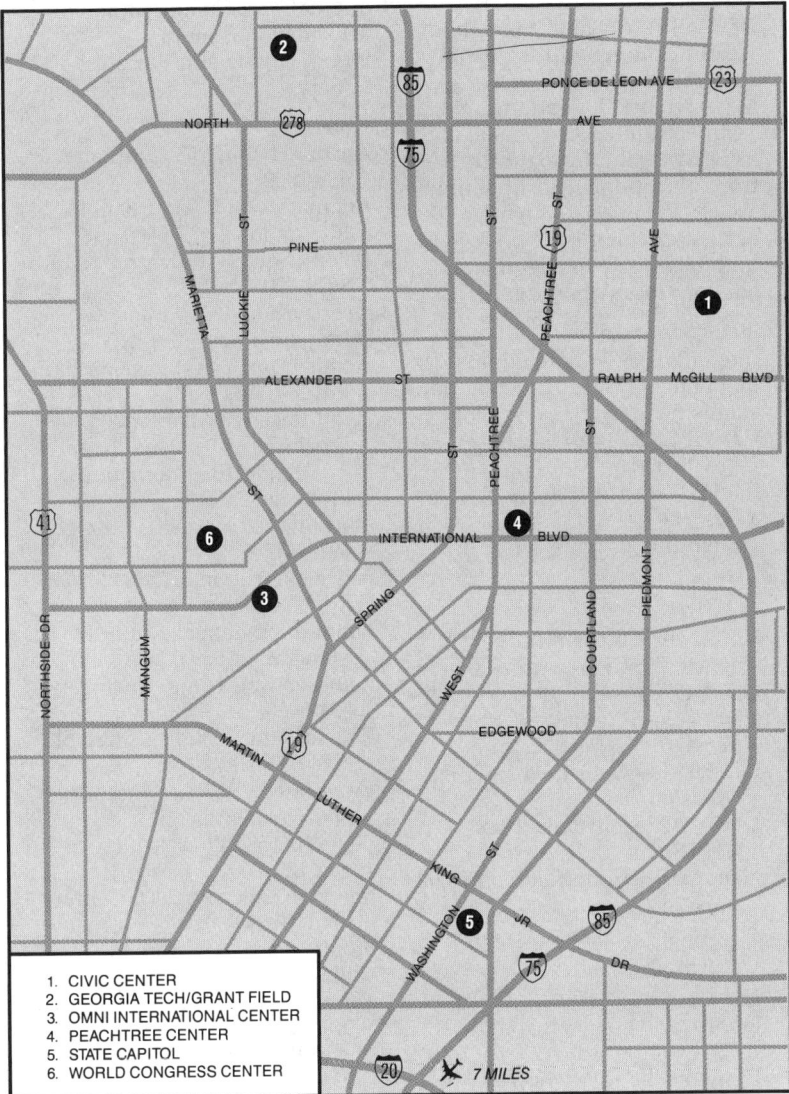

1. CIVIC CENTER
2. GEORGIA TECH/GRANT FIELD
3. OMNI INTERNATIONAL CENTER
4. PEACHTREE CENTER
5. STATE CAPITOL
6. WORLD CONGRESS CENTER

7 MILES

Atlanta

Car rental desks: Hertz, Alamo, Avis, National, Budget, Dollar, American International

Airport Taxes
$3.00 per passenger

City Information

Weather
November-April. Mild temperatures with light rains beginning in January. Temperatures between 60-75F (15-24C). Wear light to medium weight clothing with light raincoat or umbrella.
May-October. Hot and humid. Temperatures from 85-100F (30-38C). Wear light weight to tropical clothing. Most buildings are air-conditioned; guard against catching a cold. Have umbrella ready for frequent summer thunderstorms.

Transportation
Intercity taxis are plentiful and moderately priced. Catch at hotel stands on curb, or call Yellow Cab (521-0200) or Diamond Cab (521-0229). The Metropolitan Rapid Transit Authority operates a bus system and a subway system that covers part of the city.

Car Hire
Hertz, 202 Courtland 659-3000
Agency, 2951 Flowers 1-800 321-1972
Alamo, 2045 Rental Car Row 768-4161
Budget, 140 Courtland 1-800 527-0700
Dollar, 122 Courtland 1-800 421-6868
National, 122 International 1-800 227-7368
Thrifty, 527 Courtland 1-800 367-2277

Hospitals
Emory University Hospital, 1364 Clifton Rd. NE 329-7021
Crawford Long Memorial

Hospital, 35 Lindon Avenue. NE 892-4410
Northside Hospital, 1000 Johnson Ferry Rd. Ne 256-8000

Trade Fairs
Poultry and Egg Assoc. Exhibition (Jan)
Imprinted Sportswear Exhibition (Feb)
World Technology Exchange Fair (Feb)
Computer Exhibition (Apr)
International Communication Exhibition (June)
Woodworking and Furniture Fair (Sept)

Hotels
Atlanta Hilton, 255 Courtland 659-2000
Atlanta Marriott, Courtland & International 659-6500
Colony Square, Peachtree & 14th 892-6000
Holiday Inn, 4225 Fulton Industrial Blvd. 691-4100
Holiday Inn, 1810 Howell Mill Rd. 351-3831
Hyatt Regency Atlanta, 265 Peachtree 577-1234
IBIS Atlanta, 101 International Blvd. 524-5555
Marriott, 246 Perimeter Center, 394-6500
Northlake Hilton, 4156 LaVista Rd. 938-1026
Omni International, Omni Pl. & Marietta St. 659-0000
Radisson Inn, I-28 & Chamblee 394-5000
Ramada Inn, 1630 Peachtree St. NW 875-9711
Ritz-Carlton, 181 Peachtree St. NW 659-0400
Sheraton, 590 W. Peachtree St. NW 881-6000
Sheraton Century, 2000 Century Blvd. 325-0000
Stouffers Waverly, Galleria Pkwy. 953-4500
Terrace Garden Inn, 3405 Lenox. 261-9250
Tower Place, 3340 Peachtree. 231-1234

Westin Peachtree Plaza,
Peachtree Plaza. 659-1400

What to See and Do

New center of the city is the
Peachtree Plaza and Center.
Along famous Peachtree Street at
Harris, is the Visitor Information
Center. Another new center is
the Omni International Center,
near the financial district. The
Atlanta Civic Center and
Memorial Arts Center host many
art and music events, including
the Atlanta Symphony
Orchestra. East of Peachtree
Street is the state capitol with
the Capitol Dome. Outside
Atlanta is Wren's Nest, Stone
Mountain Park and Six Flags
Over Georgia. Professional
sports teams include the Atlanta
Hawks (basketball), Atlanta
Braves (baseball) and Atlanta
Falcons (football).

Useful Addresses

Embassies and Consulates
British: 225 Peachtree St.
524-5856
Canadian: 400 S. Omni Intl.
577-6810
French: 1100 Peachtree Ctr.
525-1100
German: 229 Peachtree St.
659-4760
Japanese: 1201 Peachtree St.
892-2700

Business and Commerce
Atlanta Chamber of Commerce,
1300 N. Omni Intl. 521-0845
Atlanta Convention Bureau, 233
Peachtree St. NE 659-4270
Georgia Chamber of Commerce,
1200 Commerce Bldg. 524-8481
Georgia Dept. of Industry &
Trade, Box 1776 656-3556
U.S. Dept. of Commerce,
1365 Peachtree St. 881-7000

Tourism and Travel
AAA Georgia, 1100 Spring St.
NW 875-7171

American Express, 100 Colony
Sq. NW 892-8175
Amtrak, Peachtree Station, 1688
Peachtree St. NW 688-4417
Deak International, 1795
Peachtree *110 872-0903
Uniglobe Action Travel, 3312
Piedmont Rd *110 365-8112
Uniglobe Travel Source, 1100
Ashwood Pkwy. 395-7291
Uniglobe 400 Travel, 500 Sugar
Mill Rd. 641-9900
Uniglobe Peachtree Travel, 55
Marietta St 523-3301
Uniglobe Perimeter Travel, 1100
Johnson Ferry Rd 255-6255
Uniglobe Pinnacle Travel, 10
North Pky. Sq. *100 365-9906
Uniglobe Premier Travel, 805
Peachtree St *505 885-1122
Uniglobe Prestige Travel, 5665
Northside Dr. 955-6066
Uniglobe Regal Travel, 2220
Parklake Dr. 491-7414
Uniglobe Williams Travel, 2555
Cumberland Pkwy. 438-2555
Uniglobe VIP Travel, 3 Corporate
Square 982-9100

BOSTON

Airport Information

Time
GMT -5 (Eastern)
GMT -4 (April-October)

Airport
Logan International BOS
Tel: 973-5500
3 mi (5 km) E of city
John A. Volpe International
Terminal
North-South Domestic Terminals

Airlines
Aer Lingus 1-800 223-6537
Air Canada 1-800 422-6232
Air France 1-800 237-2747
Alitalia 1-800 223-5730
American 542-6700
Avianca 1-800 284-2622
British Airways 1-800 247-9297
Canadian International 1-800
426-7000
Continental 1-800 525-0280

Delta 1-800 221-1212
Eastern 1-800 327-8376
El Al 1-800 223-6700
Finnair 1-800 223-5700
Iberia 1-800 221-9741
Japan Airlines 1-800 525-3663
KLM 1-800 777-5553
Lufthansa 1-800 645-3880
Northwest 1-800 225-2525
Pan Am 1-800 221-1111
Piedmont 1-800 251-5720
Qantas 1-800 227-4500
Republic 482-4332
SAS 1-800 221-2350
Swissair 423-7778
TAP 1-800 221-7370
TWA 367-2800
US Air 482-3160
Varig 542-5202

Transport to City

Taxis: $10-12, plus tip to downtown. About 20-25 minutes. Less expensive Share-a-Cab available at Domestic Terminal from 1530-1100 .

Coach: Airways Transportation buses leaves hourly to downtown locations for $5.25 and take 30-45 minutes. Grey Line buses leave every half-hour from 0700-1900 for $6. Some hotels have free courtesy bus services.

Transit: Take the *22 or *33 shuttle leaving every 10 minutes to the Airport Station to catch the Rapid Transittrain to downtown. Operates 0500-0100, leaves every

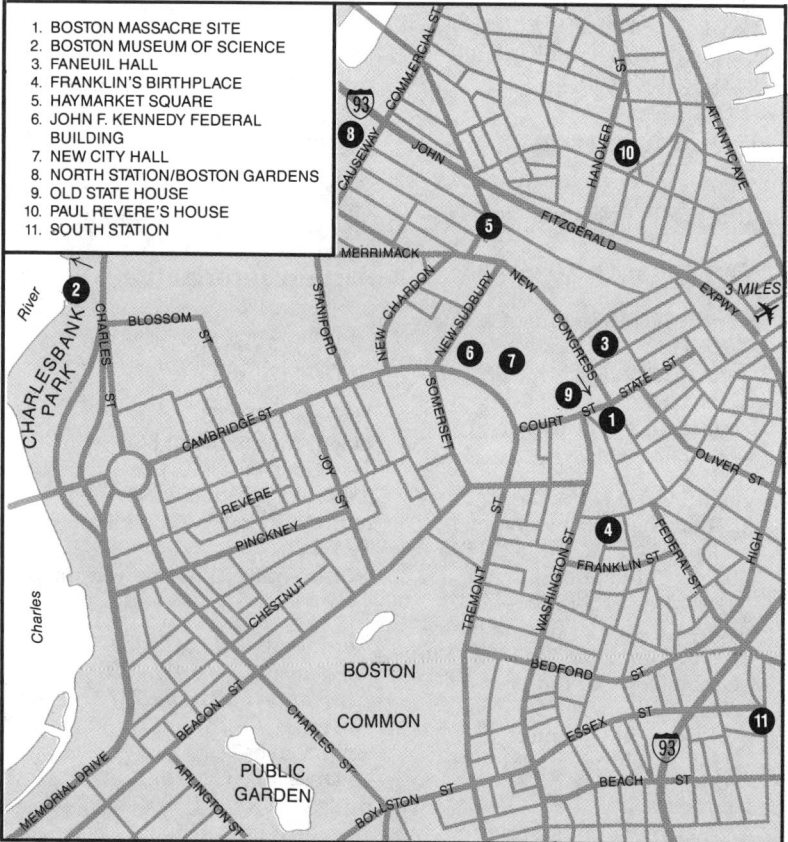

1. BOSTON MASSACRE SITE
2. BOSTON MUSEUM OF SCIENCE
3. FANEUIL HALL
4. FRANKLIN'S BIRTHPLACE
5. HAYMARKET SQUARE
6. JOHN F. KENNEDY FEDERAL BUILDING
7. NEW CITY HALL
8. NORTH STATION/BOSTON GARDENS
9. OLD STATE HOUSE
10. PAUL REVERE'S HOUSE
11. SOUTH STATION

Boston

10-15 minutes, and costs 60 cents to downtown stations.

Facilities
Currency exchange and-duty free shop (international terminal), insurance, hotel reservations, baggage deposit, restaurant and lounge, and various shops
Car rental desks: Hertz, Avis, Budget, National, Dollar

Airport Taxes
$3.00 per passenger

City Information

Weather
November-April. Cold with heavy snow. Temperatures 25-35F (-2-4C). Wear heavy clothing with overcoat, hat and boots. May-October. Hot and humid, but tempered with breezes from the ocean. Frequent brief afternoon rainstorms. Temperatures 75-90F (24-32C). Wear light clothing and umbrella.

Transportation
Taxis are plentiful and may be hailed from curb or ordered by telephone. Try Yellow Cab (787-0000). Massachussets Bay Transit Authority (MBTA) operates efficient bus, subway and trolley routes which will get you to most locations in the metro area. See transit maps at bus and subway stops.

Car Hire
Hertz, 1 Center Plaza 720-0100
Hertz, Park Square, 68 Eliot St. 482-9102
Hertz, Meridian, Marriott and Westin Hotels
Agency, 189 Squire Rd. 1-800 321-1972
Alamo, 2 Harborside Dr. 561-4100
Budget, Park Square 1-800 527-0700
National, 183 Dartmouth St. 1-800 227-7368

Hospitals
Massachussets General Hospital, 55 Fruit St. 726-2000
New England Medical Center, 171 Harrison Ave. 956-5000

Trade Fairs
Electronics Exhibition (Apr)
Tooling and Machinery Exhibition (May)
International Cargo Equip. Exhibition (May)
International Electronics Exhibition (June)
Continuing Education and Training Exhibition (June)
Industrial Security Exhibition (Sept)
Fishing Exhibition (Oct)

Hotels
Back Bay Boston Hilton, Dalton St. 236-1100
Bostonian, Faneuil Hall Market 523-3600
Copley Plaza, 138 St. James267-5300
Four Seasons, 200 Boylston St. 338-4400
Hyatt Regency, 575 Memorial Dr. 492-1234
Lenox, 710 Boylston St.536-5300
Marriott Copley Place,110 Huntington Ave. 236-5800
Meridien, 1 Post Office Sq.451-1900
Park Plaza, 64 Arlington St.426-2000
Parker House, 60 School St.227-8600
Ritz-Carlton, 15 Arlington St. 536-5700
Westin Copley, 20 Providence 262-9600

What to See and Do
Boston is a good city for walking tours. Newly refurbished Quincy Market is a complex of shops, restaurants, offices, and the historic Faneuil Hall. Walk the three-mile Freedom Trail to Paul Revere House and the Boston Tea Party ship. Other historic

areas are Beacon Hill and Back Bay. Music is much loved in Boston and the Boston Symphony and Boston Pops are institutions. Jazz and student clubs located near Harvard University and MIT in Cambridge. Boston Gardens sports arena is the home of the Boston Celtics (basketball) and the Boston Bruins (hockey).

Useful Addresses

Embassies and Consulates
British: 4740 Prudential Tower 437-7160
Canadian: 500 Boylston St. 262-3760
French: 3 Commonwealth Ave. 266-1680
German: 535 Boylston St. 536-4414
Japanese: 600 Atlantic Ave. 973-9772

Business and Commerce
Boston Stock Exchange, 1 Boston Place 723-9500
Boston Chamber of Commerce, 125 High St. 426-1250
Boston Convention Bureau, Prudential Tower 367-9275
Mass. Dept. of Commerce and Development, 1 Ashburton Place 367-1830
Massachussets Port Authority, 99 High St. 482-2930
U.S. Dept. of Commerce, 441 Stuart St. 223-2312

Tourism and Travel
AAA Massachussets,141 Tremont St. 482-8031
American Express, 10 Tremont St. 723-8400
Amtrack, South Station, Atlantic Ave. 482-3660
Deak International, 160 Franklin St. 426-0016
Deak International, Prudential Plaza, 160 Franklin St.
Thomas Cook, 113 A Summer 267-5000
Uniglobe Bay State Travel,91

91 Blanchard Rd., Cambridge 497-0400
Uniglobe Ram Travel, 325 Harvard St., Brookline 738-0500

CHICAGO

Airport Information

Time
GMT -6 (Central)
GMT -5 (April-October)

Airport
O'Hare International ORD
Tel: 686-2200
18 mi (29 km) NW of city
Terminal One (International)
Terminal Two/Three (Domestic)

Airlines
Aer Lingus 1-800 223-6537
Air Canada 1-800 422-6232
Air France 1-800 237-2747
Alitalia 1-800 223-5730
American 372-8000
British Airways 1-800 247-9297
Canadian International 1-800 426-7000
Continental 686-6500
Delta 1-800 221-1212
Eastern 1-800 327-8376
El Al 1-800 223-6700
Finnair 1-800 223-5702
Iberia 1-800 221-9741
Japan Airlines 1-800 525-3663
KLM 1-800 777-5553
Korean 1-800 421-8200
Kuwait 263-3858
Lufthansa 1-800 645-3880
Northwest 346-4900
Olympic 1-800 223-1226
Pan Am 1-800 221-1111
Philippine 1-800 435-9725
Piedmont 263-3656
Qantas 1-800 227-4500
Republic 346-9860
Sabena 1-800 645-3790
SAS 1-800 221-2350
Singapore 1-800 742-3333
Swissair 641-8830
TWA 558-7000

United 1-800 241-6522
US Air 726-1201
Varig 1-800 468-2744

Transport to City

Taxis: Plentiful but expensive. About $22-25, 30 minutes to downtown, more in rush hours. Share-a-Cab is $12 per person sharing with three persons. Coach: Airport buses (Continental) run frequently to downtown for $9, and also provide service to suburban areas and Midway Regional Airport. Departure points from all three terminals.

Transit: Elevated subway train departs from lower level of airport terminal direct to downtown (Loop) every 5 minutes during the day, and every 30 minutes at night. Fare $1.

Facilities

Currency exchange and duty-free shop (International terminal), restaurants, bars, flight insurance, baggage deposit,

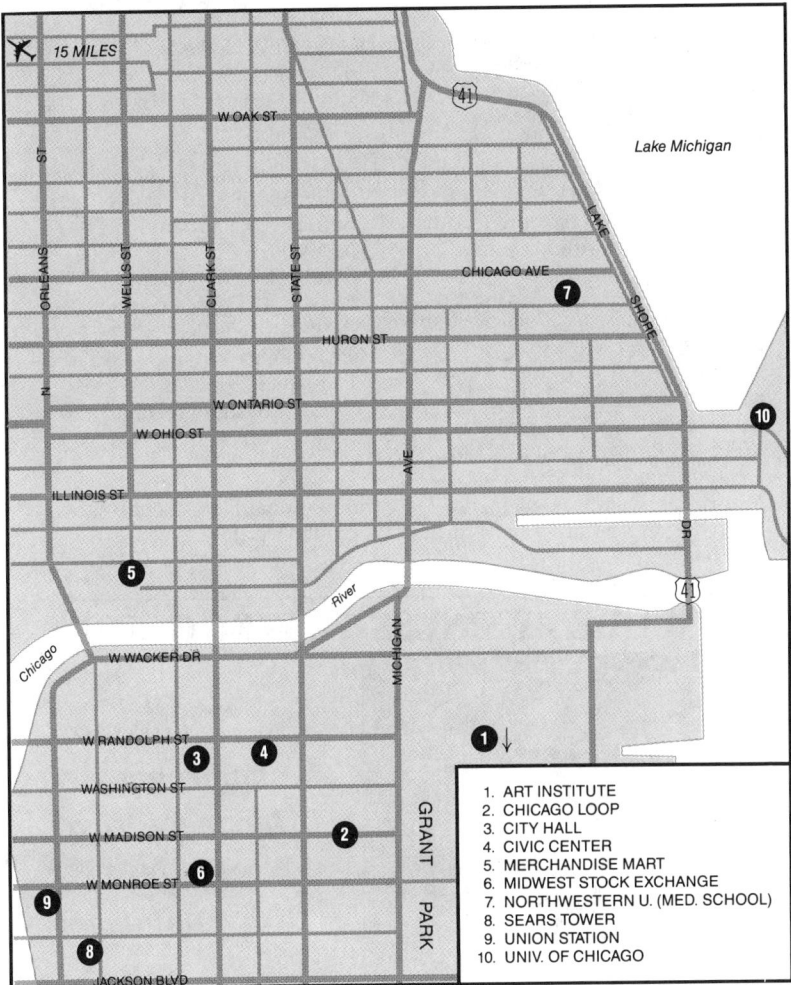

15 MILES

Lake Michigan

W OAK ST

CHICAGO AVE ⑦

HURON ST

W ONTARIO ST

W OHIO ST

ILLINOIS ST

⑤

Chicago River

W WACKER DR

W RANDOLPH ST ③ ④

WASHINGTON ST

W MADISON ST ②

W MONROE ST ⑥

⑨

⑧

JACKSON BLVD

① ↓

GRANT PARK

1. ART INSTITUTE
2. CHICAGO LOOP
3. CITY HALL
4. CIVIC CENTER
5. MERCHANDISE MART
6. MIDWEST STOCK EXCHANGE
7. NORTHWESTERN U. (MED. SCHOOL)
8. SEARS TOWER
9. UNION STATION
10. UNIV. OF CHICAGO

Chicago

NORTH/SOUTH AMERICA

barber shops, post office, first-aid, and shops.

Car rental desks: Hertz, Ajax, American International, Avis, Budget, Dollar, National, Thrifty

Airport Taxes
$3.00 per passenger

City Information

Weather
November-April. Very cold with snow and occasional blizzards. Temperatures 12-35F (-4-4C) but can fall below 0 F. Wear medium weight clothing with overcoat, hat and boots.

May-October. Hot and humid. Temperatures from 70-90F (20-32C). Lightweight clothes with umbrella or light raincoat. Chicago, known as "Windy City", experiences high winds off the lake and occasional afternoon thunderstorms during the summer months.

Transportation
Numerous taxis in Chicago. Can be hailed from curb or at taxi stands in front of hotels. Major companies include Yellow Cab (225-6000), Checker Cab (666-3700), American United (248-7600) or Flash Cab (561-1444). Metro bus system is extensive and will get you anywhere in the Chicago area. Fare $1.00 with transfers extra for extended stops. The system is tied in with the RTA subway. Same fare and structure applies.

Car Hire
Hertz, 9 W. Kinzie St. 372-7600

Hertz, Marriott Hotel, 540 N. Michigan 329-0036

Hertz, Hyatt Regency Hotel, 565-0032

Agency, 4935 N. Central 1-800 321-1972

Alamo, Holiday Inn, 5440 N. River Rd., Rosemont 671-7662

Budget, 200 N. Dearborn St. 1-800 527-0700

Dollar, 50 W. Lake St. 1-800 421-6868

National, 191 N. Dearborn 1-800 227-7368

Hospitals
Northwestern Memorial, Superior & Fairbanks Sts. 649-2000

Rush Presbyterian Medical Center, 1753 W. Congress Parkway 942-5000

Michael Reese Hospital, 2929 S. Ellis Ave. 791-2000

Univ. of Chicago Hospital, 950 E. 59th St. 947-1000

Trade Fairs
International Floor Covering Exhibition (Jan)

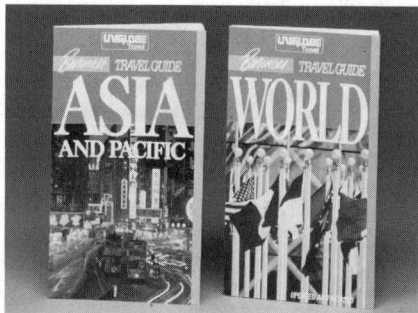

National Gift Exhibition (Jan)
International Automotive Service Exhibition (Feb)
Design Engineering Exhibition (Mar)
Houseware Manufacturers Fair (Apr)
Ceramics Technology Fair (Apr)
International Food Marketing Fair (May)
Consumer Electronics Fair (June)
National Hardware Exhibition (Aug)
International Machine Tool Exhibition (Sept)
Engineering & Manufacturing Software Exhibition (Sept)
International Marine Trade Exhibition (Sept)
Laboratory Equip. Exhibition (Oct)
International Housewares Exhibition (Nov)
Construction Equip Exhibition (Nov)

Hotels

Ambassador East and West,1301 N. State Pkwy. 787-7200
Bismark, 171 W. Randolph St. 236-0123
Blackstone, 636 S. Michigan Ave. 427-4300
Chicago Hilton, 720 S. Michigan Ave. 922-4400
Continental, 505 N. Michigan Ave. 944-4100
Drake, 140 E. Walton Place787-2200
Essex Inn, 800 S. Michigan Ave. 939-2800
Executive House, 71 E. Wacker Dr. 346-7100
Holiday Inn, 300 E. Ohio St.787-6100
Hyatt Regency Chicago, 151 E. Wacker Dr. 565-1234
Hyatt Lincolnwood, 4500 Touhy Ave. 677-5400
Hyde Park Hilton, 4900 S. Lake Shore Dr. 288-5800
Knickerbocker, 163 E. Walton Pl. 751-8100

Marriott, 540 N. Michigan Ave. 836-6128
Mayfair-Regent, 181 E. Lake Shore Dr. 787-8500
Midland, 172 W. Adams St.332-1200
Palmer House, State & Monroe Sts. 726-7500
Park Hyatt, 800 N. Michigan Ave. 280-2222
Rafael, 201 E. Deleware St.943-5000
Ritz-Carlton, 160 E. Pearson266-1000
Sheraton Plaza, 160 E. Huron 297-1234
Tremont, 100 E. Chestnut751-1900
Westin, 909 N. Michigan Ave. 943-7200
Whitehall, 105 E. Deleware Pl. 944-6300

What to See and Do

Chicago is the birthplace of the "skyscraper" and it prides itself on its many fine buildings, including the world's tallest, the Sears Tower, which has a fine observation deck on top. Also see the Chicago Board of Trade, tours Mon-Fri mornings, where the world's commodities are traded. Also the Chicago Symphony, Adler Planetarium, Field Museum of Natural History and the Art Institute of Chicago.
The best entertainment is found in the many jazz and blues clubs around town. Professional sports fans can have their choice throughout the year with the White Sox and Cubs (baseball), Bears (football), Blackhawks (hockey), and Bulls (basketball).

Useful Addresses

Embassies and Consulates

British: 33 N. Dearborn St. 346-1810
Canadian: 310 S. Michigan Ave. 427-1666

French: 444 N. Michigan Ave.
787-5360
German: 104 S. Michigan Ave.
263-0850
Japanese: 625 N. Michigan Ave.
280-0400

Business and Commerce
Chicago Assoc. of Commerce &
Industry, 200 N. LaSalle St.
580-6934
Chicago Board of Trade, 141 W.
Jackson Blvd. 435-3500
Chicago Chamber of Commerce,
11145 S. Michigan Ave.
928-3200
Chicago Convention Bureau,
McCormick Place on Lakefront
225-5000
Chicago Mercantile Exchange,
30 S. Wacker Dr. 930-1000
Chicago Regional Port District,
425 McFetridge 294-2200
French Chamber of Commerce,
55 E. Monroe 372-9200
German Chamber of Commerce,
104 S. Michigan Ave. 782-8557
Illinois Chamber of Commerce,
20 N. Wacker Dr. 372-7373
Japan Trade Center, 230 N.
Michigan Ave. 726-4390
Midwest Stock Exchange, 120 N.
LaSalle St. 368-2222
U.S. Dept. of Commerce, 55 E.
Monroe St. 353-4450

Tourism and Travel
American Express, 20 S.
Michigan Ave. 435-2595
Amtrak, Union Station, 210 S.
Canal St. 786-1333
Chicago Motor Club, 66 E. South
Water St. 372-1818
Chicago Visitor Information
Center, 208 N. Michigan Ave.
225-2323 (
Deak International, 111 W.
Washington St. 236-0042
Deak International, 500 West
Madison 993-7545
Grey Line Bus Tours, 33 E.
Monroe St.
International Visitor Center,116
S. Michigan Ave. 332-5875
Uniglobe First Travel, 360 North
Michigan 704-1118

CLEVELAND

Airport Information

Time
GMT -5 (Eastern)
GMT -4 (April-October)

Airport
Hopkins International CLE
Tel: 265-6030
12 mi (19 km) SW of city

Airlines
Air Canada 1-800 422-6232
Alitalia 1-800 223-5730
American 881-4341
British Airways 1-800 247-9297
Canadian International 1-800
426-7000
Continental 1-800 525-0280
Delta 781-8800
Eastern 861-7300
KLM 1-800 777-5553
Lufthansa 1-800 645-3880
Northwest 267-0515
Pan Am 1-800 221-1111
Piedmont 1-800 251-5720
Republic 861-4815
Sabena 1-800 645-3790
SAS 1-800 221-2350
Swissair 1-800 221-4750
TWA 781-2700
United 1-800 241-6522
US Air 696-8050

Transport to City
Taxis: From terminal to
downtown $16 plus tip, about
20-30 minutes.
Coach: Airport buses leave
terminal every hour to
downtown hotels. Fare $6-7.
Some hotels provide free van
service.
Transit: Airport/Windermere Red
Line rapid transit train leaves
from inside terminal every 10-15
minutes during rush hours, and
every 30 minutes other times.
Fare $1 to Public Square
(downtown) in 25 minutes.

Facilities
Currency Exchange, hotel
reservations, restaurant and

bar, baggage deposit, flight insurance, post office, shops Car rental desks: Hertz, Ajax, American International, Avis, Budget, Dollar, National, Thrifty

Airport Taxes
None

City Information

Weather
November-April. Cold with heavy snow and strong winds. Temperatures 20-45F (-7-7C), but can get much colder. Wear medium weight clothing with overcoat, hat and boots.

May-October. Hot and humid with occasional summer showers. Temperatures 75-90F (24-32C). Lightweight clothing with umbrella.

Transportation
Taxis are plentiful and can be hailed on the street. Call Yellow-Zone Cab at 623-1500. City bus service (orange buses marked Local) are extensive and inexpensive.

Car Hire
Hertz, Lincoln Park Garage, 708 St. Clair 696-6066

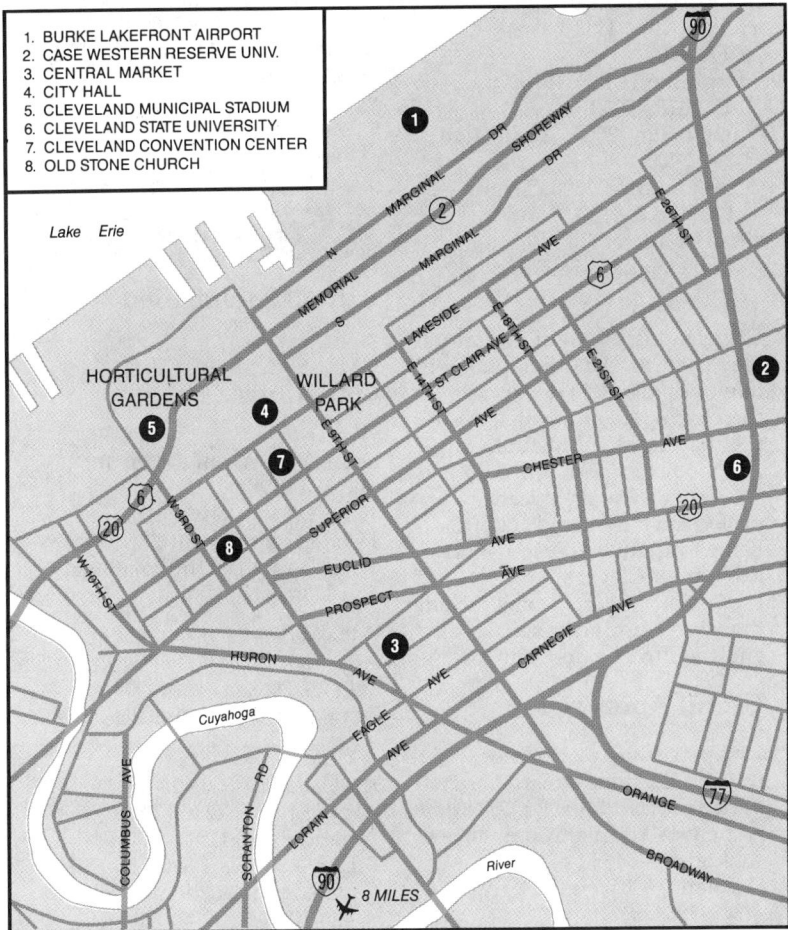

1. BURKE LAKEFRONT AIRPORT
2. CASE WESTERN RESERVE UNIV.
3. CENTRAL MARKET
4. CITY HALL
5. CLEVELAND MUNICIPAL STADIUM
6. CLEVELAND STATE UNIVERSITY
7. CLEVELAND CONVENTION CENTER
8. OLD STONE CHURCH

Lake Erie

HORTICULTURAL GARDENS

WILLARD PARK

Cuyahoga

River

8 MILES

Cleveland

Hertz, Beachwood Marriott,
3663 Park East 464-5950
Avis, 1180 Lakeside Ave. 1-800
331-1212

Hospitals

Cleveland Clinic Hospital,
9500 Euclid Ave. 444-2200
Univ. Hospitals of Cleveland,
2074 Abington Road 444-1000
Mt. Sinai Hospital, University
Circle 795-6000

Hotels

Bond Court, 777 St. Clair Ave.
771-7600
Clarion Hotel, 35000 Curtis
Blvd., 953-8000
Hilton South, 6200
Quarry447-1300
Holiday Inn, 1111 Lakeside,
241-5100
Marriott Inn, 4277 W.
150th252-5333
Ramada Inn, 28611 Euclid Ave.
944-7400
Sheraton Inn, 26300 Chagrin
Blvd., 831-5150
Stouffer Tower City Plaza ,24
Public Sq. 696-5600

What to See and Do

Cleveland is proud of its cultural
life. The Cleveland Symphony is
one of the world's finest, as is
the civic opera and ballet. Also
see the Cleveland Institute of
Art, Zoological Gardens and
Aquarium. The American
professional football Hall of
Fame in Canton is just a short
drive from Cleveland.
Professional sports teams include
the Cleveland Indians (baseball)
and the Browns (football).

Useful Addresses

Embassies and Consulates
British: 55 Public Square 621-7674
Canadian: 55 Public Sq. 771-0150
French: 1800 Union Commerce
Bldg. 687-8567
German: 1500 Terminal Tower
861-5888

Japanese: 13515 Shaker Blvd.
283-2779

Business and Commerce
Cleveland World Trade Assoc.,
690 Huntington Bldg. 621-3300
Cleveland Port Authority,
101 Erieside Ave. 241-8004
Cleveland Convention and
Visitors Bureau, 1301E. 6th St.
621-4110
U.S. Dept. of Commerce,
666 Euclid Ave. 522-4750

Tourism and Travel
American Express, 1925 E. 9th
St. 241-4575
Amtrak, Lakefront Station, 200
East Memorial Sh. 861-0105
Ohio Motorists Assoc., 6000 S.
Marginal Rd. 361-6000
Thomas Cook, Huntington Bldg.
621-3220

DALLAS

Airport Information

Time
GMT -6 (Central)
GMT -5 (April-October)

Airports
Dallas/Fort Worth Regional DFW
Tel: 574-6720
17 mi (27 km) NW of Dallas
17 mi (27 km) NE of Fort Worth
Three Terminals (International
and Domestic)

Dallas-Love Field (Regional
Airport)
Tel: 352-2663
7 mi (11 km) NW of Dallas

Airlines
Air Canada 1-800 422-6232
Alitalia 1-0800 223-5730
American 267-1151
British Airways 1-800 247-9297
Canadian International 1-800
426-7000
Continental 263-0523
Delta 630-3200

Eastern 453-0231
Finnair 387-8682
JAL 1-800 525-3663
KLM 1-800 777-5553
Korean 1-800 421-8100
Lufthansa 1-800 645-3880
Mexicana 1-800 531-7921
Northwest 988-0405
Ozark 647-8013
Pan Am 1-800 221-1111
Phillipine 1-800 630-1783
Piedmont 647-8823
Republic 988-1855
Sabena 1-800 645-1382
SAS 1-800 221-2350
Singapore 1-800 742-3333
Swissair 638-7314
TWA 741-6741
United 988-1004
US Air 1-800 428-4322
Varig 1-800 468-2744

Transport to City
Dallas/Ft Worth Airport
Taxis: From terminals to downtown, $20-23 plus tip, takes 25-30 minutes and more during rush hours. Fare is $5 between terminals.
Coach: Airport buses (Link/ Surtran) leave from all terminals at curbside on Arrival level. Fare is $8 per person. Departs every 30 minutes to downtown and makes 12 hotel stops. Also operates service to American Airlines ticket facility in North Dallas.

Dallas/Love Field
Taxis: $10 to downtown for ride of 20-30 minutes.
Coach: Love Field Bus #39 leaves every 10-15 minutes

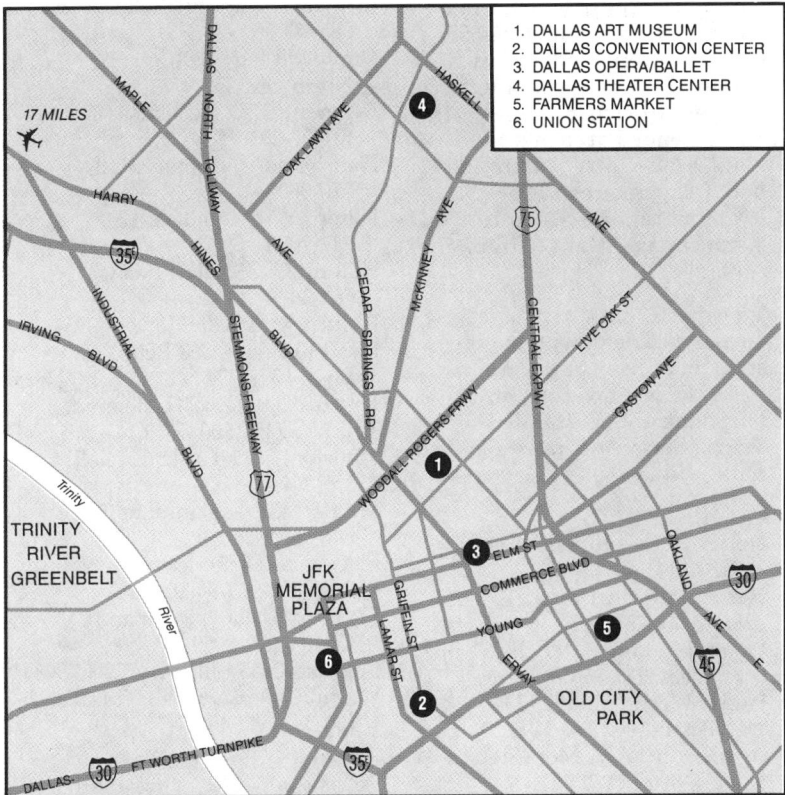

1. DALLAS ART MUSEUM
2. DALLAS CONVENTION CENTER
3. DALLAS OPERA/BALLET
4. DALLAS THEATER CENTER
5. FARMERS MARKET
6. UNION STATION

Dallas

NORTH/SOUTH AMERICA

during peak hours, and every 30-40 minutes other times to downtown for fare of 50 cents.

Facilities

Duty-free shop (Dallas/Fort Worth), currency exchange, flight insurance, baggage deposit, restaurant, coffee shop, bar, barber shop, hotel reservations, post office, shops
Car rental desks:
Dallas/Fort Worth: Hertz, Ajax, Alamo, American International, Avis, Budget, Dollar, National, Thrifty.
Dallas/Love Field: Hertz, Avis, Dollar, National, Thrifty

Airport Taxes

$3.00 per passenger

City Information

Weather

November-April. Sunny, mild and dry. Temperatures 50-65F (10-18C), dropping lower at nights. Light to medium weight clothing. Overcoat and sweaters recommended at nights.
May-October. Dry, sunny and hot. Temperatures 75-95F (24-35C), but can rise above 100F on summer days. Light to tropical clothing.

Transportation

Taxis available downtown on street or at hotel curbs. Yellow Cab is largest taxi company, telephone 426-6262. Dallas Transit Service operates a limited route within Dallas.

Car Hire

Hertz, 1933 Commerce St. 742-6814
Hertz, Marriott Hotel, 7750 LBJ Freeway 233-4421
Hertz, Summit Hotel, 2645 LBJ Freeway 243-3363
Hertz, Westin Hotel, 13340 Dallas Pkwy. 934-9494
Agency, 2626 W. Mockingbird Ln. 1-800 321-1972

Alamo, 7650 Esters Rd., Irving 621-0236
Budget, 1917 Commerce St. 1-800 442-0700

Hospitals

Baylor Univ. Medical Center, 3500 Gaston Ave. 820-0111
Methodist Hospital, 3500 Wheatland Rd. 296-2511
Presbyterian Medical Center, 8200 Walnut Hill Ln. 369-4111
All Saints Episcopal Hospital, 1400 Eighth Ave. 926-2544

Trade Fairs

Computer and Communication Equip. Ex (Jan)
Builders Ex (Jan)
Broadcasters Assoc. Ex (Apr)
Videotex Ex (May)
Intl. Electronics Ex (Sept)
Intl. Beverage Industry Ex (Oct)

Hotels

Crowne Plaza, 4099 Valley View 385-9000
Dunfey Dallas, 3800 W. Northwest 357-9561
Fairmont, 1717 N. Akard St.720-2020
Four Seasons, Colinas Blvd. 570-0800
Hilton, 1914 Commerce St. 747-7000
Hilton LBJ, 4801 LBJ Freeway 661-3600
Holiday Inn, 1015 Elm 748-9951
Hyatt Regency, 300 Reunion Blvd. 651-1234
Loews Anatole, 2201 Stemmons Frwy. 748-1200
Mansion, 2821 Turtle Creek Blvd. 559-2100
Marriott, 2101 Stemmons Frwy. 748-8551
Plaza of the Americas, 650 N. Pearl St. 979-9000
Sheraton Dallas, Southland Center 922-8000
Summit, 2645 LBJ Frwy. 243-3363
Westin Galleria, 13340 N. Dallas Pkwy. 934-9494

What to See and Do

Dallas is a wealthy city, and has

been able to build an impressive collection of cultural institutions. Among them are the Dallas Symphony, Dallas Civic Opera, Dallas Civic Ballet, Dallas Theater Center, Fair Park, Texas Hall of State, Dallas Museum of Fine Arts, and the Owens Art Center. Historic sites include John Bryan Cabin, Old City Park and the John F. Kennedy Museum, which commemorates the late president who was assassinated in Dallas.

Downtown Dallas has many fine shopping areas, headed by the famous Nieman-Marcus department store.

Events to look for are the Texas State Fair in October, the Cotton Bowl football game in January, and professional sports events featuring the Dallas Cowboys (football), Mavericks (basketball) and Texas Rangers (baseball).

Useful Addresses

Embassies and Consulates
British: 2730 Stemmons Frwy. 637-3600
Canadian: 750 N. St . Paul St. 922-9806
French: 3428 St. Johns 995-2607
German: 1530 Main St. 748-1119

Business and Commerce
Dallas Chamber of Commerce, 1507 Pacific 651-1020
Dallas Convention Center, 650 S. Griffin 658-7000
Fort Worth Chamber of Commerce, 700 Throckmorton St., Fort Worth 336-2491
U.S. Dept. of Commerce, 1100 Commerce St. 767-0546
World Trade Center, 2100 Stemmons Frwy. 655-6100

Tourism and Travel
American Express, 1201 Elm St. 748-8606
Amtrak, Union Station, 400 S. Houston St. 421-8320

Dallas Visitors Information Center, Union Station 747-2355
Deak International, 717 N. Harwood St. 953-0606
Deak International, Dallas-Ft. Worth Airport 574-2814
Southwest Motor Club, 4425 N. Central Expressway 526-7911
Uniglobe Destination Travel, 9100 N. Central, 750-4475
Uniglobe Hays Travel, 16475 Dallas Pkwy., 9312-1191
Uniglobe Meridien Travel, 9220 Skillean, 341-1268
Uniglobe Midway Travel, 4100 Spring Valley Rd. 701-9848
Uniglobe Signature Place Travel, 14755 Preston Rd. 980-2644
Uniglobe Uptown Travel, 2651 N. Harwood St. 871-1002
Uniglobe Travelsmith Travel, 729-B Preston Forest Shopping Center 368-0191
Uniglobe World Travel, 7450 LBJ Freeway, 233-6889

DENVER

Airport Information

Time
GMT -7 (Mountain)
GMT -6 (April-October)

Airport
Stapleton International DEN
Tel: 398-3844
8 mi (13 km) NE of city

Airlines
American 595-9304
British Airways 1-800 247-9297
Canadian International 1-800 426-7000
Continental 398-3000
Delta 696-1322
Eastern 623-4800
KLM 1-800 777-5553
Lufthansa 1-800 645-3880
Mexicana 1-800 531-7921
Northwest 1-800 225-2525

Piedmont 893-3567
Republic 825-6116
TWA 629-7878
United 398-4141
US Air 1-800 428-4322

Transport to City

Taxis: $8-10 plus tip. Fifteen to
20 minutes to downtown.
Coach: Airport coaches operate
every 15 minutes from 0700-2000,
and 30-minute intervals nights to
downtown hotel locations. Fare
$5 per person.
Some hotels offer free courtesy
vans from airport to their hotels.
Leave from curb at airport
terminal.
Transit: City bus #32 operates
every 15 minutes between
terminal and downtown Denver

for 70 cents, and continues to
Boulder.

Facilities

Bank with urrency exchange,
post office, bar, restaurant, first-
aid, baggage deposit, shops
Car rental desks: Hertz, Ajax,
American International, Avis,
Budget, Dollar, Econo-Car,
National, Thrifty

Airport Taxes

$3.00 per passenger

City Information

Weather

November-April. Cold with
snow, and occasional extreme
cold. Temperatures 12-30F

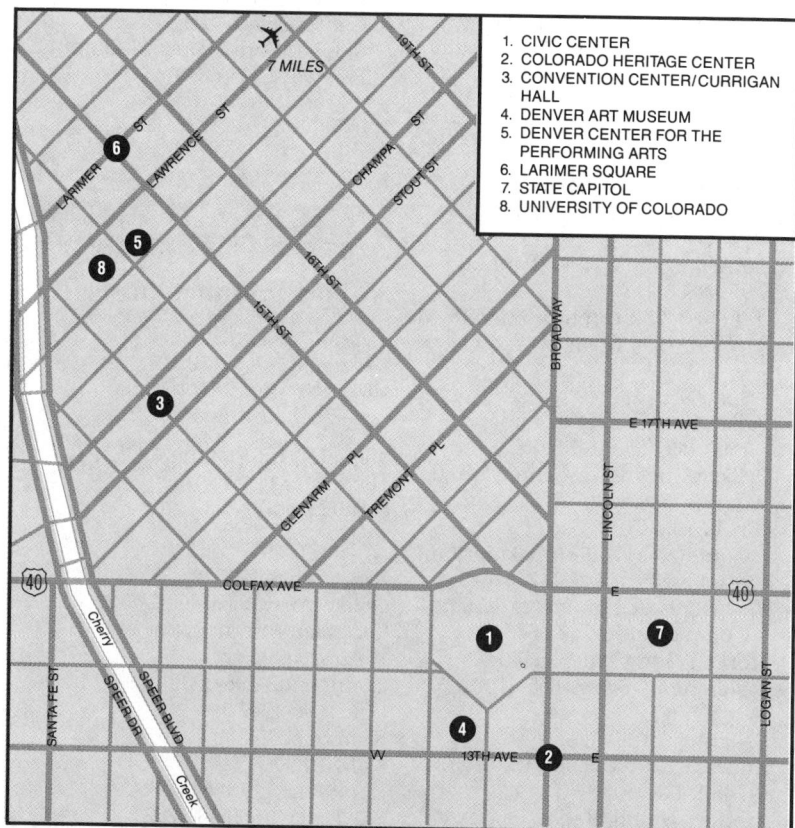

1. CIVIC CENTER
2. COLORADO HERITAGE CENTER
3. CONVENTION CENTER/CURRIGAN HALL
4. DENVER ART MUSEUM
5. DENVER CENTER FOR THE PERFORMING ARTS
6. LARIMER SQUARE
7. STATE CAPITOL
8. UNIVERSITY OF COLORADO

Denver

(-11-0C) and can drop to -30F. Wear warm clothing with overcoat, hat and boots. May-October. Warm, sunny with occasional showers and temperatures falling during the nights. Temperatures 65-90F (17-32C). Light clothing with raincoat and jacket or sweater in evenings.

Transportation
Taxis are available in downtown Denver, but are difficult to hail on the streets. Catch taxis at hotel stands or call Yellow Cab (892-1212) or Zone Cab (861-2323). RTD bus service operates in Denver and out to the suburbs.

Car Hire
Hertz, 2001 Welton St. 654-3131
Agency, 4590 Quebec St. 1-800 321-1972
Ajax, 6960 Smith Rd. 1-800 367-2529
Alamo, 3898 Monaco Pkwy. 321-1176
American Intl., 1919 Broadway 1-800 527-0202
Avis, 1900 Broadway 1-800 331-1212
Budget, 2150 Broadway 1-800 527-0700

Hospitals
Denver General Hospital, W. Eighth Ave. 893-6000
Presbyterian-St. Luke's Medical Center, 1719 E. 19th Ave. 839-6000
University Hospital, 4200 E. Ninth Ave. 394-8446

Hotels
Brown Palace, 321 17th St. 297-3111
Executive Tower, 1405 Curtis St. 571-0300
Fairmont, 1750 Welton St. 295-1200
Granada Royale, 7525 E. Hampden Ave. 696-6644
Hilton, 1550 Court Place 893-3333
Hilton South, 7801 E. Orchard Rd. 779-6161
Marriott, I-25 & Hampden Ave. 758-7000
Marriott, 1701 California St. 297-1300
Park Suite, 19th & Curtis 297-8888
Ramada Renaissance, 3200 S. Parker Rd. 695-1700
Sheraton-Greystone Castle, 83 E. 120 Ave. 451-1002
Stapleton Plaza, 3333 Quebec St. 321-3500
Stouffer's Denver Inn, 3203 Quebec St. 321-3333
Westin Hotel, Tabor Center 572-9100

What to See and Do
Denver Center for the Performing Arts is host to the Denver Symphony Orchestra and many other events. Historical sites include the Governor's Mansion, Molly Brown's House, the State Capital Building, Buffalo Bill Museum and the Colorado Railroad Museum. Elitch Gardens is home to summer theater; City Park has outdoor band concerts during the summer; the National Western Rodeo takes place in January, and Lakeside Amusement Park opens during the summer. Sports teams include the Denver Broncos (football) and Nuggets (basketball). Good hockey is also played by the local university teams, and during the winter, incomparable skiing can be found at Vail, Copper Mountain and Aspen which are short drives from Denver.

Useful Addresses

Embassies and Consulates
French: 1475 Lawren St. 595-5499
German: 1801 Jackson St., Golden 279-5383

Business and Commerce
Denver Chamber of Commerce, 1301 Welton St. 534-3211
Denver Convention & Visitors Bureau, 225 W. Colfax Ave. 892-1112
U.S. Dept. of Commerce, Customshouse, 19th & Stout Sts. 837-3246

Tourism and Travel
American Express, 555 17th St. 298-7100
Amtrak, Union Station, 17th & Wynkoop Sts. 893-3911
Deak International, 1580 Court Place 571-0808
Rocky Mt. Motor Club, 4100 E. Arkansas Ave. 753-8800
Thomas Cook, 8575 E. Orchard Rd. 694-6860
Uniglobe Advance Travel, 50 S. Steele St. 355-7926
Uniglobe Mile High Travel, 1801 Broadway, 298-0625
Uniglobe SRO United Travel, Denver 696-0564
Uniglobe Union Station Travel, 1610 Wynkoop 893-0500

DETROIT

Airport Information

Time
GMT -5 (Eastern)
GMT -4 (April-October)

Airport
Detroit Metropolitan Wayne County DTW
Tel: 942-3550
20 mi (32 km) SW of city

Airlines
Air France 1-800 237-2747
Alitalia 1-800 223-5730
American 965-1000
British Airways 1-800 247-9297
Canadian International 1-800 426-7000
Continental 963-4600
Delta 355-3200
Eastern 965-8200
KLM 1-800 777-5553
Lufthansa 1-800 645-3880
Northwest 962-2002
Pan Am 1-800 221-1111
Piedmont 962-8765
Qantas 1-800 227-4500
Republic 283-8910
Sabena 1-800 645-3790
SAS 1-800 221-2350
Swissair 1-800 221-4750
TWA 962-8650
United 336-9000
US Air 963-8340

Transport to City
Taxis: $22-23 to downtown in 30-45 minutes.
Coach: Airport buses (Commuter Transportation) depart every 30 minutes from 0600-1800, thereafter every hour. Fare $7 per person. Several hotels operate courtesy vans free of charge.

Facilities
Bank with currency exchange, hotel reservations, baggage deposit, bar, coffee shop, restaurant, post office, flight insurance, barber shop.
Car rental desks: Hertz, Ajax, American International, Avis, Budget, Dollar, National, Thrifty

Airport Taxes
$3.00 per passenger

City Information

Weather
November-April. Cold with occasional heavy snowfalls. Temperatures 20-40F (-7-4C). Medium weight clothing with overcoat, boots and hat.
May-October. Warm summers, occasionally hot and humid. Frequent summer thunderstorms. Temperatures 70-90F (20-32C). Light clothing with light raincoat or umbrella.

Transportation

Taxis can be hailed from curbside or at hotel stands. Call Radio Cab (833-1212) or Checker Cab (963-7000) for service.

Bus service (DSR) operates throughout the metropolitan area.

Detroit is one of those cities where suburban areas are important business centers in themselves. Therefore, the best way to get around is by renting a car. The highway system is good, and will get you to wherever you need to go the quickest way possible.

Car Hire

Hertz, 1041 Washington Blvd. 729-5200

Hertz, Westin Hotel, Renaissance Center 964-2678

Hertz, Hyatt Regency Hotel, Dearborn 593-4414

Agency, 9339 Middlebelt Rd. 1-800 321-1972

American Intl., 11375 Middlebelt 1-800 527-0202

Avis, 1100 Washington Blvd. 1-800 331-1212

Budget, 8715 Wickham Rd. 1-800 527-0700

Thrifty, 2911 Wick Rd. 1-800 367-2277

Hospitals

Detroit-Macomb Hospital, 7815 E. Jefferson Ave. 821-8000

Henry Ford Hospital, 2799 W. Grant Blvd. 876-2600

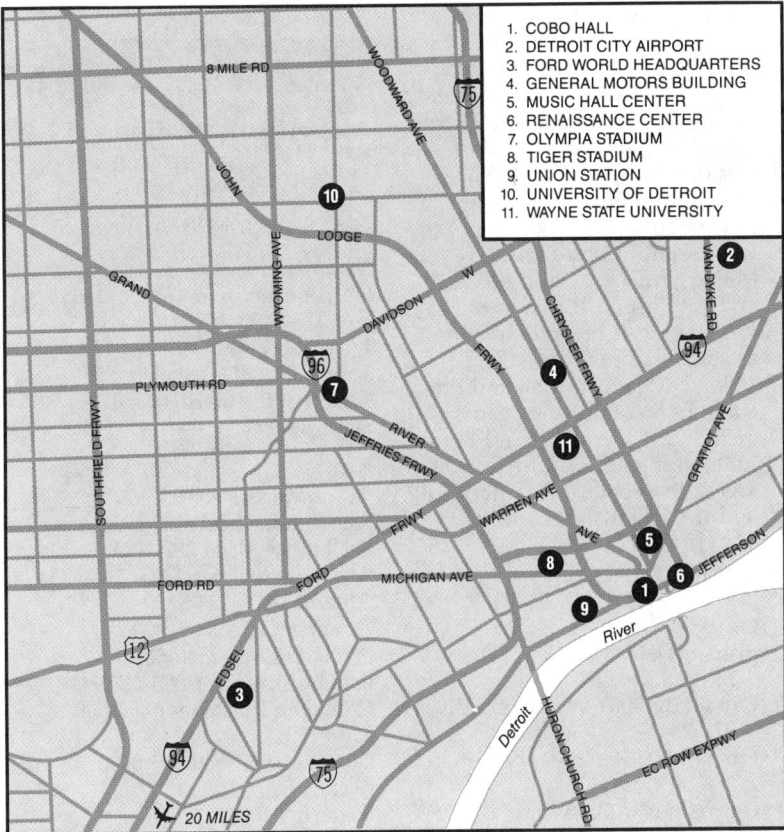

1. COBO HALL
2. DETROIT CITY AIRPORT
3. FORD WORLD HEADQUARTERS
4. GENERAL MOTORS BUILDING
5. MUSIC HALL CENTER
6. RENAISSANCE CENTER
7. OLYMPIA STADIUM
8. TIGER STADIUM
9. UNION STATION
10. UNIVERSITY OF DETROIT
11. WAYNE STATE UNIVERSITY

Detroit

Sinai Hospital, 6767 W. Outer
Dr. 493-6824

Book Cadillac, 1114 Washington
Blvd. 321-1972
Dearborn Inn, 20301 Oakwood
Blvd. 271-2700
Hilton Northfield, 5500 Crooks
Rd. 879-2100
Hyatt Regency, Dearborn
593-1234
Michigan Inn, 16400 LJ Hudson
Dr. 559-6500
Novi Hilton, 21111 Haggerty Rd.
349-4000
Omni Hotel, 333 E. Jefferson
Ave. 222-7700
Ponchartrain, 2 Washington
Blvd. 965-0200
St. Regis, 3071 W. Grand
873-3000
Westin Detroit, Renaissance
Center 568-8000

What to See and Do

Cultural activities center around
Ford Auditorium and the Detroit
Symphony, Fisher Theater,
Detroit Institute of Arts, and
the Henry Ford Museum
in Dearborn. See also the
Renaissance Center, Fort Wayne
Military Museum, and the Zoo
and Aquarium. If you have a car
you may visit the automobile
assembly plants, Greenfield
Village, Meadowbrook and Pine
Knob parks. Sporting events
include the Detroit Grand Prix in
June, and games of the Detroit
Tigers (baseball), Lions (football)
and the Pistons (basketball).

Useful Addresses

Embassies and Consulates
British: Detroit Bank & Trust
Bldg. 963-4776
Canadian: 1001 Woodward Ave.
925-2811
French: 100 Renaissance Center
568-0990
German: 660 Plaza Dr. 962-6526

Business and Commerce
Detroit Chamber of Commerce,
150 Michigan Ave. 964-4000
Detroit Convention Bureau, 100
Renaissance Center 259-4333
Detroit-Wayne County Port
Commission, 625 Lafayette
Bldg. 224-5656
U.S. Dept. of Commerce, 445
Federal Bldg. 226-3650

Tourism and Travel
American Express, 200
Renaissance Center 259-5030
Amtrak Station, Vernor Hwy, &
Michigan Ave. 963-7396
Auto Club of Michigan, 17000 E.
8 Mile Rd. 526-1000
Auto Club of Michigan, 1501
Washington Blvd. 237-5500
Thomas Cook, 300 Renaissance
Center 259-3100

HOUSTON

Airport Information

Time
GMT -6 (Central)
GMT -5 (April-October)

Airport
Houston Intercontinental IAH
Tel: 230-3100
17 mi (28 km) N of city
Terminal A (Domestic)
Terminal B (International/
Domestic)

Airlines
Aeromexico 1-800 237-6639
Air Canada 1-800 422-6232
Air France 1-800 237-2747
Air New Zealand 1-800 262-1234
Alitalia 1-800 223-5730
American 222-9873
Avianca 1-800 284-2622
British Airways 1-800 247-9297
Canadian International 1-800
426-7000
Continental 1-800 525-0280
Delta 1-800 221-1212
Eastern 1-800 327-8387
El Al 1-800 223-6700

Gulf Air 629-6320
JAL 1-800 525-3663
KLM 1-800 777-5553
Kuwait 1-800 327-2147
Lufthansa 1800 45-3880
Olympic 1-800 223-1226
Pan Am 447-0088
Piedmont 1-800 251-5720
Qantas 1-800 227-4500
Republic 868-9988
Sabena 1-800 645-1382
SAS 1-800 221-2350
Singapore 1-800 742-3333
Swissair 1-800 221-4750
TWA 222-7273
United 1-800 241-6522
US Air 1-800 428-4322
Varig 1-800 468-2744

Transport to City
Taxis: Available at both

terminals. $23 plus tip to
downtown, about 30-45 minutes.
Coach: Airport Express buses
leave for the city every 30
minutes around the clock. To
downtown stops $6.50. Some
hotels offer free courtesy vans
from airport to hotel.

Facilities
Duty-free shop, currency
exchange and bank, hotel
reservations, bar, restaurants,
post office, insurance, conference
facilities, first-aid, shops, and
helicopter service
Car rental desks: Hertz, Ajax,
Alamo, American International,
Avis, Budget, Dollar, National,
Thrifty

Airport Taxes
$3.00 per passenger

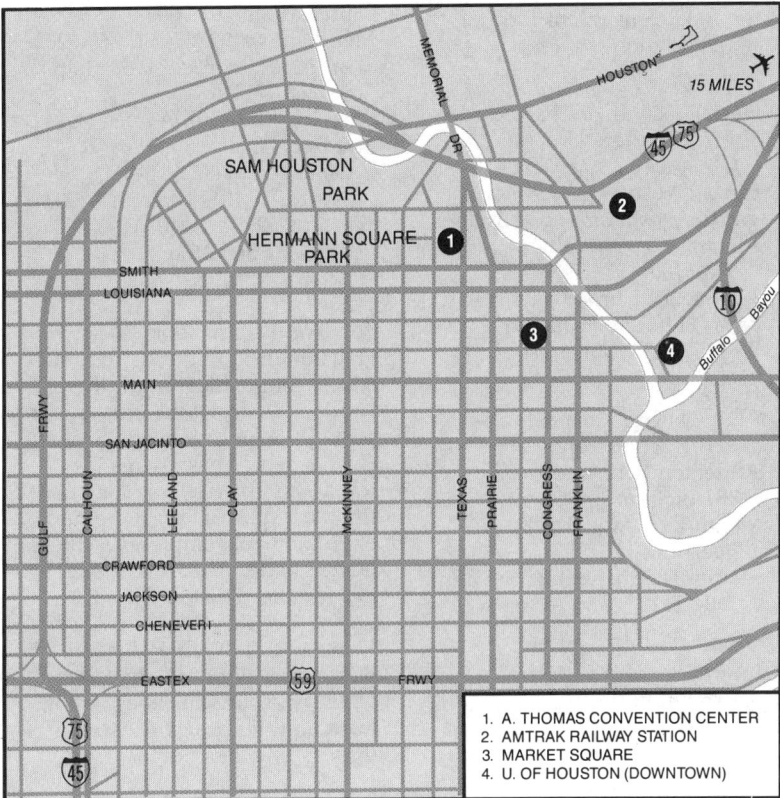

1. A. THOMAS CONVENTION CENTER
2. AMTRAK RAILWAY STATION
3. MARKET SQUARE
4. U. OF HOUSTON (DOWNTOWN)

Houston

NORTH/SOUTH AMERICA

City Information

Weather

November-April. Mild temperatures with moderating sea breezes. Light rainfall. Temperatures 60-75F (15-24C). Light to medium weight clothing with light raincoat.

May-October. Hot and humid, but moderated by sea breezes from the Gulf. Afternoon thunderstorms are frequent. Temperatures 80-95F (27-35C). Tropical weight clothing and umbrella.

Transportation

Taxis are difficult to hail in the streets. Find taxis at hotel stands, or call Yellow Cab (236-1111) or Sky Jacks (523-6080). City is served by downtown buses and a rapid transit line. Houston is a sprawling city and the most convenient form of transportation is a rental car.

Car Hire

Hertz, 2020 Milam St. 659-8190
Hertz, Stouffers Hotel, 6
  Greenway Plaza 840-8415
Hertz, Westin Oaks Hotel,
  5001 Westheimer 629-0190
Alamo, 2911 N. Beltway 8
  590-5100
Alamo, 8381 Broadway 645-2150
Avis, 2120 Louisiana 331-1212
Budget, 1925 Milam 442-0700

Hospitals

Alief General Hospital,
  11101 Bellaire Blvd. 498-0700
Anderson (Univ. of Texas)
  Hospital, 6723 Bertner 792-2121
Memorial Hospital, 7600
  Beechnut 776-5000
Methodist Hospital, 6565 Fannin
  790-3311

Trade Fairs

International Boat & Travel
  Exhibition (Jan)
International Pipe & Pipeline
  Exhibition (Jan)

Hotels

Adam's Mark, 2900 Briarpark Dr.
  978-7400
Crowne Plaza, 2222 W. Loop St.
  961-7272
Four Seasons, Four Riverway
  871-8181
Four Seasons, 1300 Larmar
  650-1300
Guest Quarters, 5353
  Westheimer Rd. 961-9000
Hilton Inn West, 12401 Katy
  Freeway 496-9090
Hilton Westchase, 9999
  Westheimer 974-1000
Holiday Inn, 801 Calhoun
  659-2222
Hyatt Regency, 1200 Louisiana
  654-1234
Hyatt West, 13210 Katy Frwy.
  558-1234
InterContinental, 5150
  Westheimer 961-1500
Marriott Astrodome, 2100 S.
  Braeswood 797-9000
Meridien, 400 Dallas St. 759-0202
Shamrock Hilton, 6900 S. Main
  St. 668-9211
Sheraton, 777 Polk Ave. 651-9041
Stouffers Greenway Plaza, 6
  Greemway Plaza 629-1200
Warwick, 5701 S. Main 526-1991
Westin Galleria, 5060 W.
  Alabama 960-8100

What to See and Do

Some of the attractions to see in Houston include the Astrodome, San Jacinto Battleground, Busch Gardens, Astroworld amusement park, Lyndon B. Johnson Space Center (which has interesting tours), and the Galleria, one of the most spectacular shopping/entertainment complexes in the United States. Cultural activities include the Houston Grand Opera, live theater at the Alley Theater, and the fine Museum of Fine Arts. Sports fans have a variety of sports to choose from, including the Houston Astros (baseball), Oilers (football), and the Rockets (basketball), all of whom call the Astrodome home.

Useful Addresses

Embassies and Consulates
British: 601 Jefferson 659-6270
French: 2727 Allen Parkway
528-2181
German: 1900 Yorktown 627-7770
Japanese: 1612 First City Nat.
Bank 652-2977

Business and Commerce
Arab Chamber of Commerce,
505 N. Belt Dr. 447-2563
German Chamber of Commerce,
2 Houston Center 658-8230
Houston Convention & Visitors
Bureau, 3300 Main St. 523-5050
Houston Chamber of Commerce,
1100 Milam Bldg. 651-1313
Houston Stock Exchange, Bank
SW Bldg. 659-3594
Japan Trade Center, 1 Houston
Center 759-9595
U.S. Dept. of Commerce,
2625 Federal Bldg. 226-4231
World Trade Center, 239 World
Trade Center 225-0968

Tourism and Travel
AAA Texas, 3000 SW Freeway
524-1851
Amtrak, 902 Washington Ave.
757-1713
Deak International, 62 Town &
Country Village 461-3325
Deak International, 5177
Richmond, 623-6177
Uniglobe Allstar Travel,12520-C
Westheimer 496-9000
Uniglobe Dynamic Travel,3555
Timmons Lane 621-3833
Uniglobe Keystone Travel, 10540
Northwest Fwy., 956-4949
Uniglobe Kirby Travel,1800
Bering Dr. 977-5455
Uniglobe Lone Star Travel,233
Greens Rd. 876-9111
Uniglobe Marco Polo, 6655
Tarvis, 528-6229
Uniglobe Northwest Travel,9433
Jones Rd. 890-8899
Uniglobe Plaza One, 2525 Bay
Area, 280-0080
Uniglobe Voyager Travel, 7001
Highway South 495-1128
Uniglobe Yorktown Travel,1900
Yorktown 623-8088

LOS ANGELES

Airport Information

Time
GMT-8 (Pacific)
GMT-7 (April-October)

Airport
Los Angeles International LAX
Tel: 646-5252
15 mi (24 km) SW of city

Airlines
Aeromexico 237-6639
Air Canada 1-800 422-6232
Air France 1-800 237-2747
Air New Zealand 1-800 262-1234
Alitalia 1-800 1-800 223-5730
American 935-6045
Avianca 1-800 284-2622
British Airways 1-800 247-9297
Canadian International
1-800 426-7000
Continental 1-800 525-0289
Delta 1-800 221-1212
El Al 1-800 223-6700
Finnair 1-800 223-5700
JAL 1-800 525-3663
KLM 1-800 777-5553
Korean 1-800 421-8200
Lufthansa 1-800 645-3880
Mexicana 687-8320
Northwest 1-800 225-2525
Olympic 1-800 223-1226
Pan Am 1-800 221-1111
Philippine 1-800 1-800 435-9725
Piedmont 1-800 251-5720
PSA 935-5005
Qantas 1-800 227-4500
Republic 772-5100
SAS 655-8600
Singapore 1-800 742-3333
Swissair 1-800 221-4750
TWA 484-2244
United 1-800 241-6522
US Air 935-5005
UTA 1-800 282-4484

NORTH/SOUTH AMERICA

Transport to City

Taxis: Taxis to downtown Los Angeles $25-30. Takes about 35-40 minutes. Fare to Burbank Airport $40.

Coach: Reserved vans (SuperShuttle) can be ordered by telephone (0-417-4974 collect). Van will arrive for pickup wherever you request. Fare is $10 to downtown Los Angeles. Airport buses are $6.50 to downtown and depart every 30-45 minutes for downtown hotels and bus depot.

Transit: Public bus system services airport from RTD City Bus Center, just outside the airport. Departs every 10-15 minutes around the clock.

Facilities

Duty-free shop, currency exchange and bank, hotel reservations, baggage deposit, bar and restaurants, post office, first-aid, and shops

Car rental desks: Hertz, Ajax, Alamo, American International, Avis, Budget, Dollar, National, Thrifty

Airport Taxes

$3.00 per passenger

1. ABC STUDIOS
2. BURBANK STUDIOS
3. DODGER STADIUM
4. THE FORUM
5. GRIFFITH PARK
6. HOLLYWOOD BOWL
7. HOLLYWOOD-BURBANK AIRPORT
8. LONG BEACH AIRPORT
9. LOS ANGELES INT'L AIRPORT
10. MARINELAND
11. MISSION SAN GABRIEL
12. NBC STUDIOS
13. PORT OF LOS ANGELES/LONG BEACH
14. ROSE BOWL
15. SUNSET STRIP
16. UNIVERSAL STUDIOS
17. VAN NUYS AIRPORT

Los Angeles

City Information

Weather

November-April. Sunny and mild with some light rain. Temperatures 60-75F (15-24C). Light to medium weight clothing, with sweater at nights. May-October. Hot, sunny and occasionally humid. Temperatures 75-95F (24-35C). Light to tropical weight clothing.

Transportation

Los Angeles is truly the city of the automobile. Its sprawling and decentralized business areas require a rental car for almost any trip. Only if you are staying downtown would you opt for a taxi or the inadequate bus system. Taxis are hard to find on the streets; call Yellow Cab (481-2345) or Celebrity Cab (278-2500). The bus system is very slow if your destination is more than a few miles.

Car Hire

Hertz, Bonaventure Hotel, 404 S. Figueroa St. 629-1498
Hertz, 1055 West 6th St. 482-5365
Hertz, Hyatt Regency Hotel, 711 S. Hope St. 680-1946
Hertz, New Otani Hotel, 120 S. Los Angeles St. 629-4572
Hertz, University Hilton, 3540 S. Figueroa St. 748-2112
Hertz, 513 West 5th St. 626-8301
Hertz, Wilshire Hyatt House, 3515 Wilshire Blvd. 732-1011
Hertz, Los Angeles Union Depot, 800 North Alameda St.
Agency, 3928 S. Sepulveda Blvd.1-800 321-1972
Ajax, 812 W. Olympics 1-800 367-2529
Alamo, 8900 Aviation Blvd., Inglewood 649-2245
Avis, Century Plaza Hotel 1-800 331-1212
Budget, 701 S. Figueroa 1-800 527-0700
Dollar, 727 S. Figueroa 1-800 421-6868

Hospitals

Cedars-Sinai Medical Center, 8700 Beverly Blvd. 855-5000
Good Samaritan Hospital, 616 Witmer 977-2121
Los Angeles County Hospital, 1200 N. Slate St. 226-2345
St. John's Hospital, 1328 22nd St., Santa Monica 829-5511
UCLA Hospital and Clinic, 10833 Le Conte Ave. 825-5041

Trade Fairs

California Boat Exhibition (Jan)
Anaheim Electronics Exhibition (Feb)
International Menswear Exhibition (Feb)

Graphic Arts Exhibition (Feb)
International Computer
  Exhibition (Apr)
Natural Gas Technologies
  Exhibition (Jun)
International Mens Fashion
  Exhibition (Sept)
International Contemporary Art
  Fair (Dec)

Hotels

Ambassador, 3400 Wilshire Blvd.
  387-7011
Bel-Air, 710 Stone Canyon Rd.
  472-1211
Beverly Hills, 9641 Sunset Blvd.
  276-2251
Beverly Hilton, 9876 Wilshire
  Blvd. 274-7777
Beverly Rodeo, 360 N. Rodeo Dr.
  273-0300
Beverly Wilshire, 9500 Wilshire
  Blvd. 275-4282
Biltmore, 515 S. Olive St.
  624-1041
Bonaventure Westin, 5th &
  Figueroa 624-1000
Century Plaza, Ave. of Stars
  277-2000
Century Wilshire, 10776 Wilshire
  Blvd. 474-3511
Hilton Midtown, 400 N.
  Vermont Ave. 662-4888
Hyatt Regency, 711 S. Hope St.
  683-1234
Hyatt Wilshire, 3515 Wilshire
  Blvd. 381-7411
IBIS Anaheim, 100 W. Freedman
  Way, Anaheim 520-9696
L'Ermitage Hotel, 9291 Burton
  Way 278-3344
Los Angeles Hilton, 930 Wilshire
  Blvd. 629-4321
Los Angeles Marriott, 5855 W.
  Century Blvd. 641-5700
Marriott, Warner Center 897-1615
New Otani, 120 S. Los Angeles
  St. 629-1200
Sheraton-Grande, 333 S.
  Figueroa 617-1133
Sheraton Plaza, 6101 W. Century
  Blvd. 642-1111
Sheraton Universal, 30 Universal
  City 980-1212

University Hilton, 3540 S.
  Figueroa 748-4141
Westwood Marquis, 930 Hilgard
  Ave. 208-8765

What to See and Do

The Los Angeles area has
enough attractions to entice
almost any businessman away
from his appointments. There is
the Los Angeles Symphony at
the downtown Music Center,
concerts at the Hollywood Bowl,
the Norton Simon Museum in
Pasadena, the Getty Museum in
Santa Monica, Huntington
Library, and the museum/
attraction in Long Beach which
contains the Queen Mary luxury
liner and the Howard Hughes
"Spruce Goose" airplane.
Amusement parks include
Disneyland in Anaheim, Knotts
Berry Farm. Stroll along
Hollywood Boulevard to Mann's
Chinese theater: walk down
Rodeo Drive in Beverly Hills or
visit Universal Studios for some
Hollywood atmosphere. Take a
day off at one of the many fine
beaches in the area.
Sports fans will not be
disappointed. There are the Los
Angeles Dodgers who play at
baseball Dodger Stadium, and
California Angeles in Anaheim
Stadium. The Lakers (basketball)
and Kings (hockey) play at
the Forum. There are two
professional football teams,
the Raiders at the Memorial
Coliseum and the Rams at
Anaheim Stadium. Racing fans
head to Hollywood Park or Santa
Anita.

Useful Addresses

Embassies and Consulates

British: 3701 Wilshire Blvd.
  385-7381
Canadian: 510 W. Sixth St.
  617-9511
French: 8350 Wilshire Blvd.
  653-3120

German: 6435 Wilshire Blvd. 852-0441

Japanese: 250 E. First St. 625-8305

Mexican: 125 Paseo de la Plaza 624-3261

Business and Commerce

British Chamber of Commerce, 1640 Fifth St., Santa Monica 384-1363

Foreign Trade Assoc., 350 S. Figueroa 627-0634

German Chamber of Commerce, 3250 Wilshire Blvd. 381-2236

Israel Chamber of Commerce, 6505 Wilshire Blvd. 658-7910

Japan Trade Center, 555 S. Flower St. 626-5700

Los Angeles Convention and Visitors Bureau, 505 S. Flower St. 489-9100

Los Angeles Chamber of Commerce, 404 S. Bixel St. 629-0711

Port of Los Angeles, 255 W. Fifth St. 548-7801

Singapore Trade Development Board, 350 S. Figueroa St. 617-7358

U.S. Dept. of Commerce, 11777 San Vicente Blvd. 824-7681

U.S.-Mexico Chamber of Commerce, 350 S. Figueroa 623-7725

Tourism and Travel

American Express, 404 S. Figueroa St. 627-4800

Amtrak, Union Station,800 North Alameda 625-2672

Automobile Club of S. California, 2601 S. Figueroa St. 741-3111

Automobile Club of S. California, 4773 Hollywood Blvd., Hollywood 666-2420

Deak International, 452 N. Bedford Dr., Beverly Hills 274-9176

Deak International, 900 Wilshire Blvd., 624-4221

Grey Line Tours, 1207 W. Third St. (At major hotels)

Thomas Cook, 9359 Wilshire Blvd. 274-7051

Uniglobe Landmark Travel, 618 7th St, 624-3215

Uniglobe Prestige Travel, 3800 Barham, 876-8981

Uniglobe Travel Center, 123 S. Figueroa, 972-0019

Uniglobe Universal Travel, 1880 Century Park E, 277-6902

Uniglobe Westside Travel, 11517 Santa Monica, 477-1531

Uniglobe Wilshire Travel, 3922 Wilshire, 480-1131

Uniglobe Carson Travel, 1007 E. Dominguez, Carson 515-0020

Uniglobe Heritage,12391 Lewis, Garden Grove (714) 971-3936

Uniglobe Ships & Trips, 301 Main, El Segundo 322-0841

Uniglobe Full Service, 1101 E. Spring, Long Beach 426-7544

Uniglobe Five Star Travel,7241 Lankershim Blvd., North Hollywood (818) 764-5544

Uniglobe Galaxy Travel, 1224 E. Green St., Pasadena (818)449-2870

Uniglobe Torrance Travel, 2377 Crenshaw, 533-6066

Uniglobe Contemporary Travel, 9100 S. Sepulveda Blvd., Westchester 216-5612

MIAMI

Airport Information

Time
GMT -5 (Eastern)
GMT -4 (April-October)

Airport
Miami International MIA
Tel: 871-7000
8 mi (13 km) W of city

Airlines
Aerolineas Argentinas 371-4800
Air Canada 1-800 422-6232

Air France 1-800 237-2747
Alitalia 1-800 223-5730
American 358-6800
Avensa 381-8001
Avianca 863-5151
British Airways 377-2051
Canadian International 1-800 426-7000
Continental 1-800 525-0280
Delta 1-800 221-1212
Eastern 1-800 327-8376
El Al 1-800 223-6700
Iberia 1-800 221-9741
Lufthansa 1-800 645-3880
Northwest 377-0311
Ozark 358-7582
Pan Am 874-5000
Piedmont 1-800 251-5720
Republic 379-7501
Sabena 1-800 645-3790
SAS 1-800 221-2350
Swissair 377-9581
TWA 371-7471

United 1-800 241-6522
Varig 1-800 468-2744

Transport to City

Taxis: $10-12 to downtown, $14-20 to Miami Beach, plus tip. Trip takes 15-20 minutes downtown, longer during rush hour.
Coach: Airport buses (Red Top) leave airport terminal every 15-20 minutes. Fare $6.75 to downtown, $8 to Miami Beach.
Transit: City bus #7 leaves for downtown every 30 minutes for 75 cents. For Metrorail service take bus #37 and transfer to metroline for downtown: $1

Facilities

Duty-free shop, currency exchange, baggage deposit, post office, bar, restaurant, shops
Car rental desks: Hertz, Ajax,

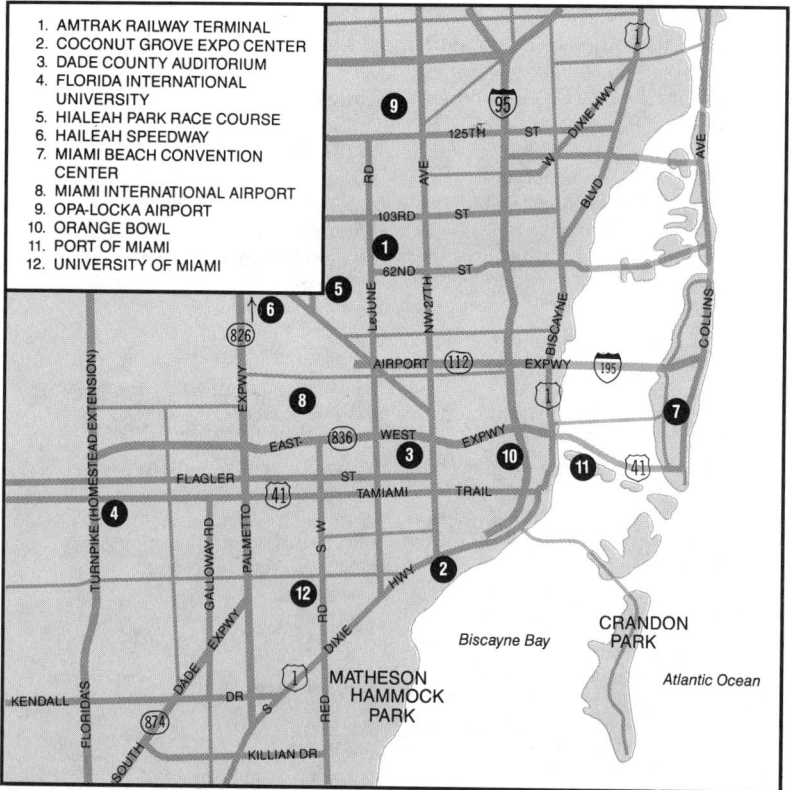

1. AMTRAK RAILWAY TERMINAL
2. COCONUT GROVE EXPO CENTER
3. DADE COUNTY AUDITORIUM
4. FLORIDA INTERNATIONAL UNIVERSITY
5. HIALEAH PARK RACE COURSE
6. HAILEAH SPEEDWAY
7. MIAMI BEACH CONVENTION CENTER
8. MIAMI INTERNATIONAL AIRPORT
9. OPA-LOCKA AIRPORT
10. ORANGE BOWL
11. PORT OF MIAMI
12. UNIVERSITY OF MIAMI

Miami

Alamo, American International, Avis, Budget, Dollar, National, Thrifty

Airport Taxes
$3.00 per passenger

City Information

Weather
November-April. Mild with light rainshowers. Temperatures 60-75F (15-24C). Light clothing with light raincoat.
May-October. Hot and humid with moderating sea breezes. Temperatures from 85-95F (29-35C). Tropical weight clothing with umbrella.

Transportation
Renting a car is the best idea for the Miami area. It is difficult to hail taxis on the street, but you can find them at hotels or you can call Yellow Cab (633-3333) or Courtesy Cab (545-6300). The bus system is adequate.

Car Hire
Hertz, 666 Biscayne Blvd. 377-4601
Hertz, Hyatt Regency, 400 SE 2nd St. 358-1234
Hertz, 17730 Collins Ave., Miami Beach 931-7904
Hertz, Fontainbleau Hotel, Miami Beach 592-5700
Agency, 7370 NW 36th St. 1-800 321-1972
Alamo, 3355 NW 22nd Street Rd. 633-6076
Alamo, 18402 Collins Ave., Miami Beach 935-5140
Avis, 225 NE First St. 1-800 331-1212

Hospitals
James Jackson Memorial Hospital, 1611 northwest 12th Ave. 325-7429
Mount Sinai Medical Center, 4300 Alton Rd., Miami Beach 674-2121

Hotels
Carillon, 6801 Collins, Miami Beach 865-4578
Coconut Grove, 2649 S. Bayshore Dr. 858-2500
Deuville, 6702 Collins, Miami Beach 865-8511
Doral Country Club, 4400 NW 87th Ave. 592-2000
Doral Beach, 4833 Collins, Miami Beach 532-3600
Eden Roc, 4525 Collins, Miami Beach 531-0000
Fontainbleau, 4441 Collins, Miami Beach 538-2000
Holiday Inn, 495 Brickell Ave. 374-6000
Hyatt Regency, 400 SE 2nd Ave. 358-1234
Inter-Continental, 801 S. Bayshore Dr. 940-4687
Marriott, 1201 NW LeJeune Rd. 649-9000
Mutiny Hotel, 2951 S. Bayshore 442-2400
Omni International, Biscayne & 16th 374-0000
Pavillon, Miami Center 577-1000
Sheraton Bal Harbour, 9701 Collins, Miami Beach 865-7511
Sonesta Beach, 350 Ocean Dr. 361-2021

What to See and Do
Miami excels more for entertainment than for culture, although the Bass Museum of Modern Art is worth visiting. Also see the Museum of Science and Space. Other attractions include the Fairchild Tropical Garden, Bayfront Park, Seaquarium, and Monkey Jungle. Deep-sea fishing boats are available for charter in Miami and Fort Lauderdale. Sports fans can watch the Miami Dolphins in their new stadium, the Orange Bowl New Year's college football game, horse racing at Hialeah Park and Gulfstream Park, jai-alai at the Fronton. And of course, there are many fine golf courses in the area.

NORTH/SOUTH AMERICA

Useful Addresses

Embassies and Consulates
French: 200 SE First St. 374-2626
German: 100 N. Biscayne Blvd.
  358-0290
Israeli: 330 Biscayne Blvd.
  358-8111

Business and Commerce
Israel Chamber of Commerce,
  3950 Biscayne Blvd. 573-0668
Latin Chamber of Commerce,
  PO Box 824 (33135) 642-3870
Miami Chamber of Commerce,
  391 NE 15th St. 350-7700
Port of Miami, 1015 North
  American Way 377-5841
U.S. Dept. of Commerce, 51 SW
  1st St. 350-6257

Tourism and Travel
AAA East Florida, 4300 Biscayne
  Blvd. 573-5611
AAA East Florida, 1435 NE
  162nd St. 949-1421
American Express, 1351 Biscayne
  Blvd. 358-7350
Amtrak, 8303 NW 37th
  Ave.638-7321
Deak International, 1 SE Third
  Ave. 381-9252
Deak International, Fontainbleau
  Hotel, 4441 Collins, Miami
  Beach 674-1907
Deak International, 3652 N.
  Ocean Blvd., Ft. Lauderdale
  566-2666
Uniglobe Prestige Travel, 8243 S
  Dixie Hwy., 665-0666
Uniglobe VIP Travel, 456
  Biltmore Way, Coral Gables
  444-1006
Uniglobe Master Travel, 2054
  Palm Beach Lakes Blvd., West
  Palm Beach 471-2726

MINNEAPOLIS

Airport Information

Time
GMT -6 (Central)
GMT -5 (April-October)

Airport
Minneapolis-St. Paul
International MSP
Tel: 726-1717
12 mi (20 km) S of city

Airlines
Alitalia 1-800 223-5730
American 332-4168
British Airways 1-800 247-9297
Canadian International 1-800
  426-7000
Continental 1-800 525-0280
Delta 1-800 221-1212
Eastern 1-800 327-8326
KLM 1-800 777-5553
Lufthansa 1-800 645-3880
Northwest 726-1234
Ozark 332-2882
Pan Am 1-800 221-1111
Piedmont 1-800 251-5720
Republic 726-7100
Sabena 1-800 645-3790
SAS 1-800 221-2350
Swissair 1-800 221-4750
TWA 333-6543
United 273-8400
US Air 338-5841

Transport to City
Taxis: $15-18 for 20-30 minute
trip to Minneapolis, and $10 to
St. Paul.
Coach: Airport buses leave every
15-20 minutes from lower level.
$6.50 to Minneapolis, $4.50 to St.
Paul. Stops at downtown hotels.
Transit: City bus #7 departs
from lower level at about 30-
minute intervals; 90 cents to
downtown Minneapolis. Transfer
from this bus to #9 at GSA
building for downtown St. Paul.
Express #35 bus to downtown
Minneapolis $1.

Facilities
Currency exchange, hotel

reservations, baggage deposit, post office, bar, restaurant, shops
Car rental desks: Hertz, Ajax, American International, Avis, Budget, Dollar, National, Thrifty

Airport Taxes
$3.00 per passenger

City Information

Weather
November-April. Very cold with snow and occasional blizzards. Temperatures from 10-30F (-12 -0C) but can fall below 0 F occasionally. Wear medium to heavy clothing with overcoat, boots and hat.
May-October. Hot and humid with moderate rainfall. Temperatures 65-80F (18-27C).

Light clothing with light raincoat.

Transportation
Good bus service in Minneapolis. Fare 90 cents. Taxis available on street, or call Yellow Cab (379-7171). Best way to get around is by car, especially if your business takes you to both the twin cities and suburbs.

Car Hire
Hertz, Hyatt Regency Hotel, 1300 Nicollet Mall 333-2500
Hertz, AMFAC Hotel, 30 S. Seventh St. 349-4000
Agency, 7200 France Ave. S. 1-800 321-1972
American International, 1400 E. 78th St. 1-800 527-0202
Thrifty, 7800 34th Ave. S. 1-800 367-2277

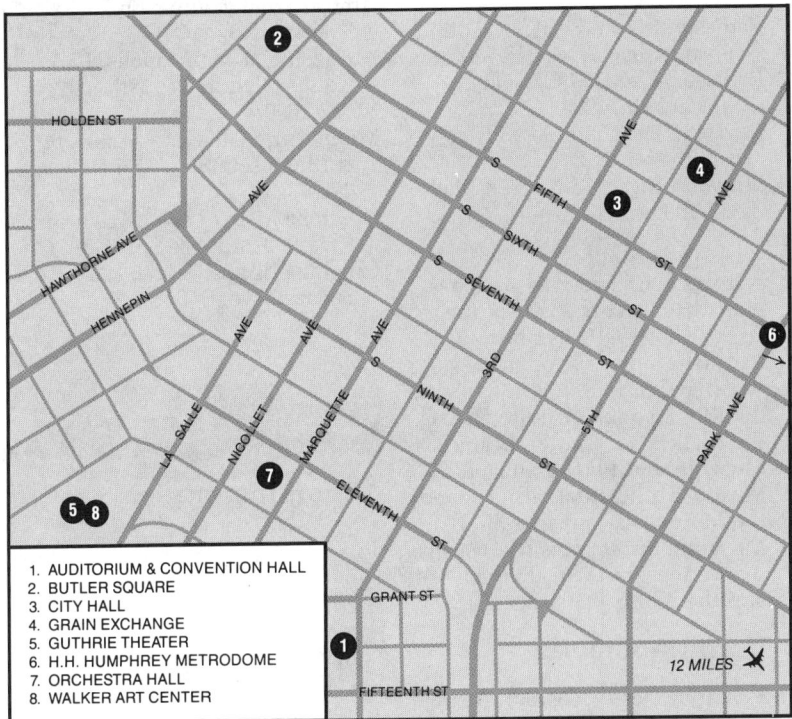

1. AUDITORIUM & CONVENTION HALL
2. BUTLER SQUARE
3. CITY HALL
4. GRAIN EXCHANGE
5. GUTHRIE THEATER
6. H.H. HUMPHREY METRODOME
7. ORCHESTRA HALL
8. WALKER ART CENTER

Minneapolis

NORTH/SOUTH AMERICA

Hospitals
University of Minnesota
Hospital, 420 Delaware St. SE
373-8484
Metropolitan Medical Center,
900 S. Eighth St. 347-4444

Hotels
AMFAC, 30 S. Seventh St.
349-4000
Hilton, 1330 Industrial Blvd.
331-1900
Holiday Inn, 1313 Nicollet Mall
332-0371
Hyatt Regency, 1300 Nicollet
Mall 370-1234
L'Hotel Sofitel, 5601 W. 78th St.
835-1900
Marriott Inn, 1919 E. 78th,
Bloomington 854-7441
Marquette Inn, 710 Marquette
332-2351
Northstar Inn, 618 Second
Ave. S 338-2288
Radisson South, 7800
Normandale Blvd. 835-7800
Radisson Plaza, 11 E. Kellogg,
St. Paul 292-1900
Registry, 7901 24th Ave. S.
854-2244
Sheraton Ritz, 315 Nicollet Mall
332-4000

What to See and Do
A tour of the Grain Exchange is
worthwhile. This is one of the
largest markets for grain futures.
Nicollet Mall is a shopping
wonder. Museum lovers can visit
the Minneapolis Institute of Arts,
the Walker Art Center, Science
Museum and Planetarium, Bell
Museum of Natural History, and
the Minnesota Transportation
Museum. Sports fans can watch
the Minnesota Twins (baseball)
and the North Stars (hockey).

Useful Addresses

Embassies and Consulates
Canadian: 15 S. Fifth St. 333-4641
French: 2629 E. Lake of Isles
Pkwy. 374-2626
German: 120 S. Sixth St. 338-6559

Swedish: 615 Peavey Bldg.
332-6897

Business and Commerce
French Chamber of Commerce,
1800 IDS Center 341-2222
Minneapolis Chamber of
Commerce, 15 S. Fifth St.
348-4313
Minneapolis Convention and
Tourism Comm., 15 S. Fifth
St. 348-4313
Norwegian Chamber of
Commerce, 229 Foshay Tower
332-3338
St. Paul Chamber of Commerce,
Osborn Bldg. 222-5561
World Trade Association,
5235 Xerxes Ave. S. 926-6202

Tourism and Travel
American Express, Pillsbury
Center 343-5500
Amtrak, Midway Station,730
Transfer Rd. 644-1127
Auto Club of Minneapolis, Park
Center Blvd. at W. 39th St.
927-2600
Minnesota State Auto Assoc., 5th
& Minnesota Sts., St. Paul
292-0323
Uniglobe Metro Travel, 120 Int'l
Ctr., 900 2nd Ave S, 339-3903
Uniglobe Riksha Travel, 330
Second Ave. S, 338-8088

NEW ORLEANS

Airport Information

Time
GMT -6 (Central)
GMT -5 (April-October)

Airport
New Orleans International MSY
Tel: 464-0831
13 mi (21 Km) NW of city

Airlines
Air France 1-800 237-2747
American 523-2188

British Airways 1-800 247-9297
Canadian International 1-800 426-7000
Continental 581-2965
Delta 1-800 221-1212
Eastern 1-800 327-8376
Lufthansa 1-800 645-3880
Northwest 1-800 225-2525
Ozark 523-1525
Pan Am 529-5192
Piedmont 1-800 251-5720
Republic 525-0423
Sabena 1-800 645-3790
SAS 1-800 221-2350
TWA 529-2585
United 1-800 241-6522
US Air 1-800 428-4322
Varig 1-800 468-2744

Transport to City

Taxis: Taxis available at terminals to downtown. Fare $18, and takes about 30-40 minutes.
Coach: Airport bus (Grey Line) leaves terminals every 30 minutes to downtown locations. $7.
Transit: City bus (Downtown Express) leaves at 10-20 minute intervals from 0530-1800 for 90 cents.

Facilities

Duty-free shop, currency exchange, hotel reservations, baggage deposit, post office, bar, restaurant, shops, conference room
Car rental desks: Hertz, Ajax, Alamo, American International, Avis, Budget, National, Thrifty

Airport Taxes

$3.00 per passenger

City Information

Weather

November-April. Mild with light rainshowers. Temperature 60-75F

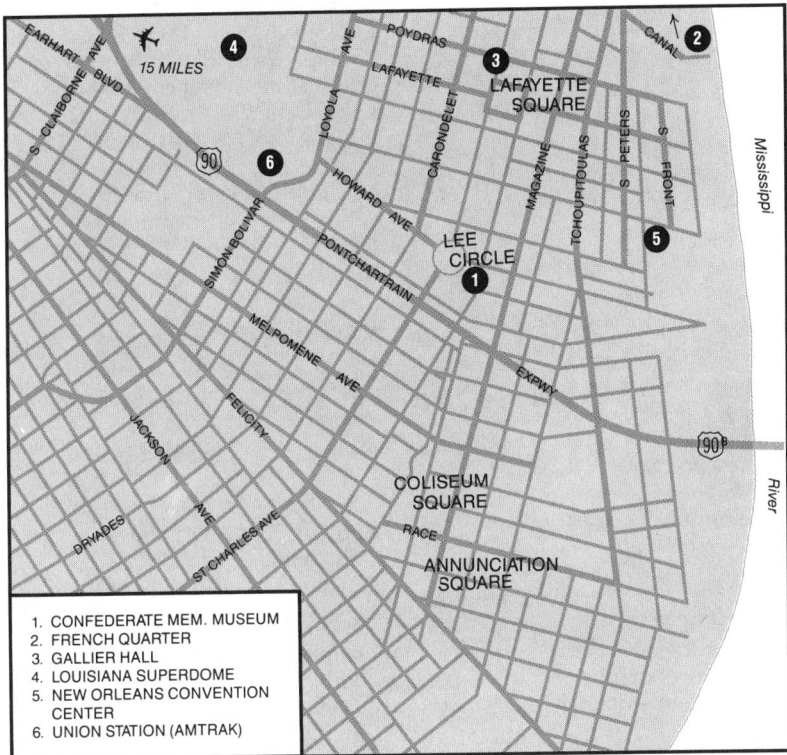

1. CONFEDERATE MEM. MUSEUM
2. FRENCH QUARTER
3. GALLIER HALL
4. LOUISIANA SUPERDOME
5. NEW ORLEANS CONVENTION CENTER
6. UNION STATION (AMTRAK)

New Orleans

NORTH/SOUTH AMERICA

(15-24C). Wear light to medium weight clothing with light raincoat.
May-October. Hot and humid with short but heavy afternoon thunderstorms. Temperatures 80-95F (27-35C). Light to tropical weight clothing with umbrella.

Transportation

Taxis are available at hotel stands and on the streets. Also call Checker Cab (943-2411), Yellow Cab (525-3311) or United Cab (522-9771).
Bus service is available downtown, and there is a streetcar line on Carrolton and St. Charles Streets beginning at Canal Street to uptown.

Car Hire

Hertz, 1540 Canal St. 568-1645
Hertz, Hilton Hotel, 2 Poydras St. 525-1646
Agency, 2240 Veterans Blvd. 1-800 321-1972
Ajax, 840 Carondelet St. 1-800 367-2529
Alamo, 1700 Airline Highway, Kenner 469-0532
Avis, 2024 Canal St. 1-800 331-1212
Budget, 1317 Canal St. 1-800 527-0700

Hospitals

Charity Hospital, 1532 Tulane Avenue 568-2311
Tulane Medical Center, 1430 Tulane Ave. 558-5471

Hotels

Bienville House, 320 Decatur 529-2345
Crowne Plaza, 333 Poydras St. 525-9444
Fairmont, University Place 529-7111
Hilton, 2 Poydras St. 561-0500
Holiday Inn, 301 Rue Dauphine. 581-1303
Hyatt Regency, Poydras & Loyola 561-1234
InterContinental, 444 St. Charles Ave. 525-5566

Le Pavillon, Baronne & Poydras 581-3111
Le Richelieu, 1234 Chartres St. 529-2492
Marie Antoinette, 827 Toulouse 525-2300
Marriott, Canal & Chartres 581-1000
Meridien, 614 Canal St. 525-6500
Pontchartrain, 2031 St. Charles 524-0581
Royal Orleans, 621 St. Louis St. 529-5333
St. Ann, 717 Conti St. 581-1881
Sheraton New Orleans, 500 Canal St. 525-2500
Warwick, 1315 Gravier St. 586-0100

What to See and Do

The main attraction is the French Quarter which is the oldest part of the city and features unique architecture, outstanding Cajun and Creole cuisine, and nightlife, principally many jazz clubs. The main event is Mardi Gras, a week-long carnival which begins on Shrove Tuesday in February. Other attractions include St. Louis Cathedral, Audubon Park, Longue Vue Gardens, New Orleans Jazz Museum, La Maritime Museum, and the sports events at the Superdome, featuring the New Orleans Saints (football).

Useful Addresses

Embassies and Consulates

British: 321 St. Charles Ave. 586-1979
Canadian: 2 Canal St. 525-2136
French: 3305 St. Charles Ave. 897-6381
German: 2834 International Trade Mart 524-0356
Japanese: 2 Canal St. 529-2101

Business and Commerce

Chamber of Commerce of New Orleans, 301 Camp St. 527-6900
New Orleans Tourist and

Convention Bureau, 334 Royal St. 566-5011

Port of New Orleans, 2 Canal St. 522-2551

U.S. Dept. of Commerce, 2 Canal St. 589-6546

Tourism and Travel

AAA Louisiana, 1223 Shreve City Center 786-0664

American Express, 134 Carondelet St. 586-8201

Amtrak, Union Terminal, 1001 Loyola Ave. 528-1600

Deak International, 111 Charles Ave., 524-0700

NEW YORK

Airport Information

Time
GMT -5 (Eastern)
GMT -4 (April-October)

Airports
John F. Kennedy International JFK
Tel: 656-4520
15 mi (24 km) SE of City
International terminal

LaGuardia Airport LGA
Tel: 476-5000
8 mi (13 Km) E of city
Domestic flights

Newark International
(New Jersey) EWR
Tel: 961-2000
16 mi (27 Km) SW of city
International and Domestic

Airlines
Aer Lingus 557-1110
Aeromexico 1-800 237-6639
Air Afrique 247-0100
Air Canada 869-1900
Air France 247-0100
Air India 1-800 223-7776
Alitalia 582-8900
American 619-6991
Austrian 1-800 854-8050

Avensa 1-800 327-5454
Avianca 246-5241
British Airways 1-800 247-9297
CAAC 656-4722
Canadian International 1-800 426-7000
Continental 1-0800 525-0280
Delta 1-800 221-1212
Eastern 1-800 327-8376
Finnair 656-7477
Gulf Air 986-4500
JAL 1-800 525-3663
KLM 1-800 777-5553
Korean 1-800 421-8200
Kuwait Air 1-800 223-6616
Lufthansa 895-1277
MEA 1-800 223-0804
New York Air 565-1100
Northwest 1-800 225-2525
Olympic 838-3600
Ozark 586-3612
Pan Am 687-2600
Philippine 1-800 435-9725
PIA 1-800 221-2552
Piedmont 1-800 251-5720
Qantas 1-800 227-4500
Republic 581-8851
SAA 826-0995
Sabena 936-7800
SAS 657-7700
Saudia Airways 1-800 472-8242
Singapore 1-800 742-3333
Swissair 995-8400
TAP 944-2800
TWA 290-2121
United 1-800 241-6522
US Air 736-3200
UTA 247-0100
Varig 682-3100

Transport to City
Kennedy International
Taxi: 35-60 minutes to downtown Manhattan, fare is $24-30 plus tolls and tip. Share-a-Ride taxi is $11-15.
Coach: Airport Express Bus (Carey) departs every 20-30 minutes from 0600-2400. Takes 60 minutes to Grand Central Terminal, $8.
Transit: JFK Express shuttle leaves terminal every 20 minutes from 0530-0050 for Howard

Station: board subway for Brooklyn and Manhattan. Fare $6.50.

City bus #Q-10 leaves every 15-30 minutes ($1) to subway and trains for transfer to Manhattan and other locations.

InterAirport Transfers: To LaGuardia take the Carey coach every 30 minutes 0630-1730, $7.

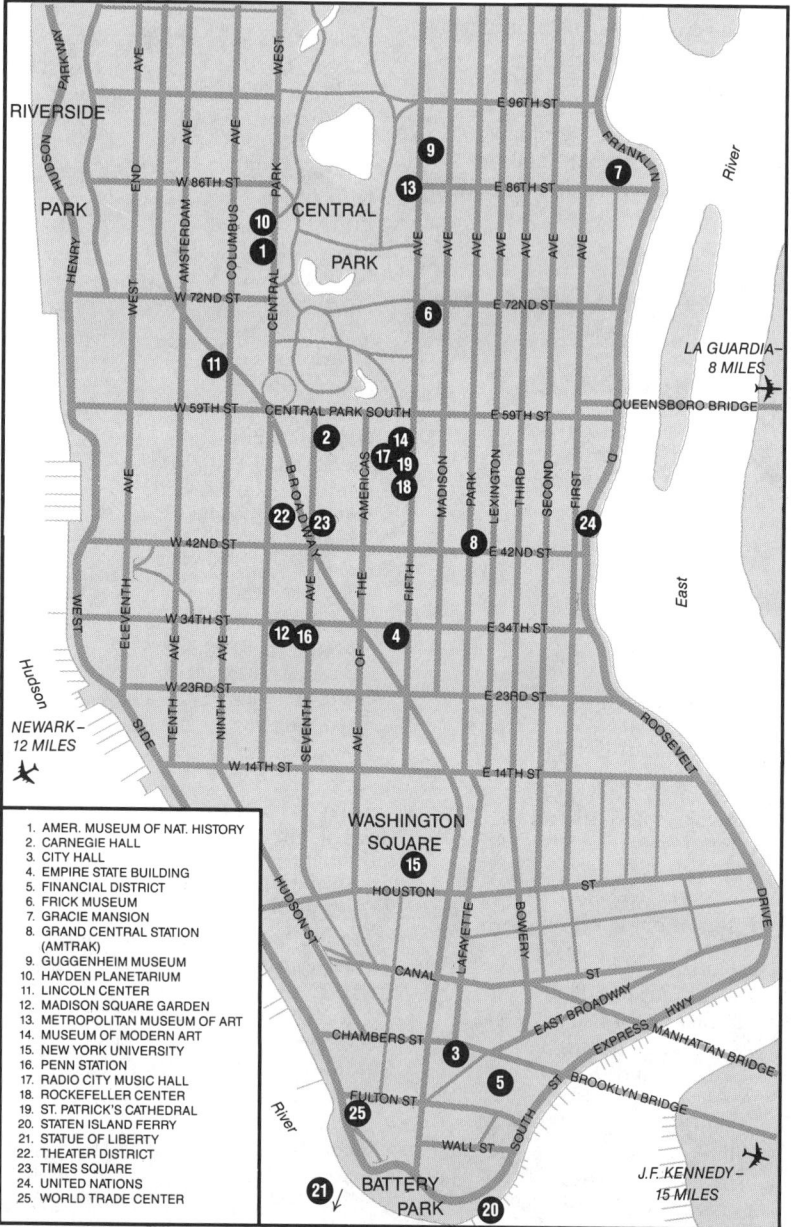

RIVERSIDE

PARK

HUDSON PARKWAY

HENRY

WEST

RIVERSIDE

HUDSON

NEWARK – 12 MILES

PARKWAY

END AVE

AMSTERDAM

AVE

COLUMBUS

CENTRAL PARK

WEST

W 86TH ST

W 72ND ST

W 59TH ST

W 42ND ST

W 34TH ST

W 23RD ST

W 14TH ST

CENTRAL PARK SOUTH

BROADWAY

AMERICAS

OF

THE

AVE

FIFTH

MADISON PARK

LEXINGTON

THIRD

SECOND

FIRST

E 96TH ST

E 86TH ST

E 72ND ST

E 59TH ST

E 42ND ST

E 34TH ST

E 23RD ST

E 14TH ST

RIVER

East

LA GUARDIA – 8 MILES

QUEENSBORO BRIDGE

ROOSEVELT

WASHINGTON SQUARE

HOUSTON ST

HUDSON ST

LAFAYETTE

BOWERY

CANAL ST

EAST BROADWAY

CHAMBERS ST

FULTON ST

WALL ST

SOUTH ST

EXPRESS HWY MANHATTAN BRIDGE

BROOKLYN BRIDGE

DRIVE

J.F. KENNEDY – 15 MILES

BATTERY PARK

River

FRANKLIN

ELEVENTH AVE

TENTH AVE

NINTH AVE

SEVENTH AVE

WEST

1. AMER. MUSEUM OF NAT. HISTORY
2. CARNEGIE HALL
3. CITY HALL
4. EMPIRE STATE BUILDING
5. FINANCIAL DISTRICT
6. FRICK MUSEUM
7. GRACIE MANSION
8. GRAND CENTRAL STATION (AMTRAK)
9. GUGGENHEIM MUSEUM
10. HAYDEN PLANETARIUM
11. LINCOLN CENTER
12. MADISON SQUARE GARDEN
13. METROPOLITAN MUSEUM OF ART
14. MUSEUM OF MODERN ART
15. NEW YORK UNIVERSITY
16. PENN STATION
17. RADIO CITY MUSIC HALL
18. ROCKEFELLER CENTER
19. ST. PATRICK'S CATHEDRAL
20. STATEN ISLAND FERRY
21. STATUE OF LIBERTY
22. THEATER DISTRICT
23. TIMES SQUARE
24. UNITED NATIONS
25. WORLD TRADE CENTER

New York City

To Newark Airport take the Salem coach hourly from 0830-2130, $16.
Helicopter: To LaGuardia and Newark, from the TWA gate #37.

LaGuardia Airport
Taxis: $12-13 to Manhattan plus tolls and tip. Takes 20-40 minutes. Group taxi and Share-a-ride also available, about $6-7 per person.
Coach: Airport buses (Carey) to Grand Central Station depart every 20-30 minutes from 0630-2400. Takes about 40 minutes, $6. Limousine service available for about $8. Some hotels offer courtesy van service.
Transit: Bus #Q-33 departs every 30 minutes around the clock. Fare $1 to Jackson Heights subway station for transfer to downtown Manhattan trains.

Newark Airport (New Jersey)
Taxis: Taxis available to Manhattan for $25-30 plus tip. Takes about 30 minutes. Share-a-Ride taxi service also available.
Coach: Newark bus service leaves terminal every 30 minutes from 0700-0100 for downtown hotels for $12.
Airport Express bus to Port Authority bus terminal takes 30 minutes and leaves every 15-30 minutes from 0630-2400. Fare $5.
Transit: Airlink bus service leaves every 20-30 to Penn Station in Newark. Transfer to the ConRail train for Penn Central Station, or the PATH rapid transit train to the World Trade Center and Penn Station.

Facilities
Duty-free shops (JFK and Newark), currency exchanges, bars, restaurants, coffee shops, conference facilities, post office, helicopter service, first-aid, barber shops, baggage deposit, and shops of all kinds
Car rental desks: Hertz, Agency, American International, Avis, Budget, Dollar, National, Thrifty

Airport Taxes
$3.00 per passenger

City Information

Weather
November-April. Cold with snow and strong winds. Temperature 25-35F (-4-2C). Wear medium weight clothing with overcoat, boots and hat. May-October. Hot, humid and brief thunderstorms. Temperature 75-90F (24-32C). Wear lightweight clothes, light raincoat and umbrella.

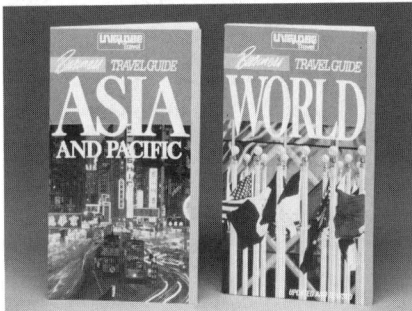

Transportation

There is no need for a rental car in Manhattan, unless you plan to drive outside the city. New York has numerous taxis which can be hailed on any street or can be found at hotel taxi stands. There are over 30,000 yellow cabs in the streets of New York.

The city bus system is extensive and reliable. Free route maps are available at the Visitors Bureau at Columbus Circle. Fare is $1 for anywhere on the system, and exact change or a subway token must be used.

Possibly the fastest way to get around Manhattan, if you don't mind the dirt and crowds, is the subway system. Its lines criss-cross the city so that you can get to within a few blocks of almost any destination. Fare is $1, and if you are going to be using the system frequently multiple tokens can be purchased at a discount. Each subway station has route maps posted on the walls for easy reference. Subway cars are patrolled by New York City police and security guards, but night rides to outer destinations are not recommended.

Car Hire

Hertz, 310 E. 48th St. 654-3131
Hertz, 150 E. 24th St. 475-2243
Hertz, 250 W. 34th St. 654-3131
Hertz, 210 W. 77th St. 654-3131
Avis, 217 E. 43rd St. 1-800 331-1212
Budget, 215 W. 48th St. 1-800 527-0700
National, 252 W. 40th St. 1-800 227-7368

Hospitals

Bellevue Hospital, 27th St. & First Ave. 561-4347
Montefiore Hospital, 1825 Eastchester Rd. 430-2000
Mt. Sinai, One Gustave L., Levy Place 650-6500
New York Hospital, 528 E. 70th St. 472-5050
New York University Hospital, 400 E. 34th St. 679-3200
Presbyterian Hospital, 622 W. 168th St. 964-2500

Trade Fairs

Mens Sportswear Buyers Exhibition (Jan)
Variety Merchandise Fair (Feb)
National Gift Exhibition (Feb)
World Tourism Exhibition (Mar)
International Fur Fair (Apr)
International Computer Graphic Fair (Apr)
International Printed Circuits Exhibition (May)
Premium and Incentive Travel Fair (May)
Electric Industry Exhibition (May)
U.S. Merchandise Exhibition (Sept)
Graphic Arts Exhibition (Sept)
International Pakcing Week Exhibition (Nov)
International Maritime Exhibition (Nov)

Hotels

Algonquin, 59 W. 44th St. 840-6800
Barbizon Plaza, 106 Central Park South 247-7000
Berkshire, Madison & 52nd St. 753-5800
Carlyle, 35 E. 76th St. 744-1600
Doral Inn, Lexington & 49th St. 755-1200
Doral Park, 70 Park Ave. 687-7050
Drake, Park Ave. & 56th St. 421-0900
Essex House, 160 Central Park S. 247-0300
Golden Tulip, 140 E. 63rd St. 838-5700
Gramercy Park, 2 Lexington Ave. N 475-4320
Halloran House, 535 Lexington Ave. 755-4000
Harley, 212 E. 42nd St. 490-8900
Helmsley Place, 455 Madison Ave. 888-7000

Holiday Inn, 440 W. 57th St.
581-8100'
Hyatt, Park Ave. at Grand
Central Station 883-1234
InterContinental, 111 E. 48th St.
755-5900
Lexington, 48th & Lexington
755-4400
Marriott Marquis, Broadway &
45th St. 398-1900
Mayfair Regent, 610 Park Ave.
288-0800
Milford Plaza, 270 W. 45th St.
869-3600
New York Hilton, 1335 Ave. of
Americas 586-7000
New York Penta, Seventh & 33rd
St. 736-5000
Novotel, 226 W. 57th St.
315-0100
Omni Park Central, 870 Seventh
Ave. 484-3300
Park Lane, 36 Central Park S.
371-4000
Parker Meridien, 118 W. 57th St.
245-5000
Pierre, Fifth Ave. & 61st St.
838-8000
Plaza Athenee, 37 E. 64th St.
734-9100
Plaza, 155 E. 50th St. 751-5710
Regency, Park Ave. & 61st St.
759-4100
Ritz Carlton, 112 Central Park S
757-1900
St. Moritz, 50 Central Park S
755-5110
St. Regis Sheraton, Fifth Ave. &
55th St. 753-4500
Shelbourne-Murray Hill, 303
Lexington 689-5200
Sheraton Center, 811 Seventh
Ave. 581-1000
Sheraton City Squire, 51st St. &
Seventh Ave. 581-3300
Sheraton Towers, Seventh Ave.
& 52nd St. 581-1000
Sherry-Netherland, 781 Fifth
Ave. 355-2800
Stanhope, 995 Fifth Ave.
288-5800
Tuscany, 120 E. 39th St. 686-1600
U.N. Plaza, 1 United Nations
Plaza 355-3400

Vista International, 3 World
Trade Center 938-9100
Waldorf-Astoria, 301 Park Ave.
355-3000
Warwick, 65 W. 54th St. 247-2700
Westbury, Madison & 69th St.
535-2000
Westin Plaza, Fifth Ave. & 59th
St. 759-3000

What to See and Do

New York confronts the visitor
with a bewildering array of
attractions. Possibly the easiest
introduction to the city is to take
one of the guided bus tours:
Grey Line (397-2600) and
Crossroads (581-2828). The Circle
Line (563-3200) tour boats leave
from 43rd St. at Pier 83 for a
fascinating 3-hour trip around
Manhattan Island daily from
April to October.
Attractions which can be
explored on foot, bus or taxi are:
the Empire State Building and its
observation deck, the Statue of
Liberty (taking the ferry leaving
hourly from Battery Park), the
World Trade Center towers and
their observation decks, and the
Wall Street financial district,
where tours of the New York
and American Stock Exchanges
are offered daily. The United
Nations is open for guided tours
each day.
Museums to visit include the
American Museum of Natural
History, the Guggenheim
Museum, the Metropolitan
Museum of Art, the Museum of
Modern Art, the Frick Collection,
and the Whitney Museum of
American Art.
The Lincoln Center for the
Performing Arts at 63rd &
Broadway, is the cultural center
of New York. Here you will find
the Metropolitan Opera, the
New York Philharmonic
Orchestra, the New York City
Ballet, the American Ballet

NORTH/SOUTH AMERICA

Theater and the Joffrey Ballet Company.

The variety of entertainment offered is so extensive it is probably best to get a copy of New York Magazine, the New Yorker or the Village Voice to see what is going on in town for jazz, concerts, live stage, movies and restaurants. New York has a restaurant for every taste and there are many good guidebooks for this purpose. Broadway offers some of the finest live stage in the world. The theater district runs from 43rd to 53rd Streets. Advanced reservations are a must for popular shows, but half-price tickets can be purchased on the day of performance at the kiosk in Times Square.

Shopping alone is one reason for a visit to New York. From the high fashions of Fifth Avenue to the bargain and resale bazaars of lower Manhattan, there is something for everyone.

Central Park is certainly worth visiting on a fine day. It is open for jogging, bicycling, horseback riding, row boating, or just plain walking. Interesting walks can also be found in the many villages such as Little Italy, Chinatown, SoHo, and Greenwich Village.

Finally, for the sports fan, there are more professional sports teams here than in any other city. Whether New Jersey claims some of these or not, the list includes the new York Giants and Jets (football), the Yankees and Mets (baseball), the Rangers and Islanders (hockey), and the Knicks (basketball). Madison Square Garden at Seventh Ave. & 33rd St., in addition to being the site of hockey and basketball, is the center for many other special attractions, such as tennis, ice shows, the circus, etc. Horse racing fans head for

Acqueduct and Belmont raceways.

Useful Addresses

Embassies and Consulates

British: 845 Third Ave. 752-8400
Australian: 636 Fifth Ave. 245-4000
Canadian: 1251 Ave. of Americas 586-2400
French: 934 Fifth Ave. 535-0100
German: 460 Park Ave. 940-9200
Japanese: 299 Park Ave. 371-8222
Swiss: 444 Madison Ave. 758-2560
USSR: 136 E. 67th St. 861-4900

Business and Commerce

American Chamber of Commerce, 200 Madison Ave. 516-2025
American Stock Exchange, 86 Trinity Place 938-6000
Arab Chamber of Commerce, 1 World Trade Center 432-0655
British Trade Development Office, 845 Third Ave. 593-2258
French Chamber of Commerce, 509 Madison Ave. 671-4466
German Chamber of Commerce, 666 Fifth Ave. 974-8830
Israel Chamber of Commerce, 500 Fifth Ave. 354-6510
Japanese Trade Center, 1221 Ave. of Americas 997-0400
Latin American Chamber of Commerce, 1 World Trade Center 432-9313
National Foreign Trade Council, 100 E. 42nd St. 867-5630
New York Chamber of Commerce, 200 Madison Ave. 561-2020
New York Visitor and Convention Bureau, 2 Columbus Circle 397-8222
New York Stock Exchange, 11 Wall Street 623-3000
Port Authority of New York, 1 World Trade Center 466-7000
United Nations, United Nations Plaza 754-1234

U.S. Dept. of Commerce,
26 Federal Plaza 264-0634

Tourism and Travel
American Express, 150 E. 42nd
St. 687-3700
American Express, 65 Broadway
344-6500
Auto Club of New York,
Madison Ave. & 78th
St.594-0700
Auto Club of New York,
Broadway & 62nd St. 586-1166
Deak International, 29 Broadway
820-2470
Deak International, Herald
Center Mall, 6th &
33rd.736-9790
Deak International, 41 East 42nd
St. 883-0400
Deak International, 630 Fifth
Ave. 757-6915
Deak International, JFK Airport
656-8444
New York Visitors Bureau, 90 E.
42nd St. 397-8222
Thomas Cook, 587 Fifth Ave.
754-2777
Times Square Information
Center, 43rd St. & Seventh
Ave. 245-1212
Uniglobe Boylan Travel, 889
Ninth Ave., 265-4800
Uniglobe Cosmopolitan Travel,
805 Third Ave. 750-5666
Uniglobe Good Life Travel,351 E.
86th St. 369-6200
Uniglobe Professional Travel,501
Fifth Ave. 490-8410

PHILADELPHIA

Airport Information

Time
GMT -5 (Eastern)
GMT -4 (April-October)

Airport
Philadelphia International PHL
Tel: 492-3000
8 mi (13 km) SW of city

Domestic and overseas terminals

Airlines
Aer Lingus 1-800 223-6537
Air Canada 1-800 422-6232
Air France 1-800 237-2747
Alitalia 1-800 523-5585
American 365-4000
Avensa 1-800 221-2150
Avianca 1-800 327-9899
British Airways 247-9297
Canadian International
1-800 426-7000
Continental 1-800 525-0280
Delta 1-800 221-1212
Eastern 1-800 327-8376
El Al 1-800 223-6700
JAL 1-800 525-3663
KLM 1-800 777-5553
Lufthansa 1-800 645-3880
Mexicana 1-800 531-7921
Northwest 1-800 225-2525
Ozark 922-7350
Pan Am 1-800 221-1111
Piedmont 1-800 251-5720
Republic 563-7501
Sabena 1-800 645-3700
SAS 1-800 221-2350
Swissair 1-800 221-4750
TWA 923-2000
United 568-2800
US Air 563-8055
Varig 1-800 468-2744

Transport to City
Taxis: Taxis are available at the
terminals for $13-15, plus tip for
30-40 minute ride to downtown
locations.
Coach: Airport limos leave from
terminals to downtown hotels
every 30 minutes from 0400-2300
at the baggage claim area. Fare
$5 per passenger. Airport
Express bus departs every 30
minutes from terminals to
downtown station for $2.25.
Some hotels offer courtesy vans.
Transit: Airport trains available
to several downtown stations
including the main 30th St.
station. The train departs from
platform adjacent to domestic
terminal every 30 minutes from
0600-2400. Fare $4.

Facilities

Duty-free shop (overseas terminal), currency exchange, hotel reservations, baggage deposit, post office, bar, restaurant, first-aid, shops Car rental desks: Hertz, American International, Avis, Budget, Dollar, National, Thrifty

Airport Taxes

$3.00 per passenger

City Information

Weather

November-April. Cold with snow with a mild early spring. Temperatures 25-50F (-4-10C). Wear medium weight clothing with overcoat, boots and hat. May-October. Hot in summer with high humidity and moderate rainfall. Temperatures 75-90F (24-32C). Light clothing with raincoat, and medium clothing in early fall.

Transportation

Taxis are plentiful and can be hailed on the streets or at taxi stands. Call United Cab (627-2225) or Yellow Cab (922-8400). The city bus system costs $1 exact fare. Transit maps can be purchased at newsstands, or acquired at the Visitor Information Bureau. Subway system interlinks with bus system and fares are transferable.

Car Hire

Hertz, 31 South 19th St. 492-2951
Hertz, 30th St. Station, 30th & Market 492-2958

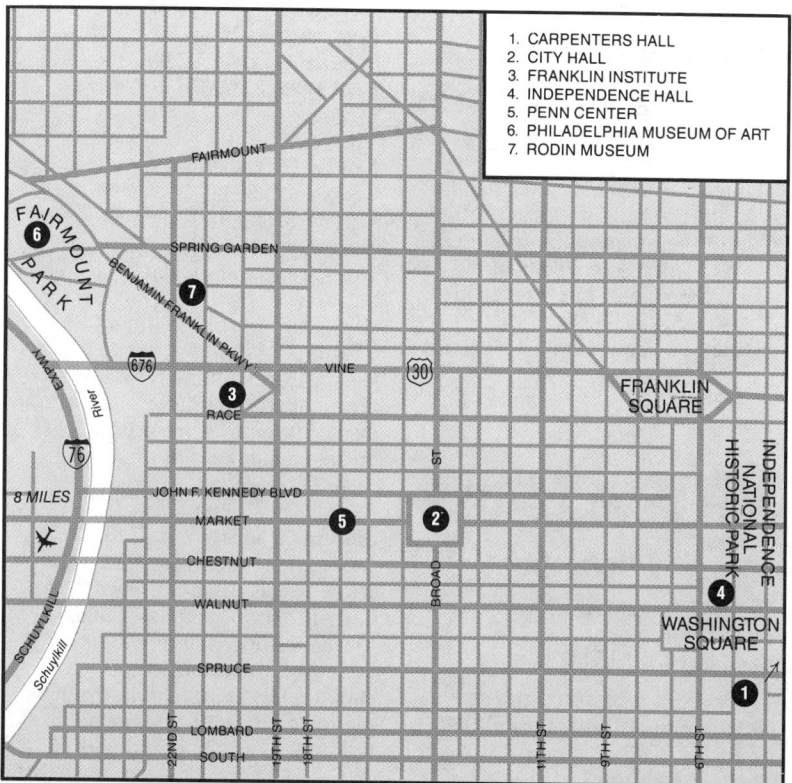

1. CARPENTERS HALL
2. CITY HALL
3. FRANKLIN INSTITUTE
4. INDEPENDENCE HALL
5. PENN CENTER
6. PHILADELPHIA MUSEUM OF ART
7. RODIN MUSEUM

Philadelphia

Agency, 3552 Bristol Pike 1-800 321-1972

Avis, 1909 Market St. 1-800 331-1212

Budget, 1800 JFK Blvd. 1-800 527-0700

Dollar, 2001 Market St. 1-800 421-6868

National, 1712 JFK Blvd. 1-800 227-7368

Thrifty, 2301 Walnut 1-800 367-2277

Hospitals

Hanneman Hospital, 230 N. Broad St. 448-7000

University of Pennsylvania Hospital, 3400 Spruce St. 662-4000

Pennsylvania Hospital, 8th & Spruce Sts. 829-3000

Thomas Jefferson University Hospital, 11th & Walnut Sts. 928-6000

Hotels

Adams Mark, City Line Ave. 581-5000

Barclay, Ritten House Square 545-0300

Four Seasons, 1 Logan Square 963-1500

Franklin Plaza, 2 Franklin Plaza 448-2000

Hershey, Broad & Locust St. 893-1600

Hilton, Civic & 34th 387-8333

Hilton Inn, 10th & Parker 755-9500

Hyatt, 2349 W. Marlton Pike 662-1234

Latham, 135 S. 17th St. 563-7474

Marriott, City Line Ave. & Monument 667-0200

Palace, Parkway & 18th St. 963-2222

Philadelphia Center, 1725 JFK Blvd, 567-3300

Warwick, 17th & Locust 735-6000

Westin Bellevue, Broad & Walnut 893-1776

What to See and Do

American history is the central attraction of Philadelphia, since it contains some of the nation's most important historical treasures. Independence Historical Park offers the Liberty Bell, Independence Hall (where the Declaration of Independence was signed), Graff House and Carpenters Hall. Also see the Betsy Ross House and Edgar Allan Poe House, and tour the U.S. Mint at 5th & Arch Sts. Museums include the Philadelphia Museum of Art, Norman Rockwell Museum, and Franklin Institute Science Museum and Planetarium. The world-famous Philadelphia Orchestra plays at the Academy of Music, which also hosts the city opera, ballet and other concerts.

Sports teams include the Phillies (baseball) at Veterans Stadium, the 76ers (basketball) and Flyers (hockey) at the Spectrum, as well as various tennis, golf and college sporting events.

Useful Addresses

Embassies and Consulates

Canadian: 3 Parkway Bldg. 561-1750

French: 3 Parkway Bldg. 525-0650

German: PNB Plaza Bldg. 922-7416

Japanese: 956 Public Ledger Bldg. 625-9900

Business and Commerce

Philadelphia Chamber of Commerce, Broad & Chestnut St. 545-1234

Philadelphia Convention & Visitor Bureau, 3 Penn Center Plaza 636-3000

Philadelphia Stock Exchange, 1900 Market St. 496-5000

U.S. Dept. of Commerce, 600 Arch 597-3311

U.S. Mint, 5th & Arch Sts.

World Trade Assoc., 1317 Spruce St., 735-0711

Tourism and Travel

American Express, 2 Penn Center
587-2300
Amtrack, 30th Street Station
824-1600
Deak International, 6 Penn
Center, 563-5544
Greyhound Bus Depot, 17th &
Market Sts.
Keystone Auto Club, 2040
Market St. 864-5000

Airport

Greater Pittsburgh International
PIT
Tel: 778-2500
16 mi (27 km) NW of city

Airlines

Alitalia 1-800 223-5730
American 771-4437
British Airways 1-800 247-9297
Canadian International
1-800 426-7000
Delta 1-800 221-1212
Eastern 1-800 327-8376
Lufthansa 1-800 645-3880
Northwest 1-800 225-2525
Pan Am 1-800 221-1111
Piedmont 1-800 251-5720
Republic 281-2088
Sabena 1-800 645-3790
SAS 1-800 221-2350
TWA 391-3600
United 1-800 241-6522

PITTSBURGH

Airport Information

Time

GMT -5 (Eastern)
GMT -4 (April-October)

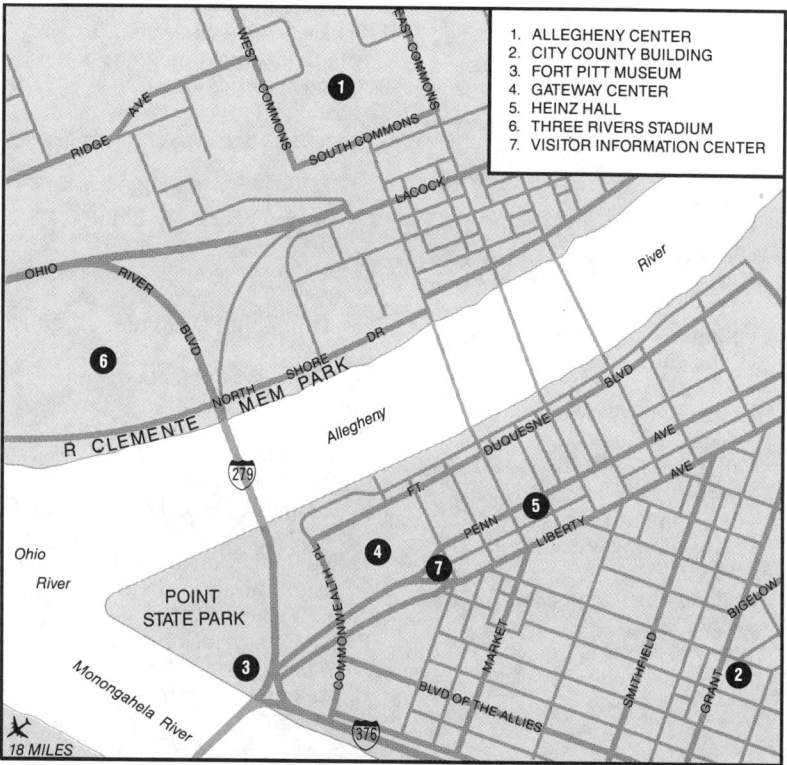

1. ALLEGHENY CENTER
2. CITY COUNTY BUILDING
3. FORT PITT MUSEUM
4. GATEWAY CENTER
5. HEINZ HALL
6. THREE RIVERS STADIUM
7. VISITOR INFORMATION CENTER

Pittsburgh

US Air 922-7500

Transport to City
Taxis: Taxis from airport terminal
to downtown cost about $27 plus
tip for a 35-40 minute ride.
Coach: Airport bus leaves from
lower level near baggage claim
every 30 minutes. Fare is $7.50
to downtown hotel stops. Some
hotels offer free courtesy bus
service.

Facilities
Currency exchange, hotel
reservations, baggage deposit,
post office, bar, restaurant,
conference rooms, shops
Car rental desks: Hertz, Ajax,
American International, Avis,
Budget, Dollar, National, Thrifty

Airport Taxes
None

City Information

Weather
November-April. Cold with
snow and heavy winds at times.
Temperatures 25-40F (-4-7C).
Medium weight clothing with
overcoat, boots and hat in
winter.
May-October. Hot, humid in
summer, with moderate rainfall.
Temperatures 75-90F (24-32C).
Light clothing with light raincoat
or umbrella.

Transportation
Taxis difficult to hail on streets
but can be found at taxi stands.
Call Yellow Cab (665-8100).
Intercity bus system basic fare is
$1 with higher charges for
further destinations.

Car Hire
Hertz, Gateway Center,
    400 Liberty Ave. 391-0362
Hertz, 1 Chatham Center
    391-0362
Agency, 3128 Library Rd. 1-800
    321-1972
Ajax, 1111 Beers School Rd.
    1-800 367-2529

Avis, 625 Stanwix St. 1-800
    331-1212

Hospitals
Allegheny General Hospital,
    320 East North Ave. 237-3131
Presbyterian-University Hospital,
    DeSoto & O'Hara Sts. 647-3000
St. Francis General Hospital,
    45th St. & Penn Ave. 622-4343

Hotels
BW Conley Inn, 3550 William
    Penn Hwy. 824-6000
Harley of Pittsburgh, 699 Rodi
    Rd. 244-1600
Hilton Pittsburgh, Gateway
    Center 391-4600
Holiday Inn, 915 Brinton Rd.
    247-2700
Hyatt Pittsburgh, 112 Wash-
    ington Place 471-1234
Marriott, 101 Mall Blvd. 373-7300
Marriott Inn, 101 Marriott Drive
    922-8400
Sheraton Station Square, Carson
    & Smithfield 261-2000
Westin William Penn, 530
    William Penn Rd. 281-7100

What to See and Do
Pittsburgh has benefited
culturally from its past as an
industrial center. It has been the
home of some of America's most
wealthy business tycoons, men
like Thomas Mellon, Andrew
Carnegie and Henry Clay Frick.
Many of the museums and
cultural centers bear their names.
The Carnegie International
Exhibit, the Frick Museum, the
Henry Clay Frick Fine Arts
Building, the Carnegie Institute,
Museum of Natural History,
Pittsburgh Center for the
Arts, and the Art Institute of
Pittsburgh are all worth visiting.
Heinz Hall, located in the
Golden Triangle, is home to the
Pittsburgh Symphony, Opera,
Pittsburgh Chamber Music
Society, and the Pittsburgh Ballet
Theater.
Local sports teams include the

Pittsburgh Pirates (baseball) and Steelers (football), who play at Three Rivers Stadium, the Penguins (hockey), and the teams from the University of Pittsburgh.

Useful Addresses

Embassies and Consulates
French: 800 Presque Island Dr. 327-6100
German: Penn Lincoln Pkwy. W 777-2000
Dutch: 600 Grant St. 566-2250

Business and Commerce
Pittsburgh Convention and Visitor Bureau, 4 Gateway Center 281-7711
Pittsburgh Chamber of Commerce, Chamber of Commerce Bldg. 392-4500
U.S. Dept. of Commerce, Federal Bldg. 1000 Liberty Ave. 644-2850

Tourism and Travel
Amtrak, Penn Station, Liberty & Grant Sts. 255-5020
Uniglobe Travel Fair, Baptist & Grove, 885-4300
Uniglobe Ultra Travel, 5000 McKnight Rd, 369-9100
Uniglobe Wings Travel, 159 Clairton Blvd., 653-9464

ST. LOUIS

Airport Information

Time
GMT -6 (Central)
GMT -5 (April-October)

Airport
Lambert-St. Louis International STL
Tel: 426-8000
15 mi (24 km) NW of city

Airlines
American 231-9505
British Airways 1-800 247-9297
Canadian International 1-800 426-7000

Delta 1-800 221-1212
Eastern 1-800 327-8376
KLM 1-800 777-5553
Lufthansa 1-800 645-3880
Northwest 1-800 225-2525
Ozark 739-1111
Pan Am 1-800 221-1111
Piedmont 1-800 251-5720
Sabena 1-800 645-3790
SAS 1-800 221-2350
TWA 291-7500
United 1-800 241-6522
US Air 421-1018

Transport to City
Taxis: Taxis take 20-30 minutes to downtown locations for fare of $18 plus tip.
Coach: Airport coach leaves every 30 minutes from 0630-1030 for downtown hotel locations for $5.90 per person. Some hotels offer courtesy vans which pick up at terminal.
Transit: Local bus service #104 operates Mon-Sat from 0800-1900 and departs airport approximately every 50 minutes for downtown: $1 fare.

Facilities
Currency exchange, hotel reservations, bar, restaurant, baggage deposit, shops.
Car rental desks: Hertz, Ajax, American International, Avis, Budget, Dollar, National, Thrifty.

Airport Taxes
None

City Information

Weather
November-April. Cold with occasional snow. Temperatures 15-45F (-10-7C). Wear medium weight clothing and overcoat, boots and hat.
May-October. Hot and humid during summer and frequent afternoon rainstorms.
Temperatures range from 75-95F

(24-35C). Light to tropical weight clothing with umbrella.

Transportation

The automobile is the best way to get around St. Louis and its suburbs, although if necessary, the city bus system (Bi-State Transit) is very good and covers the downtown area and the suburbs. Taxis are available in the streets, or you can call Checker-Manchester Cab (725-5600), Laclede Cab (652-3456) or Yellow Cab (361-2345).

Car Hire

Hertz, 400 N. Tucker St. 421-3131

Agency, 11906 Manchester 1-800 321-1972

Ajax, 9636 Natural Bridge 1-800 367-2529

American International, 10480 Natural Bridge 1-800 527-0202

Avis, 925 Washington Ave. 1-800 331-1212

Budget, 7990 Clayton Rd. 1-800 527-0700

Thrifty, 10400 Natural Bridge 1-800 367-2277

Hospitals

St. Louis University Hospital, 1325 S. Grand Blvd. 771-7600

Christian Hospital, 11133 Dunn Rd. 355-2300

St. John's Mercy Medical Center, 4201 McKibbon Rd. 427-1650

Hotels

BW Executive Intl., 4530 N. Lindbergh 731-3800

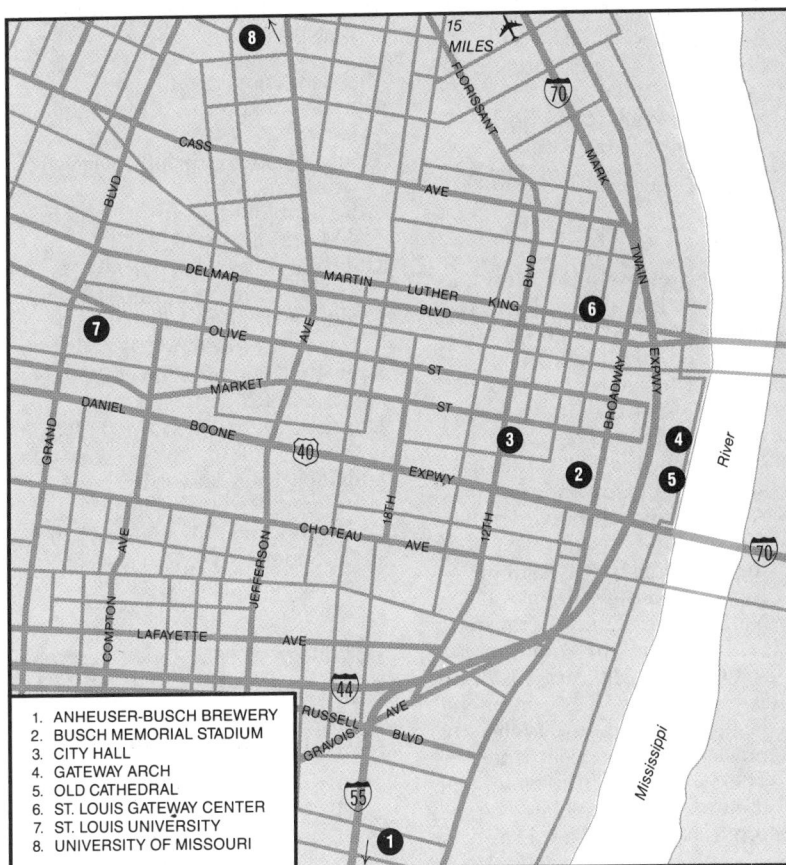

1. ANHEUSER-BUSCH BREWERY
2. BUSCH MEMORIAL STADIUM
3. CITY HALL
4. GATEWAY ARCH
5. OLD CATHEDRAL
6. ST. LOUIS GATEWAY CENTER
7. ST. LOUIS UNIVERSITY
8. UNIVERSITY OF MISSOURI

St. Louis

NORTH/SOUTH AMERICA

Breckenridge Inn, 1335 S.
Lindbergh 993-1111
Chase Park Plaza, 212 N. King's
Highway 361-2500
Clayton Inn, 7750 Carondolet
Ave. 725-1564
Harley, 3400 Rider Trail S.
291-6800
Holiday Inn Riverfront, 400 4th
St. 621-8200
Henry VIII Inn, 4690 N.
Lindbergh Blvd. 325-1588
Hilton Bel Air, 333 Washington
Ave. 621-7900
Marriott Pavillion, 1 S. Broadway
421-1776
Mayfair, 806 St. Charles St.
231-1500
Omni International, 1820 Market
St. 241-6664
Radisson, Convention Plaza
421-4000
Ramada Inn, 6926 S. Lindbergh
894-0600
Sheraton St. Louis, 910 N. 7th
St. 231-5100
Sheraton West Port Inn, 191
Westport Plaza 878-1500
Stouffer's River Front, 200 S.
4th St. 241-9500

What to See and Do

"The Gateway to the West", as
St. Louis likes to call itself, is
commemorated by the famous
Gateway Arch. Take the
elevator to the top of the Arch
for a view of the city. Nearby is
the Museum of Westward
Expansion, the Old Cathedral
and the Old Courthouse.
Anheuser-Busch Brewery offers
tours (Mon-Sat), and next door is
the St. Louis Sports Hall of
Fame. Also downtown is the
National Museum of Transport,
St. Louis Art Museum, Steinberg
Art Gallery, Missouri Historical
Society, and Powell Symphony
Hall, which is home to the city
music and dance companies.
The St. Louis Cardinals, one of
the great traditions in
professional baseball, is also the
name given to the football team.
Both play their games at Busch
Memorial Stadium. The St. Louis
Blues (hockey) play at the arena.

Useful Addresses

Embassies and Consulates

French: 210 N. 13th St. 622-2025
Swiss: 777 S. New Ballet Rd.
567-5078

Business and Commerce

Convention and Visitors Bureau
of St. Louis, 1300 Convenhon
Plaza 421-1023
St. Louis Port Authority, 1315
Chestnut 622-4711
St. Louis Chamber of Commerce,
10 S. Broadway 231-5555
U.S. Dept. of Commerce, 120 S.
Central Ave. 425-3302
World Trade Club, 111 N. Taylor
Ave. 721-8001

Tourism and Travel

American Express, 21 Mercantile
Center 241-6400
Amtrak, 550 South 16th
St.241-8806
Auto Club of Missouri, 12901 N.
40 Dr. 576-7350
Uniglobe Associated Travel,
11874 Gravois Rd. 849-6440
Uniglobe Des Peres Travel,1611
Des Peres Rd. 821-7717
Uniglobe Dynamic Travel,7750
Clayton Rd. 781-8400
Uniglobe Metro Travel, 1903 Park
Ave., 621-0010
Uniglobe Total Travel,105
Progress Parkway 878-8030
Uniglobe Travel Merchants,7730
Carondelet Ave. 727-5900

SAN FRANCISCO

Airport Information

Time

GMT -8 (Pacific)
GMT -7 (April-October)

Airport
San Francisco International SFO
Tel: 761-0800
16 mi (26 km) SE of city

Airlines
Aer Lingus 1-800 223-6537
Air California 433-2660
Air Canada 1-800 422-6232
Air France 1-800 237-2747
Air New Zealand 1-800 262-1234
Alitalia 1-800 223-5730
American 398-4434
Avianca 1-800 284-2622
British Airways 1-800 247-9297
CAAC 392-2156
Continental 397-8818
Canadian International
    1-800 426-7000
Delta 1-800 221-1212
Eastern 1-800 327-8376
Finnair 1-800 223-5700

JAL 1-800 525-3663
KLM 1-800 777-5553
Korean 1-800 421-8200
Lufthansa 1-800 645-3880
MEA 1-800 223-0804
Mexicana 1-800 531-7921
Northwest 1-800 225-2525
Pan Am 1-800 221-1111
Philippine 1-800 435-9725
Piedmont 1-800 251-5720
PSA 956-8636
Qantas 1-800 227-4500
Sabena 1-800 645-1382
SAS 1-800 221-2350
Singapore 1-800 742-3333
Swissair 1-800 221-4750
TWA 1-800 535-8780
United 1-800 241-6522
US Air 1-800 428-4322
UTA 1-800 282-4484

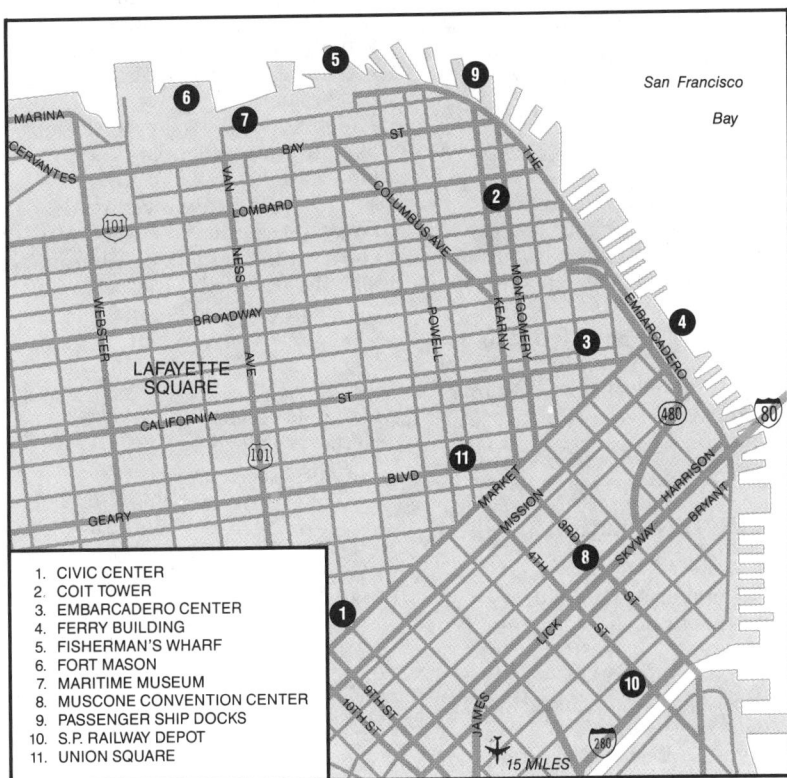

1. CIVIC CENTER
2. COIT TOWER
3. EMBARCADERO CENTER
4. FERRY BUILDING
5. FISHERMAN'S WHARF
6. FORT MASON
7. MARITIME MUSEUM
8. MUSCONE CONVENTION CENTER
9. PASSENGER SHIP DOCKS
10. S.P. RAILWAY DEPOT
11. UNION SQUARE

San Francisco

NORTH/SOUTH AMERICA

Varig 1-800 468-2744

Transport to City

Taxis: Taxis are available to downtown locations and cost about $23-24 plus tip for a 20-minute ride, more during rush hours.

Coach: Airporter bus leaves terminals at 15-minute intervals from 0600-1230, then every 40 minutes. Fare is $6.

Blue vans (SuperShuttle) offer door-to-door service to selected downtown locations for $7. Leaves from upper level and operates 24 hours a day.

Transit: City bus service (Muni) operates buses #7B and #7F daily from 0530-0130 at 30 minute intervals to downtown terminal at 1st & Mission Sts. Fare is $1.25 for 30-50 minute ride.

Inter-Airport Transport: Airporter bus leaves terminal every 2 hours from 0700-1100 for Oakland International Airport: $7 fare.

Facilities

Duty-free shop, currency exchange and bank, hotel reservations, baggage deposit, post office, bar, restaurant, first-aid, shops

Car rental desks: Hertz, Ajax, Alamo, American International, Avis, Budget, Dollar, National, Thrifty

Airport Taxes

$3.00 per passenger

City Information

Weather

November-April. Mild, with frequent rainshowers from incoming Pacific storms. Temperatures 50-65F (13-18C). Wear light to medium clothing with raincoat.

May-October. Warm, sunny and mainly dry. Temperatures 65-80F (18-27C), but much warmer in suburban cities. Frequent fog along the Pacific Ocean beach areas. Light clothing, with sweater or jacket in downtown San Francisco.

Transportation

If you are using San Francisco as a base for business in the East Bay, Peninsula or Silicon Valley, then car rental is essential. Otherwise, the taxi service and bus system (Muni) in San Francisco are excellent. Taxis can be hailed almost anywhere downtown, but if you are in the outlying districts you should call Veterans Cab (552-0300), Yellow Cab (626-2345) or Luxor Cab (552-4040).

The famous cable cars are not just for tourists. They run from downtown to Fisherman's Wharf, and up California Street. Fare of $1 is transferable to the bus system.

The rapid transit trains (BART) operate lines under San Francisco Bay to Oakland, and southward down the Peninsula. Finally, if you have occasion to go north to Sausalito or Tiburon, take the ferry, which leaves from the foot of Market St. and Pier 43 at Fisherman's Wharf.

Car Hire

Hertz, 433 Mason St. 771-2200

Hertz, 125 Stevenson St. 392-6983

Hertz, 533 Kearney St. 392-0345

Agency, 190 El Camino Real 1-800 321-1971

Ajax, 560 O'Farrell St. 1-800 367-2529

Alamo, 656 Geary St. 771-9717

Avis, 675 Post St. 1-800 331-1212

Budget, 321 Mason St. 1-800 527-0700

Dollar, 333 Taylor 1-800 421-6868

National, 500 Post St. 1-800 227-7368

Hospitals

Presbyterian Hospital,
2750 Geary Blvd. 921-6171
San Francisco General Hospital,
1001 Potrero Ave. 821-8200
University of California Hospital,
501 Parnassus Ave. 666-1037

Trade Fairs

Sports and Boat Show (Jan)
Western Air Conditioning &
Heating Exhibition (Jan)
Fancy Food and Confectionery
Exhibition (Mar)
International Trucking Exhibition
(Apr)

Hotels

Californian, Taylor & O'Farrell
885-2500
Fairmont, Nob Hill 772-5000
Four Seasons Clift, 495 Geary St.
775-4700
Handlery Motor Inn, 260
O'Farrell 986-2526
Hilton SF, 333 O'Farrell St.
771-1400
Holiday Inn, 1300 Columbus
Ave. 771-9000
Holiday Inn, 750 Kearney St.
433-6600
Huntington, 1075 California
474-5400
Hyatt Regency, 5 Embarcadero
Center 788-1234
Hyatt Union Square,
345 Stockton 398-1234
IBIS Airport, 835 Airport Blvd.
344-5500
Kyoto Inn, 1800 Sutter St.
921-4000
Mansion, 2220 Sacramento St.
929-9444
Mark Hopkins, 1 Nob Hill
392-3434
Marriott, Fisherman's Wharf,
775-7555
Meridien, 50 Third St. 974-6400
Miyako, 1625 Post St. 922-3200
Pacific Plaza, 501 Post St.
441-7100'
Ramada Renaissance, Market &
5th. 392-8000
San Franciscan, 1231 Market St.
626-8000

Sheraton Fisherman's Wharf,
2500 Mason 362-5500
Sheraton Palace, 639 Market St.
392-8600
Sir Francis Drake, Powell &
Sutter 392-7755
Stanford Court, 905 California St.
989-3500
Westin St. Francis, Union Square
397-7000

What to See and Do

San Francisco is a relatively small
city, and a good way to see it is
by walking or hopping onto a
cable car. Grey Line offers a bus
sightseeing tour. Attractions
you should not miss include
Fisherman's Wharf, Chinatown,
and Golden Gate Park, where
the DeYoung Museum, Academy
of Sciences, Aquarium and
Japanese Gardens are located. At
the Civic Center are City Hall,
San Francisco Opera House, and
the new home of the San
Francisco Symphony, Davies
Hall.
Entertainment is varied and
ranges from the opera and
symphony to the raunchy North
Beach district.
San Francisco is justly famous
for its many fine restaurants and
there are guidebooks which
adequately cover this scene.
Sports fans will find much to
watch from the San Francisco
Giants and Oakland A's
(baseball), San Francisco 49ers
(football), and the Golden State
Warriors (basketball).
Unfortunately, many events are
held at Candlestick Park, a cold
and windy stadium located 10
miles south of the city.
Shopping is centered downtown
near Union Square where you
can browse at Macys, Nieman
Marcus, I. Magnin's, and many
fine smaller stores. Near
Fisherman's Wharf are the two
factories which have been
converted into shopping

complexes: Ghirardelli Square, a former chocolate factory, and The Cannery, are both collections of unique gift stores, restaurants and specialty shops.

Useful Addresses

Embassies and Consulates
Australian: 360 Post St. 362-6165
British: 1 Sansome St. 981-3030
Canadian: 1 Maritime Plaza 981-2670
French: 540 Bush St, 397-4330
German: 601 California St. 981-4250
Israeli: 693 Sutter St. 775-5535
Japanese: 1601 Post St. 921-8000
Swiss: 235 Montgomery St. 788-2272

Business and Commerce
Arab Chamber of Commerce, 433 California St. 552-8202
British Chamber of Commerce, 3150 California St. 567-5128
Chinese Chamber of Commerce, 730 Sacramento St. 982-3000
French Chamber of Commerce, 312 Sutter St. 398-2449
German Chamber of Commerce, 465 California St. 392-2262
Japan Trade Center, 1737 Post St. 392-1333
Japanese Chamber of Commerce, 312 Sutter St. 986-6140
Pacific Coast Stock Exchange, 301 Pine St. 393-4000
Pan American Chamber of Commerce, 317 12th Ave. 752-4093
San Francisco Chamber of Commerce, 465 California St. 392-4511
San Francisco Convention and Visitor Bureau, 1390 Market St. 626-5500
San Francisco Port Commission, Ferry Building 391-8000
U.S. Dept. of Commerce, 450 Golden Gate Ave. 556-5860
World Trade Center, Ferry Building 391-8000

Tourism and Travel
Amtrak, Transbay Terminal, 425 Mission St. 982-8512
California State Auto Assoc., 150 Van Ness Ave. 565-2012
Deak International, 100 Grant Ave. 362-3452
Uniglobe Alliance Travel, 151 Union St., 421-0697
Uniglobe Complete Travel, 90 New Montgomery, 777-5225
Uniglobe Golden Gate, 130 Produce Ave, 583-1664

SEATTLE

Airport Information

Time
GMT -8 (Pacific)
GMT -7 (April-October)

Airport
Seattle Tacoma (Sea-Tac) International SEA
Tel: 433-5218
13 mi (21 km) S of city

Airlines
Air Canada 1-800 663-8370
American 241-0920
British Airways 1-800 247-9297
Canadian International 1-800 426-7000
Continental 1-800 525-0280
Delta 1-800 221-1212
Eastern 1-800 327-8376
Finnair 1-800 223-5700
Japan Airlines 1-800 525-3663
KLM 1-800 777-5553
Lufthansa 1-800 645-3880
Mexicana 1-800 531-7921
Northwest 1-800 225-2525
Pan Am 1-800 221-1111
Philippine 1-800 435-9725
Sabena 1-800 645-1382
SAS 1-800 221-2350
Thai 1-800 426-5204
TWA 447-9400
United 1-800 b241-6522
Varig 682-0999

Transport to City

Taxis: Taxis from airport to downtown take about 30 minutes. Fare $24 plus tip to downtown, less to main hotel strip.

Coach: Airport buses, Grey Line or Evergreen depart every 20 minutes from 0600-2400, for 25-30 minute ride to Seattle. Tickets can be purchased in baggage claim area for $5.

Many hotels provide courtesy vans for customers.

Transit: City bus #174 departs every 30 minutes from 0500-0300, and Express service #194 every 30 minutes Mon-Fri from south end of baggage claim. Fare 85 cents.

Facilities

Duty-free shop, currency exchange, hotel reservations, baggage deposit, bar, restaurant, shops

Car rental desks: Hertz, Ajax, American International, Avis, Budget, Dollar, National, Thrifty

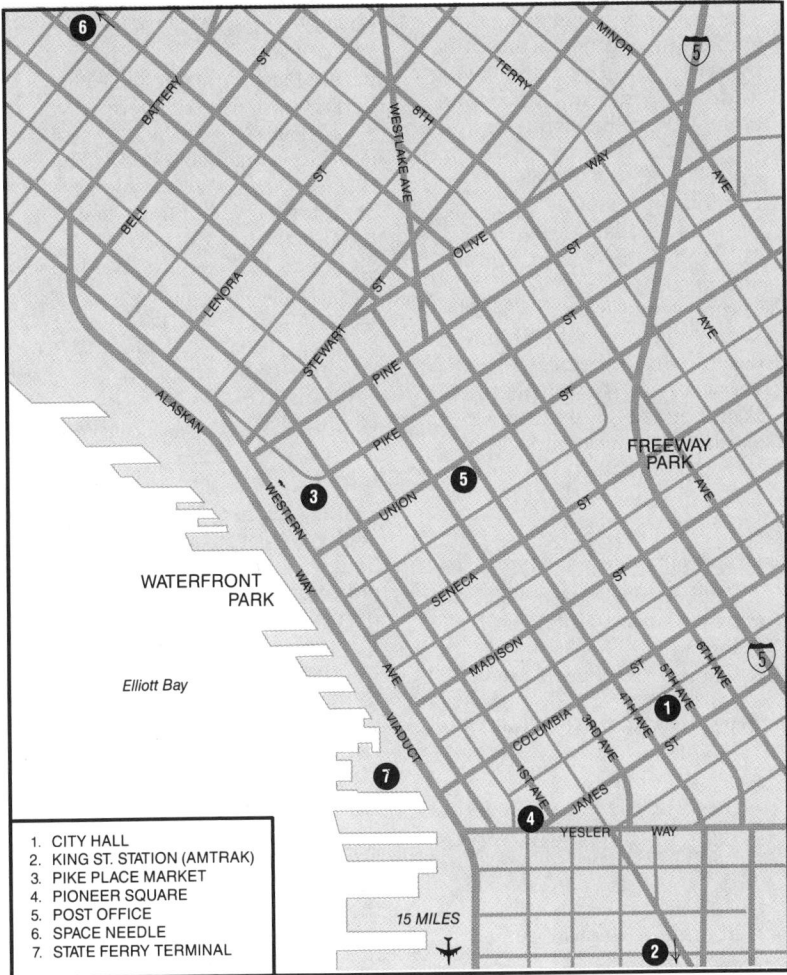

1. CITY HALL
2. KING ST. STATION (AMTRAK)
3. PIKE PLACE MARKET
4. PIONEER SQUARE
5. POST OFFICE
6. SPACE NEEDLE
7. STATE FERRY TERMINAL

15 MILES

Seattle

NORTH/SOUTH AMERICA

Airport Taxes
$3.00 per passenger

City Information

Weather
November-April. Cool with
heavy rain and occasional fog.
Temperatures 40-55F (4-15C).
Medium weight clothing with
raincoat and umbrella.
May-October. Warm, occasional
sunny days, and moderate
rainfall. Temperatures 65-75F
(18-24C). Lightweight clothing
with light raincoat or umbrella.

Transportation
The best way to get around the
spread-out Seattle-Tacoma area is
by car rental. If you are staying
in downtown Seattle, taxis can
be hailed on the streets or you
can call Far West Cab (622-1717)
or Yellow Cab (622-6500).
City bus system (Metro Transit)
services Seattle as well as the
outlying districts, and Everett
and Tacoma.
The monorail from the Seattle
World's Fair operates from
downtown to the Seattle Center.
Ferry service is available to
Whidbey Island, and from
Seattle to Victoria and
Vancouver, British Colombia.

Car Hire
Hertz, 722 Pike St. 682-5050
Hertz, Hyatt House, 17001
    Pacific Hwy. S. 433-5275
Hertz, Marriott Hotel, 3201 S.
    176th St. 433-5275
Agency, 15245 Pacific Hwy. S.
    1-800 321-1972
Alamo, 20636 Pacific Hwy. S.
    433-0182
Avis, 1919 Fifth Ave. 1-800
    331-1212
Budget, 2001 Westlake Ave.
    1-800 527-0700

Hospitals
Harborview Medical Center,
    325 Ninth Ave. 223-3000

Swedish Hospital, 747 Summit
    Ave. 292-2121
University Hospital, 1959
    Northeast Pacific St. 543-3300

Hotels
Camlin, Pine St. & 8th Ave.
    682-0100
Edgewater Inn, 2411 Alaskan
    Way, Pier 67
Four Seasons Olympic, 411 Uni-
    versity St. 621-1700
Hilton Seattle, 6th & Univesity
    St. 624-0500
Holiday Inn Crowne Plaza, 6th
    & Seneca 464-1980
Holiday Inn South, 11244 Pacific
    Hwy. 248-1000
Hyatt Seattle, 17001 Pacific Hwy.
    244-6000
Pacific Plaza, 4th Ave. 623-3900
Park Hilton, 6th & Seneca
    624-0500
Red Lion Inn, 18470 Pacific Hwy.
    246-8600
Sheraton Towers, 6th & Pike
    621-9000
Stouffer's Madison, 515 Madison
    583-0300
University Towers, 4507
    Brooklyn Ave. NE 634-2000
Washington Plaza, 5th &
    Westlake 624-7400
Westin, 1900 5th Ave. 728-1000

What to See and Do
Seattle's pioneer days are still
evident. Visit historic Pioneer
Square, where you can visit the
old underground city which was
destroyed by fire in 1889. In
this area you can walk to the
International District, and down
to the waterfront. On the
waterfront there is Waterfront
Park (Pier 59), where you can
visit Seattle Aquarium, Pike
Place Market, or take one of the
boat tours of Seattle harbor.
From downtown take the
monorail to the Seattle Center,
the site of the 1962 World's Fair.
Take the elevator to the top of
the Space Needle for the best

view of Seattle, and where there is a restaurant and the Pacific Science Center. At the center is also the Seattle Center Opera House which is home to the Seattle Symphony Orchestra. Aerospace is synomous with Seattle. Visit the giant Boeing factory in Everett, 25 miles south of Seattle, and the Museum of History and Industry, which has displays on aerospace and transportation.

The Kingdome is home to the Seattle Mariners (baseball), Supersonics (basketball) and the Seahawks (football).

Useful Addresses

Embassies and Consulates
British: 801 2nd Ave. 622-9253
Canadian: 412 Plaza 600 223-1717
French: 707 East Harrison St.
   323-6870
German: 1200 5th Ave. 682-4313
Japanese: 1301 5th Ave. 682-9107

Business and Commerce
Port of Seattle, Pier 66 382-3000
Seattle Chamber of Commerce,
   1200 One Union Sq. 447-7200
Seattle Convention and Visitors
   Bureau, 1815 7th Ave. 447-7273
Seattle World Trade Center,
   PO Box 68727 433-5291
U.S. Dept. of Commerce, 1700
   Westlake Ave. N 442-5615

Tourism and Travel
Amtrak, King St. Station, 3rd &
   Jackson 382-4120
Auto Club of Washington,330 6th
   Ave. N. 448-5353
Deak International, 906 Third
   Ave., 623-6203
Uniglobe Business Travel, 200 W
   Mercer, 282-1946
Uniglobe Gateway Travel,5518
   6th Ave. S. 763-1255
Uniglobe Paragon Travel,401 2nd
   Ave. S. 622-5410
Uniglobe Sea West Travel, 2825
   Eastlake E, 322-8334

Washington State Ferry System,
   State Ferry Terminal

WASHINGTON D.C.

Airport Information

Time
GMT -5 (Eastern)
GMT -4 (April-October)

Airports
Dulles International IAD
Tel: 471-7873
27 mi (43 km) W of city
International Airport

National Airport DCA
Tel: 557-2045
3 mi (5 km) SW of city
Domestic Airport

Airlines
Aer Lingus 1-800 223-6537
Air Canada 1-800 422-6232
Air France 1-800 237-2747
Air New Zealand 1-800 262-1234
Alitalia 1-800 223-5730
American 393-2345
Avensa 1-800 221-2150
Avianca 1-800 284-2662
British Airways 1-800 247-9297
Canadian International 1-800
   426-7000
Continental 1-800 525-0280
Delta 1-800 221-1212
Eastern 1-800 327-8376
El Al 1-800 223-6700
Finnair 1-800 223-5700
Gulf Air 1-800 223-1740
Iberia 1-800 221-9741
JAL 1-800 525-3663
KLM 1-800 777-5553
Korean 1-800 421-8200
Kuwait Air 1-800 424-1128
Lufthansa 1-800 645-3880
Northwest 1-800 225-2525
Olympic 1-800 223-1226
Ozark 347-4744
Pan Am 845-8000
Philippine 1-800 435-9725
Piedmont 1-800 251-5720
Qantas 1-800 227-4500

Sabena 1-800 645-3700
SAS 1-800 221-2350
Singapore 1-800 742-3333
Swissair 1-800 221-4750
TWA 737-7400
United 1-800 241-6522
US Air 783-4500
UTA 1-800 221-2110
Varig 1-800 468-2744

Transport to City

Dulles International Airport
Taxis: Taxis from the terminal to
downtown cost about $30 plus
tip for a 45-60 ride. To National
Airport $32; Capitol Hill, $32.
Coach: Airport bus (Washington
Flyer) departs every 30 minutes
from terminal to downtown from
0500-0300. Fare $10, 60-minute
trip. Bus to National Airport
leaves every hour for 45-minute
trip. $10.
Transit: Bus to West Church
Falls metro station departs every
45 minutes from 0600-1000.
Transfer to metro line. $7.

National Airport
Taxis: Taxi to downtown and
Capitol Hill area from $6-7, plus
tip for 20 minute trip.
Coach: Airport bus (Washington
Flyer) departs every 30 minutes
from 0530-1030, to selected
downtown stops and hotels.
Fare is $5. Fare to National
Airport $10.
Transit: Metro rail (Blue and
Yellow lines) to downtown
locations leaves from station
opposite North Terminal. Free
shuttle bus operates between
terminals and station. Trains
depart every 5-10 minutes.
Purchase tickets (approx. $1)
from automatic machine at
station.

Facilities

Duty-free shop (Dulles),
currency exchange, hotel
reservations, baggage deposit,
flight insurance, first aid, bar,
restaurant, shops
Car rental desks: Hertz, Ajax,
Alamo, American International,
Avis, Budget, Dollar, National,
Thrifty

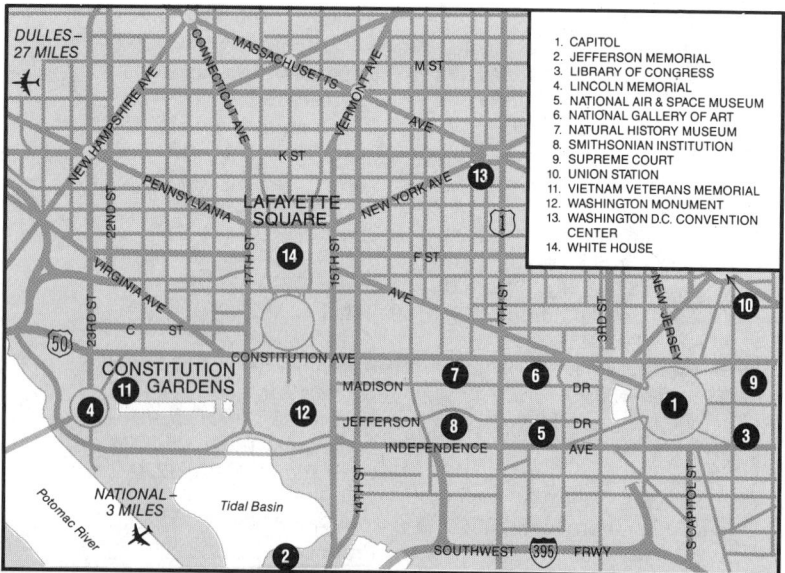

1. CAPITOL
2. JEFFERSON MEMORIAL
3. LIBRARY OF CONGRESS
4. LINCOLN MEMORIAL
5. NATIONAL AIR & SPACE MUSEUM
6. NATIONAL GALLERY OF ART
7. NATURAL HISTORY MUSEUM
8. SMITHSONIAN INSTITUTION
9. SUPREME COURT
10. UNION STATION
11. VIETNAM VETERANS MEMORIAL
12. WASHINGTON MONUMENT
13. WASHINGTON D.C. CONVENTION CENTER
14. WHITE HOUSE

Washington

Airport Taxes
$3.00 per passenger

City Information

Weather
November-April. Cold to mild, with snow and rain. Temperatures 30-45F (0-7C). Medium weight clothing with overcoat, hat and boots in winter, and raincoat during spring.
May-October. Hot and humid, with occasional rain. Temperatures 75-95F (24-35C). Light clothing with raincoat or umbrella.

Transportation
Taxis available downtown and in Capitol area on streets or at hotel stands. Taxis charge by zone system displayed on back of driver's seat. Call Barwood Cab (966-5301) or Yellow Cab (544-1212). Metrobus system provides adequate bus service for Washington and outlying areas, but not the best way to get around. The Washington Metro is one of the best and cleanest systems in the United States. Stations are marked by a giant M sign. Passengers must use an automatic ticket vending machine, which charges fares determined by the zone travelled to. Operates from 0630-2400.
If you are going to many different locations, the freeway system in the Washington area is good, and is the easiest way to get around.

Car Hire
Hertz, 1622 L Street NW 892-0003
Hertz, Union Station, 789-0460
Hertz, 1001 N. Filmore St., Arlington 276-1896
Agency, 5801 Annapolis Rd. 1-800 321-1972
Alamo, 2780 Jefferson Davis Hwy., Arlington 684-0086

Avis, 1722 M St. NW 1-800 331-1212

Hospitals
George Washington University Hospital, 901 23rd St. NW 676-2500
Georgetown University Hospital, 3800 Reservoir Rd. 625-0100
Howard University Hospital, 2041 Georgia Ave. NW 745-6100
Washington Hospital Center, 110 Irving St. NW 541-0500

Hotels
BW Regency Congress, 600 New York Ave. NE 546-9200
Canterbury, 1733 N St. NW 393-3000
Capitol Hilton, 16th & K St. NW 393-1000
Capitol Park Intl., 800 4th St. SW 479-6800
Dupont Plaza, 1500 New Hampshire Ave. NW 483-6000
Embassy Row, 2015 Massachussets Ave. NW 265-1600
Four Seasons, 2800 Pennsylvania Ave. NW 342-0444
Guest Quarters, 2500 Pennsylvania Ave. NW 333-8060
Hay-Adams Hotel, 800 16th St. NW 638-6600
Holiday Inn, 1914 Connecticut Ave. NW 797-2000
Hyatt Regency Capitol, 400 New Jersey Ave. NW 737-1234
Jefferson, 1200 16th St. NW 347-2200
Loews L'Enfant, L'Enfant Plaza E. SW 484-1000
Madison, 15th & M St. NW 862-1600
Marriott National, 1333 Pennsylvania NW 393-2000
Marriott Washington, 1221 22nd St. NW 872-1500
Mayflower, 1127 Connecticut Ave. NW 347-3000
Omni Shoreham, 2500 Calvert NW 234-0700

NORTH/SOUTH AMERICA

One Washington Circle, 1 Washington Cr. 872-1680
Radisson Henley Park, 926 Massachussets Ave. NW 638-5200
Ramada Inn, 8400 Wisconsin Ave. 654-1000
Ramada Renaissance, 1143 New Hampshire NW 775-0800
Ritz Carlton, 2100 Massachussets Ave. NW 835-2100
Sheraton Carlton, 923 16th St. NW 638-2626
Sheraton Washington, 2660 Woodley Rd. NW 328-2000
Stouffer's Concourse, 2399 Jefferson Davis Hwy. 979-6800
Washington, 15th St. & Pennsylvania NW 638-5900
Washington Hilton, 1919 Connecticut Ave. NW 483-3000
Watergate, 2650 Virginia Ave. NW 965-2300
Westin, 2550 M St. NW 955-8484

What to See and Do

There are so many historical sites, museums and other attractions in Washington, that it is a good idea to purchase a guidebook first and plan your tour. The Convention and Visitors Bureau, 1575 I St. NW, is another good source of information. If you only have a day or so, a good way to see the whole picture is to take one of the bus tours from Grey Line, Diamond, White House and others.
Attractions you should see include the White House and Capitol tours, the Washington Monument, Jefferson Memorial, Lincoln Memorial, Supreme Court, and the National Gallery of Art. If you have more time you should visit the Smithsonian Institution and its ten museums and galleries.
The John F. Kennedy Center for the Performing Arts is the cultural center of Washington, where you can view concerts, opera, ballet and theatrical performances.
Entertainment is centered mainly in old Georgetown, a residential area where many restaurants, bars and clubs are open for late-night revelry.
Sports fans can also find what they need in Washington. R.F.K. Stadium is home to the Washington Redskins (football), and the Capitol Centre in Landover, Maryland, just a few miles from downtown, is the home of the Washington Capitals (hockey) and the Bullets (basketball). And while Washington no longer has a baseball team, Baltimore (40 miles away) has the Orioles, and for horse racing fans, Pimlico Racetrack.

Useful Addresses

Embassies and Consulates

Algerian: 2118 Kalorama Rd. NW 328-5300
Argentinian: 1600 New Hampshire NW 939-6400
Australian: 1601 Massachussets NW 797-3159
Austrian: 2343 Massachussets NW 483-4474
Bahamian: 600 New Hampshire NW 944-3390
Bahrain: 3502 International Dr. NW 342-0741
Belgium: 3330 Garfield NW333-6900
Bolivian: 3014 Massachussets Ave. 232-4828
Brazilian: 3009 Whitehaven St. NW 745-2828
British: 3100 Massachussets NW 462-1340
Canadian: 501 Pennsylvania Ave., 785-1400
Chilian: 1732 Massachussets NW 785-1746
Chinese: 2300 Connecticut Ave. NW 328-2517
Colombian: 2118 Leory Pl. NW 387-8338

Czechoslovakian: 3900 Linnean Ave. NW 363-6308

Danish: 3300 Whitehaven St. NW 234-4300

Dutch: 4200 Linnean NW244-5300

Egyptian: 2310 Decatur Pl. NW 232-5400

Finnish: 3216 New Mexico St. NW 363-2430

French: 4101 Reservoir Rd. NW 944-6200

German (East): 717 Massachussets NW 232-3134

German (West): 4645 Reservoir Rd. NW 298-4000

Greek: 2211 Massachussets NW 332-2727

Hong Kong: 3100 Massachussets NW 462-1340

Hungarian: 3910 Shoemaker NW 362-6737

Indian: 2107 Massachussets NW 939-7000

Irish: 2234 Massachussets NW 462-3939

Israeli: 3514 International Dr. NW 364-5500

Italian: 1601 Fuller St. NW328-5500

Japanese: 2520 Massachussets NW 363-1935

Kenyan: 2249 R St. NW 387-6101

Korean (South): 2320 Massachussets NW 939-5600

Kuwait: 2949 Tilden St. NW966-0702

Malaysian: 2401 Massachussets NW 328-2700

Mexican: 1019 19th St NW, 293-1710

New Zealand: 37 Observatory NW 328-4800

Nigerian: 2201 M St. NW822-1500

Norwegian: 2720 34th St. NW 333-6000

Pakistani: 2315 Massachussets NW 939-6200

Peruvian: 1700 Massachussets NW 833-9860

Philippine: 1617 Massachussets NW 483-1414

Polish: 2224 Wyoming Ave.234-3800

Portuguese: 2125 Kalorama Rd. NW 328-8610

Saudi Arabian: 601 New Hampshire NW 342-3800

Singapore: 1824 R St. NW667-7555

Spanish: 2700 15th St. NW265-4939

Swedish: 600 New Hampshire NW 944-5600

Swiss: 2900 Cathedral NW745-7900

Thailand: 2300 Kalorama NW 483-7200

Turkish: 1606 23rd St. NW 429-9844

United Arab Emirates: 600 New Hampshire NW 338-6500

USSR: 1825 Phelps Pl. NW 628-7551

Venezuelian: 2445 Massachussets NW 797-3800

Yugoslavian: 2410 California NW 462-6566

Business and Commerce

AFL-CIO, 1815 16th St. NW 637-5000

American Bankers Assoc., 1120 Connecticut Ave. NW 467-4000

Export-Import Bank, 811 Vermont Ave. NW 566-2117

Federal Bar Assoc., 1815 H St. NW 638-0252

Federal Communications Comm., 1919 M St. NW 655-4000

Intl. Development Assoc., 1818 H St. NW 477-1234

Intl. Monetary Fund, 700 19th St. NW 477-7000

Intl. Trade Administration, 14th & E Sts. NW 377-5274

Intl. Visitors Service Council, 1825 H St. NW 872-8747

Organization of American States, 17th St & Constitution Ave. NW 331-1010

United Nations Information Office, 2101 L St. NW 296-5370

U.S. Chamber of Commerce, 1615 H St. NW 659-6000

U.S. Dept. of Commerce, 14th St. & Constitution 377-2000

Washington Convention and

Visitors Assoc., 1575 I St. NW
789-7000

Tourism and Travel
AAA Potomac, 1825 I St. NW
331-3000
American Express, 1150
Connecticut Ave. NW 457-1300
Amtrak, Union Station,50
Massachussets Ave.
NE484-7540
Deak International, 1800 K St.
NW, 331-7945

Deak International, 3222 M St.
NW, 338-3325
Intl. Visitors Info. Service, 801
19th St. NW 872-8747
National Visitors Center, Union
Station, 50 Massachussets
Ave. NE 484-7540
Uniglobe Full Service Travel,
4530 Wisconsin Ave NW,
244-5000
Washington Visitor Info. Center,
1400 Pennsylvania Ave. NW
789-7000

VENEZUELA

Essential Information

Type of Government
Federal Republic

Area
912,050 sq km
(352,143 sq mi)

Population
185 million

Annual Growth Rate
2.8%

Languages
Spanish (official) 98%, Indian
languages 2%

Religion
Roman Catholic 96%, Protestant
2%

Ethnic Groups
Mestizo 69%, Spanish,
Portugese, Italian 20%, Negro
9%, Indian 2%

Weights and Measures
Metric

Electrical Current
A.C. 60c 120/240V
Caracas A.C. 50c 120/208V

Major Business
Caracas (cap) 2,350,000
Maracaibo 1,400,000

Currency
1 Bolivar = 100 Centimos
Notes 10, 20, 50, 100 bolivars

Coins 5, 10, 25, 50 centimos;
1, 2, 5 bolivars

Public Holidays
Jan 1 New Year
Mar 5-6 Carnival
Apr 13-19 Easter Week
Apr 20 Independence
May 1 Labor Day
June 24 Battle of Carabobo
Jul 24 Bolivar's Birthday
Sept 24 Civil Servant's Day
Oct 12 Columbus Day
Dec 25 Christmas

Travellers Information

Entry Requirements
Passport is required by all except
certain citizens/residents of US,
and some UN document holders.
Visa not required (a tourist
landing card is fine) if arriving
by air with assured onward
ticket for nationals of US,
Canada, Britain and most west-
European countries. Otherwise a
tourist transit or ordinary visa is
required. Businessmen should
get a "transuente" visa which
requires them to declare income
acquired during their stay, and
present a tax declaration form
(Solvencia) on departure. It is
wise to inquire of your local
travel agent, tourist office, or
Venezuelan consulate what the
exact visa requirements are for

your purpose as release and tax forms must often be obtained in advance.

Vaccination Required

No immunization is required if arriving from non-infected areas. Vaccinations for yellow fever, typhoid and malaria strongly recommended, particularly for trips to Orinoco Valley. Take antimalarial tablets.

Customs and Duty Free

On arrival: 200 cigarets or 25 cigars; 2 liters alcohol; 4 small bottles of perfume or cologne; discretionary number of gift items. Meat, fruit and flowers strictly prohibited.

Currency Restrictions

There are no restrictions on the amount of foreign or Venezuelan currency or travellers checks you can take in or out.

Health Tips

The water is not purified so do not drink tap water. Buy bottled instead. Avoid raw vegetables and eat cooked ones only in places where you are sure they have been carefully prepared. Imported pharmaceuticals are available and reasonably priced. Free medical treatment is available, but private clinics, although expensive, are strongly recommended.

Climate and Clothing

Lightweight clothing is generally fine in Caracas. The dry season (Dec-Apr) has an average city temperature of 23c (74F). The rainy season is May to November. Take a lightweight coat as the temperature drops at night. In other parts of the country, the temperatures vary with the altitude.

Tipping

No tipping for taxis. Tip service persons, barbers, hairdressers, 10-15% and token tips for small services in hotels. Restaurants and nightspots include a 10% service charge but an additional 10% is appreciated.

Food and Drink

The arepa, a white corn bun available with a variety of fillings, is a very popular snack and can be bought at an Arepera. Try quesillos (yellow corn pancakes with cheese filling) and the excellent Venezuelan beef, preferably barbecued at a Parriclada. The fish and seafood is very fine as is the beer and rum. Imported wine is expensive. Fresh fruit juice, batido, is popular, and cafe con leche (coffee with milk) is recommended. In Caracas, European and Asian dishes are widely available.

Business Brief

GDP

$75.3 billion
(per capita income $4,344)

Annual Growth Rate

2.8%

Natural Resources

Petroleum, natural gas, iron ore, gold, other minerals, hydro-electric power, bauxite

Agriculture

Rice, coffee, corn, sugar, bananas, and dairy, meat, and poultry products

Industry

Petrochemicals, oil refining, iron and steel, paper products, aluminum, textiles, transport equipment, consumer products

Imports

Total $7.1 billion
Machinery and transport equipment, manufactured goods, chemicals, foodstuffs

Exports

Total $7.9 billion

Petroleum, iron ore, coffee,
aluminum, cocoa

Major Trading Partners
US, West Germany, Japan, UK,
Netherlands, Antilles, Canada,
Italy, Spain

Workforce
7 million Agriculture 18%,
industry and commerce 42%,
services 41%

Tips for Doing Business
In Caracas, a lightweight suit
and tie are necessary for all
business and government visits,
although a short-sleeved shirt is
correct in Maracaibo and other
more tropical cities. Prior
appointments are absolutely
essential and you should write
well in advance of your visit.
Once there, be direct but polite.
Business lunches are not
popular. Try for an after-work
drink or dinner. The average
businessman in Caracas is
sophisticated and has a
knowledge of languages,
including English.

Best Months for Doing Business
Business vacations are usually
taken in July and August. Avoid
the two weeks before and after
Christmas and the week before
and after Easter. Also avoid
Carnival Week in the first week
of March or whenever Ash
Wednesday falls. Best months to
visit Caracas: January-June and
September-November; for
Macaibo: March-June.

Business Hours

Government
Mon-Fri 0730-1530 to 0930-1730

Business
Mon-Fri 0800-1800 (long mid-day
break)

Banks
Mon-Fri 0830-1130, 1400-1630

Shops
Mon-Fri 0900-1300, 1500-1900

English Language Publications
The Daily Journal is main
English-language paper. Foreign
Englishlanguage newspapers and
magazines like Newsweek are
available in major cities.

Telephone and Communications
Telephone country code: 58
Telephone city code: Caracas 2,
Maracaibo 61
Telex country code: 395
Coin operated public telephones
are in restaurants, cafes and
street booths. Lift receiver, wait
for dial tone, then deposit a 25
centimo coin and dial. Direct
dialing service is available to
most countries.
Public telex service at hotels and
post offices. Telegram service is
available but slow.

Air Travel
Flying is the best way of internal
travel and almost all large towns
are connected with flights
operated by LAV and Avensa.
To ensure a seat, arrive in plenty
of time even for confirmed
bookings Call first as schedule
changes are frequent.

Other Transport
Roads are very good and car hire
is available but expensive.
Foreign license acceptable.
Insurance recommended.
Bus service is efficient between
cities and inexpensive. Book in
advance and arrive in time to
ensure a seat. Limited train
service.

CARACAS

Airport Information

Time
GMT -4

Airport
Simon Bolivar (Maiquetia) CCS
Tel: (031)551111
(International terminal)
Tel: (031)22010
(Domestic terminal) 22 km (13.6
mi) NW of city

Airlines
Air Canada 5729522
Air France 2835855
Alitalia 2840211
Avensa 5623022
Avianca 337311
British Airways 2618006
Canadian International 923632
El Al 722457
Iberia 5626666

JAL 9l2311
KLM 2831111
Lufthansa 9510044
Pan Am 2849211
Philippine 2846877
Sabena 326543
SAS 2848667
Swissair 9511211
TWA 5635544
Varig 344686

Transport to City
Taxi: some airlines provide
transport but it is more
customary to arrange for a taxi to
the city.

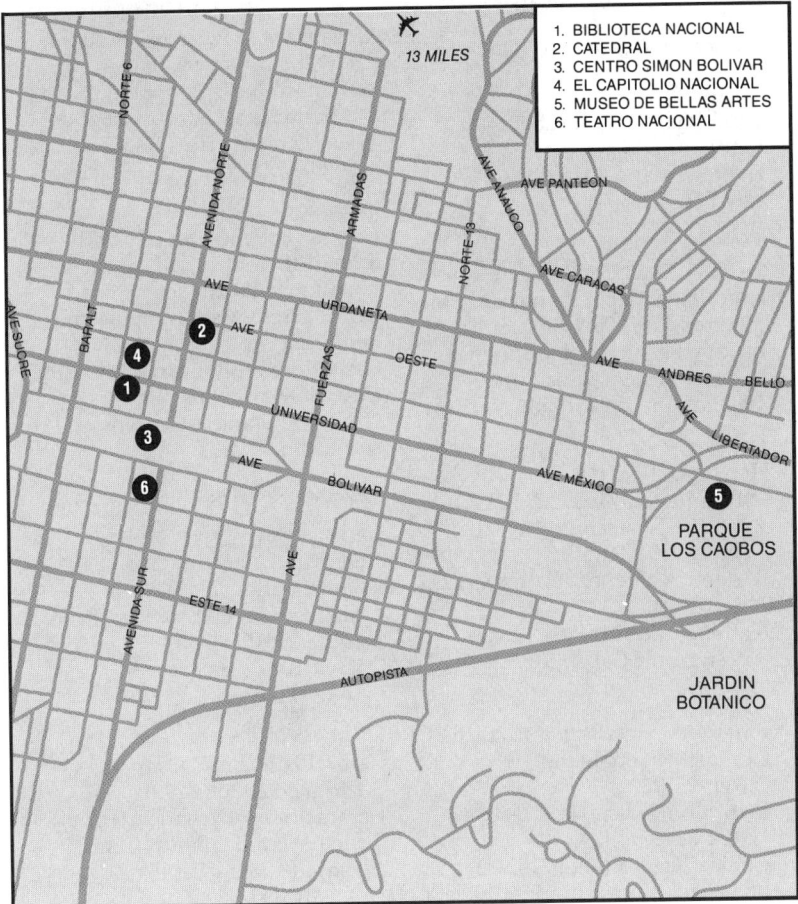

1. BIBLIOTECA NACIONAL
2. CATEDRAL
3. CENTRO SIMON BOLIVAR
4. EL CAPITOLIO NACIONAL
5. MUSEO DE BELLAS ARTES
6. TEATRO NACIONAL

Caracas

Transit: airport bus runs 24 hours a day and leaves about every 10 minutes but is not reliable.

Facilities

Bar, buffet, restaurant, bank, currency exchange, post office, barber shop, shops selling flowers, gifts
Duty-free shop sells cigarets, cigars, tobacco, wines, spirits, cameras, lighters, jewellery, glass, electronic goods. Local and US currencies accepted.
Car rental desks: Hertz, Avis, Budget, National

Airport Taxes

Per person: 460 bolivars

City Information

Weather

Oct-May is dry, Jun-Sept is rainy.
Average temps: Jan 19c (66F) July 21c (70F)

Transportation

Taxis are metered but fare can be negotiated. Tip 10% but only for metered fare. City bus service is usually very crowded. There is a subway system which opened in 1983 and is comfortable and fast.

Car Hire

Hertz, Av Ppal del Bosque(tel: 715332 & 72616)
Avis, Av Guaicaipuro 14(tel: 551190)
Budget, Av Venezuela(tel: 727177 & 32711)
National, Edifico Polar, Plaza Venezuela (tel: 9863222)

Hospitals

Emergency medical assistance at:
Clinica Metropolitano (tel: 9872222)
Instituto Medico la Floresta (tel: 2848111)
Clinica Razetti (tel: 5710211)
Pharmacies open at night have a red neon sign: "turno".

Trade Fairs

Computer and Telecommunicators Exhibition (Jun)

Hotels

There is usually no shortage of hotel space, but it is essential to book in advance.
Avila, Av Washington, San Bernadino, (tel: 515155)
Caracas Hilton, Av Libertador/ Sur 25 (tel: 5712322)
Crillon, Av Libertador/Las Acacias (tel: 714411)
Holiday Inn, Av Principal de las Mercedes (tel: 910444)
Las Americas, Calle Los Ceritos Final (tel: 729901)
Macuto Sheraton, Apdo, 65, La Guaira (tel: 91801/19)
Melia Caribe, PO Box 285, La Guaira (tel: 92401)
Tamanaco Inter-Continental, Apartado 467 Av Principal de las Mercedes (tel: 914555/ 582924522)

What to See and Do

Caracas is a modern city with little of the old colonial heritage remaining. Worth seeing are Santa Teresa, Santa Capilla and San Francisco churches: Civic Center Simon Bolivar, University City, Bolivar's Museum, El Calvario Botanical Gardens and several fine parks.

Useful Addresses

Embassies and Consulates

American: Av Miranda & Floresta (tel: 2846111)
Canadian: Av La Estancia 10 (tel: 9516166)
British: Av La Estancia 10 (tel: 911255)

Business and Commerce

Central Bank, Av Urdancta esq Carmelitas (tel: 829811)
Caracas Stock Exchange, Torre Financiera del Banco Central, Esquina Santa Capilla (tel: 815141)
Caracas Chamber of Commerce,

Av Este 2 No 215, Los Caobos
American
Chamber of Commerce, Av
Francisco de Miranda, Los
Palos Grandes, Apt 5181
(tel: 2833097)

Tourism and Travel
Touring and Automobile Club of
Venezuela, Centro Integral,
Santa Rosa de Lima, Apt de
Correos 68102 (tel: 916373)
American Express, Turismo
Consolidado Turisol CA,
CCCT-Nivel C-2, Local 53F-07,
Chuao (tel: 927922)
Thomas Cook, Av Urdaneta 33
(tel: 813657)